The Virginias,

A Mining, Industrial and Scientific Journal,

Devoted to

The Development of Virginia and West Virginia.

Edited and Published by

Jed. Hotchkiss,

Consulting Mining and Civil Engineer; Member of the American Institute
of Mining Engineers, etc.—Author of "A Geographical and Political
Summary of Virginia," of "A Physiography of Virginia," etc.—
Formerly Top. Eng. of "Stonewall" Jackson.

Volume I, 1880.

Staunton, Virginia.

Printed by S. M. Yost & Son,
Valley Virginian Office, Staunton, Va.
1880.

209262

Illustrations.

INDEX.

The Virginias.

A Mining, Industrial, and Scientific Journal:

Devoted to the Development of Virginia and West Virginia.

| Vol. I, No. 1. } | Staunton, Virginia, January, 1880. | { Price 15 Cents. |

The Virginias,

PUBLISHED MONTHLY,

By JED. HOTCHKISS, · · · Editor and Proprietor,

At 340 E. Main St., Staunton, Va.

TERMS, including postage, per year, in advance, $1.50. Single numbers, 15 cents. Extra copies $10. per 100.

Advertising Rates:

One Inch, one time, ... $2.50 | One Inch, six months, . . . $ 7.50
One Inch, two months, ... 4.00 | One Inch, nine months, . . 10.00
One Inch, three months, . . . 5.50 | One Inch, one year, ... 12.00

Address all communications to Jed. Hotchkiss, Staunton, Va.

Entered at the Post-Office at Staunton, Va., as second-class mail matter.

For Sale at Hunter & Co.'s Book-store, Main St., Staunton, Va.

Introductory.—The object of this publication is made known by its title. The development of the resources of the great territory, 67,500 square miles in extent, embraced in the States of Virginia and West Virginia, is the end we have in view. Having spent the life-time of a generation in becoming familiar with the resources, conditions and wants of these States, gathering and accumulating all sorts of information about them, we have been led to the conclusion that there is no other region, of equal extent, in the United States, having so much and such a variety of unused natural wealth, and that nothing is wanting but a development and utilization of their resources to enable them to rank with, if not lead, the first of the other States in population, industrial activity and accumulated wealth, and to acquire the power derived from the possession of an unlimited store of raw materials with skilled labor and capital to work up and market them. First in importance we place the development of their iron, coal, and a dozen other mineral resources, the extent and richness of which it is even difficult to exaggerate; that done, improvement in all other directions will follow. Therefore ours will be largely a *Mining Journal*, striving to collect and publish full and reliable information concerning the mineral deposits of these States, their location, extent and character, and how they may be made profitable; providing a medium for calling the attention of capital and skill to them, and recording the progress made in this great work. Judging from the earnest enquiries, coming from all directions and from all classes of men, for information of this kind concerning the Virginias, such a journal is greatly needed.

Supplementally, the condition, wants and growth of all other industries in these States will receive attention,—especially lumbering, which should be one of prime importance, since they have, untouched, larger and more valuable forest resources than can now be found elsewhere in the Union within the same limits.

The acreage of unoccupied planting, farming, and grazing lands, good in quality and varied in location and character, within the Virginias, is larger than can be found within the same bounds of any other region of the United States east of the Mississippi,—how to have these occupied will claim our attention.

The basis of substantial material development is scientific knowledge wisely applied, therefore we shall devote a portion of our space to the presentation of scientific facts and statements relating to the Virginias.

We invite communications and correspondence about mineral deposits, the opening and output of mines, the erection and production of furnaces; and, generally, concerning and of the resources of Virginia and West Virginia and of progress made in their development. Especially do we ask the Press of these States to aid us by collecting *detailed and accurate local information* on these subjects and so furnish the information that will enable us to make a full record of what we have and what we are doing.

The success of this undertaking will depend on the substantial encouragement we receive. We invite all that are in any way interested in the development of Virginia and West Virginia to become subscribers to this Journal. We shall do our best to render it worthy of their favor.

The American Institute of Mining Engineers, as

we learn by a circular from Dr. Drown, the Secretary (Easton, Pa.), will hold its annual meeting in New York City, beginning on Tuesday, February 17th, 1880. The local committee of arrangements will be Messrs. A. S. Hewitt, J. A. Burden, A. L. Holley, R. W. Raymond and Charles McDonald. The Secretary requests early notice of papers to be read at this meeting.

It is generally understood that the "spring" meeting of the Institute, some time next May. will be held in Staunton, Va., in response to an invitation from our City Council. We can assure our fellow members of a cordial welcome to the central city-of-the-hills and of the Great Valley, and of about as much professional sight-seeing as they generally find.

The New River and Kanawha Coal-fields, of West

Virginia, along and near the line of the Chesapeake & Ohio Railway, will be fully treated of in our next number, with maps, sections, etc., illustrating the location of this important field and the position of its many beds, of excellent coals. The Coal River basin of this field will be included in this treatment, as it is now attracting much attention in consequence of a well considered and ably sustained movement for the construction of a railway into it from the Great Kanawha River and the C. & O. R'y. We know that to be one of the richest coal and timber basins in this country.—This article was prepared for this issue, but only part of it could have been given. We prefer to have a *Great Kanawha Coal-field number of* THE VIRGINIAS.

The James River Valley is at this time attracting a large amount of attention, not only among the workers and speculators in iron but also among railway men, both contractors and exploiters, especially those of the latter class having faith in "connecting" lines, because in the development of its great mineral wealth and in its ability to furnish the missing link in a low-grade east-and-west transportation route, they see a "promise and potency" for large returns from an intelligent investmestment of capital and skill. In fact, there is more being done, in and for utilizing the mineral resources of Virginia, in the basin of the James than in all the rest of the State. In proof of this it only necessary to mention the Tredegar and other iron-works of Richmond, worked to their utmost capacity; the active granite quarrying and coal mining above that city; the mining and shipping iron ores from the iron-belt below Lynchburg and the getting ready for blast of iron and steel works in and near that city; the energetic construction of the Buchanan & Clifton Forge Railway; the making of from 3 to 4 miles of branch railway, across Rich Patch Mountain, from the Chesapeake & Ohio R'y to Callie Furnace, and the accumulation of coke and ore there, preparatory to going into blast, as well as the shipment of "red-shale" ore to Quiunimont Furnace, West Va.; the recent completion of some 5 miles of extension of the Longdale Narrow-gauge R'y, from the furnace of the Longdale Company to its great ore-beds on Brushy Mountain, and the preparations for the construction of another large furnace; the mining of "fossil" ore at Clifton Forge for the Pa. & Va. Iron & Coal Co's Quinnimont Furnace, and the extensive mining operations of that Company at Ferrol, to supply the large demands for ore at Quinnimont; the rapid growth of Williamson's, the "high" and "low" grade junction of the C. & O. R'y; and, lastly, and to the passer-by perhaps the most striking evidence of development, the progress that has been made in constructing the eighty-ton furnace at Low Moor and its accompaniments, which have already taken the form of a well-built, thriving, iron-works village.—All these things, and more too, are going on in the basin of the James, The River of Virginia, consequently, as having a present interest, we devote, in this number of THE VIRGINIAS, a large amount of space to that region, presenting full and able papers, by men of recognized authority in geological and mineralogical matters, Prof. Campbell of Washington and Lee University, and Col. McDonald of the Virginia Military Institute, to which it is only necessary to invite the attention of those that desire well presented and reliable information. These we illustrate by a map, drawn from unpublished surveys, presenting truly the main features of the region discussed.

The article by Prof. Campbell is an original contribution, in which he presents, with great force and clearness, a general view of the immense iron and other resources of parts of five of the great, Virginia physical regions,—Midland, Piedmont, Blue Ridge, The Great Valley and Apalachia,—crossed by the James. It embodies the results of years of patient, pains-taking and conscientious explorations, and its every statement is entitled to entire credence.

The article by Col. McDonald appeared about a year ago, as a pamphlet report of the Va. Military Institute. It has attracted much attention, on account of its ability; we reproduce it in full that it may reach the larger audience its merits deserve. It treats in detail of a belt, some 3 miles wide and 15 long, in the immediate vicinity of the northeast-flowing part of the James.

The catchment-basin of the James, a region 11,000 square miles in extent, (equal in area to the State of Maryland or the kingdom of Belgium,) is, beyond question, one of the largest and most important iron-bearing regions of the Union, as well as one of the best agricultural ones. The most prominent and sagacious of the iron-masters of the United States have already invested largely in its mineral lands, which, now that iron commands a fair price, they are rapidly developing by the enlargement of works already in operation or the construction of new ones. There is no better field for safe investments in iron lands, for large bodies of these are for sale at nominal prices, say from $5 to $50 per acre, and anyone guided by reliable professional advice can make no mistake in purchasing, for the mining engineer experienced in the geology and mineralogy of the region can readily distinguish the real iron lands.—Professor Thomas Egleston, of the Columbia College, New York, School of Mines, spent a month of the past autumn in the Apalachian portion of this basin, between Ferrol a' and Roaring Run furnaces, a mere corner, as it were, of the who ole; he often remarked, that in all his wide experience, in New England, the Northern and Western States and in Euro pe, he had never seen so much iron ore, and in such heavy ar d continous beds, as he had seen in this belt during that time . Professor N. S. Shaler, of Harvard University, Mass., the Director of the Kentucky Geological Survey now in progre s, spent a few days of last fall at the Rockbridge Alum Sprir gs, and incidentally, rode along the out-crop of the ores of VII on the eastern slope of Brushy Mountain, he expresse d much the same opinion.

The Mineral Resources and Advantages of the Country Adjacent to the James River & Kanawha Canal and the Buchanan & Clifton Forge Railway.[*]

By JOHN L. CAMPBELL, PROFESSOR OF GEOLOGY AND CHEMISTRY, WASHINGTON & LEE UNIVERSITY, LEXINGTON, VA.

HON. JOHN W. JOHNSTON, President, &c:—

SIR:—In compliance with your request, I proceed to give you, in as concise a form as is consistent with clearness, the impressions made upon my mind from personal observations and other sources of information, "as to the iron and other mineral interests in the James River Valley from Clifton Forge down to below Lynchburg." This I do the more cheerfully because these impressions are of the most favorable character. My explorations have been entirely voluntary and my opinions, therefore, have been formed without reference to the interests of any individual or company, but solely in the interests of science, and of the State of Virginia.

It has not been my privilege to inspect all the valuable mines and quarries within reach of your Company's line of improvements, but I have seen enough of each of the great ore-bearing belts that lie along and are crossed by them, to enable me to give you such a view of the whole, and of each separately, as may, I hope, aid others in making more detailed examinations of special localities, and give to the public a proper appreciation of the vast stores of mineral wealth lying within reach of your line of transportation.

Individual ownerships and special localities will be mentioned only when necessary to clearness of description.

At your suggestion, I shall avail myself of extracts from published documents, where they may serve to throw light upon the subject in hand.

I also wish to say, at the out-set of this communication, that I am peculiarly indebted to the kindness and valuable co-operation of Hon. Wm. H. Ruffner, Supt. of Public Instruc-

[*]Prepared to accompany the 45th Annual Report of the James River & Kanawha Canal Co., and the 3rd Annual Report of the Buchanan & Clifton Forge Railway Co., 1879, but appearing first as an original communication to "THE VIRGINIAS."

The Virginias.

A Mining, Industrial, and Scientific Journal:

Devoted to the Development of Virginia and West Virginia.

| Vol. I, No. 1. | Staunton, Virginia, January, 1880. | Price 15 Cents. |

The Virginias,

PUBLISHED MONTHLY,

By JED. HOTCHKISS, · · · Editor and Proprietor,

At 340 E. Main St., Staunton, Va.

TERMS, including postage, per year, in advance, $1.50. Single numbers, 15 cents. Extra copies $10. per 100.

Advertising Rates:

One Inch, one time,	$2.50	One Inch, six months, . . . $ 7.50
One Inch, two months,	4.00	One Inch, nine months, . . 10.00
One Inch, three months,	5.50	One Inch, one year, ... 12.00

Address all communications to **Jed. Hotchkiss,** Staunton, Va.

Entered at the Post-Office at Staunton, Va., as second-class mail matter.

For Sale at Hunter & Co.'s Book-store. Main St., Staunton, Va.

Introductory.—The object of this publication is made known by its title. The development of the resources of the great territory, 67,500 square miles in extent, embraced in the States of Virginia and West Virginia, is the end we have in view. Having spent the life-time of a generation in becoming familiar with the resources, conditions and wants of these States, gathering and accumulating all sorts of information about them, we have been led to the conclusion that there is no other region, of equal extent, in the United States, having so much and such a variety of unused natural wealth, and that nothing is wanting but a development and utilization of their resources to enable them to rank with, if not lead, the first of the other States in population, industrial activity and accumulated wealth, and to acquire the power derived from the possession of an unlimited store of raw materials with skilled labor and capital to work up and market them. First in importance we place the development of their iron, coal, and a dozen other mineral resources, the extent and richness of which it is even difficult to exaggerate; that done, improvement in all other directions will follow. Therefore ours will be largely a *Mining Journal*, striving to collect and publish full and reliable information concerning the mineral deposits of these States, their location, extent and character, and how they may be made profitable; providing a medium for calling the attention of capital and skill to them, and recording the progress made in this great work. Judging from the earnest enquiries, coming from all directions and from all classes of men, for information of this kind concerning the Virginias, such a journal is greatly needed.

Supplementally, the condition, wants and growth of all other industries in these States will receive attention,—especially lumbering, which should be one of prime importance, since they have, untouched, larger and more valuable forest resources than can now be found elsewhere in the Union within the same limits.

The acreage of unoccupied planting, farming, and grazing lands, good in quality and varied in location and character, within the Virginias, is larger than can be found within the same bounds of any other region of the United States east of the Mississippi,—how to have these occupied will claim our attention.

The basis of substantial material development is scientific knowledge wisely applied, therefore we shall devote a portion of our space to the presentation of scientific facts and statements relating to the Virginias.

We invite communications and correspondence about mineral deposits, the opening and output of mines, the erection and production of furnaces; and, generally, concerning and of the resources of Virginia and West Virginia and of progress made in their development. Especially do we ask the Press of these States to aid us by collecting *detailed and accurate local information* on these subjects and so furnish the information that will enable us to make a full record of what we have and what we are doing.

The success of this undertaking will depend on the substantial encouragement we receive. We invite all that are in any way interested in the development of Virginia and West Virginia to become subscribers to this Journal. We shall do our best to render it worthy of their favor.

The American Institute of Mining Engineers, as

we learn by a circular from Dr. Drown, the Secretary (Easton, Pa.), will hold its annual meeting in New York City, beginning on Tuesday, February 17th, 1880. The local committee of arrangements will be Messrs. A. S. Hewitt, J. A. Burden, A. L. Holley, R. W. Raymond and Charles McDonald. The Secretary requests early notice of papers to be read at this meeting.

It is generally understood that the "spring" meeting of the Institute, some time next May. will be held in Staunton, Va., in response to an invitation from our City Council. We can assure our fellow members of a cordial welcome to the central city-of-the-hills and of the Great Valley, and of about as much professional sightseeing as they generally find.

The New River and Kanawha Coal-fields, of West

Virginia, along and near the line of the Chesapeake & Ohio Railway, will be fully treated of in our next number, with maps, sections, etc., illustrating the location of this important field and the position of its many beds, of excellent coals. The Coal River basin of this field will be included in this treatment, as it is now attracting much attention in consequence of a well considered and ably sustained movement for the construction of a railway into it from the Great Kanawha River and the C. & O. R'y. We know that to be one of the richest coal and timber basins in this country.—This article was prepared for this issue, but only part of it could have been given. We prefer to have a *Great Kanawha Coal-field number of* THE VIRGINIAS.

The James River Valley is at this time attracting a large amount of attention, not only among the workers and speculators in iron but also among railway men, both contractors and exploiters, especially those of the latter class having faith in "connecting" lines, because in the development of its great mineral wealth and in its ability to furnish the missing link in a low-grade east-and-west transportation route, they see a "promise and potency" for large returns from an intelligent investmestment of capital and skill. In fact, there is more being done, in and for utilizing the mineral resources of Virginia, in the basin of the James than in all the rest of the State. In proof of this it only necessary to mention the Tredegar and other iron-works of Richmond, worked to their utmost capacity ; the active granite quarrying and coal mining above that city ; the mining and shipping iron ores from the iron-belt below Lynchburg and the getting ready for blast of iron and steel works in and near that city ; the energetic construction of the Buchanan & Clifton Forge Railway ; the making of from 3 to 4 miles of branch railway, across Rich Patch Mountain, from the Chesapeake & Ohio R'y to Callie Furnace, and the accumulation of coke and ore there, preparatory to going into blast, as well as the shipment of "red-shale" ore to Quinnimont Furnace, West Va.; the recent completion of some 5 miles of extension of the Longdale Narrow-gauge R'y, from the furnace of the Longdale Company to its great ore-beds on Brushy Mountain, and the preparations for the construction of another large furnace ; the mining of "fossil" ore at Clifton Forge for the Pa. & Va. Iron & Coal Co's Quinnimont Furnace, and the extensive mining operations of that Company at Ferrol, to supply the large demands for ore at Quinnimont ; the rapid growth of Williamson's, the "high" and "low" grade junction of the C. & O. R'y ; and, lastly, and to the passer-by perhaps the most striking evidence of development, the progress that has been made in constructing the eighty-ton furnace at Low Moor and its accompaniments, which have already taken the form of a well-built, thriving, iron-works village.—All these things, and more too, are going on in the basin of the James, The River of Virginia, consequently, as having a present interest, we devote, in this number of THE VIRGINIAS, a large amount of space to that region, presenting full and able papers, by men of recognized authority in geological and mineralogical matters, Prof. Campbell of Washington and Lee University, and Col. McDonald of the Virginia Military Institute, to which it is only necessary to invite the attention of those that desire well presented and reliable information. These we illustrate by a map, drawn from unpublished surveys, presenting truly the main features of the region discussed.

The article by Prof. Campbell is an original contribution, in which he presents, with great force and clearness, a general view of the immense iron and other resources of parts of five of the great, Virginia physical regions,—Midland, Piedmont, Blue Ridge, The Great Valley and Apalachia,—crossed by the James. It embodies the results of years of patient, pains-taking and conscientious explorations, and its every statement is entitled to entire credence.

The article by Col. McDonald appeared about a year ago, as a pamphlet report of the Va. Military Institute. It has attracted much attention, on account of its ability ; we reproduce it in full that it may reach the larger audience its merits deserve. It treats in detail of a belt, some 3 miles wide and 15 long, in the immediate vicinity of the northeast-flowing part of the James.

The catchment-area of the James, a region 11,000 square miles in extent, (equal in area to the State of Maryland or the kingdom of Belgium,) is, beyond question, one of the largest and most important iron-bearing regions of the Union, as well as one of the best agricultural ones. The most prominent and sagacious of the iron-masters of the United States have already invested largely in its mineral lands, which, now that iron commands a fair price, they are rapidly developing by the enlargement of works already in operation or the construction of new ones. There is no better field for safe investments in iron lands, for large bodies of these are for sale at nominal prices, say from $5 to $50 per acre, and anyone guided by reliable professional advice can make no mistake in purchasing, for the mining engineer experienced in the geology and mineralogy of the region can readily distinguish the real iron lands.—Professor Thomas Egleston, of the Columbia College, New York, School of Mines, spent a month of the past autumn in the Apalachian portion of this basin, between Ferrol a'id Roaring Run furnaces, a mere corner, as it were, of the whole ; he often remarked, that in all his wide experience, in New England, the Northern and Western States and in Europe, he had never seen so much iron ore, and in such heavy and continous beds, as he had seen in this belt during that time. Professor N. S. Shaler, of Harvard University, Mass., the Director of the Kentucky Geological Survey now in progress, spent a few days of last fall at the Rockbridge Alum Springs, and incidentally, rode along the out-crop of the ores of VII on the eastern slope of Brushy Mountain, he expressed much the same opinion.

The Mineral Resources and Advantages of the Country Adjacent to the James River & Kanawha Canal and the Buchanan & Clifton Forge Railway.*

BY JOHN L. CAMPBELL, PROFESSOR OF GEOLOGY AND CHEMISTRY, WASHINGTON & LEE UNIVERSITY, LEXINGTON, VA.

HON. JOHN W. JOHNSTON, President, &c:—

SIR:—In compliance with your request, I proceed to give you, in as concise a form as is consistent with clearness, the impressions made upon my mind from personal observations and other sources of information, "as to the iron and other mineral interests in the James River Valley from Clifton Forge down to below Lynchburg." This I do the more cheerfully because these impressions are of the most favorable character. My explorations have been entirely voluntary and my opinions, therefore, have been formed without reference to the interests of any individual or company, but solely in the interests of science, and of the State of Virginia.

It has not been my privilege to inspect all the valuable mines and quarries within reach of your Company's line of improvements, but I have seen enough of each of the great ore-bearing belts that lie along and are crossed by them, to enable me to give you such a view of the whole, and of each separately, as may, I hope, aid others in making more detailed examinations of special localities, and give to the public a proper appreciation of the vast stores of mineral wealth lying within reach of your line of transportation.

Individual ownerships and special localities will be mentioned only when necessary to clearness of description.

At your suggestion, I shall avail myself of extracts from published documents, where they may serve to throw light upon the subject in hand.

I also wish to say, at the out-set of this communication, that I am peculiarly indebted to the kindness and valuable co-operation of Hon. Wm. H. Ruffner, Supt. of Public Instruc-

---

*Prepared to accompany the 45th Annual Report of the James River & Kanawha Canal Co., and the 3rd Annual Report of the Buchanan & Clifton Forge Railway Co., 1879, but appearing first as an original communication to "THE VIRGINIAS."

tion of Va., in making many of the observations upon which this report is based.

Fundamental Facts.—My leading purpose is to elucidate and enforce the following two or three fundamental facts: (1) The Canal and its railway connection traverse every one of the *five great ore-bearing geological formations* of Virginia, and one of the finest limestone regions in America. (2) In these formations, or belts, we find, in great abundance and of superior quality, *every variety* of ore that is profitably worked for iron anywhere in the world, with the exception of the carbonates, like the "clay iron-stones" and "black band" ores of England, which are impure carbonates found in the coal regions. (3.) Other minerals, besides iron ores, that promise to become sources of revenue to the State as well as to the Company, abound in this valley.

Geology—The true relations and probable extent of the ores and other minerals of a region so extensive and so diversified as the James River Valley, cannot be fully appreciated without looking a little into its geological peculiarities. Viewed from such a stand-point, we find the ore-beds and limestones accompanying each other, and both conspicuous, in *five distinct formations* as many different geological ages, or epochs. These are:—

1. *The Archæan:* Which embraces numerous belts of iron ore east of the Blue Ridge and parallel thereto; each belt consisting of numerous beds, or "veins," all crossing the James at varying distances from each other, both above and below Lynchburg, and continuing to recur, in fact, to the neighborhood of Richmond.

2. *The Primordial:* The great bed of ferriferous shales and sandstones skirting the western base of the Blue Ridge from Tennessee to the Potomac; in the upper part of formation No. I. of Prof. Rogers' Apalachian series.

3. *The Hudson:* No. III. of Rogers, another and newer bed of ferriferous shales and brittle sandstones, underlying the heavy beds of hard sandstones that cap Purgatory and North mountains.

4. *The Clinton:* No. V. of Rogers, the shales and sandstones that cover much of the western slopes of Crawford's and North mountains, and constitute the upper portions of .the arch and the flanking strata on each side in the gap of Rich Patch Mountain at Clifton Forge.

5. *The Oriskany:* No. VII. of Rogers, a formation that abounds in rich ores and crops out extensively along the flanks and outliers of the ridges crossing the upper section of your railway.

Before giving a more detailed account of these several ore-bearing formations, it may be proper to remark,—1st., That the stratified rocks of this part of Virginia are rarely found in a horizontal position; but they have been arched and folded and tilted and fractured, then, subsequently, eroded, till in the Piedmont regions, and in parts of the Great Valley we see only the upturned edges of the strata; though in some parts of the Valley, and in some of the mountains west of it, occasional folds and arches of limestones and sandstones are well preserved. 2nd., The out-cropping edges and lines of folding usually run in a northeast and southwest direction, their "strike," about parallel with the general trend of the Blue Ridge, throughout the State. Their prevailing dip is towards the southeast, because, besides being folded by some powerful lateral pressure, acting from the S. E. they have been inverted until their crests turn in many places towards the N. W. In Rockbridge county the Blue Ridge is a marked exception to this prevailing inversion; there the dip is generally N. W., towards the

Valley. Along the E. margin of Botetourt county the Blue Ridge rocks, too, have been inverted. Salling's Mountain has also been inverted, but Purgatory, Crawford's and Rich Patch mountains are exceptions.

Mineral Contents of the Several Formations.—1. *The Archæan belt*, (that of the metamorphic rocks of Virginia, which have been classed as Archæan, though their relative ages have not been settled, my present opinion being that the belt in question belongs to the most recent of the Archæan rocks), is first struck by the James a few miles below Lynchburg, where the river, after cutting its way for some distance into the limestones and ores, and their imbedding shales, schists and quartzites, changes its general course towards the N. E., and, by a somewhat serpentine channel, follows the general strike of the iron-bearing rocks for many miles, to the neighborhood of Scottsville, where it resumes its S. E. course towards Richmond.

Parallel with the general course of the river, and on both sides of it, are found a number of beds of iron ores of different kinds, and several heavy ledges of limestone among the still more extensive strata of talcose, micaceous and chloritic shales and schists, and the alternating thin beds of quartzite that constitute the frame-work of most of the ridges along this portion of the river valley. This belt, with its characteristic limestones, is found traversing Virginia from the North Carolina line to the Potomac, but iron ores have not been found in it everywhere in abundance. In the N. W. part of Pittsylvania county ores are mined extensively, and from Lynchburg downward, along the margins of Amherst and Nelson counties on the north side of the river, and Campbell, Appomattox and Buckingham on the south side, numerous beds have been opened, some of which have heretofore been worked profitably and many others must become profitable under the advancing price of iron, and the increasing demand for Bessemer steel. West of this belt, especially in Amherst county, some promising beds of magnetite occur. Some are too highly charged with titanium to command any present value, but others are found of greater purity.

The valuable ores found along this belt are,—*Hematites*, in the form of specular micaceous and red ores; *Limonite* (Brown Hematite); *Magnetite*; and *a mixture* of specular and magnetic ores. The most extensive openings have been made in the specular ores. These, on account of their low percentage of phosphorus, are regarded as peculiarly adapted to the manufacture of Bessemer steel. The other varieties have also been worked to some extent and promise valuable results when they become more fully developed.

So much has heretofore been written and published about these ores, that I shall avail myself of a few extracts in relation to their extent and value. Gen. St. John and Profs. Smith and Mallet, in a communication to President Carrington, in 1875, speak thus:—"Our attention having been given to the district in question as a whole, without entering minutely into the respective advantages of individual points therein, we may say, with entire confidence, that we are satisfied of the existence of iron ore in large quantity,—quantity amply sufficient for the supply of numerous furnaces for a long period in the future. While the flattened masses, locally known as "veins," which occur conformable in dip and strike to the metamorphic rocks of the region, are found at some points to thin out and come to an end in the line of strike, they succeed each other so closely and in such number, and they attain at single localities such very large absolute dimensions, that it is safe to say,—without calculating on future developments,—that there is ore already uncovered and in outcrop, compara-

ble as to mass with the more favored localities of iron production in the United States.

"To mention one or two instances; one 'vein' with an exposure of 60 to 75 feet in width, and traceable with large, if not uniform width for two or three miles in length; one of 15 feet in width where exposed and visible for a very long distance, reliably reported as two miles; one now being worked, which at a depth of 150 feet from the surface was found to be 8 feet wide and visible, at intervals, for three miles, and probably indentifiable for five miles in length; and several other veins of 12, 10, 6 and 3 feet in width, and very considerable surface length."

Maj. Jed. Hotchkiss, in his "Summary of Virginia," p. 37, says: "Recent operations in Amherst and Nelson counties, along James River and between it and Buffalo Ridge have exposed some 25 parallel veins of iron ore, varying in width from five to sixty feet."

Col. McDonald, in his interesting and valuable report on a portion of this region, says:—"The Brown Hematites (Limonites) occur in vast quantities in the James River ore belt. They may be looked for everywhere in contact with or in the vicinity of the limestones. No special search has been made for them, the attention of explorers having been particularly directed to the discovery and development of the deposits of specular and magnetic ores, yet it is certain that in the future the brown hematites, on account of their abundance, richness in metal, and the cheapness with which they may be mined, will prove as valuable as the specular and magnetic ores with which they are so closely associated."

My own views, based upon examinations made at several points in the same region, accord with what is stated in the foregoing extracts.

To exhibit, concisely, the value of the ores of this belt, I have collected a number of the most reliable analyses within my reach of the three leading classes of ores, with reference to the percentages they contain of *metallic iron and phosphorus* respectively, giving in tabular form, 1st., the number of analyses compared, 2nd., the widest range in the percentages of iron and phosphorus, and 3rd., the average percentages of iron and phosphorus.

TABLE I.

KINDS OF ORE.	NO. OF SAMPLES.	RANGE OF PERCENTAGE OF IRON.	RANGE OF PERCENTAGE OF PHOSPHORUS.	AVERAGE PER CENT OF IRON.	Average Per Cent of Phos.
Hematite (specular)	15	30.80 to 68.34	0.01 to 0.24	51.10	0.09
Magnetite	12	53.00 to 60.42	0.01 to 0.31	42.06	0.11
Limonite	7	43.60 to 56.80	0.27 to 0.97	48.83	0.62

I have very recently analysed a sample of the specular ore of this region that yielded 66.57 per cent. of iron, with a mere trace of phosphorus.

The table shows that the magnetites are richest in iron and have the least phosphorus compared with the quantity of iron they yield, but they are sometimes injured by the presence of too much *titanium*, as is the case with some of the ores between Lynchburg and the Blue Ridge. The limonites have much the largest percentage of phosphorus, but a remedy for this will be referred to further on.

Before leaving this belt it may be well to state that some promising developments of *manganese* ore have been brought to light. I have recently analyzed a specimen from Nelson county that gave 80.78 per cent. peroxide of manganese. This is unusually rich,—perhaps a choice specimen. I have not seen the mine, but the ore is said to be abundant. Another sample, from an open vein near Mount Athos, below Lynch-

burg, gave 68.90 per cent. of peroxide; while one from a mine now open, in Campbell county, gave 67.78 per cent.,—by avoiding some small particles of silica, the same sample gave 71.42 per cent. of peroxide of manganese.

2. *The Primordial* (No. I of Prof. Rogers):—As we ascend the James to the margin of the Great Valley we find the second great iron-bearing formation, lying along the western base of the Blue Ridge and appearing first near the junction of the James and North rivers. Geologically this belt is coextensive with the Blue Ridge. Its value within the limits of Virginia (for it runs far beyond our lines) is illustrated by the fact that from it the great Shenandoah Iron Works of Page county are fed, and from it the old Mt. Torrey Furnace of Augusta, the Cotopaxi, Vesuvius, Buena Vista and Glenwood furnaces of Rockbridge, and the Arcadia and Cloverdale furnaces of Botetourt, obtained their ores.

The great bodies of ore in this belt are Limonites, though some promising beds of Hematite (Red) have been found on the Glenwood estate, in Arnold's Valley, and on the Boyd estate adjoining it, but higher up James river. This formation in the portions in Rockbridge and Botetourt contiguous to the canal, is not limited to the base of the main Blue Ridge chain, but also gives indications of ore on Salling's Mountain and its prolongation beyond the James. This broken line of outliers of the Blue Ridge is of the same geological age and structure as the northwestern ridge, or line of ridges and peaks, of the main chain; and, therefore, might be supposed to contain the same kinds of minerals. There are indications of uplifts and folds in Arnold's Valley, lying between the prolongation of the Salling's range and the main mountain, where the ores have been brought to the surface in close proximity to, and sometimes even stratified with the Valley limestones, and where they have been mined for many years.

This ore-belt is of such interest to both branches of the canal as to be worthy of a somewhat detailed examination, especially as from it are made the *neutral irons* that always command a higher price than any others. Beginning then with the portion N. E. of the Balcony Falls, or James river pass, we find, within the first two miles, extensive openings along the western slope of the mountain, from which thousands of tons of limonite ores have been mined and shipped to other points to be smelted. These beds are far from being exhausted, while there are favorable indications, at points further along the mountain, where equally productive mines may yet be opened. Near the old Buena Vista Furnace, a few miles further along the mountain, the ores of this belt were worked, extensively and profitably, in former years. This place is convenient for shipment on the North River branch of the canal. These points are mentioned as illustrations of what may be anticipated from this region whenever there is a demand for such ores, as there must be before long. The other branch of the canal traverses another extensive division of this Primordial belt lying between Buchanan and Balcony Falls. Glenwood Furnace, in Arnold's Valley, S. W. of James River, has been run, with occasional interruptions, since 1849—probably, altogether, 25 years; yet there is no evidence of exhaustion in the beds from which it has been supplied. There are, moreover, indications, at a number of points in the same neighborhood, of rich and extensive beds as yet unopened. Between this point and Balcony Falls I have seen some favorable indications of excellent ores close to the base of the mountain.

The Arcadia Furnace, on Jennings' Creek, between the James and the mountain, belonging to what is known as the "Boyd Estate," obtained its ores from this same range and its

branches that run off to some extent from the main mountain. In this vicinity, as well as high up in Arnold's Valley, there are said to be promising beds of specular ore.

Extract from Mr. Bemelman's report on the Boyd property:—"A simple inspection of the Boyd estate, combined with the actual results of workings in the neighborhood, and the analyses and tests I have made, convince me that this property contains immense amounts of iron ore of very superior quality; as to quantity, it is so great as to make it impossible to give anything like an approximate estimate, &c., &c." Ten of Mr. Bemelman's analyses are reported to have yielded the following percentages of iron: 29.1, 35.0, 40.0, 42.5, 42.5, 41.6, 47.5, 47.7, 50.0 and 52.0. These were limonite ores. He also pronounces the specular ore of this region rich in iron.

Mr. Lewellin, of Pottsville, Pa., an expert in iron ores, who examined this estate, says: "There are several veins or dips of specular ores on this property varying in thickness from 20 inches to 4 feet, and extending the whole length of the property."

From what I have seen personally and learned through others of these beds of specular ore, and from their geological position with respect to the Blue Ridge, I feel very confident that they extend into the Glenwood property on the one side, and into the Cloverdale property on the other. The position of the beds here is, in reference to the rocks of the main mountain, analogous to to that of a bed of specular ore opened and formerly worked, and where mining has again begun, near the western end of the Blue Ridge Tunnel, on the C. & O. R'y. An analysis of that ore, furnished me by Maj. Hotchkiss, gave of iron 41.41 per cent., and of phosphorus only 0.07 per cent. Analyses of the Boyd ores, made since Lewellin reported, are said to have given from 45 to 55 per cent. of iron. If they prove to be as low in phosphorus as that from the Blue Ridge Tunnel, there is every reason to anticipate from them a fine quality of steel. Extensive outcrops of the same ore are said to occur near the line between Rockbridge and Augusta counties. This ore is said to be of superior quality.

The iron obtained from all the points mentioned above stood well in the market for the manufacture of both castings and bar-iron. It is also worthy of note that on both the Glenwood and the Boyd properties there are still extensive areas of the original forests, making this a favorable region for the manufacture of *charcoal iron*, which is always in demand.

So far as I know very few careful analyses of the ores in this region, except those just mentioned, have been made; but by collating what have been made at various points along this belt we can form a very fair estimate of the average character of the whole. For they were all deposited in the shales and sandstones (chiefly in the upper shales) during the same period of geological history, and therefore under analogous circumstances. Of course there were local variations that gave rise to considerable variations in the quality of the ores, as well as in their physical conditions.

From a comparison of seven analyses I find the *range* in percentages of metallic iron to be from 40.62 to 55.84; and of phosphorus from 0.06 to 0.58. The *average* percentages are of iron 50.78, of phosphorus 0.35.*

The phosphorus here, as in most of the limonite ores, has a tendency to cause what is known as "cold shortness" in the iron; but much of the iron from this region has not been found to be "cold short" to any injurious extent; but is rather

*I am indebted to Maj. Jed. Hotchkiss, Consulting Engineer, of Staunton, Va., for the use of a very valuable table compiled by him and giving " Analyses of Virginia Iron Ores West of the Blue Ridge." Except for No. III (Hudson Epoch). I have made free use of this table, in compiling the results given here and elsewhere.

noted for its toughness,—being in demand for making wire.

The Lower Silurian limestones (No. II Rogers) that overlie, geologically, the sandstone and shales of the formation we have just been reviewing, and constitute the chief surface rocks of the Great Valley, contain some deposits of ore that have been profitably worked, but these have generally proved to be limited and uncertain as to their extent. I shall therefore pass them without further notice, as no beds of much promise have been discovered within reach of the canal.

3. *The Hudson Epoch*, No. III of Prof. Rogers, is well represented in Purgatory mountain, near Buchanan. This mountain, throughout the greater part of its length, is a pile of synclinal *troughs* standing one within another; the heavy limestones of the Great Valley forming the lowest visible trough; the Trenton limestones the next higher and extending up some distance on the lowest spurs of the mountain. Then above this is the bed of Hudson shales, extending high up on both sides of the ridge, containing the deposit of iron ore. On top of all these lie the heavy sandstones (Medina) of No. IV that cap the mountain. As this mountain approaches the river the trough-like structure of its strata is changed to a closed fold, which makes the rocks appear to dip steeply towards the axis of the ridge.

The beds of No. III shales, with their iron ores, crop out on both sides of Purgatory. On the eastern face we find the old openings from which the Etna and Retreat furnaces, near Buchanan, were fed many years ago. The ores here are not well exposed, but there is no reason to believe that they are not still abundant. Mr. Shultz, who lives near the end of the mountain, gave me a very fine specimen of ore which he said came from the west side of the ridge, where he reports an abundant out-crop of the same kind of ore. The specimen is almost absolutely pure limonite.

Prof. Rogers says:—"Here [on Purgatory mountain near Retreat Furnace] and for some distance towards the south the summit of the mountain presents the upper shales of III with a small and broken remnant of the lowest band of IV, and it is at the junction of the two that exist those ample beds of iron ore from which the Etna and Retreat furnaces were formerly supplied. Continuing south the sandstone resumes its place, and the dips now rapidly steepening, the massive strata of this rock (IV) are seen folding together, until at the end of the mountain, near Buchanan, they are pressed into a vertical position between enclosing buttresses of formation III, which, also, in a crushed state, is folded around the abrupt termination of the mountain.

"Of the extent of the deposits of iron ore above referred to, as also those situated under similar geological circumstances on the west and east flanks of the mountain, the most ample evidence has been procured. At the upper bank before alluded to, the whole top of the mountain appears to be composed of it, and in numerous other places near the junction of III and IV, indications of large deposits are to be met with."

Catawba Furnace, in Botetourt Co., was also supplied with ore from No. III; and the quantity at that place is represented as being very abundant and of fine quality.

Analyses of the ores of this age, from a number of points, as given by Rogers, show a range in iron from 48.97 to 55.66, with an average percentage of 51.91, for 5 samples. I have no analyses of these ores at hand that give their percentages of phosphorus; but they are said to have produced good iron.

4. *Clinton Formation*, No. V of Rogers, 5 b. c. of Dana's Manual. This formation is found extending high up on the western face of North Mountain and its prolongation, Crawford's Mountain; and is almost everywhere the repository of

an iron ore of a superior quality, but not usually very abundant in quantity. Its ores are generally characterized by a slaty structure with beds of ochery texture, and in some places beds of decidedly nodular and massive form. In many places beds are found that are very full of fossil remains, hence these are called "fossil ores;" in other localities the structure is decidedly shaly and the color a deep red, hence called "red-shale ores;" while in East Tennessee, where the formation is rich in ores, the texture is often finely granular, and the color so clear a red, that the ore has been used as a coloring substance, and therefore, popularly known as "dyestone ore." The ores are imbedded in the shales and sandstones, and are co-extensive with the geological formation in which they occur in this and adjoining States.

Contiguous to your line of railway it is well developed on the western slope of Crawford's Mountain, near the "pass" known as "Eagle Rock," or popularly as the "Rat Hole," where the river passes through a narrow gorge of the mountain. On the land of Messrs. Rule and Sheets, about half-a-mile from the river, a bank was opened a few years ago, and worked for a while to supply a furnace on the river at a lower point. This bed as now opened is about 12 feet thick and almost vertical in position. It would be easily mined, and, so far as it has been tried, the ore is said to be very valuable.

"Red-shale" and "Fossil" ores of the same geological age are mined at Clifton Forge, where they are found in the shales interstratified with the heavy beds of hard gray sandstones that constitute a large portion of the remarkable arch, or rather, succession of concentric arches, so strikingly displayed where the river passes through Rich Patch Mountain. The ores of this formation were extensively mined on the eastern slope of Rich Patch Mountain for some years, to supply the Roaring Run Furnace in Botetourt county. They are now highly valued for mixing with the more silicious ores of a higher formation, those of No. VII of Rogers, and, when their real value becomes better known, I have no doubt that they will be developed in many new localities along the faces and flanks of both North and Rich Patch mountains.

Analyses of seven samples, from different localities, give a range in percentages of iron from 38.71 to 57.12, and an average of 49.45; a range of phosphorus from 0.14 to 0.98, and an average of 0.38 for 4 samples.

5. *Oriskany Epoch*, No. VII of Rogers; or 8 of the general system. Of all the ore-bearing formations of Virginia, at any rate of those in the Apalachian system, this is the most remarkable for the quantity of limonite ore that it contains, and the facility with which it is mined.

In order to appreciate fully its extent, position and importance as a future "feeder" to your line of transportation, it becomes us to view it,—1st. topographically and geologically; 2nd. as to developments already made in it, and 3rd. as to the quality of its o   I shall illustrate these points by directing your attention to a limited area.

(I) Let us look topographically at the valley traversed by your railway connection between Clifton Forge and the pass of North or Crawford's Mountain. Take any good map of Virginia and w. find North Mountain and its prolongations, Crawford's and Caldwell's mountains, constituting a more or less continuous boundary on the S. E. side, while Rich Patch and Mill mountains, with their connections and prolongations, form the N. W. boundary. Between these two general boundary lines we have a somewhat broken and, throughout considerable portions of it, a sub-divided valley having a width varying from five to eight miles. Viewed lengthwise it may be regarded as extending from Buffalo Gap in Augusta county

entirely across portions of Rockbridge, Alleghany, Botetourt, and as high up as Newcastle in Craig county, a distance of about 70 miles. It is divided longitudinally by Black-oak Ridge in Augusta, Bratton's Mountain in Rockbridge, and Brushy Ridge, extending from near the Alum Springs to near Longdale Furnace in Alleghany, and by Anthony's Knobs, with some subordinate ridges in Botetourt and Craig counties.

Geologically it is a grand synclinal trough, except a part of what lies in Botetourt and Craig counties, rendered double throughout a very considerable part of its length by having portions of its bottom thrust upward by the several subordinate ridges named above. We may regard the bottom layer of this trough as consisting of the heavy sandstones appearing at Eagle Rock on the one side, and Clifton Forge on the other. Next to the sandstones lie the ferriferous red-shales of No. V, cropping out on both margins. Then, overlying these, come the very fossiliferous bed of Helderberg limestone, No. VI of Rogers, that is found cropping out at Clifton Forge, and at numerous places along both sides of the valley in the portion N. E. of James river, but limited to the middle portions and the west side in Botetourt and Craig, for geological reasons that I cannot stop to give. This limestone is a very important feature of this valley as we shall learn hereafter. Immediately over the limestone, and co-extensive with it, is found the formation, No. VII, so rich in iron ores. On top of this lie the vast masses of dark shales, Devonian, or No. VIII, that have been sculptured by the erosive action of water and frost into rounded and peaked ridges of almost every size, and found in every part of the region in question. From these shales flow the waters of the Variety, the Rockbridge and Jordan Alum, Dibrell's and other springs.

The ridges that have been thrust up from the bottom of our great trough-like valley are very important features; for they have lifted up and brought to view extensive beds of both ore and limestone for the use of furnaces; as, for example, at Longdale and California furnaces, both supplied from the same up-lift, Brushy Ridge.

To illustrate the resources of this formation it is only necessary to enumerate the principal furnaces that are now, or have been supplied from its beds of ore. Beginning at the Augusta end we have, in that county, Buffalo Gap, Ferrol (Elizabeth), and Esteline furnaces; Bath and California, in Rockbridge; Australia and Longdale in Alleghany; Rebecca, Callie, Roaring Run, and Grace, in Botetourt.

Longdale and Callie furnaces have very large and still widening developments of very fine ores; and they are both within reach of such competition as your line of transportation may offer. Then along the base of Rich Patch Mountain on the Kayser lands, and at points south of Callie Furnace, as on the lands of Messrs. Woods and Reynolds, there are promising indications of ore beds not yet opened to any great extent. This belt of undeveloped beds extends along the western and middle portions of Craig county for some miles beyond Newcastle. Then, on the western slope of North Mountain, the still unexhausted beds of the old Rebecca Furnace, near Dibrell's Springs, are only awaiting transportation and cheap fuel.

It must not be inferred from what has been said that every part of this formation is iron ore; considerable portions of it consist of a coarse gray sandstone that breaks up readily when exposed, and weathers into rounded boulders of a brown color, as may be seen near Craigsville on the C. & O. R'y. Yet it is very persistent as an ore-bearing formation along the flanks and spurs of nearly all the higher sandstone ridges of this region

and is almost invariably accompanied by the contiguous lime-stones cropping out between it and the mountain. Its ore beds are often very massive; that at Longdale is about 20 feet thick, while its length and depth have not been determined. At Callio Furnace, and at the Low Moor mines on the oppo-site side of Rich Patch, the ore-bearing beds range in thick-ness from 20 to 50 foot, composed of alternating sandstones, clay and thick deposits of ore.

The S. E. flank of Rich Patch mountain, contiguous to the river, merits a more thorough exploration than it has ever received. Here the river follows the trend of the mountain for several miles, and is therefore within reach of a long line of ore beds most of which are still unopened. There are favora-ble indications in this region not only of ores of No. VII, but also of No. V, such as were so long and successfully smelted at Roaring Run Furnace.

Analyses of 20 samples of ores of No. VII give a range of metallic iron from 36.25 to 58.29, with an average of 51.12 per cent., a range of phosphorus from 0.03 to 0.96, and an average of 0.38.

Let us now tabulate all these general results of the analyses of the ores of the four belts west of the Blue Ridge:—

TABLE II.

FORMATIONS.	Range of Met-allic Iron.	Range of Phosphorus.	Average of Iron.	Average of Phosphorus.
Primal, No. I	40.62 to 55.84	0.06 to 1.08	50.87	0.35
Hudson, No. III	48.97 to 55.66	....	51.91	
Clinton, No. V	38.71 to 57.12	0.14 to 0.98	49.45	0.38
Oriskany, No. VII	36.25 to 58.29	0.03 to 0.96	51.12	0.38

These averages present no very marked differences.

The presence of phosphorus in iron, rendering it cold-short, has proved a very serious impediment to its use for making car wheels and other pieces of machinery, and in the manufacture of Bessemer steel. But only a small proportion of the iron made in this country is consumed in that way; so that iron containing a moderate percentage of phosphorus will continue to be in demand for the majority of purposes, as long as it can be produced at low cost; when it comes into requisition for the manufacture of steel, the process for *dephosphorizing* it will doubtless be in successful operation. Methods of dephos-phorizing iron in the Bessemer process have been patented, and are on trial in England and Prussia, with such results that their ultimate success seems to be only a question of time. In a paper read before the "Iron and Steel Institute" (England) by G. J. Snelus, a prominent manufacturer, we find him saying:—"In conclusion I have the pleasure to place before the meeting what I believe to be the first sample of Bessemer steel made entirely from Cleveland iron by one operation, in which the phosphorus has been reduced to a mere trace."—[Engineering, May, 1879.]

Mr. Hahan of Pittsburg, while on a visit to Prussia, writes to the *American Manufacturer:*—"In proof of the great suc-cess and of the usefulness of this invention (Krupp's), it needs only to be cited that already several of the largest iron manufacturing firms of Europe have bought license of Mr. Krupp for the use of his patent method of dephosphorizing, for which they are erecting the necessary apparatus." Other authorities might be given, but these are enough to show that partial but promising success has already been attained in this important undertaking. Chemical science will ultimately solve this difficult problem, as it has done hundreds of others not less difficult.

Mixing Ores.—The great variety of ores found in the several belts above described, and the facility with which the railway and canal will be able to transport them from one point to another, will enable manufacturers to avail them-selves of the great advantages often derived from mixing to-gether the different varieties. Silicious ores, like those of No. VII, are often improved by being mixed with the argillaceous ores of No. V. So the ores of Nos. I and III, when very pure, may be advantageously mixed with those of Nos. V and VII.—Prof. Osborn says, in his "Metallurgy of Iron," p. 422: "It thus clearly appears that no iron ore, of whatever description, is, when melted by itself, so profitable as it would be when mixed with other ores."

"In order to produce from iron ores, iron of a certain quality and at the lowest possible consumption of fuel, the earthy components of the ore must form a fusible slag at the smelting temperature of the pig-iron, and the quantity of the resulting iron must stand in a certain proportion to the produced slag, which has to protect the iron from the further influence of the blast. * * Ores, therefore, require a suitable *mixture*, namely, a mixing of rich with poor iron ores, so that the mixture con-tains a certain average amount of iron which experience has proved to be most advantageous as regards the yield and the quality of the iron; at the same time the admixture of ores which contain different earths, and assist each other in the smelting process, is aimed at." (Crookes and Rohrig).

Limestones.—Reference has already been made to the limestones found in different parts of the James River Valley. It is worth while, however, to revert to the interesting and important fact, that limestones, heretofore employed success-fully for fluxing, are found in close proximity to the ores of every one of the five important ore-bearing belts that have been described. Fuel is, therefore, the only material to be transported for any great distance in working furnaces along this line.

Many of the beds of limestone in Rockbridge and Botetourt counties produce lime of superior quality for architectural and agricultural purposes; and I can see no reason why lime manufactured here may not compete successfully in our Southern markets, with lime brought from states farther north.

The *hydraulic* lime manufactured from the lowest and oldest of our valley limestones, is so extensively known and so highly appreciated, as not to demand more than a passing notice. Its use in this and other states has fully established its character, proving it to be unsurpassed by any other for all the purposes to which hydraulic cement is applied. If the present quarries should become exhausted others can be opened when the demand for them arises.

Other Minerals.—*Manganese ore* (peroxide) was at one time mined near the Vesuvius Furnace at the base of the Blue Ridge in Rockbridge county, and shipped on the North River branch of the canal. Instead of being exhausted, I do not think the mine has ever yet been fairly opened, although hun-dreds of tons were taken from it and shipped. There are in-dications at other points along the belt of iron-bearing shales at the western base of the Blue Ridge, of the existence of beds of manganese—especially at a point not far above the mouth of North River on what is known as the Brady property. Al-though many of these may not be pure enough to be marketa-ble as manganese peroxide, they may still serve valuable purposes in the manufacture of "ferro-manganese." There are favorable indications of manganese in some of the hills that skirt the western slopes of the Blue Ridge near Buchanan, and for some distance still farther towards the southwest. I have tested some surface fragments from that region, and found them excellent as to quality. Of the quantity little is known.

White Sand has been found in very considerable quantities

at the bottom of the shales of the Primordial bed, formed by the disintegration of the underlying bed of friable sandstones. Prof. Rogers says: "This material has every quality suitable for the *manufacture of glass.*" A bed of it is exposed near Balcony Falls, between the North River and the mountain. This sand obtained from other parts of the same formation is now employed in making glass.

The Fire-clay found in the same relations, both at the base of the Blue Ridge and on the spurs of Salling's Mountain, has been regarded as promising with respect both to quality and quantity. My impression is that it has never been fairly tested; but, with the prospect of the erection of furnaces along the line of the canal, it merits a thorough trial as to its fitness for use, either alone or in mixture with other clays found near the river at lower points, in the manufacture of fire-bricks, so extensively employed in lining furnace stacks and for coke ovens.

Barytes is found in both Botetourt and Rockbridge, but additional explorations are required to determine whether or not it exists in quantities sufficient to make the mining of it profitable. Of the excellent quality of specimens now in my possession from both of these counties there can be no question.

The slate beds of Buckingham county, on account of their extent, constitute no insignificant feature of the vast mineral resources of the James River Valley. They have been largely quarried, but their limit is not yet known. The quality of this slate must always give it a high position in market; while the demand for it will increase with the growing prosperity of the country. There are also extensive lodges of outcropping slates near Balcony Falls that have been partially opened; but, while the quantity is very great, and while they give fair promise as to quality, they have not been tested sufficiently to determine fully the position they are to occupy.

Other Mineral deposits along this line would be worthy of a somewhat extended notice, if time and space permitted. Besides iron belts not specially noticed, there are the undeveloped kaolin, and the manganese and *copper ores* of Nelson and Amherst counties; the partially worked *gold mines* of Fluvanna, Buckingham and Appomattox; the great *coal-field* intersected by the James above Richmond, and the unsurpassed *granite* quarries of the same region,—all of which either are now, or bid fair to become in the future, increasing sources of revenue to the canal and to the state. But of these, for the present, this passing notice must suffice.

Conclusions.—(1.) You have within reach of your line, as I have shown, *iron ores* in at least five great belts, intersected by the railway and canal, immeasurable in quantity, of nearly every variety, and adapted to the manufacture of iron suitable for all purposes. (2.) Lying side by side with these ores you have vast beds of *limestone* suitable for fluxing, for the manufacture of lime, or for building stone; easily quarried and convenient for shipping. (3.) An important item, not heretofore brought into this discussion, is the vast amount of *water-power* afforded by the James and North rivers. Of this I need only say that between Lexington and Lynchburg the rivers have a fall of 400 feet; and from Clifton Forge to the same point, a fall of 500 feet, while on the main trunk and both branches of the canal are numerous and powerful dams that can afford water-power sufficient for almost all conceivable purposes. The same may be said of many points below Lynchburg. (4.) Here we have at hand the *material* and the *mechanical power*. All we now want, in order to utilize these to an indefinite extent, are fuel and capital. Your railway connection -when completed will certainly bring the former, to any extent that may be demanded; while I am confident that the growing de-

mand for iron and steel, and the facilities afforded here for their cheap manufacture and transportation, will cause *capital* to seek investments at numerous points, and in large amounts along this important line of improvement. (5.) *A demand for labor* of all grades, with liberal wages, is always one of the fortunate results of drawing capital into any region of country where it can be profitably invested in extensive manufacturing operations. Such must ultimately be the case here. (6.) In the sources of revenue to the State that will thus be established every citizen will have an abiding interest.

Yours, very truly,
J. L. CAMPBELL.

WASHINGTON & LEE UNIVERSITY,
Lexington, Va., Dec., 1879.

P. S.—Since the foregoing was written a new scheme has been inaugurated for the construction of a railway line all the way from Clifton Forge to Richmond, but what has been said is as applicable to a line of that sort, as to the present canal with its railway connection in process of construction.

J. L. C.

The Nutallburg Coal,

—mined by John Nutall, Nutallburg, on New River, C. O. R'y, W. Va., of which W. A. Burke, Staunton, Va., is sole agent,—that of the upper bed of No. XII, has recently been analyzed by Prof. Thomas Egleston, of the Columbia College, N. Y., School of Mines,—the sample used being a section from the entire thickness of the bed,—with the results given in No. 1 of the following table. For comparative purposes we give, from Vol. G (1878) of the Second Geological Survey of Pa., in No. 2, McCreath's

	No. 1. Nutallburg.	No. 2. Connellsville.	No. 3. Average Standard
Moisture . . .	1.35	1.26	1.50
Volatile Matter .	25.35	30.10	26.06
Fixed Carbon. .	70.67	59.61	64.75
Sulphur	0.57	0.78	1.38
Ash	2.10	8.23	6.31
Phosphorus . .	0.08	. . .	. . .

analysis of the Connellsville Coking Coal, and in No. 3 the "Average Standard" analysis of (in the words of that Report) *"the typical coals that make make the best coke."* The Pennsylvania analyses do not give the phosphorus contained in their coals,—an important omission when the coals are to be coked for iron smelting.

The portion of the Pennsylvania Report (G) relating to coke, was written by John Fulton, the General Mining Engineer of the Cambria Iron Company. In it he says,—"From the facts hitherto submitted it has been definitely settled, that certain qualities of coal are prime elements in the production of good furnace coke. The methods of coking are secondary. If the coal is unfit for making good coke, either from impurities or lack of bituminous matter, no treatment in its coking can correct these normal defects." Also,—"Any excess of volatile matter over 25 per cent. is not a necessity."

The results obtained at Longdale in using New River Coke, where "Twenty hundred weight and three-quarters of coke are consumed in making a ton of gray-forge pig iron, the furnace producing about 185 tons of iron per week"—(H. Firmstone in Vol. VII, p. 93, Trans. Am. Inst. Mining Engs.), are doubtless due to the small amount of "impurities" contained in these coals, as above, where the Nutallburg contains only about one-fourth as much *ash* as the Connellsville and 11 per cent. more carbon. The West Virginia coal belt, in which these exceptionally valuable iron-making coals abound, succeeds, on the westward, to the iron belts, so fully treated of in this number, and the two are connected by the C. & O. R'y. Beyond question here should and will be the iron-making belt of the country.

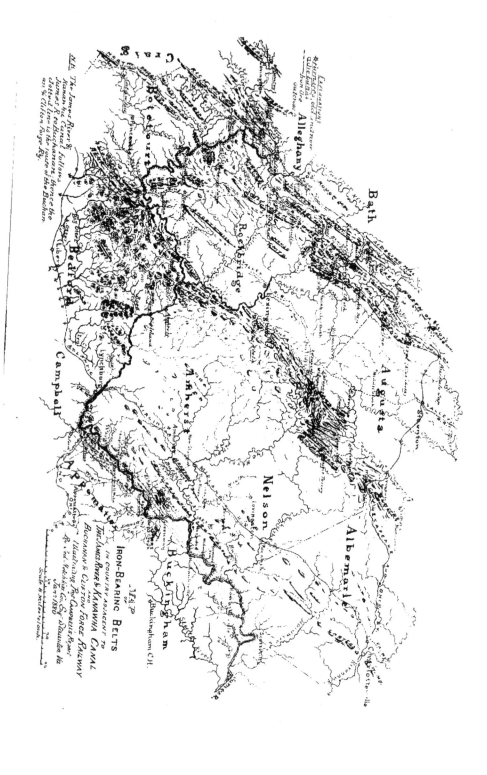

Map
of
IRON-BEARING BELTS
IN COUNTRY ADJACENT TO
THE JAMES RIVER & KANAWHA CANAL
AND
BUCHANAN & CLIFTON FORGE RAILWAY
Illustrating Rep. Pro. Campbell's Report
By A. S. Fulton Civ. Eng., Staunton Va.
Jan.? 1880

Scale 8 Miles to inch.

Explanations
*Furnaces, old & new
Quicksilver
from the
outcrops

N.B.
The James River &
Kanawha Canal follows
James R. to Buchanan, thence the
dotted line is the route of the Buchan-
an & Clifton Forge Ry.

MAP
OF
IRON ORE BELT
ON
JAMES RIVER BELOW LYNCHBURG

Illustrating the McDonald's Report

Scale 1 inch 3 Miles

GEOLOGICAL SECTION on Fork Run, Low-Moor Iron Co's Lands, Allegheny Co., Va.

By G. T. Wicks, Engr &c

Scale Feet

The Danville & New River Railroad Company, at a meeting held, Dec. 19th, 1879, decided to begin at once, the construction of its road, beginning at Danville and laying a third rail on the Piedmont Railway, the southward extension of the Richmond & Danville R. R., for several miles south and west from Danville, then grading across to Dan River, where a bridge will be erected, and thence grading to Martinsville, Henry county. The President, Major W. T. Sutherlin, was authorized to call on the city of Danville for the $50,000, and on Henry county for the $100,000, in bonds, which they had subscribed, and with the proceeds of these to begin work, as above stated, purchase an engine and "flats" and build a depot, on a lot already purchased, in Danville, thus constructing and using the road from the start.

This company was incorporated, by act of Va. Assembly, March 29th, 1873, for constructing a narrow-gauge railroad from Danville by Martinsville, in Henry county, Patrick C. H., and Hillsville, in Carroll county, to some point on the Atlantic Mississippi & Ohio Railroad "not east of Christiansburg." Its capital stock was fixed at $2,000,000, in $100 shares, which the board of directors may increase "to such an amount as may be necessary to complete the road;" they may also bond the road, to such extent as they may desire, for completing and equipping it, the bonds to bear no more than legal interest. It was allowed two years before effecting a permanent organization. It can receive lands, mines, materials, labor, etc., in payment of subscriptions to its capital stock; build lateral roads, not over 20 miles long, to connect with mines, lands, or works of any kind; and towns, cities, and counties, along its line, can subscribe to its stock. In 1877, March 20, its charter was amended, making the name of the company *The Danville & New River Railroad Company,* to construct a road to be known as the *Danville & New River Narrow-Gauge Railroad,* and giving the privilege of beginning from Danville or from some point on the Va. Midland R'y between Danville and Pittsylvania C. H., and thence as before. By act of Feb. 28th, 1878, the Governor is authorized to furnish 200 "able-bodied convicts" from the penitentiary, free of cost, except maintenance, to work on the construction of this road. By act of Jan. 22nd, 1879, it can consolidate with the Dan Valley & Yadkin River Narrow-Gauge R. R. Co., which proposes to follow the Dan into N. C. and thence across to Tenn. By act of March 31st, 1879, Henry county was authorized to levy a tax to pay its subscription to this road.

The commencement of the construction of this railway under the direction of Maj. Sutherlin is a good guarantee that it will be completed as far as the means furnished, most prudently used, will permit. It runs through one of the best agricultural districts in Virginia; the valleys of Smith's River, in Henry, and Mayo's, in Patrick, and their tributaries, which are among the best in Piedmont Virginia; Henry raised over a million pounds of tobacco in 1870, and Patrick led the State in the production of honey. The Blue Ridge counties crossed by it, Floyd and Carroll, are among the best of grazing and varied crop countries. The opening of such an inviting agricultural and grazing country to market and to an influx of population,—just the region for the north of Ireland people, and for the Scotch, suitable in climate and adaptations,—is inducement enough for the construction of this road, and Danville will find a large increase in the volume of its trade when it is completed.

This railway will make available, and therefore give value to, an important mineral region, especially if carried to a New River terminus. The *soapstone* (steatite) quarries of Henry, as in the vicinity of Spencer's Store, are of a character that can hardly be surpassed; a large trade in this, for furnace linings, domestic purposes, etc., could be easily started. The Pigg River *magnetite* belt doubtless extends along Turkey-cock Mountain and its westward prolongations. Along and in the range of Bull Mountain, partly in Henry and partly in Patrick, are the extension of the belt of fine iron ores found near Rocky Mount. Prof. Rogers (Report of 1839) remarks,—"In Patrick county a little west of Goblintown Creek and on the east side of Stewart's Knob, we find the *magnetic oxide* exposed at several places, the main deposit supplying the Union

Iron-works in the vicinity, being a bed from 3 to 6 feet wide, of a fine grained, generally black ore, sometimes having a greenish tinge from the intermixed scales of talc, and sometimes red and ochreous." Undoubtedly that western Piedmont region abounds in the best of iron ores, those most sought after, and which fact or fancy has named "Bessemer;" of forests it has an abundance, so charcoal iron can there be profitably made. In Carroll, the central county of Virginia's Blue Ridge Plateau, it will cross one of the richest mineral belts in the country, one especially abounding in iron and copper ores of various kinds, the line of road crossing more than a half dozen "leads" that appear to coincide in length with the plateau itself. Prof. R. O. Currey, of the University of E. Tenn., examined this in detail, in 1859, and gives a large amount of most valuable information concerning its resources in his rare report (which we intend to print, in full, in our next issue) He mentions a *soapstone* which in some places "constitutes immense ledges," is soft, easily worked, and soon hardens on exposure to th air; also beds of *copper-bearing "gossan"* from 8 to 250 feet wide, and "veins" of copper ore from 10 to 40 feet wide, all of unknown length and depth; and with these beds *hematite* and *magnetite* iron ores from 10 to 20 feet thick. On the borders of the Great Valley, near New River, this road will cross the immense beds of superior *iron ores, lead* and *zinc* characterizing that region.

We have been led, by the importance of the resources of the country that will be tributary to this road, to say far more about it than we intended at this time, but, in furtherance of our purpose to give full and reliable information concerning the resources of these States and the progress of their development, we shall take occasion to refer to this subject again, especially if the work so promisingly begun progresses towards completion.

The Richmond & Alleghany R. R. Co., as we learn from the *Dispatch,* at a meeting held the 22nd and 23rd. ult., in Richmond, Va., elected Gen. John C. New, of Indianapolis, Ind., formerly Treasurer of the U. S., President; H. C. Parsons, of Richmond, Va., well known from the active interest he has taken in the affairs of this road, Vice-President; and as other Directors, Cyrus H. McCormick, of Chicago, Ill., of reaper and mower fame; James R. Keene, of New York; Hon. Hugh McCulloch, of New York, formerly Secretary of the U. S. Treasury, a widely known financier; John B. Houston, President of the Pacific Mail Steamship Co., one of the strong men of New York; William Foster, Jr., of New York; George N. Bartholomew, of Hartford, Conn., President of the Charter Oak Life Insurance Co., which he has saved from bankruptcy and re-established, and who has been a successful railroad manager; Hon. James G. Blaine, of Augusta, Me., formerly Speaker of the House of Representatives; Hon. John P. Jones, of Gold Hill, Nevada; and Henry Miller, of Columbus, Ohio. It is stated that H. D. Whitcomb, formerly the chief engineer of the C. & O. R'y, during its construction, will be the consulting engineer, and that Major R. H. Temple will be offered his former position of chief engineer. Alexander and Green, of New York, will be the company's attorneys.

The re-organization of the R. & A. R. R. Co. with such a substantial board of directors indicates that active operations are intended, and lead us to hope and expect that at no distant day a railway will be in operation, at least from Richmond to Clifton Forge, either by an independent route or by way of the James River & Kanawha Canal and the Buchanan & Clifton Forge Railroad, through a consolidation of interests. There is mineral wealth enough on either route to justify the construction of a railway.

The geological section at Low Moor, which so well illustrates the conditions of relative position in which our Apalachian iron ores are found, is copied from the prospectus of that prosperous company. We know that Mr. Wickes prepared it from careful measurements. Next month a description of it will be given.

Report of a Geological and Mineral Examination of a Portion of the James River Iron Belt.*

By Col. Marshall McDonald, Professor of Geology and Mineralogy, Virginia Military Institute, Lexington, Va.

General Francis H. Smith,
Superintendent Virginia Military Institute:

General:—I respectfully transmit herewith Report of a Geological and Mineral Examination of a portion of the James River Iron Belt, undertaken by your direction and under the authority of the Virginia Military Institute.

The time that could be given the work necessarily restricted my examinations to a portion only of the belt, and I selected the section between Mount Athos and Riverville because numerous and in some cases extensive openings are found in this area, and a better opportunity for study thus presented.

I was accompanied in the examination by Mr. Donald Robertson, of Lynchburg, Va., whose thorough acquaintance with this section greatly facilitated my work and enabled me to move rapidly from point to point.

Interesting questions of speculative geology necessarily arose in the course of the examination, the discussion of which would be foreign to the object of this report, which aims to be simply practical.

The geological age of this ore-bearing series will be the subject of a subsequent paper, which, however, I do not desire to present until further investigations either affirm or disprove the unexpected conclusion to which my observations have led me.

The map which accompanies the report is constructed on the basis of the old "nine-sheet" map of the State.

The James River Belt,—Its General Features.

(a) Topographical.—The James River, in its flow from the mountains to the head of tide at Richmond, pursues a general southeast direction. At Mount Athos, about five miles east of Lynchburg, the river turns abruptly to the northeast, being deflected by the massive quartzites which carry that mountain. From this point to the mouth of Stonewall Creek, about nine miles below, the river valley is excavated in the softer slates and limestones which lie to the northwest of Mount Athos quartzites. From the mouth of Stonewall to the vicinity of Scottsville the river traverses obliquely by a series of easterly trends the iron-bearing strata. Beyond Scottsville it resumes its general southeast direction.

The valley of the James river is from 250 to 300 feet below the level of the plateau in which its channel is excavated. This plateau is intersected by numerous creeks and branches, which usually run transverse to the stratification. These and the subordinate lines of drainage have broken the surface into picturesque outlines, infinitely varied in detail, which are the visible expression of, and carefully studied, furnish the key to the geological structure.

When the more resisting quartzites enter into the stratification, they show themselves in long ridges like Mount Athos, or rounded summits like Round Top and Chestnut Mountain, which rise from 150 to 200 feet above the general level of the plateau.

(b) Geological.—The ore-bearing formation is a stratified series, limited a northwest direction by Buffalo Ridge and its extensions to the northeast. It is several miles in width, with its southeast boundary still undetermined, and extends in a northeast and southwest direction parallel to the mountains and to the stratification probably throughout the limits of the

*From a Semi-Annual Report of the Superintendent of the Virginia Military Institute, January, 1879.—Reproduced here in full, with the illustrations.

State. Whether the series is ore-bearing throughout, is a question to be determined by subsequent examinations.

In Pittsylvania county, specular and magnetic ores similar in character to those from the vicinity of Riverville are being mined and shipped to Pennsylvania, to be used in the production of Bessemer steel. These ores occur in the extension of this James River ore belt.

That portion of the ore belt subjected to personal examination is delineated in the map accompanying this report, which is a topographical and geological sketch of a segment of the belt extending from Mount Athos to Riverville.

The strata consist of alternations of quartzites, hydromica, talcose, and chlorite slates and limestones.

The principal exhibitions of specular and magnetic ores are in the quartzites and between the quartzites and the slates. These ores are evidently bedded deposits, and form an integral part of the stratified series. The distribution of the ores was mainly due to original deposition. Agencies operating subsequently may have effected some shifting and concentration, and have converted what was originally hydrated peroxides into specular and magnetic ores.

The whole of the formation is ferriferous. The chlorite slates and associated epidotes having sometimes as much as 12 per cent. of disseminated magnetic oxides. Usually the dip is nearly vertical, sometimes as low as 45°.

The vast accumulations of brown hematites and impure manganese oxides that form so conspicuous a feature of the ore belt, are not, as far as I have observed, bedded deposits. They are in proximity to and probably stand in casual relations to the numerous limestone strata which traverse the ore belt. By the percolation of surface-waters these ores have been gathered in solution from the weathered and disintegrated slates, and concentrated and precipitated in the vicinity of or in contact with the limestones. Where the chlorite slates are calciferous we have similar accumulations on the extension of their outcrops, but they are neither so persistent nor so frequent as in the vicinity of the limestones.

At frequent intervals the strata are intersected by dykes of trap which usually run in a northwest and southeast direction, and nearly at right angles to the strike of the strata. Four of these, from 100 to 200 feet in width, are located on the map. The surface out-crop of the trap weathers to rounded deposits, which are locally designated "nigger-heads," and being conspicuous surface features, where found, they furnish a ready means of locating the dykes. Two well-marked out crops of trap occur to the southwest of Chestnut Mountain, the direction of which I did not ascertain. If, as is probable, they are parallel to those already traced, they will include between them the highest portion of Chestnut Mountain, which probably owes its greater elevation to the more complete consolidation of the strata produced through the agency of the melted trap.

The extrusion of these belts of igneous rock before erosion had lowered the surface to its present level, would undoubtedly have produced a great lateral thrust, tending to crumple the prisms of strata included between two contiguous dykes. The offset in the strata at the mouth of Munday Creek and on the bench west of Captain James Dillard's, were probably produced in this way. In some cases fracture and displacement of strata, instead of simple flexure, would have been produced. My examinations have not made known the existence of any, unless the considerable offset in the quartz ledge which carries Mount Athos, has been produced in this way. There is, however, but little doubt that many displacements will be made known in the progress of mining operations. Such displacements would be approximately horizontal, and is

careful study of the surface features would generally make known the direction of the shift.

Principal Exhibitions of Specular and Magnetic Ores.

It has already been stated that the principal exhibitions of specular and magnetic ores are in the quartzites and between the quartzites and associated hydromica slates.

Examinations have made known the existence of three well defined ore belts, or *systems*, out-cropping along the railroad east of Mount Athos, which for convenience of description I have designated as follows:—(*a*). *Mount Athos System (or belt)*; (*b*). *Chestnut Mountain System (or belt)*; (*c*). *The Red Belt*.

East of the red belt there are extensive out-crops of limestone which carry on their flanks a magnificent burden of rich brown hematites; these are locally designated as,—(*d*.) *The Pot-Ore Belt*.

Fig. 3.   Section of Ore-belt at Riverville.

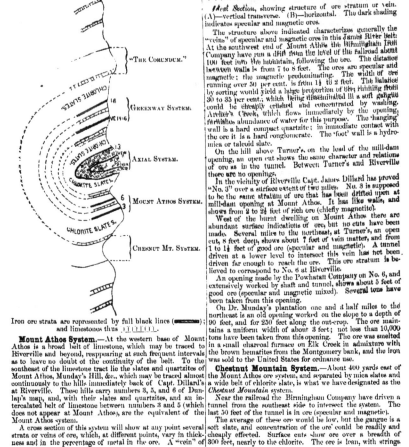

Iron ore strata are represented by full black lines (▬▬▬); and limestones thus ⊔⊔⊔⊔⊔⊔.

Mount Athos System.—At the western base of Mount Athos is a broad belt of limestone, which may be traced to Riverville and beyond, reappearing at such frequent intervals as to leave no doubt of the continuity of the belt. To the southeast of the limestone tract lie the slates and quartzites of Mount Athos, Munday's Hill, &c., which may be traced almost continuously to the hills immediately back of Capt. Dillard's at Riverville. These hills carry numbers 3, 5, and 6 of Dunlap's map, and, with their slates and quartzites, and an intercalated belt of limestone between numbers 3 and 5 (which does not appear at Mount Athos), are the equivalent of the Mount Athos system.

A cross section of this system will show at any point several strata or veins of ore, which, at different points, vary in thickness and in the percentage of metal in the ore. A "vein" of

ore, as the term is here employed, is not a single stratum of ore with undulating walls and persisting to any considerable extent in surface or in depth. Sometimes the whole width between the 'hanging' and 'foot' wall is occupied by ore; usually the stratum as a whole is made up of subordinate layers of ore shingled in with layers of talcose and micaceous slates and quartzites, carrying a greater or less percentage of ore, in the manner shown in the annexed cuts, giving horizontal and vertical sections of an ore stratum.

Ideal Section, showing structure of ore stratum or vein. (A)—vertical transverse. (B)—horizontal. The dark shading indicates specular and magnetic ores.

The structure above indicated characterizes generally the "veins" of specular and magnetic ores in this James River Belt. At the southwest end of Mount Athos the Birmingham Iron Company have run a drift from the level of the railroad about 100 feet into the mountain, following the ore. The distance between walls is from 7 to 8 feet. The ores are specular and magnetic; the magnetic predominating. The width of ore running over 50 per cent. is from 1½ to 2 feet. The balance by sorting would yield a large proportion of ore running from 30 to 35 per cent.; which being disseminated in a soft gangue could be cheaply crushed and concentrated by washing. Archer's Creek, which flows immediately by the opening, furnishes abundance of water for this purpose. The 'hanging' wall is a hard compact quartzite; in immediate contact with the ore it is a hard conglomerate. The 'foot' wall is a hydromica or talcoid slate.

On the hill above Turner's, on the lead of the mill-dam opening, an open cut shows the same character and relations of ore as in the tunnel. Between Turner's and Riverville there are no openings.

In the vicinity of Riverville Capt. James Dillard has proved "No. 3" over a surface extent of two miles. No. 3 is supposed to be the same stratum of ore that has been drifted upon at mill-dam opening at Mount Athos. It has like walls, and shows from 2 to 2½ feet of rich ore (chiefly magnetite).

West of the burnt dwelling on Mount Athos there are abundant surface indications of ore, but no cuts have been made. Several miles to the northeast, at Turner's, an open cut, 8 feet deep, shows about 7 feet of vein matter, and from 1 to 1½ feet of good ore (specular and magnetic). A tunnel driven at a lower level to intersect this vein has not been driven far enough to reach the ore. This ore stratum is believed to correspond to No. 6 at Riverville.

An opening made by the Powhatan Company on No. 6, and extensively worked by shaft and tunnel, shows about 5 feet of good ore (specular and magnetic mixed). Several tons have been taken from this opening.

On Dr. Munday's plantation one and a half miles to the northeast is an old opening worked on the slope to a depth of 90 feet, and for 250 feet along the out-crop. The ore maintains a uniform width of about 3 feet; not less than 10,000 tons have been taken from this opening. The ore was smelted in a small charcoal furnace on Elk Creek in admixture with the brown hematites from the Montgomery bank, and the iron was sold to the United States for ordnance use.

Chestnut Mountain System.—About 400 yards east of the Mount Athos ore system, and separated by mica slates and a wide belt of chlorite slate, is what we have designated as the *Chestnut Mountain* system.

Near the railroad the Birmingham Company have driven a tunnel from the southeast side to intersect the system. The last 50 feet of the tunnel is in ore (specular and magnetic).

The average of these ore would be low, but the gangue is a soft slate, and concentration of the ore could be readily and cheaply effected. Surface cuts show ore over a breadth of 300 feet, nearly to the chlorite. The ore is lean, with strings

and pockets of almost pure magnetite, assaying as high as 70 per cent. of met. iron.

Surface cuts on the side of Chestnut Mountain show about 50 feet of lean magnetic and specular ores.

In this same ore system, but west of the range above indicated, is a very rich and pure specular ore, which has been worked by the Birmingham Company, by a slope shaft, to a depth of 90 feet. A section at bottom of shaft shows 18 inches to 2 feet of rich specular ore, 6 feet of lean ore, and on the 'foot' wall a seam of very rich crystalized pyrolusite several inches in thickness.

At Whitehead's, 6 miles northeast of railroad, an open cut on this system shows two strata of ore, each from 10 to 15 feet in width, which will probably average 30 per cent. of metal.

From the mouth of Stonewall Creek the Chestnut Mountain ore belt is lost in the river valley. It will probably show in the hills on Capt. Jones' plantation, though I was not able to ascertain the fact by personal examination.

At Dr. Megginson's, 15 miles northeast of railroad, and on the west side of the river, two cuts have been made to a depth of 30 feet on the eastern and western margins of this ore belt. The western cut is in hard ore, which will run from 30 to 40 per cent. of metal. In the eastern cut, the ore is a peculiar soft ore of micaceous structure and soapy feel, and will not average over 30 per cent. of metal. The space of 180 feet between these two cuts presents everywhere abundant surface indications of ore. These ores have been traced by surface indications 1½ miles further to northeast.

The Red Belt--Lying about 500 feet to the southeast of the Chestnut Mountain ore belt, and separated by an intervening tract of slates, is what has been designated as the red belt. Near the railroad the Birmingham Company have searched for the ore with open cuts and shafts, but without satisfactory results.

On Joshua Creek, 3 miles to the northeast, a series of transverse open cuts show ore over a breadth of over 400 feet. The ores are red and brown hematites, curiously commingled and shading into each other. The red hematites are true *iron schists*. Whether the brown hematites represent portions of the original sediment, unaltered by metamorphic agencies, or are subsequent accumulations by infiltration, I have not been able to decide. The fact that they are richer in iron, and usually contain more phosphorus, would sustain the latter view.

About one mile further to the northeast, in the lead of the red belt, is an old open cut, from which vast quantities of ore were taken for the supply of Stonewall Furnace. A shaft a little to the east of this open cut, sunk by the Birmingham Company, to a depth of 20 feet, is in compact, solid ore of first-rate quality.

Further to the northeast, I know of no openings on the red belt.

Pot-ore Belt.—A few hundred feet to the southeast of the belt, we have two extensive limestone formations carrying a burden of brown hematite and impure manganese oxides. These constitute the *pot-ore belt*.

Wherever local conditions were favorable, we have, in connection with the limestones, vast accumulations of the brown hematites.

The ores to supply furnaces, long ago out of blast, were drawn from this belt. The magnificent deposit of hematites, 10 miles to the northeast, known as the Nutall openings, are believed to be in this belt, but the opinion has not been verified by personal examination.

Still further to the east there are abundant surface indications of ore, both specular and magnetic, but no openings have been made, and my examinations did not extend east of the pot-ore belt.

A section of the iron-bearing series at Riverville (see Figure 3), shows abundant indications of ore west of the Mount Athos system. Extensive workings by open cuts, shafts and tunnels have been carried on at different times, and considerable amounts of ore carried away for smelting. The principal openings have been made on veins 10½, 11 and 16 of Dunlap's map, (and so designated in section 1, figure 3.)

Vein No. 10½ has been worked at a single point, by shaft, to a depth of over 100 feet. The walls are vertical—the width

of ore from 9 to 10 feet. Several thousand tons were taken from this opening and smelted in Westham Furnace, the ore averaging from 40 to 45 per cent. of metal.

Vein No. 11 has been worked on the slope at various points over a distance of three-quarters of a mile and to a depth of 100 feet. The stratum of ore varies in width from 2 to 10 feet. The percentage of metal in the ore varies 40 to 55 per cent.

Veins Nos. 10½ and 11 I have classed together as the AXIAL SYSTEM, for reasons subsequently stated.

Vein No. 16.—To the west of the axial system, and separated from it by several hundred feet of chlorite slates and 150 feet of limestone, we have the quartzites and slates that carry No. 16. The only working upon this is at Greenway, 7 miles northeast of Riverville, yet open cuts and surface indications show continuity to Riverville and further to the southwest.

At Greenway a shaft 80 feet deep has been sunk upon the ore, and several thousand tons raised and shipped to Westham Furnace. The ore is principally soft specular, and assays very high, showing great richness and purity. The stratum runs from 2 to 5 feet in width.

The Brown Hematites occur in vast quantities in the James River ore-belt. They may be looked for everywhere, in contact with or in the vicinity of the limestones. No special search has been made for them, the attention of explorers having been particularly directed to the discovery and development of the deposits of specular and magnetic ores, yet, it is certain that in the future the brown hematites, on account of their abundance, richness in metal, and the cheapness with which they may be mined, will prove as valuable as the specular and magnetic ores with which they are so closely associated.

The Limestones of the Ore-belt constitute one of its most remarkable features. On a section of the ore-belt through Riverville there are ten well-defined belts of limestone, with an aggregate thickness of over 1,200 feet. Usually the limestones are plainly crystalline, and in no instance have I found any indication of fossils, though evidences of them were carefully sought for. Most of the limestones are magnesian; some contain a very small percentage of magnesia, and have been largely used as a flux in the old furnaces once in profitable operation through this section.

In their extension to the southwest, some of the lime-belts maintain their character to the railroad and beyond; others pass by degrees into talcoid or hydro-mica slates; the slates of this character intercalated between the Mount Athos quartzites being the representatives of the limestone at Riverville between Nos. 3 and 6 of Dunlap's map.

The Ore-belt as a whole being a series of folded strata, it is a matter of great practical as well as scientific interest to determine the axis of the fold or folds. There is the following evidence of a synclinal axis in the quartzites between Nos. 10½ and 11, in what I have designated as the axial system. On No. 10½, a shaft sunk to a depth of over 100 feet shows the ore stratum to have vertical walls. Nearly in the same transverse section, a slope shaft on No. 11, to the depth of 100 feet, shows the ore stratum dipping uniformly to the southeast, at an angle of 75° or 80°. At the bottom of the shafts, No. 10½ and 11 are about 70 yards apart, and at no very great depth below their planes would intersect if continued. To the southwest the surface indications of Nos. 10½ and 11 disappear, and the bounding tracts of chlorite slate unite. I have concluded, therefore, that there is a synclinal axis between Nos. 10½ and 11 which rises to the southwest.

If this be true, we should find on the northwest and southeast sides of this line the same alternations of strata in inverse order. This seems to be the case as far as my observations have extended, nor have I found a single fact to invalidate this conclusion. On either side of the axis we have five limestone strata, each upon the one side, having its equivalent upon the other and having like relations to the adjacent strata.

The Greenway system would be the northwestern outcrop of the Mount Athos system. The western equivalent of the Chestnut Mountain system would be found in the range of hills formed of very hard quartzites, locally termed 'corundum.' My examinations did not extend beyond this range to the northwest.

The ore-belt as a whole seems to be a closely-pressed syn clinal fold, the axis of which lies between Nos. 10½ and 11, and rises to the southwest. The strata consist of alternations of chlorite and talcoid or hydro-mica slates, quartzites, limestones and graphitose shales and slates.

Whilst compounds of iron are conspicuous elements in the whole series, there are at least three well defined horizons of ore, at which the accumulation of iron sediments was in such large proportion to other materials as to constitute true iron strata, which are essentially continuous over considerable areas, though necessarily varying from point to point, with local conditions, in the richness and thickness of the ore accumulations.

The six ore systems designated on the accompanying map are the upturned and eroded outcrops of these three ore strata.

Whether denudation has made known to us the richest areas of ore accumulation, or whether they lie deep down towards the centre of the basin, is a question of the future, to be solved only by shaft, and tunnel, and drift.

Conclusions.—It is believed, however, that the data here presented are sufficient to justify the following conclusions:

1st. That the amount of ore above the water level is vast enough to furnish the materials for the most extensive mining and metallurgical industries.

2d. That the exceptional purity of the ores and the great variety that may be brought together in the same furnace insure the production of iron of the best quality, such as will command the highest price in the market.

3d. that these ores, though of only moderate richness in the aggregate, occur under such favorable conditions for mining that the cost of ore to produce a ton of pig will be reduced to a minimum.

4th. That the whole body of ores is accessible, by short routes and descending grades, to water transportation, which leads directly by the furnace sites; consequently the cost of transportation of ores from the bank to the furnace, usually a very considerable element in the cost of production, is here reduced to a minimum.

When we further consider that the rich alluvial bottoms of the James River lie largely in this ore-belt, and that the upland soils, though now wasted and abandoned, are naturally good, and under a rational system of agriculture can undoubtedly be brought to the highest condition of fertility, it would seem as if nature had brought together every requisite to maintain a dense population under such favorable conditions, as not only to invite, but to coerce development.

The James, as if conscious of the future, at Mount Athos turns aside from its direct course to the sea to offer its vast energies to the work of development. For thirty miles it rolls its rapid tide by furnace and ore bank,—a willing servant waiting to be harnessed to work worthy of its powers. Though now condemned to ignoble tasks, the time will come when it will supply the motive power to a hundred prosperous industries.

Fuel.—The single element needed to unite in the James River iron-belt all the most favorable conditions for the establishment of vast mining, smelting, and manufacturing industries is *a cheap mineral fuel.*

When the cokes and coals of the Kanawha valley can be laid down at the furnaces at the low prices possible, then this valley of the James is destined to enter upon a career of prosperous development which we can now but faintly imagine.

Access to the coal must be *cheap, prompt and certain.* No extensive enterprises can afford to rest upon the painfully slow and precarious transportation of the canal. A railroad down the valley of the James River, from Clifton Forge to Richmond, is necessary to link the coals of West Virginia in prosperous union with the ores of this rich mineral section. The construction of this road should enlist the urgent, earnest and persistent efforts of all who are interested in the development of the valley of the James.

Until the facilities of travel and transportation which would be thus afforded are secured, the fine agricultural lands of this section will go unsought, its varied and valuable mineral resources will lie dormant, and its magnificent water powers will run idle to the sea.

Respectfully submitted,

M. McDonald,

Virginia Military Institute, } *Professor Geology, V. M. I.*
Jan. 6th, 1879

The Coal and Coke Movement over the Chesapeake & Ohio Railway, from the New River and Kanawha mines, of 1878, kindly compiled for us, from the books of the R'y Co., by its fuel agent, Mr. Charles M. Gibson, in 2240 lbs. tons, is as follows:

Year.	Coals.		Coke.	Total.
	Cannel.	Splint & Bit's.		
1879.	27,430	335,093	19,748	382,271
1878.	46,076	265,577	17,212	328,865
Increase.		69,516	2,536	53,406
Decrease.	18,646			

This shows an increase in 1879, over 1878, of over 20 per cent in the movement of splint and bituminous, of over 14 in that coke, and of over 16 in the total movement. The decrease in movement of cannel was over 40 per cent.

The Coke Supply from the New River mines is now totally inadequate to the demand, and the matter will be worse when the large furnaces, now in course of construction, are completed that expect to be supplied with that superior iron-workers' fuel. The number of ovens in that region, on the C. & O. R'y, is, taking the mines in order, from east to west, 100 at Quinnimont, 20 of them now constructing; 60 at Fire Creek, 30 of them new; 50 at Sewell, 10 new; 40 at Nutallburg, 20 new; and 6 at Hawk's Nest; or 256 in all. The output from these ovens will not be more than from 60,000 to 70,000 tons a year, while a ready market can be found for ten times that quantity,—especially when the facts are known that in 100 tons of Connellsville coke there must be nearly 13 tons of ashes, while in 100 of New River there will be but about 3. One may well wonder why the coke makers of the country do not all go to the New River region.

Mr. R. N. Pool, of Philadelphia, Pa., deserves well of both Virginia and West Virginia for the efforts he has made to introduce capital, enterprise, and skill to the development of their mineral resources, and to be congratulated for the success that has already crowned these labors. On the line of the Chesapeake & Ohio Railway, through his instrumentality, the *Davidia Iron Mines* have been opened in the superior red (specular) and brown hematite ores at the western end of the Blue Ridge Tunnel, 123 miles from Richmond, where over 50 men are now mining, under George B. Strauch, from Pottsville, Pa., as Mining Engineer,—The *Pennsylvania & Virginia Iron & Coal Co.,* (Ex-Gov. Hartranft, of Pa., President, and Maj. James F. Lewis, late of Amenia, N. Y., General Manager), has been organized and has purchased the Ferrol Furnace and its 7,000 acres of iron lands, in Augusta Co., Va., and the Quinnimont Furnace and its 7,000 acres of land in the New River Coal-fields, where iron mining and smelting and coal mining and coking are now done on a large scale,—and has organized the *Central Iron Company* which will revive the Panther Gap Furnace. Mr. Pool has also formed the James River Steel Manufacturing and Mining Company that has purchased the Iron Works above Lynchburg which are to be speedily converted into Steel Works. He has other schemes well under way, backed up by men of influence and means, that will result in large developments in other portions of the iron- and coal-fields of the Virginias.

Mr. Harry G. Blackwell, the energetic Mining Engineer of the Pennsylvania Steel Co., of Steelton, Dauphin Co., Pa., has recently paid us two visits and we have had the pleasure of taking him to see the vast beds of iron ore,—one of them having an outcrop thickness of 60 ft. of ore that analyzed 51.07 of metallic iron,—in the Cambrian foot hills of the W. slope of the Blue Ridge between the old Vesuvius and Cotopaxi furnaces, and near the line of the Valley R. R. of the B. & O.

The Pigg River Mining Co., Major Robert F. Mason, Superintendent, shipped from its mines at Pittsville, in the N. W. part of Pittsylvania county, 1200 tons of iron ore in November, and the same, or more, in December, 1879. Since June, 1878, from 20,000 to 25,000 tons of ore have been sent from these mines a distance of about 375 miles, by rail, to the Pa., Steel Co., at Steelton, near Harrisburg, Pa.; that company takes all the product of these mines. The ores of the Pigg River mines are Bessemer ores, yielding, commercially, from 55 to 60 per cent. of metallic iron, with but from 0.03 to 0.07 per cent. of phosphorus and no sulphur. They are mined at a cost of $1.50 per ton and the freightage to Steelton is $3.70 per ton. They are mixed with Spanish ores and the sulphurous magnetites of N. J. in the Steelton furnaces. The Pigg River mines are on the Pittsylvania & Franklin Narrow-gauge (3 ft.) Railway, 9 miles from Narrow-gauge Junction, 40 miles beyond Lynchburg, on the Virginia Midland Railway, and 29 miles from Rocky Mount, the county seat of Franklin Co., to which this railway will be completed by Feb. 1st, 1880, and to the large deposits of Bessemer ores near that place. The standard gauge car-bodies are shifted to and from the narrow-gauge trucks, so there is but one loading done. Great credit is given Maj. Mason for the energy and skill he has shown in the opening and management of these mines, the development of which has given new life and values to a region that before had but little of either.—These Bessemer ores are from the eastern border of Piedmont and those near Franklin are within that region, confirming in a manner the opinion of the New Jersey mining engineers that our Piedmont country contains ores similar to theirs in the same belt of metamorphic rocks.

The Geological Formations Found in Virginia and West Virginia,—classified by Times, or Eras, General Groups, or Periods, and Sub-divisions, or Formations, with their equivalents in the Numbers used for designating the formations in the Va. and Pa. Annual Reports of Wm. B. and H. D. Rogers and the names they subsequently adopted for the same, and which were used in H. D. Rogers' Final Report on the Geology of Pa.,—are given in the following table, prepared by Professor William B. Rogers, in 1877, for Macfarlane's *American Geological Railway Guide,* a most excellent traveling companion, as we can certify from its use, during thousands of miles of travel, in more than a dozen states.

It is fortunate for our States that Professor William B. Rogers, who has been identified with American geology for half a century, and who, as State Geologist of Virginia (1835 to 1841), discovered the order of their rocks, and determined their general geology for all time, has thus given us a table of *Virginia geological equivalents,* leaving no doubt as to what meaning to attach to the terms used by the famous Rogers brothers in their geological writings.

In 1876, Professor Wm. B. Rogers kindly examined the proofs of the Geological chapter in *Hotchkiss' Summary of Virginia* and approved of the statements and equivalents of that work; he also, with great labor and care, solely for the love he bore Virginia and science, delineated the geology of Virginia and West Virginia upon the Geological Map accompanying that work, giving to the world the first geological map of these States ever made based on actual surveys, presenting to us graphically, in his old age, the wonderful results of the labors of his early days in the then unknown fields of Virginia as well as of American geology. This map, though small in scale, is remarkably accurate in its outlining of great geological features; with that and this table of equivalents in hand any one may become familiar with the general geology of these

States, and especially so when he has also in hand the geological sections in *Hotchkiss' Physiography of Virginia,* now in course of publication, prepared by Professors Rogers, Campbell, and Lesley, Dr. Ruffner and others.

We advise our readers to keep this table for future reference, for they will often need it if they would read understandingly.

Table ... ne Geological Formations Found in Va. and W. Va.

BY PROF. WILLIAM B. ROGERS.

GENERAL GROUPS	SUB-DIVISIONS IN VIRGINIA AND WEST VIRGINIA.	Numbers marking the Palæozoic Formations of Va. and Pa.	Names adopted by H. D. and W. B. R. for the Palæozoic Formations of Pennsylvania and Virginia and used in H. D Rogers' Final Report of the Geology of Pennsylvania.
QUATERNARY.	20. Quaternary.		
TERTIARY.	19 c. Pliocene.		
	19 b. Miocene.		
	19 a. Eocene.		
UPPER AND LOWER MESOZOIC	(18 & 17)Jurasso-Cretac's. Upper Secondary s. s.		
	(17, 16.) Jurasso-Triassic. Mid. Secondary Sandstones and Coal Measures.		
UPPER CARBONIFEROUS	14 c. Upper Barren Group.	XVI.	Seral.
	14 c. Upper Coal Group.	XV.	Seral.
	14 b. Low'r Barren Group.	XIV.	Seral.
	14 b. Lower Coal Group.	XIII.	Seral.
	14 a. Great Conglomerate and Conglo. Coal Group.	XII.	Seral.
MID CARBONIFEROUS (UPPER SUB-CARB.)	13 b. Greenbrier Shales.	XI.	Umbral Shales.
	13 b. Greenbrier Limesto. (Carb. Limestone.)	XI.	Umbral Limesto.
LOWER CARBONIFEROUS (LOWER SUB-CARB.)	13 a. Montgomery Grits and Coal Measures. (Tuedian ?)	X.	Vespertine Sandstone and Coal.
DEVONIAN.	Names of N. Y. Survey chiefly 12. Catskill.	IX.	Ponent.
	11 b. Chemung.	VIII.	Vergent.
	11 a. Portage.	VIII.	Vergent.
	10 c. Genesee.	VIII.	Cadent.
	10 b. Hamilton.	VIII.	Cadent.
	10 a. Marcellus.	VIII.	Cadent.
SILURIAN.	8. Oriskany.	VII.	Meridian.
	7. Lower Helderberg.	VI.	Pre-Meridian.
	6. Salina.	V.	Scalent.
	5 c. Niagara.	V.	Scalent.
	5 b. Clinton.	V.	Surgent.
	5 a. Medina.	IV.	Levant.
SILURO-CAMBRIAN OR UPPER CAMBRIAN.	4 c. Hudson River.	III.	Matinal.
	4 b. Utica.	III.	Matinal.
	4 a. Trenton.	III.	Matinal.
MIDDLE AND LOWER CAMBRIAN.	3 c. Chazy.	II.	Auroral.[4]
	3 b. Levis.	II.	Auroral.
	3 a. Calciferous.	II.	Auroral.
	2 b. Potsdam Group.[5]	I.	Primal.[5]
ARCHÆAN.	Archæan. A, B, C, D.[6]		

"1. The term Jurasso-Cretaceous is chosen to designate the Upper Secondary sandstones of the Virginia reports and the associated sands and clays which in their prolongation, northeast through Maryland, Delaware and New Jersey, are found to underlie the Cretaceous greensand formation of those States, because the fossils found in the vicinity of Fredericksburg, &c., in Virginia, as well as near Baltimore, suggest the upper stage of the Jurassic period; while it is stated that the sands and clays of this belt in New Jersey are referable to the base of the Cretaceous. The whole group would seem in the main to be one of transition, and it is probably best comparable to the European Wealden.

"2. The name Jurasso-Triassic is preferred for the Mid-Secondary rocks of the Virginia reports, as it is thought to correspond best with the fossil indications thus far furnished by the several belts included in it. Of these, the most western area is in part continuous with the so-called Triassic belt of Maryland and Pennsylvania, and in part with the coal-bearing rocks of Dan River, North Carolina. The middle belt is in the line of prolongation of the Deep River coal rocks of North Carolina; and the eastern belt, including the Grits and Coal Measures of Chesterfield, Henrico, &c., is topographically without a counterpart. The middle and eastern belts in Virginia, and the western tract in North Carolina, show a close agreement in their fossil flora, which in many particulars has a decidedly Jurassic character, and all three belts are connected by certain species of Estheria, Caudona, &c., held in common. Collectively these beds represent most probably a group of deposits ranging through Upper Triassic and Lower Jurassic time, and are in large measure of a transitional character.

"3. In grouping the Lower Palæozoic formations, Sedgwick's classification is used, including as *Cambrian* and *Siluro-Cambrian,* all the formations from the base of the Palæozoic to the top of the Trenton period (4 c.), and as *Silurian* the succeeding formations to the top of the Oriskany (8.); these corresponding in limits to the Lower and Upper Silurian periods of the table.

"4. The Middle Cambrian, or Auroral group, occupying much of the Great Valley west of the Blue Ridge, and exposed in numerous anticlinals and faults in the mountain belt farther west, is marked by a great preponderance of Magnesian limestones in the lower two-thirds of its mass,

passing below in many cases into Arenaceous and Argillaceous lime stones, and followed above by o-olitic and by cherty and sandy beds, these latter giving place still higher to the more purely Calcareous and Argillo-Calcareous strata appertaining to the base of the Siluro-Cambrian, Trenton or Matinal group. The frequent faults, inversions and repetitions of the beds in the Great Valley, and the rarity of fossils in the Auroral rocks, have interfered with a precise demarcation of formations; but there can be little doubt, from fossil and other evidence, that they cover the period of the formations 3 a., 3 b., 3 c., assigned to them in the Table. Hence, and as indicating the formations ... ns well as at the localities, the designation 3 a. b. will be used for t. ... .ocks up to the the top of the Magnesian, without distinguishing between Calciferous and Quebec (or Levis), and 3 b. c., for the remaining strata up to the well defined base of the Siluro-Cambrian, Trenton or Matinal group, 4 a. b. and c.

"5. The Potsdam, or Primal group includes in Virginia, where complete, besides the Potsdam proper, the ferriferous shales next above, and the slates, shaly grits and conglomerates, below this formation. It is exposed in varying mass and completeness on the western slope and in the west flanking hills of the Blue Ridge throughout much of its length, often, by inversion, dipping to the southeast, in seeming conformity beneath the older rocks of the Blue Ridge, but often, also resting unconformably upon or against them. These older rocks, comprising masses referable probably to Huronian and Laurentian age, include also a group of highly altered beds, corresponding apparently to the copper-bearing or Keweenian series of northern Michigan, and perhaps to the lately described Dimetian rocks of Wales.

"6. The letters A, B, C, D, mark four rather distinct groups of Archæan rocks found in Virginia, of which the first three may probably be referred to the Laurentian, Huronian and Montalban periods respectively, and the fourth to an intermediate stage—the Norian or Upper Laurentian."

Marble.—Messrs. Saffer and Brahm, marble dealers, of New York city, the lessees of the quarries of the Coral Marble Co., near Craigsville, Augusta county, Va., on the C. & O. R'y., 22 miles west of Staunton, shipped, during last November, 22 car loads of 125 cubic feet each, of the beautiful, encrinal marble found there in abundance. These fancy marbles are now in great demand and shipments have recently been made, direct from the quarries, to Baltimore, New York, Boston, Cincinnati, Cleveland, Chicago and Milwaukee. More than 7,000 cubic feet have been sent to New York during the little more than a year that Saffer and Brahm have been working these quarries; they are preparing for an increased production, by opening new quarries, to meet the constantly increasing demand for these marbles.

The Coral Marble Company holds 1,115 acres of land through which the Chesapeake & Ohio Railway runs for over two miles, while nearly a mile of "switch," recently made, leads to the quarries. It is probable that more than one-third of this estate is under-laid by some 20 feet of thickness of the encrinal marble, the one most in demand, and by a larger area of a variety of hard, black marble.—The No VI, or Lower Helderberg rocks, of which these marbles are members, are here found in a synclinal trough, (the valley of the Little Calf-pasture River, along which the railway runs,) with an anticlinal ridge on each side. The quarrying is now done on the west side of one of these anticlines, the Brown Ridge.

It is gratifying to know that the persistent efforts and large expenditures of this company, through a number of years, are now being rewarded by an active demand for these highly ornamental marbles. It is entitled to the thanks of the Virginias for introducing to the great markets these "fancy," "furniture" marbles, for belts of these, aggregating hundreds of miles in length, outcrop along the sides of very many of the Apalachian valleys of Virginia and West Virginia, the Lower Helderberg limestone being the lime rock of this region, and large returns must come to these states, from this source, it proper efforts are made to meet the demand.—Especially are these marbles accessible to the lines of the Chesapeake & Ohio and the Baltimore & Ohio railways. We shall, in a future number of THE VIRGINIAS, call attention to other localities of these marbles and to the purposes for which they can be used.

The Old Trinity Mining Co., of New York, has lately purchased 74 acres of land in the "gold belt" of Virginia, 6 miles below Louisa C. H., for $13,000. It is understood that some $10,000 will be spent at once in the erection of machinery and development of mines. Parties working the placer beds of this region are making from $3 to $5 a day.

Manganese.—The Crimora Mining Company, Capt. W. A. Donald, of Waynesboro, Va., Superintendent, mined last year, at its mines near Turk's Gap of the Blue Ridge, Augusta county, Va., 7 miles northeast from Waynesboro, on the Chesapeake & Ohio R'y, over 2,000 tons of peroxide of manganese, averaging over 70 per cent. in purity. The out-put of these mines is now about 250 tons a month, all of which is shipped direct from Norfolk, Va., by the Reynold's line, to Liverpool, England. The ore-bearing belt here worked, in the Potsdam group of rocks, is from 75 to 100 feet wide, and mining operations have penetrated it to a depth of 75 feet. This company owns 200 acres of land. An iron-ore stratum flanks it on the east. About 50 men are employed at the mines, where a crusher, a washer, and a sawing machine, driven by steam-power, are in use. The ore is crushed, washed, and put in 1,000 pound casks at the mines, and then hauled in wagons to Waynesboro. The average cost of the ore, delivered at the railway, is about $12 per ton. The price for 1880 is fixed at $2 per ton over that of 1879.

This is one of the largest and most successful manganese mines in the country; its success, doubtless, had something to do with the recent lease of the Fauber mine, in the same relations, some 30 miles farther southwest, in Rockbridge county, by Cowley & Co., of Cleveland, Ohio, and ought to lead to the opening of many mines in the same manganiferous belts.

Zinc.—The Bertha Zinc Mining and Smelting Company, of Plymouth, Mass., of which Oliver Edes is President, Jason W. Mixter, Treasurer and General Manager, E. L. Edes, Secretary, and Thomas Jones, Superintendent of Works,—is now erecting zinc works at Martin's Station, on the Atlantic, Mississippi & Ohio R'y, Pulaski county, Va., 112 miles west of Lynchburg and 316 from Norfolk. This company began, the 5th of last November, the erection of eight zinc furnaces; two of these will be in blast by the first, and four by the middle of this month (January), and the others in a short time. The zinc ores it will use are mined on New River, below the mouth of Reed Creek, in Wythe county, 14 miles, by wagon road, from Martin's. Already a large stock of ore has been accumulated at the works, so that there will be no interruption in smelting, in consequence of bad roads, when once operations begin. New England "push," though, is not satisfied with such a long wagon haul, and a charter will be obtained from the present Legislature for a narrow-gauge railway to the mines, with the privilege of extending it up New River and into North Carolina, through one of the richest mineral regions in the world.

The Lobdell Car Co., of Wilmington, Del., has recently purchased the Panic, the Eagle, the Brown Hill, and the Walton furnaces and attached estates, in Wythe Co., Va., in the valley of Cripple Creek of New River, and near the western base of the Blue Ridge, there known as Poplar-camp, Ewing's and Iron mountains, where, owing to somewhat unusual geological conditions, the Potsdam (No. I) rocks out-crop extensively and their iron ores have a correspondingly large development. The publicity given by the *American Manufacturer and Iron World* (Nov. 28, 1879), Pittsburg, Pa., to the analyses of these ores by Mr. Anman, of the University of Virginia, probably had something to do with this purchase. He found what he calls the "black," the "red," and the "yellow" ores, of Cripple Creek, to contain, respectively,—of metallic iron 58.15, 55.54, and 47.82; of silica 1.09, 1.27, and 9.81; of alumina 2.32, 2.68, and 11.53; of water 12.96, 11.72, and 10.83; of magnesia, "a trace;" and of sulphur and phosphorus, "none." These are samples of the *neutral ores* of this iron-belt that runs for over 300 miles across the Virginias on the eastern border of the Great Valley.

The Peerless Lime Company, of Martinsburg, West Virginia, appears to have one of the purest limestones known. A recent analysis, by Otto Wuth, of Pittsburg, Pa., made its constituents—98.30 per cent. carbonate of lime, 0.75 carbonate of magnesia, 0.28 silicic acid, 0.07 alumina, 0.36 peroxide of iron, a trace of sulphate of lime, and 0.24 of organic matter. In consequence of the exceptional purity of the lime made by this company it is said to be in demand for use in all the plate-glass works of the country.

The articles in this issue of THE VIRGINIAS are somewhat "mixed," not in themselves, we beg to say, but in their relative positions. A condition of things almost unavoidable in a first number. A more orderly distribution will be in order hereafter. We are very well satisfied with our general appearance, for which we have to thank the excellent printers of *The Valley Virginian*. All the varied resources of the printer's art will be used to give an attractive form to this journal.

The Virginias.

A Mining, Industrial, and Scientific Journal:

Devoted to the Development of Virginia and West Virginia.

Vol. I, No. 2. }	Staunton, Virginia, February, 1880.	{ Price 15 Cents.

The Virginias,

PUBLISHED MONTHLY,

By JED. HOTCHKISS, - - - Editor and Proprietor,

At 346 E. Main St., Staunton, Va.

TERMS, including postage, per year, in advance, $1.50. Single numbers, 15 cents. Extra copies $10. per 100.

Advertising Rates:

One Inch, one time,	. . . . . $2.30	One Inch, six months,	. . . $ 7.50
One Inch, two months,	. . . 4.00	One Inch, nine months,	. . 10.00
One Inch, three months,	. . . 5.50	One Inch, one year,	. . . . . 12.00

Address all communications to Jed. Hotchkiss, Staunton, Va.

Entered at the Post-Office at Staunton, Va., as second-class mail matter.

For Sale at Hunter & Co.'s Book-store, Main St., Staunton, Va.

Subscribers and Advertisers will please note that our terms are, *invariably in advance*. THE VIRGINIAS will be sent only to those complying with these terms. Occasionally sample copies will be sent to persons as an invitation to become subscribers or advertisers; if such desire its continuance they will please remit the subscription price, by postal order where practicable, at once. Those applying for single numbers must enclose 15 cents, in postage stamps or money. The supplemental maps and sections accompanying the numbers of this Journal are each worth more than a year's subscription; they will always be sent to regular subscribers. Advertisers will find THE VIRGINIAS one of the very best mediums for advertising farms, mineral properties, furnaces, etc., for sale. We have superior facilities for furnishing maps and sections of and reports on mineral lands.—Our regular edition is from 2,500 to 4,000 copies; they are sent to all parts of the Union.

The Letter of Professor Egleston, on page 24 will attract the attention of every one in the country interested in the manufacture of iron or the consumption of coal or coke. He has seen some of our *stratified beds* of iron ore and made analyses of the ores,—he believes in the extent of the former and the quality of the latter. His positive statement in regard to the superior character of the New River coke, and the saving and advantages that would result from its use in the mining regions of the far west, should go far towards opening the way for a large trade in it in that direction. He is thoroughly familiar with the whole subject and has a right to speak authoritatively. The bullion producers of the Trans-Mississippi can well afford to look after a direct saving of 6 per cent. in their operations. We are much obliged for this strong letter; its publication will do good for these States, and we sincerely hope it may lead to the speedy making of the industrial survey he suggests. We shall do all we can to promote it, and to have Professor Egleston a factor in it.

E. Gybbon Spilsbury, of Philadelphia, announces a paper on "*The Iron Ore Deposits of James River, Va.,*" to be read at the February meeting of the American Institute of Mining Engineers, in New York City.

The Shenandoah Valley Railroad is now running trains regularly from Shepherdstown, West Virginia, on the Potomac, 43 miles southwest, up the Shenandoah Valley proper, across Jefferson county, W.' Va., and Clarke and part of Warren counties, Va., to Riverton at the Junction of the North and South forks of the Shenandoah, 2 miles from Front Royal, where a bridge across the Shenandoah is nearly completed. It makes close connection with the Baltimore & Ohio at Duffield's, with the Valley Branch of the Baltimore & Ohio at Charlestown, and witd the Manassas Branch of the Virginia Midland at Riverton. Track laying is proceeding rapidly up the south fork of the Shenandoah, and we are authorized to say that the cars will be running to Bentonville, Warren Co., some 10 miles southwest of Front Royal, during this month, and from Hagerstown, Md., where it starts from the Cumberland Valley Branch of the Pennsylvania R'y, to Luray, Page Co., Va., by June next. Grading is going on from Luray to the Shenandoah Iron Works, and doubtless the present year will witness the completion of this very important road to the Chesapeake & Ohio Railway, if not farther up the Valley.

This is one of the most important lines of railway that can be constructed for the development of the vast mineral wealth lying unused along the western border of the Blue Ridge, for more than 300 miles, in the Virginias. If it were now completed even to the Chesapeake & Ohio, and the mines near its line opened, it would be an easy matter to put upon its cars a half million tons of iron ore in a year and deliver it, by the same number of miles of railway, to the Pennsylvania furnaces that will this year use that quantity of foreign ore, the importation of which should be kept out, even if a heavy duty has to be imposed to do it, for, as *The Bulletin*, of Philadelphia, properly remarks,—"It is the worst possible policy in a financial sense, and the worst possible statesmanship, to buy ores or any other raw material abroad when the undeveloped resources of such States as Michigan and Virginia could supply all wants."

The March number of THE VIRGINIAS will devote a very considerable space to this great Shenandoah Valley line of railway, presenting several papers, by men of recognized standing, upon the resources of the country tributary to it, illustrating them by geological maps, sections, etc., prepared from actual surveys, at large expense, expressly for the purpose.—Every land owner, and every person in any way interested in the country traversed by this road should at once subscribe for THE VIRGINIAS and secure this important number, which, for its maps alone, will be well worth a year's subscription.

An invitation, of the 3rd instant, to the Editor of THE VIRGINIAS to address the Pittsburg Chamber of Commerce and the citizens, on the "Resources of Virginia and West Virginia," concludes:—"We can safely promise you a meeting distinguished for weight, character and influence in this community. Our people are very anxious to receive authoritative information as regards iron ore supplies, and are ready, we believe, to give substantial aid to any enterprise looking towards the opening up of the section with which you are so well acquainted."

A Map of Goochland County, Va., scale 2 miles to one inch, by John W. George, T. E., of Columbia, Fluvanna Co., Va., has been received. This is a pocket map of one of the richest mineral counties in the State. The gold-belt, the coal-basin, and the iron- asbestos- and plumbago-belts are all defined by boundaries. Goochland fronts 44 miles on the James River & Kanawha Canal; it is sure to share in the great development taking place on the James, and Mr. George's map will guide those seeking for mineral lands.

White's County and District Map of the State of West Virginia, scale 7.5 miles to one inch, pocket edition, has been sent us by the publisher, M. Wood White, of Grafton, W. Va.—This is, by far, the very best published map of this State, and any one needing a good pocket map of West Virginia, with the counties colored or uncolored, either plain or muslin backed, cannot do better than send to Mr. White for his.

James River, Va., will, by June 30, 1880, have a channel nowhere less than 200 feet wide and 10 deep, at low tide, from City Point down, says Engineer Whitcomb.

The iron ore beds, near Delaplane, on the Manassas branch of the Virginia Midland Railway, are soon to be worked by the Messrs. Douglas and associates.

Want of space has cut short our New River Coal-field article, as it has the one on the trial of W. Va. coals by the U. S. Navy. Both of these will be continued in our next.

The Coal Fields of West Virginia and Virginia in the Great Ohio, or Trans-Apalachian, Coal Basin; Illustrated by Maps and Geological Sections.

By Jed. Hotchkiss.

I propose to present, in a series of articles, to the readers of THE VIRGINIAS, all the information I can obtain in regard to the extent and commercial location of the Coal Fields of West Virginia and Virginia included in the Great Ohio, or Trans-Apalachian, Coal Basin, and the condition, character and adaptations of the numerous varieties of coal found in the many beds, existing in these States, of this, the largest known coal basin of the world; the one that contains the greatest amount of good coals, so disposed, level- and drainage-free, that they can be mined and marketed at the least cost. These papers will be illustrated by maps and sections and supplemented by original contributions and by extracts from whatever has been published concerning these fields, especially from the rare reports of Rogers, the Virginia Geologist, and from publications having a limited circulation,—collecting in these pages, for present use and criticism, what is known or conjectured about these comparatively unknown fields and opening the way for the complete geological and industrial survey, that it is to be hoped will soon be made under the patronage, either of the great corporations whose lines of railway cross these fields, of the States in which they lie, or, best of all, of the General Government as part of a comprehensive survey of the entire Union.

The Great Ohio Coal Basin, as a whole, is outlined on the accompanying map (No. 1), compiled from the latest surveys of the States in which it is included. It extends, in a northeast-southwest direction, parallel with the trend of the Atlantic Highlands, 750 miles from near the southern boundary of New York to near the middle of Alabama, varying in breadth, at right angles to its length, from 25 miles, in Tennessee, where narrowest, to about 200 across parts of Maryland, West Virginia, Pennsylvania and Ohio, where widest.

This is generally spoken of as the *Apalachian Coal Field,* a topographical name applied in defiance of topography, especially when the geological element of the topography is considered. If it is to be named from its relations to the Atlantic Highlands it must be called *Trans-Apalachian,* for, as a whole, it lies far beyond the Apalachian axis of elevation, far out on its westward slope, occupying a large portion of the region that is properly called The Trans-Apalachian Plateau. An inspection of the map will show that very nearly all of this great coal-bearing territory is drained by the waters of the Ohio,—that it lies within the Ohio drainage-basin. The Ohio itself, with its continuation the Alleghany, flows almost centrally through its length, in a geological drainage trough, the most depressed portion of the basin, for more than 300 miles, in Pennsylvania and between Ohio and West Virginia, where both the superficial and vertical developments of the Carboniferous formation in this basin is the greatest, before it turns northwestwardly at the Chatterawha, or Big Sandy, corner of West Virginia and Kentucky. The Tennessee, the chief tributary of the Ohio, with its continuation the Clinch, in like manner, flows more than 300 miles, in Virginia, Tennessee, Georgia and Alabama, with the length and in the drainage trough, first on the east and then centrally, of the southwestern portion of this basin before it turns to the northwest. So also the Cumberland affluent of the Ohio flows for 150 miles with the length of this coal-bearing area, on its eastern side, before it turns northwestwardly.—These topograph-

ical relations and the known geological conditions that underlie them, lead me to the conclusion that the only appropriate name for this remarkable carboniferous area is the *Great Ohio Coal Basin;* a name that locates it in reference to the ways for thoroughfares for traffic opened by the stream-valleys of the Ohio system, and that suggests to the economic engineer and the coal miner that the great market for the vast stores of fuel from the Ohio-basin grown forests of ancient times here accumulated, is westward, as the Ohio itself flows.

The extent of this Great Ohio Coal Basin is stated as 59,105 square miles, in the Statistical Atlas of the U. S. (1870), of which 12,302 are assigned to Pennsylvania, 550 to Maryland, 10,000 to Ohio, 16,000 to West Virginia and Virginia, 8,983 to Kentucky, 5,100 to Tennessee, 170 to Georgia and 6,000 to Alabama. Only from one-half to two-thirds of this area, in most of these States, is properly coal-bearing, so deep and wide are the eroded stream-valleys that everywhere trench this great carboniferous plateau.

Virginia's portion of this coal basin is from 1,000 to 1,200 square miles, in which are embraced the counties of Wise and Buchanan and the northwestern borders of Lee, Scott, Russell and Tazewell,—a region favorably situated in reference to the valley of the Clinch and the ore beds of the Silurian, V and VII, of southwest Virginia, which I propose to describe hereafter as the Clinch and Powell's River coal fields.

West Virginia's part is not less than 17,000 square miles of this coal basin, according to a careful calculation I have made of its carboniferous territory as laid down by Professor William B. Rogers on the Geological Map of Virginia and West Virginia. (See *Hotchkiss' Physiography of Virginia*). According to the same eminent authority, nearly 7,000 square miles of this area, the portion northwest of the outcrop of the Pittsburg bed and between it and the Ohio, as laid down on the same map, is underlaid by the Upper Coal Measures, as shown in lighter shade on Map No. 1, a larger portion of these measures in this basin than is found in any other State. The eastern outcrop of the Kanawha Falls Sandstone, the boundary between the Lower and the Middle Coal Measures, has never been laid down on a map; but, judging from the conditions on New River, one may roughly estimate the area, along the southwestern border of the basin, occupied by the Lower Measures alone, as from 2,500 to 3,000 square miles. From these data the area of each of the coal measures in West Virginia, much larger than in any other State, may be approximately stated as follows:

1. The Lower Coal Measures, underlying 17,000 square miles.
2. The Middle Coal Measures, underlying 14,000 square miles.
3. The Upper Coal Measures, underlying 7,000 square miles.

The general geological structure of the portion of the Great Ohio Coal Basin included in West Virginia and the States bordering on the Ohio,—the Ohio Coal Basin proper, since that river itself runs in the trough of the basin,—is a synclinal one, the rocks dipping from all directions towards the Ohio, as the streams running into this southwest flowing part of that river suggest,—those from the eastward, from West Virginia and Pennsylvania, running northwest; those from the westward, from Ohio and Pennsylvania, running southwest; those from the northward, from Pennsylvania, running southwest; and those from the southward, from West Virginia and Kentucky, running northward. The "Rough Section" across this basin, No. 1 of the accompanying illustrations, shows, rudely, how the formations rest synclinally one upon another, each thinning westwardly, in crossing the basin in a northwest-southeast direction, on the general line of the Great Kanawha. A section of the same kind, made in a northwest-southeast direc-

tion, with the course of the Ohio, would present somewhat the same appearance. In other words, the Great Carboniferous formation of this basin, using a homely illustration, may be compared to three, coal- and rock-made, shallow dishes, of different sizes and enormous dimensions, placed one within the other, the bottom one, the Lower Coal Measures, resting on the many colored Greenbrier, or Umbral (No. XI) Shales, corresponding in outline and extent to the shaded area on Map No. 1; and the top one, the Upper Coal Measures, (Nos. XIV-XVI), corresponding in outline and extent to the more lightly shaded interior portion of the basin.

The topographical, or surface features of the Coal Basin are everywhere the same, differing in size, or proportion, rather than in character. The general surface, viewed from above, is that of a widely extended, westward sloping, undulating plateau, varied, in places, with ridges, the watersheds of the main streams, trending . towards the northwest, and ribbed, at right angles to the general direction of the waterflow, by other ridges, locally called mountains, made by the outcroppings of the great sand-rocks of the coal measures. Down into this general plateau-like surface the streams of the country have everywhere furrowed out for themselves channels, more or less deep, into or through the various rock and coal beds of the Carboniferous;—as in Section No. 4, on New River, which shows how that stream has trenched a channel, nearly 2,000 feet deep, down entirely through the Coal Measures and deeply into the underlying Greenbrier Shales, making its stream-valley a mere cañoned gorge, a great, natural, river and low-grade railway cut across the country.

Without a proper understanding of these topographical peculiarities of this basin, no one can realize how easily and cheaply its many coal beds can be reached and mined. Every valley is an open drift, and every coal bed can, in one place or another, be entered from daylight, above water level, and be worked, to almost any desired extent, on a moderately ascending grade, so that, in reality, all mining here can be done level- and drainage-free, and therefore at a minimum of expense.

Having taken a general view of the Great Ohio Coal Basin as a whole, and its distribution among the States in which it is embraced, I will now proceed to treat, in detail, of the several coal-fields of that basin in West Virginia and Virginia, taking them, not in any topographical order but in the order in which they have been or are being developed and utilized. The drainage-basins of the rivers divide the entire coal-bearing areas of these States into separate and well defined coal-fields which will be worked from the stream-valleys of these rivers and their branches, therefore I shall designate the several coal-fields by the names of the rivers that receive their drainage.

1. The Great Kanawha Coal-field.

The Great Kanawha Coal-field, that portion of the Ohio Carboniferous Basin drained by the Great, or Big, Kanawha River is the largest separate coal-field in West Virginia. Its length, from southeast to northwest, from the Great Carboniferous Escarpment, locally called White-oak Mountain, near the junction of New and Greenbrier rivers, to the mouth of the Kanawha, is about 110 miles. Its breadth varies from less than 10 miles at the mouth of the Kanawha, to about 120, from the head of the Valley Fork of Elk River, near the end of Rich Mountain, in Randolph, along the escarpment and outcrop of the coal, southwest, through Pocahontas, Greenbrier, Summers and Mercer, to the head of the Bluestone, in Tazewell Co., Va. Its general form is that of an equal-sided triangle, 120 miles on each side, having its corners at the heads of Elk and Bluestone and the mouth of Kanawha, as above stated. Its area is, very nearly, 6,500 square miles. The Upper Measures occupy about 1,000 square miles of the surface 'in the northwest, the Middle Measures perhaps 4,000, across the central part of the field, and the Lower some 1,500 on the southeastern border.

This field may be divided into seven different river fields;—(1) The Kanawha proper, with about 1,000 square miles, including, Cabin, Paint and other short, creek valleys;—(2) Pocatalico, from the right, with nearly 500 square miles;—(3) Coal River, from the left, with about 1,100 square miles;—(4) Elk River, from the right, with not far from 1,500 square miles;—(5) Gauley River, from the right, with about 1,500 square miles also;—(6) New River, the prolongation of the Kanawha, with from 700 to 800 square miles;—and (7) Bluestone, of New River, from the left, with about 100 square miles.—The accompanying Hydrographic map of the Kanawha within the Coal Basin shows the location and relations of these several coal-fields, since each is coterminous with the drainage basin of the river from which it is named.

The general geological structure of the Great Kanawha Coal-field is shown in that portion of the accompanying Rough Section, No. 1, east of the Ohio, for that section is the one exposed on each side of the deep gorge of New River and of the deeply trenched stream-valley of the Kanawha, the extension of New River. (Properly speaking, New River in the coal-basin is the *Middle Kanawha*, and the Kanawha as generally known, the navigable river, is the *Lower Kanawha*.) This section shows the Upper Carboniferous general group of rocks (See p. 14 of THE VIRGINIAS) in three sub-divisions; the Upper Coal Measures, including, in descending order, formations No. XVI, XV and XIV, of Rogers' Virginia formations; the Middle Coal Measures, No. XIII; and the Lower Coal Measures, No. XII, all synclinally disposed, as before explained, and resting conformably on the Middle Carboniferous group, No. XI, the Greenbrier, or Umbral, Shales and Limestones. The full lines of the section are the portions of the formations that are above the water line of New and Kanawha rivers, those that are exposed to view to one passing up or down those rivers. The broken lines show the continuation of these formations beneath the surface.

If the Virginia geological survey of 1835-1841 had been completed and its results given to the world, there is little doubt but that the names given to the North American geological formations would have been Virginian, rather than New York and Pennsylvanian, as most of them are, not only because of priority in observation but for the weightier reason, the one accepted by leading geologists as conclusive, that here nearly all the formations have their greatest development and here their typical forms are to be seen. As it is, some of the names in common use, applied where the formations are thin, not fully developed and full grown, as it were, are not applicable to these formations with their grander proportions in the Virginian States. A good illustration of this want of fitness is found in the sub-division and naming of the Carboniferous rocks,—not only a want of fitness but a failure, through ignorance, to recognize the economic importance of some of these sub-divisions, as found in the Virginias, an importance they do not have in other States, and one destined to be far-reaching in its effects, as intimated in the letter of Professor Egleston in this number of THE VIRGINIAS. I refer especially to what I call the *Lower Coal Measures*, No. XII of the Virginia survey, and 14a., of Dana's table; the one containing the remarkable New River, coking coals. Dana, following the English geologists, calls this the *Millstone Grit ;* Hunt does not sub-divide the Coal Measures ; Lesley, in the Second Geological Survey of Pennsylvania, calls it the *Pottsville Conglomerate,* and Rogers, in the First Pa. Survey, called it the *Seral Conglomerate ;* Newberry, in his table of Ohio formations, calls it simply *Conglomerate,* but in the third volume of the Geology of Ohio he calls the Jackson and other noted Hanging Rock district coals, *intra-conglomerate ;* the recent Kentucky Reports call it the *Conglomerate Series,* though recognizing the existence of valuable coal beds in it near the Virginia border; Fontaine prefers to call it the *Con-*

glomerate Series, (for reasons stated in an able paper given in this number, page 27, of THE VIRGINIAS); and Wm. B. Rogers, in the table given in No. 1 of THE VIRGINIAS, p. 14, calls it the *Great Conglomerate and Conglomerate Coal Group*. It seems to me that we arrive at a correct understanding of the position and in many respects of the character of the coals and coal-bearing rocks (those having valuable coal beds) found in the Virginias, when we classify them according to the recognized order of their ages, beginning at the latest formed, those bearing the newest or youngest coal, and going down to the oldest, as follows:

1. The *Highest Coal Measures*,—the Jurasso-Triassic coals of Midland Virginia.
2. The *Upper Coal Measures*,—the coal beds above the Black-flint Ledge.
3. The *Middle Coal Measures*,—the coal beds between the Black-flint Ledge and the Kanawha Falls Sand-rock.
4. The *Lower Coal Measures*,—the coal beds between the Kanawha Falls Sand-rock and the Greenbrier Shales.
5. The *Lowest Coal Measures*,—the coal beds of formation X, (the Montgomery Grits and Coal Measures of Rogers' table), between the Greenbrier Limestones and the Old Red (IX) Sandstones; the semi-anthracites and anthracites found in patches, in the mountains on the western side of the Great Valley, in Va., as in Augusta, Botetourt, Montgomery, Pulaski and Wythe, and in the valley of the Greenbrier and elsewhere in W. Va.

The 2nd, 3rd, and 4th are divisions of the Upper Carboniferous great group of rocks, and the 5th belongs to the Lower Carboniferous.

These are the terms I shall use in this Journal, for the reasons above given and because these measures are here boldly and sharply defined by well known geological land-marks, conforming very nearly to the great sub-divisions of the rocks of Virginia, as first recognized by William B. Rogers and as they will continue to be recognized by every well informed and clear-headed observer through all time.—The order of sequence is the best that can be adopted in making clear the relations of a series.

All of the coal measures above enumerated, except the Highest, may be passed through and seen in the course of a few hours travel over the Chesapeake & Ohio Railway; for, the passing traveler, though descending *topographically* from the time he reaches the Kanawha waters in the Alleghany tunnel, east of the White Sulphur, until the road leaves the Kanawha at Scary, 163 miles farther west, is ascending *geologically*, because the generally westward dip of the rocks is more rapid than the descent of the water line followed by the railway. Near Caldwell, 233 miles from Richmond, the many colored shales near the bottom of XI are seen in the bluff of the Greenbrier, dipping westwardly, and under these, a little farther up the river, may be seen the rocks of the Lowest Coal Measures (X, or Vespertine), with beds of coal, dipping the same way, (See Prof. Fontaine's statements, p. 28, post.), and the same could have been seen on the eastward slope of the Alleghany Mountain at the eastern end of the Lewis tunnel, but in a nearly horizontal position.

From Caldwell to Hinton, 40 miles, the railway follows the Greenbrier, and stratum after stratum of the Greenbrier Limestones and Shales (XI, or Umbral) is seen passing under the water level in going westward. Near Hinton, 272 miles from Richmond, New River is reached and its cañon, cut down through the Great Carboniferous Escarpment, (as shown in Section No. 4 and located on the maps), is entered. There the river and railway are still in XI, but hundreds of feet up the bluff on the west side of New River the bottom of XII, the Lower Coal Measures, (the Lower Conglomerate of Fontaine's section on p. 28), may be seen, and there, said to be 800 feet above the river (See p. 29), may also be seen the most eastern outcrop of some of the New River coal beds. Near Meadow Creek, 12 miles below Hinton, the Lower Coal Measures appear in the bluffs on the right, or railway side of the river, the latter, as shown on Map No. 3, having skirted the eastern side of the Escarpment to that point. At Meadow Creek the river turns more to the northwest, and thence down the river the coal measures are seen on either hand, constantly descending towards the railway level, wherever the course of

the river is northwesterly, the railway and river in the mean time ascending through the Umbral Shales (XI), until near the water-tank below Buffalo, 301 miles from Richmond, the bottom of XII is reached and the red shales of XI go under the water level, as shown in Section No. 1. There, in the Big Bend of New River, a coal bed 3.5 ft. thick outcrops 600 ft. above the railway. From near Buffalo to Kanawha Falls, 32 miles, the railway and river rise, geologically, through XII, the Lower Coal Measures, passing over in succession each bed in the 1,000 to 1,200 feet of its thickness, the coal bed that at Quinnimont is 1,200 ft. above the railway passing under its level between West Hawk's Nest and Cotton Hill, in an air-line distance of 19 miles and a railway one of 31. Just below Kanawha Falls an air-line distance of 38 miles from the eastern outcrop of No. XII, the upper stratum of XII,—No. 57 of the strata in the admirable section (No. 2) measured by Mr. Page, given in detail on page 22,—sinks under the Kanawha, the falls themselves having cut into No. 57, the Falls, or New River Cliff, Sand-rock, 50 feet or more. From Kanawha Falls to Charleston, an air-line distance of about 27 miles, 36 by the railway, the river and railway cross the thickness of the Middle Coal Measures; the Black Flint Ledge, that at the Falls is 1,320 ft. above the Kanawha, by Mr. Veazey's measurement, passes under the water level in the shoals at the mouth of Elk River, as shown in Section No. 1. From Charleston to its mouth the Kanawha flows through the Upper Coal Measures, but they do not pass entirely under the water level, as appears in the same section, No. 1.— As the section referred to indicates, portions of each coal measure group extend farther east than the points above named.

The Five Geological Sections on the accompanying Supplements, the sections of the New and the Kanawha river coal-fields, require a few words of explanation before the special treatment of those fields. No. 1, the Rough Section across the Great Ohio Coal Basin [horizontal scale 12 miles to an inch and vertical 3,000 ft. to an inch], as before explained, exhibits the general stratigraphical condition of the Upper Carboniferous rocks on the line of New and Kanawha rivers.

No. 2, the Geological Section at Hawk's Nest and vicinity [scale 200 ft. to one inch], is that of the 1,920 feet of coal-bearing rocks exposed between the bed of New River, below the Hawk's Nest Cliff and the top of Gauley Mountain above the mine of the Hawk's Nest Coal Co., a horizontal distance of less than 3 miles. It is a complete section [See page 22] of 550 feet of the upper portion, not far from one-half, of the Lower Coal Measures, the part containing the Quinnimont and Nutallburg coal beds; of the whole of the Middle Coal Measures, there 1,049 feet thick and showing outcrops of over 66 feet of coal, in 13 workable beds ranging in thickness from 2 to 11 feet; and 321 feet of the Upper Coal Measures, above the Black Flint, the coal beds of which are not exposed.— This has been constructed, as before intimated, from the details [See p. 22] of the careful measurements and observations of William N. Page, C. & M. E., the efficient engineer and manager of the Hawk's Nest Coal Company's mines on Gauley Mountain, which he has generously furnished for this paper. It is, beyond question, the most accurate section that has ever been made of the coal measures in the New and Kanawha river fields. Its character is such that it is sure to become the standard for explorations and comparison. I take great pleasure in giving publicity to such a reliable and accurate exhibit of the geological structure of the central portion, or meeting point, of these two important coal fields, especially to such an authoritative exhibit of the location, number and thickness, by actual measurements, of the coal beds of this central and most available coal-producing part of all the Great Ohio Coal Basin. It is to be hoped, in the interests of science and development, that the other mining engineers working in Virginian fields will imitate Mr. Page's example and make like careful measurements of the rocks and their character and contents, each in his own locality, and furnish them for publication in THE VIRGINIAS, so that the data may soon be in hand for reliable, extended sections.

No. 3, a Section of the Coal Seams on Hughes Creek, nearly opposite Paint Creek station of the C. & O. R'y and midway between Kanawha Falls and Charleston. Its scale is 200 feet to an inch. It gives the thickness of the coal beds in the 1,050 ft. of section there exposed above water level, about 350 of it belonging to the Upper and 700 to the Middle measures. Of the letters given with the thickness of the coal beds, B. is for bituminous, S. for splint, C. for cannel and B. S. for black splint coal. It is from leveling and measurements by O. A. Veazey, C. E., of Paint Creek.

No. 4, is a Geological Section showing the strata as exposed on opposite sides of New River below Quinnimont. It shows the upper portion of the Greenbrier Shales [XI], and all of the Lower Coal Measures [XII]. This is from a section made by S. F.

Morris, C. & M. E., of Quinnimont, and is, essentially, the section described in detail by Prof. Fontaine on page 28.

No. 5, scale 200 ft. to one inch, is the section from the bed of Laurel Creek, at Quinnimont, to the top of War Ridge, as measured, barometrically, and observed by J. H. Bramwell, formerly the manager of the furnace and mines at that place. The section is a valuable one because it gives the places of four beds of iron ore, as well as those of the coal.—The details of this will be given in the March No. of THE VIRGINIAS.

[TO BE CONTINUED.]

What is Said of "The Virginias."—From the many notices that have come to hand concerning this Journal and its first number, we select the following, and take this opportunity of thanking all that have encouraged us with kind words, as well as more substantial favors:

"THE VIRGINIAS.—We heartily welcome among the list of our exchanges the first number of a journal under the above title, which is to be devoted to "the development of the resources of the great territory embraced in the States of Virginia and West Virginia."

The need of a journal of such a character has long been felt in West Virginia. It is a private enterprise in fact, but is in the nature of an important *public* enterprise. It will serve to do, what the State has neglected, to "advertise our wares" to the world. We will never get out of the woods till this is done. In this day of business push and competition, the world will never believe we have anything unless we talk about it ourselves. The people of our State should unite in giving THE VIRGINIAS the fullest support to which it shall prove itself entitled. It should be scattered, broadcast, over the entire country.

The next number promises to be largely devoted to a description of the New River and Great Kanawha coal-field, with maps, sections, &c., illustrating the location and position of its many beds. This will present a substantial argument in favor of the railroads projected in that section."—*Register*, Wheeling, W. Va.

"THE VIRGINIAS; A Mining, Industrial and Scientific Journal, devoted to the development of Virginia and West Virginia, is the title of a monthly paper published in Staunton, Va., by Jed. Hotchkiss, editor and proprietor, the first number of which reached us. It is a handsomely printed 16-page pamphlet, and from beginning to end is full of *Virginia* and its mineral wealth. Six pages are occupied by an article entitled 'The Mineral Resources and Advantages of the Country Adjacent to the James River and Kanawha Canal and the Buchanan and Clifton Forge Railway, by John L. Campbell, Professor of Geology and Chemistry, Washington and Lee University, Lexington, Va.' Another paper, filling more than three pages is a report of a geological and mineral examination of a portion of the James River Iron Belt, by Col. Marshall McDonald, Professor of Geology and Mineralogy, Virginia Military Institute, Lexington, Va. Both of these articles are illustrated by maps and geological sections.

We heartily wish THE VIRGINIAS success in its undertaking, and that as a result of its efforts capital may be induced to develop the long neglected mineral resources of the two States. *The American Manufacturer* has done much during the past five years to bring the mineral wealth of Virginia and West Virginia to the attention of our iron masters. The latter seem now to be waking up to the necessity of their obtaining ores from these States to compete with those of Lake Superior. Within the next few years we have no doubt the Virginias will be among the foremost ore-producing, if not the foremost iron-producing States."—*American Manufacturer and Iron Age*.

"THE VIRGINIAS.—We have received from Major Jed. Hotchkiss the first number of THE VIRGINIAS, published monthly at Staunton, Virginia, by Maj. Hotchkiss, at $1.50 per year. This is a splendid number, replete with information of the great iron-belt in Old Virginia. The range of mountains in which the ores of Virginia are found, extends through this State and into Pennsylvania. Persons interested in the iron business should send for this publication. We welcome it to our exchange list. The next number will contain a detailed description of the great Kanawha Valley.—*Examiner*, Moorefield, W. Va.

"JED. HOTCHKISS is well known as a Mining Engineer of ability, not alone in Virginia, but throughout the States. He has just started a Mining, Industrial and Scientific Journal, to be devoted to the development of Virginia and West Virginia. The title is THE VIRGINIAS, published monthly at Staunton, Va., at $1.50 year. There is a renewed activity in the development of property in the States named, and as they are rich in minerals there is a grand field to work upon in a journal such as is proposed. *The Coal Trade Journal* has from time to time called attention to this section of the Union, and long since named it the future iron centre."—*The Coal Trade Journal*, New York city.

"We welcome with pleasure the first number of THE VIRGINIAS. Such journals are invaluable in directing attention to the material resources of the State. Major Hotchkiss is fitted by years of study and practical observation for the editorial management of such a paper, and we wish him abundant success in his new enterprise. Virginians should give the journal a liberal support, for in doing so they but foster and encourage their own interests. Capitalists seeking investments in Virginia or West Virginia will find in it much useful information. Send fifteen cents for a specimen copy.—*Religious Herald*, Richmond, Va.

"THE VIRGINIAS, a mining, industrial and scientific journal, devoted to the development of Virginia and West Virginia, has just been started at Staunton by Major Jed. Hotchkiss, editor and proprietor. It is a large and handsome monthly publication, furnished to subscribers at $1.50 a year. As a diffuser of information as to our internal resources and a promoter of progress and prosperity in all our material interests, THE VIRGINIAS is calculated to do much good, and we wish it great success."—*Whig*, Richmond, Va.

"THE VIRGINIAS: A Mining, Industrial and Scientific Journal, devoted to the development of Virginia and West Virginia" is the title of a new 16-page quarto, monthly, published at Staunton, Virginia, at $1.50 per year, Jed. Hotchkiss, editor, of which we have the first (January) number before us. It is filled with very valuable matter, scientific, industrial and practical. It has a rich field to cultivate, and is the only publication of the kind ever attempted in Virginia. We wish it success."—*Kanawha Gazette*, Charleston, W. Va.

"We have received THE VIRGINIAS, which, to use its own words, will be "a mining, industrial, and scientific journal, devoted to the development of Virginia and West Virginia." Maj. Jed. Hotchkiss is the editor and proprietor, and it is but just to say that this journal could not be in better hands. Maj. Hotchkiss will be assisted by able writers, and should be heartily encouraged in his efforts to draw the attention of enterprising capitalists to the undeveloped wealth of the two Virginias.—*The State*, Richmond, Va.

"The first number, which was issued last week, and dated the 1st inst., handsomely illustrated, gives earnest that it will be quite a valuable publication, and we hope that its intelligent and enterprising proprietor and editor will meet with a success in its publication, surpassing his most sanguine expectation."—*Spectator*, Staunton, Va.

"It is elegantly gotten up, a marvel of typographical neatness and brim full of valuable information respecting the above mentioned States. The subscription price is only $1.50 per year. All those interested in the development of our State and its old mother should liberally patronize the VIRGINIAS."—*Leader*, Charleston, W. Va.

"We have placed THE VIRGINIAS on our exchange list and shall, judging from the initial number, take much pleasure in watching the exchange."—Letter from *The Engineering and Mining Journal*, of New York.

"The first number is a good one; and we have little doubt that its energetic editor will make THE VIRGINIAS a popular and valuable journal.—*The Dispatch*, Richmond, Va.

The Great Kanawha River, West Virginia, has had $2,000,000 spent in its improvement by the General Government, and the Chief of Engineers now asks for $500,000 more, which should be granted without delay. The low water of the past year was very favorable for the prosecution of this important work, and with the aid now asked it can soon be completed.

The Details of the Hawk's Nest - Gauley Mountain Geological Section, as measured and observed by Mr. Wm. N. Page, C. & M. E., taken in order from the top of Gauley Mountain, 2,700' above tide, down, separating the rock beds into the Upper, Middle, and Lower Coal Measures groups, are as follows :

1. The Upper Coal Measures, in part. No. XIV.

1. Loose material,—strata unknown,	100'
2. Laminated sandstone,	100'
3. (Unknown),	121'

2. The Middle Coal Measures. No. XIII.

4. The "Black Flint," 2,379' altitude, or A. M. T.	
5. Slate,	19'
6. Coal bed, splint; alt. 2,360' (Cannelton cannel),	9'
7. (Unknown),	
8. Coal bed, gray splint; alt. 2,310' (Coalburg splint),	3'6"
9. Soft sandstones and shales,	137'
10. Coal bed, splint, cannel and bituminous; alt. 2,163'	10'
11. Shale,	27'
12. Coal bed; alt. 2,133',	3'6"
13. Sandstone,	49'4"
14. Coal bed; alt. 2,079'	4'8"
15. (Unknown),	54'
16. Massive sandstone,	80'
17. (Unknown), Traces of coal,	20'
18. Dark shales,	15'
19. Sandstone,	60'
20. Coal bed,	7'
21. Black shale,	3'
22. Sandstone,	15'
23. Shale,	7'
24. Coal bed, clean, soft bituminous; alt. 1,822'	5'
25. Shale,	8'
26. Sandstone,	50'
27. Hydraulic limestone,	2'
28. Argillaceous slate,	21'
29. Coal bed, soft bituminous; alt 1,730',	11'
(Worked by Hawk's Nest, Eagle, Faulkner, Crescent, Coal Valley, Old Virginia, Blacksburg and Cannelton Coal companies, in opinion of Mr. Page.)	
30. Slate,	3'
31. Shaly sandstone,	27'
32. Coal bed, soft bituminous; alt. 1,697',	3'
33. Gray sandstone,	20'
34. Massive sandstone,	38'
35. Shale,	2'
36. Coal bed, soft bituminous; alt. 1,635',	2'
(Eagle steam coal, 125' under gas seam.)	
37. Shale,	4'
38. Shale sandstone,	24'4"
39. Coal bed; alt. 1,605',	1'8"
40. Shale,	35'
41. Black slate, very rich in oil,	3'
42. Black marble,	2'
43. Dark shale,	10'
44. Shale,	42'
45. Shale,	10'
46. Coal bed, soft bituminous; alt. 1,500',	3'
47. Shale,	30'
48. Black slate,	18'
49. Gray sandstone shale,	20'
50. Hard shale,	10'
51. Coal bed; alt. 1,420',	2'
52. Shale,	4'
53. Argillaceous sandstone,	32'
54. Shale,	5'
55. Coal bed; alt 1,375' (Sewell seam),	4'
56. Ferruginous shale,	45'

3. The Lower Coal Measures. No. XII.

57. Massive sandstone, top ledge of the Conglomerate,	167'
(Top of ledge 1,330' in altitude.)	
58. Shale,	10'
59. Coal bed; 1,150' alt (Nutallburg),	3'
60. Soft shale,	45'
61. Massive sandstone,	108'6"
62. Soft shale,	15'
63. Massive sandstone,	50'
64. Black slate,	5'
65. Coal bed; alt. 925' (Quinnimont),	3'4"
66. Lamniated shale,	30'
67. Coal bed, soft,	0'6"
68. Shale,	54'6"
69. Hard sandstone (to datum line 780' A. M. T.),	60'

Report of Three Chief Engineers of the United States Navy on New River and Kanawha Coals.—In 1878, by order of the Engineer-in-Chief of the Bureau of Steam-engineering of the U. S. Navy Department, three Chief Engineers of the Navy "made a careful and thorough test," at the New York Navy-yard, of *"New River coal*, from Fayette county, West Virginia," (which I am warranted in saying was from the Fire Creek mine), and of "*splint coal*. from Kanawha county, West Virginia; previously, at the same place and with the same boiler, these engineers had, in a similar manner, tested "*Anthracite* from the northeastern portion of Pennsylvania," and "*Semi-bituminous coal* from Frostburg, Maryland." "The data and results of these strictly comparable experiments on these four kinds of coal," are given in a "Report (80 pp. with inset tables) on the two kinds of coal submitted by the Chesapeake & Ohio Railroad Coal Agency. U. S. Navy Department. Bureau of Steam Engineering, Washington : Government Printing Office. 1878." From that report the following statements are drawn. "The experiments were made with a large cylindrical tubular boiler of the type and proportions commonly employed for compound steam-engines; the boiler had two furnaces." "The steam was evaporated under the atmospheric pressure, escaping freely, as fast as generated, through the steam escape-pipe 8.75 inches diameter." "The coal was fired with as much uniformity as possible, and was kept upon the grates 7 inches thick, well leveled and free from holes. The fires were cleaned at regular intervals, alternately. All the holes in the furnace doors were kept open from beginning to end of each experiment for the admission of air above the incandescent fuel."

These experiments were conducted "for the purpose of ascertaining, under the actual conditions of ordinary practice with a representative marine boiler of the type habitually employed in the generation of steam for compound engines, the number of pounds of water vaporized by one pound of Pennsylvania anthracite, of Frostburg semi-bituminous coal, of New River bituminous coal, from Fayette Co., W. Va., and of splint coal, from Kanawha Co., W. Va., in order that their respective values as steam-generating fuels may be determined, both relatively and absolutely." With the New River coal six experiments were made, and with the Kanawha four, each lasting for 48 consecutive hours, except one with the Kanawha that lasted 37.

"**The New River Coal** is a moderately caking one, apparently bituminous, but very similar in its manner of burning to the semi-bituminous coal of the Cumberland mines, in the State of Maryland. It burned freely, swelled moderately, and coked properly, proving a first-class steam-coal, and well adapted for steamers' use. It is jet-black, has an irregular fracture, and crumbles easily. It was partly in lumps and partly in dust, the latter at once cohering in the fire by coking. This coal required but little labor in the furnace to work it. It burned with a bright, dense, yellow flame of considerable length, giving off a moderate amount of brownish-black smoke and depositing a small amount of soot on the tubes."

"The specific gravity of the 'New River coal' is 1.301 ; but in the merchantable state, taking lump and dust as they come, a cubic foot weighs 48.75 ; consequently, 45.9487 cubic feet are required to stow one ton." "Of this coal there were consumed, in all the experiments, 109,392 pounds, of which 6,967 pounds, or 6.3670 per centum, were refuse, composed of ash, clinker and soot. The ash and soot weighed 5,571.5 pounds, constituting 5.0931 per centum of the coal ; the remaining 1,395.5 pounds of the refuse, or 1.2739 per centum of the coal, being composed of clinker alone. The cubic foot of dry ash, not packed, weighs 25.5. The cubic foot of clinker weighs 34.6 pounds ; the specific gravity of the clinker is 1.554, and its color is a light yellowish brown."

The following table groups some of the facts of these experiments, those named in the notes corresponding to the numbers of the columns of figures :

Coal.	1	2	3	4	5	6	7	8	9	10
New River,...	1.301	109.392	6 967	5.621 5	1.395 5	25 5	34 6	5 0931	1 2739	1.554
Frostburg,...	48.157	8.944	5,077 0	846 0	...	10.5433	1.7572	1 820
Kanawha,...	1.271	76.882	4,685	3 862 5	1.283 5	30 7	35 0	4 3d21	1.4461	...
Anthracite,...	1.500	114.021	17.583	11,509.0	5 784 0	....	49 0	10.0938	5.0407	1 931

1. The specific gravities of the coals tested.—2. Pounds of coal consumed in all the experiments.—3. Pounds of refuse from consumption, including ashes, soot and clinker.—4.

Pounds of ash and soot in the refuse,—the soot from the boiler tubes.—5. Pounds of clinker in the refuse.—6. Pounds in cubic foot of dry ash, not packed.—7. Pounds in cubic foot of clinker.—8. Percentage of ash and soot in coal consumed.—9. Percentage of clinker in coal consumed.—10. Specific gravity of clinker.

The experimentors remark that "the gases of combustion from the New River bituminous coal deposited only a small amount of soot upon the heating surfaces of the boiler during an experiment of 48 hours duration," yet they found, by comparative experiments, that "the economic vaporization by the coal" was increased 1.316 per centum by sweeping the tubes every 8 hours; in other words, when the tubes were not swept during 48 hours a pound of coal vaporized 10.8960 lbs. of water from 212° Fah. under the standard atmospheric pressure, which when they were swept every 8 hours it vaporized 11.0413 pounds. It was found that wet coal was 1.4887 per cent. less economical than dry.

TABLE of principal quantities, for a comparison of the vaporization efficiencies of the coals named,—the data and results of experiments made with the same boiler, under identical conditions, by the same Board of United States Naval Engineers, in 1877 and 1878.

KIND OF COAL.	Rates of Combustion	Rate of Combustion per hour per sq. foot of grate surface.		Pounds of water vaporized from the temperature of 212° Fahrenh't and under the standard atmospheric pressure.				Pounds of steam produced per hour.
		Pounds of the Crude Coal.	Pounds of the gasifiable portion of the Coal.	Per pound of crude coal.	Per pound of the gasifiable portion of the coal.	Per cubic foot of the crude coal.		
New River Bituminous Coal.[1]	Slow	7.9884	4.6899	10.3585	11.1047	534.9756		2425.86
	Medium	12.0534	12.1906	10.9255	11.6960	407.3628		2985.11
	Maximum	14.3654	13.4317	10.1386	10.8390	404.8587		4569.27
Kanawha Splint Coal.[2]	Slow	7.8715	7.4763	8.5200	10.6117	474.0586		2356.90
	Medium	12.9767	12.3243	9.4846	10.0807	450.3185		3690.79
	Maximum	21.1153	19.9941	7.5834	8.0893	390.1649		4625.90
Frostburg Semi-Bituminous.[3]	Slow	7.6399	4.852	10.5281	11.7955	558.1494		2491.93
	Medium	11.9542	10.33	9.9857	11.2999	586.2571		3157.69
	Maximum	13.9075	12.827	9.0816	11.0606	632.2247		4065.60
Anthracite.[4]	Slow	7.7905	8.461	9.9923	11.7751	854.5665		2357.51
	Medium	10.5799	8.728	9.9943	11.7751	859.5665		3121.50
	Maximum	12.9541	10.921	9.8918	11.7751	858.5665		3842.98

[1] Using in the same connexion those given in the next table.

[2] The coal used was perfectly dry, and the tubes were not swept during the experiments.

[3] The coal was perfectly dry, and the tubes were swept every 8 hours.

[4] The coal used was perfectly dry, and the tubes were not swept during the experiments.

"In the preceding table the rates of combustion of the gasifiable portion of the coal in pounds per hour per square foot of grate-surface are the experimental rates. The per centum of refuse in ash, clinker, and soot, is the mean of the experiments of each kind of coal, and is made constant for all."

Kind of Coal	Weights of the Coals.		
	1.	2.	3.
New River.	6.3670	48.75	45.9487
Kanawha.	5.9538	47.50	47.1579
Frostburg.	12.3005	54.00	41.4815
Anthracite.	15.1402	56.00	40.0000

1. Percentage of refuse,—ash, soot and clinker,—in the coal used.—2. Pounds of coal, taking lump and dust, the coal in a merchantable shape, in a cubic foot.—3. Cubic feet of space required to stow one ton of coal.

In regard to *the quality of the coals used in these experiments,* they remark,—"*The anthracite* was of excellent quality, and its per centum of refuse was a little less than the average in practice, which is 16⅔ per centum, or one one-sixth ;—the *semi-bituminous coal* was of fair average quality;—as the *New River bituminous* and *the splint* coals had never before been experimented with in the Navy, no opinion can be given as to whether the qualities furnished were of fair average quality, but it is believed they were."

Note by Editor.—It is now known, however, that the New River coal furnished for these experiments was from a lot of lump coal, that had been stored in New York for some time, and that it was not "the run of the mine," consequently the "stowage" comparisons are by no means as favorable to that coal as they would have been if it had been in that state, and lately mined.

"The temperature of the gases of combustion emerging from the boiler was, in the cases of the New River bituminous and

of the splint coals, higher and higher the greater and greater the rate of combustion." This temperature "in the uptake of the boiler" was, during the combustion of the preceding table (the 2nd), in the case of the New River coal, 450.°4 Fah. when that combustion was "slow," 517.°6 when "medium," and 576.°7 when "maximum." "The gases of combustion from the splint coal deposited an excessive amount of soot upon the heating surfaces of the boiler during an experiment of 48 hours' duration, which strongly affected the economic vaporization by that coal," and it was ascertained that its economic vaporization was increased 8.0332 per cent. by sweeping the tubes every 8 hours; in other words, a pound of coal vaporized 9.2709 lbs. of water when the tubes were not swept in the 48 hours, and 10.0807 when they were swept every 8 hours.

In the case of the Kanawha splint it was 391.°3 Fah. when "slow," 512.°2 when "medium" and 650.°6 when "maximum." This temperature was not observed in the experiments on the other coals. The remark is made that all the determinations of temperature "must be received with much reserve." The table "shows that an increase in the rapidity of the combustion of the New River bituminous, the splint and the semi-bituminous coals was attended with a marked decrease in their economic vaporization ; while the anthracite, on the contrary, gave the same economic vaporization at all the experimental rates of combustion. In other words, the coal (anthracite) having the least proportion of volatile constituents and the greatest proportion of fixed carbon was least affected by the rapidity of combustion."

They remark that "*the relative steam-producing efficiencies* of different coals may be compared economically in several ways," as—(1.) "by the pounds of water vaporized from a standard temperature and under a standard pressure per pound of the crude coal and per pound of its gasifiable portion ;" (2.) "by the quantity of steam produced in a given time," "undoubtedly the true practical mode of comparison, as it supposes equal quantities of heat to be generated in equal times ;"—or (3.) "the vaporization per cubic foot, or per any unit of bulk, of coal or of its gasifiable portion, in place of the vaporization per pound by them ;" the last having a practical application when the steam is used on board a vessel where space has a commercial value. The preceding table (2nd) furnishes the data for a comparison of the economic and absolute steam-producing efficiency of each of the coals experimented on by each of the ways named, as the headings of the columns indicate.

To be Continued.

We are gratified to note that the *American Manufacturer,* of Pittsburg, which has always been a true friend to Virginia development, devotes two full columns, the half of one of its broad pages, to extracts from The Virginias. We are much obliged for its complimentary notice of our first number, given elsewhere—only we would like to have our friend define "pamphlet," a term applied to The Virginias, which has pages somewhat larger than those of the substantial *Engineering and Mining Journal,* of New York, and as many pages of reading matter, and is but 3 inches shorter and 2 narrower than the full-grown *Manufacturer* itself. It may call us a "pamphlet" because our Tauchnitz-trained German binder has "stitched" us far better than any of our cotemporaries that have come to hand, not even excepting the well-done-up *Bulletin of the American Iron and Steel Association* ; or it may be because ours is "stitched together with thread," according to our standard dictionary, and not "stuck" together as some sheets we know of.

The New River Coke Company has just been chartered by the Judge of the Circuit Court of Augusta Co., Va. Its capital stock is fixed at $500,000 and it may hold 25,000 acres of land. It has been organized with M. E. Miller, of Staunton, as President, Thomas Cochran, of Philadelphia, as Treasurer. The Directors are M. E. Miller, H. M. Bell, R. H. Catlett and J. Fred. Effinger, of Staunton, and J. F. Hartranft, Thomas Cochran and R. N. Pool, of Philadelphia. It has secured a large body of land on New River, between Mann's and Keeney's creeks, including the colliery at Elm station, and will at once arrange for extensive coking operations.

List of Collieries on the Chesapeake & Ohio Railway, West Virginia, February 1st, 1880.

—In their order from east to west.

1. *In the New River District*, mining the Lower Measure, Semi-bituminous coals that are used for coking, steam and domestic purposes.

NAME OF COLLIERY, AND ALSO OF R'Y STATION.	Miles from Richmond.	COMPANY, PROPRIETOR, OR OPERATOR.	ESTIMATED YEAR-LY CAPACITY, IN 2,240 LBS. TONS.	Coke ovens.
1. Quinnimont,	394	Pa. & Va. Iron & Coal Co	6,000	100
2. Fayette Coal & Coke Co	305		(Just commencing)	100
3. Fire Creek Coal & Coke Co...	310	M E Miller,Staunton,Va,Ag't	80,000	80
4. Sewell,	313	Longdale Iron Co	81,000	80
5. Elm,	315	Beury, Cooper & Williams,	35,000	
	317	John Nutall ; W. A. Burke, }	80,000	60
6. Nutallburg,		Staunton, Va , Agent, }		
7. Louisa,	322	Byrne, Snyder & Holt,	(Just commencing)	
8. Hawk's Nest,	324	B. J. Echols & Co	do.	10,000
9. West Hawk's Nest,	324	(Not in operation.)	15,000	6

2. *In the Kanawha District*, mining the coals of the Middle Measures, which are of the bituminous class, known in the markets as Gas, Block, Cannel and Splint coals, and are used for steam, domestic and metallurgical purposes and for the manufacture of gas.

NAME OF COLLIERY.	Miles from Richmond.	COMPANY, PROPRIETOR, OR OPERATOR.	STATION OR POSTOFFICE.	Yearly Capacity in Tons.
1. Gauley Mountain,		Hawk's Nest Coal Co	Hawk's Nest,...	6,000
2. Eagle,		Eagle Coal Co	Frederick....	6,000
3. Faulkner's,		Fred Faulkner,	do.	6,000
4. Crescent,		W. R. Johnson	Crescent	30,000
5. Cabnelton,		Cannelton Coal Co.	Cannelton	36,000
6. Coal Valley,		Coal Valley Coal Co	Coal Valley P O	60,000
7. Straughan's,		George Straughan	do.	80,000
8. Mount Morris,		Mt Morris Coal Co	do.	(Opening)
9. Eureka,		Eureka Coal Co	do.	30,000
10. Kanawha Coal Co		Kanawha Coal Co	do.	15,000
11. Morris Creek Crescent,		Carver, Schupp'rt & Co	do.	30,000
12. Old Virginia,		Wilson & Lewis,	do.	36,000
13. Upper Creek,		(Not working)	do.	36,000
14. Paint Creek,	818	J Zieg e, Manager	Loc'l P O ,	31,000
15. Blacksburg,	836	Mason, Hege & Co	Fort Spice P. O. }	
16. Hampton,	850	do.	do.	50,000
17. East Bank,	852	Stuart M Buck,	Coalburg	45,000
18. Coalburg,	853	Robinson Coal Co	do.	75,000
19. Houston,	855	(Not working)	Lewistow	
20. Coalmount,	858	Consolidated Coal Co of Lin...	do.	60,000
21. Brownstown,	860	(Not working)	Brownstown	
22. Kanawha Saline,	863	(Not working)	Maldia,	
23. Bennington Coal Co.,	864	W G Corbin,	do.	80,000
24. Peytona,	841	Peytona Coal Co	St. Alban	25,000

The Gauley Mountain colliery is 5 miles, by a narrow-gauge railway, from Hawk's Nest station of the C. & O. It mines steam coal from the 11 to 12 ft. bed of the Middle Measures, which are carried by Gauley Mountain into the New River District.

The Cannelton mine is across the Kanawha from the C. & O., but its coal is ferried across to the railway. It is said the U. S. will make a wire tramway from this mine across the river that it may acquire the location of the ferry for one of the dams of the Kanawha Improvement.

Nos. 1 and 2 ship steam coal ; Nos. 3, 4, 5 and 6 ship gas and block ; Nos. 8, 12, 13, 15, 16 ship gas and splint; Nos. 9, 10, 19 and 22 ship gas; Nos. 14, 17, 18 and 20 ship splint ; and Nos. 5, 21 and 24 ship cannel.

The Peytona mines are on Coal River, at Peytona, 35 miles above St. Albans station which is at the mouth of that river. Only cannel coal is mined. It is sent in barges to the C. & O. R'y.

These estimates of capacity are based on data furnished by the Fuel Agent of C. & O. and the collieries.

3. *Collieries on the N. side of the Kanawha*, that ship below the river, in their order down stream.

1. *Enterprise*, nearly opposite Paint Creek ; H. A. Walker of Charleston. Not in operation.

2. *The Cedar Grove Co-operative Coal Co.*, above Kelley's cr., mining the soft, rich coal of the 3' bed.

3. *The Robinson Coal Co.*, below Kelley's cr., mining from 2,000 to 4,000 bushels (28 to the ton), per day, of gas coal.

4. *The Campbell's Creek*, the *Pioneer*, and *Dana Brothers* Coal Co's., mining, the first and second from 10,000 to 12,000 bushels a day each, and the last 5,000, of the noted Campbell's Creek coal.

5. *The Snow Hill* and *Boone* salt furnace mines ; not now at work.

These are all above Charleston and mine from the Middle Measures. The following are towards the mouth of the Kanawha and work on the *Pittsburgh Bed*, of the Upper Measures.

1. *Raymond City*, operated by Marmet & Co., of Cincinnati, mining from 15,000 to 16,000 bushels a day, and preparing to mine double as much, having purchased large, new tow boats.

2. *Oak Ridge*, 10 miles below Raymond City.

The Iron Ores and Coals on the Line of the Chesapeake & Ohio Railway, and the Need of an Industrial Survey of Virginia and West Virginia.

A Letter to the Editor from Prof. Thomas Egleston, of the School of Mines of Columbia College, New York.

DEAR SIR:—As you are aware, I was engaged for two months last summer making a careful geological reconnaissance of the districts of the State of Virginia, adjacent to as well as those north of the line of the Ches. & Ohio R'y. I was very greatly impressed with the value of the mineral deposits of this section, and of the desirability of a careful industrial survey being made of the whole region. The geology of the country is well settled, as you know, most of the formations having been carefully determined by Rogers and others since his time ; but the value of the different deposits, the way in which they can be worked, what special properties they possess from a metallurgical and industrial stand point, are questions which have never been carefully studied, to my knowledge.

It is well known to a few that there is a great variety both in the quantity and quality of the iron ores throughout this great iron belt of Virginia, but its real value is not appreciated at home, and is scarcely known in the North. The quality of some of these ores is very high, but they sometimes pass into a material so silicious that it cannot be used as an ore of iron. An imperfect examination of localities containing such material on the surface has given rise to the impression, announced in some of the most important local works on the geology of the U. S., that the Oriskany deposit contains no iron ores that can be worked. I have made over 60 analyses from samples collected by myself and others of these ores, and find by far the larger part of them valuable for the manufacture of iron, and many of them very rich in iron and very low in both sulphur and phosphorus. Very few of these ores, which I have analysed, would be rejected by iron men on account of their quality. The ore deposits are not, as they usually are in the North, pockets uncertain in their yield and in their extent, but are regular geological formations which can be followed for miles, and which with few exceptions can be depended upon both for quality and quantity of their iron ores. What they need is a careful exploration to determine their extent, and careful examination to determine their quality, and when this has been done, I see no reason why the State of Virginia should not be one of the largest and richest iron-producing countries in the United States. Topographically these ores are situated in such a way that they can be most easily mined. The geological accidents which have occurred in the great ore belt have turned up the strata in a series of folds, which, having been afterwards eroded on the surface, throw the deposits into a series of U shaped beds, so that at the present time the same outcrops over short distances will frequently come to the surface several times, as is particularly the case at Low Moor. Besides this, the ores are usually found high up on the hills so that they can be mined easily, and can generally be brought to the railroad by gravity roads.

There is room enough in those iron fields which I have examined personally, for from twenty to thirty very large iron furnaces. The erection of such furnaces would develop the material wealth of the State, would create many other industries and help to populate and to build up the country which is now so thinly settled.

I have had many conversations with Pennsylvania iron manufacturers, especially from Pittsburgh, since my return

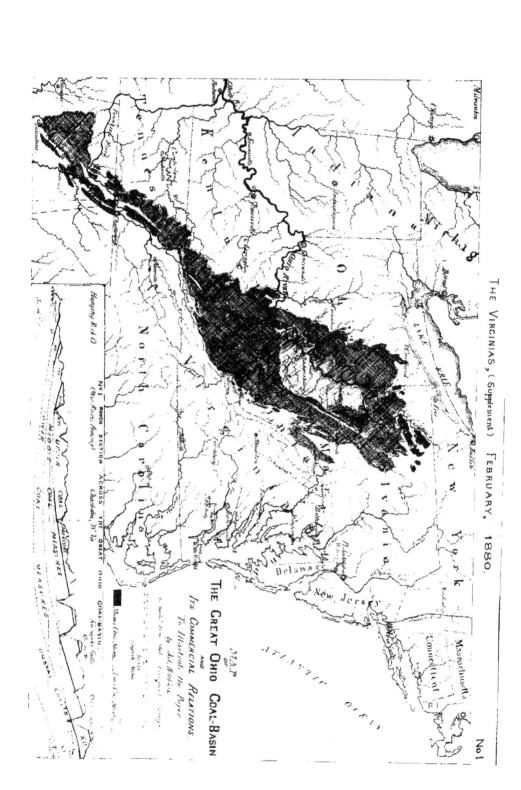

MAP OF THE GREAT OHIO COAL-BASIN AND Its COMMERCIAL RELATIONS.

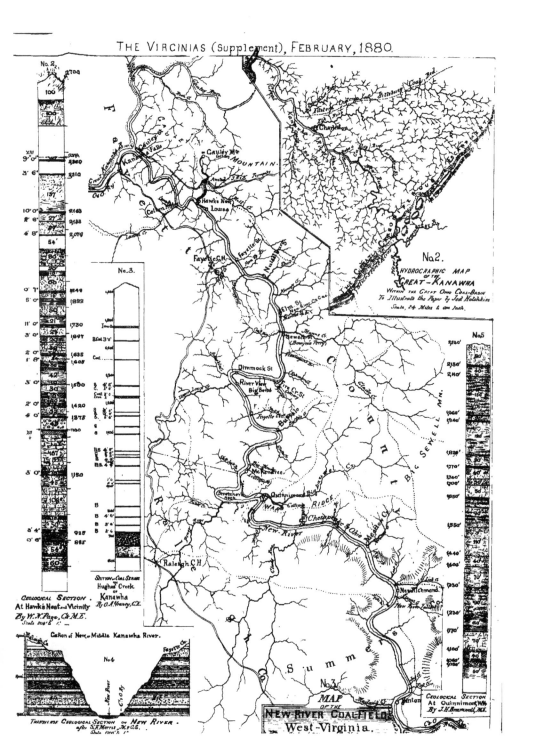

from Virginia, relative to these ores, and have been assured that if they could be delivered in Pittsburgh at a reasonable price, that city alone would take several hundred thousand tons of the ore.

The coal fields, however, have impressed me even more than the iron fields. I have examined a number of them in their different geological horizons, from the base to the top of the coal field, and found the coals which they yield exceedingly pure. None of them, so far as my examination goes, contain more than two per cent. of ash, and are besides almost free from sulphur and phosphorus. Almost all of them are capable of making a coke which is more like charcoal in its qualities, being at the same time much more tenacious and capable of resisting a very heavy charge in the blast furnace, while in other respects they act like that fuel. Some of these coals are so valuable for the manufacture of iron that it is said that at Longdale they require only one ton of coke to make one ton of iron, which is a very small quantity. The coke usually made contains only six per cent. of ash against more than double that amount as the average of the Connellsville coke. These coals are coked by only one process, but I have every reason to believe that many of the coals which do not now make a very good coke and most of those which are now considered to be impossible to coke, can be made into coke of excellent quality, with profit, if the proper kind of furnace was used. It is very desirable that this whole question should be studied with reference to the various kinds of furnaces which can be used for the manufacture of the coals of different geological positions into coke. It is well known in Europe that different coals require different furnaces for their treatment, but very little is known of this subject in the U. S. There are three general types of furnaces besides a large number of varieties of each type, but only one of them is known in your district.

Many of these coals never should be allowed to go out of the country except as manufactured into coke. If this was done there would be a double profit to the coal owner and to the iron manufacturer, since all the fine coal could be used in the manufacture of coke, and thus realize at the present time a higher profit than if sold as coal.

I noticed in the coke manufacture a serious defect, which was that the fine coke was as a general thing thrown away. This is very wasteful, as the screenings should be used for the manufacture of steam or for the calcining of iron ores. As all the ores of the mountain belt should be calcined before being used in the furnace this would be a profitable use for a material which is now thrown away.

So far as the manufacture of coke is concerned, there is a great industry to be created entirely independent of iron manufacture. The great West now depends on Connellsville for coke, for which they pay in many districts, on and off the line of the Pacific R. R., $25, $30, and even $40 a ton. Such a high priced fuel makes it impossible to treat low grade silver and gold ores. This is owing as much to the large percentage of ash in their coke as to any other cause. The amount of ash in the New River coals being reduced, from one-half to one-third of what it is in the coals which are now accessible to them, would make it possible, when these Virginia cokes become known, to treat many precious metal ores which cannot now be worked, and thus give rise to a very large coke trade in Virginia, and a much larger production of bullion in the West. I see no reason why, when the facts are known, and the different beds which can be used for making coke suitable for the western market as distinguished from those suitable for the manufacture of iron have been ascer-

tained, this coal-field should not control the entire coke trade west of the Mississippi. This would give rise at once in the coal-fields to several great industries.

There are many theories with regard to the topographical position of the coals, which are untenable, and it is quite possible that a thorough industrial examination of the region would show that certain coal lands which are now considered to be nearly valueless, would become as valuable as the best fields now worked, or even more so, if the appliances of modern engineering were extended to them. It would be exceedingly profitable to the States of Virginia and West Virginia to organize such an industrial survey; or it would be an equally profitable investment to capitalists to organize and carry into execution an industrial survey which should embrace either the iron or the coal fields, or both, determining the value of the several deposits of iron ores in the different geological ages and their value for the different purposes of iron manufacture.

The manufacture of iron at the present time is in a transition state. It is quite likely that the worst of the Virginia ores may be capable of being so worked, under some of the recent discoveries in the metallurgy of iron, as to produce an article which would sell far above the average price of ordinary iron in Virginia.

Much of the Virginia charcoal iron has been manufactured at an unnecessarily high cost. I had occasion during the last summer to ascertain that in some districts in Virginia the probable yield of the wood used for charcoal iron is not much over 10 per cent. This is a waste of valuable material, which ought not to exist in an intelligent community.

Very little is known about Virginia as a metallurgical district, and I am quite sure that if a reliable account of the industrial resources of the western part of the State, to say nothing of the other mineral deposits, were accessible to the public, the lands containing the deposits would very soon command a high price, and that some of the coals of West Virginia would take the place altogether of many of the bituminous coals now being used in the market for other industrial purposes.

It would give me very great pleasure to see some steps taken in this direction, either by the State or by capitalists. I am thoroughly convinced that should such a survey cost the State or individuals as much as $20,000 or $25,000, the whole sum would be returned to them, directly or indirectly, within a year of the time when the results of the survey became accessible to the public, and that it would be instrumental in soon placing both States in a condition of prosperity which they have never yet known.

The Coal and Coke movement from the New River and Kanawha mines

and their distribution, by the Chesapeake & Ohio Railway. during the calendar years 1878 and 1879, in tons of 2,240 lbs., compiled for THE VIRGINIAS from the books of the R'y Co., by its fuel agent, Mr. C. M. Gibson, were as follows:

WHERE DELIVERED.	Tons in 1878.	Tons in 1879.
For use of C. & O. R'y Company,	78,250	74,925
On Line of Road West of Richmond,	28,187	26,473
At Huntington for shipment on Ohio River,	10,673	69,341
At Staunton to Valley Railroad,	220	329
At Charlottesville to Va. Midland Railroad,	29,961	23,938
At Gordonsville to do do	1,031	1,020
At Hanover Junction to R., F. & P., do	3,233	4,269
At Richmond for consumption, including Steam Tugs and Dredges,	50,004	47,300
At James River Wharves for shipment,	140,921	155,827
Total.,	342,480	304,422

This shows an increase of 60,942 tons, or about 18 per cent. in 1879 over 1878. The increase of over 500 per cent. in the shipment westward, down the Ohio, is an evidence that the movement, so long predicted by those familiar with the relations of the Kanawha coal-field to the Ohio markets, has at last begun. The quantity shipped was not very large,—though it appears, when presented in the Western fashion, as 1,660,000 bushels,—but 1880 will surely present a much larger one, especially if proper energy is brought to bear on the extension of the C. & O., immediately filling up the gap of some 20 miles between Huntington and Ashland, so the deeper water of the Ohio can be reached, and then, without delay, finishing the link between the Ashland road and Mt. Sterling. If this western connection had been in operation the past year the Kanawha coals could have monopolized the Cincinnati and other river markets and secured, permanently, the position they are there entitled to. At one time as high as 30 cts. a bushel, $8,40 a ton, were paid for coal in Cincinnati, and the demand would have exhausted the capacity of every mine on the C. & O. if the way to market had been open.

The increase of about 11 per cent. in the shipments from Richmond, mainly to Northern cities, and during a period of business depression, shows that the superior steam and domestic coals from this region are meeting with increased sales in that direction.

The character of the coals moved during the same years is shown in the following exhibit:

Year.	Coals.		Coke.	Total.
	Cannel.	Splint & Bit's.		
1879.	29,697	353,133	20,592	403,422
1878.	47,699	277,041	17,760	347,480
Increase.		76,092	2,832	60,942
Decrease.	17,982			

The Nutallburg Colliery, C. & O. R'y, furnishes the following as its production of coal and coke, in 2,240 lb. tons, during the past five years. This shows a generally prosperous condition of the work there:

Year.	Coal.	Coke.
1875.	7,585	3,440
1876.	20,905	1,285
1877.	13,964	3,157
1878.	24,634	2,244
1879.	37,744	3,236

Why Rise in Freights from Europe.—A friend of ours in Richmond, writing to a friend North about freights this way from Europe, found the following in the response he got, explaining one of the reasons for the advance now prevailing: "A large house here is importing from the Mediterranean 300,000 tons of iron ores. So, you can fancy what a comparative scarcity of vessels this sudden demand for tonnage must produce in branches of trade which have heretofore looked to sending their goods to this country at merely nominal freights."

This is doubtless magnetic ore from the northern coast of Africa, and the announcement does look strange in the face of the fine deposits of this same ore in Virginia.

Mr. George W. Bramwell, who has been the mining engineer at the Gowan mines of Coxe Brothers & Co., Luzerne Co., Pa., has gone to New River to take charge of the mining and coking operations of the Fayette Coal and Coke Co., just commencing, at Flat Creek, above Fire Creek, C. & O. R'y. We gladly welcome the coming to our mining regions of mining engineers having the professional attainments and experience of Mr. Bramwell. His German technical education supplemented by mine work under the never-to-be-satisfied discipline of Eckley B. Coxe of Drifton, have doubtless made him just such a man as we want in our unexplored and undeveloped coal fields.

The International Real Estate Society, or as its chief corporator calls it, *The Swiss Commerce Society,* has recently obtained from the State of West Virginia a charter of incorporation, which we print below. This charter sets forth but in part the objects of the society. We had the pleasure of meeting Messrs. Ludwig and Kerchoff, of Switzerland, on the Kanawha. They have secured the control, at a moderate price, of some 35,000 acres of lands, lying on Loup Creek of the Kanawha, near the Chesapeake & Ohio Railway, at its Loup Creek station, which is 337 miles from Richmond and but 32 miles, by rail or the navigable Kanawha, from Charleston, the future capital of West Virginia. These are coal, timber and farming or grazing lands, every way suited to colonists from the highlands of Central Europe. Specimens of the timbers, properly labeled with statements as to the purposes for which they are used, and of the coals, from these lands, have already been sent to Germany and Switzerland.

This is a move in the right direction. There is no better region in the United States for the location of the hardy and substantial immigrants of Central Europe, chiefly of the Teutonic race, than the great Trans-Apalachian Plateau of West Virginia, a territory nearly equal in extent to Switzerland itself, (which has 15,722 square miles and a population of 160 to the square mile, while West Virginia has 23,000 square miles, in all, with but 19 to the square mile). The true policy to be pursued in this rich mining region, with its mild climate and slope towards the setting sun, is to sell the surface to a good class of people and raise on the spot a plentiful crop of hardy workers,—miners, manufacturers, farmers and graziers,—who will have an interest in the soil and homes of their own to care for. Such men will be born conservators of the peace, and we will not only see a rapid development of the resources of the country, but will hear no more of "strikes" and labor riots, the ebullitions of the passions of men that are not free-holders.

Thousands of the best citizens of the Virginias are descended from Switzers, and if the promoters of this new departure would know the policy of these States towards the capital thereof, that stock, they have but to visit them in the homes their ancestors settled more than a century ago.

We print the charter granted to this society in full, that it may obtain publicity in Europe, and show the privileges we accord to immigrants.

Charter.—"The undersigned agree to become a corporation, by the name of the "International Real Estate Society," for the purpose of acting as a medium between the citizens of West Virginia and Switzerland, Germany and Central Europe, for the purpose of procuring the immigration of Swiss, German and French settlers to the State of West Va., selecting and procuring homes for said immigrants and affording them protection in the purchase of lands and settlement upon the same, and in the procurement of supplies, and their full and complete enjoyment of civil, social and religious rights, which corporation shall keep its principal office or place of business at Charleston, Kanawha county, West Virginia, and is to expire on the 19th day of January, Anno Domini nineteen hundred.

And for the purpose of forming the said corporation, we have subscribed the sum of twelve hundred dollars to the capital thereof, and have paid in, on said subscription, the sum of one hundred and twenty dollars, and desire the privilege of increasing the said capital, by sales of additional shares from time to time, to one hundred thousand dollars in all. The capital so subscribed is divided into shares of one hundred dollars each, which are held by the undersigned, respectively, as follows,—that is to say:

Names.	Residence.	No. of Shares.
Edmund D. Ludwig,	Switzerland,	Two
Hermann Kerchoff,	Switzerland,	Two
Alexander F. Mathews,	Lewisburg, W. Va.,	Two
Charles C. Lewis,	Charleston, W. Va.,	Two
William A. Quarrier,	" "	Two
Clarkson C. Watts,	" "	Two

And the capital to be hereafter sold is to be divided into shares of the like amount.

Given under our hands this 19th day of January, 1880. [Signed by the corporators.]

Virginia Railway Items.

The Petersburg, Massanutton and Toledo R. R. Co. is the name proposed for a company now asking a charter from the Virginia Legislature to construct a railway from Broadway, on The Valley Branch of the B. & O., westward through Brock's Gap, (the Little Germany of Rockingham), and on to Petersburg, Hardy Co., W. Va., with the privilege of extending eastward to Massanutton (the New Market Gap probably) and on to Washington City. It will open a rich mineral and timber region.

The Charlottesville and Rapid-Anne Railroad, 31 miles long, the missing link in the Virginia Midland line, is in a fair way to be completed by next July, when the contract of the Va. Mid. with the C. & O. R'y for the use of its track between Gordonsville and Charlottesville expires. The work of construction is progressing rapidly. The 6 per cent. bonds for this short line were sold at par.

The Chesapeake & Ohio R'y Co. has been running experimental lines from Gordonsville to Fredericksburg, and to Potomac City, near Quantico. The question of a deep-water terminus for this road at Yorktown, Newport's News, or Norfolk, is also under discussion at the points named. It is a good sign to hear of new life at each end of this great line, and especially to know that President Huntington is giving his personal attention to the completion of its western connection, co-operating with President Echols of the Big Sandy and Lexington (Ky.) road.—We hope to see the C. & O. completed to the end of The Peninsula, to the great continental harbor of Hampton Roads, (and its connections cannot be made *complete* short of there), in time to bring Virginia's children from the farthest of her once western borders to her great Yorktown centennial.

The Staunton and West Augusta R. R. Co. has been granted a charter by the Legislature of Virginia. The corporators will endeavor to construct a railway from Staunton to Mt. Solon and the Dora coal mines, connecting at Dora with the Washington City & St. Louis line, which is partially constructed from Harrisonburg to that point and beyond, thus making a road from Staunton to Harrisonburg by the western side of The Valley.

The citizens of Waynesboro, Va., have held a public meeting and appointed a committee to do what they can to bring the Shenandoah Valley R. R. to that point. The nearer that line keeps to the Blue Ridge the better. There is where it is needed and where it will find paying freights. The people along that line have been liberal in regard to land damages. They ought to *give* the right of way and ties, if necessary to secure the road. The old stream-valley of the Shenandoah is there to follow.

Gen. John C. New and associates, a committee of the Directors of the Richmond and Alleghany R. R. named in the January VIRGINIAS, met in Richmond the 24th, ult. and asked for an option of 30 days to contract for the purchase of the James River & Kanawha Canal Company's property under the provision of the act of Assembly of Feb. 2nd, 1879. The stockholders of the Canal Co. authorized the President to give the option. Gen. New stated, in writing, that the examination made for the construction of a railway on the general line of the canal had resulted favorably, that they were in Virginia to make a final examination, and that they had associated themselves for the purpose of carrying out any agreement they might make. A decision as to whether these gentlemen will go into this enterprise is expected early in February. They have ample means to do the large thing that is to be done on this line.

The narrow-gauge railway from Bristol-Goodson, on the A. M. & O. R'y, is under construction towards Cumberland Gap, and good progress is being made in the work. Parties from Philadelphia, who own large tracts of mineral and timber lands on and near the Cumberland Mountain, Scott county, Va., and Harlan and Josh Bell counties, Ky., are effecting combinations with other owners of large tracts, of a similar character, in the same region, placing it is said some 500,000 acres of mineral lands under one management, for the purpose of making sale of the lands or of developing them, aiding in the construction of this railway for that purpose.—*Dispatch.*

The Conglomerate Series of West Virginia.*

By WILLIAM M. FONTAINE.

In the May and June numbers of the American Journal of Science for 1874, I gave some account of the strata which, on New River. West Virginia, underlie the massive sandstone exposed at the Falls of the Kanawha. This account was necessarily imperfect, since at the point examined the base of the series was not exposed, and the exposures were very unfavorable for a detailed examination.

During the summer of 1875, I revisited this field, and made further examinations at points more to the east, with such success that I am now able to present a detailed section of this field. Since the white sandstone of the Falls is the equivalent of what is everywhere called "the Conglomerate" of the Coal Measures, it might to some seem more fitting to call the rocks in question "Sub-conglomerate," or "Lower Carboniferous." In West Virginia, the strata which occupy the interval between the floor of the productive coals and the Devonian, are so greatly expanded, and so much diversified, that these terms are not definite enough to distinguish them. Besides, this New River system occupies precisely the horizon which is elsewhere commonly filled by conglomeritic sandstone alone, lying, as it does, between the red shales of the Umbral, and the lower productive coals. For these reasons I prefer to use the name "Conglomerate Series" for it. For like reasons it will be necessary to retain the names "Vespertine" and "Umbral," of the first Pennsylvania Survey, in describing rocks equivalent to those bearing these titles in the above named survey. A single instance will show this necessity. The system about to be described contains important coals. We find also far below them, in the Vespertine of Montgomery County, Virginia, near the White Sulphur, West Virginia, and elsewhere, well developed coals. To call these Sub-conglomerate or Lower Carboniferous coals would fail to distinguish them.

In my second visit to this region I made a re-examination of the strata at Sewell Station, the point at which most of the facts given in my first paper were obtained. In this last visit I found the strata quite well disclosed in the cuttings of the "Incline," made since my previous inspection. I also made a careful and detailed examination of the same strata at Quinnimont, a point on the Chesapeake and Ohio Railroad, distant by railroad twenty-one miles to the east of Sewell Station, but about ten miles by air line. While the base of the series is not exposed at Sewell Station, yet, owing to the fact that the westerly dip is more rapid than the fall of the river, even the underlying Umbral red shales are fully disclosed, and the entire series in question is contained in the lofty hills at Quinnimont, while in their summits they still retain a small remnant of the lower productive coals, with one and sometimes two coal beds.

While making my examination at Quinnimont I received valuable aid from Mr. S. F. Morris, C. E., and I take this opportunity to make my acknowledgements to him. Mr. Morris had, by levelling, determined the height of many points, and examined the character of the strata around Quinnimont, in behalf of the company owning the furnace and coal mine at that point. The data which he kindly put at my disposal were of great assistance in checking my own observations.

During the same summer I also made an examination of the country to the east of Quinnimont, especially that portion in the vicinity of the White Sulphur Springs, Greenbrier County. It will perhaps be well to give here some of the facts thus obtained, bearing on the general geology of the region, in order more clearly to define the relations of the series to be described in this paper. In order to do this I will commence at the east and proceed west along the line of the Chesapeake and Ohio Railroad, whose general course is across the strike of all the strata underlying the rocks in question.

We may for a clearer exposition commence at Lewis Tunnel, a point six miles east of the White Sulphur. Here we find Vespertine strata which run in a narrow belt along the east face of the main Alleghany range, and contain the small coal beds, and plant-bearing shales, found near the Tunnel. The main range and the country westward for twelve miles is occupied by highly disturbed Devonian strata, mainly Hamilton, Portage, and Chemung, with probably the Catskill group. In the center of the belt the Springs are situated. Six miles west of the Springs, we find, on the east side of a small creek, highly contorted Devonian strata, and on the west side within 100 yards, the upper portion of the Vespertine, dipping gently eastward toward the contorted Devonian. Just above the Vespertine, in the hill across this stream, the base of the

*From the American Journal of Science and Arts, April, 1876　At the t me of its publication Mr. Fontaine was Professor of Geology in the University of West Virginia; he is now (1880) Professor of Geology and Natural History in the University of Virginia.

Umbral or Lewisburg limestone may be seen. The contortions and other evidences of great disturbance which follow us from the east up to this point now cease, and throughout the wide belt of country lying between this point and the Ohio River, the strata undulate more and more gently, until before Quinnimont is reached the rolls cease to reverse the dip, but serve to keep the strata longer at the surface than they would otherwise remain in that position.

This sudden change in structure is not found here alone, although it seems to be more marked here than elsewhere. It may be traced far to the southwest, and probably to the north, and is to be explained by the existence of a fault, apparently the most westerly of the system affecting the Appalachian Region in this quarter. The development of this fault seems to have, in a great measure, relieved the strata lying to the west, from the disturbing force which so highly affected them on the east and it is not necessary to suppose a gradual dying away to the westward of the lateral thrust from the east. The conditions seem to imply a certain amount of unconformability between the Devonian and Vespertine, which is not incompatible with other facts observed here.

Proceeding westward along the line of the railroad from the fault, the gentle rise of the Vespertine to the west brings into view its middle or coal-bearing portion, here also containing small coal seams. This is in the vicinity of the bridge over Greenbrier River, and explains the presence near this stream, of the coal seam mentioned by Prof. Wm. B. Rogers in his reports. The Vespertine as it crosses the stream passes into a low anticlinal, which, west of the river, finally brings down the Umbral limestone to the level of the railroad, as far as Great Bend Tunnel, near the mouth of the Hungert's Creek, Summers County, where it dips under the red rocks of the Umbral series, which in this district are greatly developed. The Umbral series seems to possess a threefold character, being at bottom blood-red shales and sandstones, in the middle, grayish, bluish and brownish sandstones and shales, mainly the former; and at top brownish sandstones, blood red and variegated shales. The shales throughout the series have the texture of marlites, and the sandstones, although chiefly argillaceous are sometimes highly siliceous, forming huge cliffs along the railroad, as seen near Richmond's Falls. These three series, the Vespertine, the Umbral limestone, and Umbral shales and sandstone, thicken rapidly in proceeding from northeast to southwest. Prof. Rogers measured them in Greenbrier Mountain, Pocahontas County, a point about sixty miles northeast of Richmond's Falls on New River, where the Umbral shales and sandstones are extensively exposed. With respect to the limestone I have no data for comparison but the indications are that on the railroad it is thicker than the measurement given by Prof. Rogers, viz: 822 feet. For the Umbral shales and sandstones in Pocahontas he gives a thickness of 1,310 feet. My estimates along the line of the railroad, which, however, have not the accuracy of measurements, give for this series a probable thickness of 1,450 feet in the vicinity of Richmond's Falls, distributed as follows: 1. Lower red shales and sandstones, 320 feet; 2. Middle gray and greenish sandstones, 820 feet; 3. Upper red and variegated shales, 310 feet. If we compare this series with the character of the Umbral in the vicinity of Blossburg, as given by H. D. Rogers, we find an almost identical distribution of similar strata. The upper portion of the Umbral continues to be shown up to a short distance west of Quinnimont, where the prevailing westerly dip takes it out of sight. These upper strata form the base of the hills around Quinnimont, contrasting strongly in all their physical features with the overlying conglomerate series. This latter, whose entire thickness lies above the level of the river at this point, gradually sinks as we pass west, down stream, being kept above water level for a long distance by broad rolls. It finally passes out of sight two or three miles below Kanawha Falls, and is succeeded by the series of the Lower Productive coals in the Kanawha Region. In this latter series there is a four-feet bed of coal, about forty feet above the massive sandstone which closes the conglomerate series This is the equivalent of coal B of Lesley. This bed still remains uneroded in the tops of some of the high hills around Quinnimont.

About two miles down the river, on the Raleigh County side, Piney river empties into New River. A well graded road from the mouth of this stream, passes over the outcropping edges of the entire conglomerate series, and the numerous cuttings made in grading afford excellent exposures of almost every member of the series throughout its entire thickness. My section was made along this road. It was verified by a second section taken at Quinnimont by another road, which also passed over the entire series. These two sections were compared with observations made at Sewell Station, and with measurements made by Mr. Morris. The data in the cases in the section, marked as not seen, are given on the authority of this gentleman. The dip is northwest about fifty feet to the mile.

Section from the mouth of Piney River, Raleigh County.

21. Upper conglomerate, 150–200 feet.
20. Black slate, with thin coal partings, coal not seen, 10 feet.
19. Olive gray sandstones and shales, 100 feet.
18. Dark blue slates and sandstones, 80 feet.
17. Quinnimont coal seam, or coal No. 9, consisting of semi-bituminous coal, 4 feet; fire clay, 2½ feet; and at bottom, splint coal, 14 inches,=8 feet.
16. A thick mass of rocks not fully exposed, which may be divided as follows: 16 *e*, olive gray shaly sandstones, 40 feet; 16 *d*, coal 8, not seen, given as 20 inches thick; 16 *c*, bluish sandy shales, 60 feet; 16 *b*, coal 7, not seen, given as 2 feet thick; 16 *a*, gray sandstone, 50 feet. Total, 154 feet.
15. Fire clay and a 12-inch outcrop of coal, seen imperfectly exposed, given as 2–4½ feet of imperfect splint coal, coal No. 6, =2–4½ feet.
14. Coal system; at bottom interstratifications of coal and slate, with one seam one foot thick; (coal No. 5), and on top, flags passing into firm sandstones. Good plant impressions occur here. Thickness, 80 feet.
13. Olive marlites, 40 feet.
12. Massive firm gray sandstones, 50 feet.
11. Coal No. 4, not fully exposed, given as 2½ feet thick.
10. Firm gray flags and sandstones, 90 feet.
9. Coal system, coal No. 3; at bottom interstatifications of thin coals and strata; on top, shales, flags and sandstones, 80 feet.
8. Gray sandstones, 75 feet.
7. Ferruginous limestone, 2 feet.
6. Variegated marlites, 40 feet.
5. Bright red shales and marlites, 30 feet.
4. Coal system, coal No. 2, consisting of coal 8 inches, slate 2½ feet, coal 8 inches, sandstone 8 feet, and at bottom coal and slate 1 foot; total =13 feet.
3. Olive and reddish sandstones, passing below into olive marlites, 100 feet.
2. Black slate, not seen, said to contain 18 inches of coal, (coal No. 1), given as 11 feet thick.
1. Lower conglomerate, 80 feet. Total =1,197 feet.

Under the lower conglomerate is found a transition series, of which the following is a section, determined mainly at Quinnimont, where the strata are more fully exposed.

Transition Series at Quinnimont.

2. Black fissile slates and shales, 20 feet.
1. Thinly laminated gray flags and calcareous shales, with drifted leaves of Lepidodendra near the base; and near the top having numerous impressions of marine shells, while at the top it passes into carbonaceous shales with strings of coal, leaves of Lepidodendra and other impressions too much obscured for determination, 50 feet. Total. =70.

To complete the section of the strata exposed in the vicinity of Quinnimont, I give below a section of so much of the Umbral series as is to be seen there.

Section of the Umbral Series at Quinnimont.

3. Variegated marlites with some nodular limestone, 70 feet.
2. Gray calcareous sandstone, 20 feet.
1. Bright red shales, seen 50 feet. Total =140 feet.

Some of the above mentioned strata merit a more particular description, which I will now give.

I make in this place no further mention of the remnant of the Lower Productive coals found in this vicinity, but refer to my former paper, where some account was given of their character as found in the Kanawha Valley. It is not known how much farther east they extend, but it cannot be to any considerable distance. No. 21 of the conglomerate series is the only persistent member. As it is found everywhere throughout the Appalachian Coal Field, being in many places the sole representative of the series, and as it is always at a uniform distance below the lowest workable coal-seam of the Lower Productive coal, it would seem to be entitled to be called, as it has been, "The Conglomerate of the Coal Measures." In Raleigh County, and along New River, it is usually a coarse white sandstone, with some conglomeritic portions in its middle and upper parts. In its lower portions it is more flaggy and argillaceous. It varies in thickness from 150 to 200 feet. In the section I have in my summation taken it at the lower figure.

No. 20, near Piney River, shows at its outcrop only black slate. It has been opened near Quinnimont, and is said there to contain thin strings of coal. Nos. 20, 19 and 18, have no features of special interest.

No. 17. This is the coal-seam which is worked extensively at Quinnimont, where it is coked and used in the furnace at that place. It is the most persistent and best developed seam of the series, being easily recognized everywhere in this region by its

peculiar structure. From the flaggy sandstones over this bed at Sewell Station were obtained the plants of Devonian type mentioned in my former paper. At Quinnimont I could find none of these, and it is there remarkably free from plant-impressions of all kinds. In Raleigh also it showed no plants. At Sewell Station, this seam was at first opened for the purpose of working it, but was soon abandoned, owing to an apparent thinning out which was in fact caused by a slide.

No. 16, on the Raleigh road, was not fully exposed owing to slides, which also obscure its outcrop at Quinnimont. It presents the subdivisions founded on the character of the sandstones given in the section, but the coal beds are given on the authority of Mr. Morris, and others who claim to have opened them. I have no doubt of their existence, for at Quinnimont the black slate accompanying 16 d, or Coal No. 8, was seen.

No. 15 was only partially exposed at its outcrop on the Raleigh road. Next to the Quinnimont seam, it appears to me to be the most promising seam of the field. The fire-clay is of fine texture, and sharply distinct from the coal, features not usually seen in the coals of this series.

No. 14, (Coal 5.) This presents in a marked manner a feature very common in this field. The coal at its base exists in the form of numerous interstratifications of coal in thin partings, and black carbonaceous shales; the whole being topped by strata which become more and more siliceous, and firmer as they ascend. There is enough carbon diffused through the base of this mass to make an important bed of coal, were it collected in one mass. The condition of things here shown indicates that there was no deficiency of vegetable matter, but that the alterations of level were too rapid to permit a great accumulation of coal in one mass. The same features to a greater or less extent are shown in every coal bed of the series, and it is safe to say that the instability alone of the surface, prevented the accumulation, in this series, of coal beds as thick as those found in the more productive series which lies above it. Many good plant impressions occur here.

No. 11, from its outcrop, seems to be a promising bed of coal. Its thickness was not fully disclosed. Mr. Morris gives it as two and one-half feet thick. It shows at its base Stigmaria rootlets.

No. 10, stands out in high cliffs. Some of the other sandstones of the series also present firm perpendicular outcrops.

No. 9, is well exposed on the road in a high cliff. It presents the same features as number fourteen, even more strikingly. Numerous thin seams of coal, intermixed with carbonaceous shale, some of them four or five inches thick, form the lower portion for a space of seven feet. Vegetable matter in the form of films of coal, and impregnations of the sandstones and shales, occur to the height of thirty feet. Only a few Lepidodendron leaves were found here.

No. 8, is a massive and siliceous sandstone, forming high cliffs, and resembling to some extent No. 21.

Nos. 6 and 5, are interesting for the recurrence here, in the middle of this coal-bearing series, of the same conditions which prevailed in the formation of the upper part of the Umbral series. These two strata are most strikingly like the red and variegated marlites and shales, found in that portion of the Umbral, and might easily be mistaken for them.

No. 4, is well exposed on the Raleigh road. No plants were found in it.

No. 2, is not exposed anywhere so far as I have seen. The interval occupied by it lies between the massive rock, No. 1, and the crumbling strata of No. 3, which are especially prone to slide down over the precipitous cliffs formed by No. 1. Hence at all the places examined by me, this portion was buried under a mass which had come down from above. Its character is given on the authority of Mr. Morris.

No. 1. This member of the series I consider to be the base of the conglomerate series. It is one of the most prominent features in the hills, standing out as it does, not far above their bases, in immense precipitous ledges. It forms the first stratum, which indicates a decided change from marine to terrestrial conditions. It is much nearer a true conglomerate than No. 21, for many of the layers contain pebbles, a half inch in diameter. It is usually a coarse, open-grained, purely siliceous sandstone, lying in very thick beds. Near the bottom it is brownish in color, but above it is white, having many ferruginous stains. In many parts of this sandstone, particles of carbonaceous matter, in the condition of charcoal, are seen, produced from drifted fragments of trunks and limbs of trees. This condition of the vegetable matter is no doubt due to the ready escape of the bituminous matter from the porous sandstone. Sometimes pretty large angular fragments of the brown sandstones of the Umbral are found associated with these fragments of trees, and in some cases the pebbles of the conglomerate portions are of limestone. This rock is no doubt the heavy sandstone mentioned by Professor Rogers as found some distance to the east of

this point, forming the summit of Little Sewell Mountain. Underlying this rock is found a series of beds which are evidently the products of a period of transition. They are well exposed near Quinnimont, and exhibit some interesting features. No. 1 of this series is a thinly-laminated, argillaceous, gray sandstone in its lower part, but becomes more and more calcareous toward its upper portion, where numerous impressions of shells are found, a list of which will be given farther on. At its summit, which is not seen at Quinnimont, but is well exposed on the Raleigh road, there is a good deal of vegetable matter mixed with the shale, and which is the product of plants which have grown on the spot. This is the lowest indication of an attempt at coal formation, seen in this region. From the indications, there is little doubt that in some places this horizon may show a little coal. Professor Rogers mentions that near the top of Little Sewell, and immediately over the red shales of the Umbral, he saw a small coal-bed. It is no doubt the stratum now described. The other strata given in the sections above present no points of interest.

From this account of the coal-bearing series in question it will be seen that it occupies the horizon of the so-called "Coal-measures Conglomerate," and it would seem to be simply a greatly expanded portion of this widely extended formation. Lying between two huge plates of massive sandstone, either of which has equal claims to the title of conglomerate, the name which I have given it seems justified.

Almost no exploration has been made in the country to the east of Quinnimont, and hence the limits in that direction of this series cannot be given. That it does extend farther east is known. Since my inspection last summer, I have been informed that a five-foot bed of coal is found near Hinton, 800 feet above the level of the river. Hinton is near the mouth of Greenbrier river, about fifteen miles farther east than Quinnimont, measured in an air-line across the strike of the strata.

To the southeast and south, it is found in the counties of Wise, Russell and Tazewell, as may be seen from the account of these counties given by Professor Lesley, in his paper read before the Am. Phil. Soc., April 21, 1871. Professor Lesley shows that under the so-called "Sheep Rock"* in Wise county about 700 feet of coal-bearing rocks are disclosed, with the base not shown. The "Sheep Rock" is No. 21 of the Piney River section. In this space two coal beds are to be seen; one, a six-foot bed, lies at the very base of the hills, and the other, a two-foot bed, is a short distance above it. A similar formation exists in Russell and

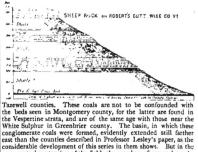

SHEEP ROCK ON ROBERT'S BUTT, WISE CO. VA

Tazewell counties. These coals are not to be confounded with the beds seen in Montgomery county, for the latter are found in the Vespertine strata, and are of the same age with those near the White Sulphur in Greenbrier county. The basin, in which these conglomerate coals were formed, evidently extended still farther east than the counties described in Professor Lesley's paper, as the more easterly extension of the field, the number of seams have diminished, especially in the upper part. On New River in Raleigh county the most important coals are found within 700 feet below the upper ledge.

As we proceed northward, along the eastern outcrop of the series, it has been more extensively affected by erosion, and has been swept off from the greater part of Monroe and Greenbrier counties, these being occupied mainly by the Umbral shales and limestone Professor Rogers mentions finding at the top of Greenbrier Mountain, in the northeast part of the county of that name, a massive sandstone resembling the conglomerate. This is no doubt a remnant of the series. North of this point, in Rich Mountain, in Randolph county, the entire series is presented, capping the mountain, according to Dr. Stevenson. But here it has undergone an important modification, from the loss of the shaly central portion, and the almost entire disappearance of the coals.

*Through the kindness of Prof. Lesley we are able to give the section at the "Sheep Rock" referred to by Prof. Fontaine.—ED.

Iron Furnaces, Mines, etc. on and near the Atlantic, Mississippi & Ohio Railroad.—The following list, prepared for The Virginias by Major Henry Fink, one of the Receivers of the A., M. & O., gives the names, names of proprietor or company, location, capacity and condition, in January, 1880, and distance from shipping points on A., M. & O., of the Iron Furnaces and Forges; Lead, Zinc and Salt Works; Copper, Coal and other mining operations on and near the line of this great trunk railway,—a line of 408 miles, across Virginia, with a tributary country abounding in untold mineral, forestal and agricultural wealth. We hope to devote some future number of our Journal to a presentation of its resources.

The list begins at Bristol, at the Tennessee line, where this road joins the E. Tenn. and Geo. R. R., and takes the works in their order to the eastward.

1. Eagle Furnace, R. & S. Stone, Bristol, Tenn. In Sullivan Co., Tenn., 5 ms. from Bristol. Capacity 600 tons a year. Out of blast.

2. Panic Furnace, Terry & D. Pierce, Wytheville, Va. In Smyth Co., Va., 6 ms. from Rural Retreat. Capacity 1,800 tons. Out of blast.

3. Speedwell Furnace, D. E. James & Son, Speedwell, Wythe Co., Va., 7 ms. from Crockett's. Capacity 1,400 tons. In blast.

4. Wythe Furnace, Sayers, Oglesby & Co., Wytheville, Va. In Wythe Co., Va., 7 ms. from Crockett's. Capacity 3,000 tons. In blast.

5. Raven-Cliff Furnace, Crockett, Sanders & Co., Crockett's Depot, Wythe Co., Va. Are working, in Wythe Co., 9 ms. from Crockett's. Capacity 3,000 tons. In blast.

6. Eagle Furnace, Crockett, Sanders & Co., Crockett's Depot. In Wythe Co., Va., 9 ms. from Crockett's. Capacity 1,200 tons. Out of blast.

7. Grey Eagle Furnace, B. Gallup, Wytheville, Va. In Wythe Co., 10 ms. from Wytheville. Capacity 800 tons. Out of blast.

8. Huddle's Forge, David Huddle, Brown Hill, Wythe Co. In Wythe Co., 11 miles from Max Meadows. Capacity 400 tons. In operation.

9. Brown Hill Furnace, J. P. M. Simmerman, Brown Hill, Wythe Co., 10 ms. from Max Meadows. Capacity 800 tons. Out of blast.

10. Walton Furnace, Howard & Sanders, Max Meadows, Wythe Co., 6 ms. from Max Meadows. Capacity 800 tons. Out of blast.

11. Cedar Run Furnace, Graham & Robinson, Graham's Forge, Wythe Co., 7 ms. from Max Meadows. Capacity 400 tons. Out of blast.

12. Graham's Forge, Graham & Robinson, Graham's Forge, Wythe Co., 6 ms. from Max Meadows. Capacity 400 tons of pig and 200 tons of blooms. In blast.

13. Reed Island Furnace, Graham & Robinson, Graham's Forge, Wythe Co., 12 ms. from Martin's. Capacity 800 tons. Out of blast.

14. Allisonia Furnace, D. S. Forney, Graham's Forge, Wythe Co., 12 ms. from Martin's. Capacity 400 tons. Out of blast.

15. Radford Furnace, Isett and Culbertson, Radford Furnace, Pulaski Co., Va., 9 ms. from Watson's. Capacity 3,600 tons. Not in blast.

16. Sinking Creek Furnace, John's Mountain Iron Co., near Newport, Giles Co., Va., 17 ms. from Christiansburg. Out of blast.

All these are charcoal furnaces and forges and necessarily of limited capacity. They are located near immense beds of the best of iron ores.

When the railway in process of construction, from the C. & O. R'y up New River, is completed, so the coke from the Lower Measure coals (the best known for blast-furnace use) can be brought cheaply to these ores, the largest of furnaces will take the place of these, and along this great belt of Potsdam iron ores there will yet be an immense and cheap production of iron.

17. The Wythe Lead and Zinc Mine Co., J. C. Raper Agent, Max Meadows, 11 ms. from Max Meadows, in Wythe Co., now working, produce 600 tons of lead and 2,000 tons of zinc ore, a year.

18. The Mercer Zinc Works, of the Mercer Zinc Co. of Trenton, N. J., 10 ms. from Max Meadows, and now at work, have an annual capacity of 1,000 tons.

19. The Bertha Zinc Works, at Martin's, Pulaski Co., are now making spelter from ores obtained from Cripple Creek, Wythe Co.

20. The Ore Knob Copper Co., of Ore Knob, Ashe Co., N. C., now working, brings its product 40 ms., to Marion on the A., M. & O., for shipment.

21. The Holston Salt and Plaster Co., at Saltville, Washington Co., Va., now produce 32,000 tons of plaster and 500,000 bushels of salt, annually.

22. The Buena Vista Co., of Saltville, Washington Co., Va., markets 1,800 tons of plaster yearly.

23. The Altoona Coal and Iron Co. is bringing anthracite coal, in moderate quantities, from its mines in the Lowest Coal Measures (No. X), by narrow-gauge railway, to Martin's. The same coal is mined near Christiansburg and Vicker's and shipped to stations near for local use.

All of the preceding works are in or near the Great Valley, between the 290th and 408th mile posts, from Norfolk, on the A., M. & O. Farther N. E., in the same section, abundant beds of iron and other ores are awaiting development. The prospect of an early completion of the Buchanan & Clifton Forge and the Valley railroads, opening the way to these for New River coke, will attract the attention of the iron-makers to them.

24. The Birmingham Iron and Coal Co., at Mount Athos, Campbell Co., Va., 6 ms. below Lynchburg, near the 198th mile post from Norfolk is now mining, and shipping to the North, hematite and magnetic iron ores from the James River Iron Belt, so fully described in the January No. of The Virginias.

Iron Items.

The Elk River Iron Company, Strange Creek, Braxton county, West Virginia, is now making from 7 to 8 tons of charcoal iron a day. It is boated down Elk River to Charleston.

The Arcadia Iron-works, usually called the Boyd Furnace, on James River, below Buchanan, Botetourt county, Va., was sold January 6th, 1880, for $125,000, to a Pennsylvania company, by Maj. John W. Johnston, commissioner. This estate includes some 20,000 acres of land in fee simple, and iron ore rights on about 4,000 acres besides. It extends for nearly 10 miles along James River and the James River and Kanawha Canal, and reaches back on the western slope of the Blue Ridge to near its crest and to the vicinity of the Peaks of Otter,—its location is shown on the map in the January number of The Virginias. There is a hot-blast charcoal furnace on the property. It has large bodies of woodland and very extensive deposits of iron ores. The mining and shipment of ore, on a large scale, by the canal, to the North, will first engage the attention of the purchasers, who have already a large force at work opening the mines. The old furnace will be put in working order at once, and arrangements are under way for constructing new furnaces. When the Buchanan and Clifton Forge Railway is completed, it is proposed to ship ores westward from these lands.

The Washington City and Virginia Mining Company, organized in Washington, D. C., under the auspices of Capt. Hugh Thomas Douglas, of Catlett's, Fauquier county, Va., will soon commence mining a deposit of iron ore on the London farm, on the James, 44 miles below Lynchburg. Prof. New, of Washington, will be the chemist of the company.

Our Advertisers.

The attention of our readers is called to our advertisements. We can endorse our advertisers, in their respective callings, as capable and reliable men. We know them all personally. No one need have any fear of buying a bad title in Virginia or West Virginia if it has been pronounced good by the attorneys and its lines have been found correct, and not "interlocked," by the engineers that advertise in THE VIRGINIAS. The farms advertised are all that they claim to be. The advertisers of mineral lands have, we very well know, some of the best in the country, and they will sell them at prices merely nominal compared with their intrinsic value. The invitation of proposals for coal and coke for the 80-ton furnace at Low Moor, rapidly approaching completion, is but the beginning. Thousands of coke ovens are needed in the New River District to supply the demands of the next two years. Coal lands can be bought or leased on favorable terms, and there is no business far a better prospect than coke-making.

We beg pardon, in advance, for making public the following extracts from some of the many letters we have received since the issue of our last number:

"I have simply given a cursory glance, and from that am convinced it is going to be a valuable paper, and should be a paying one. Staunton seems to be waking up." *Capt. W. W. Martin*, of Pittsburg, Pa., Receiver of Castle Shannon & Pittsburg R. R.

"You have my hearty wishes for the success of your paper. I congratulate you on its handsome appearance, and on the value of its contents."—*Wm. M. Fontaine*, Prof. of Geology University of Virginia.

"I congratulate you on your enterprise, and will not only subscribe for it myself but do what I can to extend its circulation. Your enterprise is one of the needs of the State and I hope that you may receive a liberal support and be encouraged to press forward in this new field of development for the growth of our Old Commonwealth."—*Maj. W. T. Sutherlin*, Danville, Va.

"I am in receipt of your new paper, which promises to be one of great interest. I will file it carefully, and have it bound for reference to the geological department of the National Museum.—*Prof. Spencer F. Baird*, Director of the Smithsonian Inst., Washington, D. C.

"The receipt of THE VIRGINIAS is as welcome as it was unexpected. Not only to fill a great want in a district of country that promises to be Staffordshire of the world, but also becoming the expectation to do a material service in a large number of the citizens of the Old Commonwealth. In addition to our subscription we would gladly aid in its circulation."—*Norris & Brother*, Baltimore, Md.

"The paper has interested me exceedingly, and if properly supported by those most interested in the development of the vast and varied resources of our respective States, will do a world of good in advancing their material prosperity."—*Hon. Alex. R. Boteler*, of West Virginia.

Manganese.—The Crimora Company mined and shipped in December, 1879, 256 gross tons of manganese, losing a week for the holidays. It is now putting up additional crushers, &c., to accommodate the increased output of its mine.

Slate.—The Red-Bud Slate Quarry, on the Valley Railway near Staunton, worked by Messrs. Owens & Buckey, quarried, shaped, and shipped to market, in 1879, 300 mantels, 1,000 hearths, 500 feet of wainscoting, 1,000 feet of steps, 30 black-boards, and some 700 feet in other forms, of the superior slates there found, near the junction of the Middle and Upper Cambrian rocks, II and III, and in the same relations as the noted slate quarries of Pennsylvania and Vermont. These Red-Bud slates have proven to be well adapted to marbleizing.

The slate quarries of Buckingham Co., Va. are said to be doing three times as much business as they have done for the past two years. The well-known superior character of these Archæan slates and the facilities for marketing them by water, ought to bring a large development to the trade in them.

Gold.—The Booker Gold Mine, Buckingham county Va., is reported as doing a good business. The gold mines of J. B. Gilliam, in that county, opened last year, has been sold to a New York company for $14,000.—Buckingham has numerous gold mines, the productiveness of which is well known, that can be bought on the most liberal terms. We are very sure that gold-mining can be made to pay well in the Virginia "gold belt" if conducted with capital and skill.

Coal.—In the Chesterfield coal basin, near Richmond, Va. after two years of constant labor, the water from the Raccoon pits has been drained into the Bright Hope pits, and so brought under control; so the Bright Hope mine will be able to again do a successful business.

Wagon lines are now running from the Dora Coal Mine, at North River Gap, Augusta county, Va., to Harrisonburg and intermediate points, delivering coal, semi-bituminous from the Saylor vein and anthracite from the Shaver vein, for local consumption. A writer in the *Valley Virginian* reports the above, and that the Shaver vein is "about nine feet thick."

The Mineral Traffic of the Atlantic, Mississippi and Ohio Railroad, from Virginia mines, for the years ending June 30th, 1878 and 1879, and the destination of the minerals conveyed, in tons of 2,000 lbs., are shown in the following table, prepared for "THE VIRGINIAS" by Mr. Henry Fink, the Receiver of that road.

DESTINATION.	Copper, Iron & Lead Ores.		Barytes.		Coal.		Pig Iron.		Pig Lead.		Marble.		Salt.		Slate and Stone.		Zinc Ores.	
	1878.	1879.	1878.	1879.	1878.	1879.	1878.	1879.	1878.	1879.	1878.	1879.	1878.	1879.	1878.	1879.	1878.	1879.
Boston		47			210	415		167	46	30	20					47		130
New York	403	768	693		1,443	1,865	210	1,234	110	70	70		11	10		30		5
Philadelphia		567	10				2,325		10	10			8,832	7,206			423	190
Baltimore		30			210			6	40	60	60		742	1,025		10	41	
Other Eastern cities		16																
Lynchburg	83				400	692		110										
Southern cities			3													47	3	
Way stations		4		4	1,735	2,250	2,684		227				1,418	1,457	1,460	30	474	
Richmond													2,433	2,450		77	847	395
Totals	711	1,368																
Totals from west of Bristol	40	67			540		625		34				10		730			1,733

The Virginias.

A Mining, Industrial, and Scientific Journal:

Devoted to the Development of Virginia and West Virginia.

Vol. I, No. 3. }
Staunton, Virginia, March, 1880.
{ Price 15 Cents.

The Virginias,

PUBLISHED MONTHLY,

By JED. HOTCHKISS, - - - Editor and Proprietor,

At 346 E. Main St., Staunton, Va.

TERMS, including postage, per year, in advance, $1.50. Single numbers, 15 cents. Extra copies $10. per 100.

This Number of "The Virginias" is largely devoted to the resources and developments of the easterly half of the Shenandoah Valley in Virginia and West Virginia, the region traversed by the Shenandoah Valley Railroad and to that railroad, in pursuance of a promise made in our last issue and of our general plan of collecting in one number detailed information concerning some particular portion of these States. In addition to a considerable space occupied editorially on this subject, we present several articles, by gentlemen of recognized ability, relating, directly or indirectly, to the same thing.—That by Prof. Campbell is spoken of elsewhere; it is the best published guide to a knowledge of the geological structure of the region in question and the location of its beds of iron ores.—Those by Prof. Prime relate especially to the mineral deposits of the Blue Ridge and its foot-hills in Page and Warren counties, and to those of the northeast group of the Massanutton Mountains in Shenandoah; they present the facts of his personal observations made in 1849. The able reports of this gentleman on "The Brown Hematite Ore Ranges" and "The Brown Hematite Deposits of the Siluro-Cambrian Limestones," of Lehigh Co., Pennsylvania, issued by the Second Geological Survey of that State, in which he was an assistant, have given him a national reputation, and prove him capable of speaking understandingly, as well as authoritatively, concerning the iron ores and other mineral deposits of the Shenandoah Valley, which is part of the same Great Valley, geologically as well as topographically, as that in which the great iron-making county of Lehigh is situated. His estimate of comparative quantities of iron ores has a special value.—Prof. Egleston adds his testimony in regard to the abundance and excellent quality of the iron ores of this region, and does not fail to say, what his personal observations have prepared him for saying, that the Shenandoah Valley Railroad will place them within easy reach "of one of the best fuels in the United States for their manufacture."—Mr. Bowron is the chemist of the Shenandoah Iron Works, and lives in the portion of this region he describes. His analysis of the pig iron made at Furnace No. 2 shows it to be one of great excellence, even good enough for the fastidious demands of the Bessemer steel makers.—The brief extract from Mr. Spilsbury shows that the large deposits of the titaniferous magnetites found along this line, can, under proper treatment, be made to produce the best of irons.

Attention is Invited to Advertisements;—Of the sale of the "Betty Martin" iron mines, in the Piedmont Virginia belt of specular and magnetic iron ores; a very valuable and most favorably located iron ore property;—To the Blackford Forge property, on the line of the Shenandoah Valley R. R., offered for sale;—To the Wire Tramways, the cheapest appliances for reaching mines of all kinds, especially elevated ones, furnished by the American Wire Tramways Co.;—To the supplies offered by the Lynchburg Iron Works;—and to the highly valuable Smithers-Gauley coal lands, now in the market.

Want of Space has crowded out many items of importance relating to our mineral development.—Lands are changing hands, prospectors and miners are busy, old furnaces going into blast and new ones being built, the railways are over-burdened by freights, existing railroads are undergoing repairs and adding to their rolling stock, and new lines, some main ones and others mineral branches, are in course of construction.—The outlook is a satisfactory and comforting one, for these Virginian States are now marching to their legitimate place, the front rank, in the mining and manufacturing world.

"The Silurian Formation in Central Virginia" the able paper by Prof. John L. Campbell of Washington and Lee University,—which through his courtesy and that of the publishers of the American Journal of Science and Arts, (for which we tender thanks) we present this month to our readers, revised and with all the costly illustrations that accompanied its appearance in that leading scientific Journal,—will amply repay a most careful study whether considered from the *scientific* or the *economic* stand-point. It might have been called The Rock Formations of the Central Valley Plateau and its Mountain Borders and the place of their included iron and other ores. It throws much light on the geological positions and relations of the several iron-ore-belts lying west of the Blue Ridge, especially in that portion of the Central Valley Plateau described in Prof. Campbell's "Report on the Mineral Resources of the Valley of the James" published in the January No. of THE VIRGINIAS, but its clear and accurate descriptions and geological section are applicable, substantially, to every part of the Great Valley and its boundary and included mountain ranges, the Archæan and Cambrian ones of the Blue Ridge on the east, and the Silurio-Devonian ones of the "North" mountains on the west and the "Massanuttons" in the middle. This is a most valuable accompaniment to this Shenandoah Valley No. of THE VIRGINIAS and we especially commend it to those engaged in developing the iron-ore deposits near the line of the S. V. R. R.

Hamilton's Metallic Paint, made from a brown ochre, mined by Captain A. M. Hamilton, of Harrisonburg, Va., from the western base of the Southwest Massanutton Mountains, near Keezletown, Rockingham county, Va., from a fine bed near the junction of formations II and III, the Valley limestones and the Massanutton slates, will soon be placed on the market by Messrs. French, Richards & Co., of S. W. Cor. York Ave. and Callowhill St., Philadelphia, Pa. Prof. J. L. Campbell recently analyzed this brown ochre, dried at 212° Fahr., and found it to consist of 52.28 per cent. of peroxide of iron (ferric oxide), 1.15 oxide of manganese, 40.22 clay (with a little very fine silica), and 6.35 combined water. Its specific gravity, powdered, was 2.82. As Prof. C. remarks: "The iron and manganese give it a clear brown color and good body, and the clay gives tenacity. Its texture is very fine."

We are pleased to announce the opening of this new ochre bed and that Captain Hamilton will very soon commence mining the crude ochre on a large scale and hauling it to Harrisonburg, where it will be ground and prepared for market. There are doubtless beds of iron ore, as well as others of ochre, on the western slope of the Massanuttons, and we expect to see a new mineral belt developed there before long. Capt. H. is a good pioneer in the work.

The Pittsburg, Pa., Chamber of Commerce was addressed on the subject of a Southern Railway from that city across West Virginia and Virginia and into North Carolina, and the iron and other resources of the country it would traverse,—by Gov. Mathews of W. Va., on the 8th, and by Maj. Jed. Hotchkiss of Virginia and Prof. W. C. Kerr of North Carolina on the 9th of the present month. A large number of the most substantial and influential men of that great iron manufacturing centre gave these gentlemen a cordial welcome and their message a most respectful and attentive hearing. The Pittsburg *Dispatch*, commenting on the meeting of the 8th, said, "The addresses were listened to attentively by those present, many of whom said, at the close of the meeting, they had had no idea of the extent of the mineral wealth of the States referred to, and the advantages Pittsburg would enjoy by increasing her railway facilities to these points."

Titanic Iron Ore.—Recently a distinguished metallurgist secretly "drew" a sample from a furnace ore pile and found in it 8 per cent. of titanium, a quantity sufficient, in the opinion of most American iron-makers, to render the ore useless; he then went to the manager and asked how they liked the ore they were using and was informed that it gave entire satisfaction. Asking whether it had been tested for titanium the reply was that it had not.

The Mineral Resources of the Page Valley.

By Frederick Prime, Jr., late Ass't. Geologist of Pennsylvania.

Brown Hematite Iron Ores.—The traveler on passing south from Front Royal will at once be struck with the series of foot-hills which lie along the western base of the Blue Ridge; separated by a valley more or less broad, they are found to be narrow in some places, while in others they are a mile or more in width. To the mining engineer these hills are of peculiar interest, as they indicate, approximately, the location of the brown hematite deposits on which the furnaces to be built along the line of the Shenandoah Valley Railroad must in great part depend for a future supply of ore.

A more or less close examination of the western crests of these foot-hills will show that they are composed of a white or straw-colored sandstone or quartzite, known to geologists as the Potsdam sandstone. This sandstone may be distinguished from the other sandstones of the region by the presence of worm-like or tubular cylinders of quartz contained in the mass of the rock and at right angles to its bedding. It may be of some practical importance to note this fact, in order to be able to recognize this sandstone deposit. The sandstones usually dip southeast or are vertical, occasionally they are found dipping northwest, the latter being the normal dip and the southeastern one due to an overthrow of the sandstone beds by the force which elevated the Blue Ridge. Overlying these sandstones when they have a northwest dip, but underlying when the dip is southeast, are a mass of slates or clays. These slates are greyish and white and pale yellow or pink in color, and are generally more or less decomposed to a white or reddish clay. The clay closely resembles kaolin in appearance, and in some cases is probably an actual kaolin in composition.

These slates and clays are of the greatest importance as being the mother-rock of the brown hematites. Where the sandstones have a high dip to the northwest, the slates, clays and ore should be looked for in the western edge of the foot-hills, close to the base of the sandstone ridges. Where there is a gentle dip to the northwest, the slates, clays and ores may rise nearly to the top of the western slope of the hills and may be looked for anywhere within a mile of the base. Shafting alone will tell their actual location, although it is well to look close to considerable quantities of surface ores for the underlying deposits *in place*. Where the sandstones have a southwest dip, then the ores, clays and slates should be looked for on the western slope of the hills and not far from the most western beds of the sandstone.

In addition to these deposits, others may be looked for through the heart of the valley, at greater or less distances from the foot-hills. These last are the débris resulting from the vast amount of decomposition of the rocks in by-gone ages. Their occurrence is uncertain and their depth limited, but while they last they yield large quantities of brown hematite of excellent quality, which can be mined cheaply. The only way to discover this last class of brown hematites is to look for rich float ore on the hill-slopes, and, where this occurs, to shaft for it. These deposits will always be subordinate in importance to those first described, as occurring near the western base of the foot-hills.

I wish here to emphasize the fact, in order to prevent any useless expenditure of money in shafting, that the brown hematite *in place* need only be looked for along that base of the foot-hills which faces the Massanutton Mountains, while there are not, and cannot be, any productive brown hematite deposits between the *western* base of the sandstone, which forms the foot-hills, and the base of the Blue Ridge. There may be and are, locally, deposits of bog-ore, but not of the genuine brown hematites belonging to the rocks of the Valley.

There can be no doubt of the existence of millions of tons of brown hematite iron ores occurring along the western base of the foot-hills of the Blue Ridge. This is only too clearly proven by such ore-banks as the Fox Mountain and Smith banks in the southern portion, the Hiestand bank in the northern portion of Page county, the mines recently opened near Front Royal by Ivins, and by the numerous occurrences of rich float ore between these localities. I do not mean to assert that there is a continuous bed of iron ore between Front Royal and Furnace No. 2 of the Shenandoah Iron Works, for such is not the case. But I do mean to say that all indications point to the presence of numerous and large lenticular deposits of brown hematite iron ores in the slates, and that there seems to be every probability of the existence of many ore-banks which will rival in extent and richness the well known Moselem and Ironton mines of the Lehigh Valley.

I am convinced that there is enough brown hematite iron ore, along the line of outcrops just described, to furnish fifty furnaces of the same capacity as those on the Lehigh with all the ore they need for more than fifty years. Nor do I know of any place where the ores can be more cheaply extracted. Labor is cheap, and the Hon. Wm. Milnes, jr., stated that he is able to extract all the ore he needs for his small furnace for 75c. per ton. As he only selects the best and richest ore, and works on a comparatively small scale, it follows that the ore all through this line of outcrop could be mined for the same price, if worked on a large scale, taking all the ore, and provided the mines are not troubled with water. On the Lehigh the brown hematites are costing at the present time from $1.62 to $2. per ton. The difference in mining, about $1. per ton, is sufficient to carry the ores about 100 to 130 miles on the railroad. I cannot doubt therefore that in the case of Page Valley alone there is a large prospective increase to the railroad company from the transportation of these. The price at which they can be mined will make it profitable to deliver the ores along the line of the Connellsville railroad and at Harrisburg and Baltimore. Nor is this all, if the data I give below are correct, as I believe them to be, pig iron can be made of as good quality as that of the Lehigh Valley, of the same character and far more cheaply. I cannot doubt that under the circumstances, shrewd iron-masters from Pennsylvania seeing that the available supply of good brown hematite iron ores is becoming limited in that State, will in the near future erect furnaces along the line of the Shenandoah Valley Railroad, thus imitating the example of that far-sighted man, the late Wm. Firmstone, Esq., of Glendon, who purchased Longdale, in Alleghany Co., Va.

In order to be safe in my calculations I have placed the outside prices on everything in the following estimate.

COST OF MAKING ONE TON OF PIG IRON.

Iron ore 2½ tons @$1,	$2.50
Limestone, 800 ℔s.,	.19
(Coke $1.50 at Connellsville) Coke 1¼ tons @$3.34,	4.28
Labor,	2.00
Superintendence, clerk hire. &c.,	.40
Repairs,	.50
	$9.87

Or, in order to cover contingencies, say $12.00 per ton. This iron can be delivered from Luray to Pittsburg at a cost of $2.48, which will make the cost of the iron delivered there on

board cars, allowing 25c. for putting it on the cars, $14.73. By reference to the prices at Pittsburg of last January, when the price of pig iron was as low as at any period for many years, I find the rate of forge pig iron quoted at $16.50, which even in a time of the greatest depression would leave a profit of $1.77 per ton. While at the present time the same irons are quoted at $29., which will leave the handsome profit of $14.27. I think that most iron-masters will allow that for the next seven or eight years the price of pig iron at the furnaces will average $19. per ton. Supposing this, however, to be the price at Pittsburg, there would be a profit per ton of $4.27, which is quite a sufficient return to pay a very handsome profit on the investment of $500,000; which would be about the capital necessary to start two large coke furnaces and the mines, tracks, buildings, &c., necessary to supply them.

The Brown Hematite Iron Ores of the Massanutton Mountains Northeast of the New Market-Luray Gap.—The Massanutton Mountain is a range of hills extending from Front Royal to Harrisonburg. Its northern portion contains a valley, in part composed of limestone and quite productive, known as the Fort Valley. Underlying this limestone and overlying the sandstones which form the crests of the hills are a series of slates and shales known to geologists as the "Clinton Formation." These slates and shales are of practical interest as containing a great abundance of iron ores; and wherever they occur between New York and Alabama the iron is found with them. In places the ore is red hematite and being composed of minute shells is known under the name of "fossil ore."

It is now a quite well known fact that there are several portions of the Clinton formation which contain beds of iron ore, and that all of them rarely, if ever, occur together. In places, as above stated, the ore is composed of fossils and according as the predominant impurities are silica or lime, the ore is known as the *hard* or *soft* fossil ore. In other localities and lower down in the formation the ore is a brown hematite, at least for a considerable distance below the outcrop. Such is the case in the Fort Valley. The brown hematites occur here not far from the bottom of the slates. They are of an excellent quality, for the most part spongy, and would work very easily and reduce rapidly in a blast-furnace; a most important consideration.

In order to show the quality of these ores I subjoin the following analyses, made, like those previously cited, from specimens selected by myself, sampled as carefully as possible, and analysed by Booth, Garrett & Blair.

	(1)	(2)	(3)	
Iron,	44.992	44.467	43.207	(1)From the Bush Mine, in the Fort Valley.—(2) From Noah's Ark Tunnel of Shenandoah Iron Co.—(3) From New Bank of Shenandoah Iron Co.
Manganese	2.599	0.995	3.331	
Phosphorus	0.401	0.146	0.129	

The ores occuring in this formation have one very great advantage over those of the Page Valley; viz: while they thin and thicken in width, the ore forms an almost continuous bed, varying in thickness from 18 inches to 30 feet, with, as I am told, an average thickness of 3 to 4 feet. The ores in the Massanutton Mountains have also an advantage over the ores of the same formation in Pennsylvania. While in the latter State the ores almost invariably occur only on one side of a mountain; in the Massanuttons four ridges of ore occur, owing to the peculiar manner in which the rocks have been folded into two synclinals, thus catching and preserving the ores from erosion. In this manner for every lineal mile we go along the Fort Valley there are four miles of ore. One on the northwest flank of the most eastern ridge, one on each side of

the middle ridge, and one on the southeastern slope of the most western ridge. That this ore is continuous is evident from its having been extensively worked at both ends of the Fort Valley—a distance of over 20 miles—and from the numerous surface indications in the intervals. I have seen no point where the ores of this formation can be more advantageously and cheaply mined.

The proper plan to work these ores is to erect a double plane from the Fort Valley to the eastern base of the Massanutton Mountains, have a stationary engine to hoist the loaded cars to the top of the ridge, and let these descend by gravity, hauling up the empty cars by their superior weight. By erecting furnaces at or near Luray the ores of the Page and Fort valleys could be mined and thus insure a first-class foundry or forge iron.

That these ores are abundant is plainly seen from an inspection of the old Bush Mine on the Eastern Ridge of the Massanutton, the Three-mile Bank on Duncan's Mountain, the Alleghany Bank on the Middle Ridge, the numerous surface indications and the banks formerly worked for the charcoal furnace at the northern end of the Fort Valley.

The mining of these Clinton ores would not cost at this time, Dec. 1879, more than from 90 cts. to $1. per ton.

The *ores of Manganese* were seen, as surface specimens, at several points. Some of these from the western slope of Round-top Mt., about 2 ms. S.W. of Marksville, analysed,—Manganese 49.613, Iron 1.050, and Phosphorus 0.310 (Booth, Garrett & Blair). This was not a fair average sample, as it had been exposed for many years. These ores will be exceedingly valuable for the manufacture of ferro-manganese, if not too high in phosphorus. Also, if pure enough, they will be valuable for the manufacture of glass.

As ores of manganese are known to exist abundantly between the Shenandoah Iron Works and the Chesapeake & Ohio Railway, I have no doubt that in time other deposits of manganese will be found to exist in Page and Warren counties along the base of the foot-hills. That found east of the western base is a very regular belt existing for a long distance, but it is so intimately mixed with quartz as to be valueless; the Jeremy's Run mine belongs to this class. Manganese is also mined near the middle of the length of the Fort Valley.

The *copper ores* of the Blue Ridge I only examined superficially, for want of time. At Overall's there are several promising localities of blue and green carbonates and gray sulphurets. Some of the land owners claim the existence of over a dozen veins. Near Marksville some ore is seen disseminated through the rock, but not showing a well defined vein. A mine was formerly worked near the Stoney-man Mt., but the ore was found too lean.

Slates for roofing and other purposes may be found along the base of the Massanutton Mts., in the thick formation of slates corresponding in geological age to the roofing slates of Lehigh and Northampton counties in Pennsylvania and of Vermont. At some points where I passed over them the indications were such as to lead me to think they might be valuable for roofing, mantles, etc.

The Clays.—In places a very soft, unctuous clay occurs, associated with the iron ores of the Page Valley. This clay is the result of the decomposition of the slates which hold the ores. As the mines are developed I would recommend having these clays analysed, to see if any of them are kaolin. I think that in places such will be the case. The discovery of kaolin would be very valuable, as giving rise to the manufactory of pottery along the line of the railroad.

The Ochre.—About three miles south of Marksville, Charles

Foote & Co. have opened an ochre bank. They are grinding the ochre and sending it to market. This deposit of ochre is an extensive one, as all the wells sunk between Foote's place and Marksville have gone through the ochre. This ochre is said to be a good one and to find a ready sale; which would seem to be confirmed by the fact that Foote pays $4 per ton for hauling the same over to New Market.—If a sufficient market exists for the sale of this ochre, I know of no place where it can be more cheaply mined and manufactured. The ochre is of a very light brown color.

Conclusions.—My conclusions as to the mineral deposits along the line of the Shenandoah Valley Railroad, in Page and Warren counties, south of Front Royal, may be briefly summed up as follows:

1st. There exist deposits of magnetic iron ore near Marksville, which may be valuable as a fettling for puddling furnaces and in time, perhaps, be used in blast furnaces.

2nd. There are very extensive and valuable deposits of brown hematite iron ore along the foot-hills of the Blue Ridge, on its western base, which can be very cheaply mined and will furnish as many as fifty blast-furnaces for many years; the iron made from them being of as high a grade as that produced in the Lehigh Valley. ·

3rd. There exist practically inexhaustable quantities of iron ores in the Massanutton Mountains.

4th. There are ores of manganese which will probably be very valuable.

5th. The copper ores should be carefully examined to see what the quantity may be.

6th. The slates at the base of the Massanutton Mountains should be thoroughly searched by a practical slater to see if there are any good roofing-slates.

7th. There is an abundance of ochre near Marksville.

8th. I know of no place where pig iron can be more cheaply made and worked into malleable iron, if coal and coke can be bought cheaply enough.

Dec. 1879. FRED'K PRIME, Jr.,
M. E. and late Ass't Geologist of Penn'a.

Many of the Prominent Mining Engineers of the country have been lately or are now prospecting in Virginia. We note that Mr. H. G. Blackwell, of the Pennsylvania Steel Co., and Mr. Hartman of the Cambria Co., have been in the vicinity of Lynchburg. Mr. E. Gybbon Spilsbury of Philadelphia and Prof. Wurtz of Hoboken, N. J., visited the ore deposits on the James not long since; the former announced a paper on these deposits for the late meeting of the American Institute of Mining Engineers in New York, which the latter would have discussed, but it was not read for want of time, very much to the regret of every one interested in Virginia, for these gentlemen could have furnished valuable information, from personal observations, concerning these ores that would help to solve the difficult problem of their origin and condition. It is to be hoped that Mr. Spilsbury will furnish his paper to the Institute or give the substance of it for publication in THE VIRGINIAS. Professors Dewees and Prime, of the Pennsylvania Geological Survey, have lately made explorations in the same region.

The New River Railroad, which, by a line 62 miles long, will connect the Chesapeake & Ohio and Atlantic, Mississippi & Ohio railways, by following the valley of New River of the Kanawha from the former to the latter, has quite a number of hands at work on its road bed both in Virginia and West Virginia. The excellent iron ores that abound in the Apalachian region crossed by this line and their almost proximity to the Lower Measures coking coals that will result when it is completed, offer sufficient inducement for the construction of this line, to say nothing of its great importance as a connection between two great trunk roads, or as a link in the chain of the Pittsburg & Southern Railway.

The James River Steel and Iron Works, above Lynchburg, now in process of enlargement, are to be managed by Mr. Catesby Jones, formerly of the Dover Works.

The Shenandoah Valley Railroad and the Mineral and other Resources of the Country Tributary to it.

BY THE EDITOR.

The Shenandoah Valley Railroad is rapidly becoming one of the most important of the numerous agencies now actively at work developing the great unused resources of West Virginia and Virginia. Only a few months ago the corporation bearing that name was regarded by most people as a dead one that had left a legacy of a few miles of unfinished railway and disconnected fragments of road-bed to mock their disappointed hopes; but today, vitalized by the energy and capital of the Shenandoah Valley Construction Company, it has fifty-four miles of first-class, standard-gauge, well-equipped railway in operation, doing a successful business, intersecting three great lines of railroad, furnishing easy access to one of the richest and most delightsome portions of the far-famed Shenandoah Valley, its charming scenery, wonderful caverns, and famous battle fields, and to the immense, far-stretching, beds of iron ores that rib with metallic wealth the sides and flanks of the mountain ranges that on either hand border that land of agricultural plenty. And,—such is the energy displayed in all the departments of its construction, so well in hand are all the needed appliances for doing and completing the work, and so frequently is section after section opened to trade and travel on the appointed day,—before the coming autumn has passed its trains will run from Hagerstown, its northern terminus (a railway centre from which lines reach to Baltimore, to Philadelphia, and to New York), for some 150 miles to the southwest, through the Lower, the Middle and most of the Upper valleys of the Shenandoah, along more than a hundred miles of the outcrops of iron ores and by scores of the best of sites, with abundant water-power if wanted, for iron-works of all kinds and other manufacturing establishments, to a connection with that great east-and-west trunk line of traffic the Chesapeake & Ohio Railway and the exhaustless and easily mined beds of coking, block and other coals that it runs through for a hundred miles.

The charter permits and the unoccupied way is open for the extension of the Shenandoah Valley Railroad for hundreds of miles still farther to the southwest through the other Valley plateaus,—those of the James, the Roanoke, the New-Kanawha, and the Holston-Tennessee,—that succeed that of the Shenandoah in that direction and with it make The Great Valley of Virginia, with its well-nigh 6,000 square miles of limestone lands of unsurpassed fertility, (larger than Saxony with its two-and-a-half million people), all bordered by massive beds of iron and other ores that can challenge comparison with those of any other lands,—but, for the present, we only propose to direct attention to the portion of this railway extending from Hagerstown, Maryland, to the line of the Chesapeake & Ohio Railway where it crosses the Upper Valley of the Shenandoah, in Augusta county Virginia, and to the character, resources and advantages of that part of the Shenandoah Valley and its boundary mountains that is naturally tributary to it, (the country shown on the accompanying map), and to the value and importance of this new railway as one of the agents for developing and building up these States and as an exceedingly valuable and important link in the railway system of the country.

The Route of the Shenandoah Valley Railroad from Hagerstown, Md., to the Chesapeake & Ohio Railway, Va., in a S. by W. and S. W. direction, is first down the beautiful valley of Antietam Creek, crossing the famous battle-field of Sharpeburg or Antietam, to the Chesapeake & Ohio Canal and the Potomac River, opposite Shepherdstown, W. Va., a distance of about 16 miles, where it crosses that river on a noble iron truss bridge of six spans. This Hagerstown-Shepherdstown section, including the bridge, is under contract, and will be completed and the road opened by the first of next June. At Shepherdstown it enters the far-famed Shenandoah Valley—the northeastern plateau of the Great Valley of Virginia, that, with an average breadth of 16 miles, stretches for 330 miles, from the Potomac to the Tennessee line, part of the Great Limestone Valley of the Atlantic Highlands, that extends for 1,500 miles from the mouth of the St. Lawrence to central Alabama, presenting by far the best railway route there is from New Orleans to New York or Boston; the line that

surpasses all other N. E.–S. W. lines in pleasantness of climate, beauty of scenery, and abundance and variety of agricultural and mineral resources.

From Shepherdstown to Front Royal, from the banks of the Potomac to beyond the forks of the Shenandoah, 44 miles, across the Lower Valley of the Shenandoah, the railway is now in operation, two trains running each way daily. This portion passes, centrally, through the entire length of the rich and picturesque counties of Jefferson, W. Va., and Clarke, Va., and into the middle of Warren, Va. Some 4 miles from Shepherdstown, at Shenandoah Junction, it crosses the main line of the Baltimore & Ohio Railway, 90 miles W. from Baltimore, connecting with its thousands of miles of far-reaching lines of trade and travel. Five miles farther, at Charlestown, the county-seat of Jefferson, it crosses the Valley Branch of the Baltimore & Ohio Railway, by which it can have access to more than 200 miles of the western half of the Great Valley of Virginia. Ten miles beyond Charlestown, after passing Ripon in Jefferson and Fairfield in Clarke, it passes through Berryville,—the Battle-town of Revolutionary days, near by the home of Morgan, the wagoner General, "Saratoga," stone-built by Hessian prisoners,—the county town of Clarke, where it will eventually be crossed by the Washington & Ohio Railway, now in operation from Alexandria to just across the Blue Ridge, and perhaps by the Baltimore, Cincinnati & Western, either of which will open a short way to the Great Ohio Coal-Basin. From Berryville to Riverton, some 22 miles, the way is not far from the Shenandoah River proper, over a charming champaign country, dotted with noble country seats, passing the venerable Old Chapel, Boyceville the station for Millwood, White Post and the remains of Greenway Court, the home in Colonial times of the owner of the millions of acres in the Northern Neck, Lord Fairfax, Baron of Cameron, where the boy county-surveyor, George Washington, had his office, Ashby and Cedarville, the last memorable as the scene of part of the battle of Front Royal, in 1863.

At Riverton the railway crosses the broad, full-volumed Shenandoah, here 453 feet above the sea-level, just below the confluence of its North and South forks, and also crosses the line of the Manassas Branch of the Washington City, Virginia Midland & Great Southern Railroad which has over 300 miles of road by which the S. V. R. R. can have eastward, westward and southward connection. Here this railway leaves the Lower Valley of the Shenandoah and enters the Eastern, or South-fork Valley (sometimes called the Page Valley from its central county), of the Middle Shenandoah Valley, the one bounded eastward by the Blue Ridge and westward by the Massanutton Mountains, and follows up the eastern or right-hand side of the South Fork, by far the larger river, reaching, 44 miles from Shepherdstown, Front Royal, the county seat of Warren county, to which the cars of this railway are now running and 10 miles beyond which, to Bentonville, they will be running by the time this reaches our readers.

This Eastern Middle Valley of the Shenandoah,—the one which, from the nature of things, will long find its outlet to market by this road,—is, as we learn from Hotchkiss' Physiography of Virginia, some 50 miles in length, averages 6 in breadth, and includes 270 square miles of undulating country ⅓ of which pertains to Warren, ½ to Page and ⅙ to Rockingham counties, inclining to the N. E. from an average altitude of about 1,200 ft. to one of 600,—the South Fork falls about 500 ft. in the 50 miles of air-line by which it winds through this valley. The Blue Ridge on the east has many lovely cove valleys carved from its western slope, like the noted ones of Elk Run and Hawksbill, Gooney Manor and Happy creeks, widening into the main valley, and nearly all of its boldly rounded crest and far-sloping sides is fertile lands adapted to grazing, to vineyards or to forest culture The Massanuttons cover 250 square miles of territory with their 3 to 5 parallel ranges of mountains, varying in elevation above the Valley from 500 ft. to 1,600, and their long included valleys, some fertile, but all rich in vast beds of iron and manganese ores and limestones, in mineral springs and forestal resources.

From Front Royal to Luray, the county seat of Page county, some 23 miles, the route is by Bentonville and Milford in Warren and by Cedar Point and Hope Mills in Page, leaving the vicinity of the river a few miles below Luray and following the parallel noted valley of the Hawksbill, one more easterly and nearer the Blue Ridge, to that town of the wonderful Cavern, one of the most remarkable known, which has attracted so many from far and near in the few months that have elapsed since its discovery;—to this point the cars will run from Hagerstown by the first of June, when thousands that have been kept from seeing the famous cave because of its distance from a railway will come to view its wonders and enjoy the lovely landscapes that surround it.

There is another phase of development that we are glad to note; that which will make these States the resort of the seekers of recreation. Few places in the Southern country will be as attractive as the delightfully located village of Luray, with its Cavern of countless wonders and its surroundings of grand and picturesque scenery, will be when the railway shall have reached it and the stately hotel, built in the contentment-bringing and guest-detaining old English style, with its fifty chambers, bath-rooms with hot and cold water, and all other desirable creature comforts that liberal souls can devise, shall be completed and complete, as it is the intention of this Company they shall be when leafy June again perfects the charms of the Valley of the Shenandoah.—The traveler loves to linger long at York Minster, because the York Station Hotel is hard by.

From Luray to the Shenandoah Iron-works, some 20 miles, the route is up the valley of the Hawksbill to near Marksville, keeping some distance from the river but near the outcrop lines of the limonite and magnetite iron ores; thence it again approaches the river and passes near the little villages of Alma (where it is crossed by the New Market and Gordonsville turnpike), Honeyville, East Liberty, Summersville and Grove Hill, not far from the iron-ore belts of the Blue Ridge foot-hills on the east and those of the enclosed valleys of the southwest Massanuttons on the west,—as shown by the accompanying map and sections. By the first of next August the cars will run to these Iron-works, 105 miles from Hagerstown, and their blomary, furnaces and vast ore beds, included in nearly 50 square miles of iron lands, will be brought within 180 miles, by rail, of Harrisburg, Pa., or Baltimore. A short distance above the Shenandoah Iron-works the road passes into Rockingham county, goes near Conrad's Store, at a distance of 5 miles, where it crosses the proposed line of the Potomac, Fredericksburg and Piedmont R. R. (a line that will probably surmount the Blue Ridge at Swift Run Gap, the one by which white men first entered the Great Valley, under Gov. Spotswood in 1716). Some 5 miles farther, near Mine Run, having passed the southern end of the Massanuttons, the route enters the broad Upper Valley of the Shenandoah, which expands to a breadth of nearly 30 miles between the Blue Ridge and the North Mountains. Following the river for some 8 miles more, and at no great distance from it, the road reaches the village of Port Republic, famed for the battle of that name fought in 1862 at Lewiston 3 miles below,—having skirted for miles the large estate pertaining to the Mount Vernon Furnace of the Abbott Iron Co. of Baltimore and not far from the great iron-ore belt that for nearly 10 miles extends through that estate.

Port Republic is most favorably located for an important manufacturing town. Its location is in the fork of the South and North rivers of the South Fork of the Shenandoah, not far below the junction of the North and Middle rivers, about 1,000 feet above the sea-level, with abundant water-power, near one of the noted passes of the Blue Ridge, Brown's Gap, and in the midst of a wide region where ores, timber and agricultural products are plentiful. To this point about 125 miles from Hagerstown, the railroad is under contract.

From Port Republic to the Chesapeake & Ohio Railway, about 18 miles, the route has not (at this writing) been fully determined, as there are three ways open for choice.—One of these, the most easterly, would be up South River to Waynesboro, passing in 3 miles the Mount Vernon Forge of the Abbott Iron Co. and its quarries of excellent limestone; and at the same place the famous Weyer's, Madison's and the Fountains caves, other caverns of wonders; and for these 3 miles and 2 more will be but a short distance from the western boundary of the Mount Vernon Furnace lands and the line of their great ore belt. A few miles farther up the river it would be but a short distance from the extensive Crimora manganese mines and from the outcrops of the Primordial or Cambrian iron-ore belt in Mike's Knob. At Waynesboro, on South River, at the western base of the Blue Ridge it reaches the line of the Chesapeake & Ohio Railway, 124 miles from Richmond, in the immediate vicinity of the thick, stratified

Continued on Page 40

The Magnetic Iron-ores of Page Valley.

Compiled by the Editor from a Report by Prof. Fred'k Prime, Jr.

Magnetic iron ores have been found at two localities, one in the valley of Hawksbill Creek, above Marksville, on the line of the old turnpike from New Market to Gordonsville by way of Madison C. H. Prof. Prime says,—"Here there are several properties that give promise of yielding a fair quantity of the magnetic oxide of iron." The exposures are far up the side of the Blue Ridge. Prof. Prime reports the bed farthest up the valley as dipping 62° N. 80° E., and having a thickness, at the surface, of 2½ ft., with a probability of widening as it descends and being richer in iron. A pit 12 ft. deep has been made on this ore. The ore is compact, with very little rock gangue mixed with it. Lower down the mountain slope, in the same valley, is an opening on a wide bed of ore, only 6 ft. of which was seen by Prof. Prime but which he was assured was 15 ft. wide. The ore here is more mixed with gangue than that higher up the mountain but, as Prof. Prime remarks, "being of a feldspathic nature it is more likely to aid than to interfere with the fluxing of the ore in a blast furnace, and its only detrimental character is to make the burden somewhat leaner." He considered this the most promising locality for thickness of ore bed in this valley.

At another place, apparently in an extension of the last named bed, openings had been made on ore said to have been 6 ft. wide at the surface and 8 at a depth of 14 ft.; the ore similar in character to the last. There are other outcrops and fragments of loose ore at other points, farther down, in the same valley. At one of these a bed of ore about 12 inches thick was exposed at a depth of 2 or 3 ft.; what is known locally as the "Maple Spring vein" is said to be 6 inches thick. At an excavation made for Prof. Prime, east of the last, the ore was found 12 inches thick, in small pieces, the bed dipping N. 38° W.,—he says, "this may widen in descending." Float ore was found southwest of the Mt. Hope Mill, near Marksville, of which Prof. Prime says,—"This ore would be a most excellent one both for the manufacture of Bessemer pig iron, as also for the fettling of puddling furnaces. The float ore has very little rock or gangue intermixed with it."

The following analyses of the above mentioned magnetic ores were made by Messrs. Booth, Garrett & Blair of Philadelphia. The samples were average ores, selected by Prof. Prime himself from the ore in sight at the mines visited:

	(1.)	(2.)	(3.)	(4.)	(5.)	(6.)
Iron,	51.026	43.883	47.353	54.598	54.547	57.225
Titanic acid,	14.560	16.860	18.560	17.360	16.760	16.470
Phosphorus,	2.097	2.025	1.547	0.025	0.096	0.013

(1) This is from the old mine above Marksville, the one first described above, Prof. Prime says,—"It is probable that this analysis does not give the full percentage of iron, and that this will increase in quantity with the depth of the bed."—(2) This is from the second locality named.—(3)this is from the third deposit mentioned above.—(4) From the Maple Spring vein.—(5) From the 12 inch bed opened for Prof. Prime.—(6) Float ore from near Marksville.

The Titanium in these ores, in the form of titanium dioxide, as the analyses show, ranges from 8.8 to 11.3 per cent. (the titanic acid ranging from 14.5 to 18.5 per cent.) Prof. Prime remarks,—"It is a commonly accepted opinion that ores containing over 7 per cent. of titanic acid cannot be used in the blast furnace, and such are the results apparently obtained by some of the iron makers in this country. It is claimed, and I think quite correctly, that with a greater percentage of titanic acid the limestone used fails to

flux it, and the result is that the furnace chills. I have been informed, however, that at Norton, England, titaniferous iron ores from Norway were very successfully treated by the use of soft red brick as a flux, or in other words that by taking a silicate of alumina, instead of using lime, as a flux for the titanic acid, very successful results can be and were attained. It is true that these ores are no longer treated at Norton, but this is said to have been due to the great expense of hauling the ores over bad Norwegian roads for long distances and not to any difficulty in the working of the furnace.' This is probably correct as laboratory experience seems to demonstrate the fact that titanate of alumina is more fusible than titanate of lime.—I see, however, little difficulty in using these ores as a quarter of the burden of a blast furnace, in those cases where the phosphorus is sufficiently low, particularly when mixed with the rich, pure and easily melting ores of the Page Valley and Massanutton Mountains. In addition, several of these ores can, I think, be used to a great extent and successfully as fettling for puddling furnaces."

I may add that I visited the Norton furnaces, referred to above, when two of them were smelting, successfully, large quantities of ores containing high percentages of titanium, and was informed by the manager that they sold their entire product to the English government, for armor plating and other purposes requiring a *tough* iron, at from $5 to $10 a ton more than any other iron made. Lately I have learned, from reliable authority, that several Canadian furnaces are now making titanic pig which is sent to England where it commands a much higher price than any other. It is simply a question of furnace construction and handling, and the purer and better iron obtained will pay well for these.

The other locality where magnetite ore is known is on Fox Ridge, some 6 miles northeast of the other. Prof. Prime saw there only lumps scattered over the surface. No developments had then been made, so no opinion could be formed as to quantity.

From the persistency of all the Blue Ridge deposits in Virginia I am of the opinion that further explorations will prove the existence of this valuable ore in other localities and in large quantities,—especially in those places where the Blue Ridge is topographically farther east than the line of its general direction, as in the 16 miles of its length drained by Hawksbill Creek, in Page, and the 9 drained by Elk Run and Hawksbill Creek in Rockingham: for these topographical peculiarities suggest wider areas of what are probably "Lower Huronian strata, the home of the iron ore deposits of Michigan" (as the Commissioner of Statistics of that State says in his 1879 report), and which, as the progress of development elsewhere in Virginia indicates, may yet be said of the same rocks here.

Specular iron ores in workable beds are not, as yet, known in the Blue Ridge northeast of the Chesapeake & Ohio Railway. They are only known by scattered fragments and as disseminated particles in epidotic rocks. But they are well known from the Davidia mines, at Rockfish Gap, southwest across the State, yielding from 25 to 55 per cent. of metallic iron and generally low in phosphorus. They have been extensively exposed at Davidia on the C. & O. R'y, and at Arcadia, near Buchanan, at which places arrangements are under way to mine them on a large scale.—I see no reason why these ores should not exists in paying quantities northeast of the C. & O. as well as southwest of it. The geological conditions are much the same, and I am confident that these ores will yet be found in paying quantities in the 100 miles of Blue Ridge between Rockfish Gap and the Potomac. Even geologists of reputation have called it "ferruginous sandstones" where it is far richer in iron than the noted "Cleveland [ronstone]" of England.

The Iron Ores Found at the Shenandoah Iron-works, Page Co., Va., and the Chemical Composition of the Iron made there,—by Wm. M. Bowron, F. C. S.

Major Jed. Hotchkiss:

Dear Sir.—In answer to yours, asking if any new developments have been made at Fox Mountain, since your visit, eighteen months since, I can report very little change. The extent of the Fox Mountain deposit, although favorable for iron making, does not help geological research, for no new territory requires proving. I have been carefully over the ground from the top of the Blue Ridge to the great limestone of the Valley, and find the following facts, viz:

1. In the Azoic rocks of the Blue Ridge, consisting mainly of epidote, mica, and quartzite, in varying proportions, no iron has been found, near here, of any commercial importance.

2. In the old Potsdam Sandstone there is a fissure vein of micaceous red hematite of no commercial value, for, though I am informed it can be traced for 30 miles northeast from here, it has only a width of a few inches.

3. The next deposits of stratification are the hydromica slates, in a state of greater or less decomposition. Through these, at irregular intervals, run beds of limonite, or brown hematite, in a direction conformable to the strike of the formation.

4. The strike of these ore-bearing lines is locally flexed by the spurs of the Blue Ridge, but they maintain, however, its general direction.

5. The dip is locally variable.

6. There are three distinct, large "leads" of ore running parallel through the formation known locally as (a) the "W. Merica bed," a bank siliceous, and not worked, but magnificent in its proportions and quality within a mile or two. (b) "Fox Mountain," a "vein" in clay, the extent and qualities of which are fully recorded in the various reports, from those of W. B. Rogers, 40 years ago, to that made by yourself lately. The deposit has the same general character and Brobdignagian dimensions for 3 miles *certainly*; being cut out by the Naked Creek depression and resumed from the spurs of Grindstone Mountain northward to the boundaries of the Shenandoah Iron-works property, beyond which I have not traced it. (c) The "Garrison" deposit has a good outcrop, but has not been proved; it lies ⅓ of a mile west of the Fox Mountain line.

7. Owing to the strictly technical nature of our operations here, no attention has been paid to the chemical composition of the ores and iron produced outside of those from Fox Mountain.

For general composition of the ores I refer you to the analyses given in your report on this property.

For analysis of the iron, I had pigs regularly drilled, during a period of eight weeks, and the borings thoroughly mixed. The analysis was as follows, using large quantities of material to satisfactorily determine traces of ingredients suspected.

Combined Carbon,	0.863
Graphitic Carbon,	4.408
Phosphorus,	0.048
Sulphur,	0.002
Lime, in cinder,	0.017
Alumina, in cinder,	0.026
Insoluble, (silica, etc.,)	3.330
Manganese,	3.809
Iron, (by difference)	87.500
Copper,	absent.
Titanium,	a trace.
Nickel and Cobalt,	a slight trace.

The blooms made from the iron had a composition as follows:

Iron,	99.450
Carbon,	.090
Sulphur,	.002
Phosphorus,	.010
Silica,	.327
Manganese and Alumina,	traces.

The iron made from these blooms was tested at the U. S. Navy-yard, Washington, for its tensile strength, and general adaptability to ship's cable purposes. I was informed by the Hon. Wm. Milnes, jr., that the elongation before breaking was 33¼ per cent.

I could, of course, duplicate these analyses materially, but it would be a needless intrusion upon your space; suffice it to say that no analysis, of recent date, is at variance with the general impressions conveyed by those above quoted and referred to.

Furnace No. 2.　　　　　William M. Bowron, F. C. S.

The Mineral and other Resources of South-western Virginia is the title of a paper read by C. R. Boyd, M. E., of Wytheville, Va., at the late meeting of the American Institute of Mining Engineers in New York. It is a resume of a volume having the same title, soon to be issued, with illustrative maps and sections.

Mr. Boyd spoke of the "broad and continuous" deposits of brown and red hematites, magnetites and semi-magnetites found in the Blue Ridge, the Great Valley and the Apalachian districts of this region. The semi-magnetites, as he calls them, of Giles county containing 69.74 per cent. of metallic iron and no phosphorus. "The great iron ore belt," that of the western slope of the Blue Ridge, in Washington, Smyth, Wythe, Pulaski and Montgomery counties, containing "millions of tons." The "long vein" of which, on Cripple Creek, furnishes ore with "58.15 per cent. of metallic iron and no phosphorus." He had measured "millions of tons in the 150 feet of depth of exposure of ore near the north end of Red-land Mountain, in Pulaski." On the Chestnut Flat, in Giles, he had examined a "vast quantity" of "blood-red ore analysing 89.55 of sesqui-oxide of iron with but 0.3 of phosphoric and 0.37 of sulphuric acid." A large number of localities where there are large natural outcrops of iron ore were named.—The *fossil ores* were said to form "continuous beds" in Walker's, Gap, Clinch, Round, Wolf Creek, Peery's and Buck-horn mountains of Apalachia; but the best beds he had examined were in Clinch Mountain, near the Washington-Russell line, and in the Poor-valley Ridge adjacent. "Three veins of magnetites, many feet thick," he had traced across Floyd, Carroll and Grayson counties, on the Blue Ridge Plateau.

The *lead and zinc ores* of Washington, Smyth, Wythe, Pulaski and Montgomery counties were quite fully treated of.—At the Kitchen, Noble and Painter mines, on Painter's Branch, the zinc blende ores dip 30° to the northwest. From the floor, or south-east wall, up, there is found, (1) heavy blende 144 ft., (2) dolomite, with spots of zinc and lead, 36 ft., (3) a stratum, with iron sulphurets and oxides, 36 ft., (4) dolomite with large veins and deposits of blende and lead sulphuret, one 18 inches thick, 90 ft., (5) iron ore, zinc and barytes, mingled, 180 ft., and (6) towards the north, or hanging wall, dolomite, charged as the last. The hill containing these deposits is from 75 to 100 ft. high from the water level.—At the Wythe lead and zinc mines (which have been worked for lead for over 100 years) there is less stratification and more folding and crushing. The ore-bearing stratum is 40 ft. thick, between walls of dolomite. In the main drift, which is reached by a 1,600 ft. tunnel, the dip is 70° towards S. 20° E. Other deposits have been proven in the same hill.—At the Bertha mine a face of silicous carbonate and oxide, about 180 ft. long by 20 feet, is now exposed and the miners are still going down on it. The continuity of the deposit has been proven by shafts.—A sample of the spelter from the Bertha Zinc Works, the first made in Virginia, was shown to the Institute.—The lead and zinc ores near the head of Walker's Creek, in Bland, were mentioned.

The *copper* beds of Floyd, Carroll and Grayson were described and the location of the "lodes" in which they are found pointed out. The iron ores and other minerals associated with these were described.

The *gold* deposits of Brush Creek and Little River, in Floyd and Montgomery counties, were mentioned.

The *coal* of the Lowest Measures (X), in Montgomery, Pulaski and Wythe were described and the statement made that beds 8 ft. thick had been opened in Montgomery, 22 at the Altoona mines in Pulaski, and 6 in Wythe, varying in pitch from 30° to 42°. Attention was called to the nearness of these coals, as well as those of the eastern border of the Great Ohio Basin, to the vast iron beds that had been described.

The paper was illustrated by a geological map and section of the region treated of, hung on the wall of the lecture room of Columbia College in which the meeting was held. The paper was favorably commented on by Prof. Egleston, Dr. T. Sterry Hunt, and Mr. Heinrich, who had made explorations in Virginia.

We shall welcome the appearance of Mr. Boyd's volume. It will supply a large amount of most valuable information concerning one of the richest mineral regions in the State, one about which very little is known,—so little that when a U. S. Senator from Virginia recently mentioned its great Washington-Smyth salt deposit to a high official of the U. S. Land Office, that functionary called its existence in question and insisted that the Senator, a native of that region, was certainly mistaken.

The Virginias.

CONTINUED FROM PAGE 37.

beds of specular and limonite iron ores that have been opened at the Davidia Mines, while not far beyond are the great ore-beds of the large Mount Torrey Furnace property and the 40-ft. thick beds of kaolin at Porcelain.—The second route would be by the line between the South and the Middle rivers, by way of Mt. Meridian, Piedmont and New Hope, reaching the C. & O. at or near Fishersville, 5 miles west of Waynesboro.—The third, deflecting from the last near New Hope, would take the shortest course to Staunton, 12 miles west of Waynesboro, an important railway centre in the middle of The Great Valley, and the county seat of the large and wealthy county of Augusta.

In a few days this portion of the route will be decided on and that done the work of construction will at once begin from the junction with the Chesapeake & Ohio and the line be finished from each end, the tracks and trains meeting, it is expected, at the Shenandoah Iron-works during the coming September.

That there will be no delay in completing the road thus located, and at the times indicated, is evidenced by the fact that the Construction Company has now on hand, paid for and ready for use, all the iron and steel rails necessary for the main track and sidings all the way from Hagerstown to the Chesa-peake & Ohio, having purchased 13,500 tons of rails, of which 6,000 are steel. Three locomotives are now at work and six more are under construction by the Baldwin Locomotive Works of Philadelphia.

We can testify that everything connected with this road and its equipment is of the very best. Only oak ties are used, and the road-bed is all being heavily ballasted with stone; the water stations are all supplied with steam pumps, and ample provision is everywhere made for the comfort of passengers and the accommodation of traffic. This railway is constructed in all respects as one should be, that, beyond any question, is to become one of the most important lines of traffic, especially mineral, and of travel in these States.

Four New Iron Companies. The Iron Company of Virginia, The Luray Iron Company, The Powhatan Iron Company, and The Shenandoah Valley Mining Company, have been chartered by the Legislature of Virginia that has just adjourned, to immediately begin operations on the Shenandoah Valley Railroad; a wise foresight and economy of administration, thus providing that when the line is opened for traffic, freight shall be ready for transportation. The steady, go-a-head activity of the Company in charge of this great work, has begotten a healthy activity in all the region it traverses; old industries are being revived, new ones inaugurated, and discoveries of undeveloped resources made daily.

The Connections Made by the Shenandoah Valley Railroad are so very important and remarkably far-reaching and competitive, considering its length, that it is worth while to repeat them.—At Hagerstown, its northern terminus, it connects with the Western Maryland, a direct line to Baltimore, with the Cumberland Valley Branch of the Pennsylvania Railroad, a direct line to Philadelphia and New York, and with the Harrisburg and Potomac Branch of the Reading Railroad, a work in course of construction that will probably reach Hagerstown the present year, furnishing a competing route to Philadelphia, New York and other northern markets.—At Shenandoah Junction, its connection with the Baltimore & Ohio system gives direct communication eastward to Washington, Baltimore, Philadelphia and New York, and westward to Pittsburg, Cincinnati and all the West and Northwest.—At Charlestown, the Valley Branch of the Baltimore & Ohio opens the way to the western side of the Great Valley, and at Riverton the Manassas Branch of the Virginia Midland leads in the same direction, and also gives a direct route to Alexandria and Washington, near tidal river ports, and to all the South and Southwest. Its connection with the Chesapeake & Ohio, at its southern terminus, furnishes a direct route to the South and Southwest and to the West and Northwest, and, perhaps, what is of more importance than through trade or travel, a direct and short line to the Great Ohio Coal Basin.—The completion of the Valley Railroad from Staunton to Salem, which will doubtless be accomplished within the next year through the co-operation of the Baltimore & Ohio, will fill the only gap in the Great Valley Route from New Orleans and the Southwest to New York and the Northwest, and place the Shenandoah Valley Railroad in that direct and most desirable of all lines of communication.

To be Continued.

Titanic Iron Ores.—E. Gybbon Spilsbury, Consulting Mining Engineer and Metallurgist, of Philadelphia, writes us,—"On this question I would say that the Titaniferous iron ores of the Province of Quebec, Canada, are being very successfully smelted in a charcoal furnace designed especially for the purpose. The ores contain from 25 to 30 per cent. of Titanic Acid, and the resulting pig is all shipped to Sheffield, England, where it is in great demand for cutlery steel, being fully equal to any Swedish iron. It is also a well known fact that at Stockton-on-Tees, Titaniferous ores containing over 7 per cent. of Titanium are being successfully worked in a 70-ft. coke furnace, and the resulting iron always obtains from 8 to 10 shillings a ton above the average market. For myself I will say that we are now using at the Coleraine Furnaces an ore containing 5.88 per cent. Titanic Acid and we do not find any difficulty with it.—In my opinion the Titaniferous ores of Virginia could be easily treated in hot-blast charcoal furnaces, and the resulting pig will soon command high prices from the steel manufacturers, after they have once tried it."

We are gratified to have this statement from such good authority. Mr. Spilsbury is an experienced metallurgist and is connected with several of the leading iron-works of the country; he is the Consulting Engineer of the Lynchburg, Va., Iron, Steel and Mining Co. There is no reason why the great beds of Titaniferous ores in the Archæan regions of Virginia should not be utilized The ores are of excellent quality, all that is wanting is skill in their manipulation in the blast-furnace,—that made of proper form, with New River coke or Virginia charcoal used for fuel, the problem is solved.

The Water-power and Manufacturing Sites at Danville, Virginia, offered for sale in our advertising columns, are worthy of the attention of capitalists and manufacturers. The Dan is there a noble river, and the great water-power it furnishes has been made available by a dam and canal. Danville is a thriving manufacturing and commercial city, having a very large tributary country rich in mineral and agricultural wealth. Three great railway lines centre there now and three others are projected and in process of construction. Cotton, iron ores of various kinds, timber, and before long coal, can all be had abundantly and cheap, making this a most desirable point for the building of cotton factories. iron works of all kinds, wagon and implement factories, flouring mills, etc. The country drawing its supplies from this city is extensive and wealthy, rendering this a most important distributing centre. You that have money, enterprise and skill to invest, go and look at the sturdy, healthy growth and business activity of Danville, and you will be convinced that it is a good place for investing and manufacturing. The entire water-power at that point can be bought if desired.

The Lynchburg Iron, Steel and Mining Company, the business of which is advertised in our columns and to which the attention of those needing such supplies as it makes and furnishes is called, has its works at Lynchburg, Virginia, and its office at 319 Walnut Street, Philadelphia. Its officers are, Gen. E. Bard Grubb, of Philadelphia, President; Gen. Thomas T. Mumford, of Lynchburg, Vice-President; Alex. Van Renselaer, Secretary; John Heins, Treasurer; and E. Gybbon Spilsbury, C. & M. E., Consulting Engineer, of Philadelphia.

This Company is enlarging its rolling-mills, building puddling furnaces and putting its foundry and machine shops in first-class condition. Its mill is now running day and night, and orders are pouring in from all directions. It has cleaned out the old Furnace Mine, on the Mundy property, on James River, and struck a very fine vein of Blue Specular Iron Ore; the hematite beds, on the same property, are opening up splendidly, with ore of a superior quality. These ores are now shipped to Baltimore.

Professor William B. Rogers, the Virginia Geologist and the venerable father of American geology, kindly writes us, "I thank you for sending me the January and February Nos. of your new periodical, THE VIRGINIAS, and am so interested in its object and so pleased with these specimens of its plan and substance that I wish you to send me regularly two copies, one for the Institute and one for myself. Authentic reports on the mineral resources and industries of the Virginias will draw increasing attention to their great fields for economic activity and your Journal bids fair to be an important aid in the work."

The Lowmoor Iron Co. has contracted with McMahon & Green, of Staunton, for the construction of 100 coke ovens at their new furnace, about 100 miles from the New River Coal-field.—This action on the part of this strong and sagacious company looks like an endorsement of the views of Mr. Bemelmans in regard to economy in coking, presented in this No.

The Silurian Formation in Central Virginia.[*]

By J. L. CAMPBELL, Washington and Lee University.

Limits.—What is known as the "Great Valley of Virginia" occupies a belt of country extending entirely across the State from the Tennessee line on the southwest to the Potomac on the northeast—including Jefferson and part of Berkeley County, now a portion of West Virginia. It has mountain boundaries throughout its whole extent. On its southeastern margin it is separated from what is called "Piedmont Virginia," by the Blue Ridge and its southwest prolongations, Poplar-Camp and Iron mountains. On the northwest side we find a somewhat irregular line of broken ridges bearing different names at different points. Through several of the southwest Valley counties it is called "Walker's Mountain." In Botetourt, Rockbridge and Augusta, it is called "North Mountain," while through the remainder of the distance to the Potomac it is called "Little North Mountain." The length of the Valley, from the Tennessee line to the Potomac, is about three hundred and thirty miles. Near its southwest extremity, in Washington County, it is about twelve or fifteen miles wide, and becoming gradually wider it extends towards the northeast. We find it in Rockbridge and Augusta varying in breadth from twenty to twenty-five miles. Its total area, embracing the contiguous mountain slopes on each side, is not much short of 6,000 square miles.

Its Topography.—With the exception of a limited belt occupied by the Massanutton range in its northeast parts, and some strip covered by outliers of North and Walker's mountains, this extensive zone has for its surface one continuous outcropping of the Lower Silurian rocks. Before examining into the geological features of this interesting region, it will be well to take a bird's-eye view of its topography. (1.) It lies between two elevated mountain ranges—the Blue Ridge on the southeast rising to heights ranging generally between 2,000 and 4,000 feet above tide-level; and the North Mountain range on the northwest, almost equally high at many points. (2.) The axial line of the Blue Ridge (which consists chiefly of Archæan rocks) has but few gaps through which streams of water can pass. Not a single outlet of any considerable size is found for the waters of the Valley through this ridge anywhere between Harper's Ferry on the Potomac and Balcony Falls on the James—a distance of one hundred and fifty miles. The only other water-gaps are the one through which the Roanoke (afterwards the Staunton) River passes towards the southeast, and the narrow, rugged ravine, by which the waters of New River (Kanawha)and some of its tributaries run down from the Plateau formed by the bifurcation of the Blue Ridge towards its southwest extremity. But along the northwest side of the axial ridge, throughout the greater part of its extent, we find a large number of short broken ridges and irregular peaks, forming sometimes double, and often triple, lines nearly parallel with the main mountain, and indicating by their position and structure that they were once continuous ridges that have since been fractured and cut into deep gorges, through which small streams of water now run down into the limestone valley below. These broken ridges consist of Primordial rocks. The mountains on the northwest are far less regular and continuous than the main Blue Ridge, and are traversed by numerous water-gaps. Here the Upper Silurian (Medina)Sandstones constitute the material of which most of the ridges are constructed, and the heavy beds are frequently arched or folded, and cut through by ravines of considerable extent and grandeur, like that through which New River makes its way towards the Ohio, or the beautiful arch at Clifton Forge, or the grand "Goshen Pass" between the Chesapeake and Ohio Railroad and Lexington.

(3.) Those who have not visited this section of the State must not imagine that the "Valley" is one vast continuous plain like some of the western prairies. It is a land of "hill and dale, of water-brooks and fountains of water." Its limestone and cherty ridges are frequently of such dimensions that in many parts of the world they would be called "mountains," and where they are cut by the bold and rapid streams that

abound here, they present many steep and naked cliffs, sometimes more than two hundred feet in height above the water. Such natural sections present features of great interest to the geologist; and afford important aid in ascertaining the real structure and relative position of the several sub-divisions of this, the most remote age of paleozoic history.

(4.) Any good map of Virginia will show that this valley is not single, whether viewed lengthwise or crosswise. From a few miles southwest of Winchester to a point nearly opposite Harrisonburg, it is divided into two subordinate valleys, by the Massanutton Mountains—a long belt of ridges of Upper Silurian and Devonian rocks that withstood the denuding agencies that uncovered so many hundreds of square miles of the Lower Silurian limestones. Less extensive ridges also interrupt the continuity on the northwest side; and some of them, like the House Mountain, (This is often spoken of as if it were a single mountain—and so it appears to be as seen from Lexington—while, in reality, there are two short parallel ridges nearly a mile apart, cut off abruptly at both ends), across which the accompanying section passes, present striking examples of mountains *left* in isolated positions by the sweeping away of the once adjacent rocky masses through the powerful denuding agencies of water and ice. That such agencies have operated in this region on an extensive scale will be considered more fully hereafter.

The cross divisions of the valley are marked by the watersheds that determine its drainage. Southwest of Wythe County we find the waters carried off by the Holston into the Tennessee River. Wythe, Pulaski and part of Montgomery, are drained by New River, which runs down from the Blue Ridge Plateau, crosses towards the northwest and makes its way to the Ohio. Thus we have "New River Valley." A small portion of Montgomery and nearly all of Roanoke County, are drained by the Roanoke River—one of the three rivers that have cut water-gaps through the Blue Ridge in a southeasterly direction. Next to this "Roanoke Valley" comes the upper "James River Valley," occupied by Botetourt and Rockbridge. Extending from the water-shed (crossing near the line between Rockbridge and Augusta) to the Potomac, we find the extensive "Shenandoah Valley."

(5.) *Elevations.*—At Harper's Ferry, where the Potomac leaves the Great Valley, the height above tide-level is only about two hundred and forty feet; but when we reach the head waters of the Shenandoah, we have arrived at a water-shed having an average height of nearly 1,800 feet. Then, in passing on to the south corner of Rockbridge, we come to the "pass" of the James, at Balcony Falls, having an elevation of about 700 feet. The Roanoke Valley has about the same average elevation as that of the James Valley, 1,200 feet; but on rising to the margin of New River Valley, near Christiansburg, in Montgomery County, we are about 2,000 feet high; and on the southwest margin, at Mount Airy—the summit of the A. M. & O. Railroad—2,600 feet. Many points on the Blue Ridge are not higher than this highest part of the great limestone valley. At the Tennessee line the height is less than 1,700 feet.

Here, then, we have a plateau, rather than a valley, with an average elevation above the sea of about 1,200 or 1,300 feet. This is much above the average elevation of the Mississippi Valley. It is in reality a part of the great belt of uplift that constitutes the Apalachian Range, but erosive agencies have stripped it of the greater part of its mountain-making masses. The Blue Ridge, which now forms its southeast border, was once the shore-line of the great primal ocean that covered the Mississippi Valley (including "Apalachia") during the remote ages of geological history.

At present the streams of water in the Valley tend towards the southeast margin all the way from the Potomac to Salem, in Roanoke County. This is most strikingly the case in the basins drained by the Roanoke and the James Rivers, thus indicating less elevation on that side than on the other. I think we shall learn hereafter that this is most probably the result of difference in the amount of denudation on the two sides.

This brief summary of the most conspicuous physical features of the Great Valley and its surroundings is deemed sufficient to give the reader a tolerably distinct, though very general view of the *present* surface formed by the outcropping of the most extensive exposure of Lower Silurian rocks in

[*]From the American Journal of Science and Arts, Vol. XVIII, 1879.—Revised for THE VIRGINIAS by Prof. Campbell.

Section of Silurian Formations, Rockbridge County, Virginia;—Crossing the Great Valley.

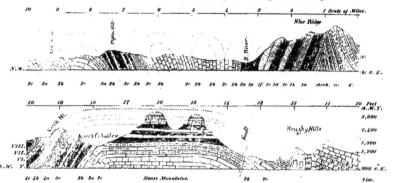

Description of the Section.—1. The leading divisions of strata are denoted by the numbers 1, 2, 3, 4; V, VI, VII. VIII, corresponding with the Pennsylvania series (Rogers). 2. Sub-divisions are indicated by letters attached to the numbers, as *1a*, *1b*, *2a*, etc. 3. On the right-hand end above (the proper place to begin the examination), the Archæan rocks are marked, "Arch *(a)*, *(b)*, *(c)*;" while an eruptive mass protruding near the crest of the Blue Ridge is marked, E. 4. The beds of sandstone are *dotted.*—coarsely when more or less conglomerate : beds of shale have closely *ruled* lines ; limestone strata are *blocked*, some having *longitudinal* and some *cross* rulings, to distinguish *epochs*. 5. The feldspathic rocks east of Blue Ridge have double longitudinal lines 6. Heights above tide level are indicated on the right of the lower division of the section.

Virginia. There are other less extensive exposures of the same rocks forming subordinate limestone valleys, but they must be left out of our present discussion.

Geology.—My purpose is to give in the first place a section extending from the Blue Ridge to the North Mountain, embracing some of the Archæan rocks at one extremity, and of the Devonian at the other. The discussion of this, with its divisions and sub-divisions, and some leading peculiarities of each, will, I think, illustrate the geology of this middle part of the State in a manner, and to an extent, not hitherto attempted by any one.

I am indebted to the partial survey of Virginia, made under the direction of the venerable and distinguished geologist, Professor W. B. Rogers, for guidance and aid in my own investigations and for many of the facts contained in this communication. The line of section here given has been carefully explored and reëxplored throughout its whole extent, several times. It crosses a portion of the Valley not heretofore represented in section, so far as I know ; and while it may be regarded, to a certain extent, as typical of this region of the State for some miles on each side of its line, it presents some peculiarities worthy of special notice. These will be discussed in future. For the present a general description must suffice.

The southeast extremity is on the slope of the Blue Ridge beyond Robinson's Gap, and extends one mile past the line between Rockbridge and Amherst counties : while the northwest reaches about a mile beyond the crest of the North Mountain to the valley of the Rockbridge Alum Springs, where it cuts the Devonian shales from which the waters of those springs flow. A subordinate ridge of Medina sandstones, however, rises in the valley between the end of the section and the Springs.

The first general division includes the metamorphic and eruptive rocks of the main Blue Ridge. The other general divisions are those adopted by Professor Rogers in his survey of the State (1836–41). Only Nos. I to VIII are included. The sub-divisions into which each of these is here divided are my own, and may be regarded as representative (with local modifications), not only of the limestones of the Great Valley, but also of the shales and sandstones of the bordering mountains and outlying ridges on both sides. They are marked, *a*, *b*, *c*, etc., in ascending order, and will be found to correspond

with many of the sub-divisions given by Professor Dana in his Manual of Geology (ed. 1875).

There is no natural section or gap through the metamorphic and eruptive rocks at this point on the Blue Ridge, but the outcrop is quite distinct, except that of a mass of syenite (E) protruded among the stratified rocks. The crest of the ridge is marked by a heavy bed of syenitic gneiss (or stratified syenite), (*b*) which might readily be taken for an igneous rock—so greatly has it been metamorphosed. This, with the thinner beds of like composition, and the interstratified slates (*c*) all dip steeply to the S. E.—or rather S. S. E. Beneath the mass of syenite we find first gneissoid rocks with considerable quantities of epidote ; and under these, slates and sandstones, all dipping conformably with those above. These are *a* of the metamorphic group on the section.

Against the upturned edges of these metamorphic strata we find the lowest of the Primordial beds, resting *unconformably*, and dipping in the opposite direction. Here begins No. I of Professor Rogers's divisions. It might be sub-divided into very many alternations of sandstones and shales, but I have preferred to limit the number to *seven*, that are quite constant in their general features for many miles along the N. W. face of the range. At the grand natural section at Balcony Falls, where the James River passes through the mountain, about fifteen miles S. W. of my line, there is a very interesting exposure of all the divisions here given—similar in relative position, similar in lithological and fossil characters, and having the same general dip.

No. I.—The group, No. I. *a*, as a general rule, has a layer of feldspathic and siliceous conglomerate near the bottom, then dark shales alternating with sandstones more or less conglomeritic. The shales, however, predominate. Next comes a bed (*b*) of very hard sandstone—quartzite ; the upper and lower layers of which are more brittle than the main mass lying between them. This is succeeded by a much thicker mass of brown, purple and yellow shales (*c*), with thin beds of brittle sandstones. This mass is extensively disintegrated at the James River where the James River pass on both sides, where its thickness is about 550 feet, including a considerable bed of sandstone which at that point seems to separate it into two somewhat distinct divisions. But at Robinson's Gap, and other places, this bed of interstratified sandstone either disappears or becomes very thin. The bed (*d*) is very constant, very hard, and has a

jointed structure so deeply marked and so extensive, that the cleavage planes thus developed have sometimes been mistaken for planes of stratification dipping S. E. The division (e) consists of shales of much lighter color than those found lower in the series. Some of the beds are decidedly kaolin in character, with numerous scales of mica disseminated through them. Up to this point we find only very faint indications of fossil remains of either plant or animal. A few scolithus borings (in b and d) are found, but they are rare, in comparison with what are found in (f). This (f) is the "typical sandstone" of the range, and constitutes the frame-work of what was once a continuous ridge, but is now crossed by numerous gorges, which have divided it into many short ridges and irregular knobs and peaks. It is a hard sandstone of white and light gray color, and jointed structure; and along this and other parts of its range it "exhibits vague, fucoidal and zo-ophytic impressions on the surface of bedding, together with innumerable markings at right angles to the stratification, penetrating in straight lines to great depths in the rock, and from their frequency and parallelism determining its cleavage in nearly parallel planes. These markings are of a flattened [many of them] cylindrical form, from 1-8th to 1-10th of an inch broad, giving the surface of the fractured rock a ribbed appearance, and resembling perforations made in sand which have been subsequently filled up, without destroying the original impression." Such is Professor W. B. Rogers's description of the character given to this heavy bed of rock by the Scolithus linearis. These fossils are so numerous that I recently counted at Balcony Falls about 150 of their extremities projecting on one square foot of surface. This may very properly be called the "Scolithus bed" of this Primordial formation. The thinner beds at the top and bottom disintegrate rapidly. Between this and the first limestone of the valley is a thick mass of ferruginous shales generally much disintegrated and covered with the debris of sandstone from the adjacent ridges just described. This is (g) on the section. It sometimes rises to a considerable height on the slope of the "scolithus bed," especially where the dip is low; and in a few cases, as at Irish Creek, I have found it reaching the crest of the ridge. It is one of the richest repositories of iron ore in Virginia—especially brown hematite—and has valuable beds of manganese, one of which, near Waynesboro', in Augusta county, is at present extensively worked. The ores of the Shenandoah Iron Works of Page county are obtained from this bed of shale. Although it abounds in iron ores, yet it has the peculiar feature of containing a layer of clay so white as to be called "chalk" by the people of the region.

This brings us to the border of the limestones of the valley, and the place of division between No. I and No. II. Thus we have passed over the Primordial Period. If it has here representatives of both the Acadian and Potsdam epochs (which I doubt) the lowest shales and sandstones must represent the former, and the upper shales and sandstones the latter. For the present, at least, I shall regard the whole as belonging to the Potsdam. The total thickness varies considerably as we ascend the ridges. This is especially conspicuous in the beds of shale, and causes such a decided variation in the dip of the sandstones as to make them present the appearance in many places of segments of broken arches; the dip varying as it does here and at Balcony Falls from 65° at the base to 30° near the upper margin, or outcrop of the beds. This peculiarity has been caused either by an original thinning out of the beds towards their margin before they were upheaved, or by a squeezing out of a portion of their material by the resistance and pressure of the more unyielding beds of sandstone above and below, at the period of upheaval.

The thrust, which was doubtless from the Blue Ridge towards the Valley, seems to have been more powerful near the base than it was near the summit. Hence the steeper dip below, which has become reversed in the limestones for several miles from the foot of the mountain.

No. II.—The first natural sub-division (a) of the Valley limestones may with propriety be called the "Hydraulic Formation," inasmuch as it abounds in hydraulic limestones throughout its whole length. It includes, however, several layers of very siliceous and argillaceous limestones separated from one another by beds of brown, bluish and purple shales, and some soft sandstones. The best bed of hydraulic stone is

near the bottom of this division, and where it has been quarried for many years, near Balcony Falls, is only about twelve to fifteen feet thick, and dips steeply to the N. W. Where our section crosses the strata of a they are nearly vertical. From this point to the Brushy Hills beyond Lexington, the strata (with one or two local and very limited exceptions), all dip towards the Blue Ridge; and, upon a superficial view of the case, might be supposed to extend beneath it. But examinations of the relative position of the sandstones and limestones at other points in the Valley, together with lithological and fossil peculiarities that prove the more recent origin of the limestones, lead to the conclusion that they are geologically above the sandstones and shales already described. The several repetitions of the sub-divisions of No. II, between the Poplar Hills and North River can be accounted for only upon the hypothesis of plications in the strata caused by pressure on the one side and resistance on the other. We conclude, therefore, that the hydraulic beds (a), as originally deposited on the ancient sea-bottom, underlie those of b, while these again were overlaid by the beds of c. Only occasional fucoid plants, and brachiopod mollusks have been seen in a. It seems to be the equivalent of the Calciferous Epoch of New York (3 a, Dana).

No. II b, embraces a series of heavy beds of dark blue limestones, with some dark brown and yellow shales intervening. A large proportion of the limestone is magnesian (dolomitic), and some beds hydraulic. The oxide of iron abounding in this formation, gives a dark brown color to the soils produced by its disintegration. These are among the best and most durable soils of the Valley. The next and upper division (No. II c), is characterized lithologically, (1) by having the greater part composed of light blue and bluish-drab colored limestones, with yellow shales interstratified, especially among the lower beds: (2) by one and sometimes two beds of coarse, brown, friable sandstone between layers of light-colored limestones; and (3) by a remarkable bed of chert near its upper limit. This hard, flinty, durable rock has so far resisted the force of disintegrating agencies, as to be left as a covering on the faces of many of the limestone hills throughout a large extent of the Great Valley. This chert bed varies in thickness from one to ten feet within the range of a few miles; but it and the brown sandstone lower down serve as well defined land-marks for this whole formation. The brown sandstone has preserved imperfect impressions of several species of brachiopod shells, while in the chert bed are found in some localities large numbers of silicified shells of gasteropod and cephalopod mollusks. This division (c) by disintegration yields light clay and sandy or pebbly soils, according to the varying characters of the outcropping strata These soils are only moderately productive—some of them very poor. Local deposits of limonite ore in this formation have been mined in past years to supply some of the iron furnaces in Augusta county.

The lithological and paleontological characters of this group of rocks, as well as its position seem to identify it with the Chazy Epoch (3 c, Dana).

The dotted lines on the section give an ideal representation of the foldings and inversions to which these rocks were subjected when turned up from their original bedding. There was not, of course, the regularity and symmetry in the foldings that these lines indicate, for there are along the line many evidences of local warpings, fractures, dislocations, etc., that could not appear on such a section. Several trap-dykes are found protruded through the rocks of No. II, in Augusta and Rockingham counties, but none, so far as I know, in Rockbridge. The Natural Bridge, from which this county takes its name, is in b—being a portion of one of its upper strata spanning a cañon or gorge, cut through its lower beds to a depth of more than 200 feet.—I incline to the belief that this gorge was originally a crevice in the strata, and subsequently enlarged by erosion—not the result of erosion alone; the arch having escaped fracture when the crevice was produced.

No. III.—In some respects this group of rocks differs so widely here from its condition in Augusta and Rockingham counties, where Professor W. B. Rogers adopted it as typical in his earlier Reports, that I feel confident that he then regarded some of the heavy, but quite irregular beds of limestone in the Lexington basin as a part of No. II, but I am equally confident that he would, upon a more detailed examination, class them as Trenton Limestones—base of III.

The lower bed (a) of this group is peculiar, as far as I have yet observed, to Rockbridge and adjacent portions of Botetourt and Augusta counties. It has all the appearance of an old coral reef very much disintegrated, stratified, and subsequently solidified by the infiltration of carbonate of lime which has given the mass a crystalline texture, and converted it into a gray limestone, very compact and admirably adapted for building purposes. The bed has well defined horizons both below, where it is separated from the chert of No. II c, by one or two thin layers of light blue limestone; and above, where it is covered with a layer that is shaly in some places and in other very hard, and full of white veins of calcite and dolomite. The upper and lower portions of this coralline bed are quite full of shells as well as fragments of coral; the middle portion is more purely coralline, more compact, and better adapted to the architectural purposes to which it is extensively applied; and to the manufacture of lime. The most easterly outcrop in this neighborhood is on Hoffman's Run, about one mile S.E. of the town, where the total thickness is about sixty (60) feet. It seems to run out somewhere beneath the synclinal fold that forms the Poplar Hills, but appears again on Buffalo Creek, six miles to the S.W. Northwest of Lexington the outcrop of this bed is finely displayed along some parts of the base of Brushy Hills, and especially on the North River, a mile above the town bridge, where it forms a nearly vertical cliff, exposing its entire thickness, which at this point is about 150 feet. This thickness is preserved in the synclinal between Brushy Hills and House Mountain, and also at other points where it appears below (b) the thicker mass of Trenton Limestone.

No. III, b, crops out extensively on both sides of Poplar Hills forms the whole of the synclinal over which Lexington stands, (This synclinal is really double—having a line of uplift running through it, but the scale of the section would not admit its insertion. There are also some local irregularities here,) and is the foundation rock of the House Mountains, around the base of which it may be seen cropping out on all sides. The general position here is horizontal, or nearly so, with some local curves. Northwest of Kerr's Creek valley it disappears beneath the North Mountain.

The general structure of b differs very widely from all the lower limestones—the beds here, except some of the lowest, being thin layers of argillaceous limestone, with interstratified shales. Near the base of b, especially along its S.E. portion, underlying the Poplar Hills, we find a bed of very compact blue limestone irregularly bedded and very full of infiltrated veins; but, as we ascend, the rocks become more and more argillaceous, with the beds of shale becoming more numerous; and finally, as may be seen on House Mountain, after passing upward through a thickness of about 850 feet, the shale become predominant, but still contains some thin beds of limestone remarkable for the profusion of fossil shells, crinoids and coral found in them. There is no well defined horizon here, between what is represented on the section as b and c, but the former seems in general characters to be the equivalent of the Trenton limestone, and the latter of the Cincinnati (Hudson) shales. It is about 750 feet thick.

Remark.—I have not seen any outcrop of the division, a, of No. III in Augusta county northeast of Staunton, nor have I seen it at all in Rockingham. If its equivalent appears in that part of the Valley, it is under quite different lithological and fossil pecularities. I might say almost as much in regard to b: for limestone beds form a very inconspicuous part of III, from Staunton (or rather a point S.E. of that place) to a point in Rockingham county, where it passes under IV in the Massanutton range of mountains.

"FAULT."—This seems to be the proper place for directing attention to the "Fault," the line of which passes in front (S.E.) of the House Mountain. It is easily traced for several miles both ways from our line of section. The newer and older rocks of No. II are found (in their own normal order) overlying the newer of No. III b, which dip beneath them. At a number of points between Kerr's Creek and Collier's Creek, two considerable streams that run out from the North Mountain at the opposite extremities of the House Mountain ridges this dipping of the newer under the older rocks may be seen along a line of very considerable regularity.

Our general description has now extended to the horizon between the Lower and Upper Silurian.

No. IV, the equivalent of the Medina group, is composed of very durable sandstones that are the chief mountain-making rocks along the northwest margin of the Valley, and throughout a belt of twenty or twenty-five miles wide, parallel with it. It may be represented under three sub-divisions. The lower one of which (a), is a very hard, light gray, sometimes white, sandstone, distinctly conglomerate in many places, and so durable as to present long lines of precipices where the strata crop out on the faces of the mountains. The middle member (b) of this group is a dark brownish purple sandstone with beds of interstratified shales of the same color. Shells in the sandstone, and fucoids in the shales, are conspicuous features of this division. A third member (c) is much lighter in color than b, but darker than a. Some of the harder layers have a pinkish hue, while the softer and more brittle especially near the top, where they border on No. V, are brown and yellowish brown in color. While this group, as it appears on the two ridges of House Mountain, rests upon a nearly horizontal base, in the North Mountain its position is changed to that of a steep northwest dip.

The general pressure that acted from the Blue Ridge side of the Valley towards the northwest seems to have lifted the House Mountain ridges somewhat above what was the original level of the surrounding region, and, at the same time, to have broken off and pushed back the edges that now form the crest of North Mountain. But while the section represents the general result, it will be found on examination, that there are a number of local and limited irregularities in the form of contortions and fractures that could not be exhibited on a scale representing so much space within so short a limit. So, also, it has here, apparently, a greater degree of symmetry on the surface, than the denuding forces to which it has been subjected, have given it. But in this regard, also, the irregularities are too numerous and limited to find a place on the section.

The strata of this group all thin off as they extend farther towards the interior basin of the coal regions. They also vary much in thickness where they crop out along the margin of the Valley. What now caps House Mountain is about three hundred and sixty feet thick, while, at the highest point, it may have lost one hundred feet or more of its original height. On the Warm Springs Mountain, in Bath County, twenty miles farther towards the great Apalachian coal basin, the thickness is very perceptibly less. At Panther Gap, two or three miles west of Goshen, where the Chesapeake and Ohio Railway passes through Mill Mountain, a very complete section of No. IV is displayed as a folded and inverted anticlinal—inverted towards the northwest so that the higher strata of V, VI and VII, seem to underlie IV.

No. V is in most places, in this part of the Apalachians, a bed of shales and brittle, shaly sandstones. In the upper part the shales predominate and have some thin bands of limestone. Valuable iron ores, some of them highly fossiliferous, abound in this formation. The development of this group is not extensive where our line of section cuts it. This seems to be the only representative we have here of the Clinton and Niagara epochs (5b, and 5c, Dana).

No. VI is not actually visible where the section passes, but its outcrops on both sides of the same valley, at points not very remote, seem to justify the hypothesis that it actually exists at this point though concealed from view by the debris of sandstone and clay from the adjacent mountain. In this part of the Apalachian range it consists almost entirely of limestones that are remarkable for the profusion of fossil coral, shells and encrinites found in them. The stone is pure enough in some of its beds to make good lime, and firm enough to make good building material for houses, railroad masonry, etc. In the prolongation of the same mountain valley, in which our section terminates, this formation is largely developed along the line of the Chesapeake and Ohio Railway, between Goshen and Buffalo Gap. At Craigsville, nine miles northeast of Goshen, it affords an extensive quarry of beautiful encrinal marble. It is the Helderberg Limestone. (7, Dana.)

No. VII is a singular bed of brownish and greenish-gray sandstone of coarse texture, easily broken, and in many places disintegrates readily under the weather. In other localities it is more durable, forms rather low flat arches, and when out

through by streams presents precipitous exposures. It has valuable deposits of iron ore at many points in Virginia. Great numbers of fossil brachiopods, especially *Spirifer arenosus* and *Rensselæria ovoides*, are found in it everywhere.

This is a remarkably well defined formation, readily distinguished by its lithological peculiarities and its fossils remains. It is cut by the Chesapeake and Ohio Railway at several places between Buffalo Gap and Goshen. On the turnpike leading from Millboro to the Warm Springs, about three miles from the station at which the stage coaches leave the railroad, this formation may be seen as an anticlinal arch, spanning the lower limestone of VI, in which the famous "Blowing Cave" of Bath County is situated. Here the Calf-pasture River has cut through a ridge and given a natural section along the base of which the stage-road passes, and where the Oriskany and Helderberg formations are well exposed, and, together with the Blowing Cave, present points of considerable scientific interest. Here, also, the meeting of the Oriskany, the upper member of the Silurian, with the Marcellus (?) shales, at the base of the Devonian, may be distinctly observed on both sides of the ridge.

The following table exhibits a comparison of the sub-divisions in this portion of the Virginia Valley, with the periods and epochs in Professor Dana's Manual:

Silurian rocks of the Great Valley of Virginia with their sub-divisions, compared with equivalent epochs of Dana's Manual, p. 142.

Ages	Periods	Epochs	Rogers' series	Virginia Valley sub-divisions
Upper Silurian.	Oriskany Lower Helderberg Salina	8 Oriskany 7 Lower Helderberg 6 Salina 5a Niagara 5b Clinton	No. VII. No. VI. No. V.	a Spirifer sandstone b Fucinal Limestone. c Calcareous Shales. b Furriferous Shales a Shaly Sandstones
	Niagara	9a Medina	No. IV	s Upper Sand rock b Purple Shales and Sandstone a Conglomerate
Lower Silurian.	Trenton	4c Hudson River. 4b Utica 4a Trenton.	No. III.	i c House Mt. Shales h Lexington Limestones. g oolitic Limestones. e Cherty Limestones.
	Canadian.	3c Chazy. 3b Quebec. 3a Calciferous	No. II.	b Dolomitic Limestones a Hydraulic Limestones. g Iron-bearing Shales f Scolithus Sandstones.
	Primordial or Cambrian.	2b Potsdam 1 Acadian	No. I.	e Kaolin Shales d Middle Sandstone. c Middle Shales b Lower Sandstones a Lower Shales
Azoic.	Archæan.	Archæan	Meta-mor-phic Igneous	c Slates and Syenitic Gneiss b Bedded Pyrite a Lower Slates Eruptive Syenite.

The Manufacture of Coke.

[Written expressly for THE VIRGINIAS by L. Bemelmans, M. E., of the Royal School of Mines, Belgium, of Charleston, West Virginia.]

A good coke contains but a small percentage of ashes and but little sulphur. It is ringing, in large pieces, as an indication of compactness, homogeneity and freedom from flaws, which, if too numerous, indicate a tendency to breakage in handling. It is hard to crush, and able to support the burden in the blast furnace. This quality supposes small, regular vacuoles and a good agglomeration. It is silvery and free from rusty spots, not only on the fresh fracture but on the surface of the pieces, an indication that it is newly made and has not been drenched with water. Rusty spots, even in the old coke, always indicate pyrites, hence sulphur. The specific gravity is a good test of value only when the percentage of ashes is known, and when the coke is fresh from the oven and has not been watered. Fresh coke soon absorbs from the air from 3 to 5 per cent. of dampness, but if it is drenched or exposed to the rain, it takes from fifteen to twenty per cent. of water and loses much of its calorific power. The tendency of moisture is to cool the zone of elaboration in the blast furnace, and that is why metallurgists often prefer to buy coal and make their own coke near the furnace, where it can be used immediately, although they pay transporation on about 30 per cent. of volatile matter, which is of no use to them. Accordingly the type of the best coke is a pure anthracite, that does not exfoliate in the fire. Indeed, anthracite is often only a coke made

from a good coking coal, under great pressure, as at Schoenfield, in Saxony, where a bed of coal has been, in places, penetrated by porphyry so that both bituminous coal and anthracite are found in the same bed.

Hence, the nearer a coke comes to anthracite in its physical properties, the better it is adapted to the wants of metallurgy. I say, in its physical properties, for the coke manufacturer, by separating the pyrites, shales, stones, and sometimes gypsum from the coal, by washing, often succeeds in producing a coke purer than the natural anthracite of that coal would be. In exceptional cases, where beds of coal, without partings and relatively free from iron pyrites, are mined under a solid roof, and without blasting, it may make little difference whether the coal is washed or not; but no one that has been impressed by the large banks of refuse separated from the coal by washing, around Pittsburg or elsewhere, can but believe that, in most cases, washing the coal greatly improves the coke. The experiment may be made, in each case, with a common sieve in a tub of water. This cleaning of the coal is especially important when a distant market is contended for, as a small per cent. of ashes becomes important by transportation. Not only has freight to be paid on ashes as well as on fuel, but at the end of the journey, they absorb heat from the fuel during the process of smelting.

Although the term *washing* has been adopted for the purifying process, it is merely a classification of bodies of nearly the same size, in the order of specific gravity, by means of water. The process, already old, is used extensively for the separation of metallic ores which cannot be separated in mining, although the difference of specific gravity between these ores is often very small. Between coal and its impurities, however, that difference is so great, (nearly as one-half), that the separation is rapid and complete, and more inequality in the size of the pieces may be allowed. The "nut" coal, however, cannot be washed with the slack. Therefore, where the "nut" is used for coking, the best practice uses a pair of rollers for crushing it. A better coke, more homogenous and compact, is obtained from fine coal than from mixed sizes, and the dampness which remains in the coal after washing eliminates some of the sulphur, although it cannot be said to insure a long life to the ovens which it cools abruptly.

When a good stream is at hand, the simplest washing process consists in mixing the coal in the stream, confined for that purpose in a flume inclined from 10° to 12°. The heaviest particles, or impurities, settle first and are collected in a fishing box; the coal is carried farther, to the foot of a dam. This process requires about 3½ cubic yards of water per ton of impure coal. A flume washes only 10 to 12 tons in ten hours, the separation is not complete and the loss of fine coal carried over the dam varies from three to seven per cent. It requires too much labor.

The concentric funnels are also a very simple washer; they effect a perfect separation but require adjustment and their individual capacity is limited to from 20 to 25 tons in ten hours. They require from 30 to 40 gallons of water per bushel of coal, according to the head. They are certainly the best washer where abundant and reliable water power can be had, as they apply it without any machinery and the whole work is automatic. If not overcrowded, the loss in pure coal does not exceed one per cent.

The most popular washers, those that use the least water, are the jigs. They are made of all sizes, to be worked by hand or by machinery, to wash successive loads or continuously; they consume, of water, from 25 per cent. of the weight of the coal up to 30 gallons per bushel of coal, according to the facilities afforded by the location of the works. Several dispositions of the jigs have been patented in the United States; but only new details can be validly patented, as a complete description of the working Berard coal washer with the results obtained, were published in the Annales des Mines 5th series, T. IX, p. 147, about 1858. These washers and others contemporaneous (see Lesoinne's Elements of Metallurgy, Liège, 1860,) embody nearly all the improvements which have been separately patented since. The Berard washer cleaned 100 tons of coal in 10 hours with 4 h. p., exclusive of raising the water (5 to 7 gallons per bushel) to the floor of the washer. Any carpenter who can build a barge and work from drawings can build an excellent coal washer to elaborate 100 tons of coal in 10 hours, at a cost not exceeding $150 exclusive of power, which may

be taken from another engine or be the same as that used for the pump.

But returning to the manufacture of coke. When a body of bituminous coal is submitted to heat with limited contact of air, it evolves gases and steam (this steam if condensed is ammonia water), the steam soon ceases to be visible and the gas becomes yellow and thick, loaded with tar. In this state and to the end of the operation the gases are very combustible, and produce, with the proper quantity of air, an intense heat, one equal to the melting of iron in a puddling furnace. The heat continuing to increase, the coal softens and agglomerates in the bitumen it evolves, and the gas, which continues to form, remaining more or less confined as the bitumen thickens and decomposes, swells the mass and leaves, by the time the bitumen is dried up at a red heat, a coke more or less cellular and more or less brittle.

This process, however, does not take place at the same time in the whole body of the coal, but begins on the surfaces most heated and gains with the heat, going deeper and deeper into the mass of the coal; so that the surface is hardened and dried into coke, while the coal below it is only swelling with the gas confined in it. Hence the rents which are always normal to the heated surface of the coal, or rather, to the surface of the swelling core. Thus imitating, on a small scale, the process of nature in the formation of mountains.

The gas escaping from the core, by the rents and through the porous coke already made and strongly heated, decomposes partially with the formation of silvery graphite, similar to that produced under the same circumstances in the retorts of gas works. It is obvious that the coal of that core, confined as it is by the weight and rigidity of the coke already made, and also, losing its gas more slowly, under slowly increasing heat, swells less, remains more compact and holds smaller cells than the layer on the top, and it has been established by direct experiments that the greater the burden supported by the coal at the period of softening, the nearer the coke approaches to anthracite.

But there is no need of separate experiments, the facts are patent in the bee-hive oven and in open pits, two processes sufficiently popular to admit of easy observation. In a good bee-hive oven, one that burns but little of the fixed carbon, the coke is made by the heat radiated from the arch only. All the rents are vertical in general direction. A small layer on the top, having no burden, is much swollen, hence offering but little resistance, it is much broken by the swelling of the coal under it. This layer turns entirely to fine coke by handling. The coke below is closer and closer, as the burden under which it has coked increases, down to 12 or 15 inches from the top (in the 24-hour work). If the thickness of the coal is greater the heat can only reach the floor after a long time of very hot fire, and, even after forty-eight hours, when 20 to 24 inches of coal are used, the coal nearest the floor remains black, imperfectly coked and unfit for the blast furnace. Besides, it all breaks into small coke under the work of the hooks while unloading. In the 48-hour work, more or less of the top coke is always burnt to ashes.

Exactly the corresponding phenomena are conspicuous in the process of open pits when the work is normal, that is, when the wind does not blow. The rents are normal to the chimnics, the top coke is light and burns easily, and the coke lowest in the pit is the heaviest, the closest and most compact.

Discarding the process of open pits, which is not suited to a regular production and which entails a loss of solid carbon amounting to from ten to twenty per cent. according to the state of the weather, we have seen that in simple bee-hive oven, the height of coke is very limited, and consequently, the coke produced is not as good as could be made from the same coal. There is also a great loss in the yield, variable with the size of the ovens and the skill of attendants, in the breakage of coke while unloading. I have seen that loss as high as 50 per cent. of the coke; however, with the best of care, this loss is always considerable. I suppose it is useless to notice here that lump coke is more in demand and commands a better price than small coke. Another depreciation comes from the water it is necessary to use while unloading. The position of the workmen, in front of the red hot coke he extracts from the oven, is a most unnecessary hardship imposed on him, and nothing but high wages and the use of too much water can

make it tolerable in summer. I know that on New River and some few other places, it is customary to introduce a stream of water right into the ovens. If the consumers and the ovens can stand it, and if the yield of coke, including water, is satisfactory, it is not for me to find fault with this practice, but the manufacturer who shall first dispense with the practice will find himself well repaid when his coke becomes known.

No wonder the iron-workers prefer to transport to their works 20 to 30 per cent. of volatile matter and then expel this volatile matter into the atmosphere, to transporting nearly the same amount of water which it takes fuel to evaporate, besides reducing the calorific power of the gas from the blast furnace. Coke need not be extinguished by water. Good coke can only burn in a large mass or with a forced blast in confined space. If spread on the yard or over the coke pile, it soon ceases to burn. All these objections to simple bee-hive ovens have been appreciated long ago; and the chiefs of metallurgical works (not regular inventors who are justly held in awe by him that is not able to judge a new thing) have slowly modified them; first, in order to increase the height of the load, then to reduce the cost of unloading, and, step by step, all successively sanctioned by experience, they have reached the ovens of rectangular form with two oppo site doors and heated sides and bottom, which, in advanced sections, have, for the last fifteen or twenty years, successively displaced all others. At first, the floor was heated by leading the fiery gases in flues under the floor before admitting them into a chimney. I hear this first step is being taken at Fire Creek. This improvement led to making the oven elliptical rather than circular. From this step to heating also the sides of the ovens, the distance was soon passed, and in order to derive an equal penetration of the heat from the sides, the ovens were made rectangular. Doors, the whole size of the section of the oven, were provided at both ends so that the coke could be pushed bodily from one door out of the opposite one. This admitted of the emptying of an oven containing from 300 to 500 cubic feet of coke in ten minutes. These ovens never cooled and therefore lasted a long time. The next step was to admit no air into the oven, but to admit it only into the flues where the gas passes. At this point the limit of theoretical yield was reached, and, with bituminous coals, 82 per cent. of coke, all merchantable and in lumps, was realized. Was that perfection? It seems not, for other considerations, to be examined farther on, allowed the making of better coke as well as the making of good coke from coals which in open pits or in bee-hives would have produced no coke fit for use. The experiment of passing the gas under the floor before sending it into the open air at once admitted, with the same dimensions of ovens, a charge from 10 to 12 inches thicker, to be coked in the same time, and the complaint of underdone soles was no more heard of. But the simple idea of heating the sides, and at the same time contracting the width of the ovens, so that the centre of the coal could be reached by efficient heat from the sides, was the richest in results, for it suppressed any limit to the height of the coal in the ovens.

These principles were applied with the greatest success in the different varieties of Belgian ovens, which are nearly horizontal, with a floor only inclined about 5° towards the exit door, also, in a number of models of inclined ovens, either plane like the ovens used at Saarbruck and my own ovens, or on the arc of a circle, like those of Eisweiler, and in vertical ovens like the celebrated Appolt.

The Belgian ovens are emptied by means of a capstan moved by hand or by a pony engine. The truck is carried on four wheels on a track which runs in the rear of the line of ovens. As an oven is emptied in 10 minutes, one truck is enough for a large number of ovens. Apart from the economical interest of this practice, it is beautiful and impressive to see an unbroken wall of red-hot coke from three to four and a half feet wide, five feet high, and from 18 to 40 feet long, issuing slowly, bodily and unbroken, from the open mouth of an oven. The process of unloading circular ovens, piece-meal, by hand hooks and drenching, and the mechanical process must both be seen to realize the difference of yield in lump coal, other things being equal.

The inclined ovens and the vertical ovens unload automatically, by gravity alone. The lower door being open, the wall of coke slides or falls bodily out of the ovens. In either case,

the doors are immediately closed, a new load of coal is put in and leveled by small apertures in the doors, and a new operation is at once under way. The horizontal ovens are used on level ground; the inclined ovens are preferred where level ground is scarce and hill sides are in the way, as on New River.

[To be Continued.]

The Smithers-Gauley Tract of Coal Lands.

By Jed. Hotchkiss, Consulting Engineer.-- Illustrated by a Supplementary Map and Sections.

The placing of the Gauley-Smithers Tract of Coal Lands on the market by Messrs. G. M. & W. B. Harrison,—as may be seen by referring to the advertising columns of this Journal,—furnishes an opportunity for presenting a description of one of the large undeveloped coal estates of the Great Kanawha Coal-field,—a typical one in location and extent and in the quantity and quality of its coal beds. This will furnish, to the general reader some idea of the resources and value of the coal lands of West Virginia, and to those seeking profitable investments or remunerative coal mining, a guide to where such may be found.

This estate is 6,256 Acres, or about 10 square miles, forming a body of land (as shown on the accompanying map) over 7 miles long and varying in breadth from three-fourths of a mile to two miles, making its average dimensions 7 miles by one and one-third. Its length is in a northeast-southwest direction, extending from near the Great Kanawha River, just above the village of Cannelton, northeast to near Twenty-mile Creek, not far above its entrance into Gauley River. It may be said to stretch across the neck between the Gauley and the Great Kanawha rivers; the watershed of these streams crosses it; about one-sixth of its surface is drained by Gauley and five-sixths by Kanawha tributaries. Smithers' Creek and its Right-hand Fork, run for over 5 miles in front of the northwestern boundary of the estate, draining four-fifths of it into the Great Kanawha and furnishing a natural, level-free outlet for about 5,000 acres of the land to that river and into the pool made by Dam No. 2 of the U. S. Improvement of the Great Kanawha,—this gives over 5 miles of available frontage on that main tributary for coal-mining operations. Twenty-mile Creek and other branches of the Gauley drain the other fifth, and 2.5 miles of frontage are available on Twenty-mile. The name of the estate, Smithers-Gauley, is derived from its chief drainage streams.

This tract is "Lot H" of a sub-division of the 19,567 A. survey granted to John Steele, March 2nd, 1795, by the State of Virginia, made by order of the Circuit Court of Kanawha county, and is held by those, or their heirs, to whom it was decreed by that court,—consequently its title is unquestioned, as the intact and continuous records of that court show. It is situated in Fayette county, West Virginia.

Its general location is in the very centre of the hydrographic basin of the Great Kanawha (See map in No. 2 of The Virginias), on the N. E. side of that river, 9 miles below its Great Falls, below its head of steamboat navigation, and 85 miles above the entrance of that river into the Ohio. It is on the line of the Chesapeake & Ohio Railway, opposite its Cannelton station, 342 miles from its Richmond, or eastern, on James River, and 79 from its Huntington, or western, on the Ohio, terminus. It occupies a nearly central position in the Great Ohio Coal-Basin.

The coal lands of C. P. Huntington, President of the Chesapeake & Ohio Railway, are adjacent to it on the N. W., above Buffalo Branch, as also those of the Cannelton Coal Co. between that Branch and the Kanawha. The village of Cannelton is at the mouth of Smithers' Creek. Public roads run along all the principal water courses.

The altitude, or height above tide-level, of this estate varies from about 640 ft., on Blake's Branch near its mouth, to not far from 2,000 ft, on the "divide" of the Gauley and the Kanawha waters,—consequently about 1,200 feet of its geological section are exposed in the slope from the top of this divide down to Smithers' Creek, as shown in the section on the line A—B, on the supplement.

Its surface, once a plateau sloping moderately to the northwest,—like the evenly bedded strata of sand-rocks, shales, slates, coals, etc., underlying it,—is the remnant of that plateau deeply trenched, by the running waters of ages, down through the successive rock- and coal-beds, into stream-valleys (those of the creeks of the map), that are now mere cañon-like gorges, as shown in the section, the narrow bottoms of which in their lower reaches are cut down to very nearly the same level as the main drainage valleys, those of the Kanawha and the Gauley, thus opening the way, by easy grades, to the outcrop edges of the coal, iron-ore and rock beds that the gorges cut through. For example, the valley of Smithers' Creek at the mouth of Blake's Branch has about the same level as the Chesapeake & Ohio Railway at Cannelton, from it the escarped faces of the ridges rise, almost abruptly, to an elevation of 700 or 800 feet, which is soon increased to 1,000, or more, on the divides of the tributary streams.

Its Coal Beds.—This property is in the central portion of the Great Kanawha Coal-field where the geological structure is exceedingly simple and well known, and where there are more thick, workable beds and more varieties of coal that can be cheaply mined than in almost any other portion of the Great Ohio Coal-Basin. The Lower Coal Measures, those of Rogers' Formation XII, those containing the remarkable New River coking coals, underlie, in unbroken beds, below the water level (but at depths not greater than those from which the lately organized Connellsville Gas Coal & Iron Co., of Fayette Co., Pa., will go for its coal) all this region. The Middle Coal Measures, Rogers' No. XIII, are all here, all (but perhaps the lowest bed) above water level, except the portions eroded by the stream-valleys,—the daylight drifts of Nature's gigantic mining operations which, free of cost, have opened the way to the outcrop edges of the 10 beds of coal, each over a yard thick, running in thickness from 3 ft. to 11, aggregating over 60 feet of coals, which Mr. Page exposed and measured in this group of rocks, as shown in his section on the supplement. Fragments of the lower portion of the Upper Coal Measures remain on the higher levels of the divide, and in these are one or two beds of coal.—It follows from the above that every part of this tract is underlaid by coal beds; the section across it shows the same.

Some idea may be formed of the value of such an estate for coal-mining purposes when the statement is made—as it can be entirely within the limits of ascertained geological conditions—that on it, under favorable conditions for working, choice can be made of almost any one of the beds of coking, splint, gas, cannel, or other semi-bituminous or bituminous coals now mined at either of the 37 collieries of the New River and Kanawha districts, now in operation on or near the C. & O. R'y, enumerated in the Feb. No. of The Virginias, since they work one or another of the beds of Page's section. For example :—

(1) The New River coking coals, which underlie the entire estate, can be reached, say from near the mouth of Blake's Branch, by shafting, as follows :—The Sewell bed, from 4' to

0' thick, that which furnishes the noted coke used by the Longdale Iron Co., at but a few feet below the water level, for by Mr. Page's measurements it is but 45 ft. above the Falls Conglomerate, the top-rock of the Lower Coal Measures, which at Cannelton is not far from the bed of the Kanawha. (This bed would probably rise above water level towards the N. E. part of Smithers-Gauley:—The *Nutallburg* and *Fire Creek bed*, a yard thick seam noted for the purity of its coal and the good quality of its coke, which Mr. Page found 222 ft. below the Sewell at Hawk's Nest, (see section), should be reached by a 250-ft. shaft, one of about the same depth as that the new Connellsville, Pa. Co. will use on the lands it lately purchased at such a large price per acre:—and The *Quinnimont bed*, from 3' to 4' thick, the equally valuable coking coal so successfully used at Quinnimont furnace, placed by the same section 224 ft. below the Nutallburg, which a 500-ft. shaft (a very short one in most coal regions) would reach.

The somewhat increased cost of mining these coals by shafts, rather than by inclines as on New River (if there would be an increased cost, which I consider doubtful), would be more than counterbalanced by having unbroken beds of coal to work in.

(2) *The Kanawha coals proper*,—the different kinds of bituminous coals that are known in the markets as gas, steam, block, splint, gray splint or cannel,—any one variety or all of them, can be mined on these lands, from the valleys of Smithers' Creek and its branches, above water-level and "on the rise," for on the sides of the hills facing these valleys the whole 1,000 feet of the Middle Measures that bear these coals is exposed, and each bed of the group can be reached, at different levels, one above the other on the same slope, as shown in Mr. Page's section, or successively by following up the valleys until by their rise they reach the levels of the several seams of coal. Among these beds, and where they can be readily opened and identified, are those mined at the Gauley Mountain, Eagle, Faulkner's, Crescent, Cannelton, Coal Valley, Straughan's, Mt. Morris, Eureka, Morris Creek, Old Virginia, Upper Creek, Paint Creek, Blacksburg, East Bank, Coalburg, Houston, Coalmont, Cedar Grove, Campbell's Creek, and other collieries of this region, and the intending miner may here select any one of these beds to mine from, confident that he will find it essentially the same in character.

The steam, gas, blast-furnace, and domestic coals shipped from the collieries named, by rail to the eastward and by rail and river to the westward, are all well known and highly esteemed, but they work only a few of the many beds here existing. Some of the thickest have never been worked, and the adaptations of a half dozen heavy beds, any one of which would be the making of a less favored region, are wholly unknown because the coal from them has never been used; their faces have been exposed, by digging away a few feet of loose material from the slope of the hill-side, and their thickness measured, and that is about all that is known of them. A dozen years ago I had a coal bed opened, on the face of the bluff on an adjacent property, which I found over 11 ft. thick, but as yet no use has been made of that great bed. I could say the same of others measured at the same time. The day will come, and before many years, when each one of the dozen or more good beds of coal here accessible will be known as furnishing each a fuel having a special adaptation, and not till then will the great value of these many-bedded coal lands be known and appreciated.

The two geological sections given on the map, while not those of this tract itself, are, essentially, the section that development will find there. They were made on opposite sides of Smithers-Gauley in the line of the general dip of the coal measures, by careful and pains-taking mining engineers, from actual measurements of the coal beds and intervening rocks in place. I consider that they fairly represent the relative location and thickness of the coal seams in this land,—The one called "a section across the land on the line A—B" is that of the coal beds, in their proper relations, as actually measured by Wm. N. Page, M. & C. E., at Hawk's Nest, a few miles southeast from Smithers-Gauley,—this shows, as before stated, in about 1,000 ft. of measures, 60 ft. of coal in 10 beds, ranging in thickness, as the figures beside the section show, from 3 to 11 ft., including beds of 5, 7, 9 and 10 ft. respectively. The section is thrown into relief form to show how the beds are cut by the cañon of Smithers' Creek and how they are inclined towards that creek, most of them above water-level, as drawn, so they can be worked level- and drainage-free.—The other was measured by O. A. Veazey, C. & M. E., on Hughes' Creek, on one of the lots of the patent from which this lot was taken, a few miles northwest from Smithers-Gauley, on the opposite side of it from Page's section, and where more of the Measures have gone down under the water level. This section shows over 49 ft. of coal in 10 beds of the Middle Measures (below the Black Flint) ranging in thickness from 3½ to 8 ft., including 4½, 5½ and 7 ft. beds. Besides this it shows 3 beds, containing 12 ft. of coal, in the 250 ft. of the Upper Measures left on the higher levels. The aggregate thickness of good coal beds in this section is over 60 ft., including cannel, splint and bituminous coals. Mr. Veazey also locates 3 beds of iron ore.

To show with more particularity the character and vast quantity of the coals on this estate I might make special mention of two or three of its beds. For example, near the mouth of Blake's Branch, just above the level of the creek valley, where it can be reached by an easy grade tramway of less than three-fourths of a mile in length from a wharf by the side of the navigable Kanawha, and without the intervention of an "incline," there has been opened and drifted on, for a short distance, a bed of splint coal, of the very best character, which I measured and found fully 7 ft. thick (I found it 8 ft. thick and about 100 ft. above the river in the face of the hill below Cannelton). Outcropping on the side of the creek valley and near the lowest levels of the property it follows that this coal bed underlies, as an unbroken stratum, almost its entire area, and represents in its solid contents (the product of 10 square miles by 7 ft.), more than 30 million tons of getable coal,—calculating by the rule that allows 1,000 tons of coal to the acre for each foot of thickness in the bed. Saying nothing about the 5 ft. thick bed of excellent shop coal lying some 70 ft. under the one just spoken of, and that I saw opened 20 ft. above the water level of the adjacent lands, I will mention the bed, about 300 ft. above the 7-ft. one, which I saw opened just below Cannelton and found, by measurement, to be 11 ft. 8 inches thick, including two or three thin slate partings. This grand coal bed, the one so cheaply and successfully mined by the Hawk's Nest Coal Co. on Gauley Mountain, and in part by a half dozen mines on the C. & O. near Cannelton station, may be fairly said to have here over 5 square miles of area,—allowing that half of it has been removed by the erosion of the valleys. This would furnish over 30 million tons of one of the most esteemed free-burning coals of the country. About 20 ft. above the last, over 400 feet above the water level, on the property below, is the 7-ft. thick bituminous and cannel coal bed, the one that furnishes the well known high-priced Cannelton cannel coal; this valuable bed doubtless will be found to hold over a large area of the Gauley-Smithers land.—The known workable beds of coal will aggregate from 12 to 15 ft. of thickness

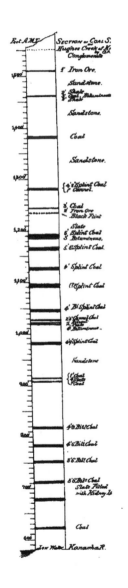

4

for the entire area of the tract for those under the water-level, and, after making ample allowance for the portions cut out by the gorges and valleys, from 25 to 30 ft. for those above water-level, for the same extent ; dimensions furnishing more than 70-million tons of the first and 150-million of the second. These very large quantities, which any one familiar with the subject and the region knows are below the actual ones, suggest the possibilities of production and profit whenever capital and labor utilize them.

The character of the coals found here is but partially known, since this is a new coal-field to most of the markets of the country, especially to the eastern ones, (for it had no railway connection with them previous to 1873); nor can it be rightly known until a properly conducted industrial survey of the field has been made; but enough is known to warrant the statement that there are no better semi-bituminous or bituminous coals, including all the varieties called for in the markets, if there are as good ones, all things considered, known in this or any other country.

The Sewell, Nutallburg or Fire Creek, and Quinnimont beds, usually called the New River coals, have been found unsurpassed for coking, steam and domestic purposes. An analysis of one of these gave to Prof. Egleston 70.67 per cent. fixed carbon, 25.35 volatile matter, 2.10 ash, 0.57 sulphur and 1.45 moisture. This is, in the main, the analysis of this group of coals, one showing that they have all the best qualities of good coking coals, a high percentage of fixed carbon, just enough volatile matter, and extremely small percentages of ash and sulphur (See also letter of Prof. Egleston in Feb. No. of The Virginias). The Connellsville coal selected by the Pa. Geol. Survey as a typical one gave 59.61 per cent. fixed carbon, 30.10 volatile matter, 8.23 ash, 0.78 sulphur, and 1.26 moisture.—The U. S. Naval Engineers pronounce the New River coals "first-class steam coals ;" the blast-furnaces make a ton of iron with less than a ton of the coke made from them.

The Kanawha coals proper have a deservedly high reputation for gas, steam, domestic, and blast-furnace purposes.—The Gauley Mountain coal, that of the "12-ft. bed," (as the 11' 8" bed of Smithers-Gauley is called), which is now used extensively in the locomotives of New England railways, contains, by analysis, 63.10 per cent. fixed carbon, 32.61 volatile matter, 2.15 ash, 0.74 sulphur, and 1.40 moisture.—The noted Cannelton cannel coal is mined from a seam 12' below the Black Flint Ledge and some 750' above the river (See map and sections), just across Smithers' Creek from the land in question, which is 7' thick, consisting of 3'.5 cannel below and 3'.5 splint above; the lower stratum analyses 58.00 per cent. volatile matter, 23.50 fixed carbon and 18.50 ash ; the "selected" cannel gives 46.50 volatile matter, 43.20 fixed carbon, and 10.20 ash. This coal commands a high price in the markets for gas enriching purposes and as a substitute for English cannel.—The semi-cannel coal, shipped also from the Cannelton mines, consists of 35.10 per cent. volatile matter, 62.90 fixed carbon, and 2.00 ash; the Coal Valley coals, mined and shipped in large quantities from the mines near Cannelton Station, have about the same composition as the semi-cannel but with less ash. These are classed with the best gas-making coals.—Of the splint coals of the Kanawha Mr. M. F. Maury says, in "Resources of West Virginia," 1876: "It is abundant, and, in admixture with more or less bituminous coal is found in seams as thick as 10 and 11 feet. For the combined purposes of steam, domestic use, and the manufacture of iron, it may be looked upon as the most useful and valuable coal of the State, and even now it ranks so high that in the New York retail market it quotes higher than any other W. Va. coal, except cannel. Its value is due to its firmness and solidity, which enables it to be handled, shifted and stored with very little loss. It burns well, leaving but little ash; has both high calorific power and intensity; is usually remarkably free from sulphur and other impurities; has little or no tendency to clinker; is *free from the danger of firing by spontaneous combustion*—a great desideratum in storage and ocean transportation ; is first-rate as a steam and household fire, and it has particular adaptability in its raw state to the manufacture of iron in the blast-furnace."

The cost of opening mines and the expense and conditions of operating them are very important factors in estimating the value of coal lands. What these are in the Kanawha coal-field is well stated in the following extracts from a report, made in 1876, by general I. M. St. John, Consulting Engineer of the C. & O. R'y:—

"Of the eighteen mines referred to, on this railway, not one has been found to require machinery for ventilation, hoisting or pumping; and there has been an unusual exemption from mine accidents. Their mining plant is of the simplest character, viz: side or branch tracks, inclines and tipples, and occasionally bins. The facilities in this Kanawha Valley for opening work at low cost are certainly exceptional. For greater precision of statement, reference is made to the Coal Valley mine, 343 miles from Richmond, which weekly ships 960 to 1,000 tons from a 7-foot vein, here 80 feet above the railway. The agent of this company states that the original outlay to open and equip the mine was $4,200, and that the entire expenditure to date, including all mining work chargable to this account, for all fixtures, rails, tools, cars, and stocks has been $6,230. This Coal Valley enterprise, one of the most successful of the Kanawha Valley, is operated on leased ground, under royalty, by an association of miners, and has supplied the Richmond Gas-works by contract during 1875 and 1876, also, shipping gas coal to more distant points. Other mines have been opened on the Coal Valley and adjoining seams for less cost where they approach the railroad more closely. The smaller mines are generally operated by miners on lease, and when examined present the most convincing evidence of the facility of mining superior coals at a very low cost. It is emphatically the field of work for men, or companies, of small means."

The facilities for reaching markets from these lands are exceptionally good since in the direction of greatest demand there is a choice of competitive modes of conveyance.—Eastwardly the way to market is by the Chesapeake & Ohio Railway; and this, though on the opposite side of the Kanawha, can be easily and cheaply reached, either by the method that has been used for a number of years by the Cannelton Co., on the lands contiguous to these, or by wire tramways, such as are advertised in this Journal. The policy of the railway is a liberal one in reference to this traffic, as is proven by its steady increase, year by year.—Westwardly, down stream, to the great markets reached by the twenty thousand miles of navigable Mississippi waters, where the demand for coals keeps pace with the wonderful growth of the country, the way is opened from the very adits of the mines, for the cheapest kind of transportation to market, now that the Kanawha Improvement by the General Government is nearly completed and that great water-way rendered permanently navigable. In a few months barges can be loaded at the mouth of Smithers' Creek, in the "pool" made by Dam No. 2 of that work, which is just below Cannelton, and transported at very low rates—about one-fourth those of railways it is estimated, to Cincinnati, Louisville, or any other of the river cities of the Ohio and Mississippi. The Chesapeake & Ohio Railway also offers facilities for shipments westward; these are constantly increasing as that great trunk line completes its western connections and enlarges the territory that can be reached with these coals,—for, notwithstanding the fact that the Western States have extensive areas of coals, there will always be in that direction a large and constantly increasing demand for the purer and better coals of the Kanawha region.

Excellent timber, oak, birch, beech, tulip-poplar, etc.. covers all this estate, so that it has not only an abundant supply for all mining and building purposes,—highly important considerations in estimating the value of a mining property,—but also a large quantity to spare.

I do not know, in the whole range of my observations, any place where investments, either for holding or working, can be more profitably made than in such abundantly coal-bearing properties as this, in the very heart of the Great Kanawha Coal-field, on the line of a great trunk railway. The price at which I am informed it is offered is merely a nominal one, bearing no sort of proportion to its intrinsic worth. Lands in Pennsylvania, not more favorably located commercially and holding not one-fifth as much coal, and what there is below water-level, have recently been sold for three times as much per acre;—a condition of values that will soon be exchanged when such facts as here stated become fully known to capitalists and miners.   Jed. Hotchkiss, Cons. Eng.

Staunton, Va., March, 1880.

Virginia Gold.—We have for a long time closely scanned the solid columns of the Engineering and Mining Journal of New York, the full and every way reliable exponent of gold as well as other mining operations, for items concerning Virginia gold mines and for some indications of a revival of interest in her great gold belt, but all we have seen has been two, standing, unchanged lines in the list of "General Mining Stocks," under the Head of "Non-Dividend Mines,"—the first, "Bertha & Edith, 645 acres, 500,000 shares, par value $1., non-assessable;" the second, "Rappahannock, 345 acres, $250,000 capital stock, 250,000 shares, par value $1., non-assessable." No sales of shares of the former have been mentioned; "sales made" of Rappahannock shares are reported regularly, the Journal of Jan. 3rd, 1880, quoting sales of 44,300 shares at from 36 to 42 cts., and that of Feb. 21st, sales of 30,700 shares at from 36 to 45 cts. The issue last named had, besides this note of sales at an increased rate, two "items" about Virginia gold, the first for a long time,—one saying, "A recent letter from the superintendent of the Rappahannock mine states that the stamp-mill will be ready for crushing ore by the 10th of March, prox.;" the other a statement from the Fredericksburg *News* of Feb. 16th, that "The purchase of the Whitehall gold mines some months ago by capitalists of Boston, Mass., has infused new life into mining interests in Spotsylvania. Several valuable mines have recently changed hands and new companies have been organized. There are now four mines in operation in the region known as The Wilderness, and new shafts are being sunk at three other places. Some of the rock from the new shaft of the Chicago-Virginia Mine has been assayed and yielded $30. per ton. The average of 12 samples was $14. per ton. One of our bankers says that a large amount has been realized during the past year from panning and sluice-washing surface dirt."

The same Journal, of Feb. 28th, says of the *Rappahannock* mine,— "Mr. Judson J. Embry, superintendent of this mine, writing under date of Feb. 20th, says : We are now sinking (at the 85-ft. shaft) to a second level, and we have not, thus far, been obliged to do any blasting. The vein continues down in the end of the shaft, nearly vertical, and of a uniform width of 2 ft. It presents the same general appearance, free from sulphurets, and containing *much* visible free gold. Our steam hoister works admirably. The mill building is nearly completed. We are now at work on the tank, and arranging the shafting and footing." On the 25th, the superintendent wrote. "Our work is progressing very favorably; we are now down 102 ft.; so far there has been no occasion to use any explosives."—In that issue sales of 21,900 shares of this mine, between Feb. 21 and 27, are noted at from 40 to 45 cts.

Gold in Montgomery Co., Va.—The discovery of gold in the lands of Brush Creek, in this county, was made last summer by J. M. Thomas, Esq., of Blacksburg, an old California miner (49-er), who suspected its existence from the similarity of the rocks, timber and soil to that of the California diggings. Notwithstanding the winter is still on us, numerous parties have been digging and washing in a rough way ever since, and now the excitement amounts to a boom, and the prospect is that a rush of adventurers will be made to this new Eldorado. The proportion of gold is from 20 to 75 cents per bushel of earth. The largest particles yet found are worth about fifty cents. Mr. H. D. Walters, jeweler, of Christiansburg, while on a visit to his father, who owns a Brush Creek farm, took three hundred and fifty pieces of gold from one pan of washings. The precious metal is found everywhere for miles up and down Brush Creek and its tributaries. Geologists have asserted the existence of gold in that region, but little did the denizens of Brush Creek suspect that they had been sleeping over mines of vast wealth.

Later.—The snow has lessened the prospecting for gold on Brush Creek in Montgomery Co., but the finding of several pieces worth as high as as $1.25 each, has made certain a rush of diggers after the ground is clear. Gold has been found to exist on many of the small streams running from Pilot Mountain into Brush Creek.— *Montgomery Messenger.*

Louisa Gold Mines.—A number of tracts of land in Louisa county, known to abound in auriferous rock or earth, have lately been disposed of to parties with capital from the North and otherwise, who have set about the unearthing of the precious metals with a vim that betokens the most satisfactory results. The gold mines of this section of the State have always been noted in the history of the Commonwealth, and have yielded more or less as they were intelligently worked. Iron and copper ought to be mined, and sulphur manufactured; in Louisa, at a profit to those engaged, and no doubt the time will soon come when such will be the case.— *The Commonwealth.*

These small signs of improvement are welcome; we hope they are the beginning of the better days for our gold belts, when skill acquired in the mining operations of the Pacific slope, supplied with the best known mechanical devices for separating the precious metals, and backed by abundant capital, shall be applied to their development. The "Great Gold Belt" of Virginia is 200 miles long and from 15 to 25 miles wide, an area of fully 4,000 square miles, crossed in every direction by hundreds of streams, bordered by "placers" and underlaid by hundreds of stratified beds of gold-bearing rocks.

The Iron Ores near the Shenandoah Valley Railroad:—A Letter from Prof. Thomas Egleston, of the Columbia College School of Mines.

To the Shenandoah Construction Co.:

Gentlemen:—I have quite recently had occasion to examine the geology of a part of the line of the Shenandoah Valley R. R., on both sides of the proposed route, in order to ascertain the probable quality and quantity of the iron ores found there, and have been greatly surprised at the value of the ores which are found in great abundance in its immediate vicinity. They are also of excellent quality, most of them containing much less than one-half of one per cent. of phosphorus. They occur in the formations known as Nos. I and V of Rogers, which contain some of the best ores of Virginia. When the road is completed to its junction with the Chesapeake & Ohio R'y, the iron ore properties will be within easy reach of a variety of other ores and of one of the best fuels in the United States for the manufacture of iron. I have made a number of analyses of the cokes of New River, and have never found them to contain as much as six per cent. of ash. They are very strong, and in some of their properties, greatly resemble charcoal. When they are used for making iron, it is said that only from one to one ton and a quarter of coke are required per ton of iron. The ores can be very cheaply mined, and the iron made from them has always borne a good reputation. If a market is found for the ores, there is sufficient in these formations to supply a very large quantity of first-class ores, the quantity being limited only by the number of mines opened. The limestones for flux and the building materials for the construction of furnaces can be had in large quantities and can be cheaply quarried near all the ore beds.　　　　　　　Yours, Respectfully,

　　　　　　　　　　　　　　　Thomas Egleston,
New York, Nov. 20th, 1879.　　　　　Engineer of Mines.

Kingwood, Preston Co., W. Va., had a meeting of its citizens a few days since and appointed a committee to prepare a report on the mineral wealth of its vicinage, and of the county, that it might be made known to the capitalists of Pittsburg who are contemplating an extension southward of the Pittsburg Southern Railroad. The preamble to the resolutions adopted says,—"Our county of Preston abounds in extensive beds of iron ore, coal, and limestone, sufficient when developed to bring wealth to the capitalist and laborer and prosperity to our people."

The Duty on Steel Rails will not be reduced this year, judging from the formidable opposition to that measure. The *Iron Age* remarks,—"It is probable that the South will give many more votes against it than were expected, as the iron manufacturing interests in that section are increasing rapidly. The panic delayed the development of these industries, as well as the furnishing of means of transportation, but the prospect is that the present condition of the iron trade will accelerate this development ; and this is leading the South to change its sentiment on tariff questions, and will make the change of tariff rates a difficult subject."

The *sentiment* has not changed, but we are quite sure the *policy* has, certainly among the people in the mineral and manufacturing regions, whither the population is moving, and among the more sagacious and horse-sense-possessing members of Congress.— The high duty on iron ore and everything made from it means the expenditure of millions in the Virginias. If the duty on iron ores were now $5. per ton it is demonstrable that not less than $5,000,000 would be spent this year in making available the iron ores of these states. It is not agreeable for the owner of millions of tons of iron ore in Virginia, lying less than 200 miles from Pittsburg, to know that is worth no more to him than so much sand-rock while the transportors of convict-dug ores from the other side of the Atlantic are reaping a rich harvest carrying those ores by his very doors to that and other Pennsylvania iron-making centres. No wonder he is in favor of a change of *policy*. In this connection we note with pleasure that the leading officials of five Virginia railways have signed the remonstrance against the removal of duty on steel rails.

P. W. Sheafer, Engineer of Mines, Pottsville, Pa., a well known geologist and anthracite coal operator, writes us concerning THE VIRGINIAS:—"I am pleased to know that these two great mineral States have an able advocate to plead their cause before the great public who are now especially on the *qui vive* for your great staples of coal, iron, zinc, salt, &c. I would advocate the consumption of your products rather than to export them and thus build up your home industries and become great manufacturing States. I was pleased to note for myself, recently, the great extent of the anthracite coal measures in the Lower Carboniferous, or Vespertine, rocks in Pulaski county, Virginia, and its proposed use in the zinc and salt works of that vicinity. Your railroads should now use it in their locomotives." He adds:—"What we want now, are large bodies of ore in small bodies of land ; not the reverse."

Mr. J. H. Bramwell, recently Manager of the Quinnimont Furnace, W.Va., now Superintendent of the Ironton (Ohio) Iron-works, was the recipient of a valuable and well deserved testimonial, in the shape of a box of costly volumes on metallurgy, mining, engineering, chemistry, etc., from the employes of the Quinnimont (W.Va.) Furnace, when he left that place, early last month, for his new post of duty. If space permitted, we would cheerfully make room for the addresses that were interchanged on that occasion, for we have personal knowledge that the words spoken were not mere compliments. Mr. Bramwell's management of Quinnimont is worthy of praise and imitation. His presence and example were a benediction to those associated with him.

Virginia Iron Furnace Notes.

The New York and Virginia Iron and Coal Company, of which H. R. Baltzer is President ; H. J. Rogers, Vice-President, and H. W. Howell, Secretary and Treasurer, has leased for three years, with the privilege of purchase, the Buffalo Gap Furnace, on the Chesapeake & Ohio Railway, Augusta county, Virginia, and is now accumulating a stock of ore and coke. It will go into blast in a few days. We are glad to note the blowing in of this favorably located furnace, and hope the lessees may be successful. There is no reason why they should not produce iron cheaply at that point. Their New York office is 54 Broad St., Room 8.

The Estaline Furnace Property, on the line of the Chesapeake & Ohio Railway, southwest of and adjacent to the Ferrol property of the Pennsylvania and Virginia Iron and Coal Company, Augusta county, Virginia, is being examined with reference to purchase. If not sold, one of its owners, Capt. Nelson Beall, of Frostburg, Md., will reopen its extensive ore beds and mine and sell iron ores.

At Callie Furnace, Alleghany county, Virginia, the proprietors report the opening in several places of what promises to be an extensive stratum of very superior red iron ore. It is said to be geologically above their large stratum of No. VII (Oriskany) brown hematite, and therefore lower down on the eastern side of the great Rich-patch Mountain arch. Three analyses recently made at the Cambria Iron Works, Pa., made the average composition of these ores 54.61 of metallic iron, and 0.0189 of phosphorus. This indicates that we may yet find the *fancy ores* wanted by Bessemer pig makers near our existing lines of railway.

Coke is rapidly becoming the blast furnace fuel of this country, because of the better production resulting from its use. The *Iron Age* reports that a Hudson River furnace, by using 25 per cent. of coke with anthracite coal, got an increase of 5 tons of metal on the 30 made with coal alone, or over 16 per cent ; a furnace in eastern Pennsylvania, by using 50 per cent. of coke, doubled its product. As a rule, the more coke used the more iron is made. The knowledge of these results has had something to do with the large purchases of coking coal lands recently made in Pennsylvania at high price per acre. For the same reason there must speedily follow a large appreciation in the value of the large areas of coal lands in West Virginia that are underlaid by the superior coking coals in the Lower Measures and not far above them in the Middle Measures.

The International Real Estate Society, noticed in our February No., has been organized by the election of Wm. A. Quarrier, Esq., President ; Alex. F. Mathews, Vice-President ; Charles C. Lewis, Treasurer and acting Secretary ; Clarkson C. Watts, Attorney and Law Adviser ; Emanuel D. Ludwig and Hermann Kirchoff, Superintendents of Immigration ; and John L. Cole of Charleston, West Virginia, and Gabriel Vuille, of Switzerland, Engineers and Surveyors.

C. R. BOYD,

Consulting, Mining and Civil Engineer,

Wytheville, Virginia.

The Mineral Lands of Southwest Virginia, in the Blue Ridge, Valley, and Apalachian Districts a SPECIALTY. Correspondence solicited

The Virginias.

A Mining, Industrial, and Scientific Journal:

Devoted to the Development of Virginia and West Virginia.

Vol. I, No. 4. } Staunton, Virginia, April, 1880. { Price 25 Cents.

The Virginias,

PUBLISHED MONTHLY,

By Jed. Hotchkiss, - - - Editor and Proprietor,

At 346 E. Main St., Staunton, Va.

Terms, including postage, per year, in advance, $2.00. Single numbers, 25 cents. Extra copies, $20.00 per 100. **Advertising Rates** made known on application. On sale at Hunter & Co.'s Bookstore, Main Street, Staunton, Virginia.

The Price of The Virginias hereafter will be Two Dollars a year, and for a single number Twenty-five Cents.—We find it necessary, to properly illustrate such articles as we publish, to accompany each issue of this Journal with cuts and supplementary maps and sections which add very largely to the cost of publication, sometimes doubling it; to meet this, in part, as well as the recent large increase in the cost of the superior paper we use, it is right to increase our subscription rate, therefore we do it. We advance the price of single copies because we find that many persons buy a single copy merely to get the map of the particular region they are interested in; they can better afford to pay twenty-five cents for such map than we can to publish it.—Of course The Virginias will be sent for the year to all that have paid for it at the former rate, but those that have not paid will be charged the advanced price.

Attention to the New Advertisements is Invited.—It is a very agreeable duty to recommend Messrs. Elder & Nelson to the numerous readers of The Virginias that we know intend to invest in real estate in these States. These gentlemen can be implicitly relied on in these matters; they are sound lawyers and experienced dealers in real estate, and one of them is a "born" farmer.——The Old Iron-Side Paint has been proven, by extensive use in this region, one of the very best preservatives of exposed metals and woods It has given general satisfaction as a roofing paint, and is especially adapted for painting all the exposed portions of large manufacturing establishments. The gentlemen offering it are skilful, energetic and reliable ——Our Liverpool, England, advertiser, Mr. Blackwell, is a well known dealer in manganese and other minerals; he handles the product of the Crimora Mines of this county. Those having manganese to sell will do well to correspond with him ——Judge Anderson offers the great Glenwood Furnace estate for sale. It is on the James River & Kanawha Canal, now in process of transformation into the Richmond & Alleghany Railroad, and by next July will be on a through line of East and West traffic Prof Campbell, who knows it well, said of this in his paper on the James River Iron Belts, in the January number of The Virginias, page 4:—"Glenwood Furnace, in Arnold's Valley, S W of James River, has been run, with occasional interruptions, since 1849—probably, altogether, 23 years, yet there is no evidence of exhaustion in the beds from which it has been supplied" An iron king in Glenwood could find a dominion worthy of his rule ——The Mountain Top Hotel and Farm, to be sold by J Thompson Brown, the 17th of April, is one of the most delightful places in Virginia. The description of this property, given in our advertising columns, is not an exaggerated one, as all that have ever visited the place will testify The line of the Shenandoah Valley Railroad is but three miles distant, and Davidia Station, on the Chesapeake & Ohio Railway, is close at hand This could be made one of the most charming of mild climate mountain homes

Recent Sales of Mineral Properties in the Virginias.—The Greenbrier White Sulphur Springs (West Virginia) for $340,000, to Wm A Stuart, of Saltville, Virginia.——The interest of J W Mixter in the Bertha Zinc Works, at Martin's, Va, to George W Palmer, of Saltville, Virginia, for over $50,000 The zinc mines are yielding well and the business of zinc smelting is proving profitable ——The Catawba Iron Furnace property, some 10,000 acres, in Botetourt county, Virginia, near the lines of the Valley branch of the Baltimore & Ohio Railroad and of the Richmond and Southwestern Railway, to J. H Bramwell, the Superintendent of the New York & Ohio Iron-works, at Ironton, Ohio. This furnace, when in operation, made a high grade ordnance and car-wheel iron ——The Powhatan Furnace, formerly known as the Westham Furnace, on James River, a few miles above Richmond, Virginia, to the Phila & Reading Coal and Iron Company, of Pennsylvania, which owns large tracts of iron lands in Piedmont, Virginia —A bed of ore, on Judge Aker's land, near Keyser, West Virginia on the Baltimore & Ohio Railroad, to Wolf & Gump, leased on a royalty with privilege of purchase. The ore is to be shipped to Pennsylvania.——In Scott county, Virginia, 4,000 acres of mineral land were purchased by Northern capitalists.——R. F. Mason has purchased the Munday tract of iron land near Stony Point, Albemarle Co, Va., near the Crickenberger lands he purchased some years ago These are on the Charlottesville & Rapid-Anne R R now under construction ——Gen John D. Imboden, of Pittsburg, Pa., bought 50,000 acres of coal land in Wise Co, Va The Richmond & Southwestern Railway is to go in that direction.

Blast-furnace Notes.—Buffalo Gap Furnace, which was put in blast the 22d of March, by the New York & Virginia Iron & Coal Company, was burned on the 30th of March. Loss, $20,000; insurance, $18,100. The work of rebuilding began at once.——The Pennsyvania & Virginia Iron & Coal Company, J F. Lewis Superintendent, is relining the old furnace at Ferrol, Chesapeake and Ohio Railway, Virginia. It will probably go into blast some time this month.——The Lucy-Selina Furnace, of the Longdale Iron Company, Alleghany county, Virginia, was out of blast two weeks in March, during which time it was thoroughly repaired and its 5- to 10-ton cadmia throat-choker, which regularly accumulates every few months, removed The furnace is making about 28 tons a day A new furnace, on much the same plan as the old one, only larger, is now under way and much progress has been made in the foundation work The new railway to the mines, some 5 miles, is now in operation.

Gold.—The Chicago and Virginia Gold Mining Company, on their tract in Orange county, are getting a fine body of ore on their dump The drift at the foot of the shaft intersects three gold quartz veins of 12½, 4, and 2 feet respectively. The ore now being taken out is from the large vein, which is 13½ feet at present depth of shaft As is characteristic of all Virginia ores, a large percentage of the gold is carried in the fine clay and gravel which fills the fissures of the veins; and the clay and gravel of this ore, by pan tests, is very rich in fine gold; the quartz carries free gold, also, with the usual percentage of sulphurets Tests have been made in the bottoms along the branch streams, and quite an area of paying placer surface has been developed This is a surprise to the company, and enhances the value of this thoroughly proved and tested property ——The Pocahontas Gold Mining Company, in Spotsylvania county, completed their tunnel on Saturday evening last. This tunnel and open-cut together are nearly 350 feet, about 220 feet of which extends through hard blasting rock This development alone has required five months of labor with large day and night force It may be ranked as one of the most noteworthy in our mining districts Work on the surface, by the most approved hydraulic methods, will be commenced this week, when we shall have further occasion to speak of this enterprising company, and of their valuable property.——Mr E. L Doyle, a practical miner and a gentleman of large experience and extensive information, has recently located several gold-bearing veins upon the Randolph mine, one of which assays $128 00 to the ton of 2,000 lbs. He will, as early as practicable, sink several shafts. He has now under his control about 1,500 acres of choice gold-bearing land, which is in this county. These properties were purchased after a thorough examination.—*Fredericksburg Star.*——It is said that a negro recently got $30 in a few days from the Brush Creek, Montgomery county, Virginia, diggings ——We were shown, on Monday, some beautiful specimens of gold, silver and lead ore from the Alley-Cooper mines in Louisa county, owned by Messrs. Joe Tyler and Isaac Cason The specimen of gold ore was estimated at $1,000 per ton, and the silver and lead ore at from $12 to $15 per ton, with traces of gold that indicated from $3 to $6 per ton About forty tons of the silver and lead ore have been raised and shipped to Newark, N J., to parties who have contracted for several hundred tons In this county there are quite a number of gold mines that are being worked with the most gratifying results —*Star*, April 7th

Iron Ore Items.—The Virginia Midland Railroad shipped 900 tons of ore from Lynchburg northward the last week in March ——In Bedford county, Virginia, west of Lynchburg, and near the Atlantic, Mississippi & Ohio Railroad, F J. Chapman is reported to have discovered, and uncovered for several miles, four large veins of specular ore ——At Ferrol, on the Chesapeake & Ohio Railway, Virginia, a large new washer has been erected, and the Pennsylvania & Virginia Iron and Coal Co., J F Lewis, Superintendent, is now sending 10 car loads of ore daily to its Quinnimont Furnace, West Virginia —- Ore is to be mined in a short time, it is said, on the Ham lands, near Barboursville, Orange Co, Va.——Dr. Morris, of Lynchburg, has leased and is mining the iron ore bed of R N Powell near Dickinson's station of the Pittsylvania & Franklin Narrow-Gauge R. R. Franklin Co, Va ——Maj. Mason expects soon to work 500 hands in mining ore from the great beds near Rocky Mount, Franklin Co, Va, that have been leased by the Pennsylvania Steel Co, of Steelton, Pa ——Several leases of iron land have lately been made by companies in the southern portions of Franklin Co., Va.

Copper.—The Theodora Copper Mine near Herndon, on the W & O R R., Fairfax county, Virginia, March 22d, shipped its first car load of ore to Baltimore. Rev. J B North, who is working the mine, it is stated, will soon erect smelting works near the mine Six men, one a Cornish miner, are now at work in the shaft ——The Ore-Knob Copper Company, of North Carolina, declared a quarterly dividend of $37,500, or 2½ per cent, March 23d. (See its location on our copper map) The yearly output is stated to be over a million dollars worth ——The Miner's Lode Copper Company, of Boston, Massachusetts, is reported to have very rich copper mines in the Page Valley, and to have passed through very rich deposits of iron ore in developing their copper mine ——A copper mine has also been opened not far from the Dark Hollow, on the Madison and New Market Turnpike, in Madison county, Virginia, on the Blue Ridge, Northern capitalists having made a purchase of land there. The ore is said to be very rich. From personal observations, made not far from this locality, we are satisfied that valuable copper mines will be developed in the Blue Ridge in Madison

Silver.—Prospectors boring for oil, in Preston county, West Virginia, on the line of the Baltimore & Ohio Railway, are said to have found paying quantities of silver ore, assaying $125.00 per ton.——Near Herndon, Washington & Ohio Railroad, Fairfax Co, Va., there is much excitement over a "rich vein of silver," reported as discovered in the Theodora Copper Mine

Professor Campbell's Paper, on the Geology of Apalachian Virginia, is one of great value It treats of and illustrates the rock structure of one of the most interesting and accessible portions of this State, the "Springs Region," traversed by the Chesapeake & Ohio Railway With this paper and its admirable section in hand, any one "having eyes to see" can very soon become familiar with the geology of this region, and get the key for understanding that of most of the Virginian Apalachian country, for this section is a typical one. We again thank the *American Journal of Science* for the use of its illustations and Professor Campbell for the revision of this paper. The wide publicity The Virginias is giving to such substantial papers, is creating an increased interest in these States ——Colonel Wm Allan, the head of the McDonogh Institute, near Baltimore, writes us,—"I have read The Virginias with the greatest pleasure. You have entered on a most useful and needed work. The articles published are many of them of great value in giving an insight into the wealth of the Old Dominion. Professor Campbell's article, in the last number (March) is the best and clearest statement of the geological structure of the Valley I have seen, and is alone worth the subscription."

A Report on the Iron Ores near Cumberland Gap, Virginia, by P N. Moore, from the Kentucky Geological Survey, now in progress under Prof. N. S. Shaler as Director, will appear, in full, in the May number of The Virginias The geological sections accompanying that report are given on one of the supplements of illustrations in this issue.——This Virginia report, by the Kentucky geologists, will have a present interest and value now that three lines of railway are heading in that direction from the eastward.

The Advantages of Advertising in our Widely Circulated Journal are well illustrated by a statement recently made by an advertiser that he had received letters from Liverpool, New York, Baltimore and Chicago, as well as from other points, in reference to what he here offers for sale, each stating that the writer's attention was called to it by the advertisement in The Virginias

The Geology of Apalachian Virginia.*

By J. L. CAMPBELL, Washington and Lee University.

CONTINUED FROM PAGE 45

In the number of this Journal for July last, a general outline of the geology of the Great Valley of Virginia was given, and illustrated by a section embracing the several epochs represented in the Valley proper, and in the two mountain ranges forming its boundaries on the southeast and northwest. That section may be regarded as a typical representation of the several varieties of rock that come to the surface for many miles on both sides of it.

In the present paper I propose to give what may be regarded, in part at least, as an extension of the same section—the results of observations made in the same general direction, but not exactly on the same line. Moving the line of section about eight miles toward the northeast of my former route, I shall fall back and begin again within the limits of the Great Valley; the reasons for which are, first, to renew the connection with the Lower Silurian limestones, that will again make their appearance in an interesting anticlinal valley at the other end of the section; and secondly, that we may pass through or near a considerable number of points of no little interest, and easily accessible to the scientific traveler or the student of geology.

What is here presented is, in its main features, the result of a survey made several years ago, in conjunction with the Hon. Wm. H. Ruffner, LL.D., the present Superintendent of Public Instruction in Virginia, and who is a gentleman of no mean attainments in geological science. Some important details that are introduced, as well as some of the generalizations, are the fruits of subsequent observations made by myself in review of our original work. The main conclusions, however, stand as originally agreed upon.

It would hardly be proper to call this an "ideal" section since some of the most interesting portions of it represent *real* sections that nature has opened up to our view on a grand scale—where the geologist may revel, or the student of science find interesting and profitable employment for many days together. It passes through or near several mountain gorges of considerable depth and extent, as well as many points of minor interest, where mountain streams have cut their channels through the lower hills and thus exposed the various formations along its lines.

On my former section the series of Professor Rogers was given with sub-divisions; and a table appended to present a comparison of these with the corresponding periods and epochs given in Professor Dana's Manual, so far as the equivalents have been definitely determined in this part of the Apalachian chain. On the section accompanying the present paper, the numbers and letters refer to Professor Dana's system.

Beginning, then, with the southeastern extremity, near the Rockbridge Baths, we find a natural section cut by the North River through a part of $3 a$ and the whole of $3 b$ and c, etc. (Calciferous, Quebec and Chazy=No. II Rogers). In the immediate vicinity of the Baths these formations are very much obscured by the Quaternary deposits of drift from the mountains above, but they may be studied conveniently at points a while lower down on the river cliffs, or on the neighboring hills a little remote from the river, on the southwest side, where the section passes. For a description of the rocks of this period, the reader is referred to the number for July.

The line of fault presented on the former section continues, with a single interruption, some distance beyond the present section, crossing the river a short distance above the Baths (N.W.)—the older (3) being still thrust upward over the edge of the newer (4 a.) This junction of the disturbed strata can be seen distinctly along the river banks at low water, but may be more distinctly traced in the hills southwest of the river, and on Hays' creek northeastward.

This fault has doubtless much to do with determining the temperature of these thermal Baths, the waters of which have a temperature of 72° F., and are kept in gentle but constant agitation by escaping bubbles of gas, consisting largely of nitrogen and carbonic acid. The remedial virtues of the Baths have been long recognized. As we pass up the river in a northwesterly direction we soon find the Trenton limestones forming the bottom of the river-bed where the strike of the strata can be distinctly seen crossing the stream nearly at right angles. The same rocks also crop out on the neighboring hills, which generally have a rounded shape and are strewed with quantities of local drift from the adjacent mountain gorges. There are no cliffs here; for these argillaceous limestones and overlying shales were too fragile to withstand the denuding force of the vast floods of water and masses of sandstone bowlders that have, at some past past period of time, come down with violence from the neigh-

From the American Journal of Science and Arts, Vol. XVIII, Aug. 1879. Revised for THE VIRGINIAS by Prof. Campbell.

boring mountains and the valleys beyond. Both the lithological and fossil characters of these rocks show that they are the same as those on which Lexington stands; but here, as well as along the base of House Mountain, they are softer, and not so extensively permeated with white veins, as they are around Lexington, where the crushing forces to which they have been subjected have not tended to harden many of the beds, but have produced innumerable fissures that have been filled up by infiltration, and now present beautiful veins of calc spar. But the underlying coraline bed that forms the base of this epoch, and crops out so conspicuously near Lexington, is not brought to the surface at this point, yet is found at the distance of a few miles on both sides of our present line of section. I have, therefore, included it.

At the distance of two miles above the Baths, we come to the base of Hog-back Mountain, (This and Wolf Ridge, immediately in rear of it, have evidently been once connected with the two ridges of House Mountain, represented on the former section; though now separated by a beautiful valley three miles wide.) at its northeast terminus, and about a mile northeast of where our section crosses. Here the North River cuts it off from what was once its northeast continuation, called Jump Mountain. The Medina sandstones (Rogers, No. IV) that crop out along the faces of the two ridges sink gradually as they approach the river—showing a marked depression at the point where the river has found its way through. Such, however, is not the case with the contiguous and nearly parallel ridge of North Mountain farther west.

The spurs of Hog-back and the face of the main ridge, to the height of several hundred feet, display an extensive outcrop of $4 b, c$ (Utica and Cincinnati shales.) These appear occasionally beneath the hard sandstones of $5 a$, as we pass up through the wild, winding canyon that here gives passage to the waters that come down from the mountain valleys above, and meet at the upper entrance of the gorge to form the North River. Just where the river issues from the mountain pass, the stream separates into two parts, forming a small island, in the middle of which rises a spring of sulphur water, now known as Wilson's Spring. It evidently rises from the shales of $4 b$, that here form the bottom of the river.

This is the point at which the turnpike leads us into the "Goshen Pass," through which we follow the winding course of the river for several miles.

In pursuing his course through this crooked gorge the geological student will find a problem to solve of no little complexity, arising in part from the windings of the river, and in still greater part from the rupturing and faulting of the mountains themselves. After passing the ends of both Hog-back and Wolf ridges (see section) at the distance of about a mile and a half above Wilson's Spring, he will find the course of the river nearly coincident with the strike of the Medina sandstones that here dip so steeply on the N.W. face of Wolf Ridge as to pass the lower beds beneath the stream, while those higher up are cut through in the direction of their strike. Within view of this point, and on the opposite side of the river, a great downfall from the next ridge (N. Mt.) has occurred, around which the stream makes a loop of half-a-mile in extent; this slip, however, is quite limited; for above, and on the right and left of the fallen mass the Medina sandstones again crop out along the face of the North mountain ridges with a moderate northwesterly dip, displaying their full thickness of about 500 feet along the southeast face, and, with one slight undulation, and subsequently increased dip passing beneath the Little Goshen Valley beyond.

After careful and repeated examinations of this portion of the "Pass," Dr. Ruffner and myself agreed that the phenomena presented could be accounted for only upon the hypothesis of a *fault* running parallel with the axis of the mountain chain. Repeated observations since our general survey have tended to confirm the conclusions originally formed.

In following the course of the loop in the river, mentioned above, we travel a short distance with the strike of the rocks toward the southeast, then turn and cross the fault (filled up with the debris from the face of the broken mountain,) and finally change our course to the northeast again following the line of strike in nearly an opposite direction, and passing beneath the outcropping sandstones that rise far above our heads. But we soon deviate from this course to one at right angles to the mountain, and by which we are conducted through another natural section of $5 a$, b and c, and apparently pass out, right upon the beds of Devonian shales. At the base of the mountain, however, from the gap of which we have just issued, 7 and 8 are concealed from view, as evidenced by the fact that they crop out at many points along the base of the mountain at some distance from the road on both right and left. In this Little Goshen Valley there are indications of extensive beds of limonite ores some of which were worked many years ago. They are found in both $5 b$, c, and in 8.

This valley offers no special facilities for studying the Devonian shales, which are found much more fully and favorably exposed

Section of Silurian and Devonian Rocks, in Rockbridge and Bath Counties Virginia ; — Crossing Apalachia.

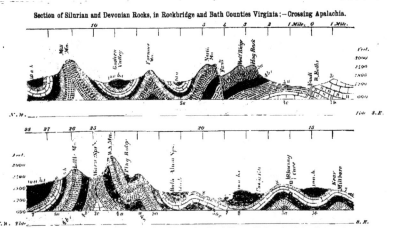

Explanation of the Above Section.—1. General bearing of the section N. 40° W.   2. Horizontal scale in miles, numbered at top; vertical scale in feet, numbered at right and left extremities   3 Limestone strata are *blocked*, sandstones *dotted*, and shales *ruled*. 4. The periods and epochs are indicated, the former by *numbers*, the latter by *letters*, in accordance with the system found in Professor Dana's Manual of Geology.

farther west, but along its western border for a distance of four or five miles from the turnpike, in a northeasterly direction, some interesting developments of 7 and 8 are found along the foot of what is here called Furnace (or Knob) Mountain, through a gorge of which the Big Calf-pasture, the chief fork of North River, comes down from the Great Goshen Valley on the west. In this gap tolerably well-defined arches of 5 *a*, are displayed on the right as we pass up the river, while on the left (Bratton's Mountain) the same rocks are overlaid by a bed of 5 *b*. The arch on the right hand is the one represented on the section

Between this and Mill Mountain lies Goshen Valley, a beautiful agricultural region, and one that presents some points of scientific interest that are readily reached by the student of geology. The section passes near the Cold Sulphur Springs about 1½ miles southwest of Goshen depot on the Chesapeake & Ohio Railway. The waters of these springs flow from exposed strata of 10 *a*, dipping slightly toward the Mill Mountain on the northwest. In this valley, as well as throughout this whole region, the Salina Period (6) is but indistinctly represented, if at all, while the Corniferous Group (9 *a*, *b*, *c*), appears to be entirely wanting. But the very fossiliferous limestones of the Helderberg (7), and of the sandstones of the Oriskany Period (8) are well exposed at Craigsville, nine miles northeast of Goshen on the railroad, where a beautiful encrinal marble is quarried from 7, and also at points nearer to Goshen. Just west of Panther Gap in Mill Mountain (through which both railroad and turnpike pass), at several points a short distance from the base of the mountain, good exposures may be found. The mountain itself, at this point, is cut by Mill Creek, and its Medina sandstone axis is exposed in the form of a closed anticline pushed over toward the northwest so as to give all the strata a southeasterly dip.

Before leaving Goshen Valley we must observe the fact that, about the depot and the Cold Sulphur, the upper member of 10 has been swept off, and in many places a large portion of the middle member (*b*) has also disappeared. There is a ridge, however, beginning a mile or less north of the depot, on which all the members (10 *a*, *b*, *c*) appear. I have not found what remains of this group to exceed 450 or 500 feet any where in this valley.

Resuming our line of section west of Panther Gap we find the thickness of 10 *a*, *b*, *c* to have increased and the lithological characters to have undergone some modifications. Beds varying from siliceous slates to argillaceous sandstones are found cropping out, especially in *b*, as may be seen both on the railroad and the turnpike. Large quantities of these rocks have been brought from the tunnel near Milboro depot. Calcareous concretions of a disc-like form, full of veins of infiltrated carbonate of lime (*septaria*), in-

crease in size and number; while thin beds of fossil limestone, especially in *a*, are occasionally exposed to view.

At Milboro depot a line of stages leaves the railroad for the Warm Springs, fifteen miles to the west. At the distance of two miles we reach the old Millboro Springs where we again find sulphur water rising from the Devonian strata (10). Another mile brings us to the famous "Blowing Cave," where it is well worth while for the explorer to allow himself at least one full day. He is now upon the banks of the Cow-pasture River, one of the upper forks of the James. Here the river cuts through a ridge (Cave Hill), exposing to view an arch of Helderberg limestone (7) into which a cavern of unknown depth extends from which a breeze of considerable force issues continually in warm weather. Above the limestone is a second arch of Oriskany sandstone [8], in which are numerous Spirifer shells well preserved. These two formations may be studied here with great convenience; and, if an additional exposure is desired, it may be found two miles farther toward the northeast, where Stuart's Creek exposes a similar arch in the same hill, and where fine specimens of Favosites are easily obtained.

Exposures of the members of 10 may be studied along the banks of the Cow-pasture both above and below the passage through Cave Hill. A short distance below, in what is called "Alum Bank," we found a thin bed of limestone remarkably full of fossil shells. At other points higher up and lower down the river similar exposures occur.

Near this place is one of the numerous so-called "Alum Springs"— the *Wallawhatoola*, an old Indian name. The waters here, as at the Rockbridge and Bath Alum Springs, collect slowly from the crevices of the dark pyritous shales of No. 10. Springs of this class are very numerous among the Devonian shales in Virginia; and waters of similar character sometimes issue from shales of earlier and later dates. Their chief mineral constituents are sulphates of alumina, lime, magnesia, potassa, soda, iron [*ferrous* sulphate], with more or less *free* sulphuric acid. In the Wallawhatoola I found, with the spectroscope, a decided trace of lithia.

The shales of this region, and especially in this valley of the Cow-pasture River, present three tolerably well characterized beds; the equivalents, no doubt, of the three recognized epochs of the Hamilton Period [This is No. VIII of Professor Rogers' series.]— Marcellus, Hamilton and Genesee. The lower member consists of dark—sometimes black, sometimes bluish-black—shales that split readily into thin layers, and even fine scales or slender columnar fragments. The middle member has a decidedly greenish tint— olive in many places, especially where it appears along the public roads, and in cuts on the railroads. The highest division is much variegated in color and texture; the beds of shale are yellow, brown

and red, while considerable strata of sandstone of argillaceous character are found alternating with the shales.

Among all these are found beds of very calcareous shales passing often into impure limestones that abound in Encrinites, Atrypas, Spirifers, etc. The upper member has generally more calcareous beds in it than either of the others. This whole region has been greatly denuded, but the sharply rounded, and often cone-like hills that are left standing, with deep ravines cut out between them, present a striking feature of the landscape, and, at the same time, afford the means of an approximate estimate of the thickness of the whole series of shales, which cannot be less than seven hundred feet.

Along the faces of many of the hills that have been recently denuded by floods in the river and its tributaries, the planes of stratification, and of slaty [metamorphic] cleavage, are both well displayed—the latter so distinct that an unpracticed eye might readily mistake them for the planes of original stratification.

About four miles west of the Blowing Cave the turnpike crosses a ridge called Mair's Mountain, topped by a low arch of Oriskany sandstone [8], beneath which are exposures of the Helderberg limestones [7] where a small stream has cut its way through the ridge. Beyond this ridge we find another synclinal trough filled with the shales of No. 10, out of which rise the waters of the Bath Alum. Near this watering place is a cave formed by the washing out of the softer bed of Medina rocks so as to leave a regular arch which becomes narrower and lower toward the rear of the cavern, giving the whole cavity the shape of a semi-cone with the dividing plane for the floor. This is an object of interest to visitors. Its location is beneath the ridge, marked "Piny Ridge," on the section.

A mile beyond the Bath Alum, our line begins to ascend the lofty ridge of the Warm Springs Mountain. To the structural geologist this presents an object of the highest interest. As we follow the windings of the turnpike we find ourselves surrounded first by the debris of the Clinton sandstones and shales [6 and 7 are concealed], and as we approach the crest of Piny Ridge the Medina sandstones [5 a] make their appearance in situ. We are thence conducted by a spur across to the face of the main ridge, where the road is cut out of the sandstones, exposing their lithological and fossil features in a very interesting way. Ripple marks and casts of shells in the brown and purple sandstones, and fucoids in the shales, are of frequent occurrence.

On reaching the depression of the summit where the road crosses, we turn to the left and follow the crest of the ridge for half a mile toward the southwest to the top of what is known as "flag rock"— the highest outcrop of Medina sandstone on this mountain, having a steep southeasterly dip. From this point, 3,340 feet above tide level, the mountain scenery on all sides is very grand. Along the base of this ridge, on the northwest side, lies the Warm Springs Valley—a narrow strip of the Lower Silurian limestones of the Great Valley again brought to the surface. On the opposite side of this narrow valley another ridge, Little Mountain, rises to a less elevation, but is composed of the same kind of rocks as the main mountain, but dipping toward the northwest. [Along some parts of this broken ridge the sandstones are vertical or even inverted.] The olive-colored sandstones, generally found at the base of the Medina group in this region, appear near the summit of both these opposing ridges, and are succeeded by the fragile sandstones and shales of the Cincinnati and Utica epochs that form the steep slopes of both mountains. These are succeeded by the Trenton [4 a] limestones that dip beneath them, but form more gradual slopes toward the middle of the valley, where the older Chazy [3 c] limestones make their appearance. The latter are not largely developed where the tepid waters of the Warm Springs rise, but widen out considerably toward the southwest. A short distance to the northeast of the springs we found Trenton fossils in abundance, like those we had found just below the entrance of Goshen Pass.

In this anticlinal valley the Lower Silurian rocks come to the surface for a distance of several miles on both sides of the section, the general range being parallel with the Apalachian chain.

The two ridges that here face each other were doubtless parts of a great open anticlinal fold that was formed, when, by powerful lateral pressure from a southeasterly direction, the strata were pushed up from their original horizontal bedding. But it is hardly probable, judging from the present condition of things, that they ever formed complete arches across the valley. It is certainly more reasonable to suppose that such masses of strata of varying hardness and strength, and with an aggregate thickness of more than two thousand [2000] feet, were so ruptured at the time of upheaval as to form a rugged gorge, extending for many miles along the crest of the fold, and that subsequent erosions and denudations by ice and water widened it out, and shaped it into the beautiful valley as we now find it. This is a valley of thermal waters; for, besides the Warm Springs, near which our section crosses, the baths of

which range in temperature from 95° to 98° F.; the Hot Springs, five miles to the southwest, with temperature varying from 100° to 108 F., and the Healing Springs in the same neighborhood, with a temperature of 85°, rise in the same anticlinal fold.

About half a mile southwest of the Warm Springs the collected waters of this portion of the valley find their way out in a north-westerly direction through a deep ravine, in which are found exposures of all the formations from 4 to 8.

General Remarks.—[1.] Throughout the whole region represented on the accompanying section, conformity of strata prevails, and so continues till we reach the Carboniferous in West Virginia. [2.] The Medina sandstones that are from 450 to 500 feet thick along the North Mountain thin out to about 350 on Warm Springs Mountain. Here, too, the structure is less conglomerate, and the marks of shore-line formation are less numerous and distinct than they are farther east. [3.] It may be well to mention some of the prominent points along the line of section convenient for observation. At the lower entrance of Goshen Pass, and in Warm Springs valley, exposures of 4 may be readily found. No. 5 [Medina] may be successfully studied in Goshen Pass and on Warm Springs Mountain; while the region around Millboro Springs affords to the explorer some of the finest exposures of 7, 8 and 10. But the accompanying section may serve as a key to a wider range of observation. Perhaps the best point of departure would be Goshen, on the C. & O. Railway. If he wishes to extend the section farther toward the northwest, the turnpike from Warm Springs to Huntersville, in West Virginia, affords a favorable route for horseback explorations.

The Resources of the Shenandoah Valley near the Line of the Shenandoah Valley Railroad.

SUPPLEMENTED BY MAP AND SECTIONS.

BY THE EDITOR.

CONTINUED FROM PAGE 40.

The Basin of the Shenandoah River, shown on the accompanying map, is generally called the Shenandoah Valley; in reality it is the Northeastern Plateau of the Valley of Virginia, rather more than one-third of that great limestone trough, 16 miles by 330 in dimensions, that extends from the Potomac southwest to Tennessee. The general altitudes of its undulating, or "Valley" lands, varies from 500 to 2,000 feet above tide, averaging about 1,200,—making it a plateau of Guyot's third class, between 1,000 and 4,000 feet above the sea. Its average length is 136 miles. The breadth of the Valley proper, from the base of the Blue Ridge to that of the North Mountains, exclusive of the Massanutton Mountains, varies from 12 to 24 miles, averaging 18. The area of the entire drainage-basin (including the small portion drained into the Potomac by minor tributaries) is about 3,000 square miles; 1,000 of this is occupied by mountain chains; 2,000 of it is undulating valley plateau. The Blue Ridge, a tangle of two geologically different mountain chains, makes a wide belt of fringes and bars on the southeast; the North Mountains, variously named, marshaled like echeloned lines of battle, band and border it widely on the northwest: while the Massanuttons, with their two groups of triple or quadruple ranges, divide its middle portion into two parts. The mountain chains are from 500 to 3,000 feet higher than the general level of the Valley.

The Mineral Resources of this Basin of the Shenandoah are remarkably varied and abundant, because a half dozen or more of the great groups of geological formations, those generally rich in mineral wealth, have here not only an exceptionally large development but are exposed, some of them several times, in broad parallel bands of outcrops, many of which coincide in length with basin itself.—The kinds and character of these resources, the conditions under which they are found and their relations to each other, and to lines of transportation will be best understood, in the absence of a detailed geological map, by first considering the general geological structure of this region with the aid of the accompanying

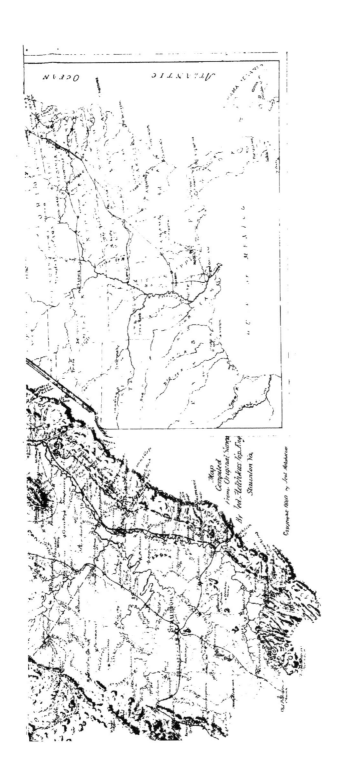

topographic and partially economic map and geological sections.

The general geology of this country is very simple, but the details are complicated, as a study of the sections given on the supplement, or of those on page 42 of THE VIRGINIAS (which are, in a manner, typical for the Great Valley), will show.

The general groups of the rocks here exposed, in belts of northeast-southwest stretching country, taking them from the east and crossing the basin, towards the west, following Rogers' subdivisions (page 14 of THE VIRGINIAS), are,—(1.) *The Archæan Belt*, that of the old Metamorphic or Archæan rocks, forming, as the Blue Ridge proper, the high eastern rim of the basin, a belt of mountains of irregular forms, greatly varied in its surface features, underlaid by steeply dipping granitic, shaly and slaty rocks. (2.) *The Lower Cambrian or Primordial belt*, that of the No. I or Potsdam and associated formations, a belt of mountain forms flanking with their somewhat regular outlines the western foot of the Blue Ridge as broken mountain ranges and foot-hills of sandstones, slates and shales bordered by narrow sandy or stony valleys or terraces; it is the "piney woods" region of the Blue Ridge. (3.) *The Middle Cambrian belt*, that of the Valley limestones (the Lower Silurian of some), here the valley of the South River, and that of its prolongation the South River, and the Shenandoah proper, rightly described as the *eastern limestone belt of the Valley*, varying in character as the hard dolomitic lower beds or the softer and more calcareous upper beds of the group come to or near the surface, as shown in sections and explained by Prof. Campbell on page 43. (4.) *The Siluro-Cambrian, or Upper Cambrian belt*, the central slaty belt of this basin, a broad band of broken country, made from the slates of No. III. The Valley slates, that extends almost the entire length of the basin making this *the central slaty belt*, the one that divides the Valley lengthwise into two parts. In the Upper Valley, Augusta and part of Rockingham, it is a belt of slate lands threaded by very crooked streams; in the Middle Valley it is a much twisted synclinal trough, as shown in the sections, on which are sustained the sand-rocks that from the Massanutton Mountains and on each sides of which are belts of slaty country; in the Lower Valley the mountain masses have been denuded and there, as in the Upper, it becomes a central slaty belt of broken country, including the Opequon basin, that extends from the Massanuttons to the Potomac and beyond. (5.) *The Massanutton belt*, that of the two somewhat oval groups of mountain ranges, a southwestern and a northeastern, that make the chain of the Massanuttons; a detached belt that extends only the length of the Middle Valley, embraces the Silurian (often called Upper Silurian) ranges and their included valleys, those made from formations IV to VIII inclusive, of the Massanutton Mountains, and which divide the Middle Valley by a mountain chain into an Eastern (the Page Valley of some) and a Western Middle Valley. (7.) *The western limestone belt*, a western and more extensive outcropping, in a wide belt, equal in length with the Valley, of the same Siluro-Cambrian (Lower Silurian) rocks, formation No. II, that make the eastern limestone belt, these rocks passing under those of III, as shown in the Massanutton sections, and coming up again on the western sides of the Upper and the Lower and along the central part of the western of the Middle valleys of the basin. On the western side of this limestone belt there is, in places, a western slaty belt, one of Formation III; but it is not as continuous as the others. (8.) *The Apalachian belt*, a region of generally parallel mountain ranges and included, small, broken valleys, formed from Silurian, Devonian and the Lowest Carboniferous rocks, IV to X or XI inclusive, the North Mountains portion of the Shenan-

doah basin, its western rim the most westerly part of which is the Great North or Shenandoah Mountains, is generally from 500 to 1,000 feet higher than the Blue Ridge opposite, and from 1,500 to 3,000 higher than the Valley, forming a barrier against the cold winds and storms of the northwest.

It results, from the above, that this Shenandoah basin has some eight distinct, parallel belts of country, most of them extending its entire length, included within its limits,—belts that differ, more or less, both geologically and topographically, and therefore in resources and adaptations. The first, second, third, fourth and fifth of these are in the immediate vicinity of the line of the Shenandoah Valley Railroad throughout the length of this basin; its route is, for most of the way, in or along the third belt, *the eastern limestone one*, that of the drainage-trough of the entire basin, the one towards which nearly all the streams of this Valley flow, since its surface slopes to the southeast more rapidly than it does to the northeast,—consequently all the resources of the basin, from one side to the other, can be brought by gravity alone to the line of traffic that follows this trough.

The ores and other mineral resources of the five geological belts near the route of the Shenandoah Valley Railroad are the only ones that can be noticed at this time. The red lines upon the map, showing the known and exposed outcrops of the iron ore beds of this region, give the best expression possible concerning the location, continuity and wide range of distribution of this most valuable of minerals in this part of the Shenandoah basin. The geological sections, in like manner, show as it were the horizontal distribution of these ores, and prove, from sound scientific deductions based on careful explorations, the vast extent of these ore deposits, showing how they underlie a large portion of the entire region, suggesting the iron producing capabilities of this portion of the Shenandoah basin when these now comparatively hidden and unknown resources shall be developed.

1. The minerals of the Archæan belt; the Eastern or main Blue Ridge.—*Copper ores and native copper*, are found throughout its length in Virginia and in some places in very large quantities. Some developments have been made at Overall's, in Stoney-man Mt., near Marksville, and at Fischer's Gap; but nowhere sufficient to warrant any definite conclusions. Near the Fairfax Corner Gap, at the head of Naked Creek, on the eastern side of the Blue Ridge, in Greene Co., quite extensive explorations have been made exposing three veins of copper ore, one 7 ft. thick, for over 3 miles, proving, by *shafts and tunnel*, the existence of an abundance of excellent ores and native copper. These mines are not far from the line of the S. V. R. R.—*Specular and magnetic iron ores*, as described on page 38 of THE VIRGINIAS.

2. The minerals of the Lower Cambrian or Primordial belt, the Western Blue Ridge.—The rocks of this belt, Rogers' No. I, are among the most productive known in excellent *iron ores*, chiefly *limonites* (brown hematites), described by Prof. Prime on page 34. These are found in thick stratified deposits so persistent in character that they may properly be called continuous. These ores are found in the hydro-mica or damourite slates that lay between the Calciferous sand-rock and the Potsdam sandstone, that is, geologically, above the Potsdam and below the Calciferous. Rogers considered these ore-bearing slates the top of Formation No. I,—the metal plating that finished the Lower Cambrian rocks. Their geological position and relations in the Eastern Middle Valley (Page) are shown in sections No. 1 and 2 on the map of the Shenandoah basin (constructed by Prof. Campbell from our joint observations). They rest on the western slopes of the Cambrian foot-

CONTINUED ON PAGE 60

The Next Census and Virginia's Iron Ores.—Mr. E. It. Benton, an Expert Special Agent of the 10th Census and Assistant of the Division of Mining Geology of the United States Geological Survey, in charge of the Department of the Interior and having its headquarters at Newport, Rhode Island, will soon visit Virginia for the purpose of obtaining samples of its different iron ores. Of course every Virginian will give to this gentleman (and to others connected with the special information section of the Census) all the information he can, that this "sampling" may be as well done as it can be in a few weeks by those that have never studied in the field the geology of our great State.

And yet we are bound to say, no matter what may be the standing of the "Expert Special Agents," that it is much to be regretted that this work has not been entrusted to some one of a half dozen men that could be named, citizens of the State, who are already familiar, from years of exploration and study, with the location and extent of our iron-ore deposits,—men who *know* where these ores are and how to sample them by groups, so that their general character may be fairly ascertained, and who could not be misled by the representations of the ignorant or the designing, or deceived through lack of knowledge of the special conditions under which our ores are found. Some of our great iron-bearing formations are not the iron-bearing ones of other States, and some of our richest deposits, as now developed and in use, have been condemned by experts who drew their conclusions from geological conditions with which they were familiar in other States. Some ridiculous (there is no other word that will express it) *finds* have already been made in a neighboring State; let us hope to escape from such "sampling."

If our great geological iron-belts could be taken up one after another, and each be properly sampled throughout the hundreds of miles in which each is exposed, there can be no question but that the result would be every way advantageous to the State. Again we say, let us do all we can to make the best of what we consider a bad arrangement, with the promise that we will see this matter through and scan closely the results. We want no such farce as the "mining" showing of the 9th Census was.

The County Superintendents of Schools in Virginia will help along its development very materially if they comply with the requirements of the following law which went into operation March 4, 1880.

1. Be it enacted by the General Assembly of Virginia, That the Commissioner of Agriculture be required to receive, in the name of the state, from the county superintendents of schools, and preserve in proper form in his cabinet, any charts, maps, geological sections, mineral specimens, specimens of woods, specimens of the productions of their respective counties, and any written descriptions illustrating or pertaining to the physical structure and mineral or other resources of said counties, which the above officers may be able to furnish; and that the said Commissioner of Agriculture shall include in his annual reports so much of the information thus furnished him as may in his judgment be conducive to the public interest.

2. That the county superintendents of schools be instructed to combine with their regular official visits such examinations of the mineral deposits and geological structure of their respective counties as may be practicable and which in their judgment will not materially interfere with their official duties and which might increase their usefulness by means of information thus collected and imparted to school teachers, school officers, and the people generally in regard to the geology, mineralogy, and geography of their respective counties and of the State.

3. That at least once a year the county superintendents of schools shall report to the Commissioner of Agriculture, giving the results of their observations and explorations of their respective counties.

The Iron-makers of Wythe County, Virginia, and Vicinity, and their Forges and Furnaces.

By EDWARD SHELLEY, OF WYTHEVILLE, VA.—MARCH 15, 1880.

(1) The makers of forged iron and the forges where they operate:

1. David Pierce, at High Rock, Reed Island Creek.
2. David Forney, at Reed Island Creek.
3. Graham & Robinson, at Graham's Forge, Reed Creek.
4. Alex. Pierce, at Pierce's Forge, Cripple Creek.
5. John P. M. Simmerman, at Chadwell, Cripple Creek.
6. David Huddle, at Lockett's Forge, Cripple Creek.
7. William Bell, at Raven Cliff Forge, Cripple Creek.
8. Stephen Porter, at Porter's Forge, Cripple Creek.
9. James White, at Speedwell Forge, Cripple Creek.
10. Kincannon's Forge, Rye Valley.
11. J. F. Kent's Forge, Reed Creek.

(2) The pig-iron makers and their furnaces:

1. David Pierce, Fancy Gap Furnace.
2. Graham & Robinson, Old Furnace.
3. Graham & Robinson, New Furnace.
4. Howard & Sanders, Walton Furnace.
5. Abraham Painter & Co., Brown Hill Furnace.
6. Graham & Robinson, Eagle Furnace, Cripple Creek.
7. Crockett, Tate & Co., Raven Cliff Furnace, Cripple Creek.
8. Sayers & Oglesby, Wythe Furnace, Cripple Creek.
9. David James & Co., Speedwell Furnace, Cripple Creek.
10. Lobbell Car-wheel Works, White Rock Furnace, Cripple Creek.

(3) Furnaces building or projected:

1. By Graham & Robinson, at Reed Island.
2. By Crockett, Tate & Co., on Percival estate.
3. By Crockett, Tate & Co., on Wm. Pierce estate.
4. By Wythe Iron Co., near Porter's Forge.
5. By Hendricks & Co., on Wm. Porter property.
6. By James M. Clayton & Co., at Martin's Station.

The mineral properties that have been sold and bought in this region, within the last three months or so, as far as I am informed are:—The John S. Noble Zinc, Iron and Lead estate, bought by Messrs. Hendricks, Van Liew and Judge S. Sherrard; the Callie Kitchen Zinc, Lead and Iron property, sold; the Wm. Porter and the Quesenberry properties, besides timber lands, sold; the Lobdell Car-wheel Co., of Delaware, has bought the Walton Furnace, the Painter or Brown Hill Furnace, and the Panic Furnace (the last they have rénamed White Rock) and the estates belonging to them, and some timber properties; Graham & Robinson have bought some small tracts of land: Robinson, Tate & Co., have bought the Wm. Pierce estate and the Percival farm; the Bertha Zinc Company has bought the Robert Calfee Zinc Mines and property, and a site for zinc works, at Martin's Station; the Wythe Iron Company (John S. Noble & Co.), has bought part of the Iron Mountain, 15,000 acres. These purchases, including that of James M. Clayton & Co., at Martin's, amount to over $225,000, and it is supposed that as much more will be spent in erecting works and putting them in operation. Several of these are already under way; the Bertha Zinc Works are finished.

The Iron Trade Moving Westward? is the title of an elaborate statistical article in the *Iron Age* (Feb. 28). It groups Va. and W. Va. with the Southern States, all those S. of the Ohio, showing that the Eastern and the Middle States are falling behind in the percentages of production of iron in the U. S. while the Western and Southern States are advancing. In 1878 the Southern States produced, of the U. S. product, some 27 per cent. of the charcoal pig; 12 per cent. of bituminous coal and coke pig, (remarking that in this production during the last 6 years "notably the S. States have secured a marked advance"); 10 per cent. of the rolled iron exclusive of rails, and 11 per cent. of the iron rails,

Iron-making in Virginia a Hundred and Fifty Years Ago.—In September, 1732, Col. William Byrd, F. R. S., of Westover, on the James, the owner of vast possessions and the foremost man of the Colony of Virginia in his day, in order that he might learn "the Mystery of making Iron," visited a furnace that was then in operation at Fredericksville, Spotsylvania county, Virginia, in charge of Mr. Chiswell, an account of which he left, in manuscript, under the title of "*A Progress to the Mines,*" which has been published in a rare and costly volume called the "Byrd Papers." From that the following interesting extracts are taken. They will be read with interest, and, perhaps, with profit by the iron-makers of our time.—There is an abundance of Col. Byrd's "Oar" still left at the old site, which is not far from the line of the Chesapeake & Ohio Railway and its New River coke; it has been a long time, too, since the forests of that region have been vexed with the ax, and coaling timber is abundant. It is time for a new "Fredericksville."

Mr. Chiswell had his home in the forks of the "Pomunky," having reached which, Col. Byrd says :—

"I found Mr. Chiswell a sensible, well-bred Man, and very frank in communicating his knowledge in the Mystery of making Iron, wherein he has had long Experience. I told him I was come to Spy the Land, and inform myself of the Expence of carrying on an Iron work with Effect. That I sought my Instruction from Him, who understood the Mystery, having gain'd full Experience in every part of it. Only I was very sorry that he had bought that Experience so dear. He answer'd that he would, with great Sincerity, let me into the little knowledge he had, and so he immediately entered upon the Business. He assured me the first step I was to take was to acquaint myself fully with the Quantity and Quality of my Oar. For that reason I ought to keep a good Pick-ax Man at work a whole Year to search if there be a Sufficient Quantity, without which it would be a very rash undertaking. That I shou'd also have a Skilful person to try the richness of the oar. Nor is it great Advantage to have it exceeding rich, because then it will yield Brittle Iron, which is not valuable. But the way to have it tough is to mix poor Oar and Rich together, which makes the poorer sort extremely necessary for the production of the best Iron. Then he shew'd me a Sample of the Richest Oar they have in England, which yields a full Moiety of Iron. It was a Pale red Colour, smooth and greasy, and not exceedingly heavy; but it produced so brittle a Metal, that they were oblig'd to melt a poorer Oar along with it. He told me, after I was certain my Oar was good and plentiful enough, my next inquiry ought to be, how far it lyes from a Stream proper to build a furnace upon, and again what distance the Furnace will be from Water Carriage; Because the Charge of Carting a great way is very heavy, and eats out a great part of the Profit. That this was the Misfortune of the Mines of Fredericksville, where they were oblig'd to Cart the Oar a Mile to the Furnace, and after twas run into Iron, to carry that 24 Miles, over an uneven Road to Rappahannock River, about a Mile below Fredericksburgh, to a Plantation the Company rented of Colo. Page. If I were satisfy'd with the Situation, I was in the next place to consider whether I had Woodland enough near the Furnace to Supply it with Charcoal, whereof it wou'd require a prodigious Quantity. That the properest Wood for that purpose was that of Oyly kind, such as Pine, Walnut, Hiccory, Oak, and in short all that yields Cones, Nuts, or Acorns. That 2 Miles Square of Wood, wou'd supply a Moderate furnace; so that what you fell first may have time to grow up again to a proper bigness (which must be 4 Inches over) by that time the rest is cut down. He told me farther, that 120 Slaves, including Women, were necessary to carry on all the Business of an Iron Work, and the more Virginians among them the better; Tho' in that number may be comprehended Carters, Colliers, and those that planted the Corn. That if there should be much Carting, it would require 1600 Barrels of Corn Yearly to Support the People, & the Cattle employ'd; nor does even that Quantity suffice at Fredericksville. That if all these Circumstances shou'd happily concur, and you cou'd procure honest Colliers

and Firemen. which will be difficult to do, you may easily run 800 Tuns of Sow Iron a Year. The whole charge of Freight, Custom, Commission; and Expences in England, will not exceed 30 Shillings a Tun, and twill commonly sell for £6, and then the clear profit will amount to £4,,10. So that allowing ten Shilling for Accidents, you may reasonably expect a clear Profit of £4, which being multiply'd by 800, will amount to £3200 a year, to pay you for your Land and Negroes. But then it behooved me to be fully inform'd of the whole Matter myself, to prevent being imposed upon ; and if any offered to put tricks upon me, to punish them as they deserve. Thus ended our Conversation this day."

Having ridden from Mr. Chiswell's house to the mines, some 25 miles, and partaken of a lunch, Col. Byrd continues :—

"When our Tongues were at leisure for discourse, my Friend told me there was one Mr. Harison, in England, who is so universal a dealer in all Sorts of Iron, that he cou'd govern the Market just as he pleased. That it was by his artful Management that our Iron from the Plantations sold for less than that made in England, tho' it was generally reckon'd much better. That ours wou'd hardly fetch 6£ a Tun, when their's fecht 7 or 8, purely to serve that Man's Interest. Then he explain'd the Several Charges upon our Sow Iron, after it was put on Board the Ships. That in the first place it paid 7s 6 a Tun for Freight, being just so much clear gain to the Ships, which carry it as Ballast, or wedge it in among the Hogsheads. When it gets Home, it pays 3s 9 custome. These Articles together make no more than 11s 3, and yet the Merchants, by their great Skill in Multiplying Charges, Swell the account up to near 30s a Tun by that time it gets out of their Hands, and they are continually adding more and more, as they serve us in our Accounts of Tobacco. He told me a strange thing about Steel, that the making of the best remains at this day a profound Secret in the breast of a very few, and therefore is in danger of being lost, as the Art of Staining Glass, and many others, have been. He cou'd only tell me that they us'd Beech Wood in the making of it in Europe, & burn it a Considerable time in powder of Charcoal ; but the Mystery lies in the Liquor they quench it in. After dinner we took a walk to the Furnace, which is elegantly built of Brick, tho' the Hearth be of Fire-Stone. There we saw the Founder, Mr. Derham, who is paid 4 Shillings for every Tun of Sow Iron that he runs, which is a Shilling cheaper than the last Workman had. This Operator lookt a little Melancholy, because he had nothing to do, the Furnace having been Cold ever since May, for want of Corn to Support the Cattle. This was however no neglect of Mr. Chiswell, because all the Persons he had contracts with had basely disappointed him. But having receiv'd a small Supply, they intended to blow very soon. With that view they began to heat the Furnace, which is 6 Weeks before it comes to that intense heat required to run the Metal in perfection. Nevertheless, they begin to blow when the Fire has been kindled a Week or ten days. Close by the Furnace stood a very spacious House full of Charcoal, holding at least 400 Loads, which will be burnt out in 3 Months. The Company has contracted with Mr. Harry Willis to to fall the Wood, and then maul it and cut it into pieces of 4 feet in length, and bring it to the Pits where it is to be coal'd. All this he has undertaken to do for 2 Shillings a Cord, which must be 4 foot broad, 4 foot high, and 8 foot long. Being thus carry'd to the Pits, the Collier has contracted to Coal it for 5 Shillings a Load, consisting of 100 Bushels. The Fire in the Furnace is blown by 2 Mighty pair of Bellows, that cost one Hundred pounds each, and these Bellows are mov'd by a great Wheel of 26 foot diameter. The Wheel again is carry'd round by a small Stream of Water, conveyed about 350 Yards over Land in a Trough, from a Pond made by a wooden Dam. But there is great want of Water in a dry Season, which makes the Furnace often blow out, to the great prejudice of the Works. Having thus fill'd my Head with all these Particulars, we returned to the House."

"Over our Tea, Mr. Chiswell told me the expence which the Company had been already at amounted to near Twelve Thousand Pounds ; But then the Land, Negroes, and Cattle were all included in that Charge. However, the Money began now to come in, they having run 1200 Tuns of Iron, and all their heavy disbursements were over. Only they were stil forc't to buy great Quantitys of Corn, because they had not

Strength of their own to make it. That they had not more than 80 Negroes, and few of those Virginia born. That they need 40 Negroes more to carry on all the Business with their own Force. They have 15000 Acres of Land, tho' little of it rich except in Iron, and of that they have a great Quantity. Mr. Fitz Williams took up the mine tract, and had the address to draw in the Governor, Capt. Pearse, Dr. Nicolas and Mr. Chiswell to be jointly concern'd with him, by which contrivance he first got a good price for the Land, and then, when he had been very little out of Pocket, sold his Share to Mr. Nelson for 500£; and of these Gentlemen the Company at present consists. And Mr. Chiswell is the only person amongst them that knows any thing of the matter, and has 100£ a year for looking after the Works, and richly deserves it. After breaking our Fast we took a walk to the principal Mine, about a Mile from the Furnace, where they had sunk in some places about 15 or 20 foot deep. The Operator, Mr. Gordon, rais'd the Oar, for which he was to have by contract 1s 6 p. Cart-Load of 26 Hundred Weight. This man was oblig'd to hire all the Laborers he wanted for this Work of the Company, after the rate of 25s a Month, and for all that was able to clear 40£ a-year for himself. We saw here several large Heaps of oar of 2 sorts, one of rich, and the other Spongy and poor, which they melted together to make the Metal more tough.

To BE CONTINUED

The Paper on the Copper and Other Resources of the Floyd-Carroll-Grayson Plateau,—part of which, with map and geological sections, is given in this number,—is one of very great value, not only because of its rarity, very few having seen it or even known of its existence, but because it is the only known publication that gives any detailed, authentic information concerning one of the richest mineral regions of Virginia, one embracing some 1,300 square miles of her territory, that included in the counties of Floyd, Carroll and Grayson, lying on the expanded top of the Blue Ridge in the southwestern part of the State.—The full title of the rare pamphlet from which this paper is reprinted, *in full*, (and for which we are indebted to Dr. C. M. Stigleman of Floyd C. H., one of the most efficient of Virginia's County Superintendents of Schools) is, "A Geological Visit to the Virginia Copper Region. By Richard O. Currey, A. M., M. D., formerly Prof. Geology, &c., East Tenn. University: late Prof. Medical Chemistry, Shelby Medical College, Nashville, Tenn.: Author of 'Geology of Tennessee,' Report on Alleghany Mining Co.,' 'Report on Copper Hill Mining Co.,' &c., &c. Knoxville, Tenn.: Printed by Beckett, Haws & Co., Book and Job Printers, Gay Street. 1859." The colored map and sections, in two sheets, accompanying it are imprinted, "Lith. of L. F. Oitti, Richmond, Va." A "dedicatory preface," the only portion we omit, is addressed to L. H. Anderson, M. D., of Gainesville, Ala., who accompanied Dr. Currey during his explorations. In that Dr. C. says they spent a month examining Floyd, Carroll and Grayson counties, Va., and Ashe and Alleghany, N. C., "traversing these 5 counties throughout their length and breadth, and traveling in them a distance of 480 miles. Each important mineral lead was taken up by us in order, and traced its entire length; and every mine, and opening, that had been made on these leads, were personally visited and examined, our desire to read these mines thoroughly inducing us to descend many shafts and explore many tunnels that had been abandoned, and where more cautious feet would have refused to follow." This preface is dated, "Knoxville, Tenn., Dec. 1st, 1859,"—a date that explains why this valuable contribution to the scientific and economic geology of Virginia is so little known; for just as it must have been issued the whole country became involved in a gigantic civil war and in the devastation that followed, at his home, most of the copies of this pamphlet must have been destroyed; the one we have is the only "survival" we know of: the learned Doctor has himself gone to his reward and his "relict" cannot find a copy of this his last work.

No better use can be made of our columns than to grace them with this unknown, important record of original observations; that honor may be accorded to one that labored earnestly and honestly, as his work shows, to aid in the development of Virginia, and that those now striving to carry on that work may have the benefit of his observations and deductions.

CONTINUED FROM PAGE 57

hills and undulate in the swells of Fox Mountain and other ore-bank ridges where their ores are exposed and mined, and then pass from sight, to the westward, under the higher rocks of the westward belts. Sometimes the outcrop edges of these slates are overturned and they appear dipping to the eastward: if the miner follows the foldings of the strata he will eventually find them resuming westward dips, as a mass, as shown in the sections. The eastward outcrop edges of these ore-bearing slates once rode higher up the foot-hills than they do now, (as shown in Section No. 5, copied from Lesley); in the course of time the exposed outcrops crumbled down on the drainage slopes and made "banks" of ore, masses of mingled clays, shales, iron ore, manganese, etc.—the slates and whatever they contained having decayed in confused heaps. Such ore-banks may be seen scattered all along this iron-bearing horizon, especially where the Cambrian hills are mere swells, as on the Mount Vernon property and at the Fox Mountain bank of the Shenandoah Iron-works. These wastings are often deposited beyond, generally westward of the slates in place, and so it often happens that the miner and the iron-master, knowing only of "pockets" of ore, lose their "veins" and, after floundering for awhile, without guide or clue, conclude that the "pocket" is exhausted and abandon the lands. It is a common thing to hear such views expressed, and yet every well informed mining engineer knows that they are incorrect. The only proper view, the one that furnishes a substantial basis for development, is that of Prof. Wm. B. Rogers, who, in 1838, after a thorough examination of this Cambrian belt entirely across Virginia, wrote. "Its iron ores are both rich and of inexhaustible extent. The continuity of this iron-bearing series of rocks, bordering our Great Valley on the east throughout its entire length, is calculated to add largely to our estimate of the manufacturing resources of that Valley. For although numerous localities of the ore have long been known and resorted to, it is only by the evidence of this continuity derived from a careful geological examination that just views of the extent of this item of our mineral wealth could be obtained." The value of every iron estate in this belt will be greatly enhanced when the conditions and relations of this great ore-bearing belt are understood.

—*Manganese Ores* are among the abundant products of this belt; they almost invariably accompany the iron ores, as a manganese-bearing stratum, sometimes in the ferro-manganese proportions, and in some places, as at the Crimora mines, the slates become manganiferous rather than ferriferous and the result is deposits of manganese of remarkable extent and purity. Having the same geological range as the iron ores, of course they may be expected to have a like extension from their outcrop to the westward. I am satisfied, from the known exposures, that a vast quantity of this valuable mineral can be obtained from this belt.—*Beds of Kaolin, Fire-clays,* some of them proven to be of great extent, are found associated with the iron ore outcrops of this belt; they have resulted from the decay of the slates that bear the iron. Analyses and tests that have been made show that these clays are as good as any known for the purposes of the potter and the brick-maker.—*Blue, yellow, and red ochres* are plentiful in the same relations, as any one can see that will inspect the old ore banks of this belt. They are now manufactured in Page, says Professor Prime (see page 35).—*Glass-sand* of a superior quality, fine and pure, can be had in any quantity in the vicinity of the Potsdam sand-rock, a product of the weathering of that rock. The sandstone itself could be crushed for the same purpose.—*Building stones,* some of them excellent for furnace construction, are found in the formation No. 1.—(For details of this formation see Professor Campbell's paper, page 42.)

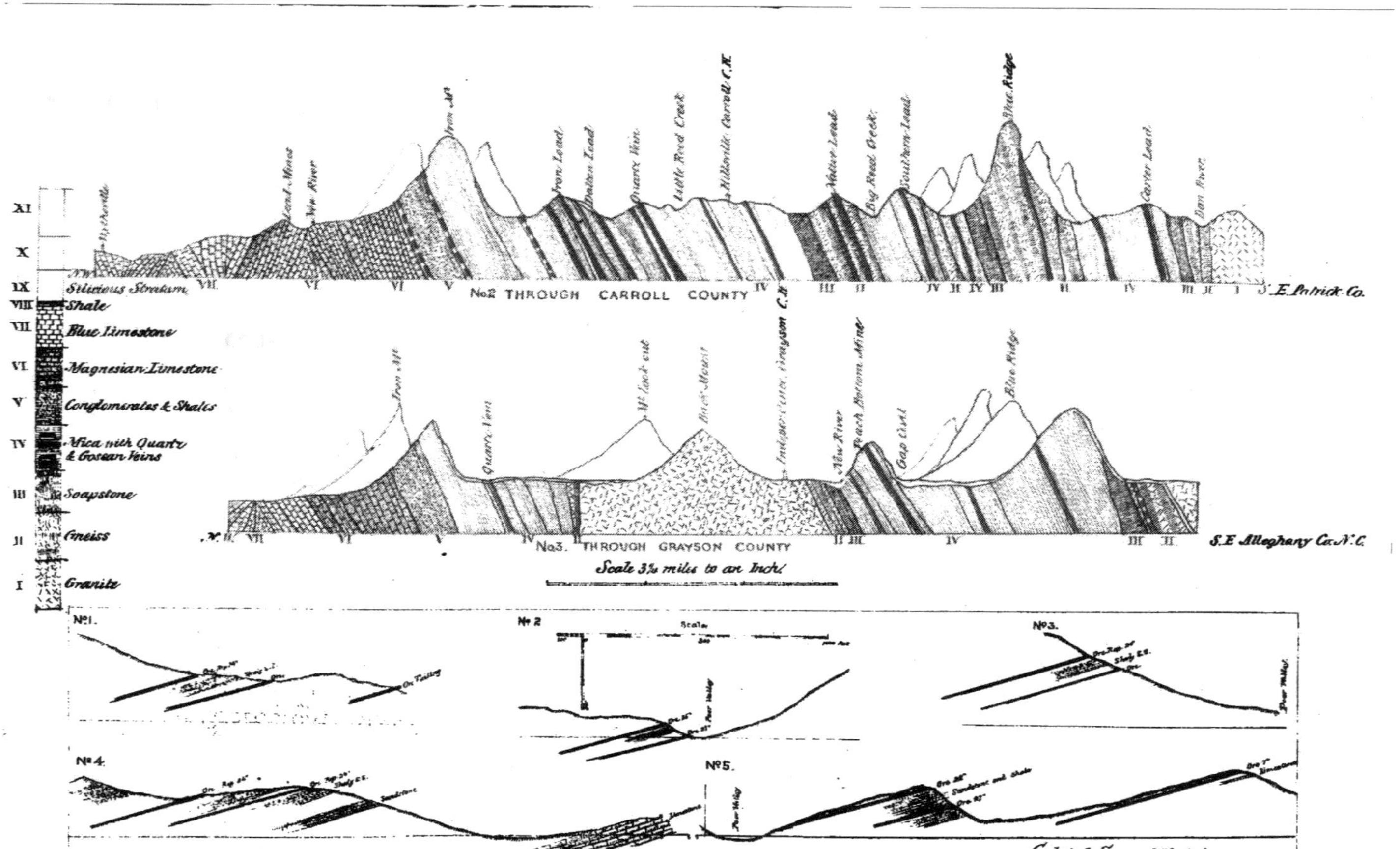

SECTIONS SHOWING THE POSITION OF THE FOSSIL ORE BEDS IN THE VICINITY OF CUMBERLAND GAP.

Geological Survey of Kentucky.
Part V. Vol. IV. Second Series.

Scale 3½ miles to an inch.

I Granite
II Gneiss
III Serpentine
IV Mica with Quartz & Garnet Veins
V Conglomerate & Shale
VI Magnesian Limestone
VII Blue Limestone
VIII Shale
IX Siliceous Sandstone
X
XI

No. 2 THROUGH CARROLL COUNTY

No. 3 THROUGH GRAYSON COUNTY

S. E. Hughery Co. N. C.

S. E. Arnick Co.

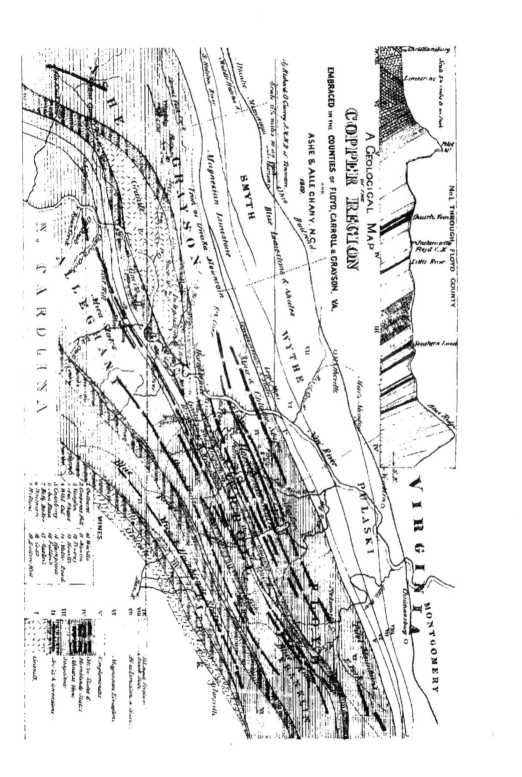

A Geological Map of the COPPER REGION

EMBRACED IN THE COUNTIES OF FLOYD, CARROLL & GRAYSON. VA.

AND ASHE & ALLE CHANY. N.C.d

1859

3. The minerals of the Middle Cambrian (Lower Silurian) belt, the eastern limestone belt.—*Limestones* of various kinds are the special resources of this belt. (See No. II, page 43.) These are perfectly inexhaustible in quantity and all the qualities desired for any purpose can be had from one or another of the many thick beds that enter into this formation. One bed furnishes a stone containing 98.30 per cent. of *carbonate of lime* (page 15 of THE VIRGINIAS).—*Cement* of the best quality is made from the lowest beds of the formation (p. 43), and dolomites of the right kind for *basic bricks.*— *Colored marbles* are quarried in places in the Valley and good *building stones* are furnished by some of the beds.—*Zinc and lead* are found associated with the lower beds of this formation in many places ; these have not been proven in this part of the Valley except that there are outcrops of zinc ore near Waynesboro. Pockets of *brown hematite iron ore* are of frequent occurrence where the limestones are wasted ; some of these have proven quite extensive, and the ores very valuable for mixing with others.

4. The minerals of the Siluro-Cambrian or central slaty belt.— Beds of excellent *iron ore* are found associated with the upper beds of Formation III. Professor Rogers makes frequent mention of "heavy beds of valuable iron ore, of which extensive exposures have been traced for great distances along the borders of the slate subjacent to the massive sandstone (IV) in this region." The ore of this formation makes an iron of remarkable toughness, one much sought after for car-wheel and ordnance purposes.—*Slates,* admirably adapted for marbleizing, good for flagging, etc., are quarried from this belt near Staunton. I see no reason why the same ones should not be found further east. Prof. Prime refers to these slates (p. 35).

5. The minerals of the Massanutton belt, formations III to VII or VIII.—The Massanutton Mountains, as the map shows, are in two well-defined groups, a northeastern and a southwestern, each of these has the general form of a long, somewhat canoe-shaped, synclinal trough, as shown by the sections. In consequence of the structure of the mountains and their included valleys the geological formations from II to VIII inclusive, are there exposed in one place or another : therefore this detached belt is a great compact storehouse of mineral wealth. The *limonites* of formation III, ores held in great estimation, are especially abundant and very accessible in the northeast group; some of the beds are *manganiferous* and deposits of *manganese* are associated with them. Prof. Rogers says of this ore in the Big Fort Valley. "It presents a spectacle truly imposing, from the magnitude of the deposit in which the workings are carried on." *The limestones* of II also outcrop in the Big Fort Valley of the northeastern group where they have a special value for blast-furnace flux.—Of special importance to this region are the *Clinton* or No. V. iron ores, that are found in great abundance, and where they can be cheaply mined, within each of the Massanutton groups ; for these, under the names of *red shale* or *fossil ores,* are everywhere in great demand for mixing with other ores to improve the quality of the iron made. The iron outcrop line in the southwestern group, on the map, is that of these ores ; the red members in sections 2 and 3 show how these ores outcrop on the sides of and under-run the valley of Cub Run. Prof. Campbell and myself concluded that this ore-bearing syncline of V occupies from 8 to 10 miles of the length of this trough-like valley between the Middle and the South mountains, with an outcrop from 30 to 100 feet thick, (the ore yielding 55.24 of metallic iron and but 0.10 of phosphorus) ; dimensions that guarantee a vast quantity of ore. The same sections show that the central part of this syncline is a bed of No. VI or

Lower Helderberg *limestone,* an arrangement that places a superior flux in proximity to these excellent ores. There are other exposures of ore in this group but I do not now know their relations. It is worthy of mention that the water-gaps to these valleys open towards the South Fork.

The ores of the northwestern group are described by Prof. Prime on page 35. Prof. Rogers, in his Virginia Reports, mentions the limestones of II and VI as occurring in the Big Fort Valley while the red shales and ores of V are on its sides; the Little Fort Valley he says is occupied by III. He writes, "In both these valleys iron ore occurs in great abundance not only in connection with III, but with V, and is procured from both these formations to supply the 2 furnaces near by. The ore of V is found to be peculiarly rich and valuable and may be traced for several miles. Manganese occurs abundantly in the Little Fort Valley. Viewing the abundance and excellence of its ores, and the facilities of transportation which it is to be hoped will ere long be afforded this part of the State, this mountain region would seem to be destined, at no remote day, to become a busy scene of manufacturing industry,"—a vision that, after the lapse of 42 years, this famous Geologist may perhaps see become a reality through the agency of the Shenandoah Valley Railroad.—*Building stones* abound in formation IV of this group.—The Forts-mouth is open towards the line of the railway and these ores may be brought out by gravity if desirable.

The section (No. 4) of the North Mountains, by Joseph Lesley, reveals the structure of the western side of this Valley. It shows how the same iron-bearing formations, III and V, outcrop again, but associated with VII another of Virginia's great iron-producing rocks.

Space forbids mention of the agricultural and forestal wealth of this basin, of its abundant water-powers, of its all-the-year round agreeable climate;—it is enough to say that these will not be dwarfed by comparison with its mineral resources as here briefly sketched.

The opening of this line of railway to a connection of these vast stores of mineral wealth to the coals beyond, and to the great markets on either hand, will doubtless soon make a reality of another thought of Virginia's great Geologist, born when contemplating these very riches,—"Anticipation, confiding in the certain deductions of cautious scientific research, already begins to sketch the gladdening picture of successful industry—crowding population and wide spreading improvement, which, at no remote day, it will be its happy lot to realize."

The Resources of South-West Virginia, by C. R.
Boyd, E. M. of Wytheville, Va.—is a work announced, by John Wiley & Sons, Scientific Publishers, 15 Astor Place, New York City, as soon to appear. It will be sold by the publishers, to whom subscriptions may be sent, at $2., postage or expressage extra.

We spoke of this forthcoming book in our last issue (p. 39). We hope every one in any way interested in Virginia will subscribe for it. Mr. Boyd has been for a long time engaged in exploring and surveying the region he describes, and is thoroughly competent, from training and experience, to prepare an exhaustive and reliable work on its vast resources.—In the circular sent us by the publishers they describe Mr. Boyd's volume as "A work designed to show the mineral and other resources of this section of country, which to enterprising men one of the finest fields for investment in the world. Here are found immense deposits of Magnetic and other Iron Ores, Bituminous Coal, Zinc, Copper, Lead, Salt and Gypsum; all being of great purity and easily worked. The work will also show the staples of the various counties, the methods of transportation and access, and contains some ten full page sketches made by the author. The whole book will be exemplified by a large and finely made map, showing the Geography, Geology and Topography of this region. It will be well printed and appear in 8vo size."

The Copper and Iron Region of the Floyd-Carroll-Grayson Plateau of the Blue Ridge in Virginia, etc.

[By Richard O. Currey, formerly Professor of Geology in the University of East Tennessee, etc.—Illustrated by a map and sections.]

1. INTRODUCTORY.—When, during the summer of 1859, it was proposed to me to undertake the examination of the geology and mineral wealth of the Copper Region of Virginia, embraced in the counties of Floyd, Carroll and Grayson, the request was cheerfully complied with, for the reason that the field was comparatively new and I was desirous of examining the relation between these mines and those at Ducktown; at the same time to contribute to the development of a mineral region that stands second to none in the Union, not only for its supply of ores, but also for their richness and extent.

In the performance of the duties of the survey, the three counties mentioned, together with Ashe and Alleghany, in North Carolina, were traversed in various directions; the leads traced out, and the strata crossed, requiring a travel of 480 miles in the five counties.

Desirous of constructing a geological map of this region, I labored under the disadvantage of not being in possession of an accurate geographical map, having frequent occasion to correct the existing maps, especially with reference to the water courses, which serve an important purpose in mineral regions in affording power for mills and blast furnaces. Any errors therefore upon the map, geographically, must be attributed to this fact.

In delineating the geological formations I have endeavored to be as accurate as the survey could make it. The sections were drawn as each county was traversed, and illustrate the order in which the several strata lie upon each other.

In this "Visit," I have deemed it proper to set forth the agricultural resources of this district, as also its climatology, for a mining region must possess the necessaries of life to render it desirable or profitable.

2. PHYSICAL GEOGRAPHY.—AGRICULTURAL RESOURCES.—CLIMATE.—The Copper Region, described in this survey, is embraced in the counties of Floyd, Carroll and Grayson, in the southwestern part of Virginia, and in the adjoining counties of Ashe and Alleghany, in the northwestern part of North Carolina. Composed themselves of a series of ridges and mountains, they are confined between the ranges of the Iron Mountain on the west, and the Blue Ridge on the east, both of which in their northeast course gradually approximate, until they merge into one chain at the northeast corner of Floyd.

The Iron Mountain presents a regular course N. 54° E., while the Blue Ridge is not so much inclined to the east, its bearing being about N. 10° E. The Blue Ridge is the more elevated of the two ranges, and impresses itself on the general physical features of the entire adjacent country.

Although thus enclosed by mountain ranges, this region is not a valley, but composed, as stated, of numerous ridges and mountains with their intermediate valleys, which observe no regular direction, and consequently the smaller streams, which so abundantly drain this entire region, are very tortuous in their course: the entire drainage of the country, however, being from the base of the Blue Ridge westwardly to New River. This stream, coming from North Carolina, flows through the counties under examination, receiving several tributaries, and finds an outlet through Iron Mountain on the western boundary of Carroll county. Thus in Floyd, Little River takes its rise by three branches in the Blue Ridge, and running westwardly through Iron Mountain, empties into New River. In Carroll, Big Reed Island Creek heads up in Patrick county, on the eastern side of the Blue Ridge, near the head waters of Dan River—makes its way through the gorges of the Blue Ridge, receives into its bosom the waters of Laurel Fork, Big and Little Snake Creeks, Greasy Creek, Beaverdam, and, lastly, Little Reed Island Creek, and then forces its way through Iron Mountain to the channel of New River. This is an important point in any railroad enterprise that may hereafter be undertaken, affording the only practicable route from Danville to this Copper region. Crooked and Chestnut creeks in the southern part of this county pursue the same western course to New River. In Grayson, New River may be said to afford the basin, as it traverses the center of the county, into which the waters of both ranges of mountains are drained off. Thus on the east we find Little River, while on the west are Elk, Peach Bottom, Fox and Wilson creeks, coming from the base of the Iron Mountains.

Passing into North Carolina we find the same drainage flowing in from the east and the west as just noticed in Grayson.

These water courses are important features in the prospective developments of this region, for no better water power can be desired than is to be found upon these tributaries for all kinds of manufacturing operations.

Along these mountain ranges are many elevated peaks, affording most extensive and beautiful views. Buffalo Mountain, in the Blue Ridge, is one of these well known points. From its towering hump may be had a view of the Peaks of Otter to the east, and of Pilot Knob in North Carolina: while just as extensive and as splendid a view is obtained from Point Lookout, in Buck's Mountain, not far from Independence, Grayson county.

However, notwithstanding the ruggedness of many portions of this district, there are enclosed between the ridges and mountains fertile valleys, in a high state of cultivation; the grassy meadow, with grazing herds, surrounding comfortable country mansions, while the burdened orchards and promising fields of corn on the declivities indicate thrift and comfort, as well as skill in husbandry.

This entire region is admirably adapted for agricultural purposes, and for stock raising. The soil produces abundantly Indian corn, wheat, buckwheat, tobacco, oats and rye—while for grass they are scarcely excelled. Hence its adaptation to the culture of the cereals, to which the farmers are beginning to direct their attention. It was with surprise that we were informed that they were dependent upon other portions of the country, especially upon East Tennessee, for flour. *There is no country better adapted for wheat, and no better water power can be found anywhere, for converting it into flour.*

Buckwheat is cultivated very extensively, at the time of the visit, being in full bloom, the distant fields on the mountain tops presenting the appearance of a covering of snow. The yield is from 40 to 70 bushels per acre. While the valleys are given up almost exclusively to grass, the mountains are cultivated almost to their summits in corn and grain. No valley, however small, is permitted to grow up in thickets or weeds. Many of the worn-out hill-sides, however, are neglected, and are washed away by every rain, while the sowing of grass would produce as fine pasturage after a few years, as is to be found in the meadows. Judicious cultivation, and grass after the soil is exhausted, would keep these mountains in perpetual vigor.

The tobacco crop is the pride of Virginia. Every man has his patch of greater or less size, according to his means, and yet it was surprising to see such limited arrangements for curing the leaf. Its culture is well understood, judging from the appearance of the crop.

Although corn is cultivated extensively, yet it was diminutive in size. I am disposed to regard this soil as better adapted for the different grains than for corn, and believe that more would be gained by directing attention to the cultivation of such products, for which it may be suited, than to force it beyond its capabilities. For there are not in the soil the elements for maturing the Indian corn, while the same labor bestowed upon wheat and grass would more than doubly remunerate. But let it be borne in mind, that while such a change is advocated, it is not intended that only the valleys should be cultivated. The hills on the contrary are sometimes more fertile and more productive than the valleys: the forest growth on the summit of these elevated places clearly indicating the strength of the soil there: some of the highest mountains producing chestnut trees, measuring 25 feet in circumference, while the oaks and poplars are of like gigantic size. The natural growth of the forests are oak, chestnut, beech, hickory and walnut.

In many places are to be seen forests of crab apple trees, of large size and great height, heavily laden with their native fruit, a strong evidence that this is naturally a fruit region. As an evidence of this, it was only necessary to glance at the orchards to be found on every farm, at this season freighted to their utmost capacity with choice golden fruit.

The climate is delightful, and with the exception of an occasional case of typhoid fever, sickness is scarcely known

among the population; and this would be a stranger to them, were the proper precautions used in those habitations where it is accustomed to prevail.

The variety of freestone, sulphur and chalybeate waters, has already attracted visitors from abroad. Altogether this region is well adapted for sustaining a dense and thriving population. There are here all the elements necessary for the successful prosecution of the various industrial pursuits, whether connected with agriculture, or with manufacturing operations. Flour mills, copper smelters, wool factories, steammeries and manufactories, could here find the material for successful operation, and ample water power for propelling the machinery.

All these sources of wealth still lie dormant, awaiting the wand of the monied magician to call them into existence.

3. THE GEOLOGICAL FEATURES OF THE VIRGINIA COPPER REGION.—Although embraced within the limits of the Primary System of rocks, yet the diversity of slates which compose this district, and the appearance of a granite upheaval in its very center, render its study very interesting, and its mineral prospects very important.

The series of rocks consist of granite, gneiss, olivine, greenstone, mica slates, hornblende slates, chlorite slates, talcose slates and quartz veins, in some of which are found beautiful crystals of garnet, tremolite, prehnite, actinolite, amethystine quartz, staurotide, tourmaline, rutile, and others, only of a mineralogical importance.

The regular series in which these strata occur, containing also two extensive deposits of metalliferous minerals, render this a very important region to the economist, as well as to the mineralogist. For in these strata are to be found veins of the ores of copper, hydrated oxide of iron, magnetic oxide of iron, lead with an important trace of silver, while some of the chlorite slates may yet be found to be the resting place of gold deposits.

By reference to the map, the order of the rock strata will at once be seen.

East of the Blue Ridge, along whose elevated crest runs the boundary line between the counties composing this district and those on the east, there is found a granite ledge coursing N.E. and S.W. This granite is very massive, and is quarried and worked up into millstones. Such is its compactness and suitableness for the purpose that I was informed by Col. M. D. Carter, of Patrick, near whose residence the ledge is found, that a pair of these millstones had been in constant use in his grist mill, on the waters of Dan River, for fifty years, and that they had worn away only six inches during that interval.

This granite presents the appearance of having been subjected to a lateral pressure at the time of its upheaval, for it over-rides the succeeding strata of gneiss and syenitic granite. The dip of the gneiss rock varies from forty-five to eighty degrees, being most vertical nearest the granite. It is of a dark color, very compact and tough, and has a course N. 54° E.

Next in order of occurrence is found a thin stratum of soapstone, which, on account of its refractory nature, is used for hearthstones and other purposes.

Then follows a narrow belt of micaceous and hornblendic slates, occupying the eastern declivity of the Blue Ridge, and in which is deposited the ore of the Carter Copper Mine, near the Danville Turnpike, in Patrick county.

The crest of the Blue Ridge again presents the gneiss rock with olivine, and large veins of quartz, imbedded in which are beautiful crystals of tourmaline. The course of the strata along this ridge is N. 45° E., dipping to the S. E. at an angle of 60°.

This is again succeeded by a narrow strip of talcose slate blending into micaceous, chloritic and hornblendic slates, constituting the eastern half of the copper region. In these strata is found the southern copper lode, reaching from the northeastern part of Floyd to Ore Knob, in Alleghany county, North Carolina. Numerous quartz veins are to be found among these slates, some of which contain fragments of gossan, and may lead to the development of important copper mines beneath. Some of these quartz veins are very extensive, constituting immense ledges of a pure white color and very compact, their course partaking generally of that of the stratum through which they are injected.

In the midst of these slates, there occurs a limited stratum of gneiss, interstratified with a trappean rock and greenstone, in which are found the magnetic oxide of iron. Course N. 54° E., and dip almost vertical.

These micaceous slates, in the northern portion of the district, have a course N. 54° E., whilst to the south in Alleghany and Ashe counties, North Carolina, they deflect at a greater angle to the west, partaking of an almost east and west course. At Ore Knob, for instance, the strata run N. 70° E., while on Roane Creek, and as they approach Jefferson, they run N. 85° E. Beyond Jefferson they are again turned towards the south, the lateral pressure which produced the uplifting of the strata, here impinging upon the granite upheaval in Grayson county.

With a narrow band of talcose slate, there next occurs the gneiss and olivine rock extending from Floyd through Carroll and into Grayson, where it is singularly ruptured by a protrusion of granite, around which it encircles and reunites at the termination of the granite in Ashe county. In this gneiss rock, possessing all the characteristics, in portions of its stratum, of a Trap rock, occurs the *Trap or Native Lead*, as it is called, consisting in the impregnation of the vein rock with particles of native copper, ranging in weight from one grain to five pounds. The vein rock is of a beautiful olive color, very dense, and filled with radiating crystals of tremolite of a greenish color.

Sometimes the particles are so finely disseminated through the rock that their existence is only proved by hammering it into dust, when they are aggregated and flattened into scales. In Carroll this gneiss stratum is one-half mile wide, dipping at an angle of 70° S.E., and running N. 54° E. It surrounds, in Grayson, the upheaval of granite.

This upheaval adds interest to the geological and mineral character of this region. Beginning at Elk Creek, in Grayson county, it extends, gradually widening, a S. W. course into Ashe county, North Carolina, and terminates near the north fork of New River. The main portion of the granite upheaval is west of New River, its central action to all appearances being in Buck's Mountain, some five or six miles S. W. of Independence. From the most elevated summit in this range—Mount Lookout—there is a gradual descent, the altitude of the mountains, north and south gradually diminishing towards the extremities of this upheaval. Near its edges the granite is found injected into the crevices of the slates. It presents an inclination to the S. E., apparently, as in Patrick, over-riding the gneissoid rock on the west.

In Carroll, the gneiss and trappean rocks are skirted with a soapstone stratum, which, beginning near Greeneville, runs N. 54° E. within two miles of Hillsville, the county seat of Carroll; thence through Floyd, within two miles of the copper mines on the west fork of Little River; thence it deflects more to the east, passing within two miles of Jacksonville, the county seat of Floyd; thence deflecting still farther east, crosses the Blue Ridge near Howell's mine, and may be traced near to Rocky Mount, Franklin county. This soapstone, in some places, constitutes immense ledges, its greatest outburst being near the Toncrey mine, in Floyd, and near Jacksonville. It is of a reddish color, soft and easily worked. It soon hardens on exposure to the atmosphere. It will be invaluable in the construction of furnaces for smelting operations.

Between this soapstone stratum and the Iron Mountain, the western boundary of the copper region, lies an extensive stratification of micaceous and hornblendic slates, alternating on the mountain with chlorite slates. As in the former slates, here are also found numerous quartz veins lying near to, and sometimes connected with the gossan leads of the copper mines. These slates afford the bed for the great *northern copper lead* with its lateral branches, extending from the northeast corner of Floyd, through Carroll and Grayson, to Elk Knob, North Carolina. They dip at an angle of 45° to the S. E., and possess a course N. 54° E., varying in certain localities to a greater or less angle of inclination, from their proximity to some elevated ridge or mountain. The upper portion of these slates, in Grayson, are less elevated than in some parts of Carroll or Floyd; the mineral veins acquiring importance according to the altitude of the country.

The blending of quartz and chlorite slate on Poplar Camp Mountain is beautifully displayed.

We have already remarked that the existence of these vein-

ings of quartz in chlorite slate afford strong grounds for believing that auriferous deposits may be found in them, a belief which acquires importance from the fact that small particles of gold are said to have been washed out from the soil at a locality about seven miles N. W. from Jacksonville. It is in the same order that gold occurs on Coqua Creek, in Tennessee, to the west of the copper region, in the midst of the chlorite and quartzose slates.

This description of the geological formations so far appertains to the copper region of Virginia. It is not irrelevant to the objects of this "Visit" to extend our description farther to the west for the purpose of showing its contiguity to the coal fields of Wythe and Montgomery. To this end two of the geological sections are extended to that deposit, showing the intervening strata. [Not extended in THE VIRGINIAS, because Dr. Currey evidently did not himself examine the country far west from the Copper Region.—EDITOR.]

After descending Poplar Camp Mountain, the conglomerates and slates of the semi-metamorphic formation occur, succeeded by the magnesian limestone, sandstones and shales of the Cambrian System. In these limestones are found valuable deposits of lead, which have been profitably worked for many years. The ore occurs in the forms of sulphuret and carbonate—the former being found in veins of rotten or decomposed limestone, the latter generally in beds or pockets at the intersection of the veins.

The limestone strata at the ferry on New River form an anticlinal axis, the course of the strata being N. 50° E.; the dip from thence gradually increasing to the N. W. One mile west a synclinal axis is formed, the strata again assuming a S. E. dip. At this place appear the limestones and shales of the Lower Silurian System, which are folded in a series of axes, and are succeeded by the coal measures west of Wytheville, which lie, as it were, in a basin formed by the depression of the limestone strata.

The extent of these coal measures is not yet fully ascertained. It is known that they exist in Montgomery county, near Christiansburg, and that they may be traced southwest through Pulaski and Wythe. They are of a bituminous nature, and in the future development of this country will bear an important part. Their contiguity to the coal mines is an important fact, being distant from them not farther than thirty miles. Thus nature has been lavish of her stores, placing in close juxtaposition, inexhaustible mineral wealth and an abundant supply of coal to prepare it for market.

While, therefore, we may readily infer that the metamorphic slates were subjected to a strong lateral pressure, causing them to overlap each other at the time of that great volcanic action, when the elevated crest of the Blue Ridge was upheaved, so these limestones and shales, westward of the Iron Mountain, were so lifted and depressed as to constitute folded strata, becoming less marked westwardly, till the last fold or depression forms the basin in which the Wythe and Montgomery coal fields are found. Among the metamorphic slates, the lateral pressure from the southeast broke the continuous strata, and caused them to overlap each other, thus presenting a dip to the southeast, and a uniform course to the northeast. Whilst westward of the mountains, although the same upheaving and lateral pressure acted in a line parallel to the former, the limestone strata were simply folded in wave-like lines, the summit of each wave being denuded, and exposing a series of anticlinal and synclinal axes.

The relative position of these strata is readily seen by reference to the geological sections accompanying this "Visit."

In view, then, of the discoveries of copper which have been found in the mica slates of this region, the question presents itself, Is this a true mineral region? As far as the geology of the district is concerned, it may be readily answered in the affirmative. De LaBeche in his Geological Observer states, that the most valuable mineral deposits of copper and tin are always regarded as belonging to those metamorphic slates which have suffered the greatest volcanic action, and which are nearest to the primary rocks; and that it is customary for those engaged in mining to prefer certain rocks above others, as affording the most reliable indications. Now we have such a region in this Virginia Copper District. The existence of two granite upheavals, with the surrounding gneissoid and trappean rocks, stamps the metalliferous character of the lodes

found in the adjacent mica slates. It is said that "Mountains are the mothers of minerals," and it is well verified in this district, the most valuable veins being found in those parts of the lead where there is the greatest altitude.

TO BE CONTINUED.

The Richmond & Southwestern Railway; its Route and the Resources of the Country it Traverses.

By Prof. N. S. SHALER, of Harvard University.

CAMBRIDGE, MASS., March 22, 1880.

GENTLEMEN :—

It will give me great pleasure to set about the preparation of the preliminary and final reports concerning the geological and other resources of the proposed Richmond and Southwestern Railway which you request from my hands. The work is the more satisfactory to me from the fact that I have, at one time and another, seen nearly all the line to be traversed by your road, and the most important parts of it I have traveled over more than once. Moreover, these journeys have been made in connection with my work on the Kentucky geological survey, and with the especial object of determining the practicability of a road that should open the mineral districts of Western Kentucky to the central and seaboard markets, from which they are now absolutely sealed. These travels long ago satisfied me that the section from Central Kentucky to the tidewater region of Virginia not only affords the easiest set of grades for the track of a railway of any route south of New York, but that it traverses a region, on the whole, richer in mineral, timber and agricultural resources than any existing trans-Alleghanean railway. Of the desirableness of this road, from a commercial point of view, and the facilities the district offers for its construction, I have made frequent notes in the various publications of the Kentucky survey, especially in a report "On the Transportation Routes of Kentucky," Vol. III, New Series, p. 319. So I am only repeating convictions that have stood the test of years, when I say that the line you have chosen, from the Mississippi to tide water, combines more natural advantages than can be secured by any of the existing lines. Briefly stated, these advantages are as follows: In the distance between the seaboard and the Mississippi, this line will traverse more miles of coal area than any existing east and west road. It is about nine hundred and fifty miles by the meanders of the road line from Gloucester to the Mississippi. Of this distance over four hundred miles will be in contact with coal. This includes the largest cannel coal basin known to me in this country, in the great cannel coal basin of the upper Kentucky. This stretch of four hundred miles lies in two distinct areas, that of Eastern and Western Kentucky. Besides the cannel coal, this field includes some coals that can be worked raw, and very good coking coals; there is also a small undeveloped area of anthracite coal.

If the road should pass through Pennington Gap, or, if passing through Pound Gap, a branch twenty-five miles long should be laid as far as Pennington Gap, it would enter an undeveloped field of dye-stone iron ore which has been worked for years for local consumption. This is certainly the best field for cheap iron ores of high grade, awaiting development, in all the Apalachian region. Three other iron ore belts of proven quality are traversed by the proposed line, viz., those of the Red River district, the Edmonson district, and the Muddy River district, all in Kentucky; you also traverse the iron district of the Valley west of the Blue Ridge, which is now furnishing some of the best iron ores of this country.

The proposed road will traverse the best untouched forests of hard wood timbers that this country now affords; I believe that the road would find in these forests a basis of profit for many years to come. From the time you enter the Blue Ridge until you pass the eastern confines of Madison county, Kentucky, a distance of not far from four hundred miles, the forests of white-oak, walnut and poplar are as yet essentially untouched.

The other mineral resources of this district are numerous and valuable. In the Blue Ridge there are extensive but little developed deposits of copper. For at least fifty miles of its course your line passes through the Virginia gold field, where for many years mines have been worked in a desultory and speculative way, and where I believe legitimate mining will yet find a large reward. The whole of the eastern coal field of Kentucky, indeed the area from Clinch River to Kentucky, is underlaid by deposits which yield abundant salt wells. If your road should take the southernmost of the lines proposed, you would traverse the Southern Kentucky petroleum district, where there is an abundant supply of high-grade lubricating oils which are now cut off from effective transportation, though their products find their way to market in small quantities by wagon.

At various points you pass extensive deposits of high-grade build-

ing stones, including the well-known Tennessee marble and dolomites of Kentucky.

The agricultural resources of this district are more varied than those along any of the other east and west railways. In Virginia, you pass the northern part of the cotton belt, and for one hundred or more miles are in the tobacco region. The valleys of the Upper Clinch are limestone lands and contain excellent grain fields. In the coal belt you have thinner soils, yet they are excellent for tobacco, the culture of which has been hindered by want of transportation. In Central Kentucky, a limestone district, are the richest and most permanent of all soils; they have long given large exports of grain and hemp. In Western Kentucky you again enter upon a tobacco region that alone exports enough tobacco to afford a very fair business for a railway in the shipping season.

The price of lands along this line is, on the whole, cheaper than in any other part of the continent where there are no disabilities arising from the climate. Leaving out the seaboard of Virginia and the central agricultural district of Kentucky, the average price of lands, which are almost all arable, will not now exceed about three dollars per acre, and this where the mineral and timber resources are of great prospective value. By getting possession of lands through purchase or a gift, or on condition of the construction of the road, I believe that a million of acres of mineral lands, immediately adjacent to the railway, could be secured at a cost not exceeding five hundred thousand dollars. Taking the value of similar lands along the Pennsylvania or the Baltimore and Ohio Railway, such a body of land would, soon after the construction of your road, be worth about as much as the road would cost.

The climatal conditions of this region are excellent. Between the Blue Ridge and Western Kentucky the line runs at an elevation of one to two thousand feet above the sea, and so escapes the heats its southern position would entitle it to. Statistics show it to be the healthiest part of the United States. It is not a plantation country, but one that favors small farming and manufacturing industry. Its sparse population is of good material, and the low prices of labor will make the work of railway construction moderate.

Presuming that your road will be built in successive sections, from the coast line towards the Mississippi, I may say a word concerning the resources the line will find open to it during the years of its advance westwardly. When the line is completed to Lynchburg, you should secure a share of the large tobacco shipping interests to and from that point. The timber adjacent to this section of the railroad is of good quality and should furnish an export of considerable value. The general agricultural value of the lands is fair, much of it is excellent in quality, and the road would open a district that is now rather remote from transportation. In Buckingham county, the line traverses a valuable gold field which before the civil war had yielded, if reports may be believed, over two millions of dollars in bullion. From Lynchburg west to the Kentucky line would be the next natural section. Although in this section, for a part of the distance, your line runs parallel to the Virginia and Tennessee Railroay, it is separated from it by one or more difficult mountain ranges, and opens up a new region to transportation. The agricultural value of this range of territory is good, the valley of the Clinch especially being excellent land. In passing the Blue Ridge, or on its flanks, you cross a belt of iron and copper bearing rocks that on your line, or by short feeders, will give you access to valuable elements of commerce. When you enter the coal fields of Wise county, you at once obtain access to a source of fuel supply that is greatly needed by all Eastern Virginia. These coals are of good quality, and being above the drainage line can be worked to advantage. Near this line you have, in Botetourt and Montgomery counties, some fields of anthracite coal which have not yet been sufficiently worked to determine their full value; I am, however, very hopeful of their future usefulness, especially for smelting purposes. In the valley of the Upper Clinch you pass some admirable building stones. The Chesapeake and Ohio Railway is only about fifty miles from this part of your line. The admirable success it is winning with the same set of resources gives good promise of success for your project in this section.

The section from the Kentucky line to the populous centres of that State traverses the best undeveloped coal area in this country. I know of thirty levels of workable thickness, including two excellent cannel coals. The unculled hard-wood timber of this district will find a ready market in Central Kentucky and the large manufacturing districts adjacent to it. The more valuable of these woods will find a market in the East as well as the West.

From the point where you cross the Tennessee and Nashville Railroad west to the Tennessee River, your line will traverse the Western Kentucky coal and iron fields. This is the best part of the so-called central coal field of this country, and it contains the largest known stores of iron ore between the Mississippi River and the Alleghany Mountain system. This is also an excellent region for hard-wood construction timbers, and is also the largest tobacco-

raising district for its area in the world.

In the section from the Tennessee to the Mississippi we have again a fair agricultural country, beneath which we find some valuable glass sands and pottery clays.

The whole of the line you propose to build, whichever of the several routes you may finally determine upon, extends through lands fit for settlement. At least ninety per cent. of the soil within ten miles of the way will be found arable, and that not fit for plough culture is good timber land. Your line is on the average, by road distances, at least twenty-five miles away from any existing railroad.

The whole of this district is exempt from droughts, yellow fever, and peculiar insect pests. The land is, on the average, of better quality than in any other district known to me that possesses the same advantages of mineral wealth.

The good-will of the people in the section to be traversed is assured in advance. I know, by much contact with them, that they are very anxious to have such means of communication with the outside world. Nothing in their history has led them to a factious opposition to such enterprises. I believe that you will find nothing but hearty co-operation from all the people in the sections you propose to traverse.

The point selected by you for your port is, in my judgment, the best place for harborage of modern cargo ships on our coast. That no point between the James and the Rappahannock was taken for a principal harbor in the early days of the country is, I suppose, due to the fact that the ships of the last century required less water, and the needs of defence demanded more landlocked conditions than this affords. All the harbors at the mouth of the Chesapeake Bay are favored by nature, and this section seems to me to combine more advantages than are afforded by any other part of these waters.

The preliminary report on the line of your road will, I hope, be ready by the middle of April.

Very respectfully yours,
N. S. SHALER,
State Geologist of Kentucky.
To the Directors of the Richmond and Southwestern Railway.

The American Institute of Mining Engineers will probably have its next meeting in the Lake Superior mining region, for two weeks at some time during the coming summer, that taking the place of the spring meeting. We had expected the next meeting to be held in Staunton, but members have long desired to go to the great mining region of Michigan and only lately could arrangements be made to go there.—Staunton will come in for the meeting after that, the opinion being that the Virginias will by that time be more developed and in a better condition for showing their vast resources.

At the last meeting W. N. Page, Hawk's Nest, W. Va., and J. E. Johnson, Longdale, Va., were elected members.—The Institute itself is honored by having such active and intelligent mining engineers in its membership.

A Map of the Catskill Mountains, by A. Guyot, for sale by Charles Scribner's Sons and B. Westermann & Co., New York, has come to us "with the kind regards of the author." This map by Prof. Guyot, of Princeton, the first of living geographers, is, like everything that comes from his hand, extremely welcome, because it is good, honest, and reliable work. The map, on a scale of 3 miles to an inch, is a real picture of the topography of one of the most noted groups of American mountains; it is accompanied by four pages of altitudes (elevations above tide) of points on the mountains and places near, for our author always, and rightly too, insists that we must know the facts of the relief of any region if we would understand it. Having given us a map of the northeastern group of the Apalachians proper, we hope our geographer will now turn his attention to the middle group of that system in the Virginias.

The Fayette Coal and Coke Co., of which George F. Stone of New York is President, is now actively at work at Stone-Cliff station, on New River, W. Va., on the line of the Chesapeake & Ohio Railway. 305 miles West of Richmond, putting up 100 coke ovens and the necessary buildings for the company's and laborers accommodation, under George W. Bramwell, M. E. as superintendent. This Co. has secured 1,040 A. of New River coal lands at this point. As soon as 100 ovens are completed as many more as the locality will accommodate, say from 100 to 200, will be constructed.

The Manufacture of Coke.

[Written expressly for THE VIRGINIAS by L. Bemelmans. M. E., of the Royal School of Mines, Belgium, of Charleston, West Virginia]

CONTINUED FROM PAGE 45

All these ovens, heated by the floor and mainly by the side walls, are from three to four and a half feet wide. With three feet the penetration of heat is more regular, but the nature of the coal to be coked may require more.

Among the coals which agglomerate by heat, good coke can be made with those containing from eighteen to forty per cent. of volatile matter. It may be said also that this coke may be made in almost any of the known kinds of ovens, provided the method of working is suited to the coal. For instance, a coal which produces only the amount of bitumen necessary for its agglomeration, must be brought to a red heat as rapidly as possible, so as to lose as little as possible of that bitumen, by distillation, before it can produce its useful effect. A rich coal, on the contrary, yields a closer and stronger coke. if it is heated gradually.

In the simple bee-hive it is not easy to regulate the heat in a practical manner, but much may be done at starting. When coking a coal having none too much volatile matter, it ought to be an object to keep the oven as hot as possible while loading. Hence there should be quick unloading, no water or steam in the ovens, they having too great a capacity for heat, chimney closed, thick walls able to act as a reservoir of heat, rapid loading and leveling, and good doors that can be closed rapidly. The pores of the coke so produced may be somewhat larger, but the coke is much stronger and more resistant. With a rich coal, some points might be gained by allowing the oven to cool more, or even by raising the arch.

For the ovens with flues, and especially when the sides of the oven furnish the heat, the best results have been obtained from a poor coal by giving only three feet width and by heating each oven by the gas of the next one, timing the work so that each oven is refilled when the gases which heat it are most abundant and hottest. For a rich coal, it is preferable to allow each oven to heat itself with its own gas and therefore more slowly, and the oven may be made somewhat wider. Sometimes a portion of the gas is allowed to escape for a time, without passing through the heating flues. In short, any device that will delay the coking, within certain limits, is favorable, with a rich coal, to the production of a dense coke.

In the first case, when working comparatively dry coal, the ovens are usually coupled two by two, each one yielding fuel for the other, so that for repairs it is only necessary to stop two ovens. In the case of a coal yielding 25 to 30 per cent. of volatile matter, it is always preferable to build ovens heating reciprocally each other, because timing the moment of loading allows of regulating the initial heat at pleasure, so as to obtain the strongest coke any given coal is able to yield. Besides, if provision is made for regulating the air admitted into the flues, the gradual increase of heat in the oven is also under perfect control. It is probably owing to a neglect of these precautions that Belgian ovens when new in this country did not justify expectations.

In all cases the gases evolved in coking are more than sufficient for the demands of the operation, and with coal rich in volatile matter the loss of heat is very important. And just more so when the heat for coking is produced by the combustion of a part of the fixed carbon, as in open pits process. The escaping gas, if mixed with a proper proportion of hot air before it is chilled, is able to generate an amount of heat, variable with the quality of the coal, but which, with rich bituminous coals, is in no way inferior to the heat produced by the amount of gas from gas-generators.

However, there is not always in proximity to coke ovens a profitable use for this gas, and when there is it is not even then always utilized, probably because of the practical difficulty encountered in regulating two operations dependent on each other; still the gas from bee-hives has been successfully applied to roasting ore, sometimes in kilns similar to small lime kilns. It has, also, been used for evaporating saline solutions in pans under which the gas is made to circulate. The small supplementary draught required by this additional flue is supplied by a small chimney. With rectangular flue ovens of the horizontal type, steam boilers, put crosswise of the ovens, over a

battery, raise steam very economically, although it is a doubtful policy to put heavy loads over strongly heated walls.

In all these applications the gas is utilized in close proximity to if not on the ovens which generate it. The yield of gas varies in quality and quantity while coking and the evolution of combustible gas is stopped during the period of loading and unloading. These facts make it difficult to use with advantage the gas from each oven separately, and the danger of introducing fresh air in the collecting flues, during loading and unloading, militates against using mixed gas from several ovens so as to produce a more regular supply. This difficulty has been overcome, in at least one case, by the use of valves, which are so connected with the doors of rectangular ovens that when the door opens all communication is closed between the oven and the collecting flue. This flue may be made of any length and the small draught of each oven is controlled by a steam jet.

In particular cases gas, either for lighting with special burners or only for heating, is made at the expense of the coke and its quality is somewhat sacrificed to the yield and quality of the gas, at least in this that the heat necessary for coking is produced, as in open pits, by the combustion of a portion of the carbon.

Hon. W. H. Ruffner, Superintendent of Public Instruction in Virginia, writes of THE VIRGINIAS, in the March *Educational Journal*:—

This is an important addition to what may be called the literature of physical development. With all the glowing generalities about Virginia's mineral resources, and all the puffing of special properties, which have been vexing the public eye for generations past, the capitalists of New York and London know much better what is in Colorado than what is in Virginia. Time was when moneyed men bought mineral lands as men buy lottery tickets. But land speculation, mining, and even prospecting, are becoming exact sciences. If lands are offered for a trifle men will buy, trusting to luck ; but if venders want good prices they must furnish a scientific demonstration that they have something good to sell. And just here is Virginia's trouble. She is like Sinbad the sailor, begirt with diamonds on a lonely desert. Had she allowed Wm. B. Rogers to tell the tale to a listening world, the aspect of the old State would have been as different from what it now is, as that of Cinderilla at the ball and Cinderilla after the ball. The cost of a good geological survey is the merest trifle, compared with the results.—But Maj. Hotchkiss is doing the best thing that can be done under the circumstances. He is publishing to the world, in readable form, all the physical information that exists about Virginia's mineral and industrial resources. Besides the great work done by Rogers, quite a number of scientific men, such as Professors Campbell, Fontaine and McDonald of our own State, and Messrs. Shaler, J. P. Lesley, Currey and others of other States, have made valuable observations and publications concerning particular localities in Virginia ; and the readers of THE VIRGINIAS will get the benefit of all these. And Major Hotchkiss has himself collected a great amount of useful material, which of course he will freely use in his journal.—The publication is likely to possess permanent value as the repository of solid physical information about the two Virginias, whose future is largely dependent upon systematic expositions of their wealth and facilities. Every intelligent citizen would do well to read and circulate this journal.

South Branch, W. Va., Iron Ores.—The Iron Age of Feb. 26, says,—"The miners sent by the Cambria Iron Co. to explore the Moorefield region have finished the examination, which has not been as successful as anticipated. Mr. Fulton, of the Cambria Co., will make the final report in a few days."—We await the appearance of this report, and in a future issue will have something to say about this region the ores of which have lately been pronounced the best and the worst of the State by different mining engineers. The Cumberland *News* stated that "the ore so far found is of good quality, but its extent has not yet been fully ascertained." In the meantime the "Hardy County Iron Co." ought to have other reports, from competent geologists and mining engineers, before coming to conclusions.

Mineral Resources of the Virginias.—Prof. Egleston lectured on Monday evening before the New York Academy of Sciences on the mineral resources of Virginia and West Virginia. The lecture was of a sort to explain the recent renewal of railroad building in those sections. Virginia produces iron ore in great abundance, while West Virginia is full of coal beds. The Virginia iron ores are of remarkable quality, stretching in veins between the Blue Ridge and the Alleghanies, and extending from the Potsdam on the east to the Clinton on the west. The iron-beds are sometimes continuous, sometimes in folds numbering from three or four up to twelve, and some of the specular ores were as rich in metallic iron as those of Lake Superior. These ores have not been developed, owing to difficulties in access and transportation. Fuel is scarce, connection not being yet closely made with the coal-beds further west. But the time was now coming when these ore-beds would be worked. They were too rich to be longer neglected, few of them containing more than a fifth of one per cent. of phosphorus. Virginia is richer in iron than Pennsylvania, says Professor Egleston, and it is a store of wealth for coming generations. If, he added, the prosperity of the iron trade continued, an industrial survey would have to be made of the country, and such a survey would show so much industrial wealth in Virginia that capital must inevitably flow into the State.—*Baltimore Sun.*

Harvey Edward Fisk, of No. 5 Nassau street, New York, desires to acknowledge the receipt, from Capt. Thomas D. Ranson, of Staunton, of samples of *kaolin*, from the Virginia Porcelain and Earthen-ware Company's property, and of *mineral paints* from S. H. Steele's, in Augusta county, Virginia. Mr. F. is collecting, at the office of Fisk & Hatch, New York, samples of the minerals and other products of the country on the line of the Chesapeake & Ohio Railway, to call attention to them. We hope all persons having mines, &c., will send samples to him. These will be forwarded, free of charge, from any station on the Chesapeake & Ohio Railway.

West Point, the Port Richmond of the *State*, is improving rapidly. Since the connection of the Richmond York River & Chesapeake Railroad, with the Piedmont Air-line, or Richmond & Danville Railroad, it has become the shipping port of a great far southward-reaching line of railway.

Col. J. C. Shields, now of the Lynchburg *Virginian*, formerly editor of the Richmond *Whig*, writes us.—"You deserve well for the valuable service you are rendering our material interests, for you are putting reference in such a form as to render information at all times easy."

The Virginias.

A Mining, Industrial, and Scientific Journal:
Devoted to the Development of Virginia and West Virginia.

Vol. I, No. 5. }　　　Staunton, Virginia, May, 1880.　　　{ Price 25 Cents.

The Virginias,

PUBLISHED MONTHLY,

BY JED. HOTCHKISS, - - - Editor and Proprietor,

At 346 E. Main St., Staunton, Va.

Terms, including postage, per year, in advance, $2.00. Single numbers, 25 cents. Extra copies, $20.00 per 100. Advertising Rates made known on application. On sale at Hunter & Co.'s Bookstore, Main Street, Staunton, Virginia.

"Iron is on the March Downward, and in spite of lower card rates had a fall of mill from $43.00, net cash, March 3rd, to $37.00, net cash, April 20th, or $15.00 per ton in six weeks; it is difficult to make sales, and $28.00 to $34.00 will be the June and July rate, I think. The nail mills have decreased the quantity of nails on the market 800,000 kegs in their 3 months stop, and even these will have to cut their rate 50 cts. to $1.00 per keg to make sales. The boom is over and those who came in on top will drop hard and burst unless they are well fixed."—So writes us a leading iron-master from one of the great iron producing centres of the West.

We consider this "drop in the price of iron" one of the best things that could have happened for the benefit of the Virginias. As long as pig iron brought $42.00 or even $32.00 a ton men could afford to manufacture it almost anywhere, regardless of the cost of the raw materials that entered into it, these costing in some manufacturing centres, we have been informed, as much as $20.00 to the ton of iron. Capitalists have been "planting" wildly in the erection of new furnaces where there were already too many, because too far from a supply of ore, and in relighting old ones where raw materials are hard to get and therefore costly. But now that a halt has been called all along the line, and when the Cleveland correspondent of the *American Manufacturer* writes, April 21, (after stating that there had been no arrivals of ore from Lake Superior as the lakes are pretty full of ice), "There is considerable talk in regard to the inability of the furnaces to pay the price for ores at which some of them have contracted and meet the metal market," the capitalists and manufacturers, will come to their senses and when ready to start again, as they soon will be, they will be in a condition to listen to the facts that can be presented in reference to the facilities existing in the Virginias for the continual making of cheap iron,— for the making of iron at a profit under the worst conditions of demand. The potentiality of economy in iron-making now becomes a vital business question.

We now look for an increased interest in our great ore and coal fields and to see many more doing what Mr. F. A. Bates of Cleveland, Ohio, has done; he recently sold out his Munday Creek Furnace, in the Hocking Valley, and is now seeking a site on which to erect one in Virginia.

We will conclude this matter, for the present, with one or two reliable statements as to what a ton of pig iron can be made for in Virginia.—The Engineer and Managing Director of the Low Moor Iron Co., whose extensive works are on the Chesapeake & Ohio Railway, in a report dated Oct. 1st, 1878; makes this estimate-

COST OF ONE TON (2,240 LBS.) PIG IRON AT LOW MOOR.

1.5 tons coke at $2.85 per ton	$ 4.27
2 26 tons ore at $2.03 per ton	4.61
1 ton limestone, at 40 cents per ton	.40
Labor $1.75; extras 47 cts.	2.22
Total	$11.50

The Hon. Wm Milnes, Jr., gave, in 1878, to the Editor, the following as the actual cost of producing a ton of hot-blast, charcoal pig at the Shenandoah Iron Works, Page Co., Va., now on the line of the Shenandoah Valley R. R. that will in a few months become part of the connected railway system of the country.

ACTUAL COST OF ONE TON (2,240 LBS.) PIG IRON AT SHEN. IRON WORKS.

2.1 tons ore at $1.66 per ton	$ 3.50
110 bush. charcoal at 5 cts. per bush	5.50
450 to 500 lbs. limestone	.18
Cost of raw materials	$ 9.18
Labor, wear, interest, and hauling 5 miles to forge	6.82
Total cost at forge	$16.00

When the Shenandoah Valley R. R. is completed, next Sept., and the New River coke can be taken to these works, Mr. Milnes estimates the cost of a ton of pig iron at his furnace as follows :

2.1 tons ore at $1.66 per ton	$ 3.50
1 ton New River coke	5.00
450 to 500 lbs. limestone	.18
Cost of raw materials	$ 8.68
Labor, incidentals, &c.	2.07
Cost per ton at furnace	$10.75
Freight to Baltimore	2.25
Cost per ton of pig, delivered in Baltimore	$13.00

Immigration.—It is estimated that 400,000 immigrants, from nearly every European State, will reach this country this year. In one week, lately, 5,800 embarked at Bremen. Those coming are unusually well off, both physically and financially, and very many of them are skilled laborers. These States, especially west of Midland, are well suited to the Scandinavian, Scotch, German, Swiss, English, and other north country people now coming this way in such numbers, and we hope the great railway companies which traverse thousands of unoccupied acres and boundless resources, that if developed would bring them vast revenues, will move in some efficient way to turn hither this great incoming tide of industry. They alone can do it. The railways of the Great West have built it up by their unremitting looking after immigrants. There is not a railway in the Virginias that should not have ten times as many people on its line as it has now. Good lands are as cheap here as they are in the West, and we have almost every variety to choose from. We repeat it, there is no existent power but the railway companies to do this work, and they can do it, if they will, and reap their reward in largely increased resources. Our long lines of railway do not pay because they all run through sparsely settled regions. Take any one of these and count up how many people live withing 10 miles of them and you will see that the population, and therefore the production, is out of all proportion to the carrying capacity of the rails. The plenty of pay is to be found in an abundance of local freight, human and that which comes from human labor. Whoever organizes for these immigrants will get them, for as a rule they go as they are led. Which one of our railways will become the leader and, instead of joining in the mad rush to carry everybody *through* and *west*, at rates that do do not pay, make it a business to settle up and develop the country naturally its own and furnish an example for the others to follow ?

The Swiss is perhaps the only European government that takes any interest in the colonizing of its surplus population. Most of the others hinder rather than help. That country can spare, to its own advantage, limited as is its capacity, some 20,000 people yearly. We are pleased to note that its commissioners are now inspecting West Virginia as a field for its emigrants, and that they have been cordially welcomed by Gov. Mathews and the citizens of Wheeling. Through the efforts of Mr. Diss Debar, and others, a goodly number of hardy Swizers have already settled in that State, and it would be a great thing for us if many more would come. We have too many people that seem to have been born tired, or lazy, and it will do them great good to have an infusion from an industrious race.

The *Wheeling Register*, a paper alive to the wants of these States, furnishes the names of the gentlemen comprising this commission: They are: Otto Bruner, President of the National Agricultural College at Zurich; Charles Chappuis of Geneva, President of the Anthracite Coal Works of Willis, Switzerland; Walter von Muller, President of Hofwyl University, near Berne, and Emanuel D. Ludwig and Hermann Kirchoff, of the Swiss Commerce Society, noticed in THE VIRGINIAS for February. The *Register* says: "The object of the visit of these gentlemen is a most important one. They are sent by the Swiss government to West Virginia to enquire into the practicability of establishing a Swiss American Commercial Society. The plan is to operate a system of direct commerce between Switzerland and West Virginia, and Mr. Ludwig has estimated that fifty million francs, or about $10,000,000, will be necessary for the enterprise. It is proposed to establish trade depots along the Great Kanawha river for the purpose of buying cattle, grain, etc. for diret exportation to Switzerland. Norfolk is thought of as the probable point of embarkation. Messrs. Ludwig and Kirchoff have formed a co-partnership and have purchased a tract of land near Gauley Bridge, upon which they will begin operations. The plan is an important one to this State and its projectors should meet with every encouragement at the hands of our people."

A late number of the *Railway Review*, of Chicago, states that 1,049 bona fide settlers recently passed over the Northern Pacific to Minnesota and Dakota, in 10 days. That the Union Pacific sold 16,475 acres to settlers in Central Kansas in March. That thousands of Canadians are now coming to settle in the United States. That the Harvey monthly excursions, taking settlers from the Eastern States to the West, that began with 10 in a party, now takes from 300 to 500 each time.— *The railways do it.*

The Copper and Iron Region of the Floyd-Carroll-Grayson Plateau of the Blue Ridge in Virginia, etc.

By Richard O. Currey, formerly Professor of Geology in the University of East Tennessee, etc.—Illustrated by a map and sections.

CONTINUED FROM PAGE 64

[The following is the portion of Dr. Currey's report that describes in detail the character and condition of the copper and iron resources of the counties of Floyd, Carroll and Grayson, those that occupy Virginia's part of the New (Kanawha) River plateau of the Blue Ridge. This is the larger portion of this able paper and we give to it much of our space in this issue so that it may follow the colored map and sections illustrating it which accompany the last (April) No. of THE VIRGINIAS.—This portion is continued from page 64.]

4. MINERAL WEALTH OF THIS REGION.—DESCRIPTION OF ITS LEADS.—NORTHERN LEAD.—DALTON LEAD.—NATIVE LEAD.—SOUTHERN LEAD.—Such being the geological character of this district, what deductions are we to make with reference to its mineral resources?

The most casual observer in passing over this district can scarcely fail to be struck with the peculiarity of the rock formations observable in certain localities. He will see a series of quartz veins, in some places composed of loose fragments scattered profusely over the surface of the ground, in others the quartz-rock rising in large masses, each traceable as far as the eye can reach. On tracing out these quartz veins, although they may disappear occasionally, yet he will find them to prevail over a large extent of country, and regularly interstratified with all the rock formations composing the district. It is, in fact, one of the prevailing rocks of the region.

In some of these quartz veins he will find fragments of oxide of iron filling the crevice, while in other localities the ore of iron will be found cropping out in large masses, and covering the surface of the ground. The iron ore will be of a porous character, and of various shades from red to yellow. On breaking some of the fragments, he will find some of the cavities filled with a greenish mineral, which the usual tests will reveal to him to be one of the ores of copper, and in regions where copper deposits may be supposed to exist, it will serve as a valuable surface indication of the lodes found beneath. This ore of iron is termed *gossan*, and was orignally a combined sulphuret of iron and copper, but through the agency of the atmosphere and surface waters, it has been decomposed and sulphuric acid formed, which attacks the ore and produces sulphate of copper. This then is removed by leaching, the ore of iron being left of a spongy, porous nature, forming a hydrated oxide of iron. The soluble ore of copper thus formed undergoes other changes, resulting in the formation of beds of carbonate and the various oxides, with sometimes chinks of metallic copper, produced, as is done in an electrotype process, by the precipitation of copper from its ores.

A constant examination of such surface leads will induce him to set a greater value upon some than upon others. Thus he will find that the porous, high colored, light varieties of gossan will invariably lead to ore of a high per centage, while the compact, dark colored and heavy gossans are generally indicative of ores of a low per cent.

These so-called leads constitute the surface indication for the existence of copper veins.

There are three principal leads in this region from which some three or four others branch off, constituting lateral leads, though no less important than those from which they come. They are designated the Northern Lead, the Native or Trap Lead, and the Southern Lead. In connection with the Northern Lead, there is the Dalton Lead and one or two others of no inconsiderable importance. What we would therefore designate as the North Lead is all that mineral region lying east of the Iron Mountain, while in the same way the Southern Lead embraces all those immediately west of the Blue Ridge. The Trap or Native Lead thus divides the Northern and Southern from each other.

In sinking a shaft either upon the Northern or Southern Leads, the position of the ores is found to occur in the following order: First, the gossan from the surface down from twenty to forty feet deep, dipping at an angle varying from 40 to 70 degrees. Second, beneath which occur the oxides, red and black—not very abundant in some of these mines—together with the carbonates in seams in the gossan. Third, then follows the lode consisting of the grey and black sulphurets—the upper vein or portion being invariably richer than the lower grey ores. Beneath these is found the mundic rock, the depth of which has not been ascertained, as no company has yet undertaken deep mining so as to reach the yellow ores. This mundic rock is a sulphuret of iron and copper of the same nature as the surface gossans.

The practiced miner possesses two modes of ascertaining the quality of the ores he is lifting, by *striping* and by the *green flame*. If he is working in a compact ore, the stroke of his pick will impart a metallic lustre to the ore if it be rich—the best quality of ores giving a stripe as brilliant as polished brass—soon tarnishing and changing to blue. The second test is used for ores that are soft and friable. The miner moistens it into a paste and places it upon the wick of his candle, while the depth of green tinge imparted to the flame indicates the richness of the ore.

5. HISTORY OF THE DISCOVERY OF COPPER IN THIS REGION.—COPPER MINING.—During that intense excitement for copper which prevailed so extensively through the South in 1854, owing to the discoveries made at Ducktown, it was remembered by some that they had noticed singular appearances in some of the rocks of this region, and that the same difficulties had attended the smelting of iron from these ores, as had been experienced at Ducktown. Under such impressions, deepened by the appearance of individuals prospecting through the mountains, with hammer and test glass, an excitement was soon aroused in this region upon the same subject.

The first step was directed to the mining of the native metal found in the olive colored rocks constituting what is now called the Native Lead. Here leases were made and work begun, but not meeting with any encouraging results, owing to the compactness of the rock, attention was soon turned to the gossan leads. Leases were made upon these for leagues by a few leading spirits, mostly from Tennessee, and in 1854 the Cranberry, the Bettie Baker, and the Toncrey mines were projected and opened.

In 1833 the Peach Bottom mine was opened by a company for its lead and silver, but soon passing into the yellow sulphuret of copper, and believing that no good would result from it, the works were suspended.

Outcropping over the Cook and Wistar lodes, and over the Great Outburst, are immense ledges of the hydrated oxide of iron, called gossan. Seventy years ago, it was supposed that this ore of iron could be smelted and converted into merchantable metal, and accordingly a furnace was erected on the waters of Chestnut Creek, and operations continued for several years. But the metal would not weld, it was too brittle and fell into such disrepute among the blacksmiths of the country as led to its abandonment. A heap of slag from this old furnace lies near the ruins, the fragments of which, when broken open, present a beautiful cupreous appearance, like the matt, and would yield at least 5 per cent. of copper. The iron-monger, who erected this establishment, selected the ore from different localities, in the vain endeavor to find some that would not be so objectionable. The works have, for several years, been abandoned, and have almost gone to ruin.

The Toncrey mine was formerly the Shelor or West Fork Furnace. Here there are immense deposits of gossan, the crevices of which are filled with the green carbonate of copper, with which it is so highly impregnated that the metal run from it appears to be equal admixtures of iron and copper. "It has been worked for iron upwards of sixty years, and is celebrated for the tenacity of the metal it makes. There are, at this time, castings in the neighborhood, made at the first blasting of this furnace.

"An anecdote is current about this old Furnace, which was related to me by Mr. Toncrey, himself. It runs thus:—The former owner, Squire Shelor, some fifty years ago, feeling anxious to introduce his hollow-ware through the country, concluded to take a wagon load to a military training ground, where most of the planters, from many miles around, had gathered together. The squire arranged his kettles about his wagon, and commenced descanting upon the superiority of his ware over that of any other. This collected a crowd around him, and the great praise bestowed by him upon his kettles, the still greater roughness of their appearance, created great laughter which had the effect to call a still larger number to the scene, all of whom seemed disposed to have a little sport at the expense of the squire and his hardware. This ebullition greatly irritated his honor, and he immediately commenced a violent cursing, which resulted in the throwing of the pots and pans violently against a stone heap, which, to the astonishment of the bystanders, and even the squire himself, would rebound high into the air, ring like a bell, and return to the earth unbroken. This wonderful phenomenon dumbfounded the whole assemblage, who stood motionless with astonishment, when presently the whole body of spectators made a rush upon the squire, and, at a considerable advance upon prices previously asked, bought him out, and to his entire satisfaction.

"At this time most of the car wheels running on the Virginia and Tennessee Railroad are made from this iron: their

tenacity, there is no doubt, is owing to the copper contained in the iron.

"The outcrop of the Toncrey, is an immense body of gossan, under some eight feet of which lays a bed of brown hematite, varying from ten to twenty feet in thickness."

These works continue in good repair, and for a small outlay the old iron furnace can be converted into a copper smelter. The gossan at this mine is similar to that at Ore Knob.

At Peach Bottom Creek, Grayson county, are found the ruins of the old Pine Hope Iron Forge and Furnace. The ore used to supply this furnace was obtained from the adjoining ridge, and is also highly impregnated with carbonate of copper. The same ill-success attended the smelting of this ore as elsewhere.

At the present Howell mine, Franklin county, east of Jacksonville, the gossan was used some years ago for the manufacture of iron, but abandoned for the same reason.

And so at other places, all these facts tending to the discovery of the copper found beneath these iron ores. The testimony deduced from the examination of the Ducktown gossans, led to the conclusion that these iron ores were but surface indications of a more precious metal beneath them. This fact, forcing itself upon the minds of the community, led to the opening up of these immense beds of decomposed ores, and to the confirmation of the valuable metalliferous character of this region.

With this general description we proceed to a more particular account of each lead.

1. THE NORTHERN OR IRON LEAD.—We designate, as one lead, all those found in the western portion of this district. There are several divisions, a few of which seem separate and distinct, showing no connection with each other, yet their occurrence was simultaneous, and it will be found that cross veins connect the several leading ones, adding increased value to this mineral district. Such cross veins have already been slightly developed in two instances.

The northern lead developes itself at Elk Knob, Ashe county, North Carolina, and there are sufficient connecting links on the line of this great lead, to show that it is a continuation of the Ducktown leads. Going north from Elk Knob we trace it to Meat Camp Mine on the northern branch of New River, 20° E. of north; thence passing into Virginia, it deflects more to the east, the course then being N. 45° E. In the western part of Grayson it is only observable in isolated localities, upon which no developments have been made. But on approaching New River the surface indications increase rapidly in importance, beyond which the gossan leads swell up into immense masses on the properties of Cook & Wistar, the Great Outburst of W. J. March, the properties of Yarnell & Co., the Limeberry and the Wilkerson. On entering the property of Cook & Wistar, the lead is found to possess four branches about two hundred yards apart, each of which may be traced to their union in the Great Outburst of W. J. March—a property of ten acres—through which it passes in one continuous line but again subdivides about the centre of the Yarnell & Co. fifty acres, into two branches. Thus far the course of the leads have been N. 45° E., but in passing into the Wilkerson property, these two leads were so acted upon as to change their course, the western branch obtaining a course N. 25° E., while the eastern is again subdivided; the middle branch running N. 25° E., while the other bends round through the J. Limeberry, and re-unites with the other in about half-a-mile. Thus continuing to the line between the J. Limeberry and the F. Limberry, at or near the "Monkey Grave," a reunion also takes place with the western branch, which has been traceable all the way through the M. Wilkerson property. Thus re-united in one lead, it continues uninterruptedly through the T. Blair property to Copperas Hill, on the banks of Crooked Creek, another piece of property belonging to Cook & Wistar. The divisions and reunions of this lead are strongly developed for a distance of five miles, each division presenting equally valuable surface indications.

At Copperas Hill, another division takes place, the two branches running off nearly parallel N. 45° E. One arm constitutes the Dalton Hill Lead, along which to Reed Island Creek, about eight miles, there are several fine surface indications, but none comparable to those which are found on Dalton

Hill, near the Wytheville Turnpike, and from which the lead takes its name.

The other arm constitutes the Northern or Iron Lead, traceable and finely developed as far as Big Reed Island Creek, a distance of 14 miles. Although no developments are made on this lead southwest of the M. Vaughn property, about 4 miles from Copperas Hill, yet here and there indications are found, proving its existence. Developments are made on this lead through the properties of M. Vaughn, Kirkbride, J. Shockley, M. Shockley, Early, Brown & Stevenson, Kincannon, Hale and Bettie Baker or Carter. Beyond the Bettie Baker mine no developments have been made along this lead, which is only traceable here and there through the western part of Floyd, until it reaches the northwest corner of that county, where it is slightly developed. The course throughout, although varying in some points, has generally been N. 54° E.—except in the northeastern part of Floyd, where it deflects to N. 65° E.

Intermediate between the Dalton and the Iron Leads, is found another short lead branching off doubtless from the main lead, and there is a probability that several such cross leads may be found, seeming to connect together by a network, this great mineral region.

With this general description of the Northern Leads, we proceed more particularly to describe each mining property:

The *Cook & Wistar property* is embraced in three tracts, one of 200, a second of 400 acres, adjoining each other, and the third of 450 acres, containing the famous Copperas Hill. This property has been well tested in all of the leads which pass through the southern tracts of 600 acres, affording ore of excellent quality, yielding as high as 35 per cent. No shaft has been sunk deeper than 35 feet, and no tunnel driven farther than 40 feet. One of the gossan leads through this property may be estimated at 250 feet wide. We have already remarked that there were four leads traceable through it, all converging towards one point. Between these leads are mica and hornblende slates, which form the *hanging wall* of the shafts. The five tunnels driven in upon this property, and the five shafts fully establish its value.

The 450 acre tract, containing *Copperas Hill*, lies on Crooked Creek, about four miles farther along the lead. The developments made on the property, consist of two tunnels and one shaft, and from the outcropping of sulphuret of iron and copper, there is every reason to believe that it will justify still further openings.

Then comes the *Great Outburst Mining Company* with their property of 10 acres. The property is of a triangular shape, and so situated that it possesses within its limited territory the union of all the leads coming from the Cook & Wistar. It takes its name from the great upheaval of gossan found capping the summit of this high ridge, and from which to the waters of Chestnut Creek, flowing at its base, is a precipitous descent of 300 feet. On this almost abrupt bluff Mr. W. J. March has driven in four tunnels across the mineral lode, and then followed it, excavating ores of a superior quality, the total drivage of tunnels being 306 feet. The vein is found to dip to the southeast at an angle of 50 degrees, but at one point it forms an arch, dipping also to the northwest with the same angle. A cross tunnel, run in at this point, shows the width of this vein to be not less than 30 feet. In driving these tunnels, several "horses" were encountered, but on passing beyond them, the ore was always found to be of a more superior quality. He began work on this property in 1856, and so far has shipped 300 tons of ore, ranging from 10 to 30 per cent., consisting principally of the bisulphuret, though at the time of the visit he had opened upon the red oxide in the cross-cut made from the main tunnel. The ore was found about 20 feet below the surface, and the width of the veins is supposed to be about 60 feet.

The *Yarnell Mining Company* owns 50 acres, adjoining the Great Outburst Mine on the northeast, besides having leases on the Limeberrys, the Wilkerson, and the T. Blair properties, all lying on the divisions and subdivisions of the lead.

The 50 acre tract, situated along the ridge leading from the Great Outburst Mine, presents large ledges of gossan. A shaft has been sunk 100 feet deep on the lead, and a tunnel driven in 150 feet, from which ores of good quality were being re-

CONTINUED ON PAGE 74.

The Developed and Undeveloped Mineral Wealth in North Carolina.—In the Raleigh *Observer*, of April 30th, we find the following letter, with this heading, from Dr. W. C. Kerr, the thoroughly efficient and able State Geologist of North Carolina, in reference to his recent visit to Pittsburg and his address to the Chamber of Commerce of that city in reference to the extension of the Pittsburg Southern Railway across West Virginia and Virginia into North Carolina. We had the pleasure of participating in this visit, and the honor of presenting to the Pittsburg Chamber of Commerce some facts concerning the topography and the mineral and other resources of the portions of West Virginia and Virginia that the proposed extension of that railway will traverse and bring within the reach, at moderate distances, of that great manufacturing city. We have not, as yet, found time to make our report—not to "Their Excellencies," the Governors of the Virginias, for we hold no official relations to those gentlemen—to the general public that we address here and elsewhere, but we propose to do it very soon. In the mean time, we commend to the thoughtful consideration of our readers, especially to those interested along the line of extension, what Prof Kerr says about the industries of Pittsburg and their enormous demands for just such raw materials as we have in qualities and quantities equal to any demand that can be made. The prizes that North Carolina offers to Pittsburg as the rewards of "extension," the merits of which her representative so well presents, and which we know are but truthfully stated, can only be reached by crossing the entire breadth of both of these States;—so we say to Pittsburg, Finish your Southern Railway to the head springs of the Great Kanawha in North Carolina; it will pay you, in every way you can think of, to do it:

His Excellency T. J. Jarvis, Governor of North Carolina:

Sir:—With your approval I accepted an invitation to visit Pittsburg last week to promote an enterprise of much interest to North Carolina. You are acquainted with the character and drift of the correspondence between the State Geologist and parties in that city in reference to a narrow gauge railway, called the "Pittsburg Southern." This road is projected and partly built, and runs due south, with the view of penetrating the middle coal and iron region of the Virginias and the iron and copper region of western North Carolina. It takes the course, first, of the valley of the Monongahela to its source, then of the Greenbrier to its confluence with New River, where it meets the narrow gauge road now building up the valley of that river towards Wytheville and Ore Knob. Through the courtesy of Mr. W. L. Nicholson, Topographer of the United States Post Office Department, I obtained the sheet of the Post Office Department maps of this and the intervening States to Pennsylvania, and mounting these in a wall map six feet square, I was able to lay down and present in one view the entire line of the proposed road and its connections, and to locate the lines of the narrow gauge system of roads of this State which converge upon the same objective point, Ore Knob, in Ashe county, viz : Chester and Lenoir (graded to the latter point, 110 miles, and finished half way); the Cape Fear and Yadkin Valley road, with its terminus at Patterson; the Dan River road, pointing in the same direction, and the Cranberry and Patterson road. Along these several lines were also laid down the ranges of iron, copper and gold ores from the great beds of Cranberry and the Roan Mountain, through the deposits of Ashe, Watauga and Caldwell to the extended ranges of the King's Mountain belt, of the the great bend of the Yadkin and the Saurætown Mountains and of the Guilford and Rockingham. Maj. Jed. Hotchkiss, the distinguished civil engineer and geographer of Virginia, and myself addressed the Chamber of Commerce of the city of Pittsburg on the subject of the practicality and advisability of the proposed road, *from their point of view*, and in the two fold aspect (1) of its probable success as a business enterprise on account of its feasibility in a physical and engineering sense, and of the various and abundant sources of freight; and (2) of its bearing, immediate and immense, on the great and growing industries of that city and region. After Major Hotchkiss had conducted the audience, composed of representative business men and capitalists, in his graphic and masterly way, (with which, happily, very many North Carolinians are familiar), through the successive coal beds of the Alleghanies and the Kanawhas and the reduplicated iron ore beds of the folded and crumpled and faulted and over-turned strata of the Great Valley and its mountain wallings on both sides, they were shown, by means of the map above described, how this State would be reached by the completion of the several sections of the narrow gauge road now building along the course of New River, entering it in Ashe county, and passing, by the way of Ore Knob and Gap Creek, to Cook's Gap in the Blue Ridge, and so on to Patterson, meeting here at their junction the two great arms of the narrow gauge system of this State, a third arm making off at some point on new River in the direction of Dan River Valley and Danville, thus bringing the Pittsburg Southern into immediate communication with many of the greatest iron ore ranges of the State. Attention was called to the fact that, on leaving the Valley of Virginia and crossing the Iron (or Smoky) Mountain into the upper valley of New River, near the North Carolina border, the older geological formations are encountered, in which the high grade Bessemer ores are commonly found, and to the number, localities, magnitude and chemical purity of the magnetic and hematite deposits along these several routes, on both sides of the Blue Ridge and of the Smoky Mountains, in Ashe and Watauga and Mitchell, on the head waters of the Yadkin, on this side and in Caldwell, and of the King's Mountain ores extending from the southern border of the State to the Western North Carolina Railroad in Catawba, and from the great bend of the Yadkin, by the Ararat River and the Pilot Mountain to Danbury in Stokes; and lastly, of the Guilford and Rockingham thirty mile range of titanic magnetic hematites, of absolute purity, and producing the very best iron known under proper management. And this region of abundant and pure ores was shown to be within 400 miles of Pittsburg by the course of the Pittsburg Southern Railway, and the connections it will meet southward, a considerable part of which are completed or under contract.

Your Excellency will appreciate the importance of these facts to the business of that city, and their interest to North Carolina from the following statement, viz : That the Baltimore & Ohio Railroad is now delivering, under a single contract, 500,000 tons of iron ore from Africa, and that 400,000 tons are to be brought out the present year from the west coast of England; that a single blast furnace, and that one of the smallest capacity which I visited, was consuming weekly over 1,200 tons of ore, and that the total capacity of the furnaces here is 500,000 tons of pig iron, requiring 1,000,000 tons of ore per annum and over 800 car loads of coke daily; that there are 800 puddling furnaces and 95 rolling mills in operation, and that the annual consumption of iron of all sorts in the various mills and manufactories here is equivalent to more than 800,000 tons of pig, or more than one third of the product of the United States. A single Bessemer steel establishment—the Edgar Thompson—is producing nearly 500 tons of steel daily, and making about one Bessemer rail a minute through the whole 24 hours, which is equivalent to 4 miles of railway a day; and other furnaces and mills are building continually. I found at the furnaces of this one establishment (and by the courtesy of the superintendent brought away samples, which your Excellency will find in the museum alongside of ores of the same quality from many places in North Carolina), iron ores from Africa, Spain, England, Ireland, Missouri, Lake Superior and South Virginia, but not a ton from North Carolina. Here, within a distance far less the length of the State, is an absolutely inexhaustible deposit of the best ore in existence—iron ore, which it lays three continents under contributions to supply; that is, North Carolina is practically further off than the whole breadth of the Atlantic, and this notwithstanding the fact that the State has been for two generations damming rivers, digging canals and building railroads, for the express purpose of developing its resources of raw materials and getting them to market or into forms of value. There are those who think that North Carolina expends too much in making known her material resources; but these enterprising and intelligent people of Pittsburg, who are scouring the planet for raw materials for their countless manufactories, had scarcely heard of them.

And I have only instanced one industry of this busy and pushing city. I found that they make here more than half of all the glassware produced in the United States, and some of the raw material is brought from a great distance, for example, at present, from the middle of Massachusetts. A neighboring town of six thousand people devotes itself wholly to the manufacture of porcelain and stoneware, keeping fifty furnaces in blast and loading ten to twelve cars a day with their products, and they draw their kaolins, quartzes and feldspars from all over the continent, with, of course, one exception, from Delaware, Maryland, Maine, Middle Missouri and Indiana, &c., &c. And yet there are not two states that can show so fine, or so large, or so many veins of kaolin and feldspar as North Carolina. Even the Indians "packed" it from the Smoky Mountains to the coast, and exported it to England under the name of "unaks," (their word for *white*, and for that chain of mountains in which it was found), before North Carolina was even a province. The Pittsburg Southern will penetrate the region of these deposits. The various manufactories of wood consume more than 50,000,000 feet annually, which is drawn largely from the forests of Canada and Lake Superior; so that this railway would give a high value to every acre of the now useless abundance and luxuriance of the 10,000 square miles of primeval forests of the mountain counties, and would ultimately develop numberless manufactories throughout that region. The single item of barrel staves for the city of Pittsburg (where 6,000,000 barrels of oil were refined last year) would enrich half a dozen counties. And they manufacture half as much cotton as the whole of this State. And yet, although we are nearest to them of all the cotton States, we do not furnish them a single bale. The proposed road would soon change all that and, by facilitating the transport of that staple, would rapidly enlarge the demand and, what is more important, would bring these enterprising capitalists into contact with the superior facilities which this State offers for that industry in its abundance of raw material and of cheap labor and water power, and favoring climate.

I have named only a few of the leading manufacturing industries of this thriving city and region, selecting those for which we might be furnishing the raw material, at least. The aggregate in money's worth of the manufactured products of this single city far exceeds that of our whole State. What we need, in order to develop our wonderfully varied and abounding, but hitherto unavailable resources and facilities for such productions, is just this sort of direct and immediate and cheap communication with the accumulated capital and skill and manifold appliances which alone can give them value. So that it is not less important to us than to them that the proposed road should be built.

For further sources of freights and business, which this road will speedily develop, attention was directed to the abundant deposits of gold and copper bearing sulphurets of Gaston, Mecklenburg, Cabarrus and other midland counties, and to the recent correspondence with parties in Charleston in reference to the transport of these ores to that point to be used in the manufacture of superphosphates, thus furnishing great quantities of freights both ways, and to the great demand which would be at once stimulated by the revived agricultural interests of the region for the plaster and salt and lime of Southwest Virginia. So that the road could not fail to pay dividends on every mile as fast as constructed, and this the more certainly from the fact that the first cost of building it will be less than half that of the common broad gauge, as has been demonstrated by the actual grading (ready for the cross ties) of about thirty miles of one of the branches of this very road (near Pittsburg) *for* $1,000 *a mile*. North Carolina would be twenty millions richer today if every mile of railway in it were of the narrow gauge, for almost all our roads would pay dividends on one-half their stock if their running expenses were also halved.

Then as to results. Your Excellency will be gratified to learn that very great interest was manifested by the substantial business men who constitute the Chamber of Commerce, the president and several members declaring that "They had no idea before of the extent of the mineral resources of the regions to be traversed by this road, nor of the advantages Pittsburg would enjoy by increasing her railway facilities to these points." You will see from the enclosed Pittsburg paper and journal that they are favorably considering a proposition which I made them, to appoint a committee of their own number to travel over and explore the whole region described, and see for themselves. And I knew, from the ready and cordial endorsemnt which your Excellency gave to my proposal to accept the invitation to Pittsburg, that my promise to meet them on the borders of Ashe county and conduct them through the mineral region adjacent would meet your approval. I do not know how I could more appropriately close this report than by the expression of my appreciation of the liberal and enlightened spirit in which your Excellency has met both this and every suggestion I have had the honor to submit, with a view to the speediest and fullest accomplishment of the important purposes of the survey.

I have the honor to be, your obedient servant,

W. C. Kerr, State Geologist.

Railway Notes.—The Buchanan & Clifton Forge division of the Richmond & Alleghany R. R., is to be finished by July 1st. About 1,000 hands are now worked on it by Mason, Hoge & Co., the contractors. H. D. Whitcomb is President of this division. The Board of Directors has recently gone over the line from Clifton Forge to Richmond. By its charter this Co. must finish 56 miles above and 50 miles below Lynchburg in 10 months.——The railways centering at Danville are doing a good passenger and a heavy freight business——The Richmond & Alleghany Co. has recorded a mortgage deed for $5,000,000, George M. Bartholomew has resigned the office of President of the Co , and F. O. French of New York, has been chosen in his place. Mr. Bartholomew remains in the directory and is a member of the Executive Committee.——Work has been begun on the southwestern end of the Shenandoah division of the Shenandoah Valley R. R. at Waynesboro, where it connects with the Chesapeake & Ohio Ry., so the whole line from Hagerstown to Waynesboro is now under contract.——The Richmond & Petersburg R. R. is doing a heavier freight business than it ever did before ——The Chesapeake & Ohio contemplates the construction of an air-line, "cross-lots," from Shadwell to Louisa C. H., making the line 15 miles shorter than it now is by Gordonsville.—[News and Farmer.——Work on the "Missing Link," (the newspaper name for the Charlottesville & Rapid-Anne R. R.) is making satisfactory progress; the grading is nearly completed and rails, &c., are now being delivered at Charlottesville and Orange C. H. It will be finished early in July.—[Piedmont Virginian.——The Richmond & Southwestern Railway will soon have a corps of young men at work gathering detailed information, on the ground, in regard to the resources of each county on its line.——The Franklin & Pittsylvania Railroad, narrow-gauge, was completed April 23rd to Rocky Mount, the county seat of Franklin county. On that day a train of cars took Pres. Barbour of the Va. Midland, Pres. S M. Felton, Supt. Bent and Mining Engineer Blackwell of the Pa. Steel Co., Steelton, Pa., Maj. Mason the Supt. of the Pittsville iron mines, and others to Rocky Mount. It is understood the road will be leased to the Virginia Midland for a term of years, and that it will take possession May 1st. This opens a new Virginia iron field to market. It runs from the Va Midland, at Ward's Spring, Pittsylvania county, 21 miles beyond Lynchburg, to Rocky Mount, Franklin county, a distance of 41 miles. It was commenced in June, 1879.——Senator C. T Smith and others are presenting the merits of the Richmond & Southwestern R'y to the people of the Apalachian counties it traverses, and Senator H. A. Atkinson and others are engaged in the same work in Midland Va. County subscriptions, to be paid after the railway is finished through the county, are to be voted on. The notices for meetings are signed Parker C. Chandler President, Benj. Kimball Sec'y.——The Virginia, Kentucky & Ohio R. R. to extend from New River bridge on the A. M. & O through Giles, Bland and Tazewell to the Ky system of roads was begun near Big Walker's Creek bridge in Giles Co , Va., a few days ago, says the Pearisburg Virginian, Mr. C R. Boyd, the Vice-President, holding the plow.——Two mortgages, one containing 38 and the other 43 printed pages, have been admitted to record in the clerk's office of Clarke county. They are given by the Shenandoah Valley Railroad Company to the Fidelity Insurance Trust and Safe Deposit Company of Philadelphia. The first dated April 1, and provides for issuing $2,500,000 of bonds—or $15,000 per mile—to retire the bonds issued under a previous mortgage, and the other, dated April 2, provides for issuing $1,000,000 more of bonds, and in addition thereto $20,000 per mile for each mile of single track and $10,000 per mile for each mile of double track. These mortgages will place an indebtedness of $35,000 per mile of single track on the S. V. Railroad, which is independent of its stock subscriptions, amounting to something like $10,000 per mile. The same mortgages have been recorded in all the counties traversed by the road ——Maj. W. T. Sutherlin is canvassing Henry county for subscriptions to the Danville & New River R. R. on which work is progressing favorably.——A deed conveying all its property and franchises has been made by the James River & Kanawha Canal Co to the Richmond & Alleghany R R. Co. and recorded in all the counties along the line of the canal.——The Washington & Ohio R. R., leading from Alexandria to the Blue Ridge via Leesburg, has been declared insolvent by the Circuit Court of Richmond, Va , and a decree for its sale, after 60 days notice, is made ——The Directors of the Washington City, Cincinnati & St. Louis Narrow-gauge Railroad, at a recent meeting in Harrisonburg, Va., elected J. W. F. Allemong President, and J. S. Loose Vice-President, both of Bridgewater. An effort is to be made to complete the road from Harrisonburg to the Dora Coal Mines via Dayton and Bridgewater.——Powhatan county, Va., votes, May 20th on the question of subscribing $50,000 to the Richmond & Southwestern R'y.——A hundred men are at work on the S. V. R. R. bridge over the Potomac at Shepherdstown, W. Va.; one pier, 70 feet high is completed and two others are half done. The work is progressing rapidly —[Register, April 24.——Gen. John Echols, President of the Lexington and Big Sandy R. R., has closed the contracts for the grading, etc., of the entire line of this road, the whole to be finished this year. All the contractors are at work and large numbers of negroes pass daily over the C. & O. to augment the number of laborers. This "missing link" will soon be completed and the C. & O R'y become a grand trunk east-and-west line.——The Virginia Midland R. R. is to be sold, at Alexandria, Va., May 13th; the main line and branches make 346 miles of railway.

Recent Sales of Mineral, &c., Lands.—Some 18.000 acres coal lands, on New River, W. Va., between Piney and Loup creeks, nearly opposite Quinnimont, to John White, of New York, and Charles Parrish, of Wilkesbarre, Pa.——A tract of 1,250 acres of iron land in Page county, Va., on the line of the Shenandoah Valley R. R., for $4.10 an acre, to John Donovan and others, Harrisonburg gentlemen.——The Danville Water-power, advertised in The Virginias, was sold to Wm. Crews and J. D. Corbin for $14,000.——The Wytheville *Dispatch* says the party that agreed to sell his interest in the Bertha Zinc Works wishes to recede from the sale. ——The Fincastle *Herald* says Capt. C. M. Reynolds, Treasurer of Virginia, has sold to Hileman, Cook & Co., of Callie Furnace, Botetourt county, Va, for $36,000 the Reynold's homestead. The Callie Furnace property of 500 acres was sold from the Rich-patch Mountain end of this homestead a few years ago. This purchase extends the Callie property to the James and to the Richmond & Alleghany R. R., and also gives it more of the length of the great iron belts on the eastern slope of the Rich-patch Mountain, and makes this one of the best furnace estates in the country, one having vast quantities of two or three varieties of ore, ample room for the largest of operations and connection with two lines of railway, as it lies between the C. & O. and the R. & A.——H. C. Parsons, Vice President of the Richmond and Alleghany R. R., has purchased from Samuel Wood, for $18,000, a large tract of land on the Rich-patch Mountain, Botetourt county, Va., containing iron ores.—*Fincastle Herald, April* 15.—D. A. Kayser, of Staunton, Va., has sold for $20,000, to the Richmond & Alleghany Railway Co.. 500 acres of his Clifton Forge farm, advertised in The Virginias.

This gives that Company not only fine alkaline and chalybeate springs and an unsurpassed site for aspring's hotel, but also the best of grounds for shops and other purposes near its junction with the C. & O. In consequence of this purchase the line of the R. & A. R'y will probably be changed to the S. W. side of Jackson's River, and it will connect with the C & O. beyond Williamson's without crossing the river. Mr. Kayser still holds for sale the large body of timber, iron and farming land forming the rest of the estate, which is made more desirable by this sale to the Railway Company.——The Mountain-top Hotel, advertised for sale in The Virginias, was sold to Messrs. Cochran, Ross & Massie, of the University of Virginia, for $3,900. They will improve and make more attractive this delightful summer resort. ——The Lobdell Car-wheel Co., of Wilmington, Del., has purchased the E. E. Early and the Thos. Wilkinson tracts of mineral land on New River, in Wythe county, Virginia.

Iron Ores.—New beds of specular and brown hematite ore have been discovered in Botetourt, at Cloverdale and vicinity, near the line of the Valley R. R.——Heavy beds of magnetite have been discovered between Peake's Cross-roads and Tolersville on the C. & O. R'y, passing by Holladay's Mills and Twyman's Store. The veins are said to be very rich and well located for mining.——A deposit of iron ore has been opened by Carter Shepherd on his farm near the Shenandoah in Clarke county, Va., in a large hill. It is probable this is in one of the outcrop lines of the Primordial ores located on the The Virginias' map of the Shenandoah Valley in the April No.—*Courier*.——Col. Jos. F. Kent has found, by analyses made by Prof. Mallet of the University of Va., that iron ores on his extensive property in Wythe Co., near the A. M. & O. R. R. are of a superior quality.—*S. W. Va. Enterprise*.——The Pennsylvania Steel and & Iron Co. has closed an indefinite lease on the immense iron ore beds some 2 miles from Brosville, Henry Co., Va., says the Danville *Daily Post*.——The narrow-gauge railway being completed to Rocky Mount 200 tons of magnetic iron ore are to be shipped thence daily, says the Lynchburg *News*.——The Bedford Iron, Mining & Manufacturing Co. has elected Maj. A. Lewis, of Salem, its President.——Iron ore has been discovered on Bolivar Heights, Harper's Ferry, W. Va.——John F. Sowers is about to send a car load of iron ore to Harrisburg, Pa., from his farm in Warren Co., Va., where recent developments indicate a large body of ore.

Personal.—The recent death of Gen. I. M. St John, the Consulting Engineer of the Ches. & Ohio R'y, has deprived us not only of a genial and accomplished gentleman but of one that has, for a number of years, been ardently devoting his talents to the development of the resources of the Virginias. He prepared for the C. & O. a number of able papers on the mineral and forestal wealth of the region it traverses.——C. F Conrad, M. E. of Winchester, Va., but for several years past in charge of anthracite coal mines in Pa., has taken charge of the New River Coke Co's operations at Elm, on the C. & O. R'y, as Superintendent and Engineer. Mr. C. has acquired an excellent reputation as a mining engineer in Pennsylvania. We are glad to welcome back, to aid in the development of our resources, the sons of Virginia that have become better fitted for their work by contact with the practical workings of the extensive mines of other States. They can speak knowingly of our advantages. William Bos. Johnson of Staunton, lately from Texas, has become Mr. Conrad's assistant, and an active and intelligent one he will be.——Mr. S. H. Charlton, the traveling industrial correspondent of the bright and newsy Evening Telegraph, of Pittsburg, Pa., gave us a call the other morning that was as pleasant and cheerful as that of the spring morning on which he came, or as that of the business outlook along the Chesapeake & Ohio as reported by him. The Telegraph is to be congratulated upon having such an observing and intelligent representative and our States upon having him to represent their resources and conditions of developement to the great manufacturing city that sits queen at the head of the Ohio and draws upon the resources of all lands to supply the vast quantities of raw materials demanded for the daily consumption of her gigantic industries. Mr. Charlton's letter to his paper from the Great Kanawha Coal-field is of such an excellent character, and does such justice to that coal-producing rival of Pittsburg, we are constrained to reproduce it, although it has already been widely circulated by the Coal Trade Journal of New York.——Col. Alex. Montgomery of Lewisburg, W. Va., has resigned as teller of the Bank of Lewisburg to become a division engineer on the Richmond & Alleghany R. R.

CONTINUED FROM PAGE 71.

moved when the property became a matter of litigation, and an injunction issued stopping further operations. About 50 tons of the bisulphuret of copper, averaging 12 per cent., has been shipped from this mine.

The *M. Wilkerson tract*, of 450 acres, contains in its southern portion two branches of the lead, on which there are three air shafts of no considerable depth, connecting a tunnel of 200 feet, from which 50 tons of the bisulphuret of copper (blue ore,) averaging 12 per cent., has been taken and shipped to market. Work was commenced on this property in 1857. The ore was found about 20 feet below the surface.

Through the *Jerry Limeberry*, one branch of the lead may be traced, uniting with another just before passing into the F. Limeberry tract. The course of the lead here is N. 20° E. One shaft has been sunk on this property, from which the grey sulphuret was obtained, at a depth of eighteen feet.

The *F. Limeberry* contains the combined veins of the lead, on which six shafts have been sunk, yielding good ores of the several varieties. The "monkey grave," as it is called, (but more properly the monger's grave, from the iron monger who first opened it) is on the line of this property, and was originally opened for its iron ores, in order to supply the old Forge located on Chestnut Creek. The remains of this forge still stand, and the same ill-luck attended the manufacture of iron from the gossans at this place as elsewhere. The gossan lead continues for two miles through this property, and is an important one.

The *T. Blair property*, of 300 acres, next succeeds, and is traversed throughout its entire length, for one and a-half miles, by a single lead. It has but one shaft and one tunnel, from which ore of good quality was obtained. The surface of this property is very rugged, especially along Crooked Creek, the overhanging cliffs being 400 feet high. The ore taken from the tunnel on the south side of this ridge consists of oxides and bisulphurets, with indications of the yellow sulphuret, in the mundic rock. At the water's edge, on the north side of the ridge, a small vein of yellow sulphuret was seen in the slate, a circumstance which should render the existence of this ore beneath the decomposed ores "a fixed fact."

Opposite to this place, on the north side of Crooked Creek, rises *Copperas Hill*, alluded to as belonging to the Cook & Wistar tract.

The country, which is very rugged south of this hill, now gradually subsides into less elevated ridges, along which no special surface indications are found until the M. Vaughn property is reached. The lead is here found to be N. 54° E., showing that at Copperas Hill, where it is N. 10° E., it has deflected to the east. Between Copperas Hill and Vaughn's property there is a distance of four miles.

This brings us to the properties of the Tennessee and Virginia Mining Co., consisting of the Ruggles tract; the Sarah Ellen mines, on the Vaughn tract; Ann Phippe, on the J. Shockley tract; Wild Cat, on the M. Shockley tract; Cranberry and Fairmount mines, on the Early tract; besides the Davis and the Stone properties on the Dalton Lead, embracing in all 2,900 acres. This company was one of the first to enter upon the mining of copper in this district.

The *Sarah Ellen* was opened in 1856, and work is yet being actively pushed forward in its tunnels. At the southern portion of the tract, a tunnel has been driven in at right angles to the vein, which was thus reached at 100 feet, from whence it was carried northeast and southwest along the lode. The northeast branch has been driven 300 feet, exposing a vein of 40 feet with an unknown depth, the ores of which are soft and friable and easily mined. Each hand from this vein delivers two tons of ore per day upon the ore floors at the mouth of the adit. The blue ore found here is a sulphuret, being in these mines the lowest of the veins. The average per cent. is 14. There are some two or three ventilating shafts let down upon the tunnel: the floors are dry and all the works in good condition.

Going to the southwest, along the vein, we find the same rich exposure, this southwest branch being driven in 250 feet. There are cross-cuts along the width of the vein, along which it is found to dip at an angle of 50°. These cross-cuts, with the parallel tunnels, afford intervening walls, through which the lode passes, and which, when stoped out, will yield a

handsome supply of ore. At the termination of those two tunnels there is quite a bold forehead of ore, there being no decrease either in width or depth of the lode.

Under the ore sheds were large heaps of ore awaiting the completion of the smelting furnace, as these mines have all suspended the transportation of ore, and are reserving them for the one now being erected near the Cranberry mines, an account of which may be found in another part of this "Visit."

On the northern portion of this tract Mr. Heiskell has driven in a tunnel 450 feet in length. At 100 feet, the vein was struck, dipping 30° S. E., and thence for 200 feet one of the side walls of the vein has been stoped out, obtaining ore of a grey color and soft. By cross-cuts he has also ascertained the vein to be 30 feet wide. The average per cent. of the ore obtained from this portion of the tract is the same as that just described. Several tons were heaped up under the ore sheds. In these mines I found a large force at work, and everthing carried forward with skill and energy. Up to this time the Sarah Ellen has shipped 300 tons of the blue sulpuret. The average depth of the lode beneath the surface of the ground is 40 feet, along which there has been driven about 1,000 feet of levels, with seven ventilating shafts, no one exceeding a greater depth than 40 feet, the total depths of shafting being 175 feet. The Vaughn property contains 700 acres, and runs one mile on the lead.

On the extreme southern portion of this tract, Mr. Vaughn is also at work. Laboring under the inconvenience of having to deliver his ores by lifting through a shaft, he is, however, vigorously pushing forward his work, taking out ore of the same quality as that just described. One of his tunnels opens into the southeast branch alluded to above. He has let down three shafts, each about 40 feet deep, connected by tunnels, along which he finds no decrease in the ore, either in width or depth. In addition to the blue ore he had also opened upon bunches of the red oxide, which lay under the shed in an assorted heap.

Intervening between the Sarah Ellen mines and the Ann Phippe, on the J. Shockley tract, lies the *Kirkbride property*, of 327 acres, running for one mile along the lead. It is worked by a different company, but as it occurs in regular order, it is deemed best to introduce an account of it at this place.

The name of this company is the *Kirkbride Mining Co.* The mine was opened during the present year (1859,) and consequently not much ore has been raised, the principal work, so far, having been directed towards opening the lode. The vein, where opened, is found to lie within ten feet of the surface, and more horizontal than any other vein in the district. The blue ore is raised from a vein from two to three feet in thickness. This company has shipped 30 tons of ore, averaging 14 per cent., the total drivage of levels amounting only to 40 feet, and the total depth of shafts 50 feet, no shaft being deeper than 10 feet.

There is along the lead a heavy gossan outcrop, which would indicate more valuable results than have, as yet, been attained.

The *Ann Phipp mine*, on the J. Shockley tract, worked by the Tennessee and Virginia Mining Co., may be ranked as one of the most valuable properties examined, not only on account of its advantageous location for mining, but also for the depth, and width, and the richness of the lode. Its ores present a beautiful display along the levels, fully confirming the evidence of its wealth afforded in the surface indications. It lies on the lead immediately adjoining the Kirkbride, along which it may be traced for three-fourths of a mile.

This mine was first opened in 1855, and though there is work sufficient to keep a strong force constantly employed in raising ore, yet we found only a few hands at work, sinking a new shaft on the southern portion of the property for the purpose of ventilating the levels. This effected, there will be no obstacle to the continued success of this mine.

The gradual manner in which the lode sinks, below the surface, is well illustrated in this mine. In the preceding properties we had the blue ores near the surface. On this property they are reached on the southern portion, but disappear beneath the black and green ores along the northern portion of the lode. To give a correct representation of the surface of this property, it may be compared to a wave-like line, alternately hill and vale, there being four such undula-

tions. From the northeast and southwest slopes of these knolls the lode has been reached by tunnels, some of which are driven to the right and others to the left of the vein, so that the two walls are fully exposed at different points, presenting an entire width of not less than 20 feet, with a dip of 45 degrees to the southeast. At the mouth of one of the tunnels was a mass of red oxide, weighing not less than one ton, taken just from beneath the surface, and covered only by a light coat of gossan.

There has been shipped from this mine 300 tons of ore, averaging about 15 per cent., though the red oxides possessed a value of 30 per cent.

Only in a few places has the mundic rock been reached, and no attempt has been made to penetrate it, as a sufficient quantity of decomposed ores yet remain to afford vigorous mining for years to come.

The total drivage of levels amounts to 1,000 feet, into which shafts have been sunk, the deepest not exceeding 30 feet, the total shafting being 150 feet.

In many places the floor, roof and walls consist of solid ore, the tunnel being driven immediately through the lode, while occasionally the floor is composed of the mundic rock.

The ores taken from this mine consist of the blue and black sulphurets, the green carbonate, and the red oxide, altogether averaging 15 per cent.

The *Wild Cat mine* is situated on the M. Shockley tract of 400 acres, being about one-half mile on the lead. This mine presents the same attractions as were seen in the Ann Phipps, though it is not so extensively developed. We found but one set of hands on this property, engaged in opening an adit on the southern portion, so as to drain the upper tunnels. This adit is being driven across the lode, and being below the mundic rock, has already begun to present indications of the existence of the yellow sulphuret. On Babbit's Creek, another tunnel has been driven in some 200 feet across the lode, and just above the water level, for the purpose of exploring for the yellow sulphuret; and it has resulted in breaking in upon some small veins in the compact mica slate and quartzite. This fact is highly important, as establishing, without the shadow of a doubt, the existence of this *ultima thule* of copper mining also at this point.

The Wild Cat mine was first opened in 1855, since which time there have been shipped 300 tons, consisting of oxides, carbonates and bisulphurets, averaging 14 per cent. The width of the mine is found to be 20 feet, its depth unknown, as nearly throughout the whole length of its levels the ore forms the floor. The greatest depth to which the mining has been carried does not exceed 40 feet, the vein itself being reached at a depth of 30 feet. The total drivage of levels amounts to 700 feet, and the total depth of shafts 250 feet, no shaft exceeding 40 feet.

As in the other mines, the ores are easily picked out, and the drifts being high above the water level, with one exception, the tunnels are not greatly troubled with an accumulation of water.

The *Cranberry mine*, on the J. Early tract, containing 100 acres, and extending one-half of a mile on the lead, was opened in 1854, and the work of mining pushed to a greater extent than any other property. This property is composed of an elevated ridge, which rises like a crest, overlooking the Wytheville Turnpike, and well adapted to the tunneling, to which it has been subjected. The total drivage of levels amounts to 800 feet, opening upon a mineral vein about 60 feet below the surface, and running N. 54° E. with a dip of 60 degrees to southeast. The entire vein, in all its length through this property, is estimated at not less than 10 feet thick and 25 feet wide. There are about nine shafts sunk on the lead, for ventilating mainly, their total depth being 250 feet, though the deepest only reaches 45 feet. Neither the depth nor the width of the mineral vein has been fully ascertained. Cross-cuts have been made from the main tunnels, and parallel levels, driven, but still along the mineral lode. The works on this property exhibit very markedly the order of superposition of the various ores of these mines. After penetrating through the gossan crust, which here is strongly deposited, the carbonates are found occupying the upper portion of the veins. To these succeed, in the second galleries, the decomposed bisulphurets or black ores, and in the lower gallery, the grey and blue bisulphurets, beneath which lies the mundic rock. These galleries are separated by thin floors of hard rock or of plank, and beautifully illustrate the system of mining in following the vein downward.

A deep shaft has been also sunk in the valley at the base of the ridge, and near the turnpike, which, after passing through a hard quartzose slate, opened upon a vein of the yellow sulphuret. This shaft, in our opinion, would have yielded handsome results, had it been located a few paces farther to the south. It also establishes the fact that below the mundic comes the yellow sulphuret in the vein rock, which would grow richer as the depth increased. A strong force is at work on this mine.

There have been 700 tons of ore shipped from this mine, consisting of the usual varieties of carbonates, oxides and sulphurets, and averaging 15 per cent. All the ores to be raised in future from these properties are be reserved for the Baltimore and Cuba Smelting Furnace, now being erected near this mine.

The establishment of these smelting works is calculated to stimulate the mining operations to a degree heretofore unknown, and as by the new process of chemical decomposition, ores of one per cent. can be as easily treated as the richer, there will be nothing lost at these mines. I refer the reader to a description of the smelting works on another page.

The *Fairmount mines*, on the southern portion of this property, were opened in 1855, the vein being found to be 25 feet, and only 40 feet below the surface. The gossan indications are strongly marked, and the yield consists of ores of good quality, being green carbonate and blue sulphuret. The total drivage of levels amounts to 700 feet, with a total depth of shafts of 150 feet.

Following the lead northwards, after passing the Fairmount, we come upon the property of *Brown & Stevenson*, on the waters of Little Reed Island Creek, on which we find a heavy gossan outcrop on the summit of the ridge, on the western side of which an exploring tunnel has been driven in 250 feet, the ore being reached about 60 feet beneath the surface of the ground. The falls on this creek are admirably adapted for any purpose of manufacturing or smelting. This tract is very advantageously situated for the delivery of the ores by railway on a descending grade from the mouth of the level to the ore floors.

The *Kincannon property*, adjoining, also affords the same good prospects, the testing which has been made on it resulting very favorably. There is no doubt that a tunnel driven in from the water level would develop strong lodes of the yellow sulphuret.

The *F. L. Hale properties* are next entered on the lead, the two embracing an area of more than 3,000 acres, the lead being traceable four miles through the tracts. Throughout their whole extent, the surface gossan indications are well marked, and exploring shafts have been sunk at various points with good results. On the northeast end of this property, and just adjoining the Bettie Baker mines, the *Ann Eliza and Anna Mary mines* have been opened, and successfully worked. These properties form a part of the mining lands of the *Meigs County Tennessee & Virginia Mining Co.*, to whom also belong the Bettie Baker mine, and the properties to the northeast on the northern lead, and several properties on the Native lead, in Carroll, said to embrace an area of 100,000 acres, along these three leads, and in a direct line on them of forty seven miles.

The *Anna Mary* is supposed to be on a different vein from the Bettie Baker. It is, however, only 50 yards to the north of it, and may very properly be regarded as an offshoot from this great lead. We doubt not, when explorations are carried sufficiently far, this opinion will be satisfactorily established, and add no little to the intrinsic value of this mining region. Cross veins, often richer than those from which they emanate, indicate the intensity of the volcanic action which produced them. In advancing the opinion, therefore, that these lateral veins are branches of the main lode, there is imparted an additional interest to this mining region. These branches sometimes strike off laterally and then again they are thrown upward from below.

The drivage of tunnels on the Hale properties amounts to 300 feet, with a total depth of shafts of 200 feet. The greatest depth of any one shaft being 60 feet. These tunnels are driven to the centre of the ridge, both from the southwest slope and from the northeast. Seventy tons of ore, averaging 14 per cent., were shipped from these mines during the time they were in operation. A portion of the ore was very rich, consisting of the oxides and black smut ore, in which were found crystals, and occasionally large masses of native copper. One mass, lifted out of this bed of smut, weighed 100 pounds. The width of the vein is estimated at 20 feet, and is found 60 feet beneath the surface. This mine is only opened sufficiently to show that it possesses great attractions; for if it opens so beautifully on the 300 feet developed, what must it not possess still deeper in the lode.

The *Bettie Baker mine* is entered on the side of the hill, opposite to the Hale mines. On this property is to be found the famous Paint Bank, from whence was obtained, for many years, ochreous iron for domestic purposes. Here was done probably the first work in this mining region.

Entering the levels, opposite the Anna Mary mines, we pass in for 40 feet at right angles to the lode, where it is reached. It is then followed 300 feet, with some two or three cross-cuts and parallel drifts, exposing, throughout its entire length, a splendid view of the vein, from which the red and black oxides are mined, yielding 22 per cent. Since the first day of May last, 130 tons of

20 per cent. ore has been taken out and shipped to Baltimore, Here, as in the Cranberry mines, the richer ores occupy the upper vein, while the poorer lie upon the mundic rock, beneath which no explorations have been made. Whenever a "horse" intervenes, the ore beyond is found of richer quality and in greater quantity justifying the conclusion that deep mining would here, as well as in the other mines, be productive of the most brilliant results.

On the eastern side of the ridge, a tunnel has also been driven in with the same good results; while on a second hill, the old "paint bank," extensive openings are found, being the original works on this property. Since 1854 there have been shipped from this mine 595 tons, mostly of the black ore, with an average of 16 per cent. The width of the vein increases to 30 feet, and depth unknown. The amount of drivage in tunnels is 800 feet, while no shafting of any consequence has been required. The lode has been reached from the slopes of the ridges, and the tunnels driven in along the lead.

Northward from the Bettie Baker, with an inclination of 54° to the east, the vein may be traced to Big Reed Island Creek, through several properties belonging to this company. But as at the Bettie Baker it was found to tend downwards as it advanced north, it may be that deep mining would be required to reach the lode, in which case the ores would partake of a different yet richer character; and such an inference is sustained from the fact that on Big Reed Island Creek, on the Sutphan property, an exploring shaft has reached the yellow sulphuret. Here, then, is another point established, from which the owners of these properties may be fully assured of the inexhaustible nature of their mining properties. For when the decomposed ores are exhausted, a thing not likely to occur for many years, then they have reached a basis of operations that will know of no limits.

Passing through the western part of Floyd, along the course of the lead, there are, as far as I could ascertain, no special indications, until the northeast corner is reached, where an outcropping of gossan occurs, which has been opened with a shaft by Mr. Howell, of Jacksonville, and with good results.

This is the extreme northern limit of this iron or northern lead. We have traced it from Elk Knob, N. C., into Virginia, through the counties of Grayson, Carroll and Floyd. Let us now retrace our steps to examine one of the lateral leads branching off from the main trunk, the gigantic character of which has much importance attached to it.

I have stated that the *Dalton lead* branched off from the northern lead at Copperas Hill. Gradually diverging at the Wytheville Turnpike it is nearly one mile to the east of the northern lead, there being found intermediate to the two a large quartz lead, assuming at some points a gossan character. The purity of this quartz and its associating slates, naturally suggest the idea of a *gold-bearing vein*, and we would not be surprised to hear of this precious metal being found in it. At any rate, it would be well for those interested to examine closely the gossan connected with it. For when there is gold or any other metal in the original sulphuret of iron and copper, that gave birth to the gossan, notwithstanding its decomposition and its conversion into an ore of iron.

Reasoning from the immense masses of gossan found upheaved for miles along this lead, and the ore obtained from those shafts and tunnels which were judiciously located, I would not hesitate to select the Dalton lead as one of great value.

There have been only two properties developed upon this lead—the Stone property, belonging to the Tennessee & Virginia Mining Co., and Dalton Hill, belonging to the Dalton Mining Co.

There was only one shaft opened on the *Stone property* as a prospecting shaft, which after passing through gossan and slate, reached the vein, affording ore similar in every respect to that found on the iron lead.

But on *Dalton Hill*, near the Wytheville Turnpike, there have been 30 shafts sunk, and 6 tunnels driven in from the side of the ridge; out of the whole number of which only two or three appear to have been judiciously located. From two of them, sunk to a depth of 50 feet, ore of good quality was raised, the vein being found to be about 25 feet wide, yielding the blue and green ores, at a depth of 35 feet only below the surface. The total depth of shafting amounts to nearly 700 feet, and the total drivage of tunnels to 500 feet. Fine indications of the yellow sulphuret were observed in the tunnel on the north side of the ridge, at 80 feet from the surface, in a heavy quartz lode. The width of this sulphuret vein was estimated to be 13 feet.

Had all the work bestowed on this property, been expended in running in two cross tunnels from the south side of the ridge, across the lodes, the better to reach the decomposed ores and the lower at the water level to strike the yellow sulphuret below the mundic rock, the intrinsic value of this mine would be inconceivable.

The property of the Dalton Mining Co. reaches to Reed Island Creek, along the whole length of which the lead may be traced.

Additional value is attached to this property from its proximity to the smelting works, erected at the Cranberry mines.

We hope to learn that work has been re-commenced on this property at an early day, under the management of a skillful mining captain; and we are convinced that the results will not disappoint the most sanguine expectations that can be entertained with reference to it.

There is another lead, called the Jenning's Lead, to the east of the Dalton, but as no explorations have been made on it, it was not particularly examined. It is moreover a quartz lead.

2. THE NATIVE LEAD.—By reference to the Geological Map, it will be seen that the Granite upheaval of Grayson county is surrounded by a gneiss and greenstone formation, which extends northward to Floyd county. This stratum affords the bed for the second great lead through this mining region, entirely different from that just described, and of such a character as to be properly designated the *Native Lead*. It is just such a formation as this that contains the mines of Lake Superior, a trap and gneissoid rock; hence the blocks of native copper obtained from these mines. The Native, or as it is sometimes called the Trap Lead, is about half a mile wide and may be traced for 16 miles. The series or rock strata consist of gneiss with quartz, crystals of native copper being minutely disseminated through the mass, and interstratified with an olive colored rock resembling olivine, and with greenstone. The course of the strata is N. 54° E., changing to 70° towards it northern termination. Its inclination is S. E., varying from 40 degrees to a position almost vertical towards its western limit.

Several openings have been made upon this lead, on lands formerly owned by John S. Sutphan, but now the property of the Meigs County, Tennessee, & Virginia Mining Co. Work was begun early in 1854, since which time but little more has been done. Thirty-two tons of the native ore and native rock were shipped to market, yet as it yielded only 8 per cent., of course it did not pay at that time. The rock thrown out from the shafts consisted of olivine and sandstone laminated with gneiss, containing radiating crystals of tremolite, through which crystals of native copper were profusely distributed. The carbonates found among them are due to the action of the carbonic acid of the atmosphere upon the oxidized metal, and therefore do not exist to any great depth.

This is, without doubt, an important lead, independent of the value which may be attached to its proximity to the other mines of this region. It will require heavy work to open this lead, yet, when opened, it would be productive of valuable results. The metal being disseminated through the vein rock, it would necessarily have to be subjected to the stamping process, by means of which the minute particles of copper may be aggregated together.

3. THE SOUTHERN LEAD.—Although somewhat similar to the northern or iron lead in its general characteristics, the southern lead presents many points entirely different. Its gossan lead is not so uniform, as it is frequently replaced by a silicious and highly ferruginous stratum, even the mica slate itself partaking of this ferruginous character. It is, however, none the less valuable.

Situated in the southern portions of Floyd, Carroll and Grayson counties, Va., and in Alleghany county, N. C., it lies between the gneiss and greenstone of the native lead on the north, and the gneiss and olivine of the Blue Ridge on the south.

The slates, in which the lode occurs, are alternately hornblende and mica, interstratified with immense ledges of pure white quartzite.

The mines which have been opened on this lead, are Ore Knob and Peach Bottom, in Alleghany county, N. C.; Hampton's, Cox's and Fulton's, on Little River, in Grayson county, Va.; Whitmore mine in Carroll and Hylton's, the Nowlin, Weddle and Toncrey mines in Floyd, and Howell's mine in Franklin.

We are aware of the fact that some of these belong to lateral veins, but they all may be placed in the same great lead, and designated the *Southern Lead*. Some of the lateral leads run into the main one, as was observed with reference to the Northern lead. This is, however, not so regular in its course as the northern lead. In N. C. it possesses nearly an east and west course, but in Va. it strikes N. 45° E. till it reaches Floyd, when it deflects again towards the east, as it crosses the Blue Ridge into Franklin county.

At Ore Knob, the surrounding slates are similar in every respect to those at Peach Bottom mine, 12 or 14 miles distant, except that there is also an abundant out-cropping of gossan, containing beautiful crystals of carbonate of copper, and closely resembling that at Toncrey mine, in Floyd, and Howell mine, in Franklin, The surface indication at the Peach Bottom mine, on Elk Creek, is a decomposed mica slate, a rusty iron color pervading its mass. The ore obtained beneath this is the undecomposed yellow sulphuret; whereas at the Ore Knob there is a heavy vein of decomposed ores lying above the mundic, in which the yellow sulphuret is to be found.

Going northwest from the Peach Bottom mine, several openings near the mouth of Little River, with gossan indications, the gossan yielding crystals of the green carbonate of cop-

per in its cavities as in that at Ore Knob. I must confess my inability, however, at present, owing to the ruggedness of the country, to locate the lead upon which they are situated. They present the appearance of belonging to the southern lead, yet they are to be found in a gneissoid rock, similar to that of the native lead, and are also bounded on the east by a soapstone stratum, intervening, it seems, between this lead and the southern lead, and isolated; or they may be the continuation of the native lead, occurring under such circumstances as to afford the yellow sulphuret instead of the native copper.

I had learned of the existence of this gossan outcrop near the mouth of Little River, and observed similar indications on the road from Jefferson, before reaching the mouth of the North Fork of New River, both of which are doubtless a continuation of this new lead, occurring in the gneissoid rocks, and affording the yellow sulphuret of copper, but no decomposed ore. They are interesting localities, and their proximity to the gneiss and granite afford strong evidence in favor of their value.

Proceeding northward through Grayson, there is nothing to be seen until the Whitmore works, in Carroll, are approached. Here we find large masses of gossan out-cropping, near the waters of Snake Creek. The openings made in the ridge, afforded fair evidence of the vein of ore to be found there, but it is not yet fully tested. Passing thence into Floyd, the surface indications become very important; and at the Toncrey mine, such is the quality of this hydrated oxide of iron, that for 70 years it was used to supply an iron establishment erected on the waters of West Fork. This has already been alluded to in a previous chapter.

From thence to the Howell mine, in Franklin county, the lead may be traced through the Blue Ridge, its course hence being N. 70° E.

With this general description of the lead, we proceed to consider its developments, as they occur, beginning at the southern extremity.

Ore Knob is in Alleghany county, N. C., and near the waters of Cranberry Creek. It is east of New River, distant about 6 miles, and consists of an elevated ridge, the crest of which runs N. 65° E., and as the vein is N. 60° E., it passes diagonally across its summit. The rock strata composing this ridge consist of hornblendic and micaceous slates, very compact, and interstratified with a talco-mica slate. The outcropping of gossan is very heavy, containing beautiful crystals upon a brown surface, throughout its cavities.

Extensive works have been constructed, 4 shafts having been sunk upon the lode, and a tunnel driven in across the vein at the water level. The upper shaft is 90 feet deep, the second 40, the third 30, and the fourth, half way down the declivity 40 feet, from all of which ore of good quality and very abundant has been raised. The upper shaft was carried through solid beds of gossan to the depth of 70 feet before the lode was reached, while in the two lower, situated on the declivity 65 and 70 feet beneath the upper, the vein was reached at 24 feet, clearly showing the importance of working this mine by means of a level run in from the slope of the ridge. In these shafts the wall rock on the north side was flint, and on the south hornblendic slate.

From this mine sufficient ore was shipped, during the time it was in operation, to realize $9,500, after paying the expenses of transportation. The first work was begun in 1855, and suspended in 1856, one-half of which time was employed in opening dead ground. When the lode was opened, a hand could raise 2 tons per day, the ore averaging 19 per cent. The width of the vein was not ascertained, though supposed to be not less than 20 feet. Large heaps of ore are yet lying exposed under the ore sheds, and scattered over the surface of the ground, which, though it would yield 10 per cent., was not considered of sufficient value to bear transportation. The ores consist of the red and black oxides, carbonates and the yellow sulphurets.

Effectual work was done while it was in operation, such as the construction of sheds, three whims, dwelling-houses and stables.

This mine is 63 miles from the nearest point on the railroad, and over a rough country, a fact which doubtless caused its suspension, for the ores certainly speak for themselves. I regard the place as appropriately named, Ore Knob.

Another prospecting shaft has been let down on the south side of the knob, and with like good results.

The successful working of this mine demands the erection of furnaces, for which an abundant water power is afforded by Peak Creek flowing near the base of the knob.

Pursuing a course N. 60 E. to the waters of Elk Creek, 14 miles distant, we come to another mine.

Peach Bottom Mine was opened in 1832 for its lead and silver, known to be found here. But when, along with it the yellow sulphuret of copper turned up, it was regarded as worthless and was abandoned. Within the last twelve months, some of the original owners have renewed their leases and commenced operations for copper.*

The course of the lead here is N. 54° E. Two shafts have been let down upon the vein rock, both located on the side of the ridge, the upper being 66 feet and the other 30 feet deep. On a level with the mouth of the lower shaft, a tunnel has been driven in till it intersects with the upper shaft, and is then continued 50 feet along the vein. From the floor of this tunnel, an inclined shaft, dipping at an angle along the vein, has been sunk for more than 30 feet, till it reaches a point opposite the second shaft, from which it is intended to connect the two together, and to run an adit to the surface. The width of the vein in the upper tunnel is 6 feet, and is found gradually to increase in value with the depth. The dip of the vein is 86°, a fact very favorable for mining, and indicative of the richness of the mineral lode.

In sinking these shafts there was found the following regular stratification: After penetrating the surface decomposed slate, the hanging wall is composed of a dark hornblenic rock, very compact, beneath which lies the softer and lighter colored mica slate, 6 feet thick, interspersed with veins and pockets of sulphuret of copper. In this is sometimes interposed a hornblende containing copper, which is regarded as the "horse" of the mine, 6 inches thick; then follows a rotten slate, called by the miners *selvidge*, from 1 to 4 inches thick, beneath which lies a stratum containing argentiferous lead ore, 6 inches thick; then follows a greenish semi crystalline felspar, lying upon the foot wall of hornblende slate. Confident of success in the further developments of this mine, the company has erected very substantial works for crushing and washing the ores. This establishment is carried by the waters of Elk Creek, and runs two pair of fluted and four pair of smooth crushers. This being completed, a strong force will be put into the mine, and work pushed forward vigorously. Should that success attend them, which every indication guarantees, there will arise an absolute necessity for a smelting furnace, still further to reduce the ores to a regulus before shipping to market, for which the waters of Elk Creek will afford ample power.

The lead on which this mine is located may be traced N. E. and S. W. from this point, along which other developments have been made, and with like good results, but leases having expired, the operations were suspended.

This lead may be regarded as belonging to the Southern or Toncrey lead, though some are disposed to regard it as being intermediate between it and the Native lead. The ruggedness of the country would not admit of its being traced throughout.

These ores have a greater resemblance to those of the Canton mine, Ga., than any that I have heretofore examined, especially in their association with ores of lead.

Going northward, three miles south of Independence, there are found excellent surface indications of gossan, on the property of Mrs. Austin, also at Mr. Fulton's, three miles east of the old Pine Hope Furnace, on Peach Bottom Creek. This lead may be traced through Haywood Cox's property, and through Andrew Hampton's.

---

*GRAYSON C. H., VA., Oct. 31st, 1859.

Dr. R. O. CURREY

Dear Sir—The information you desired may now reach you too late to be embodied in your Report, but be that as it may, I will give you such facts in regard to the discovery of copper in this region as have come to my knowledge. With the iron ore, and its admixture with copper, at the Toncrey works, formerly the Shelor's, in Floyd county, and the fact that copper was known to exist there for many years past, seems to have been communicated to you, and therefore I shall say nothing in regard to that. The iron ore, or gossan, on the Iron Ridge, 5 miles north-east of this place, was first discovered in the year 1785, by the persons who subsequently erected iron works on Chestnut Creek, with a view to the manufacture of bar iron from it. They soon found, however, that the ore contained too much copper to make good bar iron, and they were obliged to procure more suitable ore for that purpose from other and more distant points; but until after the discovery of copper at Ducktown, they never dreamed that by sinking a shaft on their iron lead they would find a body of the oxide of copper. I had faith in it myself, and in the year 1857 proposed to Mr. John Blair, the owner of a part of the lands, to join him in a search for copper, but he had no faith in finding a copper mine, and declined my proposal.

I did not commence work at the Peach Bottom mine, in Ashe county, N. C., in search for lead, as you suppose. In the spring of 1832, Col James Maxwell, who then claimed the land, brought me a piece of slate rock, which he said, was something new to him, and asked me what it was, and whether it contained mineral of any valuable kind. I informed him at once that it was copper, and that in my judgment a valuable copper mine would be found at the depth of 80 or 100 feet. At his request I went and examined the place, and obtained a lease for 99 years, and commenced work with a few hands from the lead mines in Wythe, in the month of October, 1832. I continued my operation as long as I had a dollar, and until, by writing to gentlemen in most of the northern cities, I ascertained that the process of washing and smelting copper ores was not then understood in the United States. I had struck the sulphuret of copper at the depth of 57 feet from the surface, had assayed it myself, and knew it to be good and paying ore, but for the want of means, and hands or miners, who understood mining for copper and preparing it for market, I was compelled to abandon the work, and did not commence work at that place again until about 12 months ago.

The piece of rock brought to me by Col. Maxwell, as above mentioned, was found at the bottom of the ditch he had cut to convey the water to his mill, which you will remember, is yet standing a short distance below where we have put up our machinery.

Our crushing mill is now in successful operation, grinding up from 70 to 100 tons of the rock containing the ore, per day, and with 20 hands we can wash and prepare for market 3 to 5 tons per day, worth, at present Baltimore prices, $135 per ton.

I sent a sample of our ore, as we had washed it, to Mr. H. McKim, of Baltimore, who by letter of the 18th inst., informs me that the yield was 32 14-100 per cent. copper, and worth $135 per ton.

I had forgot to say that the vein of argentiferous lead is still going down with the copper lode and becoming richer.

The works of the Baltimoreans, at the Cranberry mine, in Carroll, are now in operation, and successful in producing copper even beyond their own expectations.

I am, very truly, your friend, S M'CAMANT.

P S—If I am not the first discoverer of copper in this region, I am unquestionably the first person that ever cut an adit or sunk a shaft in search of it.

[CONTINUED ON PAGE 80.]

The Iron Ores near Cumberland Gap, Virginia.

BY P. N. MOORE.

The iron ores of economical importance in this region lie on the southeast of Cumberland Mountain, usually in the range of foot-hills known as the Poor Valley Ridge, which is almost always seen at the base of the mountain. Occasionally, this ridge disappears, and we find the ores on the flank of the mountain proper, near its base; but their occurrence in this position is exceptional.

The ores are, consequently, in Virginia and Tennessee; but as they occur so close to the Kentucky line, and are so intimately connected with Kentucky interests, in that they cannot be fully developed without the use of Kentucky fuels, an examination was made of them for a few miles up and down the mountain, from Cumberland Gap, to ascertain something as to their method of occurrence, quantity and quality, and to determine the capabilities of the region to sustain an iron-manufacturing industry.

The manufacture of iron from these ores from charcoal fuel has been, for a long time, carried on in this vicinity in a small way, at a number of places; both pig iron and blooms having been produced. It is, however, upon coal as a fuel that the permanent iron industry must be founded, and the coal which will, in the future, smelt the ores along the mountain for a considerable distance below, and for a still greater distance above Cumberland Gap, must come from Kentucky. There is no coal to the southeast in either Tennessee or Virginia, and Cumberland Gap affords the most feasible passage by railroad through the mountain from the ore to the great Kentucky coal-field.

Such being the case, these ores become of almost as much importance to Kentucky as to the States in which they are situated, especially when we consider that their development is dependent largely upon a Kentucky railroad enterprise to give them access to market. Either of the projected railroads through Kentucky to Cumberland Gap, will find in the transportation of these ores, and of the iron made from them, one of the most important sources of revenue.

The ores of this region are stratified hematites, belonging to the Clinton Group of the Silurian formation, a group which has been designated as the Dyestone Group by Prof. Safford, in his report on the geology of Tennessee. The ore is variously known as the Dyestone or Fossil ore, and sometimes simply as the Red ore. It is called the Dyestone ore from the fact that it is sometimes used for dyeing purposes by the residents of the region where it is found.

The rocks with which it is associated are usually shales, sometimes calcareous, which occasionally pass into thin-bedded sandstones. There are also occasional unstratified thin beds of limestone, which increase in frequency towards the lower part of the series, and below the ores.

The thickness of the group in Tennessee, as stated by Prof. Safford, varies from two hundred to three hundred feet. In this vicinity it is usually thicker, ranging from three hundred to five hundred feet. These rocks pass almost imperceptibly into the Medina sandstone below. This sandstone is here thin-bedded, and less marked in every way than it is further southeast, where it is the massive determining rock of Clinch Mountain; but it is still heavy enough to form, with the lower portion of the Clinton beds, the Poor Valley Ridge, or foot-hill range of Cumberland Mountain. The "Poor Valley," between the foot-hill and the mountain, is excavated in the thin-bedded, soft, and easily eroded Clinton rocks, and it is to their silicious nature, and the soil resulting from them, that the infertility of the valley is due. The Devonian shale and the Waverly also help in the formation of the valley to a certain extent, but the Clinton shales are particularly the valley rocks. Usually the shale above the ore occurs in the valley, and the upper ore (of the three to be hereafter described), with a thin but hard sand-stone immediately above it, is the highest and crest-forming rock of the Poor Valley Ridge.

As before stated, the ore occurs in beds or layers, interstratified with shales and lime-stones. It differs much in quality in the different beds; but when at its best, is an oölitic, greasy-feeling, fossiliferous hematite, formed at places almost entirely of fragments of crinoid stems. Other fossils are numerous, but by no means reach anything like the proportion of the crinoidal remains.

The ore has not been studied in sufficient detail over a large area, where it has been opened in depth, and the overlying rocks are fully exposed, to enable the writer to form a theory of its formation satisfactory in every respect; but the structure of the ore, in most cases, indicates, beyond reasonable doubt, that it was originally a bed of fossiliferous limestone. The original limestone has been dissolved and removed by the solutions which brought the iron and deposited it in the form and place of the limestone. The iron has probably been derived from the rocks above, and has been gradually removed by a process of leaching.

This ore is by no means a local deposit. It is characteristic of the rocks of this period, from New York to Alabama, and it is also found in the same formation in Wisconsin, of a quality that can hardly be distinguished from the New York or Tennessee ore. This marked uniformity of quality and position of the ore show that the waters, at the time of the deposition of these rocks, must have been very uniformly charged with iron over an area hundreds of square miles in extent. There is no similar formation in which iron ore is distributed with anything like so great a uniformity, or of which it is so characteristic. Other ores are found usually connected with rocks of a particular formation, but they are by no means coëxtensive with that formation; they are, on the contrary, "pockety" and erratic. This, however, both in quality and position, maintains its identity along the parallel mountains of the Apalachian series for hundreds of miles. In the aggregate, therefore, it presents a mass of ore which is practically inexhaustible, and is unequaled by any other deposit in the country.

In New York and Pennsylvania ore of this age is largely worked for the supply of blast furnaces; but south of those States it is almost untouched, although in Virginia and Tennessee a number of small charcoal furnaces and forges have been using it for many years past. Their consumption is so small that, in comparison with the vast amount remaining, what ore they have used is too small for notice.

There are usually found in the region under consideration three beds of ore. These have been found to extend with considerable regularity for five or six miles each side of Cumberland Gap. Whether they are persistent at a greater distance above the Gap than this is not yet known. Ore is found in good thickness at many places above; but the sections taken have not been detailed enough to prove the existence of more than one bed, although there is no reason to doubt that the others will be found when properly sought for. Below Cumberland Gap, at Speedwell Furnace, two ores have been worked, apparently corresponding to the middle and upper of the three above mentioned, with the distance between them considerably increased.

The positions and relative distance apart of the three ores are shown in the sections of the accompanying plate.* These sections were all taken within a few miles of Cumberland Gap, and the most of them within one mile and a half. It will be seen from them that the ores are sometimes found at the foot of the mountain proper, and sometimes in the Poor Valley Ridge. They are of the most value when they occur in the ridge, for the reason that there is then a larger amount of the ore above drainage level, where it can be much more easily and cheaply mined. It is also probable that, at a certain depth below the drainage level, the soft fossiliferous ore becomes hard, calcareous, and poor in iron; in other words, that it approaches the condition of the original limestone, and is no longer profitable to work in the furnace. This opinion is not founded upon observations in this immediate region, for mining has not yet been carried deep enough to ascertain the fact; but it is based upon reports of mining operations upon the same ores at other and widely separated places. When the ore occurs in the Poor Valley Ridge, it dips nearly with the slope of the ridge on the mountain side, so that there is a large amount of it at a uniformly small depth below the surface; while, when it is in the mountain, it dips directly back from the surface; and even if it does not change its character, and become lean, it will soon be difficult and expensive to mine.

*Republished from Part V. of Vol. IV., second series of Geological Survey of Kentucky.—N. S. Shaler, Director.

*The sections referred to are on a supplement to the April No. of THE VIRGINIAS.

It will be seen from the accompanying sections, that the distance between the upper and middle ores varies from seventy to one hundred and five feet. The distance between the middle and lower ores is from two hundred to two hundred and fifteen feet.

The upper ore is the most valuable of the three in this region. It is soft, very fossiliferous, and much richer in iron than the middle ore, although it is not nearly so thick. It has been seen by the writer varying from fifteen to twenty-two inches in thickness, and is reported on good authority at one place, where a full measurement could not be obtained at the time of visit, to be twenty-six inches thick. It is the only ore that has been worked in the furnace at Cumberland Gap. There is such an abundance of it in the neighborhood, and it is won so cheaply, that there has been no inducement to attempt to utilize the middle ore, which is both thicker and leaner than the upper. It is hard, silicious, and not very fossiliferous. It has been seen by the writer twenty-seven inches thick, and is reported, at other places, to be thirty inches. It seems to have been originally a silicious limestone, which is now impregnated with iron. It apparently corresponds to the "hard ore" of this same period in Pennsylvania, while the upper ore seems to be the counter-part of the "soft ore" of the same State.

At Speedwell Furnace, about twenty miles below Cumberland Gap, the middle or hard ore has been used in considerable quantities to mix with the soft ore, a purpose for which it is well adapted. This is the way in which the two ores can be profitably utilized. The hard ore, although richer and more valuable than is now commonly supposed by iron-makers in that region, is yet too silicious to work easily in the blast furnace alone. Mixed with the soft ore, however, it can be used with very good results.

Owing to its greater thickness, there is a larger quantity of this ore in a given area than of the upper ore, although its specific gravity is not so great.

The lower ore, which occurs about two hundred feet below the middle, is but little known, and never, to the knowledge of the writer, has been mined in this region. In quality it very much resembles the soft upper ore; so much so, that specimens of it can scarcely be distinguished from the upper ore. It is, however, thin, not having been seen by the writer more than six or seven inches in thickness. Where this ore occurs in the mountain proper, and dips away from the surface, it will be of little value, as it is too thin to be profitably mined at present under such circumstances; but where, as shown in the lowest section of the accompanying plate, it lies near the surface of the ridge for a considerable distance, it can be worked at very reasonable rates, and a large amount of ore be obtained; as, with a thickness of from six to seven inches, each square yard covered by the ore will yield nearly half a ton.

The lowest section of the accompanying plate shows the position of the ores in the Poor Valley Ridge, at Cumberland Gap, just below the Tazewell road. It will be seen that both the lower and the upper ores lie here in the most favorable position possible for easy and cheap mining, as they are both near the surface, and only covered by a slight thickness ot overlying material. The upper ore has been mined for the furnace at the Gap, beginning down in the valley and working upwards towards the crest of the hill, throwing the earth behind as each successive bench of ore is raised. In this way the pits or benches are easily drained. The cost of mining the ore here is only fifty cents per ton.

This fortunate position of the ores in the ridge is continued for several miles below Cumberland Gap, interrupted occasionally by changes in the topography, where longer spurs than usual put out from the mountain, between streams, but returning again to their position on the ridge as soon as these are passed.

The section just referred to shows the slope of the ridge on which the ore lies to be about six hundred feet in width. At places below, on the ridge, it will exceed this measurement by nearly one half. It will, therefore, be safe to estimate the breadth above drainage of the ore stratum running along this slope of the Poor Valley Ridge at six hundred feet, or two hundred yards. The ore varies in thickness from fifteen to twenty-four inches, and it is probably under rather than over the average for this region to place it at eighteen inches; but

in the following estimate of the quantity of ore in this ridge it is essential to keep within limits of safety. The ore has, according to the determination by Mr. Talbutt of two samples, a specific gravity of 3.94 and 3.91. Assuming a specific gravity of 3.9, a thickness of eighteen inches, and a breadth of ore belt of six hundred feet, there will be present, for each mile of the ridge holding the ore in this position, 538,319 gross tons. This estimate is, however, too great, in that it assumes the ore stratum and the suface of the ridge to be continuous, unbroken by ravines, gullies, and streams. No accurate estimate of the amount lost in this way can be made without a detailed contour map; but it is believed that one fourth will be more than ample to cover it. Deducting one fourth as lost in this way, we still have 403,740 tons of ore present per mile of the ridge. This estimate is made exclusive of any ore below drainage at the foot of the mountain proper, for the reason that it as yet uncertain to what depth the ore will be found soft and rich; and it will be a long time before there is any demand upon it in this position. It is simply desired to show how vast an amount of excellent and easily obtainable ore there is lying almost at the surface.

Where the belt of the ore is two hundred yards in width, there will be in the same ridge above drainage one hundred and fifty yards in width of the middle or hard ore. This, with a specific gravity of 3.1, and an average thickness of twenty-seven inches, will contain for each mile of the ridge 462,404 gross tons of ore. Deducting one-fourth, the same proportion as in the former case, for ore lost by ravines, streams, &c., and there remain 349,303 gross tons per mile. The estimate of one-fourth loss in this case is much larger than in the other, as the ore lies so deep that it is not reached by many ravines, which have cut the upper ore.

It is impossible to give accurate estimates of the quantity of available ore above drainage, where it does not lie in this favorable position on the Poor Valley Ridge, without a most minute study along the whole outcrop of the ore, and a contour line map showing its elevations at different points, as it varies for every mile of the distance, running out on the ridge when that is high enough to hold it, and again setting back at the base of the mountain as the ridge falls way in height.

Prof. H. D. Rogers, in Volume I, of the Geological Reports of Pennsylvania, in giving an estimate of the quantity of ore of this kind, eighteen inches thick, present in the region around Danville and Bloomsburg, Pennsylvania, places it at fifty thousand tons for each running mile of outerop. This is based upon the assumption that the soft ore will not be found of more than an average depth of thirty yards, ere it changes to hard, lean ore, which cannot be profitably mined. This assumption does not, however, prove true in every case, as Prof. J. P. Lesley states that mining operations at Bedford, Pennsylvania, have yielded the ore in perfect condition, at a depth of several hundred feet below the outcrop. It is probably safe to assume that the amount of available soft ore will average two hundred thousand tons, per mile, for the whole distance, and at many localities will much exceed this, as it grows thicker further up the valley.

About eighteen miles above Cumberland Gap, above where Martin's Creek cuts through the Poor Valley Ridge, an exposure was seen, which showed the ore, slightly tumbled and broken, as follows:

Hard silicious ore	10	inches
Good ore, somewhat broken	21	"
Solid ore	21	"
Total	52	"

The position of the ore at this point was such that it is barely possible there may have been a repetition in the measurement as it lay on a hill-side in a considerably disturbed position. It is not believed that such is the case, however, for it was examined very carefully. A single block of ore was seen lying near, twenty-seven inches in thickness.

At lower Pennington's Gap, the ore was found standing nearly vertical (dip 80°) in the Poor Valley Ridge, and thirty-five inches in thickness. It is commonly spoken of in this region as three feet thick, and probably does reach that thickness at many places. The ore at this point is unusually coarse in structure, being formed of large rounded globules, and containing numbers of small quartz pebbles. It is difficult to account for the presence of these in the ore on the commonly received theory of its formation by replacement of limestone.

At many other places between the above mentioned points

the ore has been seen, but it was usually only in loose out-crop, not in position where its thickness could be measured. It was seen often enough, however, to prove that it extends with great persistency all along the valley, although it may vary in thickness.

The quantity of ore, per mile, increases by many tons for each additional inch of thickness of the ore bed, so that when the above noticed increase in thickness is considered, it will be seen that the estimate of the amount of ore is considerably under, rather than over, the probabilities.

Where the middle or hard ore is present, it is safe to estimate an amount of it above drainage, for each mile, fully equal to, or greater than the soft ore. It should be distinctly remembered, however, that these last estimates are mere approximations, and are not based upon sufficient data to render them worthy the credit due to the first estimates, which were founded upon more detailed observation.

Quality of the Ore.—The soft ore is of excellent quality, producing about fifty per cent. of iron, and working easily in the furnace. The hard ore is more silicious and poorer in iron, and will probably require admixture with the soft ore to enable it to be smelted successfully. The quality of three samples of ore, from the immediate vicinity of Cumberland Gap, is shown by the following analyses by Dr. Peter and Mr. Talbutt, from samples collected by the writer:

	1	2	3
Iron peroxide.............................	72.905	77.880	47.905
Alumina...................................	8.776	3.941	9.120
Lime carbonate............................	4.510	.490	1.290
Magnesia..................................	.305	......	.194
Phosphoric acid...........................	.319	.319	.075
Sulphuric acid............................	......	......	trace.
Silica and insoluble silicates............	11.796	12.980	42.490
Combined water............................	5.886	2.505	4.000
Total...................................	100.596	100.920	99.784
Metallic iron.............................	51.734	54.166	39.575
Phosphorus................................	.140	.140	.561
Specific gravity..........................	3.914	3.945	3.190

No. 1 is the upper or soft ore from the valley near the Virginia road, a short distance above Cumberland Gap.—No. 2 is the same ore from the ridge below Cumberland Gap.—No. 3 is the middle or hard ore from the ridge near the same place as last noted.

The above analyses show in all the samples a workable percentage of iron. The amount of phosphorus present is decidedly less than is usually characteristic of the ore at other places. As a rule in other States, this ore is decidedly phosphatic, and produces a cold-short iron; but it proves to be exceptionally pure in this vicinity.

For comparison, there is herewith appended the following analysis of the hard ore of the same geological period from Dysart's mine, Huntingdon county, Pennsylvania, by Prof. Persifor Frazer, Jr., of the University of Pennsylvania:

Sesquioxide of iron...	38.44
Protoxide of iron.....	4.27
Silica................	37.99
Alumina...............	9.26
Lime..................	2.66
Magnesia............a trace.	
Alkalies..............	2.34
Phosphoric acid.......	1.44
Sulphur...............	.05
Loss by ignition......	4.70
Total.................	100.54
Metallic iron.........	30.54

It will be seen that it is very similar in constitution to No. 3 of the analyses just before given, except that it contains a larger proportion of alumina and phosphorus.

There is also herewith given an analysis, by Dr. Peter and Mr. Talbutt, of the pig iron made at the Cumberland Gap Furnace from the soft ore of the upper bed. It is a cold-blast charcoal iron, of excellent quality and great strength. It is used for car-wheel purposes.

Analysis of cold-blast, charcoal pig iron, Cumberland Gap Furnace:

Iron..................	92.895
Graphitic carbon.....	3.950
Combined carbon......	.340
Silicon..............	1.058
Slag.................	.480
Manganese............	.162
Aluminum.............	.700
Calcium..............	.112
Magnesium............	.070
Phosphorus...........	.148
Sulphur..............	.088
Total...............	100.590

This iron is hauled to Powell's River and boated down to market at Chattanooga at times of high water. It is manufactured very cheaply at the furnace; but the expense, risk, and uncertainty of the transporation to market, greatly reduce the profits on its manufacture, and leave only a narrow margin at present prices for iron.

The cheapness with which iron can be manufactured at this place will be realized when it is understood that the ore is de-livered at the furnace throat for one dollar per ton, thus costing only two dollars to the ton of iron for the ore.

Furnaces lower down in Tennessee and in Alabama, smelting ore of this kind with coal or coke, produce iron at as low or lower prices than in any other part of this country. It is stated, on very competent evidence, that the Roan Iron Furnaces of Rockwood, Tennessee, make iron for less than fifteen dollars per ton.

With a railroad from the central part of the State through the mountain at Cumberland Gap, so that the Kentucky coal can be used with this ore, this locality can produce iron as cheaply as any other point in this highly favored valley, and can place it in market at lower rates—It is destined to be one of the great iron-manufacturing regions of the country, and only awaits facilities for the transportation of its product to inaugurate a wonderful development of its resources in this direction.

Copper, etc.—Continued from Page 77.

On these properties, prospecting shafts have been opened, from which ores of different qualities were obtained. At Peach Bottom Creek, the ruins of the old Pine Hope Forge and Furnace are still to be seen, where, 60 years ago, the iron ores of this vicinity were converted into metal, but meeting with the same ill-success as at other places wherever this cupriferous gossan has been used, it was ultimately abandoned. Some of the gossan broken open at this place, contained beautiful crystals of carbonate of copper.

Passing thence N. 54° E., no opening has been made on the lead until the Whitmore mine is reached, 6 miles southeast of Hillsville, where it crosses the Volunteer Road. The rock strata here consists of talcose and mica slates, with imbedded garnets. The gossan lead is an important one, cropping out on the north-east declivity of a steep ridge. To these slates succeeds a heavy stratum of hornblenic slate, in which a vein of quartz and manganese is to be found, south of which comes another stratum of trappean rock, very compact, almost vertical, and fracturing into rhomboidal blocks.

Passing thence along the lead, there are no other developments in Carroll, though here and there the gossan indications are found well displayed.

Passing thence into Floyd county, we find the lead opened at the Hylton, Nowlin, Weddle, Bear Bed and Toncrey mines.

The *Hylton mine* is about 10 miles south of Jacksonville. It has been but recently opened, and so far presents a fair showing for ore.

The other properties just mentioned belong to the *Meigs County, Tennessee, & Virginia Mining Company.* They embrace an area of 1,000 acres, extending along the lead about three miles.

Beginning with the *Toncrey mine*, although the most northern, we first notice the old and neglected iron furnace. Erected 70 years ago, as the Shelor Furnace, it was continued in blast until within a few years past. The copper contained in the gossan, rendered the iron unfit for ordinary purposes, and it was abandoned. This furnace is driven by the waters of the West Fork of Little River, which affords abundant power at all seasons. The establishment is in good order, and, for a sum not exceeding $500, could be easily converted into a copper smelting furnace, as scarcely anything is to be done but to reconstruct the furnace, the blast and other machinery being in good condition. I have learned that a mason, who has been engaged at Ducktown in such work, offers to put the establishment in perfect order for that sum. Here are all the necessary ore floors, coal houses, blacksmith shops, &c., so that with this small outlay these mines can be stimulated to their full extent in keeping it in operation. I am confident that these mines are capable at once of keeping two blast furnaces in constant operation, reducing each 10 ton per day. From the Toncrey mine, it is down grade to the furnace, distant one-fourth of a mile.

The *Toncrey mine* is six miles south-east of Jacksonville. Work was begun upon it in 1854, though nothing has been done towards excavating the ores for shipment, the work being mainly directed towards opening the mine. This has been effectually done. There is an immense outcropping of gossan on the surface of the ridge, which led to its use for the iron works, the depth of the iron ore reaching 30 feet. A shaft which has been sunk through it, reaches the copper vein only 2 feet beneath it—that is at a depth of 32 feet below the surface. This gossan outcrop is 60 feet wide, and serves to indicate great width in the copper vein, which, on running in the tunnels, was found to be the case.

There are two tunnels driven in upon the vein, situated upon the declivity of the ridge. The upper tunnel is driven in from the north side S. 40° E., so as to cross the lead, which has a course N. 54° E. This tunnel reaches 245 feet, through a hard gneiss rock with quartz veins. Through the crevices of the quartz, there are found small clusters of native copper. The main object had in view in excavating this tunnel was to obtain a drift for the upper

gallery, expecting too, that it would intersect the vein at a lower depth.

The upper tunnel is situated about 70 feet above the lower, and has been driven in through gossan and vein rock to a depth of 300 feet. When this upper tunnel was first opened, it was injudiciously driven in too far to the left of the vein, but in carrying in a cross-cut to the right, about 40 feet from the entrance, the vein was reached at a distance of only 20 feet. It was then followed for 250 feet, through a soft talco-mica slate, several cross-cuts being run off to the right and left, so as to test the width of the vein. Throughout this whole length, the vein is traced without any intermission—increasing in richness and width as the depth descends. The cross-cuts and the tunnels, driven in parallel to the main drift, expose the vein in a most beautiful manner—the intervening partitions, which have never yet been stoped out, consisting of solid banks of ore, in all its varieties, but mostly the oxides and black sulphuret. As only 32 tons of ore have been shipped from this mine since it was first opened, and as the ores exist in such rich abundance all along its walls and roofs, it may be readily inferred that the company had but one object in view—to open their mine to its fullest extent before raising their ores. Consequently, they have been content to drive a tunnel of 6 feet width through a 30 foot vein, only bringing out such ore as they had necessarily to excavate in driving forward the tunnel. Thus they have exposed sometimes the centre of the vein; then by a cross-cut, they have run to its northern side; then by another, to the southern: and from each of these branches carrying along tunnels parallel with the main trunk. They have thus exposed this vein for 300 feet, proving it to be one of great depth, with a width of 30 feet, the dip being to the S. E., at an angle of 45 degrees. The average per cent. of the ores raised is found to be 16. As soon as the lower tunnel is completed, and has effectually drained the upper, there will be no limit to the ores which may be excavated from its tunnels and chambers. In many of the mines these chambers are already formed by the continual raising of ores; here, however, the intervening partitions between the tunnels yet remain, and will afford, by stoping, an incalculable supply of rich ore. Leaving out of consideration the worthless tunnels run in upon the side of the hill, and only estimating those which have led to the vein, there is a drivage in levels of about 500 feet, into which three shafts are sunk, so as to ventilate the mines perfectly.

Capt. Hanley regards this as being a cross vein, the main lead being to the south of it across the ridge. If so, it adds not only to the interest of this region, but to its value and permanence.

The *Nowlin mine* is situated about two miles to the S. E. of the Toncrey, "across the ridge," which is composed of a hard hornblendic rock. On it a shaft and tunnel have both been opened, the shaft being 60 feet deep and the tunnel 50 feet in length. The width of the mineral lode is estimated to be 60 feet, from which ores of good quality were raised. The gossan outcrop is still found to be large, and lies adjacent to a massive quartz lead. I obtained at this mine some fine, large specimens of magnetic oxide of iron.

The *Weddle mine* is opened three-fourths of a mile south of the Nowlin, being about three miles from the Toncrey, and ten miles from Jacksonville. From a shaft, 68 feet deep, and passing 30 feet through the gossan, ores of good quality, consisting of carbonates, oxides and smut ores, had been obtained, lying between walls of gneiss and mica slate. As it has been several years since work was carried on at this mine, I had no opportunity of examining anything beyond the rock to be found around the shaft. There are substantial buildings erected for ore floors and whims, and laborers' houses, and the shaft is well-timbered. The country is not so favorable for mining as it is either at Toncrey or Nowlin, being more level, and consequently not admitting of tunneling, unless at great expense.

The surface indications are very good, consisting of quartz and gossan.

To the north-east of these mines is the *Bear bed* of Capt. Hanley, which I propose to designate as the *Laurel mine*. On a prospecting jaunt, Capt. Hanley crept in underneath the thickly clustered laurel branches, through which the rays of the sun could scarcely penetrate, and found a bear bed, freshly made, and near to it a fine outcropping of gossan. The denseness of the laurel bushes has not admitted of any farther examination into the lead, but there is every reason to believe that it is the same with those just described, being to the N. E. of the Toncrey mine.

Continuing the examination of this lead N. 54° E. from this interesting locality, it may be traced till it crosses the Blue Ridge into Franklin county, being immediately south of the soapstone stratum. Just as it passes into Franklin county, Mr. Howell, of Jacksonville, has opened the lead, sinking a shaft about 40 feet through gossan and mica slate, and running in a tunnel some 200 feet on the side of the ridge, with fine prospects for a valuable lode of ore. This gossan, like that at Toncrey and elsewhere on this

lead, is highly impregnated with carbonate of copper The heavy outcrops of gossan existing here had led to their use, in former years, for supplying an iron furnace and forge in their vicinity; but the same objection being had to the metal, that it would not weld, caused them to be abandoned.

[*To be continued.*]

The Richmond and Southwestern Railway Company was incorporated by the Legislature February 2d, 1880; it has also been incorporated by the Legislature of Kentucky. The corporators named in the "Act" are:—Wm. Amory, Jr., Walter M. Sweet, Parker C. Chandler, Wm. Frazier, Francis H. Manning, Otis Kimball, and Edward C. Ellis; these are also the first board of directors. The annual meeting of the Company may be held at Washington City or elsewhere. This company is authorized to build a railway "from any point they may select at or near Pound Gap, or Cumberland Gap, on the southwestern boundary of the State of Kentucky, passing through the counties of Tazewell, Bland, Giles and Craig by the city of Richmond to such point as may be selected by said Company at tidewater in said State of Virginia," provided it does not interfere with the franchises or privileges of the James River & Kanawha Canal Company, or the Buchanan & Clifton Forge Railway Company.—It is authorized to connect or consolidate with other roads, and other roads connecting with it may subscribe as much as a million dollars to its stock; to borrow money at 7 per cent. or less, to mortgage its property, etc. It may receive property of any kind in payment for subscriptions to its stock; mining and manufacturing companies may subscribe thereto, It may acquire title to and hold, manage, mortgage, sell, etc., real estate to any extent, the same as a natural person, only it must dispose of all such (except what railways may hold in Virginia) within 30 years from the completion of its road. It may also construct branch roads from its main line, not over 25 miles long, and may extend its road into other States, under the authority of those States.

The railway company thus clothed with unusual powers,—but not greater than are necessary for a company to have that must look largely to the development of the regions it traverses for remuneration for its outlays,—we have good reasons for believing has already secured a deep-water terminus at Gloucester Point, opposite Yorktown and on the same noble harbor, and that, sustained by Boston capital, it contemplates the immediate construction of a double track, narrow gauge railway from that point up the Gloucester Peninsula to West Point, thence to Richmond, and thence by an air-line to Lynchburg, from which it will cross the Blue Ridge, probably by way of the Peak's Gap, into Botetourt and then through Craig, Giles, Bland, Tazewell and Russell counties, and on to Pound or Cumberland gap, and thence, by the shortest route, across Kentucky to near the mouth of the Ohio.—This line will cross every grand division of Virginia and every one of its geological formations. To catalogue the economic resources of the region it will traverse would fill an issue of THE VIRGINIAS; and yet we may have that to do, in the interest of development, at no distant day.

The Washington and Virginia Mining Co. has leased the David Combs farm, Stafford Co., Va., on which is a deposit of magnetic iron ore. This is on the head waters of Aquia Cr., 2 ms. below Tackett's Mill and 12 above tide-head This is on the eastern iron ore belt of the Archæan region of Virginia. As analysed by the chemist of Schoenberger, Blair & Co., of Pittsburg, Pa., its composition is 2.31 per cent. silicic acid, 0.003 phosphorus, 62.73 metallic iron, and about 10 per cent. of titanic acid.—The lessees believe this will prove a good ore for "fix," or "fettling," ores which now command $16. per ton at Pittsburg. We had something to say about the Virginia titanic ores last month.

This is on the *Quiyough* (of which Aquia is but a corruption) Creek of Capt. John Smith of famous memory, and it may be is. the very mine he went to see in his remarkable voyage of discovery in 1608, when, having rowed up the Quiyough as far as he could go in his "bote," "he marched 7 or 8 myle before they came to the mine," which he describes as "a great Rocky mountaine like Antimony; wherein they (the Indians) digged a great hole with shells and hatchets; and hard by it, runneth a fayre brooke of christal-like water, where they wash away the drosse and keepe the remainder, which they put up in little baggs and sell it all over the country to paint there bodyes, faces, or Idolls; which makes them look like Blackmoores dusted over with silver."—Newport had told him this stuff was half silver, but his description is that of micaceous ore, the basis of the fashionable spangled paints of our day. May it prove silver to the iron-workers is our wish.

Iron-making in Virginia in 1732.

By Col. WM. BYRD, F. R. S., of WESTOVER.

CONTINUED FROM PAGE 60.

The way of raising the oar was by blowing it up, which Operation I saw here from beginning to End. They first drill'd a hole in the Mine, either upright or Sloping, as the grain of it required. This hole they cleansed with a Rag fasten'd to the End of an Iron with a Worm at the end of it. Then they put in a Cartridge of Powder containing about 3 Ounces, and at the same time a Reed full of fuse that reacht to the Powder. Then they ramm'd dry Clay, or soft Stone very hard into the Hole, and lastly they fired the fuse with a Paper that had been dipt in a Solution of Saltpetre and dry'd, which burning Slow and Sure, gave leizure to the Engineer to retire to a proper distance before the Explosion. This in the Miner's Language is call'd making a Blast, which will loosen several hundred Weight of Oar at once; and afterwards the Laborers easily separate it with Pick-axes and carry it away in Baskets up to the Heap. At our return we saw near the Furnace large Heaps of Mine with Charcoal mixet with it, a Stratum of each alternately, beginning first with a layer of Charcoal at the Bottom. To this they put Fire, which in a little time spreads thro' the whole Heap, and calcines the Oar, which afterwards easily crumbles into small pieces fit for the Furnace. There was likewise a mighty Quantity of Limestone, brought from Bristol, by way of ballast, at 2s 6 a Tun, which they are at the Trouble to Cart hither from Rappahannock River, but contrive to do it when the Carts return from carrying of Iron. They put this into the Furnace with the Iron Oare, in the proportion of one Tun of Stone to ten of Oar, with design to absorb the Sulphur out of the Iron, which wou'd otherwise make it brittle. And if that be the use of it, Oyster Shells wou'd certainly do as well as LimeStone, being altogether as strong an Alkali, if not Stronger. Nor can their being taken out of Salt water be any Objection, because tis pretty certain the West India LimeStone, which is thrown up by the Sea, is even better than that imported from Bristol. But the founders who never try'd either of these will by no means be perswaded to go out of their way, tho' the Reason of the thing be never so evident. I observ'd the richer Sort of Mine, being of a dark

Colour Mixt with rust, was laid in a heap by itself, and so was the poor, which was of a Liver or Brick Colour. The Sow Iron is in the Figure of a half-round, about two feet and a half long, weighing 60 or 70 Pounds, whereof 3000 weight make a Cart-load drawn by 8 Oxen, which are commonly shod to save their Hoofs in those Stony ways. When the Furnace blows, it runs about 20 Tuns of Iron a Week. The founders find it very hot work to tend the Furnace, especially in Summer, and are oblig'd to spend no small part of their Earnings in strong Drink to recruit their Spirits. Besides the Founder, the Collier, and Miner, who are paid in proportion to their Work, the Company have several other Officers upon Wages, a Stock-taker, who weighs and measures every thing, a Clerk, who keeps an Account of all Receipts and Disbursements, a Smith to Shoe their Cattle, and keep all their Iron work in repair, a wheel-Wright, Cartwright, Carpenter, and Several Carters. The Wages of all these persons amount to one Hundred Pounds a Year; so that including Mr. Chiswell's Salary, they disdurse 200£ p. Annum in standing Wages. The Provisions too are a heavy Article, which their Plantations dont yet produce in a Sufficient Quantity, tho' they are at the Charge of general Overseer. But while Corn is so short with them, there can be no great Increase of Stock of any kind.

"Having now pretty well exhausted the Subject of Sow Iron, I askt my Friend some Questions about Bar-Iron. He told me we had as yet no Forge erected in Virginia, tho' we had 4 Furnaces. But there was a very good one set up at the head of the Bay in Maryland, that made exceeding good work. He let me know that the duty in England upon Bar Iron was 24s a Tun, and that it sold there from Ten to 16 pounds a Tun. This wou'd pay the Charge of Forging abundantly, but he doubted the Parliament of England would soon forbid us that Improvement, lest after that we shou'd go farther, and manufacture Our Bars into all Sorts of Iron Ware, as they already do in New England & Pennsylvania. Nay, he question'd whether we shou'd be suffer'd to cast any Iron, which they can do themselves at their Furnaces. Thus Ended our Conversation, and I thankt my friend for being so free in communicating everything to me. Then, after tipping a Pistole to the Clerk, to drink prosperity to the Mines with all the Workmen, I accepted the kind offer of going part of my journey in the Phaeton."

Manufacturing.—A. M. Hamilton & Co. are putting in order a paint mill in Harrisonburg, Va., to prepare for market the Massanutton Mineral Paints, noticed in our March issue——The Harrisonburg Tannery of Houck & Wallis, is turning out 800 sides of leather weekly. The superior Virginia tanning materials at their command enable them to make a class of leather that is much sought after by Eastern manufacturers.——The *Times* says that two Northern men are looking at the Danville water-power as a good place for a silk factory, working 200 hands.——The Fredericksburg Woolen Mill has been rented by Kern, Bently & Co., of Winchester, The property will be improved and put in operation by May 1st.—*Star*.——A new shoe factory is going into operation at Charlottesville, Va.—*Jeffersonian*.

Kaolin.—A large deposit of white clay has been opened on the land of Carter Shepherd, on the Shenandoah, in Clarke county, Virginia, in a large hill in which there are beds of iron ore. This is the fire-clay that results from the waste of the hydro-mica slates of Formation I, as stated in our April number.—*Courier*.

Petroleum.—Another oil well has been opened in Wood Co., W. Va.

Virginia Gold.—The Rappahannock mine has a 100-horse-power boiler.——The Chicago-Virginia mines have a 60-horse-power boiler on the way from Chicago, and a 10-stamp mill under construction at Fredericksburg.——The four companies now operating in The Wilderness region are managed by careful men who are persuaded that gold-mining here can be made to pay.——The gold washings at the Alley-Cooper mine are now paying well.——The Mansfield-McGehee mine is not worked at this time, but the rich "pickings" at its placers are much visited by depredators.——Report says the Walton mine is soon to be worked.—Near Tolersville, on the Chesapeake & Ohio Railway, a new gold mine has been discovered, and a stamp mill is already at work there.——Miners from California, Utah, the North and Northwest, are now prospecting the Virginia gold fields.—*Louisa News*.——The gold diggers on the John Walters farm, Brush Creek, Montgomery county, Virginia, have struck placers that pan out $2.00 to the cubic yard. the particles of gold become larger and more numerous as they go up the creek.—*Montgomery Messenger*.——The Chicago-Virginia Gold Mining Company at Mine Run, Orange county, have just completed several cabins for their miners, a substantial office and house, and placed a new shaft-house over the shaft from which they are raising ore from the large fourteen-foot vein, which is perfectly defined at their sixty-foot level This company have purchased their engine and boiler, and they are now *en route* to the mine. Mr. Bowering, whose extensive experience in building machinery for the mines in this section, is too well known to make more than simple mention, is now erecting and building the stamp-mill for this company. The enterprise shown by this company is worthy of the Garden City; and the fine showing in the drift and cross-cuts, is a guarantee that the company have an inexhaustible supply of rich ore. The President of the company is Mr. Floyd B. Wilson, an enterprising attorney of Chicago.——The Pocahontas Gold Mining company, of Andrews, Spotsylvania county, is another Chicago enterprise The development on this mine will rank among the very first in the State. The placer workings comprise some 150 acres, which are being worked by sluicing in several sets of boxes with water supplied by a large steam pump. One rich vein has been crossed by the tunnel, and a large vein located and prospected to some depth above this tunnel——At the Randolph Mine, Mr. E. L. Doyle, has recently located a gold-bearing vein of a very promising character, and will at once sink a shaft. He has also resumed operations upon what is known as the Trigg property, and we are glad to learn that the prospect for a handsome yield of gold is quite encouraging. Already a shaft has been sunk 40 feet, which will be carried much deeper, and a cross-cut formed.——It is very gratifying to learn that the gold-mining interest in this section is on the increase, and that those who are operating the various mines are greatly encouraged.—*Star*, Ap. 24

Copper.—The mine near Tolersville is to be worked again. Sulphur works are being erected by Mr. Hummer, who will use the excellent pyrites that are so very abundant at the "Copper," the "Jenkins-Controy" and the "Victoria Furnace" mines in Louisa Co., Va.——The Ore Knob, N. C. Copper mine has 500 men on its pay roll. The daily capacity of its mines is 7,200 lbs. of copper. Its depot is Marion, Va., on the A. M & O., 40 miles distant.——The Blue Ridge Mining Company, the principal stockholders of which are Gen. John E. Mulford, Wm. Duryea and James F. Preston, of New York city, and Rev. Thos Heywood, of Elizabeth, N. J., is, we are pleased to learn from J. E. Fletcher, of Stanardsville, Va., about to resume operations at its valuable copper mines, on the spurs of the Blue Ridge, near the head of Conway River, Greene County, Va. In 1877 this company, under the superintendence of R. M. Eames, M. E., expended considerable money in developing three veins of copper on property it had purchased and leased; but since that time no work has been done.——A fine vein of copper ore has been discovered near Alleghany Springs, Montgomery county, Va. *Messenger*.

Recent Sales of Farming Lands.—On Shenandoah River, Rockingham Co., 347 A at $3.50 per A., and 123 A. for $974,77.—*Old Commonwealth*.——In Roanoke Co. the R A. Brown farm, 282 A., to J S Peery of Tazewell Co., at $47.45 per A.

Manganese.—Veins have been discovered near Twyman's Store, Spotsylvania county, Virginia.——D. S. Forney, at Allisonia, Furnace, Pulaski county, Virginia, has found extensive deposits associated with his iron ores, the Primordial of the Blue Ridge.

Blast Furnaces.—It is rumored that two are soon to be erected at Buchanan, Botetourt Co., Va——Victoria Furnace, Louisa Co., Va., is to be put in blast soon.——The rolling mill above Lynchburg is now at work——The construction of a blast furnace in Lynchburg has been begun by the Lynchburg Iron, Steel & Mining Co, which now has a rolling mill and foundry in operation at Lynchburg and works mines on the James below that city.——Callie Furnace, Hileman, Cook & Co., Botetourt Co., Va., will probably go into blast about July 1st, says the *Fincastle Herald*.——The Capon Iron Furnace, Hardy Co., W. Va., is now in the hands of a Philadelphia Co. and machinery for putting it in working order is being made at Winchester, Va.—[*Times*, April 21.

Educational.—The Educational Association of Virginia will have its next annual meeting, the 15th, at Hollins Institute, Botetourt Springs, July 13-16, 1880. Twelve standing committees are appointed "to report upon any important reforms or novelties in text-books or methods that may seem to them worthy of attention," on twelve named studies; and twelve subjects are proposed for discussion, in papers or addresses. Among these subjects we note one that we hope to hear fully discussed; it is: "The new education, or education adapted to the new era."——The Educational Association of West Virginia will meet at Hinton, on the Chesapeake & Ohio Railway, July 6th, 1880, and continue in session for 3 days.

Recent Prices Obtained for Farms in Virginia.—In Warren county $11 25 and $12 per acre.—'Woodbury,' the old Hon. Hy St. Geo. Tucker farm, Berkeley county, W. Va., 357 acres and a fine, costly old mansion for $39.95 per acre.—The Wilson farm, Loudoun county, Va., 303 acres for $8.25 per acre.——An A. S. Dandridge farm, near Kearneysville, Jefferson county, W. Va., 250 acres for $30.25 per acre.——The John Whitmore farm on James River, Botetourt county, Va., 96 acres for $650.——The lists of deeds recorded monthly in the several counties of Virginia and West Virginia are now very long, showing that there is much activity in the real estate market.

The Condition of the Blast Furnaces of the Virginias, April 1st, 1880, as compiled for the *Iron Age*, is: In Virginia, 27 charcoal stacks of which 13 are in blast; 1 anthracite, not in blast; and 5 bituminous or coke, of which 2 are in blast;—In West Virginia, 6 charcoal stacks of which 2 are in blast; and 6 bituminous or coke, all of which are in blast. Totals;—In Virginia 33 of which 15 are in blast;—In West Virginia 12 of which 8 are in blast. These states have 33 of the 200 charcoal blast furnaces in the U. S. and 15 of the 102 in blast; they have 11 of the 206 bituminous or coke, and 8 of the 140 in blast.

Slate.—A good slate trade has been started between Buckingham county, Va., and the city of Nashville, Tennessee. The slate is brought here by the canal, and then transferred to the cars of the A. M. & O. R. R., by which route it is shipped. So far this week a hundred tons have been shipped to Nashville.—*Lynchburg Virginian, April 9th*.——Slate suitable for roofing and other purposes is reported to havebeen found on Jacob Minnick's land near Broadway, Rockingham county.

Attention is Invited to the Danville Water-power offered for sale in this issue. New iron mines are being opened, almost daily, within a moderate distance of this city and in a few months via. the Richmond & Alleghany Railway, it will have cheap transportation for coke from the New River coal-fields. We advise those contemplating the erection of iron-works where they can *always* make iron cheaply. to examine this property.—Ed.

Mica, in splendid blocks, has been found on the farm of W. D. Walker, near Green Spring, Cumberland county, Va.—*Mercury, April 7th*.

Lead.—There is a rich lead vein worked to some extent, at the Alley-Cooper gold mine, Louisa county, Virginia.

Plumbago has been discovered on the farm of Walker Blanton, Cumberland county, Va., says the *Farmville Mercury*.

Silver.—The excitement in the lower part of Preston Co., W Va., continues and there is a favorable yield of ore.

Silver.—The Silver vein at the Alley-Cooper mine is quite productive; a good quantity of ore has been raised.

The Virginias.

A Mining, Industrial and Scientific Journal:
Devoted to the Development of Virginia and West Virginia.

Vol. I, No. 6. }   Staunton, Virginia, June, 1880.   { Price 25 Cents.

The Virginias,

PUBLISHED MONTHLY,

By Jed. Hotchkiss, - - - Editor and Proprietor,

At 346 E. Main St., Staunton, Va.

Terms, including postage, per year, in advance, $2.00. Single numbers, 25 cents. Extra copies, $20.00 per 100. Back numbers, from the first, can be had at 25c each.

Advertising, per inch of length of single column (3 columns to a page, 56 on advertising pages), one month, $2.00; two months, $4.00; three months, $5.50; six months, $7.50; nine months, $10.00, and twelve months, $12.00; payable in advance.

Specimen Numbers of this journal are sometimes sent to parties supposed to have an interest in the development of the Virginias, or a desire to be informed in reference to their resources, improvement, etc.; they will please consider this an invitation to become subscribers and so help to sustain a paper devoted to their interests.

On sale at Hunt. r & Co.'s Bookstore, Main Street, Staunton, Virginia.

Mining Statistics of the Tenth Census of the U. S. in Virginia and West Virginia.—Having been appointed special agent for the preparation of the mining statistics of Virginia and West Virginia for the Tenth Census, I will be obliged to the owners or lessees of mines of every description—Coal, Iron, Manganese, Baryta, Lead, Zinc, Mica, etc., etc.,—in these States, if they will at once send me, on a postal card their addresses, and kind and location of mines, in full, that I may send them "special schedules of mining" to fill up, and may learn where to go and whom to seek when I start on my round of inspection and verification. I hope all the newspapers in the Virginias will give publicity to this notice, and more, that each one will prepare a complete list of all mines in the county where it is published, as a check on information otherwise derived, and send me two copies of same. I intend to do my best to make as full and complete an exhibit of the mining industries of these States as I can, and invite the co-operation of all concerned. I invite correspondence. Address

Jed. Hotchkiss,

Special Agent U. S. Census, Staunton, Va.

Attention is Invited to the New Advertisements.—*Ford's Hotel,* at Richmond, Virginia, as we know from years of experience, is a thoroughly well kept, comfortable and agreeable sojourning place, in one of the most pleasant parts of what, in our opinion, is one of the most attractive cities on the Atlantic slope of the United States. One of the geological sections given in this number shows the location of the Capitol, at Richmond, on the border of the granite terrace of the Midland plain, about 170 feet above the tide level of the James, which it overlooks; on the same level, facing the Capitol and its inviting park, is Ford's Hotel.—*The Chesapeake & Ohio Railway,* considered from our standpoint, was constructed for the especial benefit of the geologist and mining engineer; and, we may add, if it fills the measure of their requirements it will also fill that of most mortals. The colors on the Geological Map of the Virginias, on which the course of this railway and its Virginia connections is laid down, show that in the 430 miles of its line, from tide-end, at Richmond, on the James, to Huntington, on the Ohio, it traverses, where most of them have grand proportions, a dozen geological formations,—in fact its geological section is that of the American Continent, and the man that has not seen it has not seen the largest and best displayed one of that Continent. There is not a more invigorating and enjoyable ride to be had than one over this road; it crosses plains, valleys, mountains, and Piedmont lands, and runs through canyons, and its track is on all gradations of levels, between that of the sea and near 3,000 feet above it; and then, strung all along its pathway, there are dozens of health-giving fountains, in cool and breezy mountain valleys, where even midsummer is a delightsome season. We advise all that travel, or go from home for the summer, to try a trip to the mountains of the Virginias.——*The Mineral Lands* in Wythe county, Virginia, offered for sale, are in one of the best mineral districts in the Union, one where very desirable investments can be made. This property is sold to settle the affairs of an estate and will doubtless be sold cheap. Anyone that would buy it, and has not time to go and see it, can get Capt. C. R. Boyd, M. E., who lives near it, to give a reliable report on its value.—*Mr. Charles E. Dwight* is an Analytical Chemist of deserved high standing. He has done the chemical work of the Wheeling iron works for the past ten years, and refers to their proprietors in reference to the character of his professional work. He also made most of the analyses for the West Virginia Report of Maury & Fontaine and so is already familiar with the coals and iron and other ores of the Virginias.——*Washington and Lee University* offers the best of advantages for the acquirement of a collegiate education. It has distinct schools of Ancient and of Modern Languages, Moral Philosophy and Belles-Lettres, of Mathematics, Natural Philosophy, of Chemistry, Mineralogy and Geology, of Law and Equity, and of Engineering. The student elects his course of study from these, and may graduate in one or all, according to his requirements. It has a full and able corps of professors, all appliances for illustration that pertain to a first-class institution of its kind; an ancient and honorable record in its founders (including Washington) and its alumni of almost a century—for its charter dates from 1782; and, above all, a reputation for sound scholarship and good morals and manners. Lexington is in the heart of the Great Valley of Virginia, in sight of and surrounded by grand scenery, and has a finely tempered climate. We may add that the School of Geology, etc., is in charge of Prof. Campbell, whose able papers on Virginia geology are so familiar to our readers, and that no other professor of this important subject has such grand natural sections at hand to refer to.——*McCreary & Lowry* live in the coal and timber region of West Virginia and on the Chesapeake & Ohio Railway. They are competent and reliable gentlemen, and can direct to most profitable investments.——*The Residence and Grounds* in Staunton, offered by Messrs. Hudson & Patrick is what they state it to be in their advertisement. We do not know of as delightful a home for the money that this will be sold for. Staunton, with its four female colleges, its 1,500 feet above sea elevation, and its location in the wide, rolling, historic Valley of the Shenandoah, is a very desirable place of residence.——The *coal* and *timber lands* that Mr. Bristor has for sale are well known to us. We can endorse his statement that they are among the best (and that is saying a great deal), in the Kanawha coal and timber fields.

The Geological Map of Virginia and West Virginia, that accompanies this number of The Virginias, was constructed by Prof. Wm. B. Rogers, chiefly from data obtained from the Geological Survey of Virginia, which he, as State Geologist, so ably conducted from 1835 to 1841, and from his later observations. This graphic presentation of the outlines of the surface exposures of the principal groups of rock formations in the Virginias,—a work of wonderful fidelity to nature, embodying the results of years of labor by Prof. Rogers and his assistants, and representing the expenditure of large sums of money by Virginia,—was, gratuitously and with a noble generosity, furnished to the editor of this journal, in 1873, to accompany a Geographical and Political Summary of Virginia, that he had prepared for the Board of Immigration, and illustrate a chapter on the Geology of the State. It is *Rogers' Geological Map of the Virginias,* as it came from his own hand,—one that will forever remain a monument to his genius as one of the fathers, if not *the father,* of American Geology,—and the editor's only claim to it is that of ownership resulting from its copyright publication, and from the preparation of the topographical map on which it is based. This much by way of explanation, lest anyone should misunderstand the title to this map as it is printed. This map will be referred to in some future issues of The Virginias to illustrate some chapters on the geology of Virginia and West Virginia.

The Pittsburg-Virginias Excursion.—Wytheville, by her General Improvement Association, has moved with commendable spirit in arranging for an excursion of the iron and other business men of Pittsburg to see the mineral wealth of Virginia that can be reached by the Pittsburg Southern Railway. Whenever these gentlemen are ready to come, we are ready to see that they are hospitably received and arrangements made to show them the mineral wealth near the Chesapeake & Ohio Railway and in the Valley of the James, just as our Wytheville friends are ready to do the same thing for the Atlantic, Mississippi & Ohio country. Gentlemen of Pittsburg, when may we expect you?

The Geology of the Blue Ridge, etc., at James River Gap, Virginia.*

By J. L. Campbell, Washington and Lee University.

Among the many localities in the mountains of Virginia that are peculiarly interesting to the geologist, very few offer attractions superior to those found in the great natural section of the Blue Ridge at Balcony Falls, where the James River passes from The Valley to Piedmont Virginia. The canal from Lynchburg to Lexington passes through this mountain gorge, and renders the exposures of the rocky formations easily accessible. Here both the Archæan and Primordial formations are displayed in their relative positions, and their contact laid bare to inspection. Reference was made to this point in a former paper (July No. of Am. Journal, pp. 22, 23), by way of illustration. I now propose to discuss some of its interesting features more in detail.

Topography.—The accompanying map and section will serve to throw light upon both the topographical and the geological features of the locality. Leaving out of view a number of irregular footridges on the southeast side, we may regard the range of mountains here, known as the "Blue Ridge Range," to consist of (1) the real Blue Ridge on the southeast border—the long water-shed between the Valley and the Piedmont counties—between Rockbridge on the northwest and Amherst and Bedford on the southeast. Here and for some miles along its line both ways, this ridge is flanked by Archæan rocks on the southeast and Primordial rocks on the northwest—the latter resting unconformably upon the former.

Y-shaped lake, through which they seem to have flowed at some former period of their history.

The two rivers above mentioned, traverse the little valley obliquely, and meet at a very obtuse angle just where their waters, as one united stream, enter the deep gorge or canyon by which they pass through the mountain range. Just below their junction are mills for grinding hydraulic lime, burnt from the ledges that crop out a little higher up the James River. "Balcony Falls" is the name given to a succession of "rapids," beginning about half-a-mile below the Cement Mills, and continuing to the southeast limit of the gorge. The river here is 700 feet above tide level.

Geology.—The foregoing outline of the topography of the region will enable the reader to undestand more clearly its geological peculiarities, and to interpret more readily than he otherwise could, the ideal section accompanying the map.

Conceive a vertical plane with its edge resting on a line represented by the broken line of the map, marked "S. E.," and "N. W.," and having a height of 1,500 feet above the bed of the eroded rocks of the gorge, and all that the plane itself would cut (including those of Salling's Mountain), to be pictured on the plane, and you will have a mental conception of what the section is designed to represent.

The student of geology will find here a somewhat intricate, but a very interesting problem for solution. By a series of careful observations along the canal and bed of the river, and also by the turnpike that crosses the mountain near the canal, very satisfactory conclusions may be reached. In the gorge we have the rocks of

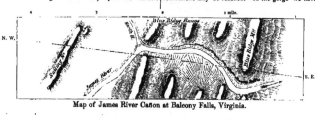

Map of James River Cañon at Balcony Falls, Virginia.

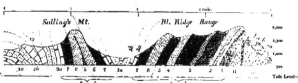

Section of Blue Ridge at Balcony Falls, James River, Virginia.

(2) Skirting the northwest side of this leading ridge, and parallel with it, are two well defined lines of broken ridges that have evidently been once continuous, but now consist of short, abruptly terminating mountains, of rounded dome-like hills, and of rugged conical peaks. These all have a frame-work of Primordial sandstones, with the less durable shales of the same period lying along their flanks or filling the depressions between them. Of these lines of ridges the one bordering on the great limestone Valley, heretofore described, (see July No.), is by far the most conspicuous, and the most uniform in its physical features. It consists essentially of the durable masses of the Upper Potsdam sandstones, so durable that many parts of it have maintained a height almost equal to that of the main ridge, the average height of which, in this region, somewhat exceeds 2,500 feet. The mean bearing of this portion of the range is about N. 35° E.

Salling's Mountain, seen on the left of the map, is an outlying ridge of Primordial sandstones and slates, cut off at its northeastern end by the North River, and at its southwestern end by James River. It is separated from the principal chain by a narrow synclinal valley of limestone (Lower Silurian), most of which is concealed from view by an extensive bed of *alluvium*, accumulated by the two rivers that meet here; but accumulated originally in a

two distinct eras so meeting as to enable us to study not only their composition and structure, but also their relative positions, and some of the metamorphic influences they have exerted upon one another. These two eras are, (1) the Archæan, represented on the accompanying section by the rocks on the right marked G, S, and 1 *a, b;* (2) a portion of the Lower Silurian covering the remainder of the section.

Let us begin at the base of the Archæan. Here we find two masses, or a sort of double mass, marked G. and S.—the former a mass of Granulite, and the latter of Syenite. These are usually regarded as igneous, or, perhaps with more propriety, aqueo-igneous rocks. They underlie the stratified rocks of this era; but, considered as solid rocky masses, they are probably of more recent date than any other rocks represented on the section—having been thrust upward beneath the over-lying stratified beds in a plastic (semi-fused) condition, and subsequently hardened into their present condition.

G. is "granulite" (So classed by Professor Dana, to whom a specimen was submitted.)—a granitoid rock, eruptive in its origin. It is composed of granular quartz mixed with feldspar, both white and pale flesh-colored; and has numerous crystals of garnet, and occasional crystals and blotches of epidote disseminated through it, giving it a spotted appearance. This is about 100 feet wide at the base, and seems to be separated from the larger mass of syenite (S.)

*From the American Journal of Science and Arts, Vol XVIII, Dec. 1879.—Revised for The VIRGINIAS by Prof. Campbell.

by a crushed and greatly metamorphosed bed of gneissoid rock, in which distinct traces of the original bedding can be seen. The syenite is well exposed from a short distance below the limit of the granulite, as far down the canal as to lock No. 15. It also forms a rugged bed for the river in this part of its course, and rises to the height of several hundred feet beneath the mountain on the opposite side. Syenite is a granitoid rock composed essentially of quartz, feldspar and hornblende, in varying proportions. Besides these constituents we find the mass at Balcony Falls containing, in some places, considerable quantities of epidote, both crystalline and amorphous, giving the rock a green color, and in others numerous crystals of garnet.

The bedded rocks (1 *a*, *b*,) that rest upon the syenite, are very much metamorphosed, are gneissoid in character, and dip toward the southeast. These are succeeded by beds of red and brown slates. Then follows a bed of forty or fifty feet of conglomorate quartzite, bearing some resemblance to the conglomerate sandstones on the opposite side of the ridge, but so unlike in composition, texture, position and thickness as to preclude the idea that they have any historical connection. Over this again we find another bed of slate. These beds all dip towards the southeast, while their upper margins reach beyond the underlying syenite and granulite, and with their edges support the lowest beds of Primordial rocks where they extend high up on the ridges, beyond the limit of the igneous beds. The two series here, and at other points along the ridge, are entirely unconformable. Such are the Archæan rocks.

Starting again on the northwest side of the granulite, let us briefly sketch the remarkable beds that make up the remainder of this massive range. In the Archæan rocks we have just described there are no traces of fossil remains, nor do we find any in the lowest beds or what we call Primordial. If organic remains have ever been imbedded in them here, they have either been obliterated or remain yet to be discovered.

Subdivisions.—On the section illustrating a former article (July No.), the classification of Professor Rogers in his reports was employed, and subdivisions of my own introduced. In a second article (August No.), the classification and notations of Professor Dana's Manual were introduced. (Professor Rogers himself has partially adopted this system in his article on the Geology of Virginia, in Macfarlane's Geol. R. R. Guide.) This latter system I shall employ in this paper—introducing subdivisions only in the Primal period, numbered, 1, 2, 3, etc.

The Primal or Potsdam period is often divided into Acadian and Potsdam epochs—2*a* and 2*b*—but as it is very doubtful whether both of these, as they occur farther north, have equivalents here, or if they have, where the horizon between them is to be found, I shall designate the whole period as 2*ab*, and its subdivisions 1, 2, 3, 4, etc. These will correspond with the subdivisions, 1*a*, 1*b*, 1*c*, etc., on my former section. As these were then regarded as only of secondary importance to my main object—the Silurian limestones—a very brief description of them was deemed sufficient ; but now they become of prime importance in our discussion, and demand a more full and detailed examination.

Without repeating in each case the notation, 2*ab*, the several subdivisions will be referred to by the simple numbers, 1, 2, 3, etc. All the beds of this period, with some local and limited exceptions, dip toward the northwest. The slight alternations and variations of dip are confined almost entirely to the thinner beds of sandstone, and the shales contiguous to them (especially in 3), and are limited apparently to points near the margin of the river. Variations in the steepness of dip in the heavy beds of sandstone as they rise toward the crests of the ridges, are, however, common throughout the whole range. The limited irregularities may, with much plausibility, be referred to the undermining action of the river; for there are abundant indications that the water once stood several hundred feet higher in this pass, and in the little valley west of its entrance, than the present height of the river bed.

Subdivision 1 is a bed of conglomerate about 50 feet thick, resting unconformably against the Archæan rocks, and composed of sand, rounded quartz pebbles, fragments and worn crystals of feldspar, with some fragments of epidote, all firmly cemented together, and hardened by the action of heat from the contiguous igneous rocks ; followed by several alternations of slates and conglomeritic sandstones, with an aggregate thickness of about 120 feet. This division has been considerably affected by heat throughout. Its position, too, has protected it against the erosive action of the river which has been far less here than it has been among the slates higher up in the series.

Number 2 is a heavy mass of sandstone fully 350 feet thick, and so hard that we may call it "quartzite." It consists of three tolerably distinct beds varying in hardness and color ; the lowest being very hard and of a light gray, sometimes pinkish color ; the middle one of coarser texture, partly conglomerate and mostly of a greenish gray color ; the upper bed is more brittle than either of

the other two, and of darker color. These heavy beds of hard sandstone seem to have presented one of the most durable barriers to the passage of the river through the mountain, and doubtless obstructed its flow to such an extent as to keep the water in contact with the higher beds for a period long enough to cause some modifications already mentioned, and others to be noticed hereafter. Before the canal was constructed the steep rugged outcrop of this massive ledge projected considerably over the left margin of the river, and was known as "Balcony Rock"—hence the name of the falls. For some little distance on the west side of this sandstone the river runs nearly with the strike of the strata, exposing in succession the rugged edges of the several beds.

Number 3 consists of two heavy beds of slates separated by a stratum of hard conglomeritic sandstone about 60 feet thick, and greenish gray in color. The slates are of brown, purple and yellow colors, with some thin beds of argillaceous sandstone interstratified. At this point the river has left some marked traces of its former action in eroding the softer, and undermining the harder strata. The most conspicuous irregularity has been caused by the undermining of the interstratified bed of sandstone just mentioned, so as to give it a low, and sometimes waving dip, and to cause a mass of it to slip from its normal position and modify both dip and strike, as seen just above the margin of the canal. This seems to me the only rational way of accounting for the anomalous position of this bed of sandstone at this point, compared with its position at several other points remote from the river. It also explains its want of conformity with the general structure of the whole Primal period, as exhibited all along this part of the Blue Ridge range. These local irregularities are not represented on the section.

It is a little difficult to determine, even approximately, the thickness of this double bed of slates with its enclosed sandstone, but the aggregate must be at least 600 feet.

Number 4 is not well defined below, since 3 becomes more and more siliceous and blends gradually into it; but the greater part of it is a bed of brownish gray sandstone with a well defined upper surface. It crosses the river at the Cement Mills, and its highest ledge forms the abutment of the dam on the opposite side of the river. Where a deep channel was washed out by a freshet a few years ago, this rock is well exposed on the lower margin of the turnpike, and its upturned edges may be conveniently examined. A considerable exposure of it also crops out above the turnpike between the houses of Messrs. Locker and Campbell, while the corresponding ledge may be seen on the cliff beyond the river. It has a very regularly jointed structure—the cleavage planes being so distinct as to have been mistaken by an unpracticed observer for planes of stratification dipping to the southeast, while the true planes of stratification dip with considerable uniformity and great constancy toward the N.W.

In this and some of the lower beds of sandstone, very faint impressions of fucoids and occasional Scolithus borings are found ; but the conglomerate structure is much less prominent here than in the older beds.

Number 5 is made up of numerous thin beds of slate quite different in color and texture from any that we find lower down. They exhibit, where recently exposed in repairing the canal, a great variety of color from nearly pure white kaolin to various shades of yellow, red and brown, and abound in fine scales of mica ; but no distinct traces of fossil remains have been found in them. In the portion near the river their dip varies from 25° to 50°. I estimate their thickness at 180 feet.

Number 6 is, in some respects, the most interesting of all the subdivisions of this Primal group. It is the sandstone that "constitutes the type of this formation." It differs from the beds already described in both its lithological and fossil peculiarities, (see July No., p. 22). It may well be called the "Scolithus sandstone," if we call the primal worms (?) that had their millions of habitations in this rock the "*Scolithus linearis.*"

Its entire thickness (including some quite brittle beds that underlie and overlie the more massive portion), is about 340 feet. The dip at the base of the ridge, where the two rivers meet at the entrance of the gorge, is fully 65°, while it falls gradually to 40° before it reaches the summit—looking as if it might once have been one leg of a grand natural arch, which still stands up with one exposed face forming an almost perpendicular cliff nearly 800 feet in height. There is, however, no point in this portion of the range where I have found it reaching beyond the northwestern line of ridges, of which it generally forms the crest and the greater part of the western slope, as represented on the accompanying section. A part of this sandstone, with the next beds of slate and sandstone below it, has broken loose from the upper outcrop of the ledges on the S. W. side of the river, and slipped down the eastern face of the ridge without any great change of dip. This displaced mass

CONTINUED ON PAGE 94.

All of Virginia's Representatives in Congress, as well as all of Kentucky's approve the project of a railway traversing their States from the mouth of the York to the mouth of the Ohio, as the following letter shows:—

HOUSE OF REPRESENTATIVES, April 7, 1880.

To the Directors of the Richmond & Southwestern Railway Co.:

GENTLEMEN,—We take pleasure in saying that the enterprise projected by the Richmond and Southwestern Railway Company, under charters from the States of Virginia and Kentucky, will, in our opinion, be promotive of the commercial, mineral, and agricultural interests of these States and of the whole country. We are satisfied that your road, from the deep water of the York River, through the capital of Virginia, with its great manufacturing capacity and its growing population, thence up the James River to Lynchburg, into the heart of the tobacco region of Virginia, and striking there and thence westward; traversing mineral beds of vast and undeveloped wealth, and passing through the southwestern counties of Virginia, with their products of lumber, minerals, and agriculture, into the State of Kentucky, with its large resources in all the departments of industry, and terminating at its commercial metropolis on the Ohio River, promises to do a large and useful work in bringing the products of the great West, as well as of the intermediate region, to the waters of the Chesapeake, for export to foreign lands and to every part of the Union.

We do not doubt that such an enterprise, supported by Northern capital, and directed by the skill and with the energy of the company, will be greeted with friendly feelings by our people, and will be aided by their hearty sympathy and co-operation.

We are, very respectfully,

ROBERT E. WITHERS, JOHN W. JOHNSTON, Senators from Virginia.

J. RANDOLPH TUCKER, JOHN T. HARRIS, JAMES B. RICHMOND, EPPA HUNTON, R. L. T. BEALE, JOHN GOODE, JOSEPH E. JOHNSTON, GEORGE C. CABELL, Representatives from Va.

JOHN S. WILLIAMS, JAMES B. BECK, Senators from Kentucky

JOHN G. CARLISLE, THOMAS TURNER, JOHN W. CALDWELL, PHIL. B. THOMPSON, JR., JAMES A. McKENZIE, ELIJAH C. PHISTER, J. C. S. BLACKBURN, ALBERT S. WILLIS, J. PROCTOR KNOTT, OSCAR TURNER, Representatives, from Ky.

Gold in Montgomery County, Va.—Maj. Wm. G. Guerrant, of Pilot, writes us, May 28th.,—"I was at the location where gold is now found in paying quantity on Brush Creek two days ago. Eight parties are at work on leases. The gold is found on a branch heading in a low ridge which runs through the middle of this valley. The branch is about 700 yds. long and runs nearly due south; the flat along it, averaging 50 yds. wide, is a dark loam to the depth of 18 inches, then blue (sometimes yellow) clay, with white flint of all sizes, is struck, and that rests on a bed of dark slate and granite. Some quartz rock containing gold has been found, and a nugget that sold for $2.35 on the spot. The gold found is bright yellow and has every conceivable shape. Gold is also found on the opposite of the ridge and explorations are being made on the ridge to find the mother vein if such exists. Leads of quartz run through this valley; some beautiful specimens of galena have been found, also pyrites in flint, 3 miles below here on the mountain. Gold is also found in the branches 5 miles above this, on Laurel Creek and in localities to the northeast."—Others state that the Brush Creek placers improve in richness the farther they are worked; That the gold hitherto found is "drift" and with an occasional "nugget"; and that parties are now regularly at work, "sluicing" and "panning," with satisfactory results. Two men with only a tin pan, lately, in 5 days, "panned out" $100 worth of gold. There is considerable excitement all along the western border of the Archæan rocks in Montgomery where these developments are being made. It will be seen, by reference to page 63 of THE VIRGINIAS, that Dr. Currey thought gold would be found in this region.

Gold.—Wm. E. Gilliam has re-opened an old mine in Buckingham county, and found new veins of rich ore. Large offers have been declined.——The Snead gold mine in Fluvanna, has been sold to Willson & Kennedy of Philadelphia, Pa., for $15,000.—— In Spotsylvania county, a negro washing for gold lately found a nugget weighing 10½ pennyweights, which he sold to Minor & Co., of Fredericksburg. Surface washing in this county is paying well, as it ought to.——Gold mining is now an exciting topic in Buckingham county, and new deposits have been discovered.——A nugget of pure gold, weighing more than an ounce, was found, several feet beneath the surface, by a miner in one of the Louisa county mines a few days ago.

The Coal and Coke Movement over the Chesapeake & Ohio Railway, for the three months ending March 31st, 1880, and for the corresponding period of 1879, in tons of 2,000 lbs., by Mr. Charles M. Gibson, Fuel Agent of the Company, is as follows:

	1879.	1880.
Fuel for use of Company	17,875	26,515
Shipped at Huntington on Ohio River	5,447	35,671
Delivered on line of road west of Richmond	9,099	6,862
Delivered at Staunton to Valley Railroad	198	76
Delivered at Charlottesville to W. C., V. M. & G. S. R. R.	6,796	10,537
Delivered at Gordonsville to do do	81	75
Delivered at Junction to R. F. & P. Railroad	654	8,903
Delivered at Richmond for consumption, including steam tugs and dredges	13,326	14,229
Shipped at James River wharves	30,084	34,334
Total	73,298	127,202

The character of the coals moved during the same period is shown in the following exhibit:

From 1st January to	Cannel.	Splint & Bit's.	Coke.	Total.
March 31, 1880	7,559	111,698	7,945	127,202
Same period, 1879	1,026	67,704	4,563	73,293
Increase, 1880	6,533	43,994	3,383	

The Iron Mines on the James in Piedmont-Midland.—The following letter from the *Lynchburg Virginian,* of May 28th, furnishes most valuable information in reference to the present condition of mining interests along James River, below Lynchburg, in the adjacent borders of Piedmont and Midland. It is a timely contribution to this number of THE VIRGINIAS, and furnishes evidence that the resources of the region that will be traversed by the Richmond & Southwestern Railway are being developed. We regret that its author has withheld his name from so creditable a communication:

GALT'S MILLS, AMHERST COUNTY, VA., May 25th, 1880.

While here on a professional tour, engaged in making a topographical and mineral survey of the valuable lands belonging to the estate of the late Thomas Warwick, I have taken the time to visit some of the valuable iron ore deposits along the river, and from observation and inquiry, am enabled to give through your valuable paper a brief description of this valuable mineral belt and the operations now going on in this section.

GALT'S MILLS.—Our party, consisting of Mr. A. D. W., J. W. M. and myself, have our headquarters at these well-known mills, now operated by Mr. S. J. Turner, a true, whole-souled old Virginia gentleman, by whom we were entertained in Old Virginia style. The mills are situated on the north side of the James River, 14 miles below Lynchburg, at the mouth of Stovall's Creek, which supplies the necessary water-power. The large brick mills were built in 1813, have a present capacity of 60 barrels of flour per day and power enough, if the water from the canal was also used, equal to 250 horse-power. The fall at this place being over 20 feet.

I refer to these mills particularly because this point is the principal centre of the iron deposits of this section, which, beginning on the south side of the James at Judge Robert Davis' place, six miles below Lynchburg, extend from that place down the valley of the James to the Greenway mines, on the north side, 30 miles below Lynchburg. The approaches to Galt's Mills from the Amherst as well as the Appomattox side are good and the roads both up and down the river are first rate. The mills are in the centre of one of the most productive agricultural regions of Virginia, and if progress in the opening and working of iron ore and the manufacture of that metal shall continue for the next few years, as it now promises to do, Galt's Mills will be the site of one of the most flourishing and important manufacturing towns in Virginia. A party of engineers of the Richmond and Alleghany Railroad, in charge of Captain Dade, are now locating the road at this place. The location made at this place is upon the tow-path, up to a point a half a mile above Galt's Mills, where it crosses the canal and goes over on the farm land of Warwick's estate and thence into the lands of Paul Campbell, thence crossing the river some two miles below Joshua dam to the south side, in the lands of Neville Mundy, Esq.

The first important depot on the railroad to Richmond will be located at Galt's Mills, or just above it. Having described this

future centre of this important iron region, I now proceed to refer to the operations now going on in iron mining.

THE NORTH SIDE MINES.—1. The "Lone Pine Mine," 14 miles below Lynchburg, adjoining the Warwick farm, 1½ miles from Galt's Mills, on Stovall's creek, operated by Col. Thomas Dunlap, on land leased from Wm. Keet's estate, now employing a force of 40 hands—ore shipped north via Lynchburg.

2. The mine on the property leased from Mr. Bailey, one mile down the canal from Galt's Mills, operated by J. E. Adams & Co., ore mines now being opened—some 10 or 12 hands employed.

3. The property leased from W. H. Turner, 6 miles from Galt's Mills, operated by J. E. Adams & Co., with a force of 8 or 10 hands—mine now being opened.

4. Property of A. R. Boteler, formerly belonging to Col. Walker, 7 miles below Galt's Mills and 21 below Lynchburg, operated by Mr. Boteler, who has a large force, now in charge of an old miner, making a large tunnel in the mountain, taking out ore of very fine quality—a force of 12 hands employed in the mine ½ mile from the canal.

5. The celebrated "Maude View," on land purchased by Col. Thos. Dunlap, who purchased from Mrs. Dillard, named by Col. Dunlap "The Maude View," as a compliment to Miss Maude Dillard, is situated 1½ miles from the canal and 2½ miles below Galt's Mills. Col. Thos. Dunlap is now working at this mine about 50 hands and building a tram road from the canal to the "View"—ore shipped North via Lynchburg.

6. Mine at Riverville, operated by Col. Thos. Dunlap and Naylor & Co. of Philadelphia, 20 miles below Lynchburg, land bought from J. J. Dillard, ore shipped to Richmond—about 30 hands employed.

7. The 2nd mine at Riverville, land bought of Wingfield's estate, is operated by Col. Thos. Dunlap, one mile from canal and 20 miles below Lynchburg, force of 50 hands employed. This mine has a standard gauge railroad constructed from the canal to the mines of the Dover Company, adjoining the Wingfield estate, and over this road ores are now being shipped to the canal. This enterprise is under the management of Mr. Reid of the Dover Company—ore shipped to Richmond.

8. The 3rd mine at Riverville, operated J. E. Adams & Co., on land bought from Watts, one-half mile from the canal. Force of thirty hands employed; ore shipped via Lynchburg.

9. Mine ten miles below Watts' Mills, operated by Messrs. Munford & Grubb, of the Lynchburg Iron and Steel Company, on land leased from Dr. J. C. Mundy, located one-fourth of a mile from the canal, and employing a force of forty hands.

10. The celebrated Greenway mines, sixteen miles below Galt's Mills and thirty miles below Lynchburg, operated by Col. Thos. Dunlap, one and one-half miles from the canal, on land bought from DeWitt and Horsley. Force employed, 45 hands, and ore shipped via Lynchburg to Pennsylvania.

The above list embraces all the mines now being operated on the north side, but prospecting parties are sinking shafts and pits, and examining the deposits on the lands of Thomas Warwick and others.

MINES ON SOUTH SIDE.—11. Mines on the old Robertson place just below Six Mile Bridge, owned and operated by Messrs. Williams, Parsons & Co., known as the Bessemer Iron and Steel Company, about one-half mile from the canal, operating a force of about 20 hands.

12. Mine operated by Barksdale & Co., on land leased from Neville Mundy, seven miles below Lynchburg. Twenty hands employed, one-half mile from the canal—ore being shipped via Lynchburg.

13. Mine worked by Messrs. Williams & Co., of the Bessemer Iron and Steel Company, land bought by them from Webb, eight miles below Lynchburg, one mile from the canal, operating a force of 10 or 12 hands.

14. Mine operated by the Bessemer Iron and Steel Company, on land bought from Drikell, nine miles below Lynchburg and one mile from the river, working a force of eight or ten hands.

15. The old Stonewall mine and property, bought by the Bessemer Iron and Steel Company from Legrande, about 9 miles below Lynchburg—operating a force of about 10 hands.

16. Mine worked by this same company, about a mile below Stonewall—bought from Mr. Ingram.

17. Mine worked by the same company, 2 miles below No. 16— bought from Mr. Whitehead.

18. Mine owned by the same company, bought from Mr. Turner, situated on the river just opposite Galt's Mills.

19. Mine operated by Dunlap & Co., on land leased from Mr. Plunkett, situated on the river, just below the farm of Chas. Mundy.

At all of the above named places, 19 in all, work is being pushed forward with vigor, and already in the purchase and development of these mines and lands, not less than $600,000 have been expended, and at this time not less than 500 men are employed in

these mines, to say nothing of those engaged in transportation.

The trade from most of these mines centres at Galt's Mills, where our friend Mr. Turner also keeps a well stocked supply store.

I found that among the country people everybody spoke in the highest terms of Mr. Dunlap, who has invested more money, and done more in that section than any other party. He is described as a thoroughly prompt, liberal and pushing business man—generous, kind and polite to all those with whom he meets. The people of the neighborhood are rejoicing in the fact that he is now building, for himself and family, a commodious residence near the river, some few miles below Galt's Mills, which is an evidence that he likes our people as much as they like him. May he have the success that his enterprise and energy deserve.

These mines, now being opened, will, in a few years, necessitate the building of furnaces, and we may reasonably expect ten or more furnaces to be established in this section during the next two or three years.—These mines and furnaces, when fully developed, will give employment to not less than 10,000 people.

Yours truly.   E. S. H.

Prof. David Thomas Ansted, F.R.S., who recently died in England at the age of 66, was an eminent writer on scientific subjects, especially on physical geography and geology, and mining engineering. He was knighted, as Sir David, by the Greek government, for his able report on the Larium mines, the silver of which enriched ancient Athens and the lead of which, that the Athenian miners threw away, came near being the cause of a war between France and England. In the pursuit of his profession as a consulting mining engineer, Prof. Ansted has twice visited the Virginias, and spent some time in their coal and iron regions, and well informed himself in regard to them, for he was an indefatigable and clear sighted explorer ; he always wrote and spoke of their great extent, superior character, and of the cheapness with which they could be exploited, in the most enthusiastic manner, both in England and in this country, for what he had seen of them, though mostly in an undeveloped state, had made a wonderful impression on his mind concerning their great value.

In 1854 Prof. Ansted spent a number of weeks in the Great Kanawha coal basin, making a special examination of the great "Wilson Survey," which embraced most of the region on the south side of that river, drained by Armstrong's, Paint, Cabin, and some other creeks, (now the most developed part of this field on the Chesapeake & Ohio Railway), and his published report and the coal section that accompanies it, known as the Armstrong's Creek section, were, until very recently, the most detailed and reliable ones in reference to that field. On his return to England he published a volume of travels, in which he gave an account of his observations in Virginia, commenting on its resources and condition.

In February, 1873, when, by invitation, Major Jed. Hotchkiss addressed the Society of Arts, of London, England, on the Agricultural, Mineral and Commercial Resources of the Virginias, Prof. Ansted followed with a hearty endorsement of what had been stated, saying, among other things, that "there was no coal-field which was more important than the Virginian, and none where the coal seams were more accessible or of a better quality, and they might be looked upon as inexhaustible ;" that "Virginia was also rich in iron fields of every variety and quality, and he saw no reason whatever why, if the same amount of energy and intelligence were applied to the manufacture of iron as in England, Virginia should not take precedence in that important manufacture. No country had greater resources of wealth, and he looked forward to Virginia being one of the countries of the future."

In 1873, Prof. Ansted spent three months in West Virginia and Virginia, chiefly on the line of the Chesapeake & Ohio Railway, again investigating their coal and iron resources, an account of which he gave to the Society of Arts, of London, January 28, 1874. His special mission at that time was to advise the Gauley-Kanawha Coal Company, which had been inaugurated by Gen. J. D. Imboden, in reference to working coal lands it had purchased near Hawk's Nest ; and we owe him a debt of gratitude for demonstrating, by actual construction, the feasibility of working profitably the elevated coal beds of the Kanawha field by high grade, narrow-gauge railways. During that visit he appeared before a committee of the U. S. Senate and urged the improvement of the Great Kanawha ; he also reported on the Cabin Creek coal lands, the Kanawha Falls coal lands and water-power, the Ferrol iron property, and on other mineral lands in these States.—His able papers have been of very great advantage to these States, for his eminent standing among men of science, attested by his being a Fellow of the Royal Society, secured attention to whatever he had to say.

Several important articles, now in type, are crowded out of this issue.

The Resources of the Virginias on and near the Proposed Route of the Richmond & Southwestern R'y.

BY THE EDITOR.

The proposed Richmond & Southwestern Railway, as chartered by the legislatures of Virginia and Kentucky and as described in the prospectus of its company, promises to be an agent of the first importance in the development of a very large portion of Virginia and of a very considerable part of West Virginia.

Beginning just above and under the shelter of Gloucester Point, on the northern side of the noble harbor of Yorktown, where it has already secured a site, of ample proportions, for a great railway terminus and seaport town to be known as Chandler, in honor of the President of the railway company, the proposed route of this line of improvement will be westerly across Virginia, on or near the location of the red line on the accompanying Geological Map of Virginia and West Virginia, (constructed by Prof. William B. Rogers, as elsewhere stated) as surveys, now in progress, may determine, either to Pound Gap or to Cumberland Gap, probably, by branching, to both of these passes in the Great Carboniferous Escarpment known as the Cumberland Mountains, on the eastern border of Kentucky, whence it will cross that State, by routes indicated on the accompanying Route Map, to Cincinnati, Louisville, Paducah and Cairo and to connections with lines of railways, similar in gauge (three feet) leading to Chicago and other great centres of trade in the West and Southwest, making a double track railway, some 900 miles in length, nearly half of which and its Atlantic seaboard terminus will be in Virginia.

An inspection of the map shows that in Virginia this railway will traverse, in whole or in part, the counties of Gloucester, King and Queen, King William, New Kent and Henrico, in Tidewater; Chesterfield, Powhatan, Cumberland, Buckingham, Appomattox and Campbell, in Midland; Bedford in Piedmont and on the Blue Ridge; Botetourt on the Blue Ridge and in The Valley; Craig, Giles, Bland, Russell, Scott and Lee, in Apalachia and along the eastern border of Trans-Apalachia; and along Buchanan and across Wise and Dickenson in Trans-Apalachia;—thus traversing some twenty counties of Virginia and passing near twenty others of that State, crossing each of its seven grand divisions, and passing near a half dozen counties of West Virginia. The extent of this belt of country, allowing that 15 miles on each side of the line will be tributary to it, is fully 12,000 square miles, an area larger than that of Maryland or Massachusetts and equal to one-third of the land surface of Virginia.

An inspection of the geological map shows that this railway will cross or skirt, in its course through Virginia, extensive outcrops of each of the dozen great groups of rocks found in that State, embracing nearly all those known in North America. Its seaboard turminus is near the eastern outcrop of the Miocene or Middle Tertiary and thence, for some 60 miles to the westward, it crosses the Miocene and the Eocene (or Lower) groups of the Tertiary to its western outcrop on the western side of the Tidewater division of the State; there, in the vicinity of Richmond, it crosses a narrow belt of the Jurasso-Cretaceous, or Upper Secondary of the Mesozoic; thence, for over 120 miles, across Midland, Piedmont and most of the Blue Ridge its way is over the several groups of metamorphic rocks of the Archæan, passing through two and near a third of the detached areas of the Jurasso-Triassic, or Middle Secondary areas of the Mesozoic. The Lower Cambrian rocks, the Primal, or No. I, of the Paleozoic, are crossed on the

western slope of the Blue Ridge, and the Middle and the Upper, or Siluro-Cambrian (Lower Silurian), Nos. II and III in The Valley for 20 miles. Entering Apalachia the line winds through and along outcrops of Cambrian, Nos. II and III, Silurian (Upper) Nos. IV to VII; Devonian, VIII and IX, and Lower and Middle Carboniferous, X and XI (the Lowest Coal and Carboniferous Limestone groups of the map), for over 200 miles; here also, in passing through Tazewell, Russell, Scott and Lee, a distance of 130 miles, the line skirts the eastern border of the Great Carboniferous, Nos. XII to XVI, in Virginia and West Virginia, and the route through Pound Gap crosses it for 30 miles or more.—It necessarily follows that a belt of country having such a variety of geological formations, well developed as they are here, must have a great variety and abundance of mineral wealth;—the statements hereafter made will fully confirm this. It also follows that a railway traversing these several outcrops of rocks for such long distances will have great facilities for developing their mineral resources.

It appears from the above, and will more fully appear hereafter, that the natural grand divisions of Virginia where crossed by this railway, as well as elsewhere, differ very greatly in their geological structure and therefore in their soils and in the adaptations and productions that depend on variations of soil. For 60 miles the course of this railway is across the marly, sandy and alluvial soils of the Tertiary plain of Tidewater, a low-land country; then for 100 miles it crosses the undulating Midland plain resting on the upturned edges of the old Metamorphic or Archæan rocks, from the decay of which that plain has been formed, including 14 miles, in two parcels, of Jurasso-Triassic, or New Red Sandstone country; thence, for some 40 miles, its way is among the hills and spurs and intermediate valleys that run out from the Blue Ridge to the eastward, forming the greatly varied Piedmont region, and across the Blue Ridge, both underlaid by and derived from members of the same Archæan group rich in all the elements of fertility; and thence, for more than 200 miles, its course will be across and along valleys of Lower Silurian (Cambrian) limestone, with rich calcareous soils, bordered by mountain ranges and table lands and with adjacent valleys derived from more than a dozen different geological formations and having the varieties of soil implied in that fact.

One more general statement must be made before the greatly diversified and complex character of this belt of country and its adaptation to a wide range of wants and productions can be fully understood.—As it appears on the map the belt of country pertaining to this railway is a narrow one, ranging but about half a degree on each side of 37° N. latitude, making 1° its climatic breadth if bounded by lines of latitude, while its real climatic breadth, that bounded by isotherms, or lines of temperature, is that of 14° or near 1,000 miles, 14-times that of its sea-level latitude width, because its habitable and cultivable areas vary in altitude from the sea-level to fully 4,000 ft. above that level, making its range of climate, adaptations and productions that of the sea-level from North Carolina to Nova Scotia, omitting the influence of the sea.

The altitude of the Tidewater country, the Tertiary of the map, along this line, varies from tide level to 150 feet above it; that of Midland, the country between Richmond and Lynchburg, from about 200 feet to 850; that of Piedmont, between Lynchburg and the Blue Ridge, from about 500 in its stream-valleys to 1,000 on its divides and near 3,000 on its detached mountains; while the Blue Ridge rises to 4,014 in Flat-top of the Peaks of Otter and 4,258 in Apple Orchard Mountain near by. The Valley in Botetourt varies from

about 800 feet of altitude in the valley of the James to 1,500 on the divides; while the valleys of Apalachia range from 1,000 feet to 2,700, or more, and its mountain table lands rise to over 4,000.

The terminal harbor at Chandler, says the U. S. Coast Survey Report of 1857, "is one of the first-class" * * "sufficient for the largest navy and commercial marine," and is, next to Newport, R. I., "the safest and the most commodious harbor in the United States;" which is equivalent to saying it is the best harbor in the Union for commercial purposes, because Newport is so situated that it is not and probably never will be an entrepot for commerce.—"York River at Yorktown affords the best harbor in the States for vessels of the largest size," said Jefferson in his Notes on Virginia.

The capacity of a harbor that is to accommodate an extensive commerce and meet all its demands must be very great, and fabulous sums are expended on the harbors of great commercial cities to meet the requirements of trading ships,—requirements that the uninformed do not know. For example, about one-third of all sailing vessels have a draught of over 20 ft. and 95 per cent. of them draw over 16 ft.; of the largest sailing vessels 16 per cent. draw 24 ft. Coast-wise coal-laden steamers usually draw 16 ft. and coal-laden schooners 12 ft. Roominess of length and breadth are almost as important as depth, for a first-class ship requires a half-mile, and a medium schooner 600 ft. of way, or sea-room when beating to windward, and in a straight channel steamers and vessels in tow of steam-tugs must have at least 100 ft. In anchorages 2.7 acres of swing-room, beyond the 18-ft. curve, are needed for each ship of a coasting fleet, and 32 acres, and for some 44, in not less than 10 fathoms of water, for a man-of-war. These requirements are from the Coast Survey Report for 1871,—the following facts of some of its dimensions will show how the Chandler-York harbor meets them.

The upper York, from the Yorktown-Gloucester Point narrows to West Point, is so wide, deep, and straight as to entitle all of it to be called a harbor that is, as a whole, 26 miles long and has an average breadth of 1.5 miles; for 15 miles, from Yorktown to Portan Bay Point, its average width is two miles. Its ship-channel is 3 miles wide at the entrance and from 18 to 30 ft. deep; for 8 miles, from Yorktown to Queen's Creek, it is from ½ to ¾ of a mile wide and from 21 to 66 ft. deep; thence for 15 miles farther it is ¼ of a mile wide and from 20 to 39 ft. deep. This harbor is easy of ingress and egress, for the course of the York extended leads to the entrance to the Chesapeake, and in its mile-wide channel the largest ship afloat can beat up and down or ride at anchor with perfect ease and safety. The average depth across the entrance to this harbor is 65 ft. and the mean rise and fall of the tides about 2.5 ft.,—there is no bar at the mouth of the York, and its least depth is 33 ft.—The low water depth to New York harbor is 25 ft. and to Boston 23 ft.

The scale and shell fish resources of the York and the thousands of square miles of adjacent oceanic waters, embraced in Chesapeake Bay and its hundreds of arms and in the Virginian Sea outside of it, are great in variety, noted in quality, and, under proper regulations, exhaustless in quantity. More than two million dollars worth of scale fish are annually sent to market from these waters, and from 12 to 15-million bushels of oysters that have a money value of nearly as many million dollars.—In 1869, the last census year, over 5,000 boats and 1,000 vessels of over 5 tons burthen were employed in taking oysters from these waters, and 502 vessels, 18,876 tons of burthen, were engaged conveying them to market.—If the facts of transportation were accessible it would be found that a very large portion of this "catch" of fish and "take" of oysters finds its way, by railroad, far into the interior.

The mineral resources of the country traversed by the Richmond and Southwestern Railway are exceptionally great

and exceedingly varied since, as before intimated and as Professor Rogers' Geological Map, accompanying this, shows, it crosses, either at right angles or diagonally, each of the geological formations found in Virginia—which is equivalent to saying it crosses nearly all those found in the United States—where most of them have their largest development, and where, as a consequence of that development, those formations most abound in the valuable minerals that are generally associated with them.

In the Tidewater country.—Associated with the Tertiary strata that underlie the alluvium, etc., of the Quaternary that forms the surface of this region, and exposed on the banks of its streams, are several beds of *marl*, some valuable for fertilizing and others for building purposes, and *plastic* and other *clays* such as, found in the same relations, have proven so valuable in New Jersey.—Rogers mentions extensive beds of *pulverulent white marl* in Gloucester, New Kent, etc., "all of them largely abounding in calcareous matter," some with as much as 97 per cent. and "in general the proportion exceeds 80 in the 100." In a table of Miocene marls from Gloucester, from nine different localities, the per cent. of carbonate of lime ranges from 37.1 to 96.8; and in one of three from New Kent it is from 76.1 to 93.6.

A *blue marl* is found in beds, generally below the white, that has proven valuable for fertilizing sandy lands. In places are beds of hard *ferruginous marls*, consisting of shells, more or less broken, which are rich in calcareous matter, also *shell-rock*, approaching limestone in composition, some of which Rogers found to contain 87 per cent. of carbonate of lime. *Green sand, sulphate of iron* and *sulphur* are also found in the marly beds of the Miocene, or Middle Tertiary. All of these are valuable not only for improving the lands of Tidewater but especially for improving those of Midland to the westward.—In the Eocene or Lower Tertiary belt,—the eastern boundary of which, where in its eastward dip it passes under the Miocene, or Middle Tertiary, is indicated by the dotted line A---B on the map,—some 16 miles wide on this line, are thick beds *green-sand marl* abounding in fertilizing elements.—The transportation of these Tidewater marls and clays will in time become a large business here as it has in New Jersey. Prof. Rogers thought it by no means improbable that some of the ferruginous beds of this region might prove valuable sources for *iron ore.* At Richmond is exposed a remarkably thick bed of *infusorial* or *diatomaceous earth*, lying near the boundary of the Middle and the Lower Tertiary; elsewhere such beds have a commercial value. *Brick clays* and *molder's sand* are abundant in Tidewater.

In Midland and Piedmont.—From the western border of Tidewater to the western slope of the Blue Ridge, for 125 miles of air-line distance, the route is mostly across the Archæan or *Old* Metamorphic and Primary rocks that here as elsewhere abound in mineral wealth. In the vicinity of Richmond outcrop abundantly massive beds of *granite*, gneissoid in character, furnishing a building stone of unsurpassed excellence, as attested by the use of millions of dollars worth of it in the construction of the public buildings at Washington.

Ten miles beyond Richmond the line reaches and for 10 miles crosses the Jurasso-Triassic area (shown on the map and in section No. 1) known as the Chesterfield or Richmond Coal-basin, some 189 square miles in extent. This contains two beds of superior *bituminous coal*, one of them from 20 to 40 ft. thick, the other from 3 to 5 ft., and also a heavy bed of *carbonite* or *natural coke.* Macfarlane, in "The Coal Regions of America," says of this coal-field, "It was one of the earliest opened by the miner. It is the solitary one at tide-water, and

near a State capital. It contains several beds of coal, and one of these is sometimes of great thickness; it is mined by shafts, on the English plan, and affords a variety of fuels, ranging from gas coals to native coke." O. J. Heinrich, M. E., in his very able paper on "The Mesozoic Formation in Virginia," in the Transactions of the American Institute of Mining Engineers, Feb. 1878, (to be reproduced in full in THE VIRGINIAS) giving the results of extensive explorations with the diamond drill and with shafts, undertaken "for the purpose of establishing the existence and continuity of the coal deposits in the Richmond coal basin," says, "At least two workable seams of coal are known to exist in that basin: the lowest seam from 3 to 5 ft., and the big, or upper seam, from 20 to 40 ft. and more in thickness and occasionally developed in two seams divided by a series of slates and sandstones 5 to 10 ft. thick. The distance between the upper and the lowest seam is about 50 ft. There is no doubt whatever that these carboniferous deposits, geologically speaking, are continuous. Mr. H. states that of the 121,000 acres in this basin not over 500 have been worked, (these in six different localities) and from them some 6-million tons of coal were taken from 1822 to 1877. In 1873, from one acre, at Midlothian, 19,057 tons were taken. He places in contrast with this the statement that in 30 years the big 14-ft. seam of the Cumberland basin produced from 2,525 acres but 13-million tons of coal. He concludes by saying— "This field yielding an excellent gas coal, as well as coking coal, steam coal and blacksmith coal, its revival in the markets of the United States, which it commanded before the late civil war, will only be a matter of time, because its accessibility to sea-going vessels of 500 to 1,000 tons's capacity will fairly counterbalance the moderate cost encountered by deep mining. Therefore this oldest of our coal-fields is yet to see its best days."—This field, with its millions of tons of getable coal will be less than 70 miles from the deep water harbor of Chandler.

The bituminous coal of this field contains, on an average, from 30 to 38.5 per cent. of volatile matter; 59 to 66 per cent. fixed carbon; 2 to 10.8 (average of 21 analyses 5.58) per cent. of ash; 0.6 to 1.7 per cent. of sulphur; its specific gravity is from 1.246 to 1.292; and it weighs 2,075 lbs to the cubic yard. The carbonite contains about 11 per cent. volatile matter, 80 per cent. fixed carbon and from 9 to 22 per cent. ash (Heinrich).

The *fire-clay* and *shale* of this Mesozoic area "would form an important item in *ceramic manufactures*," remarks Mr. Heinrich in the paper above referred to, "as various qualities, from a light yellowish-gray, or nearly white, to those of a red color are found, and the manufacture of pottery, fire-brick, or common brick and terra-cotta, in connection with a low-priced fuel, would be remunerative, and at the same time furnish a new source for the use of coal. The *sandstones* of this formation have been used *for building purposes*, and if selected with proper care furnish a sufficiently firm material." He also mentions that some of the thicker *limestone strata* could be quarried for the same use, and that "a great source of lighting and lubricating material is stored away for future generations in the highly *bituminous slates*, which frequently occur in very heavy strata, and near the surface," and that the *pyritiferous* slates here occurring "would be used in other countries probably for the manufacture of copperas, alum, etc., as, for example, at Pardubitz in Bohemia.

In his second report Prof. Rogers calls attention to the *iron ores* accompanying the coals of Chesterfield and gives the analysis of a sample from near Trabue's pits that in 100 parts contained 85.15 peroxide of iron, 4.20 silica, 4.00 alumni and 6.50 water.

In the 38 miles across Powhatan and Cumberland and along Amelia and between the Chesterfield and the Bucking-

ham, etc., New Red Sandstone areas, the line crosses numerous undeveloped beds of *iron ore* and near well known deposits of *plumbago*. Near Willis' River its way, for 3 or 4 miles, is across a smaller Mesozoic area having the same general character as the one in Chesterfield. Coal beds have been opened in this near Farmville, but they have not been worked to any great extent.

In the next 40 miles, crossing Buckingham, Appomattox and part of Campbell, to the western border of Midland this road passes one of the most remarkable belts of mineral wealth in Virginia, if not in the whole country. The Archæan rocks in this belt have a rather uniform N.E.—S.W. strike and a steep dip either to the N.W. or the S.E., consequently the country is divided, by bands of outcropping strata, into bands trending with the strike, so we find bands of *gray gneiss* of *magnetic iron ore*, of micaceous and talcose slates bearing *gold, copper* and *ochreous* and *brown iron ores*, of *roofing slates, limestones* and *marble*, all, of which will be cr'ssed, where more or less naturally exposed, and nearly at right angles, by the Richmond & Southwestern Railway. The numerous gold mines, iron and copper mines, and slate, limestone and marble quarries that have been opened and worked in this belt of country have fully proven the abundance, variety and excellence of its mineral deposits.

In an article on "The Natural Wealth of Virginia" in Harper's Magazine, Dec., 1865, the writer says—"In Buckingham, Goochland and Fluvanna alone we visited no fewer than twenty-five rich and well known mines, teeming with gold, copper, silver, roofing slate, copperas, granite and many other valuable materials."

The *gold belt* where crossed by this line in Buckingham is from 10 to 15 miles wide, consisting of repetitions of outcrops of gold-bearing rocks, dipping at high angles, the character and richness of which have been abundantly proven by the shafts and drifts of a dozen mines, in different localities, from which large amounts of gold have been taken. The writer above referred to makes these statements in reference to Buckingham mines visited by him:—At Ford's Mine an extremely rich gold vein was discovered, in 1835, but on shafting rich *copper pyrites* formed so much of the gangue they could not by their methods extract the gold profitably; they might have taken out great quantities of excellent copper. The Duncan or Apperson mine has "several large and valuable veins." At the Lightfoot mine, "one of the oldest, most valuable, and celebrated in the State," there are "four well-known and very rich veins," where one lessee made from $300 to $400 a day by stamp-crushing for gold; a copper mine on the same estate, has been successfully worked and its gray and green carbonate and sulphate ores and native copper been found abundant. The Buckingham, Loudoan, Rumpus, Hobson, Ayres, and Booker, are some of the other noted mines of this county, and to this region may be confidently applied this remark of Overman, the celebrated mineralogist and metalurgist, in his work on Practical Mineralogy:—"There are gold-bearing localities in Virginia and North Carolina which, if not equal to those of California at present, will be of greater importance in the future, and, I predict, more sure and lasting." The same eminent authority,—after asserting that all native sulphurets, particularly iron, contain gold, and that sulphurets can only penetrate rocks from below, as confirmed by the fact that all pyritous veins invariably improve in quantity and quality with the depth,—says "We have here (in Va., etc.) a belt of gold ores of unparalleled extent, immense width, and undoubtedly reaching to the primitive rock, which, on an average, cannot be less than 2,000 ft. deep. Here is a mass of precious metal, inclosed in the rock, which cannot be exhausted for ages; and, in this respect, the region in question is the most important of all known gold deposits, California not excepted."— In this connection attention may be called to the fact that the streams of this county, which are numerous and generally abounding in water, have from 600 ft. downwards of fall within its limits.

The *slates* of Buckingham are among the best known for roofing, marbleizing, flagging, school and all other purposes for which slates are used, as has been proven by 60 years of use in Virginia, by "honorable mention" of the London

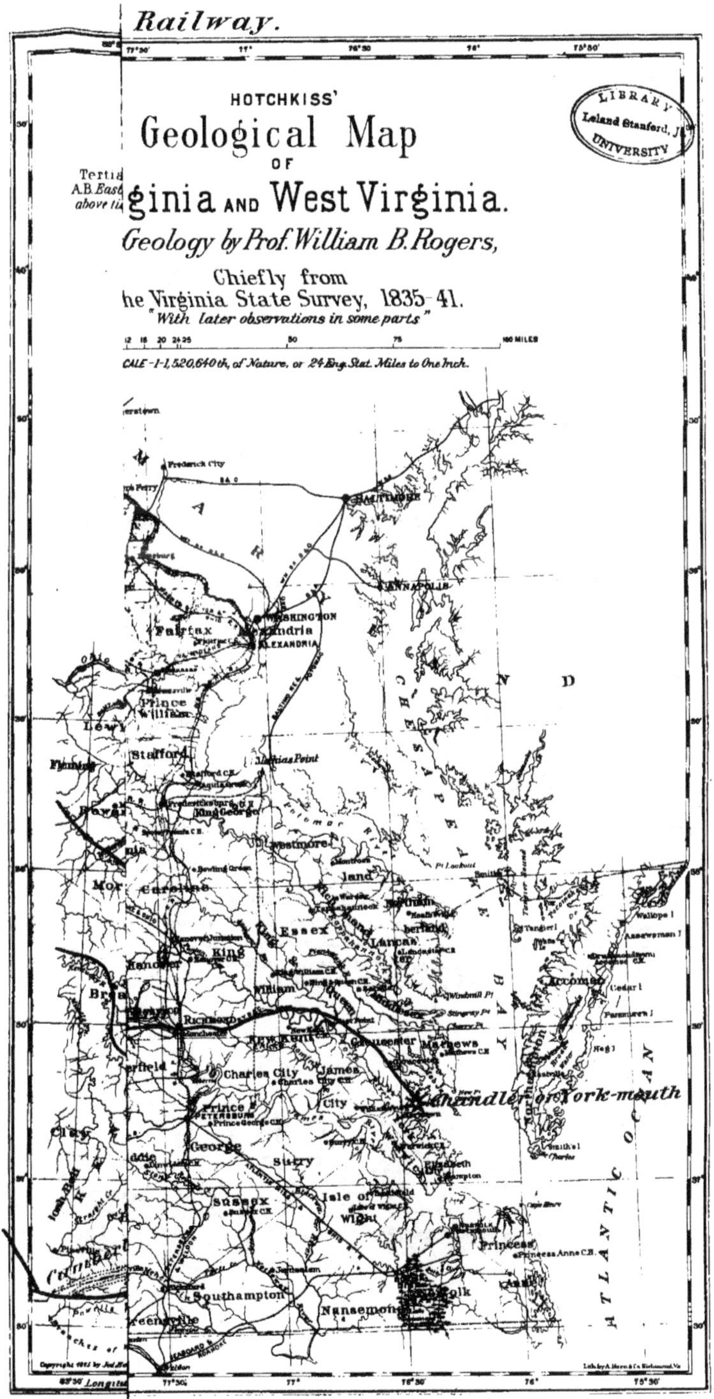

Railway.
HOTCHKISS'
Geological Map
OF
ginia AND West Virginia.
Geology by Prof. William B. Rogers,
Chiefly from
he Virginia State Survey, 1835-41.
"With later observations in some parts"
CALE-1-1,520,640th of Nature, or 24 Eng. Stat. Miles to One Inch.
LIBRARY Leland Stanford, Jr. UNIVERSITY
Frederick City
BALTIMORE
ANNAPOLIS
WASHINGTON
ALEXANDRIA
Fairfax
Prince William
Stafford
King George
Westmoreland
Caroline
Essex
Hanover
RICHMOND
Charles City
James City
Prince George
Surry
Sussex
Isle of Wight
Southampton
Nansemond
Norfolk
Princess Anne
Gloucester
Mathews
Accomac
CHESAPEAKE BAY
ATLANTIC OCEAN
Chandler or York-mouth
Lith. by A. Hoen & Co. Richmond, Va.

No. 21

S.E.

No. 24

S.E.

No. 25

S.E.

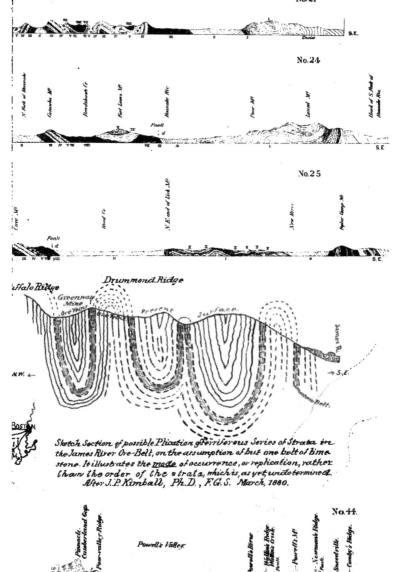

Sketch Section of possible Plication of Ferriferous Series of Strata in the James River Ore-Belt, on the assumption of but one belt of lime-stone. It illustrates the mode of occurrence, or replication, rather than the order of the strata, which is, as yet, undetermined. After J.P. Kimball, Ph.D., F.G.S. March, 1880.

No. 44.

Geological Section from Cumberland Gap Va. S.80 E. to Sneedville Tenn. 25.5 Ms. After Safford Geol. Tenn. (See p. 59)

World's Fair of 1851, and by its present standing in the markets of the country. The *slate belt*, in which the "Buckingham," "Welsh," "Old Dominion," "Ordway," "Nicholas," and other companies have quarried successfully, has been developed for 5 miles on each side of Hunt's Creek, a 9-miles long tributary of Slate River flowing parallel to that river on the S.E. and entering it a mile above its mouth. This belt undoubtedly crosses the county parallel to the course of Slate R. and its S. Branch extension, and not far from the watershed of that river on the S.E.—It wil' be an easy matter to build up an immense trade in these superior slates, both in this country and abroad, when facilities are afforded for transporting them directly to the sea coard whence they can be distributed; for they may be had in almost any dimensions that can be required, and even in grain and tough in structure. I have used them for years for three purposes and speak from experience. An industrial survey of this region, such as the R. & S-W. Ry. has already inaugurated, will doubtless bring to light other belts, or outcrops, of these same slates in the successive foldings of the rocks with which they are associated

Copper has already been mentioned as one of the abundant products of this region, it is found in the various forms of its ores and as native copper associated with the rocks ot the gold belt. From the Lightfoot Mine ores were formerly shipped to Baltimore for smelting. A new impulse will be given to copper mining here when the limestones of The Valley and the pure Lower Measure coals and their coke from the Clinch basin can be brought to aid in the reduction of its ores, and when its sulphurets will be in demand for the soda-ash works that in the future will be erected at the Holston salt deposits,—contacts that the R. & S-W. R'y, will make possible and results that its construction will render probable. The ancient dwellers in this land worked its copper and gold mines, for their rude and curious tools and crucibles are now found in working its mines.

Willis' Mountain, in Buckingham, near which this road will pass, is a remarkable object in the lanscape of the Midland plain, but it is still more remarkable for the abundance and variety of the minerals in and around it, of which Rogers makes frequent mention. Its rich *pink* or *purple gneiss*, of which nearly the whole of the principal peak, several hundred feet high, is composed, "from its hardness, and the indestructible nature of its materials," wrote Prof. Rogers in 1835, "will some day possess a value independent of that founded upon its color, which will bring it into use as an article for building." In this abundant "beautiful rock," with a "brilliant aspect," we probably have the best of *scotch granite*.—Here also are *schorl*, *asbestus*, a *whetstone rock*, and *kyanite*.

Kaolin occurs in extensive beds in the neighborhood of the feldspathic rocks of all this region, and *feldspar* and the purer forms of *silica* abound, furnishing materials that are in demand elsewhere and that suggest local manufactures of all forms of earthenware, fire-bricks, &c., in the future.

The *iron ores* of Buckingham, Appomattox and Campbell counties, on the Midland side of the James Basin, and of Nelson, Amherst and Bedford on its Piedmont side, are well known to be exceptionally large in quantity, numerous in variety and of the best known in quality. The James and many of its tributaries have trenched for themselves narrow stream-valleys down deep into the many folded but nearly vertically disposed rocks that underlie this region (much as shown in the accompanying theoretical section, copied from a report by Dr. J. P. Kimball), the beds of their streams lying some 500 ft. below the general level of the Midland and Piedmont plains, thus exposing, on the tops or in the flanks of the watershed ridges, in hundreds of feet of section and hundreds of miles of outcrop, the numerous beds and veins of iron ore that accompany these Archæan rocks, and making it an easy matter, by open cut, shaft and drift, to mine them above the general drainage level of the region. When Jefferson, in 1781, wrote his Notes on Virginia Ross', Ballendine's and Calloway's iron-works were in operation in this part of Midland on the south side of the James; making, annually, the first 1,600 tons of pig and 150 of bar iron, the second 1,000 tons of pig, and the third 600 tons of pig and 150 of bar,—large products for that day; and he states that the metal made at Ross' was so tough that "pots and other utensils, cast thinner than usual, of this iron, may ue safely thrown into, or out of the waggons in which they are transported." These

and other old furnaces here ran successfully until the forests near were all "coaled," then most of them were abandoned for want of cheap fuel. In the past few months,—during which the Lake Superior ores, of precisely the same character, and derived from the same geological formation, have been held at $12. per ton of ore at Cleveland,—$26. for the ore for a ton of iron at Pittsburg,—attention has been directed to this region, and already a score or more of mines are in operation (as stated, in part, elsewhere), sending ores to the North, and even to Pittsburg, though by roundabout ways, and furnaces and other iron-works are being constructed at and near Lynchburg.

Prof. Wm. B. Rogers, during his Geological Survey of Virginia (1835–1841), explored this region thoroughly, and in his several reports he often calls attention to its mineral wealth.—In his 1835 report he mentions "several veins or beds of *hematite iron ore* in N. E. Buckingham of which, 15 ft. in average thickness where it had been uncovered, had been proven a *continuous bed* for 2 miles, by the owners of a furnace at New Canton, and traced for 7 miles, and parallel to that, and but 100 yards distant, is another bed, dipping steeply to the east, as did the other bed and the associated rocks. Mention is also made of a bed of "*magnetic iron ore*" of a very valuable quality" at the base of Willis' Mountain, which I have myself since visited and had analysed and found to be as stated. In his report for 1839 the details of an exploration of this region are given in which attention is called,—to beds of an abundance of the best of *porcelain clay* in a belt passing a little east of Cumberland C. H.; to abundant localities of *sulphate of baryta (barytes)* in the ridge between Beaver and Opossum creeks near Lynchburg, and in Bore-auger Mt. in Bedford; to an abundance of *garnet*, in Buckingham, which, containing 20 per cent. of lime and 16 per cent. of oxide of iron, he suggests might prove a valuable auxiliary *flux* for iron ores; a belt of *true unstratified granite*, a mile or two wide, in Campbell county, a little east of Falling River; of *syenite*, "in almost every variety," in solid masses, in Campbell and other counties "quarried for *millstones*, formed of a single piece;" *a grey granitic gneiss*, at various places, adapted for building purposes, that had been "largely explored in these quarries" in Cumberland; *kyanitic gneiss*, in massive ledges, *kyanite*, *schorl*, etc. in Willis Mt.; the *slates* of Buckingham, before mentioned; beds of *marble* and *limestone*, in places 50 ft. thick, in a belt along and near the James, and crossing Campbell county to the S.W., of excellent quality for architectural, agricultural and furnace uses; a *quartzite* or *quartz slate*, near Leesville, Bedford county, that "easily rives out in masses or slabs of any required thickness and length," some of which can be easily dressed, and that "besides its beauty and durability as a building material would appear to possess such a power of resisting intense heat, as to fit it for employment in furnaces;" a bed of *blue limestone*, also, near Leesville; a bed of *soapstone* or *steatite*, exposed 2 miles west of Lynchburg and traced for many miles each way; a belt of *limestone*, over 300 ft. thick, in "contiguity to extensive beds of *rich iron ore*," below Ross' furnace, in Appomattox; a "bed or vein of fine granular *sulphate of baryta* of a pure white color," near Beaver Creek in Campbell. By experiment Prof. Rogers found that some of the limestones above referred to made a good, slow-setting, hydraulic cement. In this report Prof. Rogers summarizes his observations on the iron ores of this region, mentions again the bed of *brown* and *ochreous ore* of N. E. Buckingham, "that from its continuity and thickness, and from the general richness of its contents deserves to be considered as of high economical value;" also calling attention to the *brown ore*, "extensively exposed" in a nearly vertical bed from 10 to 15 ft. thick, on and near Stonewall Creek, and to a parallel bed, a *yellow ochreous oxide of iron* to the eastward of the last; and to "a prolonged bed of ore" 8 ft. thick, and probably 16 in places, that ranges through Campbell and other counties; and "a heavy bed of *magnetic oxide*," that may be traced some distance in a N.E.—S.W. direction, in a line with Willis' Mt., in Buckingham, "from 6 to 8 ft. in width, solid and dense, generally bright and specular." This report also notices the magnetic iron ores of Franklin county, those that have recently become accessible by the construction of a narrow-gauge branch of the Va. Midland. The iron ores that are now being developed in the eastern part of Bedford county are probably a N.E. extension of the Frank-

Continued on Page 96.

CONCLUDED FROM PAGE 87.

may be seen as a very conspicuous object nearly opposite, though a little below the Cement Mills. It is apparently one of the effects of undermining by high water in the remote past.

Division 7—the upper Potsdam shale—usually extends some distance up the slope of 6, where the normal dip has been preserved, as may be seen at the iron mines a short distance to the N.E., or opposite the Cement quarries, a short distance S. W. of the entrance of the gorge; but just at the entrance it has been eroded by the river and then concealed very much from view by the drift and diluvium of the Valley. Its dip increases toward the Valley. As nearly as can be determined here, the thickness is fully 600 feet. A sufficient additional description of it may be found in the July number, p. 23. This brings us to the top of the Primordial Period.

The next is the Canadian Period [3]—sometimes called, "Middle Cambrian"—and, like the Primordial, belongs to the Lower Silurian Age. It has three epochs, Calciferous [3a], Quebec [3b] and Chazy [3c]. The first of these, named from the prominent character of its rocks in New York, might well be called "Hydraulic," in Virginia, as it is generally characterized by the presence of one or more beds of hydraulic limestone. Where our section crosses, this limestone is quarried from a bed 12 to 13 feet thick, interstratified with shales and other beds of impure limestone. It dips steeply to the northwest, and again crops out at the base of Salling's Mountain, on the west side of the little valley in which the two rivers meet. Over it lies a part of the Quebec [3b], that has escaped the denuding agencies that have operated so extensively over the whole of the Great Valley. It crops out at a number of points along the James River near the cement quarries, and along the base of Salling's Mountain. We have thus a synclinal trough of limestone resting upon the Primordial shales and sandstones, which we find rising again on the west side and forming the mass of the bordering mountain.

In a depression of Salling's Mountain, about half-a-mile to the right of the point cut by the section, and where the turnpike leading from Balcony Falls to the Natural Bridge crosses, we find the shales and thin beds of sandstone of 2ab, 7, extending to the top of the ridge, but where the mountain is more elevated, the heavy beds of Scolithus sandstones [2ab, 6], form the core of the ridge, all dipping steeply to the southeast; while beyond, the mountain shales of 7 again appear, dipping toward the mountain and apparently beneath the sandstone which elsewhere underlies them. Then as we descend into the valley beyond the mountain we again meet with the limestones and interstratified shales of 3a and 3b, dipping under 7. These facts lead to the conclusion that the mountain is a closed fold of Primordial strata pushed over toward the northwest, so as to invert all the strata on that side, and place the older above the newer. But on crossing a low ridge half-a-mile from the mountain and parallel with it, the limestones appear again on its western side still dipping southeast, but in their normal order. From an examination of this limestone ridge at different points, the conclusion to which my mind is drawn is, that it consists of a closed synclinal fold, the middle portion of which is the lower part of the Chazy [3c], all higher beds having been pressed out and subsequently swept off. This part of the section will be readily understood from simple inspection.

Salling's Mountain will serve as a type of a considerable number of nearly parallel outliers of the main Blue Ridge chain, extending for thirty miles toward the southwest; and consisting of arches of the upper Primordial strata of sandstones and slates, as may be seen on the road leading from Buchanan to the Peaks of Otter, or of closed and inverted folds, a conspicuous example of which may be found in the ridge that separates Buford's Valley in Bedford from the Great Valley in Botetourt county, and is here called Blue Ridge, because it is the geographical watershed between the two counties—not because it is a continuation of that ridge geologically.

Ridges of this class generally lie off from one to several miles from the main range, and seem to have been thrust up beneath the limestones of the Canadian Period, breaking them up of which were probably much shattered at the time, and subsequently worn or swept away, so as to leave the ridges of more durable sandstone naked for some distance down their steep sides, and flanked along both bases by slates and limestones—the latter often occupying narrow valleys or troughs, like the one above described, or like Buford's Valley in Bedford county, traversed by the A. M. and O. R. R., in going from Lynchburg to Salem.

Theoretical considerations.—1. The Primal strata, as well as all those of later date, given on my two former sections, [July and August Nos.], are of an oceanic origin, and the sandstones and conglomerates have evidently been deposited over the bottom of shallow water, and most heavily along the margin of an ancient ocean whose shore-line was the Blue Ridge. The earliest of these beds—those found at the very bottom, and for some distance upward in the series, are composed of the debris of still older rocks

that composed the ancient shore land, and that seem to have been metamorphosed before they were worn down as material for the Primordial strata; for in the latter we find fragments of metamorphosed slate, with both fragments and crystals of feldspar, epidote, etc., more or less water-worn, mingled and cemented together, but not otherwise differing from the same material, as we now find it broken down by the weather from the metamorphic rocks of the Archæan land.

2. The irregular, unbedded masses of syenite and granulite that constitute the base of the Blue Ridge, have evidently been erupted since the deposition of the Primordial strata. This is evident from the mode of contact of the two classes of rock—the stratified resting at a high dip against the igneous masses; and also from the influence the heat of the igneous rocks has exerted upon the slates and sandstones overlying them. Again, the higher we ascend in the series the fewer traces we find of the metamorphic changes.

3. As far as we can read the records left upon the Silurian rocks from the Primordial upward, mechanical force seems to be entirely, inadequate alone, without the aid of heat from other sources, to produce any very great amount of metamorphism. The extent to which the rocks represented on the several sections I have given—especially on the first—have been subjected to bending and pressure, and consequent friction, ought, according to the mechanical theory of metamorphism, to have made the Great Valley of Virginia one vast mass of metamorphic strata. But no such effect has followed. The limestones have their fossils beautifully preserved. The sandstones have not been changed to quartzite. The shales are still nothing but fragile shales [with a few exceptions]; while the embedded limonite iron ores still retain their water of crystallization. There has been metamorphism, but only limited, not general, except so far as it has been produced through other agencies than heat, or even super-heated water under pressure.

4. Such closed folds as we find in Salling's Mountain, and in many localities among the Lower Silurian limestones, seem to have been great wrinkles in the strata, pushed upward [or downward in the case of synclines], and then pressed together by mechanical force acting from a southeasterly direction and in a horizontal plane. This is the only way we can plausibly account for the numerous troughs and arches and folds found along the lines of the several sections we have had under discussion.

5. The flexures and folds of course produced numerous fractures, especially in the limestone beds, and thus prepared the way for the action of the denuding agencies that stripped this great limestone valley of thousands of feet of its original covering. As the pressure was most powerful on the margin nearest the Blue Ridge, so we should expect to find there the flattest folds and the most numerous fractures, and consequently the greatest amount of denudation. Such we find to be the case; for in the first place, we find the higher—the Trenton—limestones from the James to the Potomac nearly all gone from that side of the Valley; and in the second place, all the waters in this region flow toward that side, until they approach the base of the mountain near which they continue till they find an outlet by some one of the great streams that carry them through the mountains and finally to the Atlantic Ocean.

Water acting alone could hardly have been the cause of the vast amount, and peculiar kind of denudation we find extending over nearly the whole 6,000 square miles of this limestone valley, unless it had swept over it in one vast torrent sufficiently deep and powerful to have carried whole mountain chains before it. A much more probable hypothesis is that ice as well as water was an important agent in bringing about the great changes of surface that have given this valley its wonderful fertility.

There are indications throughout this whole region of two great flood periods, since the close of Paleozoic time, when the great Apalachian revolution left the vast accumulations of stratified rocks of that remote age in essentially the same relative position they now occupy. But further notice of these must be postponed for the present.

The Copper and Iron Region of the Floyd-Carroll-Grayson Plateau of the Blue Ridge in Virginia, etc.

By Richard O. Currey, formerly Professor of Geology in the University of East Tennessee, etc.—Illustrated by a Map and Sections.

CONCLUDED FROM PAGE 81

STATISTICS AND GENERAL REMARKS.—Thus minutely we have described these important mineral leads, tɔgether with the mines opened on them, in this highly interesting mineral region. In order, however, to present the facts and figures, deducible from the workings of these mines in as small compass as possible, I have gathered them together in the following statistical tables, which being obtained from the superintendents themselves, may be regarded as accurate.

STATISTICAL TABLE OF THE MINES AND MINING OPERATIONS IN THE VIRGINIA COPPER REGION.

NAME OF MINE.	When Opened.	Tons Shipped.	Average per cent.	Kind of Ore.	Width of Vein.	Total Driftage of Levels.	Total Depth of Shafts.	Depth of Ore Beneath Surface.
					Ft.	Ft.	Ft.	Ft.
NORTHERN LEAD.								
Cook & Wistar....	1856	5	30	Bi-sulphuret	30	150	180	20
Coppras Hill......	1857					50	20	
Great Outburst...	1856	300	14	Bi-sulphuret	60	306		20
Yarnell Co., 50 A ..		50	12	Bi-sulphuret	10	150	100	
Jerry Limeberry...		ore obtained.					18	10
F. Limeberry......							30	10
M. Wilkerson.....	1857	50	12	Bi-sulphuret	20	200	80	20
T. Blair..........	1857			Sulphuret		50	30	
Sarah Ellen........	1856	300	14	Bi-sulphuret	30	1,000	175	40
Kirkbride..........	1859	30	14	Blue & Green	30	40	50	10
Ann Phipps........	1855	300	13	Blue & Green	20	1,000	150	25
Wild Cat..........	1855	300	14	Brown&Grey	30	700	180	20
Cranberry.........	1854	700	15	Black	35	800	250	40
Fairmount........	1855			Blue & Green	36	700	150	40
Brown & Stevenson	1855					250		60
Anna Eliza........	1855	70	14	Black	20	300	60	60
Bettie Baker.......	1854	595	16	Black	30	800	25	60
NATIVE LEAD.	1853		8	Native.	0		35	25
SOUTHERN LEAD.		Value of						
Ore Knob (N. C.)..	1855	$9,500	19	Oxide	20		210	24
Peach Bottom (N.C.)	1859			Sulphuret	6	100	96	
F. Novlin.........	1855			Black	60	50		50
Weddle..........	1855			Black	20		60	60
Toncrey..........	1854	33	16	Black	30	500	50	50
DALTON LEAD.								
Stone............	1855			Bi-sulphuret			20	20
Dalton Hill.......	1855			Bi-sulphuret	25	500	700	35

I regard the mineral resources of these mines as inexhaustible, and deserving of every facility that can be afforded them for their successful working and easy transportation to market. They have so far labored under great disadvantages. They have not altogether been managed with that skill which they merited, and hence there has been in many instances a wasteful expenditure of labor and money. Many who have engaged in them, finding no speedy profits resulting therefrom, have become disheartened, and abandoned work just at a moment when, probably, a little more labor might have been crowned with success. There is necessarily such a heavy outlay to be made in breaking dead ground, and in making the necessary preparations for mining, that many become discouraged and sell out at a sacrifice to others, and thus lose the reward of their toil.

Moreover, had the companies entered earlier upon the construction of smelting works for reducing their own ores before shipment, enough would have been saved on the transportation, not only to have paid for the erection of the furnaces, but also to have left a snug little sum for dividends.

It is confidently believed that the importance of smelting has not impressed itself upon the owners of these valuable mines. Nature has deposited her treasures in these mountain ranges, and by the side of them she has dug out the channels of the mountain streams, providing that power calculated to call forth man's ingenuity and to develop his physical faculties, in the construction of furnaces and manufactories, while every hill and mountain top is burdened with gigantic forest trees for such industrial as well as domestic purposes. In view of all the facts in the case, it is highly important that smelting furnaces be erected at the Toncrey mine, on the waters of the west fork of Little River; at the Bettie Baker, on that excellent waterfall of twelve feet in Big Reed Island Creek; at the

Great Outburst, on the site of Blair's old iron forge, where a cut-off has been made in the bend of Chestnut Creek, producing a fall of ten feet; at the Peach Bottom, on the waters of Elk Creek; and at Ore Knob, on Peak Creek. There is already an establishment about being finished at the Cranberry mine, on the new chemical process of Moniere, the success of which will stimulate this entire mineral region and prompt others to go and do likewise.

If the German blast or the Reverberatory furnace should be used, there is a fine soapstone stratum running the entire length of the district, as indicated on the map, which would afford the best material that could be used for the jambs and the hearth-stones.

A common German blast furnace, with two smelters, can be erected at a cost of $5,000, all complete, each of which will run out ten tons of ore per day, reducing 10 per cent. ores by one smelting, after having undergone two calcinings, to 40 per cent. matt, which, after being roasted three times, and again run through the smelter, may be brought up to a standard of 90 per cent. regulus or black copper, with a clear profit on the entire process of 100 per cent. ores. It costs no more to ship this regulus than it does 10 per cent. ores.

For these processes, *coal* is an important article. The source from whence this can be obtained is amply sufficient for a score of years to come. Three cords of wood will produce 100 bushels of coal. Each acre of these mountains will cut 60 cords, so that we may estimate each acre as having upon it 2,000 bushels of coal. The cost of cutting each cord, coaling and hauling, will be about $1.00, or 3½ cents per bushel of coal, delivered at the coal house.

But suppose the supply of charcoal should fall short in the course of time, then there are, in the adjoining counties of Montgomery, Pulaski and Wythe, extensive beds of bituminous coal, distant only 30 miles from the centre of the copper region.

The outlet for these ores has heretofore been at Wytheville, at Mac's Meadows, at Christiansburg, on the Virginia & Tennessee Railroad (now A. M. & O.), thence to Richmond. From the Cranberry mines to Wytheville the distance is 24 miles; from the Great Outburst to Mac's Meadows 22 miles, at which ores are delivered by wagon at a cost of $7.00 per ton; from Betty Baker to Mac's Meadows 16 miles, ore being delivered at $6.00 per ton; from Toncrey to Christiansburg 28 miles, ore being delivered at $8.00 per ton, and from Ore Knob, the distance is 63 miles to Wytheville with a proportional increase on cost of transportation.

In the development of these mines, the entire southwestern portion of the State is deeply interested. The increase of population will necessarily stimulate the farmers to supply the increased demand for provisions—all the mechanical trades will be called into requisition—the commercial interests enhanced, and this entire region present a scene of industry and a realization of wealth heretofore unkrown to it. But, to secure this desirable result, it is absolutely essential that there should be provided some more expeditious outlet for these resources. In the present age, railroads alone can produce this result. Those concerned should therefore see to it that there is secured, during the present session of the Legislature of the State, such aid as will bring about the construction of a railroad through the length and breadth of this region at an early day. I have already said that the channels cut through these mountain ranges would afford easy grades for such a road from Danville to Wytheville, and from Jefferson, N. C., to Christiansburg. Let two such roads be constructed, intersecting at or near Hillsville, the centre of the region, and there is every reason for believing that the mines will pour forth such treasures, and in such rich abundance as to return to the State in a few years all that she may expend in the construction of such roads.

NOTE.—The communication relating to the smelting works erected at Cranberry mine, and to the new process of reducing ores by chemical decomposition, and to which allusion has been made, has not been furnished me in time for insertion in this report. I will state, however, that the process consists, so far as I can understand it, in mixing and crushing all the ores with the sulphurets, and then calcining them so as to expel the sulphur, after which they are subjected to some chemical action with one of the salts of soda in the vats, and the metallic copper precipitated by means of scraps of iron. So that, in all probability, the ore obtained is the precipitated copper. The success of this process, on an extensive scale, is yet to be demonstrated. One advantage it will possess over other furnaces is the readiness with which it will reduce poor as well as rich ores, even ores of one per cent. being easily acted upon.

THE VIRGINIAS for May has been issued, and, like all its predecessors, is a compendium of valuable information with reference to the minerals,&c.,of the two States. There is no publication in the United States more ably conducted, and none calculated to accomplish more good to this section than THE VIRGINIAS. It is reliable, enterprising, and essentially useful, and certainly every Virginian should feel it his duty to encourage the work. We are glad to know that its worth is being appreciated. It started with a circulation of 4,000, and will probably double that number for the June issue.—*Shepherdstown (W. Va.) Register.*

lin ores, while those found near Buford's and along the E. foot of the Blue Ridge belong to another and more westerly belt of ores. The report for 1839 concludes with analyses, among which are 22 of limestones from the Archæan, one of which, from Appomattox, shows 88.4 per cent. of lime carbonate.

Rogers' report for 1840 contains 6 analyses of iron ores from Buckingham, Appomattox and Campbell, showing a range of metallic iron of from 50.40 per cent. to 58.94, (the last from the 8-ft. stratum mentioned above as ranging through Campbell county); of alumina from 0.28 to 4.00; of silica, etc., from 4.20 to 16.47; and of water from 6.50 to 11.10.

This wide Archæan iron belt, to be traversed for 120 miles by this railway, has been, considerably explored by geologists and mining engineers of repute in the last few years, and most of them concur in representing it as one having an abundance of various kinds of rich ores. But all the explorations that have made have covered but a small portion of the Midland, Piedmont and Blue Ridge region that is iron-bearing. There is no doubt of the fact that well nigh continuous beds of *hematite* (including its *specular, micaceous, red* and other varieties), *magnetite, limonite* (including its *brown hematite, brown* and *yellow ochre, bog ore*, and other varieties), as well as *manganic* and the other kinds of ore found in Archæan regions, run through all this belt of country, for they are found, wherever proper search has been made, from the eastern to the western outcrop of these rocks, from the head-of-tide to the western slope of the Blue Ridge, as shown on the map.—Messrs. Wurtz, Egleston and Kimball of New York; Genth, Booth, Garrett & Blair, and Platt of Philadelphia; McDonald, Campbell, Smith and Mallet of Virginia, all well known geologists, chemists, &c., are some of those that have examined, in place, or analyzed the ores of this region, and a volume could be filled with favorable testimony in regard to them. For example, they show that some of its ores with 69.86 per cent. of metallic iron contain but 0.034 of phosphorus, while some with 67.81 contain none.

In the Blue Ridge and The Great Valley.—Having crossed the Eastern or Archæan Blue Ridge, the Blue Ridge proper, this railway will wind among the Cambrian foot-hills that make the Western Blue Ridge and then cross the Lower Silurian or Great Limestone Valley of Virginia. These are embraced in the blue band of the map, which represents Rogers' Virginia formations Nos. I, II, and III, as numbered on his geological sections.

No. I is here the equivalent of the Potsdam or Primal Group, 2 b, of the Lower Cambrian, including the abundantly iron-bearing shales, Prof. Campbell's 2 a b. No. II represents the Middle Cambrian rocks, the 3 a. Calciferous, 3 b. Levis, and 3 c. Chazy of N. Y. and the Auroral of Pa. No. III stands for the Upper Cambrian (Siluro-Cambrian or Lower Silurian of some) the 4 a. Trenton, 4 b. Utica, and 4 c. Hudson River rocks of N. Y., the Matinal of Pa.

This belt is here rich in minerals, especially *iron ores, ochres, limestones, fire-* and *brick-clays*, and *manganese*, that are developed and well known; and there is but little doubt but that *zinc, lead, barytes*, and other minerals that are abundant elsewhere in this Valley and in these formations will yet be found in paying quantities.—We have only room for brief mention of the localities where and the relations in which these are found, and of their character. Reference to the sections on the back of the map and on page 86 will aid in obtaining correct ideas in reference to statements made.

A stratum of *specular iron ore*, from 2 to 6 ft. (and even more in places) in thickness, ranging in metallic iron from 25 to 55 per cent. and generally low in phosphorus, has been proven along the W. side of the Blue Ridge for the whole length of Botetourt county; it appears to be a regular member, somewhere near the bottom of No. I, and is probably in 1 of 2 a b of Campbell's section. It has been proven, as continuous and very thick, for some 15 miles through the Cloverdale estate.—The *limonite* (brown hematite) ores of No. I, the Primordial ores, have here an enormous development. The heavy beds of shales on the top of formation No. I, (t of 2 a b, p. 86) which throughout Virginia abound in the best of iron ores, those from which the high-priced *neutral irons* are made, are here extensively exposed in consequence of the foldings of the rocks, in the general form shown in the section on page 86, where 7 is the iron-bearing stratum. The continuity and great thickness of these ores has been established, beyond question, all along the

Blue Ridge of this part of the Valley, at Glenwood, at Arcadia, at Cloverdale and other furnaces, and from them have been made, for generations, irons that have stood above all others in their good qualities, the U. S. Navy Department specifying that its cables, and the War Department that its guns should be made of the iron produced here. In his report for 1838 Prof. Rogers mentions an outcrop of a belt of this ore, near where the R. & S-W. Ry. will cross the Blue Ridge, "where the whole surface seemed to be covered with the ore, projecting frequently in large masses," that is about three-fourths of a mile wide and nine miles long; while another rich belt of a different ore of the same formation runs between the first and the Blue Ridge.

The beautiful *white sand*, derived from the decay of the upper white sandstone of I, was found here in abundance by Rogers in 1838, and he then recommend it as "*a material having every quality suitable for the manufacture of glass*." In a recent visit to Virginia Prof. R. informed the writer that the best plate glass made in America is made from these No. I sands. The white sandstone that forms the principal member of this group furnishes one of the most beautiful and durable of *building stones*, and from another member many of the furnaces in this range obtain excellent *hearth stones*.

"The continuity of this iron-bearing series of rocks, bordering our Great Valley on the east throughout its entire length, is calculated largely to add to our estimate of the manufacturing resources of that valley. For it is only by the evidence of this continuity, derived from a careful geological examination, that just views of the extent of this item of our mineral wealth could be obtained," wrote Rogers in 1838, when there had been no development worth mentioning. Now we know, from natural outcrops that have been discovered and mines that have been opened, that this belt of Primordial ores is one of the most, it not the most remarkable known; for it is no exaggeration to speak of *strata of solid ore*, averaging over 50 per cent. of metallic iron, and over 50 feet in thickness, for such may be seen in this portion of the James Basin, as well as elsewhere in Va, where hundreds of feet of steeply dipping ore stratum appear on the sides of the gorges of the ravines of the Blue Ridge which pass from the sight, to unknown depths, beneath the Valley to the westward. It is an *iron belt*, almost undeveloped, that could supply the world's demands, stretching for hundreds of miles along one side of a limestone valley, averaging 15 miles in breadth, of unsurpassed fertility and salubrity, and that has room for and can sustain a hundred times its present population.—Any railway that reaches its arms from the sea to this belt of iron and limestone, and has sense enough in its management to know what can be done with these two things, and then does it, need go no farther for an abundance of paying business.

To be Continued.

Richmond & Southwestern Railway.—The able and alert Washington correspondent of the *Richmond Dispatch* started this item, which has gone the rounds of the papers : "Maj. Jed. Hotchkiss says the Richmond & Southwestern Railway will bring ten million dollars into Virginia." Maj. H. desires to "correct" that item, so it will read five times ten million, in fact he thinks an "amendment" would be in order, making it ten times ten; judging from the course of events.—Mr. F. B. Deane, of Lynchburg, has been employed by this railway to go over Buckingham county and investigate its mineral deposits ; especially gold, iron and copper, says the *Farmville Journal*.—Two engineering parties will soon be in the field in Bland and Tazewell, says the *South and West* of May 27th.—Mr. Wm. Frazier, President of the Commercial Company, that will construct this railway, writes to Tazewell county, that the narrow gauge railways can accommodate cattle as well as the broad-gauge, and that they propose to make more comfortable arrangements for them than the broad-gauge does.—Pres. Parker C. Chandler, of Boston, Mass., writes to the *Clinch Valley News* that the directors of the Richmond & Southwestern Railway are much gratified at the endorsement of their plans in Virginia and Kentucky, and says they intend to give an increased value to interior lands and their products, by furnishing them a cheap outlet to market, and to make it a primary consideration to promote the welfare of the people along the line of the road.—The Virginia counties to be traversed by the Richmond & Southwestern Railway are voting subscriptions to it with great unanimity, as they well may. *Craig*, by 357 to 28, voted $23,150 ; *Cumberland*, by 777 to 127, voted $50,000 ; *Gloucester*, by 1,295 to 40, voted $50,000 (Dr. Ruffner having "impulsed" that people with a description of the mineral wealth, "from beyond," that would enrich them when this railway should be completed) ; *Tazewell*, by 1,300 to 85, voted $48,000 ; *Bland*, by 440 to 11, voted $20,000 ; *Powhatan*, by about 10 to 1, voted $50,000.

Something about the Minerals of Southwest Virginia.

By Hon. W. H. Ruffner, Supt. Public Instruction in Virginia.

Maj. Jed. Hotchkiss:—You have asked me for some endorsement, from personal observations, of the statements made by Lesley, Shaler, Rogers and others in reference to the mineral deposits in that part of Southwest Virginia which lies on the Kentucky side of the State somewhat remote from the existing railroads. This would embrace most of the country lying west of Walker's (or North) Mountain, and southwest of James River, beginning, say, about New Castle, in Craig county, including the upper end of Rich Patch Mountain, which carries more iron ore than any other mountain known to me. I have seen the prolongation of the Low Moor and Callie bed at different points along this mountain and its extension, Barber's Ridge, one exposure of which is within 5 miles of New Castle. The arched structure of this mountain with its flanking waves of the iron-bearing shales and sandstones gives confidence that the Clinton hematites as well as the Oriskany limonites are continuous from Clifton Forge to New Castle.

Not having studied Potts' Creek or Peter's Mountain opposite to the latter point, I can only surmise from the geological structure that these ores would be found there also. The rising of that remarkable axis, which begins close to New Castle, known as Sinking Creek Valley, adds notably to the reduplication of the best iron-bearing strata, and a section carried across this valley by Prof. Rogers to the west base of Peter's Mountain shows numerous waves, and six or seven basins of formation No. V, which bears the red fossil ore, or dyestone ore as it is called further to the southwest. And this is a notable fact characteristic of Southwest Virginia. It abounds in the red ore which is so important for mixing with the cold-short limonites. All the mountains from a cross line at New Castle to New River are iron-bearing mountains. And there are said to be fine deposits of iron ore in Sinking Creek Valley; in fact near Newport there is a furnace. I have never had an opportunity of examining the position of the ore beds, but inasmuch as this valley is an anticlinal of the Silurian beds similar to the Warm Springs, Rich Patch, Crab Bottom and Sweet Spring valleys, it seems probable that the ores are found in the chert band of the limestones, as is the case with a rich bed near Pearisburg, or that the bed lying at the juncture of III and IV is here accessible. I think it will turn out also that the lead-bearing dolomites are exposed in this valley, as they are in its continuation beyond New River, where it is known as the Valley of Walker's Creek. I have myself seen this galena in Walker's Creek Valley a few miles southwest of Bland C. H.

The vast pile of mountains about the Salt-pond (or Mountain Lake) is of the same material as those hitherto described. From New River to the Tennessee and Kentucky lines the mineral wealth increases and becomes more diversified. There are two natural railroad routes through this country, with a block of tangled mountains between. One of these skirts along the base of Walker's Mountain, following Walker's Creek to its head, and descends the North Fork of the Holston. If the object were to reach Cumberland Gap, the road would leave the river valley at Moccason Gap, ascend Moccason and Little Moccason creeks, cross to Clinch River, pass up Stock Creek through the Natural Tunnel, cross Powell's Mountain at a sag above Pattonsville, and enter Powell's Valley. The other, or more westerly route, would ascend Wolf Creek, following the Clear Fork, and descend the North Fork of Clinch River. When reaching the mouth of Guest's River the question would be whether the road should ascend this river, or run farther down Clinch and fall into the line of the route first described. Iron and coal chiefly characterize the latter route, with possibly some copper and other things. The former or Holston route in addition to these, will offer lead, gypsum, salt, and Tennessee marble—to say nothing of Kimberling and Sharon springs. The limestones in Walker's Creek Valley, especially near the watershed, so resemble the lead-bearing limestones of Wythe county (which are the same geologically), that I was not surprised to observe diggings along the roadside, and to have specimens of galena handed to me. The proto-carboniferous (No. X) coals which flank the western side of this valley have not yet been shown to possess any commercial value. But there can be no doubt

as to the immense deposits of superior gypsum and salt in the Holston Valley. Although the salt, so far as discovered, is confined to one small basin, gypsum has been found for say 20 miles along the line of this valley, which follows one of the great geological faults characteristic of Southwest Virginia. Deposits of Tennessee marble are found about Estillville, in Scott county.

But the two great minerals of the world are coal and iron, and these are to be found in this region in endless abundance. The coal underlies the whole of three counties and parts of several other counties in Virginia, and large portions of West Virginia and Kentucky. The reports of Profs. Owen and Lesley but especially those of Prof. Shaler (not yet published) will give exact information on this subject. My impression is that the iron deposits will turn out to possess remarkable value on account of the abundant supplies of the fossil ore or red hematite, the transportation of which I have already adverted to. Indications of its presence abound, not only in the numerous repetitions of the rock strata enclosing it, but in surface exposures. A remarkable example occurs between the North Fork of Clinch and Pattonsville, where a flat topped ridge is crusted with it, and the ore held in place at both sides by the Helderberg (VI) Limestones. W. H. Ruffner.

The Mineral Traffic of the Atlanta, Mississippi & Ohio Railroad

for the months of November and December, 1879, and January, 1880, in tons of 2,000 pounds, kindly furnished by Col. E. E. Portlock, the Auditor of the road, is given below. That for the years ending June 30, 1878 and 1879, was given on page 31 of The Virginias:

DESTINATION.	Barytes.			Ingot Copper.			Pig Iron.			Pig Lead.			Coal.			Plaster.			Salt.		
	Nov.	Dec.	Jan.	Nov.	Dec.	Jan.	Nov.	Dec.	Jan.	Nov.	Dec.	Jan.	Nov.	Dec.	Jan.	Nov.	Dec.	Jan.	Nov.	Dec.	Jan.
Boston............								10	20	10											
New York.......	81		121	62		31			10	19	10										
Philadelphia ...	58		34			78	67	168	10											
Baltimore........							258	466	168	10											
Lynchburg......	108					10	21				108	30	42							
Williamson......	31					1					206	223	146	50	23	100	358	179	11
South'rn States													16	11	80	1242	2614	912
	130	187	156	62		21	347	492	336	40	30	20	401	263	100	50	34	210	1366	3152	923

*In January, 1880, 13 tons of copper, lead and iron ores were transported to Boston.

In addition to the above, there were received from beyond Bristol, in November, 57 tons pig iron, 206 tons marble, and 77 tons coal; in December, 50 tons barytes, 107 tons pig iron, 125 tons marble, and 395 tons zinc ore; and, in January, 148 tons marble, 264 tons zinc ore, 14 tons pig iron, and 44 tons coal.

The aggregates for the three months from Virginia mines, &c., were 431 tons barytes, 83 tons ingot copper, 1,177 tons pig iron, 90 tons pig lead, 844 tons coal, 304 tons plaster, 4,596 tons salt, and 23 tons copper, iron, and lead ores; in all 7,548 tons. The quantity, from beyond Bristol was 1,487 tons; so the entire mineral traffic of the road was 9,035 tons.

The report does not specify whence these products came, but it is probable that of those credited to Virginia, the barytes was mostly from Smyth county, the ingot copper from the Ore Knob, N. C., mines, the product of which is shipped at Marion, Virginia; the pig iron and lead were from Wythe, the coal from Pulaski and Montgomery, and the plaster and salt from Saltville, Washington and Smyth counties.

Prof. Campbell's Illustrated Paper on the Geology of the Blue Ridge at James River Gap,—which is given in full in this issue, with illustrations, for which we return thanks to the *American Journal of Science*,—is the record of a pains-taking and intelligent study, in detail, of one of the most interesting of the many natural geological sections found in Virginia. It is wholly unnecessary for us to commend to our readers the work of this able scientist. He that with observing eyes looks upon the great rock structures that Prof. Campbell describes, sees and feels that he has read aright their origin, conditions and changes. But we desire to direct attention to two points: (1.) That the Richmond & Alleghany R'y, now in process of rapid construction, will soon give a thoroughfare for travel through this grand, water-gap, mountain pass; and the scientific, as well as the observing traveler, will find in this article and its map and section a valuable guide in studying the features of this, perhaps, the finest section of the Blue Ridge in Virginia. (2.) That it shows clearly the geological position of the beds of the Primordial (No I) shales, described by Prof. Campbell in his report on the Mineral Resources of the James River Valley, in the January number of The Virginias, as one of the great repositories of iron and manganese ores all along the western base of the Blue Ridge. This ore-bearing shale is subdivision 7 of 2 *a b* in the section on page 86. It is difficult to estimate the economic value of this guide to the location of th vast stores of iron, manganese, zinc, lead, and other ores that exist, sometimes with regular, but oftener with confused outcrops, near the western base of the Blue Ridge and the eastern border of the Great Valley.—The owners of this mineral wealth owe a large debt to Prof. C. for placing the facts of its existence on a sound basis, and so do the mining engineer and the miner for having a safe guide to operations furnished them.

The Richmond and Southwestern Railway as a Trunk Line from the West.

—The prospectus issued by the Richmond & Southwestern Railway Co. contains tables, compiled from the "Official Guide," of "Comparative Distances of various competing points from the Atlantic Ocean by existing trunk lines and by the Richmond & Southwestern Railway," from which we gather the following, that our readers may have at hand the advantages of distance which this proposed railway presents as one of the reasons why it should be constructed.

It is enough for us to know that this railway will traverse almost the entire length of Virginia, through an air-line distance of about 400 miles, from Chandler (Gloucester Point), to Cumberland Gap, and become the agent that will develop more than ten thousand square miles of our territory, an area larger than the State of Massachusetts, abounding in undeveloped resources, crossing more than 300 miles of iron-bearing and along more than 150 miles of coal-bearing formations, (as Professor Rogers' map shows and as we have stated in detail elsewhere in this issue), but the investors in railway securities are so accustomed to consider the *through-line* aspects of the question it becomes necessary to present the facts of "comparative distances." This presentation is the more necessary when such influential journals as the *Chicago Railway Review* (of May 8) comments *doubtingly* on this scheme as follows :

We chronicled last week in our news columns the formation of a company to build a double track, steel rail, stone ballasted, narrow-gauge railway from tide water through Virginia and Kentucky to Louisville, with an ultimate extension to the Gulf. The idea appears to be to afford an eastern outlet to the existing narrow-gauge system of Ohio, Indiana and Illinois. While naturally indisposed to decry anything in the way of progress in the railroad interest, we can hardly approve this present undertaking. In the first place our East and West trunk lines and water ways are as yet quite able to take care of the traffic coming to them. The recent opening of the Grand Trunk line will more than supply any deficiency in transportation facilities, if indeed such deficiency has existed. Then, for another reason, is the scheme available : it is too "gilt edged." The construction of a plump 900 miles of double track railroad with first class accessories is rather too ambitious for even Boston wealth and enterprise. Especially does this appear true when we reflect that the scheme is of rather doubtful utility after all. The projectors have, however, secured the confidence of Kentucky and Virginia, and the Legislatures of those States have granted them very liberal charters and seem disposed to afford the fullest aid to the enterprise. This is but natural, for the road, if ever constructed, would open up some very fine mineral and timber regions in both States.

The comparative distances we select are from St. Louis, Chicago, Cairo, Paducah, Louisville and Cincinnati, by railway, to the Atlantic, (1) to the Capes of Virginia, the entrance to Chesapeake Bay, *via* the Richmond & Southwestern, or the Chesapeake & Ohio, or the Baltimore & Ohio; (2) to the Delaware Breakwater, at the entrance to Delaware Bay, *via* the Pennsylvania Railroad ; (3) to Sandy Hook, the entrance to New York harbor, *via* the N. Y., Lake Erie & Western, or the N. Y. Central & Hudson River, and (4) to the entrance to Boston harbor *via* the N. Y. Central & Hoosac Tunnel.

Distances from St. Louis to the Ocean:

	Miles*	Miles*
Via Richmond & Southwestern R'y.	1,029 Miles*	
" Chesapeake & Ohio R'y. and Ohio R.	1,034 "	5 saved
" Pennsylvania R. R. - -	1,083 "	54 "
" N. Y. Central & Hudson R. R. R.	1,188 "	159 "
" N. Y., Lake Erie & Western R. R.	1,222 "	193 "
" Hoosac Tunnel & N.Y. Central R. R.	1,237 "	208 "
" Baltimore & Ohio R. R.	1,303 "	274 "

Distances from Chicago to the Ocean:

		Miles
Via Richmond & South-western Railway {	Via Cincinnati 1,005 Miles " Louisville 1,016 "	
" Pennsylvania R. R. - -	930 "	75 less
" N. Y., Lake Erie & Western R. R.	991 "	14 "
" N. Y. Central & Hudson R. R. R.	1,000 "	5 ".
" Chesapeake & Ohio R'y. and Ohio R.	1,003 "	2 "
" Baltimore & Ohio R. R. -	1,035 "	30 saved
" Hoosac Tunnel & N.Y. Central R. R.	1,049 "	44 "

Distances from Cairo to the Ocean:

	Miles	Miles
Via Richmond & Southwestern R'y.	883 Miles	
" Chesapeake & Ohio R'y. and Ohio R.	1,208 "	325 saved

Distances from Paducah to the Ocean :

	Miles	Miles
Via Richmond & Southwestern R'y.	853 Miles	
" Chesapeake & Ohio R'y. and Ohio R.	1,163 "	310 saved

Distances from Louisville to the Ocean:

	Miles	Miles
Via Richmond & Southwestern R'y.	666 Miles	
" Chesapeake & Ohio R'y. and Ohio R.	847 "	181 saved
" Pennsylvania R. R.	885 "	219 "
" N. Y., Lake Erie & Western R. R.	991 "	325 "
" N. Y. Central & Hudson R. R. R.	997 "	331 "
" N. Y. Central & Hoosac Tunnel R.R.	1,046 "	380 "
" Baltimore & Ohio Railroad -	1,074 "	408 "

Distances from Cincinnati to the Ocean:

	Miles	Miles
Via Richmond & Southwestern R'y.	695 Miles	
" Chesapeake & Ohio R'y. and Ohio R.	693 "	2 less.
" Pennsylvania Railroad -	775 "	80 saved
" N. Y., Lake Erie & Western R. R.	881 "	186 "
" N. Y. Central & Hudson R. R. R.	887 "	192 "
" Hoosac Tunnel & N.Y. Central R. R.	936 "	241 "
" Baltimore & Ohio Railroad -	964 "	269 "

*The miles of the first column are the distances to the ocean by the railways named ; those in the second column are the differences, more or less, by the Richmond and Southwestern Railway.

The *savings of distance* indicated by the above tables show very clearly the advantages the Richmond and Southwestern Railway will have, as a route for *through traffic*, over some of the " grand trunk" lines from the West regarded from the mileage stand-point alone, saying nothing about the advantages of climate of a route near 37° 30' of N. latitude, of the advantages of a line built from the beginning in reference to terminal points, and of one having harbor facilities of unsurpassed excellence, both of approach and anchorage, in sight of the ocean and near its great highways, and where ice never obstructs.

The Virginias.

A Mining, Industrial and Scientific Journal:
Devoted to the Development of Virginia and West Virginia.

Vol. I, No.7. }   Staunton, Virginia, July, 1880.   { Price 25 Cents.

The Virginias,

PUBLISHED MONTHLY,

By JED. HOTCHKISS, · · · Editor and Proprietor,
At 346 E. Main St., Staunton, Va.

This Edition is 12,000.

Terms, including postage, per year, in advance, $2.00. Single numbers, 25 cents. Extra copies, $20.00 per 100. Back numbers, from the first, can be had at 25c each. Advertising, per inch of length of single column (3 columns to a page, as on advertising pages), one month, $2.00; two months, $3.50; three months, $5.50; six months, $7.50; nine months, $10.00, and twelve months, $12.00; payable in advance.

Specimen Numbers of this journal are sometimes sent to parties supposed to have an interest in the development of the Virginias, or a desire to be informed in reference to their resources, improvement, etc.; they will please consider this an invitation to become subscribers and so help to sustain a paper devoted to their interests.

On sale at Hunt F & Co.'s Bookstore, Main Street, Staunton, Virginia.

The Iron and Steel Statistics for the Tenth ensus, those of the manufacture of iron and steel in the U. S. for the year just preceding June, 1880, are to be collected by James M. Swank of 265 S. 4th St., Philadelphia, Pa., he having been appointed Special Agent of Census for that purpose. There is no question but that Mr. Swank is the best man in the Union for this special duty, for, as Secretary of the American Iron and Steel Association, he has, to some purpose, made iron and steel statistics a study, and, through the publications of the Association, has furnished to the world more reliable information in reference to the production of iron and steel in the United States than any other man. In the circular he has issued Mr. S. urges all manufacturers of iron and steel in the U. S. to at once fill up, completely, the schedules he sends them and return to his address, as above; and he would be glad to have the address of every such manufacturer that does not soon receive such schedules sent to him. He says he wants his report to be the *first one completed* of the industrial reports of this census, and we hope it may be, and then be immediately published. Send in the schedules at once and help to gratify this laudable ambition.

And just here a word in reference to the questions in the industrial schedules of the census. Mr. Swank says (and so must say every agent of the census,) *"It is especially desired and insisted upon that every interrogatory shall receive a definite and complete answer."* The law requires it, and anyone refusing to answer may be fined from $500 to $10,000.—No one need hesitate about answering these questions, for, as Prof. Raphael Pumpelly, of Newport, R. I., who has charge of this whole matter, remarks in one of his circulars: "Be assured that the information conveyed will be received and kept as strictly confidential. The officers of the Census are all sworn to secrecy and the final publication will be made by aggregates and averages only, and individual names are used only for the purpose of making sure that the entire field is covered and no omissions made."

The education of our own people to a knowledge of the resources of our states and of the conditions in which those resources exist, was one of the objects had in view in establishing this journal. It is gratifying then to be informed, as we were a few days ago, that we have not missed the mark in our aim. A gentleman in Rockingham, who is the owner of mountain lands, lying not far from a railroad, that he had many times searched over for iron ore, but with no satisfactory results, recently received from a friend a copy of the March No. of THE VIRGINIAS, in that he found and carefully read Prof. Campbell's excellent article on the "Silurian in Central Virginia" and, by the help of the information derived from it and its section, he at once found the place of the iron ores of VII and proved the existence of a heavy stratum of the same extending for miles through his land.—We intend to make THE VIRGINIAS a standard for reference in all geological and mining questions, as well as in others relating to the physical condition of the Virginias, and we would be glad to have it in the hands of all classes of our people, and especially in the hands of the teachers and where it can be referred to and studied by the generation of Virginians now attending our schools." *The Commonwealth*, of Richmond, in commenting on the collection of the mining statistics of these states for the census, concluded its forcible comments with this suggestive remark.—"What we have under ground is to make us rich—our fathers pretty thoroughly stripped the surface."

Coke Yield.—The Quinnimont, W. Va., coke ovens, in charge of S. Fisher Morris, M. E., in 18 days of the latter part of last May made 1,874 tons of coke; a yield, by actual weight, of 65.8 per cent. from all the coal put into the beehive ovens.

Personals.—Prof. Thomas Egleston of the Columbia College School of Mines, N. Y., will, we are greatly gratified to learn, probably take a trip this summer to the copper region of the great plateau of the Blue Ridge in Va. and N. C. The visits of Dr. Egleston to Virginia and West Virginia, last year, were of very great service to these states; his position is a commanding one and he has generously given a metropolitan publicity to the great facts of our mineral resources that he learned from personal observation. We hope to hear from him again.——Prof. J. J. Stevenson, who was connected with the 2nd. Geol. Survey of Pa., working out the geology of the coal-fields of the S.W. part of Pennsylvania, and who has more recently been connected with the U. S. Geological Surveys, has lately visited W ise, Dickenson, and other S. W. Va. counties, with Gen. Imboden, examining their mineral resources. Prof. S. has also done much geological work in W. Va., of which more hereafter.——Dr. Joseph Leidy, of Philadelphia, the famous paleontologist, Prof. Porter, of Yale, and other scientists of note, accompanied by their wives, have gone on a scientific and pleasure tour to the mountains of Western North Carolina; thence they will go through the Great Valley in East Tennessee and Southwest Virginia, to New River, and then down that stream to the Chesapeake & Ohio Railway, in West Virginia. It would be difficult to arrange elsewhere in this country a trip that in the same distance combines so much of absorbing scientific interest with so much of scenic attraction.——Assistant A. T. Mosman and party, of the United States Coast and Geodetic Survey, have occupied Kreny's Knob, near the Chesapeake & Ohio R'y, in West Virginia, as a station in the triangulation that is being extended across the continent. The stations they will observe upon to the westward from this are those that overlook the Ohio, while those they will observe upon to the eastward are on the mountains near the Va. and W. Va. line; so most of this season's work will be in West Virginia, and go far towards carrying the triangulation across that State. We trust Assistant Mosman will observe upon as many points as possible in our mountain region and make, as he always cheerfully does, further contributions to the geographical knowledge of these States.

The Shenandoah Valley R.'R.—"Work on the Shenandoah Road, built in Virginia to carry ore and iron, has been suspended," says the Philadelphia *Record*, in telling what the Reading Receivers are doing. This reference is not to the Shenandoah Valley Road, as many suppose,—for work is pushed as actively as ever, all along its line, and there is little doubt of its completion, as a *standard-gauge railway*, from Hagerstown, Md., to Waynesboro, Va., at the before-specified time,—but probably to the railway the Reading Co. was constructing from its lines to Hagerstown. The S. V. R. R. has arranged for business connections with the Pennsylvania R. R. and the Western Md. R. R., so that as soon as its line is finished to Hagerstown it will become part of lines to the Northern cities from the Chesapeake & Ohio R'y, as we have before stated.—The *Warren Sentinel*, whose editor is one of the directors of S. V. R R and ought to know whereof he writes, stated in a late issue that on the 17th of June officers of that company would start to examine the Piedmont slope of the Blue Ridge southwest of the Chesapeake & Ohio, in reference to the feasibility of an extension of their road through the Rockfish tunnel of the C. & O. and thence S. W. into N. C., keeping as near the E. base of the Blue Ridge, in Va., as possible. This would open an extensive region, abundant in mineral and agricultural wealth, that is now without railways, and open a new N. E.-S. W., trunk railway line.—The shipments by the Shenandoah Valley R. R. during May last from the Riverton and Front Royal depots, embraced among other articles, 1,020,000 lbs. of lime, 40,000 lbs. of mill feed, 48,000 lbs. of corn, a double-decked car-load of sheep, a car-load of cross-ties, 35 car-loads (30,000 lbs.) of tan-bark, 19 tons of ground bark, 208 bbls. of flour, 1,191 sides of sole leather, and 10½ tons of sumac; besides wool, wine, brandy, dried fruit, etc.—all products of the Great Valley.—*Sentinel.*

The Pittsburg & West Virginia Railway Co. has been chartered to construct a railroad from the Pa. and W. Va. line, in Monongalia Co., W. Va., through Monongalia, Preston, Marion, Taylor, Barbour, Randolph, Pocahontas, Greenbrier, Summers, Mercer and Monroe counties to the Va. line. Its chief office is to be at Grafton. The stock is $5-million, in $100 shares.

Coal Lands Sold.—S. B. Elkins of Arizona has bought for $16,000, from Judge Armstrong of Romney, W. Va., his third of the 6,000 A. of the coal lands of the Preston Coal and Iron Company—lying in Mineral and Grant counties, W. Va.

The New River Coal-Field of West Virginia.*

BY S. FISHER MORRIS, M. E., QUINNIMONT, W. VA.

The New River coal-field embraces that portion of the Apalachian coal formation which lies on the waters of New River, principally in Fayette and Raleigh counties, West Virginia, covering a strip of territory about forty miles in length along the line of the Chesapeake and Ohio Railway from Quinnimont to Kanawha Falls, where New River empties into the Kanawha, the railroad following the banks of the river the whole distance. (See map.)

Between Kanawha Falls and the Valley of the Ohio lies the great Kanawha region, and these two coal-fields possess a greater variety of coal than can be found in any other portion of the country, enabling them to furnish the best fuels for any of the various demands of manufacture or domestic use, the Kanawha region possessing many varieties of gas, hard splint, and cannel coal, and the New River region bituminous and semi-bituminous, steam and coking coal.

New River, in its westward course towards the Kanawha, has cut its way entirely through the Seral conglomerate or No. XII of the Pennsylvania Reports, the Umbral red shales of No. XI appearing at the foot of the mountains at the eastern end of the region at Quinnimont, one of the upper ledges of the Conglomerate forming the summits; while at the western end, at Kanawha Falls, the top of the Conglomerate is nearly down to the level of the river, a portion of the "Lower Productive Measures" forming the greater portion of the mountains.

These mountains rise abruptly from the banks of the river to a height of from 800 to 1,200 feet, leaving only here and there narrow strips of bottom land, a few acres in extent; and as the measures consist principally of hard sandstones, shales, and conglomerates lying in a nearly horizontal position, the mountain

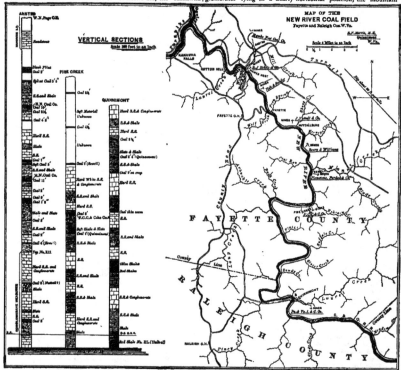

sides are very precipitous, with many long and high cliffs, which, with the great height of the mountains, give the country a very rugged appearance.

Along the sides of these mountains fronting on New River and its many tributaries there are exposed the outcroppings of several veins of bituminous and semi-bituminous coal, varying in thickness from a few inches to over four feet, five of them being workable, or containing three feet of coal and upwards. Of these seams only two appear to crop out with a workable thickness at or near the river front, the highest seams being in the high hills a short distance from the canyon of New River.

The geological position of these coals is in the Conglomerate (No. XII), and the name "Inter-conglomerate" by which they are known was proposed, I believe, by Professor Fontaine, of the University of West Virginia, (now of the University of Virginia).

The thickness of the conglomerate on New River is not yet certainly known, but from the top of the red shale of XI at Quinnimont to the top of the conglomerate shown on the Hawk's Nest section it is about 1,450 feet, of which 1,300 feet is to be seen at Quinnimont.

The elevations on all the accompanying sections were obtained by the leveling instrument, with the exception of the two upper coal seams on the Fire Creek section, which were ascertained by aneroid barometer. For the very complete section at Hawk's Nest and Ansted I am indebted to Mr. W. N. Page, superintendent of the Hawk's Nest Coal Company, who has proved all the coal

*From the Transactions of the American Institute of Mining Engineers.—Read at the Montreal Meeting, September, 1879.

veins shown on the section, and carefully measured all the intermediate rocks. This section exhibits the "Lower Productive Measures" (from the Conglomerate to the Mahoning sandstone), which are here 1,200 feet thick and contain sixteen veins of coal, having an aggregate thickness of 67 feet, and of these sixteen veins, eleven are workable or contain 3 feet of coal and upwards.

These measures have a dip of from 75 to 100 feet per mile to the northwest, and the regularity of dip and strike is of great value in determining the proper location of new mines, in laying out the workings, and providing for permanent and cheap means to secure ventilation or drainage. The coal is soft, is easily and cheaply mined, and no expensive machinery is required for handling the coal, or for ventilation or drainage. The amount of dead work in the mines is small, as the coal veins have excellent roofs, and all the mining expenses can be brought to as low or a lower figure than in other regions.

The coal has a high reputation as a steam coal, and is fully equal to the best-known steam coals in the country, but it is the *coking* property which makes it very valuable, and which is rapidly bringing it into use in the great iron region of the Ohio Valley, several of the largest and best-known furnaces on the Ohio having used the New River coke for nearly two years with the best results. It will "stand up" under a heavy burden in the furnace, it contains a high percentage of carbon with very little ash and sulphur, and extended use and experience have proved it to be one of the best and most economical furnace fuels in use. Mr. J. H. Bramwell, who has used this coke in the Quinnimont Furnace for over five years, says: "In using the Virginia brown hematites, the quantity of fuel required will vary with the percentage of metallic iron, silica, and alumina contained in the ore. From 1¼ to 1½ tons of 48-hour coke is a usual average. Using 72-hour coke and an ore with 50 per cent. metallic iron, 5 per cent. silica, and of an aluminous nature, one ton and even less has produced a ton of iron at Longdale Furnace."

The hematites occurring in juxtaposition to sand-rock, and imbedded in a matrix derived from this source, contain on an average, however, 45 per cent. metallic iron and from 15 to 20 per cent. silica. These require a high percentage of lime to flux them, and fully 1½ tons of 48-hour coke for their reduction. The introduction of Whitwell stoves and more carefully prepared ores will reduce this high consumption of fuel to 1 or 1¼ tons 48-hour coke.

The increasing demand thus is developing the region, and new mines are being opened and new ovens under contract at several places, and in a short time the New River district will rank among the most important coke-producing districts in the country, and will attain this position by reason of the superior quality of its coke, which specially adapts it for metallurgical uses, and the improved transportation facilities, which will enable the coke manufacturers to furnish a regular supply to consumers in the great market of the Ohio Valley.

The coke is made exclusively in beehive ovens, and experience and experiment seem to have proved thus far that coke thus made is superior for furnace use to that made in any other form of oven. It is made in the usual manner by dumping about 3 tons of coal into the oven through a hole in the top, spreading it evenly over the floor, and coking it 48 hours, except on Fridays and Saturdays, when a larger amount of coal is charged, and the coking continued for 72 hours. The coal yields from 63 to 64 per cent. of coke, one manufacturer claiming a yield of over 65 per cent., which is a very high yield for beehive ovens.

Below is a table of analyses of several New River cokes and an analysis of standard Connellsville coke, by which it will be seen that the New River coke contains about 5 per cent. more carbon than the Connellsville, and only one-half as much ash:

	Carbon.	Ash.	Sulphur.	Moisture.	Chemist
Connellsville	87.26	12.00	0.74	.....	2d Geol. Survey of Pa.
Quinnimont	93.85	5.85	0.30	.....	J. H. Britton.
Quinnimont	93.11	5.84	0.89	.....	Prof. Egleston.
Fire Creek	92.18	6.68	0.61	0.11	Dr. Ricketts.
Sewell	93.00	6.73	0.17	.....	C. E. Dwight.
Nutallburg	92.27	7.54	0.92	.....	C. E. Dwight.

The largest works in the district are those of the Pennsylvania and Virginia Iron and Coal Company, at Quinnimont. These works were begun in 1873, and consist of a blast furnace, 15x60, 100 beehive coke ovens, the coal mines, and all necessary shops and buildings, including a small foundry. The furnace was blown in in the latter part of 1874, and has been running ever since, except when blown out for necessary repairs. The output for the mines this year will be about 60,000 tons of coal, and of the ovens 30,000 tons of coke, that portion of the coke which is not used in the furnace being shipped to Western markets.

The coal mined is from a seam a little over 3 feet thick, with no slate partings, lying high up in the mountain, over 1,000 feet above

New River, and is brought down the mountain on an incline, 2,100 feet long, to the coke ovens. It is a soft, semi-bituminous coal, makes a very bright, hot fire, leaving but little ash, and is an excellent steam coal. Nearly all the coal mined is used in the coke ovens to supply the furnace with fuel, the coal yielding 63 per cent. of coke.

This coal has been analyzed by Professor Egleston and J. B. Britton, with the following results:

ANALYSIS OF QUINNIMONT COAL.			
	No. 1. Britton	Lump coal No. 2. Egleston	Slack, No. 3. Egleston
Fixed Carbon..	79.89	79.76	79.40
Volatile Matter	18.19	18.65	13.57
Ash	4.68	1.11	2.99
Sulphur........	0.30	0.13	0.18
Water	0.94	0.76	0.83

Ten miles down the river below Quinnimont, Mr. J. H. Bramwell has a very good opening on the Quinnimont seam, and has contracted for the construction of coke ovens to supply fuel for a large furnace on the Ohio.

Six miles further west are the works of the Fire Creek Coal and Coke Company, which were opened in 1876, and have been running ever since. This company has an excellent plant of 60 coke ovens, and also ships a considerable amount of coal for steam purposes. This coal is in a higher seam than the Quinnimont, and is not so friable. Its analysis is as follows:

ANALYSIS OF FIRE CREEK COAL.	
Fixed Carbon...........	75.00
Volatile Matter........	22.34
Ash	1.43
Moisture	1.00
Sulphur	.38
	100.00

Two miles beyond Fire Creek, at Sewell Station, are the works of the Longdale Iron Company (Firmstone, Pardee & Co.), who here have a plant of 40 ovens to supply their Longdale Furnace with fuel. Preparatory to the erection of another furnace this company is engaged in building 60 more ovens, and by the first of June will have 100 ovens in operation. They are working a vein of excellent coal, and their coke does remarkably good work in their furnace at Longdale. An analysis of their coal by C. E. Dwight gave the following result:

ANALYSIS OF LONGDALE COAL.	
Fixed Carbon...........	72.32
Volatile Matter.......	21.38
Ash	5.03
Water	1.03
Sulphur	0.27
	100.03

Two miles beyond Sewell is the mine of Beury & Williams, who have a very good opening, showing in several places four feet of coal free from slate and of excellent appearance. No analysis has been made of this coal, which is shipped to Eastern markets for steam purposes.

Three miles further on is the Nutallburg mine of Mr. John Nutall, of Pennsylvania, who is also an operator in the Clearfield region. Mr. Nutall opened this mine in 1873, and ships his coal to Eastern markets, and he also has a plant of 50 coke ovens, the coke being shipped down the Ohio River for use in blast furnaces. Two analyses of this coal are given, one by C. E. Dwight, made two or three years ago, and one by Professor Egleston, made recently. The ash in Mr. Dwight's samples is unusually small.

ANALYSIS OF NUTALLBURG COAL.		
	No. 1. Dwight.	No. 2. Egleston.
Moisture.............	0.34	1.35
Volatile Matter......	29.59	25.35
Fixed Carbon.........	69.00	70.67
Sulphur	0.78	0.57
Ash	1.07	2 10
Phosphorus	-----	0.08

About four miles west of Nutallburg a new mine is being opened by Holt & Snyder on the Nutall vein, about 300 feet above the level of the railroad. No analysis of their coal has been made; but it probably does not differ materially in its composition from the Nutallburg. At Hawk's Nest, two miles further west, and thirty miles from Quinnimont, the railroad crosses New River, and the Nutall vein is worked on both sides of the river, this seam being here only about 75 feet above the railroad, having fallen fully 1,500 feet in the 30 miles from Quinnimont. The following analysis was made in 1877 by Professor J. W. Mallet, of the University of Virginia:

ANALYSIS OF HAWK'S NEST COAL.	
Moisture...............	0.93
Fixed Carbon...........	75.37
Volatile Matter........	21.83
Ash	1.87
Sulphur (in ash)......	0 20

With these mines at Hawk's Nest we have completed the list of the coking-coal mines on New River, nine in all, the output for 1880 being estimated at 200,000 tons coal, and by midsummer there will probably be 350 coke ovens in operation, with every indication of a rapid growth of this important industry

At Ansted, about three miles northeast of Hawk's Nest, is the mine of the Hawk's Nest Coal Company, which was opened in 1873 by the Gauley-Kanawha Coal Company. This company ships about 200 tons per day to Eastern markets, where it meets with much favor as a locomotive fuel. Although this mine is in the New River region, the coal is mined from a vein in the Lower Productive Measures, about 400 feet above the Conglomerate, the seam being 11 feet thick, with a very thin slate partings. The following analysis of this coal is taken from *Resources of West Virginia*, by Fontaine and Maury:

ANALYSIS OF ANSTED COAL.	
Carbon	63.10
Volatile Matter.......	32.61
Water	1.40
Ash	2.15
Sulphur	0.74
	100.00

The **Arcadia Furnace Iron Property**, which embraces over 39 square miles of the northeast corner of Botetourt county, Va., has of late become an object of interest to iron manufacturers and also to scientists, mining engineers, and economists, because of the remarkable developments of iron ore that have been made upon it; therefore, an opportunity offering, we recently visited it and inspected these developments, and learned, from a personal examination, the character and condition of its resources, that we might be prepared to speak advisedly concerning them, as well as of the advantages there presented for the cheap manufacture of iron on a large scale.—That our readers may be fully informed in regard to this very large and important mineral property,—a typical one, in many respects, as it presents, on a grand scale, the conditions under which the iron ores of the Western Blue Ridge are often found,—we give in this number:—(1) An accurate topographical map of this large property and its surroundings, by Col. (now. Br. Gen.) T. H. Williamson, of the Va. Military Institute, on which Walter N. Johnston, Esq., the Supt. of Arcadia, has laid down the outcrop lines of the iron ores,—the limonites, or brown hematites, designated by the letter L, the speculars by S, and the magnetites by M,—from the mining operations and explorations conducted by him. (2) A letter from Prof. J. L. Campbell, undoubtedly one of the first of American stratigraphists, on the Geological Features of this property, accompanied by a Geological Section of the Western or Primordial Blue Ridge, in the southwestern part of this estate, which, in a masterly way, interprets to the eye and to the understanding the structure of this range of the Blue Ridge chain at this point, and shows the geological place and vast extent of its strata of specular, or red hematite and limonite, or brown hematite iron ores,—this section is given on the map sheet. (3) On page 110, a somewhat detailed report on this property by Mr. Leonard Forbes Beckwith, M. E., of New York, which describes the character and modes of occurrence of the iron ore deposits of Arcadia, the developments that have been made, the accessibility of the ores, the quantity already mined and the cost of mining, an estimate of the cost of making pig iron at Buchanan, etc. (4) Extracts, on page 112, from a report by L. Bernelmans, M. E., and from J. B. Britton, each giving analyses of the ores, and from a report by Mr. L. E. Lewellen.—All of these gentlemen present fairly and correctly, each from the stand-point of his own observations, the obvious facts of the resources of this property, judging from what we saw in two days of examination.—The extended natural outcrops of the iron ores and the extensive exposures that have been made of them at numerous points, as indicated by the broken red lines of the map, leave, in the mind of one familiar with the conditions in which the iron ores of the Western Blue Ridge are found, no room to doubt the existence here of vast qauntities of limonite and hematite iron ores, in manner, quality, and quantity, as set forth in these documents; and several natural outcrops of magnetites furnish, by their location among the Archæan rocks of the Eastern Blue Ridge and by their character, strong assurances that they will also be found abundant in the unexplored southeastern half of this estate.

The *limonites* seem, from the map, to occupy a N. E.-S. W. belt of the property, on its N. W. side next to James River, about a mile wide and 8 miles long, or eight square miles in area; the ores appearing in 4 lines of outcrop in the S. W., in consequence of the disposition of the ore-bearing stratum in two synclinals, as shown in Prof. Campbell's section. Towards the middle of the belt only 2 outcrops are as yet known, but 4 appear again in the N. E., though in relations suggesting a change in stratigraphical relations. At the western foot of Pine Mountain, especially near Sprout's Branch, this ore outcrops in massive ledges similar to those that elsewhere in the Western Range of the Blue Ridge indicate its presence in great quantities. As stated elsewhere, these ores have not yet been developed to any great extent. These limonites can be mined and transported very cheaply to any point along or near the dozen miles of the railway and river frontage of this estate, for they outcrop near the river and from to a very considerable elevation above its levels and where the river is made navigable and deep by the dams and locks of the canal.

The *specular ores* appear, from the map, to occupy a belt of the property that is about 7 miles long and varying in breadth from near 2 miles in the S. W. to a half mile in the N. E., lying along the S. E. side of the limonite belt, some 8 square miles in area. The map shows 6 lines of outcrop of these ores in the S. W., but Prof. Campbell represents but 4 of these, though in grand proportions, in his section, very properly omitting the most easterly and its counterpart as being merely a highly ferruginous sand-rock and not an ore. In the N. E., at Jennings Creek, only two lines of outcrop have hitherto been found and developed. The mining operations on the easterly one there, at and near the mouth of North Fork, indicate an ore of a superior quality. As the map shows these heavy beds of ore are cut across by Stone Run, Jennings Creek

and Sprout's Branch, and where cut by these streams and their branches, their edges appear with almost vertical dips, rising from the stream levels to many hundred feet above them, so that millions of tons of these ores can here be mined level- and drainage-free, where they can be transported by gravity over short tram-ways of moderate grade, cheaply constructed along stream valleys to the banks of the James, or to the lines of the Richmond & Alleghany or the Valley railways, and probably to the Richmond and South-Western Railway.

The limestone strata associated with the limonites will furnish an abundance of cheap and excellent flux.

It seems to us that here, at or near Buchanan, is one of the places where iron-works on the most extensive scale, embracing furnaces, rolling mills, foundries, nail mills, etc., could be put up, that would have secured to them, under proper management, a certainty of profit from their operations under almost any condition of the markets of this country that can be imagined. Abundant ores and forests for fuel, and water-power are here in close proximity, suggesting the cheap manufacture of high-priced charcoal iron. Ores in at least two, and perhaps in three varieties, can here be delivered at the furnace, at a railway centre, in any quantity that may be desired, at a cost of less than $3 00 for the ton of iron, and the best of coke (such as is described on page 103 of this issue) can be had on most favorable terms. There the best of labor for iron-works operations is plentiful and cheap, food is produced in great variety and abundance, and the climate is suited for all the-year-round work. Two lines of railways, leading directly to good markets and connecting with others that lead to all markets, will be in operation to this point before works could be constructed. If anything is wanted to insure success and profit to such works located here, under proper management, we cannot see what it is. And we hope the sagacious and full-handed northern capitalists, that have demonstrated by development the existence here of such vast quantities of excellent iron ores, will now proceed to erect beside these ores the best of modern furnaces and other iron-works, and demonstrate, as we are certain they can, that iron can be made here as cheaply as it can anywhere in the United States.

Geological Features of the Arcadia Iron Property.

By Prof. J. L. Campbell.

Walter N. Johnston, Esq., Supt., Buchanan, Va.

Dear Sir:—It has recently been my privilege and pleasure, in company with yourself and Maj. Jed. Hotchkiss of Staunton, to examine the developments of iron ores on the Arcadia property, to determine their real characters and probable extent. The chief task assigned me was to determine the geological features of the whole region, so far as these might throw light upon the position and probable extent of the ore beds.

For the general topography of the region covered by these lands; for the quantity of ores available, and for analyses of the ores (which I presume are reliable), you are referred to other reports and the accompanying map.

The portion of the property along the James River borders on the Silurian (or Cambrian) limestones of the Great Valley. The greater part, however, rests upon the Primordial shales and sandstones that make up the great mass of ridges, out-lying knobs, and winding ravines that constitute the N. W. slope of the Blue Ridge range. The Primordial is, geologically, the lowest and oldest of the periods of Silurian age. A considerable area, however, about the head-waters of Jennings Creek, is underlaid by Archæan rocks, still older than the Primordial. The upheaval of the Peaks of Otter caused here a widening of the Blue Ridge proper on this part of its line, and a consequent thrust of the Archæan rocks much farther towards the Great Valley than at points southwest of this. In fact, at the point where our section crosses, no Archæan rocks come to the surface; nor will we find any along the same line of section, till we pass entirely across Buford's Valley.

The Geological Section.—After a careful comparison of all the observations and notes taken at various points, I have concluded to give you a section extending from Buchanan

A REDUCTION
of
The Topographical Map
of the
Arcadia Furnace Iron Property.

ne; while
infer from
connected
metamor-
Mountain,
old, as ex-

shales in
of sand-
limestones
in an in-

n this re-
ore to be
l features.
n are in-
ed condi-
continuity
untain oc-
d crushed
immense
ting force,
he moun-
ually dis-
boulders,

limestone
was cut
belonged,
onnection

as limon-
amorphic
them of
r present
are real
ith their
ral miles

gorge of
the fur-
own hem-
earer the
lly when

extended
its south-
nd in the
rocks a
o be un-
these old
y, and in
nd thor-

mportant
inion as
res. As
ak most
id to you
supply."
lated for
s ravines
which to
cend to-
a down-

FRELL.

in part
lend and
e in the
a at the
features.
details,
ntortions
. L. C.

Manganese Ores.

BY W. A. DONALD, SUP'T. OF THE CRIMORA MINES.

To the many people who have manganese ore, or so imagine, it may be of interest to know something of the relative supply and demand, as indicated by the following tables, lately received from our London correspondent. Manganese ore is shipped to England from Spain, Portugal, Germany, Turkey, Sweden, Nova Scotia, New Brunswick, Cape Colony, New Zealand, the United States, and Canada. The English mines also furnish ore. Virginia, Georgia, and California furnish the bulk of that sent from the United States.

The annual consumption in England and on the Continent is about 25,000 tons. Of this amount, New Zealand furnishes from 3,000 to 4,000 tons of high grade ore. Sweden and New Brunswick will this year furnish from 6,000 to 8,000 tons of rich ore.

The bulk of the ore for chemical purposes comes from Huebra, Spain, where there are from 50 to 60 mines, large and small, at work. These mines this year will furnish at least 8,000 tons, or nearly three-fourths of what the trade will demand. The latest information is that most of this is now held in store awaiting a rise in price. The practical effect of this holding back is quite depressing on the market.

Manganese Ore Shipped from Various Sources During 1879.
(All the following tables are given in tons.)

New Zealand, 2,812; Cape Colony, 141; Virginia, 2,175; Georgia, 820; Canada, 1,112; Sweden, 350; Turkey, 125; Greece, 140; Spain (Salagia), 965; Spain (Lisbon), 2,264; Spain, (Huebra), 5,547; Portugal, 1,357:—Total, 17,808 tons.

Note by correspondent.—"This quantity will be much increased during 1880. We estimate the quantity required for 1880 at 25,000 tons. All of the sources above mentioned can supply more, and will furnish the quanity required without difficulty."

Stock of ore on hand in Great Britain, Jan. 1st, 1880:—

Portuguese, 1,396; Spanish, 25; Turkish, 261; Virginian, 165; Georgian, 331; New Zealand, 690; German, 100; English, 218; Sundries, 128; Total, 3,314 tons.

On the way to England Jan. 1st, 1880:—

Portuguese, 270; Virginian, 131; New Zealand, 1,231; Turkish, 75; Grecian, 148; Canadian, 329; Total, 2,184; In store and on the way, 5,498 tons.

Approximate stock of Manganese ore awaiting shipment January 1st, 1880:—

Spain (Huebra), 7,500; Portugal, 1,000; New Zealand, 1,750; Turkey, 1,300; Sweden, 300; English mines, 250; Virginia, 200; Georgia, 500; Canada, 200.—Total, 13,000. Add to this, stock on hand, 3,314 tons; add also stock in transitu, 2,136 tons.—Total, 18,450 tons.

It will be seen from this last table that about three-fourths of all that was likely to be needed for the year 1880 was already mined, and more than 5,000 tons of it were in stock and in transitu on the 1st day of last January. Much of this surplus may still be held over, but, as said before, the practical effect is to depress the market, as its being so held is known to all dealers.

I have shipped, direct to Liverpool, via Richmond and Norfolk from the Crimora mines, in May last, 293 tons, and in June, to the 15th, 171 tons.

Waynesboro, Va., June 16, 1880.   W. A. DONALD.

Gen. John D. Imboden, from his adopted home in Pittsburg, Pa., wrote us, some time ago, a letter of encouragement in which, among other kindly things, he said—"THE VIRGINIAS is 'opening the eyes of the blind and making the deaf hear' in regard to our resources. Keep it up to the standard of the first and second numbers and it will yet remove, literally, mountains as well as prejudice." And now we are greatly gratified to learn (from our spirited and enterprising neighbor, *The Chronicle* of Charlottesville) that the General is about to return to his native State and locate permanently in Southwest Virginia making Estillville, in Scott county, his home and devoting himself to the management of collieries, coke and iron-works in Wise and Scott, for a wealthy Pitts-

burg Co. for which he has purchased 35,000 A. of mineral lands in those counties and is about to purchase 1,500 more. *The Chronicle* says "iron furnaces and coke ovens will be in operation very shortly, and the General thinks his company has secured the most valuable property in the United States. The iron ores are of the very finest quality, and the varieties of coal equal in grade to the best of the Kanawha Valley, while the supply is absolutely without limit. The capital which will be brought into that section of Virginia by this enterprise, which Gen. Imboden inaugurated and will supervise, will put a new face on everything in that hitherto undeveloped section of Virginia." General Imboden has, with untiring energy, devoted most of his life to active efforts to provote the development of Virginia and in so doing has become thoroughly familiar with her vast resources. The company that has secured his services is to be congratulated and so is the State that so loyal and able a son has returned and is giving his wide experience and well known skill to the development of one of the richest but least known portions of the Commonwealth.—Will not Gen. I. favor our many readers with some notes of conditions and developments in Southwestern Virginia?

The Resources of the Virginias on and near the Proposed Route of the Richmond & Southwestern R'y.

BY THE EDITOR.
CONCLUDED FROM PAGE 96.

NOTE.—Since the issue of the June No. of THE VIRGINIAS, I have visited the Arcadia Iron Property, in Botetourt county, through or near which the line of this railway will pass, and inspected the extensive mining operations that have lately been carried on there under the very intelligent and skillful direction of Walter N. Johnston, Esq., of Buchanan. These operations have fully proven the existence of four or more *continuous beds of specular iron ore* (red hematite), averaging a yard in thickness, that outcrop, in N.E.-S.W. lines, in the Western or Primordial Blue Ridge, for 9 miles, from near Buchanan to the N. E., in a 3-mile wide belt of mountain chain parallel and adjacent to James River. Many thousand tons of this ore, proven by analysis and furnace test to be of good quality, have already been mined from mountain side adits and open cuts. Vast quantities of this specular ore can here be cheaply mined; while from the western side of the same belt, almost on the banks of the James in its eastward bends, *brown hematite ore* (limonite) can be had in abundance from the broad band of that ore that here, as elsewhere accompanies and caps the Potsdam. I have never before seen such a development of specular ores in Virginia, and am satisfied that the inducements offered by their abundance and consequent cheapness in the immediate vicinity of four or five other varieties of ore that are also abundant, and at a moderate distance from the best coking coals of the great Ohio Basin, must go far towards making Botetourt one of the great iron-producing centres of the country.

(Cross Section. No 8, on the Map)

SHOWING THE ABB'S VALLEY DOWNTHROW.

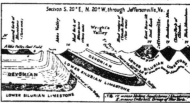

Section S. 20° E, N. 20° W, through Jeffersonville, Va.

The *Valley limestone*, the Lower Silurian, II and III, of the geological map (See THE VIRGINIAS for June, 1880), will be traversed by this railway for more than 200 miles after it leaves the Blue Ridge and before it passes into the great coal field. In the seven divisions and more than a mile of thick-

ness of the rocks of these formations we have limestones of almost every variety and composition. *Hydraulic limestones* are the characteristic ones of the lowest bed of No. II ; most excellent *cement* has for a long time been made from this at Balcony Falls, in the Blue Ridge gap of the James. The *dolomitic* beds that succeed the hydraulic ones, outcrop abundantly, especially on the eastern side of the Valley; these can furnish the best of materials for the *basic bricks* that are now so much in demand for metallurgical purposes. Others of these limestones make the best of lime for agricultural and architectural purposes, and the burning of these has for some time been an important industry on the James in Botetourt. The opening of the R. & S.-W. R'y. will make lime-burning a thriving industry, for it will supply cheap fuel to the lime burners and will traverse a wide region in which there will be a large demand for lime. Superior *building stones* are supplied by some of the members of this group, especially the coralline one, from which Lexington obtains quarry stones of a superior character, such as would be in demand elsewhere if known. No region can furnish more cheaply than this any or all of the varieties of *limestone* that may be needed *for fluxing* in the blast-furnace; some of these contain 98.30 per cent. of carbonate of lime, others abound in alumina. One furnace near the base of the Blue Ridge pays but 18cts. to the ton of iron for its limestone.

Marbles of various kinds abound among these Lower Silurian rocks, but as yet they have not been quarried to any extent. A *gray marble* is mentioned by Rogers, on Stone Run, near Buchanan, lying very near the junction of I and II, solid, massive, fine-grained, and in a bed 50 yds. wide. A fine grained *white marble* is met with in the Valley, especially in Rockbridge. A *dove-* or *dun-colored* marble is quite common. In the Apalachian valleys a fine grained *red marble* is found near the top of No. II, says Rogers, as at the base of Angel's Rest Mountain, near Pearisburg, Giles county ; and in Scott, near Estillville, this reddish, variegated, fossiliferous marble, known in market as *Tennessee marble*, is so abundant it is used for common foundations, and broken up for road metal. The trade in the last mentioned is a very large one from Tennessee, and an increased demand for this beautiful stone is sure to follow an increased supply of it.

Limonite ores are found in pockets, some of them very large, in all portions of the Valley. They are generally imbedded in clay and more or less intimately associated with the cherty or flinty beds of II (Campbell's 3c, p. 86) overlying the dolomitic beds. These ores are generally soft or honey-comb in character, and are noted for producing a remarkably tenacious and durable iron. *Lead* and *zinc* ores and *barytes*, as before stated are common products of formation No. II in Virginia, and, in places, *fluor spar* and a good *buhr-stone.*— Large quantities of barite (barytes) are now shipped to market from the Valley, and the demand for the superior white article here found is sure to increase, since it is used to make from one- to two-thirds of the body of nearly all the "white lead" used, as it adds to the opacity of the paint and protects the lead from being speedily blackened by sulphurous vapors (Dana).

The *brown hematite* (limonite) *iron ores* that accompany the shales in the upper portion of formation III (Hudson River) have not only a remarkable development in Botetourt county, but they are so disposed, in thick, continuous beds and extended outcrops, that they can be cheaply mined on a large scale. Purgatory and Garden mountains that boldly flank the county for a dozen miles on the northeast and nearly cross the Great Valley; and Bigg's (Rat-hole), Crawford's, Caldwell's and North mountains that are in its northwest border for more than 20 miles; and McAffee's and Tinker mountains

that flank it on the southwest for near 10 miles, also nearly crossing the Valley ; are all banded on their flanks or around their crests by a well-nigh continuous outcrop of a thick stratum of these ores of III. A sample of this ore from Crawford's Mountain, near Catawba Furnace, gave Rogers 81.16 per cent. per-oxide of iron (56.80 metallic iron), 4.90 silica, 0.40 alumina, 13.27 water, and 0.26 loss. An analysis that explains why the iron made from these ores at Catawba, Etna and other Botetourt furnaces had such an excellent reputation. An inspection of the sections shows that there are many exposures of the junction of III and IV, the place of these ores; and the bordering of the Lower and Upper Silurian areas of the geological map indicate the same thing.

CONTINUATION OF SECTION No. 8 (OF THE MAP) SOUTHWARD.

In Apalachia and Trans-Apalachia.—After crossing the Great Lower Silurian (Silurio-Cambrian) Valley, the line of this railway enters, in the western border of Botetourt, the Apalachian system of mountains proper; the one which Lesley describes as composed of "interminably long and narrow barrow mountains, with level summits, seldom a thousand feet in height, looped and gophered in an intricate and artificial style (see geological map), with lens-shaped coves in the northern part; and on the other hand, in the Southern States, terminating in pairs of perfectly straight ridges, cut off by short faults." This belt of mountain-and-valley country, lying northwest of and alongside the Great Valley, is boldly carved, in high relief, from all the geological formations from II to XII or XIII, inclusive, from the Siluro-Cambrian to the Great Carboniferous, and its mineral wealth has all the variety and abundance implied in numerous and repeated out-crops, in horizontal, vertical, inclined, and all forms of anticlinal and synclinal disposition, of the eighteen or more groups of rocks here naturally exposed.

Explanatory.—The upper Silurian area of the geological map, that in reddish-brown, that which Rogers now prefers to call simply *Silurian*, embraces the Virginia formations IV, V, VI, and VII. In the system of the New York Survey, or of Dana's Manual, IV is the equivalent of 5a. Medina ; V of 5b. Clinton, 5c. Niagara, and 6. Salina ; VI of 7. Lower Helderberg ; and VII of 8. Oriskany. In the First Pennsylvania Survey, IV is called Levant, the bottom member of V Sargent, and the middle and top Scalent, VI Pro-Meridian, and VII Meridian ; in the 2nd Survey, VI is called Lewistown Limestone, and VII is put as the lowest member of the Devonian group.

The Devonian area of the map, the light brown, includes VIII and IX of the Virginia formations ; VIII, the Cadent of the 1st Pennsylvania Survey, including 10a. Marcellus, 10b. Hamilton, 10c. Genesee, 11a. Portage, and 11b. Chemung of the New York Survey ; and IX the Ponent of the 1st Pennsylvania Survey, representing 12. Catskill of New York, the rocks that form the base of the Catskill Mountains, the Catskill Red Sandstone.

The white, or uncolored patches of the map represent outcrops of formation X, that of the *Lowest Coal Group* in Virginia, which Rogers now makes the Lower Carboniferous general group, or 13a. Montgomery Grits and Coal Measures ; the Vespertine Sandstone and Coal of the 1st Pennsylvania Survey, and the Pocono Grey Sandstone of the 2d.—In this formation, as shown in sections 24 and 25 (see back of geol.

map), are found beds of anthracite and semi-bituminous coal, described hereafter.

The Carboniferous Limestone Group, that of the pinkish area of the map, is that of formation XI, the 13b. Greenbrier Limestone (sub-carb. limestones), and 13b. Greenbrier Shales, of the Middle Carboniferous; the Umbral Limestones and Shales of the 1st Pennsylvania Survey, and the Mauch Chunk Red Shale of the 2d.

The Great Coal Group, the Upper Carboniferous, the dark, or slate colored area of the map, is that of the Virginia formations XII to XVI, inclusive, the Seral of the 1st Pa. Survey. The equivalents in Pa. are, of XII, 14a. Great Conglomerate and Conglomerate Coal Group; of XIII, 14b. Lower Coal Group; of XIV, 14b. Lower Barren Group; of XV, 14c. Upper Coal Group; and of XVI, 14c. Upper Barren Group. In the 2nd. Pa. Survey XII is 14a. Pottsville Conglomerate, and the rest of the group is 14b. Alleghany River Coal Series with Lower Barren Measures above, and 14c. Monongahela River Coal Measures with Upper Barren Measures above. As stated in the Feb. No. of THE VIRGINIAS we prefer, as best suited to the geological conditions found in Virginia and West Virginia, to call X the *Lowest* Coal Measures, XII the *Lower* Coal Measures, XIII and XIV the *Middle* Coal Measures, and XV and XVI the *Upper* Coal Measures. Sections 21 and 25 show how the outcrops of XII, those containing the *Lower* or New River coals, form the eastern border of the Great Ohio Basin Coal-field.

The mineral resources of the Lower Silurian areas of Apalachia are the same as those of the Lower Silurian of The Valley, as above detailed. Those that almost invariably accompany the Upper Silurian, Devonian and Carboniferous rocks of this region, and their place in those rocks, may, at first, be mentioned briefly; for a study of the geological sections by Prof. Rogers, Nos. 24 and 25 on the back of the map in the June No. of THE VIRGINIAS, and of those by Prof. J. P. Lesley, now the State Geologist of Pennsylvania, (for the use of which we are indebted to his kindness), in connection with these statements, will show very clearly that all portions of this region must have large stores of very accessible mineral wealth. The sections are real ones that represent the actual condition in which the rocks of this region are found, so that anyone that has these in hand and is possessed of the art of seeing can soon learn to trace out the exposed lines of each formation and know where to look for the outcrops of their beds of iron ore, coal, etc., and to have some conception of their extent.

Formation No. V always has two, and sometimes has three or more, beds of *red-shale* or *fossil iron ore* as regularly stratified members of its calcareous shales. One of these beds is near the bottom of this Clinton formation, consequently these highly esteemed ores are often found held in shallow depressions, synclinal troughs, of the hard sandstones of IV, the underlying formation, where most of V has been denuded, as in section No. 24 (See back of map in June No.), the grand one seen in looking N. E. from Pearisburg, where Rogers shows nine such depressions in the elevated, Mountain Lake, or Giles-Craig plateau, that of John's Creek, Middle and Peter's mountains; and in each of those troughs, the valleys of the head waters of Potts' and Craig's, and Big and Little Stony creeks, are found those ores. In section No. 25 it will be seen that in Wolf Creek valley V is the top of an anticlinal, or arch, and there this ore is found. These sections also show how formation V outcrops on or along Catawba, Craig's Creek, Cove, Big Walker's, Wolf Creek, Buck-horn and East River mountains; the sections from Lesley, in this paper, show how it is held on Paint lick and Deskin's mountains; those from the

Kentucky survey (see March No. of The Virginias) show their disposition in Poor-valley Ridge, the eastern foot hills of Cumberland Mountain, so-called; and that from Safford, No. 44 (see back of map in June No.), exhibits its outcrops, in the stratum designated as 5c., or the Dyestone Group, in Poor-valley Ridge, Powell's Mountain and Newman's Ridge on the east of Powell's River valley, in Lee and Scott, all suggested by the Upper Silurian belts of the geological map. In all these exposures of V are the beds of its peculiar ores, holding a thickness ranging from 1 to 6 ft.

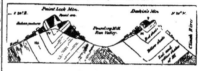

CROSS SECTION AT THE ROAD FROM THE CHURCH TO CLINCH RIVER ABOVE CEDAR BLUFFS; AT LYLE'S GAP.

Prof. J. P. Lesley, in a brief report on this Apalachian region, made in 1870, says:—"This mountain belt is rich in iron ores (of two varieties), in gypsum, in salt, and in bituminous coal. Its valleys run in pairs, the northwesternmost of each pair being always a *limestone valley*, resembling in all respects (except in size) the valley of the Shenandoah ; equally fertile, growing naturally the blue grass, and sending large herds of cattle to market ; long settled with a hardy, intelligent, virtuous and enterprising population, and abounding in brown hematite iron ore deposits.

The southeasternmost of each pair is always a *shale and sandstone valley*, or, as the inhabitants of the limestone valleys call it, a 'poor valley.' It is made by the erosion of the Upper Silurian and Devonian formations interposed between the two sandrocks, No. IV and No. X (Shawangunk and Catskill), which are left as its bounding mountains.—(See section, page 107.) Every such 'poor valley' has a co-extensive outcrop of the famous 'dyestone,' 'bloodstone,' 'paint' or 'fossil ore,' of the Frankstown, Hollidaysburg, Lewistown, Danville and Bloomsburg iron districts of Pennsylvania, the Clinton ore of New York (formation No. V), and the ore which furnishes the mineral for the furnaces in Tennessee, and the iron-works about Chattanooga.

The whole belt is a direct prolongation of the iron-making Juniata region of Middle Pennsylvania, and is sure to become equally famous for its iron-works, when a railroad is once built to encourage the opening of its mines and the erection of furnaces, forges and rolling mills."

And in a paper on "The Geological Structure of [Tazewell,"Russell and Wise Counties, in Virginia," read April 21st, 1870, before the American Philosophical Society, by the same eminent geologist, based on personal observations the paper from which the cuts here given are taken, by permission of Prof. Lesley, it is stated :—"The valleys of Tazewell and Russell, in Virginia, being geological as well as geographical prolongations of the interior limestone valleys of Pennsylvania, such as the Nittany, Morrison's Cove, and Kishicoquilis, contain necessarily the same kinds of ore, in the same formations and in the same conditions. I mean that the unbroken ground is at present covered with patches of brown hematite 'blossom,' just as the ground used to be where our charcoal furnaces stand ; and that the color of the road and field soil is the same as that of our best iron ore banks ; the limestone rocks project in the same style, have the same internal composition, and exhibit the same corroded and dissolved surfaces ; and pot-holes, caverns and sinks abound along certain lines of outcrop. All these things are now known to bear an intimate relationship with both the original setting free of the mineral iron from the lime-rocks and its subsequent deposit as

dation. And it seems to be becoming clear to our geologists, that while there are regularly stratified beds and belts of the ore at two or three distinct horizons in the Lower Silurian Limestone Formation, which may be traced for many miles along the strike of the rocks, there are also vast accumulations of this brown hematite ore along anticlinal axes, especially wherever these are fractured; or degenerate into pure upthrow faults. It stands to reason that such a line of fracture, with a high wall on one side of it, should, in the course of thousands of ages, have collected vast quantities of the peroxidized iron which was being, through all these ages, set free in the slow dissolution of the limestones and the reduction of the whole mass of upheaved country to its present level. To say nothing of the facility afforded by such fissures to the decomposing and recomposing agency of drainage waters. It is along the great upthrow fissures, then, that we are first to seek the iron ore deposits of this section of Virginia.''—Prof. Lesley then mentions the ''large masses of blossom'' on the hills bordering the N. bank of the Clinch in Russell Co., in the hills S. E. of Jeffersonville, in the cove of Wolf Creek, behind Buckhorn Ridge, in the different valleys of Wolf Creek and its branches, etc.

Prof. Lesley, writing of this ore of V in this very region, after he had examined it, says;—''But the ore is there; and, as in Pennsylvania and Tennessee, it will run for miles together in a workable condition as to size and posture and prove a source of wealth.—The principal use of this ore is to mix with other varieties,—with the blue carbonate lean ores of the Coal Measures, especially; but also with the inferior grades of brown hematite. The time will come when it will be smelted in connection with the primary ores of the Blue Ridge Range and Smoky mountains.'' He saw this ore as held in the singular synclinal forming the crest of Paint-lick Mountain (see section and view here given); a deposit of ore from

.PAINT LICK MTN, FROM THE SOUTH; CLIFFS AND ORE.

the outcrop of which the Indians obtained paint for their faces and lodges, and with which they painted on the solid rock wall of IV, on the face of that mountain, where they remain, ''numerous pictures and symbols of men and animals in red paint, fresh as when first made, and older than the settlement of the country by the whites.''—Lesley.

''There are extensive outcrops of the fossil ore of No. V along Poor Valley; in fact the deposit (whether rich or not remains to be discovered) runs uninterruptedly more than a hundred miles in an almost mathematical straight line along the south flank of the Clinch Mountain, from Tennessee, past Moccason Gap, back of Saltville, past Sharon Alum Springs, to Hunting Camp and Kimberling creeks, and so on, eastward, across New River towards the James River country.''—Lesley.

The quality of these ores may be inferred from an analysis of one from Poor-valley Ridge, in Lee, by the Kentucky Survey (see p. 80 of THE VIRGINIAS), which gave 54.16 per cent. metallic iron, 0.14 phosphorus, 3.94 alumina, 0 42 lime carbonate, 15.96 silica and insol. silicates, 0 31 phosphoric acid, and 2 50 combined water.

Formation VI, the Lower Helderberg of N. Y., is an abundant heavily bedded limestone in Apalachian or northwestern Botetourt, but it appears to thin to the southwestward. Prof. Rogers found a bed of it in Botetourt that proved, by analysis, an excellent hydraulic

limestone, from which superior cement could be manufactured; it is used for a blast-furnace flux in this region, with satisfactory results, and from it are obtained beautiful encrinal marbles, that have of late become very popular for furniture and other purposes.

Formation VII, the Oriskany, as sections 24 and 25 (on map in June number) show, outcrops as one of the components of Catawba, Craig's Creek, John's Creek, Cove, Big Walker's, Wolf Creek, East River, and other mountains, on and near the line of this railway. Its outcrop is the one that most attracts attention, a rusty yellow, decaying sandstone, may generally be found along the borders of the Upper Silurian areas of the geological map, for it is the upper member of that group of formations. Formation VII is here one of the great iron-bearing ones. I have never found in the central portion of Apalachian Virginia any considerable exposure of this formation that was not accompanied by one or more heavy beds of excellent limonite; and often nearly the whole thickness of the formation, sometimes as much as 100 feet, is either a series of beds of solid ore, varying in purity, but most of them rich enough for use, or a decayed mass of mingled soft and hard ores, clay and other materials. Often a solid bed of ore, 12 ft. or more thick, containing as a mass 50 per cent. or more of metallic iron, rests immediately on a limestone bed of No. VI that will furnish the best of flux for mixing with this ore in the blast-furnace, while beneath that VI, in the gorges and on the slopes of the same ridges, outcrop the red shale and fossil ores of V, a yard in thickness, that are so desirable for mixing with those of VII to produce the best grades of iron.—These conditions may be seen at many points along the chain of Rich-patch Mountain and its extensions in Botetourt and Craig counties, at Callie, Roaring Run, and Grace furnaces, and their existence,—at moderate distances from the Lower Measure coking coals, such as are described by Mr. Morris on page 103, and such as the Richmond & South-Western Railway will reach some 75 miles southwest of these places,—clearly indicate the localities where iron making can be easily conducted on a large scale, with a certainty of remunerative returns under all conditions of trade, whenever lines of transportation to coal and to markets reach these localities.

Formations No. VIII and No. IX, the Devonian ones, as the map and sections indicate, do not occupy a very large proportion of this region. The former is the shales and slates of the poor valleys and the lines of broken, slaty hills that border them; the latter is the hard sandstone that underlies and sustains the bolder poor ridges and mountains back of the slaty hills. Pockets of iron ore are here sometimes found in VIII, but so far none of any great extent. The aluminous shales of the same formation may yet be utilized in the manufacture of alum. Mineral springs, especially those called alum springs, abound in the areas of VIII. No minerals of value are known to be in IX, unless its massive sand-rocks prove to be good for masonry.

Formation No. X, the Lowest Coal Group, as the white strips and patches of the geological map and the sections show, has a larger development on this line than elsewhere in Va. This formation is of interest because it generally contains two or more workable beds of semi-anthracite or semi-bituminous coal; those at New River (according to Lesley in the Trans. of Am. Philosophical Society for 1862,) are, the lower bed 3 ft. and the upper one, in places, 9 ft. thick. The quality of the coal is excellent, that from near Catawba Furnace, in Botetourt, was found by Rogers to contain of Carbon 78.80 per cent., of Bitumen 16 20, and of Ash 5.00; and that from Brush Mountain, in Montgomery, on the bank of New River, yielded 80 20 per cent. Carbon, 13.60 Bitumen, and 6 20 Ash. The disposition of this formation and its coal beds in the Brush and the Brushy Mountain ranges is shown in sections No. 24 and 25 of our June number and in one of the accompanying sections from Lesley. Most of these coal beds are cut off by the ''faults'' made by the great up- and down-throws of this region, and they are generally badly crushed; but they contain large quantities of superior coal, that may prove of great value in the development of this region.

The Arcadia Iron Property.

By Leonard Forbes Beckwith, m. e.

General Description.—The Arcadia Iron Property is situated in Botetourt county, Virginia, on the south side of the James River, along which it stretches eastward for a distance of about 7 miles, or almost 12 miles if the windings of the river are followed, from the small town of Buchanan, the western terminus of the James River and Kanawha Canal, which extends from Richmond to Buchanan.

The property extends south of the river some 6¼ miles and covers 24,000 acres, of which 20,000 are held in fee, and 4,000 in mineral right, the surface having been sold

The general character of the property is very mountainous and it is cut up by heavily wooded ridges nearly 2,500 feet high, above tide, running parallel to the main chain of the Blue Ridge, the Peaks of Otter of which, about 4,400 feet high, are just beyond the lines of this property.

Part of the land in the valleys is fit for cultivation and can be sold later to advantage reserving the mineral rights. There is a great deal of fine timber on the property, suitable for charcoal, mine timbers, ties, &c.

There is a small charcoal blast furnace on the estate; this will be described later.

The main value of the Arcadia Iron Property consists in its extensive deposits of iron ore, Red Hematite, Brown Hematite or Limonite, and Magnetic. These have been opened at different points on the property.

The investigations made by the writer were confined to the northwestern quarter of the estate, comprised between Stone Creek valley, the James River, Jennings Creek, and the ridges about three miles back from the river. The chief deposits of red hematite lie in this district, where they are well developed, as well as some brown hematite and magnetite. In the remainder of the estate it is presumed that considerable deposits will be developed, as it is known to contain brown hematite ore.

Red Hematite Ores.—These ores have been chiefly developed in the *Stone Creek valley.* They lie in beds which will average 3 feet thick, varying from 2 ft. 9 inches to 3 ft. 6 inches. They are bedded in slates underlying the Potsdam sandstone, to which they are non-conformable. The ore beds and slates dip to the S.S.E., near the outcrops from 25° to 40° with a final regular dip of 27° where the excavations and tunnels penetrate the hills. The underlying sandstone dips N.N.W. across the edges of the slates.

Seven beds of ore have been discovered of which four have been proved by openings at different points. The highest beds have been proved at points between 7 and 8 miles apart, as well as at intermediate points. Stone Creek cuts these beds, almost at a right angle, and enables them to be mined from below by tunnels and stoping, affording natural drainage to the mines, and avoiding the expenses of hoisting and pumping. All the beds are above the waters of the creek, and crop out on each side of the valley. The handling of ore from the time it is mined, is therefore down hill, and a tram-road along the bottom of the valley can convey the cars of ore to the James River. The cars can be loaded from shutes at the entrance of the cuts and tunnels. Power is therefore required only for hauling the empty cars up to the mines, the loaded cars descending by their own weight.

The ore beds all lie with a solid standstone or quartzite roof as hanging wall, and soft clay slates as a foot wall or floor. This presents advantages in mining, as the height for tunnels is cut in the slates; and in removing the ore, the soft slates are cut away below, and the solid bench of ore is blasted down in large masses. This enables the mining to be cheaply conducted, the roof being very firm and not requiring heavy timbering.

The ore breaks up into cubical blocks, jointed, and presents a very hard compact body, with numerous siliceous particles. It is observed that the latter diminish in quantity as the tunnels penetrate into the beds. The ore by careful measurement weighs 168 pounds per cubic foot, a block of about 10½ cubic feet weighing 3,800 pounds.

A good country road ascends the west side of the Stone Creek valley and crosses the outcrops of the different beds.

The first bed opened is at a point about 1½ miles from the the mouth of the creek, at an elevation of 1,060 feet above the

James River (This measurement and that of the following heights were taken by Prof. Platt with a barometer). The bed is 3 feet thick, well defined, good ore. The same bed is opened on the opposite or east side of Stone Creek valley and shows the same thickness and character of ore, as well as geological formation.

A short distance further south a second bed is opened, at a height of 1,160 feet above the river level. This bed has probably some 400 feet difference in level with the first bed in the geological formation, owing to the dip. The ore is about 2 ft. 6 ins. thick near the outcrop, but widens to nearly three feet at the breast in the tunnel which is driven some 60 or 70 feet into the hill. This tunnel shows, as does also the succeeding one on the upper bed, the remarkably solid character of the whole formation, and the small timbering required.

About half a mile further south a third bed is opened by a tunnel, 1,390 feet above the river level, with 2 ft. 6 ins. of ore at the outcrop, widening to about 3 feet further in. The ore in these beds are all identical in character.

Further south, a mile distant from the third bed, is the fourth bed, the highest of all, 1,660 feet above the James River. This opening is therefore about 3 miles from the latter. The crest of the ridge is about 2,000 feet above the river. This bed has a greenish colored slate for the roof and floor, and the general direction of the outcrop is W.S.W. The outcrop of this bed is cut at right angles by a number of small ravines running down into Stone Creek valley, and in a length of half a mile five open cuts have been made on this outcrop at the points of intersection with the ravines. These cuts have been driven right and left along the outcrop at each point into the hillside, and a very considerable quantity of fine compact ore taken out and stacked in heaps ready for removal. At some openings as much as 3,000 tons of ore are collected, and a fair estimate of the total quantity of ore already mined at all the openings would be 20,000 tons. This ore is ready for shipment. The ore of this upper bed is not so siliceous as that of the other beds; its streak is very red, and the general character of the ore is excellent. The bed presents a thickness varying from 2 ft. 6 ins. to 3 feet. 6 inches. and the general formation as shown by the breast in the cuts is much distorted, the ore forming a double fold or S, with an almost vertical dip at the outcrop, and finally tending to a regular dip of about 27° as the bed sinks into the mountain. Between the open cuts, the ore would rise about a couple of hundred feet to the outcrop. The mining of the upper or 4th. bed has the great advantage of this double fold in the ore collecting large masses of some 9 or 12 ft. of ore in a very small section, and it can be therefore worked very cheaply.

The outcrop has been followed to the S.W. of the Stone Creek valley, and also on the mountains to the N. E. The same ore has been proved, it is assured, between 7 and 8 miles N.E. of these openings.

Between the bottom of the Stone Creek ravine and the outcrops of the beds of ore lower down the valley, there are several hundred feet in each instance, all of which being above water level and being easily mined from the ravine by tunnels at different levels is therefore available.

As previously mentioned the preferable way to transport the ore to the river would be by a tram-road or narrow-guage railway. Much of the grading for this has been completed, with a grade of about 300 feet to the mile, and 2,000 ties have been cut and are ready for use. About 3,000 ties in all are needed. The total length would be 3 miles, and the cost of transportation would be in the neighborhood of 10 cents per ton. At present for cartage by the ton 50 cents is asked, but it can be probably done for half this price.

One hundred thousand tons of ore can readily be mined per annum from the mines on Stone Creek alone, without making any great inroad on them for many years. Admitting an average thickness of 3 ft. for each of the four beds, and a weight of 358 lbs. per cubic foot, an acre in area of the four beds together would give about 98,000 tons of ore. Taking an average distance of a couple of hundred feet (300 feet would be nearer the reality) between the outcrops and the lowest point at which each vein can be worked above water level, which in this case is the bottom of Stone Creek, a mile of outcrop corresponds to about 2¼ millions of tons. This average of two hundred feet is a minimum, the distance being

frequently much greater, and further the additional folds of the upper vein are not taken into account, all of which would swell the above total.

The cost of mining so far has been 75 cents per ton, delivered on the dump at the entrance of each mine. This figure is based on 20,000 tons mined, and includes the cost of all prospecting and permanent improvements, such as roads, tools, workmen's houses in the Stone Creek valley for 150 men, 1,800 cords of wood cut, repairs to furnace, &c. It may therefore be taken as an outside figure, although on the other hand, much of the ore already mined is from outcrop and open-cut work. It is presumed the cost of mining will not exceed 75 cents even when more tunneling and timbering may be required. This low cost is due to the fact that colored labor at $1. per day of 11 hours is employed with white foremen. As to the cost of delivering in canal boats on the James River the writer believes that at present it can be done, by teaming, at a price not to exceed $1. per ton, inclusive of mining.

In the valley of Jennings Creek, several miles east of Stone Creek, there are several openings of ore-beds which are identical in character of ore and general formation with the ore-beds of Stone Creek.

About 2 miles above the mouth of Jennings Creek, a bed of red hematite ore is opened 3 feet thick, dipping 'S. and E. about 50°. The elevation of this opening is 250 feet above the James River.

At a distance of about ¼ mile above the old blast-furnace, at the intersection or junction of the North Branch and Jennings Creek, a red hematite ore-bed is opened, about 1 ft. 4 in. thick, with a hanging wall of quartzite and a foot-wall of soft, smooth, steatitic and talcose slate rocks. Continuing up the hill, the ore is opened at four places on the strike, the highest opening being 450 ft. above the lowest one. These different openings show the iron ore bed with an average thickness of 3 ft. as before. The ore is identical with that of Stone Creek, the resemblance being so striking as to preclude the idea that it is any other ore. The lowest opening of these ores is 100 ft. above the James River.

On account of the proximity and low elevation of the Jennings Run ores, they would cost less to deliver on the canal-boats, at the James River, than the Stone Creek ores.

Analyses of these ores have been made by several parties, as follows :

	(1)	(2)	(3)	(4)
Metallic Iron	44.90	49.95	55.80	43.30
Phosphorus	0.48	0.40	0.39	0.47
Sulphur		0.06	trace	
Silica	26.80	19.69		38.30
Manganese		trace		

(1) By McCreath, Chemist of the 2d Pa. Geol. Survey, April 13th, 1880, an average of samples from the outcrops of different openings, on Stone Creek, selected by Prof. Platt.——(2) By Prof. Thos. Egleston, of the School of Mines of Columbia College, New York, March 27th, 1880, of sampl selected by Prof. Platt from outcrops in Stone Creek Valley.——(3) By Prof. Fred. W. Taylor, of the Smithsonian Institution, Washington, D. C., an average of 9 samples from 8 openings, 3 ft. under surface, from Stone Creek Valley. Kindly furnished by Dr. E. N. Wood, who owns lands adjacent to Arcadia, on which he has developed the continuation of the stratum of ore worked in tunnel No. 1. Prof. Taylor says of this : "I consider it a valuable ore, and do not think the small amount of phosphorus will prove injurious."—— (4) By McCreath, of Pa. Survey, April 13th, 1880, an average of samples from different outcrops on Jennings' Creek.

The analyses of these ores, as well as their physical characteristics, formation, dip, &c., and the way in which they are met in parallel beds in similar measures, show very conclusively that they are continuous ore-beds, and it is perfectly safe to rely on them to afford an enormous quantity of iron ore along the outcrops and between the points where they are opened.

Professor Franklin Platt, of the Pennsylvania Second Geological Survey, after a close examination of the property in April, 1880, and before the developments had shown as conclusively as they do at present the large amount of ore, had reached the opinion that the quantity of ore was immense, and one "that an ordinary furnace plant would make but little impression on."

It will be noticed that this ore is strong in silica; it is fit for mixture with the aluminous ores, limonites, (brown hematites,) of the estate with which it would give very satifactory

results. It would be beneficial, also, for mixture with hematites found along the whole eastern half of the Chesapeake & Ohio R'y, and its tenor in iron is higher than the average of these hematites, its fluxing qualities would make it very valuable. The writer also believes that the length of the campaigns of the furnaces along the above railroad, would be increased by its use, and probably less limestone required as a flux.

Magnetic Iron Ore.—On the southern slope of the ridge, which runs parallel to the James, about 2 miles back from the latter, a strong outcrop of magnetic iron ore is met, very rich in alumina, and between 6 to 7 feet thick. The outcrop can be followed some distance. It is imbedded in slates which are parallel to it and enclose it, and the dip at the outcrop is almost vertical. The outcrop has been simply opened by a blast, but no work done beyond this.

Brown Hematites, or Limonites, exist at several points on the property, and were mined quite extensively during the Rebellion to supply the small charcoal furnace which ran on them exclusively. The writer understands that there are considerable quantities of these ores at the openings made, but did not investigate them. Near the old furnace are heaps of ore showing that some of the brown hematites were roasted before use.

The Charcoal Blast Furnace, on the property, not far from James River, and near the mouth of Jennings Creek, was built in 1862, and run by the Confederate Government, but has been out of blast since the war. The furnace is of stone, 36 ft. high by 9 ft. bosh, and supplied by blast from two cylinders driven by a breast-wheel, supplied with water from Jennings Creek, across which a dam was thrown. Only one tuyere was used, and a *very small* hot-blast stove placed at the throat of the furnace.

The furnace is already being put in repair, another tuyere added, a new breast-wheel is already cut out and ready to be put together. The furnace remains to be relined and the stock house, as well as water-way, to be rebuilt. It is estimated that the total expenses of putting the furnace in full running order will amount to $2,600, and that she will be able to make from 10 to 12 tons per day, at a cost of about $12 per ton. The writer is informed that 1,300 cords of wood for charcoal are already cut, and considerable charcoal made.

Market for Ores.—The present outlet is from Buchanan, by the James River & Kanawha Canal to Lynchburg, 50 miles, and thence to Richmond and to the eastward by canal or railroad. The freight by canal-boat to Lynchburg is 70 cents per ton, by the cargo. At that point the ore can be shipped either North to furnaces in Maryland and Southern Pennsylvania, or Westward by the Virginia Midland and Chesapeake & Ohio railroads to Huntington on the Ohio River. At that place it is understood it can be sold for not less than $6 per ton, which would leave a good return on its cost.

The Richmond & Alleghany Railroad Company is now building a line from Buchanan to Clifton Forge, on the Chesapeake & Ohio R'y, 34 miles distant. This will be opened by the autumn of this year, and will afford a short outlet for the ore to the West, and to furnaces along the Chesapeake & Ohio R'y, with a return freight for coal and coke, which will then preferably come to Buchanan for distribution along the line of James River.

The balance of the Richmond & Alleghany Railroad, from Buchanan to Richmond, is to be built along the canal, which is ceded to the company by the State of Virginia, and which affords an easy grade to tide-water. It is expected that this main part of the line will be built in 20 months, but until then the canal will be available for freights eastward. The railroad runs for miles along the northern boundary of the property, and will be of much advantage in developing it. The rate of ½ of a cent per mile can probably be obtained from the railroads on large contracts for transportation.

Blast Furnace Plant.—There are two sites, at the mouths of Stone Creek and Jennings Creek, where there is a never-failing supply of water and room for extension, which are particularly favorable for a blast furnace plant for which the Arcadia property presents numerous advantages.

Inexhaustible supplies of iron ore and limestone are at hand, and the completion of the railroad to Clifton Forge connects it with the New River coke district, at Quinnimont and beyond, in West Virginia.

The cars carrying coke to Buchanan can have a return freight of ore for the Ohio Valley.

The market for the pig metal can be sought west in Cincinnati, where the price averages $5 a ton higher than east of the Alleghanies, or it may be sought east in Lynchburg and Richmond, or by water-freights access can be had to Baltimore, Philadelphia and New York.

The new rail mill of the James River Steel Manufacturing and Mining Company, at Lynchburg, would be a good customer, to the mutual advantage of both works.

The following estimate of the cost of making pig iron at Buchanan is believed to be a safe estimate; it is based upon the supposition that the owners of the furnaces own also their own coal lands and coke ovens in the New River district. The coke in that case would cost them $1.75 per ton, and about $1.25 freight, or about $3.00 at Buchanan. If the coke was bought in the open market, it would be worth at least $3.00 at the ovens, which with the freight added would make $4.25 per ton at Buchanan.

2¼ tons ore at $1.,	$ 2.25
1 ton limestone at 50 cents,	.50
1½ tons coke at $3.,	4.50
Labor	2.50
General expenses 50 cts.; taxes 8 cts.; insurance 10 cts.; repairs 25 cts.; management 25 cts.; total,	1.18
Total cost at the furnace,	$10.93
Freight to New York, or to Cincinnati,	3.50
Commission 2 per cent.; discount and interest 50 cts.,	1.06
Total cost at market,	$15.49

These figures show that pig metal can be made on this property in the dullest times to advantage. Pig metal, No. 1 foundry, is very seldom below $20. in New York, or $25. in Cincinnati.

For charcoal iron, substituting 125 bush. of charcoal for the coke, most of the other items remaining the same, it will be seen that as long as charcoal can be obtained inside of 10 cts. a bushel, on account of the extra price of the pig metal, $32 to $35, there is every advantage in making it. The present price of charcoal is said to be 5 cts. a bushel, cost price.

Summary.—The Arcadia property presents, in the quarter of the area investigated, enough iron ore to supply several furnaces on the spot, and to supply a large quantity of ore for shipment. Havii g plenty of timber, limestone, running water, and advantages of location in being able to reach a Western or Eastern market, it can, in my judgment, rely on making money in the most depressed times, with large returns in the usual conditions of the markets. In the balance of the estate, three-fourths of the whole area, there is every probability of developing additional ore deposits.

LEONARD FORBES BECKWITH, M. E.

New York, May 31, 1880.

L. Bemelmans, M. E., of Charleston, W. Va., whose paper on "The Manufacture of Coke" appeared in the March number of THE VIRGINIAS, made a report on this property in 1873, after having carefully explored it for its whole length and analysed its ores. His analyses of 11 samples of iron ores which he collected from different localities, from natural, surface outcrops, (for there had been no development at that time), gave the following percentages of metallic iron, viz: 29.1, 35.0, 40.0, 42.5, 42.5, 42.5, 41.6, 47.5, 47.7, 50.0, and 52.0.

He says:—"Here it is but seldom that any indications of sulphur can be found, but most of the ores are remarkably pure and contain manganese." "A simple inspection of this estate, combined with the actual results of workings in the neighborhood, and the analyses and tests I have made, convince me that this property contains immense amounts of iron ore of very superior quality. As to quantity, it is so great as to make it impossible to give anything like an approximate estimate, as estimates of this character cannot be made with any approach to accuracy until excavations have been made, conclusively showing the length, breadth, and depth of all the deposits. I have no hesitation in saying that I regard the question of the successful working of this estate, as an iron property, to depend simply on two things, viz: ordinary facilities for fuel and transportation. I regard the supply of iron ore abundant, and durable for several generations of miners at least. I would recommend the purchaser of this estate to also secure a coal property on the line of the Chesapeake & Ohio Railway."

J. B. Britton made two analyses of Arcadia iron ores in April, 1879, that from mine No. 3, now the 2nd tunnel, contained 42.98 metallic iron; and that from mine No. 5 contained 47.86. The samples analysed were from the surface.

L. E. Lewellen, of Pottsville, Pa. (now dead), a practical miner of large experience and a very skillful and reliable explorer, spent some time on the Arcadia estate, in the fall of 1874, and made a sensible report of his explorations, from which the following extracts are taken:

"The greater portion of the property is covered with the original growth of *timber*, the most of which is very heavy for mountain timber. *Chestnut-oaks* form a large proportion of this and their bark could be made useful for tanning purposes."

"A vein of *hematite ore* runs the whole length of the lands, forming two dips; the one dipping towards the Valley, and the other towards the mountain. At some points they are connected, forming an anticlinal axis; at other points they are some distance apart. Shafts or holes have been dug on this vein in several places from one end of the property to the other."

. . . "I am confident from the surface indications, and from the trials already made, that this vein contains an abundance of good brown hematite ore. Along the line of this vein, but separate from it, there are several deposits of very rich hematite ore, the extent of which cannot be ascertained except by actual working. There is also a deposit of hematite ore on Sprout's Run, which, from surface indications and what little digging has been done, looks favorable. The ore is of a very fine character and so situated that it can be raised and put to the furnace at a small cost. While a great many holes have been dug on the hematite vein, at different points, and more or less ore found in them, still I do not think they were generally dug in the proper places, and, at some points, to a sufficient depth to test the ore."

"About a half mile above the furnace, on Jennings Creek, there is a very fine *flag-stone quarry*, where stones of any size and thickness can be very easily quarried; and from there to the river is not a mile, over a good road of easy down grade."

"There are several veins or dips of *specular ore* on this property, extending its whole length, varying in thickness from 20 inches to 4 ft. I found 3 dips of this vein on the Buchanan and Peaks of Otter Turnpike. The first is about 2½ miles from James River and two-thirds of the way up the mountain; it is 4 ft. thick and can be easily opened so as to carry the ore down grade to the river. The second dip of this vein is about ¼ mile farther up the same road, and has same thickness. The third is about ½ mile farther up and is about 2½ ft. thick. These all contain the same kind of ore which I think will yield from 45 to 50 per cent. I consider these veins good workable ores that can be mined at a fair cost, as they are continuous. I have no doubt but they will be found at other points nearer the river and probably thicker. I am confident there is another dip of this vein, and probably there are two, between those described and the base of the Ridge, but I had not time to examine. I also opened 2 dips of the same vein, about 400 yds. apart, on Cove Mountain, dipping towards each other, forming a synclinal or basin. The ore on the W. side, dipping E., is 20 inches thick as far as I followed it, which was only 2 ft. under the surface; the other, dipping E., is 30 inches thick at about the same depth. These veins extend from the Bear-wallow to within about ¾ of a mile of the furnace. Another dip of specular ore crosses Jennings Creek above the furnace and extends across Sprouts Run to the end of the property. Still another dip of specular ore crosses Jennings Creek about 2¼ miles from the river and extends to the N. F. end of the property. The ore in these veins is about the same as in those on Cove Mountain. About 4 miles from the river I found traces of a very rich specular ore in the gneiss rocks, but did not find a vein of the ore."

The Coal and Coke movement over the Chesapeake & Ohio Railway, for the month ending April 30th, 1880, and for the corresponding period of 1879, in tons of 2,000 lbs., by Mr. Charles M. Gibson, Fuel Agent of the Company, is as follows:

	1879.	1880
Fuel for use of Company	7,584	10,713
Shipped at Huntington on Ohio River	10,399	11,483
Delivered on line of road west of Richmond	1,881	1,831
" at Staunton to Valley Railroad	12	....
" at Charlottesville to W. C., V. M. & G. S. R. R.,	2,085	2,410
" at Gordonsville to do. do.	33	76
" at Junction of R., F. & P. Railroad	176	1,391
" at Richmond for consumption, including steam tugs and dredges,	4,005	2,949
Shipped at James River wharves	11,340	15,479
Total	37,345	47,332

The character of the coals moved during the same period is shown in the following exhibit:

From 1st April to	Cannel.	Splint & Bit's	Coke.	Total.
April 30, 1880	4,593	38,695	4,044	47,332
Same period, 1879	2,171	32,053	3,021	37,345
Increase, 1880	2,422	6,642	1,023	10,087

The James River Steel Manufacturing and Mining Company's Works.

BY THE EDITOR.

We recently had the pleasure of visiting the rolling mill and other works of this company, situated on James River and on the James River and Kanawha Canal (soon to be the Richmond and Alleghany Ry.), four miles northwest of and above Lynchburg, Va., which have just been remodeled and, as it were, entirely rebuilt, and which, by the time this reaches our subscribers, will be in operation turning out steel rails, railroad spikes, fish plates, etc. On page 116 we present a view of these works engraved from a photograph that we had taken while there.

It is with very great satisfaction that we chronicle this commencement of the work of manufacturing steel rails *in* the iron-bearing region of Virginia,—this thorough placing of the first link in the chain of first-class iron and steel works that must extend along the whole 200 miles of the length of the James and its Jackson's River, that crosses the iron belts, soon after the completed track of the Richmond and Alleghany Railway joins that of the Chesapeake and Ohio, making communication rapid and cheap between these ore-belts and the W. Va. beds of coking coals.

The officers of the James River Steel Manufacturing and Mining Company are, J. F. Hartranft, President; R. N. Pool, Vice President; W. S. Morris, 2nd Vice President; J. P. Richardson, Sec'y and Treas., and T. C. Jones, Superintendent. The directors are J. F. Hartranft, R. N. Pool, S. A. Caldwell, Thomas Cochran, Gorge N. Allen, Theodore M. Allen, J. P. Richardson, and Wm. T. Kirk. All of Philadelphia, Pa., except Maj. Jones, who is from Virginia. The general office of the company is at 417 Walnut St., Philadelphia, Pa.; its branch office is at Lynchburg, Va.

The real estate on which these works are located is 71 acres of land extending along the west or right-hand bank of James River for over a mile on one side, and for three-fourths of a mile along, and for one-fourth of a mile on both sides of the James River and Kanawha Canal and the Richmond and Alleghany Railway on the other. The land between the river and the canal is level, and varies in width from 300 to 1,500 ft., furnishing ample room for a large expansion of the works, and where the great water-power pertaining to these lands can be used. The land on the hill-side, beyond the canal and railway, can be utilized for dwelling sites.

The water-power here used and available, is that of the entire volume of James River, controlled by the Big, or Ives Dam of the James River and Kanawha Co., a structure, chiefly of solid masonry, in places 32 ft. high, that gives a constantly available head of 21 ft. at the works, and a supply of water, for which the canal itself furnishes a race-way, regulated by a lock at the dam, far beyond the present, and probably any future wants of the company. This valuable water-power, which saves a large annual expenditure for

fuel for motive purposes, is secured to this company, for a long term of years, for a rental, on a sliding scale, of from $300 to $1,000 a year, or the company may keep the dam in repair instead of paying a rental. The change of the canal to a railway will leave the undisturbed use of the water-power to this company. At present only about 500 horse-powers of this water are used, while 1,000 are available if wanted.

Two turbine wheels, of the most approved pattern, from Allentown, Pa., one 5 ft. 6 in. in diameter, of 256 H. P., and one 4 ft. 8 in. in diameter, of 149 H. P , (nominally 400 H. P. but really 500 if required), are placed in the bottom of a heavily walled well, to which an arched, masonry water-way leads from the canal, which gives them 21 ft. of clear fall of water, or head, and from which an arched waste-way leads to the river. All the appliances connected with the utilization of the water-power are of the most substantial and durable character; the foundations reach down to the granitic rocks in place.

The main building at these works is 242 ft, by 72, and 20 ft. high, in the clear, under the eaves, and 30 ft. high to the ridge; at one end is an annex 72 ft. by 45, the same height as the main building. A shed 30 ft. wide and 12 ft. high in the clear, with its roof 3 ft. below the eaves of the main building, extends the whole length of its canal front. The river front of this building is also shedded, part of its length to a width of 40 ft. The buildings are substantially constructed, of wood, the posts resting on stone piers, and covered with slate roofs supported by wooden trusses strengthened by iron rods. The covered-in space is near 25,000 square feet.

The equipment of this establishment consists of 4 double puddling furnaces, (the equivalent of 8 single ones), and 6 heating furnaces; 2 of the latter, placed in the annex, for reheating blooms for rails, and 2 for use with the merchant train. The furnaces are constructed with air circulation, for cooling, in their sides, between the cast iron plates and the brick work, and their stacks are supported on iron columns. The "rail trains" are, one 18-inch puddle train, 3-high, with 6 housings 8 ft. high by 4 wide, and one 18-inch rail train of same dimensions; they are driven by the larger turbine; the fly-wheel between them is 18 ft. in diameter with 11 in. face. A "crocodile" squeezer, for squeezing puddle balls, is connected with the puddle train. There is also a 10-inch "merchant train" driven by a 5-inch underground shaft connected with the smaller turbine. This shaft also runs, by belting, a line of shafting, on one side of the mill, by which are driven the accessory machinery, such as 8 spike machines, 2 rail punches, rail straighteners, bolt headers (4" by 30"), fan blower, grindstone, large cold shears, small hot shears and a pump ; and a line on the other side of the mill that drives a large roll lathe, a machine lathe, a planing machine, 3 bolt machines, and rail saws.—The fly-wheel on the smaller turbine shaft is 8 ft. in diameter, and two 5-ft. pulleys transmit the power to the lines of shafting on each side of the mill.

The 2 sets of rolls on hand can turn out 56- and 60-lb. rails. The merchant mill is supplied with rolls for spike rods and for the usual sizes of merchant bars. The rail mill housings are large enough to receive 21-inch rolls in place of the 18-inch train, if necessary. The floor of the mill is well supplied with cast iron race plates, 181 in number, each 4 ft. square. There are cast iron bosh troughs for cooling tools, and the mill is amply supplied with rail carriages, vises, anvils, tongs of all kinds, barrows, iron furnace buggies, capstan, turn-table, 5-ton chain pulley, 4 new Fairbanks scales that can weigh from 400 to 4,000 lbs., belting, etc. etc. The coal bin 32 ft. by 24 and 8 ft. high, is filled with 750 tons of coal from Quinnimont, in the New River coal-field. There is a well of pure water at the east end of the mill.

The production here, it is claimed, will be 40 tons of rails per day with a single "turn" and 80 with a double "turn." With a 21-inch train and steel blooms, it is claimed that 120 tons of steel rails can be made in a day, with two "turns." By reheating Bessemer

CONTINUED ON PAGE 116.

James River Steel Works, Near Lynchburg, Virginia.
(See Page 113.)

blooms for steel rails the cost per ton of rails for coal, labor, wear and tear, is put at about $6., and the charge for rolling and heating at about $15 , so that when Bessemer blooms cost $48 at the mill rails will cost from $65. to $70.

A large store, with a good stock of merchandise, and office and bed-rooms attached, 28 excellent dwellings for laborers, each with a neatly enclosed yard and garden, with an abundant water supply at hand, a stable, etc., are some of the other improvements connected with these every-way well ordered and appointed works, where everything has a thrifty, attractive and business-like look. A cooper shop supplies all the kegs, etc. that will be used, and a fully equipped repair shop is attached to the main building.

This company has a 20-years lease on 3,000 acres of iron ore land, in Pittsylvania and Franklin counties, convenient to the Virginia Midland R'y. and its branches. It has a contract with the canal by which all its freight is carried to and from Lynchburg for 5cts. a ton; at that city is the connecting and competing point for three lines of transportation to market that are now in operation, and there is every reason to believe that a fourth will soon be added, giving to these works unsurpassed facilities for securing cheap freight rates, and especially for reaching and supplying with rolling-mill and iron-works products the great and rapidly developing Southern and South-western country, every portion of which is reached by the railways radiating from Lynchburg.

Some $70,000 have been expended in putting these works in the excellent running order in which they now are; and farther improvements, such as the erection of a foundry, and probably a blast-furnace, are contemplated. Employment will be given to 300 laborers, 150 on a turn. All the common labor will be negro, which here is not only plentiful and satisfied with moderate wages, but is well known to be the very best and most reliable for most iron-works and mining purposes. The skilled labor will be white, drawn at first, necessarily, chiefly from the Pennsylvania mills.

New River coal, of which 750 tons are on hand to begin with, now costs $4.25 per ton, delivered; this will be reduced $1., or more, by the opening of the Richmond & Alleghany R'y., allowing $1.25 a ton for it at the mines. The adaptability of this coal to metallurgical purposes may be known from the reliable statements concerning it in Mr. Morris' article in this issue of THE VIRGINIAS. It is needed here only for *heating and puddling purposes*, water sup-

plying the power. Pig iron can now be obtained from the line of the Chesapeake & Ohio R'y. and before long Bessemer pig will be one of the abundant products of the James River Valley, both above and below these works.

The mill is already well supplied with orders for rails, especially some large ones for narrow-gauge sizes, fish-plates, spikes, bolts, etc. Its prospects for doing a good business are excellent; and situated as it is, where raw materials of every kind that it requires, and food and labor are abundant, where the climate is favorable for continuous operations, and where there are many large consumers of its products near at hand, there is no reason why, under good management, *which it now undoubtedly has*, these works should not be everyway successful.—We hope this company may have as many orders as it can fill, and urge our people to buy from it.

We cannot close this notice without calling attention to the fact that Mr. R. N. Pool, now of Philadelphia, is entitled to a large credit for the revival and complete restoration of these works, as well as of others in these states. He has overcome difficulties, apparently unsurmountable, that have deterred others from attempting the work of restoration and development in our iron and coal regions, and, by his persistent presentation of the facts of our mineral wealth, he has succeeded in inducing a large number of the most wealthy, influential and enterprising men of Philadelphia, Hartford and other Northern cities, to invest their money and talents in developing the resources of these states. We are all placed under many obligations to him for what he has already done, and we can but wish him and his associates abundant success in that which they are doing and proposing to do. Mr. Pool has been a successful pioneer in the developments of recent years in the Virginias.

WASHINGTON & LEE UNIVERSITY.

GEN. G. W. C. LEE, President.

Full courses in Classical, Literary, and Scientific Studies, including those of the professional degrees of Civil Engineering and of Law.

TERMS:—Tuition and other fees in the Academic Departments and in Law, $100; in Civil Engineering, an additional charge of $15. Board, Lodging, &c., per month, from $12 to $20.

The next session begins September 16th, 1880, and ends June 2nd, 1881.

For other particulars apply to

J. L. CAMPBELL, Jr.,
Clerk of Faculty, Lexington, Va.

The Virginias.

A Mining, Industrial and Scientific Journal:
Devoted to the Development of Virginia and West Virginia.

Vol. I, No.8 . }　　　　　Staunton, Virginia, August, 1880.　　　　　{ Price 25 Cents.

Vhe Virginias,

PUBLISHED MONTHLY,

By JED. HOTCHKISS, · · · Editor and Proprietor,

At 346 E. Main St., Staunton, Va.

Terms, including postage, per year, in advance, $2.00. Single numbers, 25 cents. Extra copies, $20.00 per 100. Back numbers, from the first, can be had at 25c each.
Advertising, per inch of length of single column (3 columns to a page, as on advertising pages), one month, $2.00; two months, $4.00; three months, $5.50; six months, $7.50; nine months, $10 00, and twelve months, $12.00; payable in advance.

Specimen Numbers of this journal are sometimes sent to parties supposed to have an interest in the development of the Virginias, or a desire to be informed in reference to their resources, improvement, etc.; they will please consider this an invitation to become subscribers and so help to sustain a paper devoted to their interests.

On sale at Hunt r & Co.'s Bookstore, Main Street, Staunton, Virginia.

The Mining Statistics of Virginia and West Virginia for the Tenth Census.

—Recent instructions from Prof. Raphael Pumpelly, who has charge of the mining statistics of the 10th Census, direct me to gather the statistics of the following substances in Virginia and West Virginia:

Alum Mass, Apatite, Asbestos, Arsenic, Antimony,— Barytes, Buhrstones, Borax, Bismuth,— Chrome, Coal, Cobalt, Copper, Corundum and Emery, Cements (Hydraulic),— Fluor Spar, Feldspar (for potash),— Gold, Grahamite, Graphite, Gypsum and Plaster, Grindstones, Millstones, Honestones, (Novaculite, &c.),— Glass Sand, Green Sand,— Infusorial Earth, Iron Ores, Iron Pyrites,— Kaolin,— Lead, Lignite, Lithium,— Manganese, Mica, Molybdenum, Mercury,— Nitre, Nickel,— Ochres, Peat,— Quartz,— Roofing Slates,— Serpentine, Slate, Silver, Slate Pencils, Soapstone (Steatite), Soda,— Talc, Tin, Tungsten,— Zinc.

This list, of over fifty mineral substances, greatly enlarges the field of enquiry and investigation in these states and makes it necessary to renew my request for information, by postal card or otherwise, as to ownership and localities where any of those substances have been mined during the census year, from May 1st, 1879, to June 1st, 1880, or at any time since 1870, or where they exist in considerable quantity but have not been mined.' I will be under renewed obligations to the newspapers of Virginia and West Virginia if they will give the same general publicity to this request that they gave to one issued last June.

The statistics already gathered show a large and most gratifying increase in these states over those of 1870, and if all persons in any way interested in our mineral wealth will aid me with the information desired I will be able, with that already in hand, to make a "return" that will be everyway creditable to the mining industries of these states and that will lead to a proper appreciation of their great and varied mineral resources.

The statistics of "Mining, in all its branches, which includes the production of Coal and Petroleum," east of the Mississippi is in charge of Prof. Pumpelly. In the "instructions" to his assistants he says—"It is the wish of the Census Office to gather all the information relative to the mining industries that is necessary to a full and exact understanding of their magnitude and their characteristics. The results will be a valuable addition to the data on which political economy is founded, and *will be the basis from which to estimate the increase of mineral production in the future. As they are gathered under the direction of the United States they will be* taken *as authoritative everywhere*, and no pains should be spared to make them worthy of the consideration they will receive. The preparation of these statistics is an honorable and instructive task, but one which calls for industry, tact and patience. The co-operation of owners and operators is essential to the success of the work, and they should be made to understand that the work is undertaken in their interest."

The essential points of information desired are: (1) Name and exact location of mine or quarry; (2) Amount of product for census and previous years since 1870; (3) Value of product at the mine or place of shipment; (4) Average number of persons employed, distinguishing between those over and those under 16 years of age; (5) The amount of wages paid during the census year; (6) The amount of and value of materials, powder, lumber, etc., consumed in the census year; (7) The power used in mining operations, preparing ores, etc.; (8) Broad details of machinery, its horse-power, &c.; (9) No. of horses and mules used and their value; (10) The markets for the products and the routes and freight rates to them.—Information of every kind, the more detailed the better, in reference to the extent and character of mineral deposits, the cost of mining and marketing them, their development or why undeveloped, the cost of labor, living, etc., is very much desired.

Finally, those that receive schedules will greatly facilitate the work if they will fill them out, fully, and return them promptly,—some that were sent out two months ago have not as yet been returned.

Jed. Hotchkiss,
Expert Special Agent.

Staunton, Va., Aug. 1st, 1880.

Acts of the last Va. Legislature.

—The General Assembly of Virginia during the session of 1879-80 passed 309 "Acts and Joint Resolutions" that became laws. Those relating to or organizing mining, manufacturing, railway and other improvement companies were: 1. To legalize the organization of the Bristol Coal and Iron Narrow-gauge RR. Co. 2. Allowing the Richmond, Fredericksburg & Potomac RR. Co. to change site of its Richmond terminus. 3. Amending charter of Richmond & Mecklenburg RR. Co. so it can become a corporate body when $5,000 are subscribed to its stock. 4. Providing for continued use of convict labor by James R. & Kanawha Co. on canal and its railway extension. 5. Incorporating the Richmond & Southwestern Railway Co. 6. Amending the charter and enlarging the powers of the Royal Land Co. of Va., allowing it to extend its railway to the Potomac and to Richmond, etc. 7. Incorporating the Va. & N. C. Mining & Transportation Co. to mine, transport and manufacture iron and other ore in Pulaski, Wythe, Carroll or Grayson counties, and build railways to A. M. & O. at or west of Martin's. 8. Incorporating Mt. Vernon RR. Co. to build railway from Alexandria to Mt. Vernon. 9. To incorporate the Va. Angora Co. to stock a part of the mountain region of Va. with pure Angora, Mexican and Maltese goats and other stock, &c. 10. Amending charter of Richmond & Alleghany RR. Co. in reference to borrowing money. 11. Incorporating the Chesapeake and Idaho Gold and Silver Mining Co., to mine, &c., in Idaho but have its office in Norfolk, Va. 12. Authorizing Potomac & Ohio RR. to record

mortgages, etc. 13. Authorizing consolidation of James R. & Kanawha Co. and Buchanan & Clifton Forge R'y. Co. 14. Incorporating Mineral Land Co. of Va., Ky. and Tenn. 15. Incorporating Staunton & West Augusta RR. Co. 16. A free telephone or telegraph law. 17. Amending charter of Bristol Coal & Iron Narrow-gauge RR. 18. Incorporating the Mt. Alto Mining and Land Co. of Va., with office in Richmond. 19. Incorporating the U. S Commercial Co., with limited liability. 20. Authorizing tax on assessed value of railway property in counties. 21. Amending law in reference to chartering companies by circuit courts. 22. Amending charter of Buchanan & Clifton Forge R R. Co. 23. Incorporating the Luray Iron Co., one of the companies proposing to operate one the line of the Shenandoah Valley RR. 24. Incorporating the Norfolk Knitting and Cotton Mfg. Co. 25. To incorporate the Petersburg, Massanutta & Toledo R'y. Co., to build railway from Brock's Gap, Rockingham Co., to Petersburg, Va., and Washington, D. C. 26. Incorporating Jeffersonville & Marion Turnpike & Telegraph Co. 27. To incorporate Shenandoah Valley Mining Co., to operate on Shenandoah Valley RR. 28. Authorizing Richmond, York River & Chesapeake RR. to borrow money. 29. To incorporate Broad Creek Toll Bridge & Turnpike Co., in Princess-Anne. 30. Amending charter of New River RR., Mining and Manufacturing Co. and changing its name to New River RR. Co., and allowing it to branch into any part of S. W. Va. 31. In reference to sale of J. R. & K. Canal to a railway Co. 32. Authorizing Chesapeake & Ohio R'y. Co. to construct a branch from near Hanover Junction, etc., to Chesapeake Bay, etc. 33. Allowing railways to build branches 20 miles long. 34. Amending charter of Valley RR. Co. 35. Authorizing James R. & Kanawha Co. to sell out to Richmond & Alleghany RR. Co. 36. Requiring Co. Supts. of Schools to make reports of minerals, &c., to Commissioner of Agriculture. 37. Incorporating Seaboard Manufacturing Co., to make leather, cotton goods, &c. 38. To incorporate Warrenton & Fauquier White Sulphur Springs Turnpike Co. 39. Amending charter of Broad Creek Toll-Bridge and Turnpike Road Co. and changing name to Broad Creek & London Bridge Turnpike Co. 40. To incorporate Mineral & Lumber R'y Co. to build railway from Clover Hill in Chesterfield to Hardwicksville in Buckingham, etc. 41. Authorizing James R. & Kanawha Co. to build railway along its line. 42. To incorporate the Barboursville (Orange Co., Va.) Mercantile and Manufacturing Co. 43. To incorporate the Virginia Mineral R'y. Co. to operate in Pulaski, Wythe, Carroll and Grayson counties. 44. Incorporating Walker's Creek Bridge and Turnpike Co's, in Giles Co. 45. To incorporate Seaboard Cotton Compress Co. 46. Authorizing consolidation of Richmond & Alleghany and Buchanan & Clifton Forge railway companies. 47. To incoporate Baltimore Cincinnati & Western R'y. Co. 48. Amending charter of Dan Valley & Yadkin River Narrow-gauge RR. Co. 49. Authorizing purchasers of Va. Midland RR. to issue stock. 50. To incorporate Richmond & West Point Terminal R'y and Warehouse Co. 51. Incorporating Iron Co. of Va., to operate on line of Shhenandoah Valley RR. 52. Incorporating Halifax & Pittsylvania RR. Co. 53. To incorporate the Southwest Virginia Improvement Co. of Pulaski Co. 54. Incorporating Portsmouth and Deep Creek Turnpike Co. 55. Amending charter of Warm Springs Valley RR. Co. 56. Authorizing voting a tax in Augusta county to macadamize its roads. 57. Amending turnpike law. 58. Amending charter of Va. Angora Co. 59. Incorporating Alleghany Coal and Iron Co. 60. To incorporate White Rock RR. Co. (Wythe, Smyth and Grayson counties). 61. To incorporate Norfolk & Portsmouth Terminal R'y., Wharf and Warehouse Co.

It appears from this list that over one-fifth of all the laws enacted by the last legislature had reference to railway, turnpike and mining and manufacturing companies.

The Gold Region of the Atlantic Slope, from Maryland to Alabama, is to be mapped by the U. S. Coast and Geodetic Survey. This map will be based on the already completed triangulations of that region by the Coast Survey. The first section of the map will embrace the country extending from Hagerstown, Md., southwesterly to beyond Lynchburg, Va., and will embrace most of the developed Virginia "Gold Belt," especially if the map includes Halifax and Montgomery counties, as it ought to. This a move in the right direction, one that will aid in directing attention to this great gold region, and one that will, incidentally, help to bring about a Geological Survey of the State by the General Government. This work is in good hands and Supt. Patterson will have it well done.

Personals, Geological, etc., for July.—Prof. Wm. M. Fontaine, of the University of Va., has been making observations in the Mesozoic regions of Chesterfield, Buckingham and Prince Edward, in the Montgomery gold field, the Pulaski coal and iron beds near Martin's, the Wythe iron, lead and zinc mines, and the salt and plaster belt of Smyth and Washington.——Prof. J. L. Campbell, of Washington and Lee University, has worked out a geological section of Little North and Church mountains and vicinity in N. E. part of Rockingham, showing location and relations of lead and zinc ores and of Clinton (V) and Oriskany (VII) iron ores; he has also made a geological reconnoissance of the Montgomery gold field, and the Wythe and Pulaski iron, lead, zinc and coal regions, and is now at work on the general and economical geology of Purgatory and Garden mountains in Botetourt.——Prof. J. J. Stevenson (who has had charge of the geology of Greene, Fayette, Washington and Westmoreland counties, the southwestern ones of Pa., in the bituminous coal field, for the 2nd. Geological Survey of Pa.) has finished careful measurements and explorations in Virginia's part of the "Great Ohio Coal Basin" in Lee, Scott, Dickenson, Wise and Buchanan, and prepared an elaborate paper on the same which he will publish through one of the learned societies of Philadelphia. Prof. S. has had a large experience in the study of the northern portion of the Great Ohio Coal Basin, in Pennsylvania and Ohio, where it is most developed, so his conclusions on the Va. part of this basin will be exceptionally valuable and conclusive We learn that the analyses of the coals he collected, made by McCreath of the Pa. Survey, show surprising results in purity and calorific properties. This report will be eagerly looked for.——Prof. Shaler, of Harvard University, the Director of the Ky. Geol. Survey, and his corps are at work on the geology of the country traversed by the Richmond and Southwestern R'y, working westward from Gloucester. We hear of them in Chesterfield, Powhatan, Cumberland and Buckingham. If this distinguished geologist can complete the exhaustive survey of the belt proposed, one 25 miles on each side of the R. & S-W. R'y., he will give the world the most extensive detailed geological survey yet made in Virginia, one covering over 2,000 square miles of her territory and crossing, more or less, all of her grand divisions and geological formations.——Profs. Leidy and Willcox of the University of Pa., Prof. Porter of Lafayette College, and Mr. Meehan of the Gardener's Monthly, representing the Pa. Academy of Sciences, in a tour for scientific observation and collection, called upon us on their return from North Carolina and we had the pleasure of accompanying them over portions of the Chesapeake & Ohio and of the Valley railways and calling their attention to the grand geological sections there displayed. They were delighted with the geological and botanical wealth, the charming scenery and the general fertility and thrift of the portions of Virginia and West Virginia that they saw. Prof. Porter was especially pleased with the vicinity of the Hawk's Nest, on New River, W. Va., as a field for the botanist.——Prof. W. C. Kerr, the State Geologist of N. C., has been visiting the "bright tobacco" counties of Virginia along the Carolina border, collecting samples of soils and making observations for a "Tobacco Production" report and a "Tobacco Soil Map" that he is preparing for the Tenth Census,—duties for which he has eminent qualifications.——Maj. T. L. Ragland of Halifax county, Va., the highest authority in this country in

reference to the cultivation of tobacco, and who, very properly, has been made an Expert Special Agent of Census for the collection of the statistics of tobacco and whatever pertains to its production and manufacture in Virginia and West Virginia, has been on his round of observation in Midland, Piedmont and The Valley, in Virginia, and has now gone to Trans-Apalachia in West Virginia, visiting all sections where tobacco is grown. Maj. R. examines the soils on which the various kinds of tobacco are raised and takes samples of them for analysis, and when done he will have the materials in hand for the construction of "Tobacco Production" and "Tobacco Soil" maps of Virginia and West Virginia which he will have prepared to accompany his report.——P. W. Sheafer, Engineer of Mines, of Pottsville, Pa., (one of Prof. H. D. Rogers' assistants in the First Geological Survey of Pa.), a greatly esteemed authority in all matters pertaining to anthracite coal in his state, has recently examined the coal and iron deposits of Pulaski Co., Va., near ·Martin's on the A. M. & O. RR. He has favored us with a copy of his "Report on the Altoona Coal and Iron Co." (9 pp. 8vo.), dated July, 1880, containing the results of his observations and analyses of some of the iron ores there found. Of this report we shall have somewhat to say in a future issue.—— Mr. E. R. Benton, Expert Special Agent of Census, has been very busy collecting, for analysis, samples of the ores of Virginia. We have heard of him all along The Valley and the people commend his industry and energy in the very important work he has in charge. It is of the utmost importance that the *quality* as well as the quantity of our mineral resources shall be fairly and fully shown in the forthcoming census reports. He has (August 18th) sent his last samples of Virginia iron ores to Professor Pumpelly, having spent four months in sampling the Virginia iron ores. He will now sample those of West Virginia.——Major Jed. Hotchkiss, Expert Special Agent of Census in charge of the Mining Statistics of Virginia and West Virginia has been visiting the iron, coal, lead and zinc mines along the A. M. & O. RR., in Bedford, Roanoke, Montgomery and Wythe, noting their topographical and geological location, characteristics, condition, etc.; collecting information of all kinds in reference to the mineral deposits of those counties, and verifying, on the spot, the "returns" of operations. He has already sent in a considerable number of "completed returns" and many "General Notes."——Hon. W. H. Ruffner, Supt. of Public Instruction in Va., has been delivering a course of lectures on geology to the 500 teachers assembled at the 6-weeks Normal School now in session at the University of Virginia.——J. Blodget Britton of the "Iron-Masters Laboratory," Philadelphia, is at his summer home in Warrenton, Va., where he has recently established a well appointed branch of his laboratory for technical and experimental work.

The Excelsior Iron Mine,

on the lands of Mrs. Deane on the western slope of Peter's Mountain, Alleghany Co., Va., about 2½ miles from Excelsior Switch of the Chesapeake & Ohio R'y, 217 miles west of Richmond, has, in the last few months, been successfully opened and well developed by Mr. T. G. Trice, the lessee,— he has not only exposed a large body of ore but has constructed an excellent wagon road to it and mined and hauled a thousand tons of lump ore to Excelsior Switch of the C. & O. R'y, where it is now piled up ready for shipment and awaiting a purchaser, as Mr. Trice states in our advertising columns.

We visited this mine on the 14th inst. and found it some 450 ft. above the valley of Dunlap's Creek in a bench of the western slope of Peter's Mountain, as a stratified bed from 8 to 10 ft. thick, dipping moderately to the eastward, the ore resting on a solid sandstone stratum and generally overlaid by about a yard of fire clay and a few feet of soil, but outcropping at the escarpment and on the surface of the bench and where cut by ravines, so that large quantities of it can be readily mined. From its position and general characteristics this appears to be an extensively developed stratum of high grade Clinton (No. V.) ore.—J. Blodget Britton analysed a surface sample of it, in May, 1880, and found it to contain in 100.39 parts, 13.73 silica, 0.63 alumina, 73.14 iron sesquioxide, 0.21 manganese protoxide, 1.09 phosphoric acid, 0.08 sulphur, 0.49 lime, 0.24 magnesia, and 10.81 water; its metallic iron was 51.20 per cent. and phosphorus 0.48.

We have rarely seen a pile of ore the size of the one Mr. Trice has at the railway so equally good and uniform in character, and would advise anyone wanting a superior article of brown hematite to correspond with him.

The Bedford Iron Mining and Manufacturing Company

owns and controls several thousand acres of mineral lands lying on the eastern slope of the Primordial or Western Blue Ridge, there the more prominent mountain range, in Bedford county, Va., the lands extending from southwest of the Atlantic, Mississippi & Ohio RR., just east of where that railway crosses the Blue Ridge, the Western one, near Blue Ridge Springs station, across that road and for several miles to the northeast of it,—in fact they include most of the eastern slope of the mountain, here consisting of spurs, foot-hills and intermediate ravines and narrow valleys, drained by Goose Creek of the Roanoke, that lies between the Arcadia Iron Property (so fully described in the July No. of THE VIRGINIAS) and the A. M. & O. RR.; the country traversed by the extension of the iron ore belt of that property to the southwest. Through the courtesy of some of the officers of this company the Editor, about the middle of last month, had an opportunity for visiting its mineral lands and inspecting the very remarkable exposures that, by the expenditure of a few hundred dollars, have been made, of massive stratified beds of specular iron ore (red hematite, or hematite proper), through more than a mile of N. E.-S W. strike, across the spurs and ravines of the eastern slope of the Primordial Blue Ridge.

The stratum of ore here revealed by the removal of a few feet of earth, generally less than three, appears, from the imperfect sections of it that have been cut, to be from 3 to 6 feet thick and in the crest of an anticlinal or arch. It has been exposed at a number of points both in the hollows and on the spurs of the mountain, and through a range of over 300 feet of elevation, as between the hollows and spur-crests, and of from 600 to 700 from the water level of the little valley traversed by the railway, near at hand, which is the drainage trough of these lands. So the ore exists in vast quantities above water level and in the most favorable conditions for mining by open cut or level- and drainage-free drift, and where gravity roads, from one-fourth to three-fourths of a mile long, can be made to carry it to the railway.

The ore of this stratum, so far as exposed, is massive, compact, and quite uniform in appearance. Thirty pounds of it, a sample from near the surface, were sent to J. Blodget Britton, and his analysis of May 6th, 1880, gave the following composition in 100 parts:—45.27 pure metallic iron; 19.04 oxygen with iron; 26.53 silica; 2.48 water; 4.98 alumina; 0.29 lime; trace of magnesia; no sulphur; 0.494 phosphorus and 0.636 oxygen in phosphoric acid; 0.12 oxide of manganese, and 0.16 loss and undetermined matter. Another sample, analysed May 18th, 1880, contained 48.12 per cent. pure metallic iron, 23.57 silica, and 0·628 phosphorous, the only ingredients for which it was examined. The silica in this is largely "free."

Near and on each side of the railway, on the same estate, brown hematite iron ores, of a superior quality, are abundant, as are also beds of excellent limestone suitable for flux.—Under all circumstances it seems to us that here is one of the very best of locations for immediate operations in the mining and shipping of iron ores and for the erection of blast furnaces. The A. M. & O. RR. runs through the property and its policy is one that fosters new enterprises by giving them favorable rates for transportation. We hope some of the strong iron men of the North will join this company and help to develop its great stores of iron. We shall hereafter have more to say about this matter.

A Combined Cooking-Can and Dinner-Pail,

chiefly for the use of workmen and others who have to take their meals with them to be eaten away from home, has just been patented by Rev. John B. Haskell of Staunton, Va. We helped to eat a warm supper of meats, biscuits, corn bread, coffee, etc., taken from some of these dinner-pails seven hours after these articles had been put hot into them, and can testify, from the proof of the eating, that we had an excellent *warm meal*.—This invention will prove a great blessing to the laborer and help materially in promoting his comfort and his health and in giving him the continual feast that comes from a well digested dinner. We welcome this Virginia invention and commend it to our miners and laborers of every kind.

The Mesozoic Formation in Virginia.*

By Oswald J. Heinrich, Mining Engineer.

During the last twenty years much has been done to investigate and define the Mesozoic formation of the United States along the Atlantic States, as well as in the Territories. The investigations of Professors Hitchcock, Emmons, Hayden, H. D. Rogers, and those now in progress in connection with the geological surveys of Pennsylvania and New Jersey, under the various eminent leaders, have given decided answers to many questions formerly existing, and will throw, as they have already done, much light upon the character of this interesting formation. It is much to be regretted that this formation, existing in the State of Virginia, and first defined there nearly forty years ago, by Professor W. B. Rogers, has since received no public attention. This is the more to be regretted, because Professor Rogers pointed out the economical value of some of its deposits. In order to preserve the results of a series of observations and explorations conducted there during the past few years, and furthermore to preserve the almost inaccessible public records of the former investigator, I beg to submit the following remarks to the Institute:

I. Geographical Distribution of the Mesozoic Formation in Virginia, its Outlines and Area.

Probably more than in any other of the Atlantic States, or in the Territories, this formation occurs in Virginia in isolated tracts and patches of greater or less magnitude, some being of very limited extent. They appear so now, at .least, but by observing them upon the map, a former connection between the tracts may be traced out, by considering the lines of bearings, and comparing the geological structures in Virginia amongst themselves, as well as with those extending into the border States, North Carolina and Maryland. It is also indispensable to take into consideration the elevation now presented by the topography of the country (see Map, Plate I).

For a clearer conception of the facts it will be necessary first to define the outlines of the various tracts, and for a guide we will follow the statement in the various annual reports of Professor W. B. Rogers, which, unfortunately, are now almost inaccessible. They may be enumerated as consisting of four divisions or two double ranges, their main axes running very nearly in parallel lines to each other, and also parallel to the main course of the Blue Ridge mountains, with a bearing from S. 30° to 37° W., the ranges being also nearly the same distance from each other. Proceeding from the east to the west, and also from northeast to southwest, in the line of trend for each, we may designate the following divisions, viz : A., the Eastern ; B., the Middle-eastern ; C., the Middle-western ; D., the Western division; each consisting of numerous tracts.

A. The Eastern Division.

1. *Petersburg deposits.* Extending from Richmond to Petersburg, Chesterfield County, and further south to Greensville and Brunswick counties.

Its shape, rather irregular in outline, is nearly that of a right-angled triangle, stretching in its western irregular boundary from Richmond to Petersburg in a nearly meridional line, thence in a northeast course, defined by the overlapping rocks of the Tertiary formation, towards City Point, on the south bank of the James River, and from there in a northwest course across the James River about one mile east of the neck at Dutch Gap, thence in a course a little less northwest to Richmond, where it is exposed in the ferruginous sandstones, the lowest stratum in the valley of Shockoe Creek. It can also be noticed upon the top of the table-land stretching beyond the city along the James River to within two or three miles west of Richmond, in isolated patches, in Henrico County.

Its entire length would be about 33 miles from north to south, and 8 miles from east to west at City Point, comprising an area of about 95 square miles.

2. Further south the formation occurs in Greensville County, west of Hicksford, and also in the adjoining county of Brunswick, east of Lawrenceville. None of these regions have yet been accurately defined.

*From the Transactions of the American Institute of Mining Engineers Read at the Philadelphia Meeting, February, 1878.

B. The Middle-Eastern Division.

1. *Taylorsville deposits.* Containing the territory of sandstones and slates, underlying the Tertiary strata about the South Anna River, from the North Anna River to Ashland, Hanover County.

This tract, which is not well defined, is of a somewhat trapezoidical shape. In consequence of the easy decomposition of its constituent rocks, and the difficulty of distinguishing the Mesozoic debris from that of the underlying Eozoic rocks, which are almost identical with the Mesozoic in material, the lines of demarcation are often obliterated.

Beginning at the head of Mechump Creek, near the C. and O. RR., south of Hanover Courthouse, the boundary extends in a nearly westerly direction to the headwaters of Beech Creek, thence in a variously curved northern line to near the mouth of Beaver Creek, at Newfound River, thence in a northeasterly direction to the neighborhood of Chesterfield depot. The tract, comprising nearly all the area between this boundary and the North Anna River, is about 8 miles wide between the extreme east and west points, and 10 miles long in its northeast and southwest course, and has an area of about 60 square miles. Taylorsville is situated nearly in its centre.

2. *The Springfield deposits,* or Springfield coal basin, a small isolated basin, near Hungary Station, on the R. F. and P. RR., in Henrico county, a short distance south of Chickahominy River.

It is a basin of elliptical shape, and extends southwest to the head waters of Deep Run. It is situated northeast of the main body and east of the northern spur of the next tract, No. 3, but entirely isolated from it by nearly three miles of Eozoic formation. Its length northeast and southwest of the main axis is about 2 miles, and its width about one-fourth of a mile ; its area is about 1.6 square miles. The old Deep Run coal mines have been worked in this basin.

3. *The Richmond deposits,* or Richmond coal basin. This, generally known as the Richmond coal field, is by far the most important of the deposits. It extends from the northern county lines of Goochland and Henrico counties across the James River to the Appomattox River, lying in Powhatan, but mainly in Chesterfield County.

About 11 miles west of Richmond it extends upon both sides of the James, but mainly upon the south. Its shape somewhat resembles the contour of a plum, with its peduncle pointing north, formed by a narrow branch extending northwards from Tuckahoe Creek for about six miles, averaging about one mile in width.

We will commence to trace its boundary at its northern extremity in the northeast corner of Goochland County, above the head waters of Little Tuckahoe Creek at the northern apex of the triangle formed by the "Three-chopped," the Manakin Ferry, and Pounce's Tract, or Westham roads. It here crosses the first mentioned road, about half a mile east of Little Tuckahoe Creek, intersecting the main Tuckahoe Creek near the Carbon Hill pits, and running almost due meridionally, forms the east boundary of the spur. It now bears southeast, towards the James River, crossing the same a little above the United States Arsenal, turning again in a nearly due meridional course in an irregular line (in consequence of some smaller outlying patches) to the R. and D. RR. about half a mile east of Coalfield Station, and a little west of Falling Creek, where we come into the neighborhood of the oldest coal mines in the country, the old Black Heath, Ætna, and Midlothian. Then continuing nearly in the same direction, and maintaining a course a little east of the road leading from the pits south to the Genito road, and passing through the western part of St. Leger's farm, the boundary line crosses Swift Creek a short distance below the mouth of Dry Creek ; continuing in this direction, and a little east of Dry Creek, for a short distance, it bears now into a course about S. 22° W., striking the headwaters of that creek ; turning still more westward, about, about S. 57° W., it strikes the Clover Hill Railroad about half a mile west of Summit Station, and resuming again the former less westerly course, it passes about half a mile east of Winterpock Creek, crossing the Bevil's Bridge road about five-eighths of a mile east of the creek, and maintaining nearly the same course it strikes the Appomattox River about one mile above Eppes's Falls.

From this point the boundary nearly coincides with the

course of the river as far as Winticomack Creek. This forms the southern extremity of the deposits, there being very few exposures of the sedimentary rocks south of the river. Now, abruptly turning to the northwest and following very nearly the course of the river, the boundary line strikes obliquely across it, as is shown by the Eozoic rocks about one mile below Bevil's Bridge, whence it passes to the mouth of Sappony Creek, following the course of the river to near Goode's Bridge, presenting one or two small patches of the sedimentary formation on the south side.

Assuming now a course nearly due north, the boundary crosses the road from Colesville to Genito, about half a mile east of Skinquater Creek, and continuing a little east of that creek, it crosses the road from Chesterfield Courthouse to Genito, about half a mile from the creek; thence it is extended so as to intersect Swift Creek about one mile below the road from Genito to the main Buckingham road, crossing the latter about one mile east of their junction. Bending more eastwardly, pursuing the Dittoway branch of Jones' Creek, and then the creek itself for some distance, it crosses the James River in a line east of northeast, about a mile and a quarter west of Manakin Town ferry. Passing northeast on the north side of James River by Dover Church, the boundary line intersects the broad branch of Tuckahoe Creek a short distance above its mouth; turning then abruptly northwards, even a little west of north, and forming the western boundary of the spur, it crosses, the Three Chopped road a little east of Big Tuckahoe Creek, and after keeping its course almost due north rounds off and strikes the point at which we started to trace the boundary.

The main body of this area, as delineated above, is accompanied by a number of smaller branches and outlying basins, which either are entirely separated from the main body, or, as it is frequently the case, form only branches of the main body, produced by local anticlinal ridges of greater or less magnitude. Among the most important on the eastern boundary are those which occur south of the James River and the R. and D. RR., in the neighborhood of the National and the old Black Heath mines, the Union mines (Greenhole), east of the Midlothian, and some still less extensive at the Clover Hill mines, near the southern extremity at the Appomattox, all of them in Chesterfield County. Upon the western margin we notice a branch west of Sampson's Hill on the north side, and west of Jones' Creek upon the south side of the James. Extending from a short distance north of the river, this prong unites with the main body near the Dittoway branch and the upper part of Jones' Creek in Powhatan County.

Including the northern spur the length of this basin will be about 31½ miles, over 24 miles of it in the main body. The width varies from 7½ to 10 miles, comprising in all an area of about 189 square miles.

C. The Middle-Western Division.

1. The Aquia deposits. Including the sandstones and slates underlying the Tertiary strata about the western bank of the Potomac, from Mount Vernon across Fredericksburg to the Massaponax River, in the counties of Fairfax, Prince William, Stafford, and Spotsylvania, Aquia lying near the centre of its western boundary.

Its shape is that of a narrow border, about four miles broad along the Potomac, widening out abruptly at its southern extremity by bulging westward as the area progresses southward. The more northern tract skirts the Potomac from the upper extremity of the cliffs at Mount Vernon, which forms the northern termination. Its western margin, in a southwest course, is observed a little to the east of the old road from Fredericksburg to Colchester and Alexandria; passing east of Colchester it crosses Neabsco Creek a little east of the road; also Occoquan River, about three and a half miles west of High Point at Gilly Creek. Extending to Dumfries, on the Quantico Creek, an eastern indentation from the main course will be observed, pinching the margin about two miles eastward. Bearing again more westwardly until it assumes a course about S. 15° W., crossing Aquia Creek about three-quarters of a mile above Aquia, and below the mouth of Beaverdam and Cannon Creek, and gradually turning more to the westward it passes within about a mile and a half north-

west of Stafford Courthouse; turning now more abruptly to S. 67° W., it crosses Potomac Creek about one mile west of Wallace's mill, arriving at its most western extremity. From this point it gradually rounds off through a southerly bearing into a course about S. 37° E., towards Fredericksburg, crossing the Rappahannock about one mile west of Falmouth; thence it curves again westward to about S. 30° W., so as to intersect the R. F. & P. RR., about three miles from town, and passing along Hazel Run it crosses the same still further west, nearer its headwaters, forming another extreme western boundary. It now assumes a northern bearing, crossing Massaponax River about three and a half miles west of R., F. & P. RR., and curving first east to form the southern margin of the formation, it crosses that railroad about one mile south of Massaponax River, running N. 60° E., nearly with the course of the river towards the Rappahannock, to a point below the mouth of Massaponax.

From here, crossing the Rappahannock, the eastern margin of the formation is formed in a nearly north course by the irregular boundaries of the Tertiary formations overlying it. About three and a half miles below Fredericksburg it crosses the road to Belle Plain, bearing more to the northeast to Potomac Creek, a little above the church, and bearing still more in that direction it crosses Accakeek Creek at Brook's mill. From here the course changes again to nearly due north, crossing Aquia Creek about half a mile below the mouth of Austin's Run; turning more to the eastward it crosses Meadow Branch. The balance of the eastern margin to the beginning is formed by the river banks.

Its greatest linear extent from Mount Vernon to the Massaponax is therefore a little over 40 miles, and its greatest width at Potomac Creek, or at the Massaponax River, about 8½ miles, comprising in all a superficial area of 174 square miles.

2. The "Farmville" deposits, containing the two isolated basins upon the north and south sides of the Appomattox at Farmville, in Cumberland and Prince Edward counties, known as the Farmville coal basin. One, the larger and most northern of them, has nearly the shape of a half moon, with its concave side eastward; the other, much smaller, has an elliptic shape, with the major axis bearing southwest. Farmville is situated just between them, the former stretching from the north bank of the Appomattox River nearly due north in its main extension, the latter from the south side of the same river in a southwest course.

To trace the boundary of the main basin we commence in the fork of Buffalo Creek and Willis' River, as its most northern extremity. Bearing in a southwest direction it crosses Ca Ira road about a mile and a half from Ca Ira, and east of Willis' Mountain, intersecting Great Willis' River about one mile east of Curdsville, in Buckingham County, passing immediately east of Mrs. Hendrick's, and then taking a nearly due south direction to a point below Sandy Ford bridge, it bears southeasterly towards the mouth of Buffalo and Appomattox River, just on the edge of Farmville. Passing through the Bizarre estate in a northerly course, it crosses a westward road to Dry Creek, about one mile west of its intersection with the Forest road. Bearing again more to the northward it passes about three-quarters of a mile west of Raine's tavern, in Cumberland, to near the intersection of Little and Great Willis' rivers, thence in nearly a northeast couse it extends west of Ca Ira about a quarter of a mile, crosses Raine's Creek near its mouth, and reaches the northern extremity mentioned in the beginning.

The whole length of the deposit measured on its curved axis would be about 13 miles, and being on an average about 2 miles wide, its area is computed to about 20.5 square miles.

The first small basin south of the Appomattox extends over the area from the river southwestwardly along the road from Hampden Sidney College to the river, to about half a mile north of King's tavern, its easterly boundary running nearly parallel with, and and about half a mile east of Buffalo Creek, terminating again at the Appomattox river at the edge of Farmville. It is, in fact, but a part of the main tract north of the river, but nearly separated from it for a distance on its western boundary just above the junction of the Buffalo and Appomattox, by the exposure of the Eozoic rocks, from which the formation has been removed by denudation.

The Virginias.

The length of the tract being about three miles by 1 mile wide, its area would be about 2.4 square miles.

About two miles further southwest, near Prince Edward Courthouse, we approach the last of the basins, which is of an oval shape. Its northern margin is visible a short distance south of the courthouse. Its western boundary ranges from half to three-quarters of a mile east of the main road from Charlotte Courthouse to Farmville for about two miles to its southern terminus; the eastern boundary being marked by the course of the Briery River, which flows along and sometimes a little within its margin.

Less than 2 miles in length and nearly 1 mile wide, its area would be about 1.6 square miles. All the Farmville basins together comprise, therefore, an area of about 24.5 square miles.

D. *The Western Division.*

In linear extent, as well as in superficial area, the western division is by far the most important. Extending in two large tracts from the Potomac River southwestward for 80 miles, and from the Dan River northeastward for 60 miles, with several exposures of the formation in the interval of 7½ miles, it may be said that it can be traced, more or less, across the whole State of Virginia.

1. *The Potomac deposits* form the most northern part of this division. Commencing in the State of Maryland it extends from the north side of the Potomac above the falls through the counties of Fairfax, Loudoun, and Fauquier, to Robertson's River, in Culpeper. Its shape in Virginia is that of a prolonged, nearly equilateral triangle, with its base along the Potomac, its apex in the forks of Robertson's and Rapid-Anne rivers, passing uninterruptedly through the counties named above. Beginning at its northwestern extremity about Noland's Ferry, and the mouth of Clark's Run upon the south bank of the Potomac, the western boundary extends along to the headwaters of Clark's Run and Limestone Creek, in a course nearly southwest. Following the east flanks of the Kittoctin Mountain it passes a little west of Leesburg, crossing Goose Creek at Oatlands or Carter's mill, the W. & O. RR. about a quarter of a mile east of Aldie, and extending along the base of Bull Run Mountain in nearly a uniform course, it crosses the Manassas Gap Railroad about a quarter of a mile east of the mill at the end of the Gap. It continues close to the eastern flanks of Pond Mountain and Baldwin's Ridge, crossing Cedar Run a little below Blower's Branch, about two and three-quarter miles east of Warrenton, whence it bears more southwestward towards the headwaters of Licking River, about a mile and a half west of Germantown and Fayetteville, crossing the Hodgman's River a little below Freeman's Ford, and Aestham's River above the mouth of Muddy Run. Passing a little west of Fairfax it intersects Cedar Run a little to the eastward, where it is crossed by the road leading from Fairfax to Orange Courthouse; bearing now a little more southwestward it terminates at its southern extremity at the mouth of Robertson's River, and the south fork of the Rapid-Anne.

Tracing the eastern boundary from this point we have a variously interrupted exposure of the formation along the Rapid-Anne River, for about three-quarters of a mile to Raccoon Ford. It now diverges from its former due east course, leaving also the river until it touches the Courthouse road, between half and three-quarters of a mile towards the south; it then bends a little northwards, curving around so as to strike the river about one mile above the mouth of Brook's Run, and crossing the Rapid-Anne in a northeasterly direction, it passes Brook's Run a short distance above its mouth, intersecting the road leading from Germanna Ford to Stevensburg, at a point a little west of the fork near the meeting-house. Thence bending slightly towards the north it crosses Mountain Creek, about two miles above its mouth, and strikes the north fork of the Rappahannock a short distance above the mouth of Marsh Run. Now pursuing a course almost due northeast it strikes the head of Elk Run a short distance east of Hickerson's, at the crossroads, and, turning rather more towards the north passes west of Brentsville, and east of New Market, so as to cross the Va. Mid. RR., just west of Centreville. From this point, continuing in nearly the same direction, it intersects the A. & W. RR. east of the headwaters of Salisbury Plain Run, about four and a half miles west of Fairfax Courthouse, the G. & L. RR. at Dranesville, striking the Potomac River at a point about one

or two miles below the mouth of Seneca Creek in Maryland. Of its prolongation into Maryland it may be stated, that while the western boundary keeps nearly the same course, as the boundary in Virginia, about parallel with the Monocacy River to Frederick, Maryland, the eastern boundary, after passing across the Potomac, quickly bends around to the north, and then to the northwest, so as to pass over the Seneca, between the mouth of the Dry and Little Seneca, and to intersect the Little Monocacy some distance above its mouth, whence, turning to the north, afterwards the northeast, it crosses the Big Monocacy very obliquely, and shows itself on the B. & O. RR. towards Frederick, and farther northeast, in a much contracted area.

Its entire length, measured along the western boundary, from the northern extremity on the Potomac to its extreme southern point on Robertson's River is 74 miles, its width upon the Potomac (being the widest part) about 14½ miles, making the entire area of country covered by this formation about 651 square miles.

2. *The Barboursville deposits* is a small area, in Orange county, on the south side of the Rapid-Anne, of an elliptical shape. It commences at the Rapid-Anne River, near the mouth of Baylor's Run, thence bearing to the southwest it passes a short distance east of the mill where the Orange Courthouse turnpike touches the river, and continues on a little westward of the meeting-house about one mile beyond Barboursville. From this point, the most southern extremity, it may be traced a little east of the headwaters of Blue Run, and running nearly parallel with, but east of that stream, passes the mill below Beaver Branch. Continuing in the same direction parallel to the west flank of the Southwest Mountain, it passes a little west of Montpellier, striking the road from Orange Courthouse to Stanardsville at the eastern crossing of Baylor's Run; by bearing a little northwest it terminates at the beginning.

About 9 miles long and 2 miles wide at its widest part, its area would be about 14 square miles.

3. *The James River deposits* contain several occurrences of the formation about Warminster, on both sides of James River, extending into Nelson, Buckingham, and Fluvanna counties. They are situated in the wide internal between Barboursville and those at Danville to be traced below. They are less defined, and consist of more isolated narrow patches, stretching for about eighteen miles from the southwest corner of Fluvanna county, about the Hardware River, with a width of about five miles, to a distance of about one mile below Warminster on the James, where the formation is much narrower, showing exposures west of Scottsville, below the mouth of the Rockfish River, upon the north side, and higher up upon the south side of the same, and also below Warminster. Its area cannot yet be computed correctly, but would be about 40 to 45 square miles.

4. *The Danville deposits* extend from Falling River, in Campbell county, across the Staunton River, through Pittsylvania county, to the north side of the Dan River, just above Danville. Its shape is that of a long and narrow strip, wider at its southern than northern extremity, with an expansion in its contour along the western margin nearer the centre of the tract, extending to the headwaters of Stinking Creek.

Beginning at the northern extremity near the mouth of Rattlesnake Creek, in Campbell county, taking a southwest course, it crosses the road from Campbell Courthouse to Reid's Bridge on Falling River, about a mile and a half west of the bridge, crosses Molley's Creek, at the lower mill, and continuing in a nearly straight southwest course, crosses Staunton River, a short distance above the upper end of Long Island. Bearing now more westward to Chalk Level, it passes near the main road to Lynchburg at George's Creek. Thence in a southeasterly and afterwards nearly southerly direction, it passes one mile east of the White Thorn Tavern at the creek of the same name to within two miles east of Competition, and taking now a westerly turn crosses Cherrystone Creek about two and a half miles above its mouth, and the Banister River about one mile east of the mouth of White Oak Creek. From here it follows the western flank of the White Oak Mountain, passing about one mile east of Chestnut & Fitzgerald's store, and crossing Sandy River about one mile east of Dalla's Bridge arrives at the southern extremity of the line at the end of White Oak Mountain. Here it is inflected by

the mountain, and passes round its southern edge in an easterly direction to a point about a mile and a quarter north of Bachelor's Hall, and continues on to within three-quarters of a mile of Dan River, and within about two miles of Danville.

It now assumes a northeasterly course nearly parallel with its western boundary, and intersects the road from Danville to Pleasant Gap, in the White Oak Mountain, about five and a half miles north of Danville, crossing Sandy Creek near the road to Charlotte Courthouse and the headwaters of Shockoe Creek it passes within half a mile west of Riceville. From here its eastern boundary is almost a straight line across the Staunton River, about half a mile below Pannel's Bridge, in a general course N. 30° E., almost parallel with its western boundary to the west of Nowlan's, and after passing about three-quarters of a mile east of Reid's Bridge it curves gently round to the beginning. Its extreme length northeast and southwest is 54 miles, its greatest width at Brusby Mountain 8 miles, but its average width will not exceed more than 4 to 4½ miles. The area of the formation thus delineated may therefore be computed to be from 260 to 272 square miles.

5. *The Dan River deposits* comprise the small portion of the tract a little west of the former at Smith's River, passing across the Dan River into the State of North Carolina, and known there as the Dan River coal basin. Its whole extent is about 40 miles long, of which only about 8 miles, the extreme northern end, is situated in Virginia, the balance being in the counties of Rockingham and Stokes, in the general direction from Leaksville to Germantown. The width of the basin var'es from four to seven miles.

The outline of the portion in Virginia may be traced by beginning at the State line about one mile east of Cascade Creek, passing northeast in a course nearly parallel with the creek to a point a little east of the village of Cascade, thence turning westward so as to cross the creek about five miles from the State line, and sweeping around to a southwesterly direction, intersecting Smith's River near the State line in its western boundary. The area of this small portion may be about 14 square miles.

The whole area of the Mesozoic formation, as existing and distinctly traced out in Virginia, amounts, according to the areas given, to 1,495 square miles. But including the tracts at Hicksford and James River, it will amount to over 1,500 square miles. Of this, over 1,150 square miles would be comprised in the western, and over 345 square miles in the eastern localities; 329 square miles occur immediately along and ultimately overlaid by the Tertiary, and 1,166 square miles in the isolated tracts surrounded entirely by Eozoic rocks.

II. DESCRIPTION OF THE ROCKS CONSTITUTING THE FORMATION.

The principal rocks constituting the formation are sandstones and slates of various grades and colors; occasionally conglomerates and limestones, shales or fireclays, and seams of bituminous coal, as well as a number of accessory minerals and igneous rocks are met with. The latter are occasionally found to have penetrated the series of sedimentary rocks, which display a great variety of color, texture, and solidity in rapidly changing strata.

1. *Conglomerates.*— With the exception of the occasional occurrence of rather coarse sandstones, the conglomerates are apparently very few in number. One occupies the lowest position in the series, and therefore forms the bottom of the basins, although its outcrop is not always perceptible. It consists of large pebbles of quartz, granite, and other crystalline rocks, such as epidote, also gneiss and hornblendic rocks, and the Eozoic slates, which formed the borders of the valleys in which the deposition occurred. Even the rocks of the Blue Ridge have given their contingent at some of the localities. The boulders vary much in size. No doubt, from vestiges found at the surface, they sometimes attain very large dimensions, while pieces of the size of a nut and egg are quite common. The cementing mass varies from a silicious to a highly calcareous and argillaceous material, but in many instances must be of a very friable nature; highly ferruginous cements are also found, particularly in the upper strata of the series. Again, as in the Potomac marble, the pebbles are largely of a calcareous character, differing in that respect materially in various portions of the State.

The color of the conglomerates must consequently differ greatly. Gray and greenish-gray shades, or brown and ochreous tints are the most frequent. The large boulders of granite and other crystalline rocks being set free from their cement by decomposition, occur close up to the Eozoic base rocks, and may sometimes be confounded with them.

2. *Sandstones.*—These rocks are represented by a great number of varieties. In general they are either of a gritty silicious or of a friable argillaceous character. The former furnish a tolerably firm, and occasionally even a good material for building.

a. Psephites—silicious and feldspathic sandstones. Most of them are entirely composed of quartz and feldspar, the larger grains not exceeding generally the size of peas, and diminishing to fine particles of sand. In many instances it is the perfect *arkose*, or feldspathic sandstone, in others, of rarer occurrence, the silicious material (in appearance almost a quartzite) predominates. This is particularly the case in the lowest strata of the formation. Mica, principally muscovite, in small silvery scales, occurs not unfrequently.

The quartz is either milky, smoky, or of a bluish-gray opal color; it is also frequently colorless. The feldspar is principally white, or light gray, and often decomposed into kaolin. Most of these sandstones, particularly those in which the decomposition of the feldspar has not progressed so far, effervesce strongly with acids, showing the presence of carbonate of lime, indicating probably the presence of various varieties of feldspar as, for instance, labradorite. It is a remarkable fact, at least in the Richmond deposits, that while in the upper strata of the formation *only* the white or gray-colored feldspar occurs, from a certain horizon lower down the flesh-colored orthoclase begins to make its appearance.

The consistency of the sandstones is more or less hard and durable; according to the condition of the feldspar, some of them presenting a hard and good building material, others decaying fast by exposure.

The colors of these sandstones are generally white, light-gray, and buff. In the eastern range these colors predominate in the upper strata. In the lower, some red-colored sandstones of a ferruginous character are found to exist in more or less thick strata. Particles of specular iron ore may be detected in them, while the coloring matter consists of the hydrous oxide of iron.

In the western deposits, the red-colored sandstones are far more frequent, indicating in each instance whence the material has been derived to form the secondary deposits.

Occasionally very dark gray sandstones of the psephitic description occur, which by all indications must have undergone a considerable change through igneous action. They are distinctly but very closely grained, containing also crystals of feldspar, generally of a highly vitreous appearance, imbedded in a silicious and apparently vitrified aluminous paste. Even the impressions and carbonized remains of vegetables are noticed in it. The rock has frequently a great degree of tenacity, and at first sight has a close resemblance to some of the porphyritic rocks. They are frequently met with at disturbed locations, near the saddles of anticlinals.

Very few indications of organic remains are met with in the psephites beyond some small carbonized vegetable particles of the nature of mineral charcoal. Some few strata, generally more porous, are either of a light color, with yellowish-green spots, or of a uniform dark brownish-green tint. They contain *mineral oil*, which may be readily perceived by its smell, when the impregnation is strong, or occasionally even by drops of oil collected in small caverns of the more porous rock; they also have the greasy appearance and feel. When the oiliness is not marked it can still be perceived by moistening with some liquid, which will not soak into the pores, as in other rocks, but accumulate as a fixed globule. In stronger oil-rocks water is sufficient, in the weaker a drop of acid is preferable. The drop of water or acid let fall upon the rock, from the point of a glass rod, will remain for a shorter or longer time, as a perfect globule on oily rocks, while on non-oleiferous rocks it will be soaked up immediately. There are various strata of oil-rocks at certain fixed horizons in the formation. So far, their only practical value will be as a landmark for the seams of coal.

b. Psammites. This subdivision of sandstones is also largely

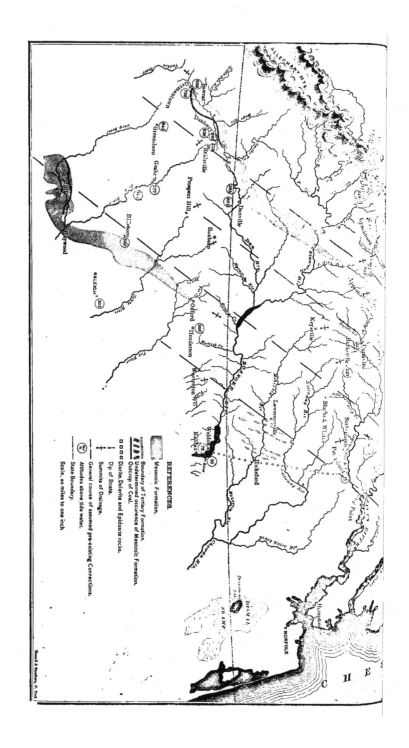

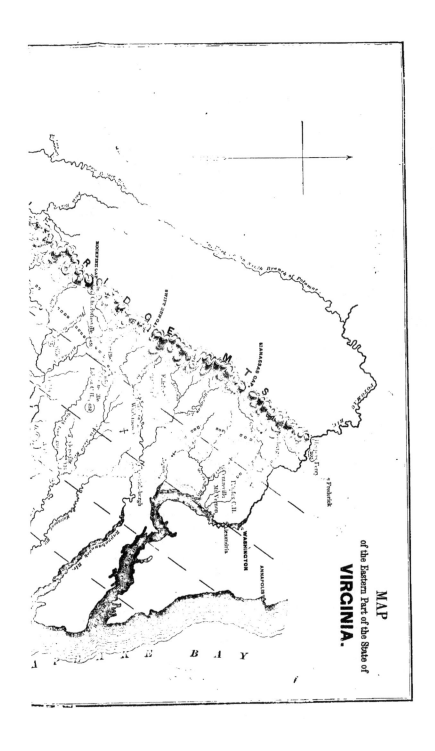

MAP
of the Eastern Part of the State of
VIRGINIA.

represented in the formation, particularly in the western localities. They are largely composed of argillaceous matter in which fine silicious sand, and, but sparingly, larger grains of quartz, and even feldspar, are found more or less regularly disseminated. Mica, principally in the fine silvery scales of muscovite, but sometimes the black variety, or biotite, is found invariably in them, sometimes so largely as to form micaceous psammites, which being generally finely laminated, appear as micaceous slates. Chloritic minerals also sometimes take part in their composition. The principal colors of these sandstones are again various shades of rather dark gray, greenish and yellowish gray, red and buff. When they contain much carbonaceous matter, which is frequently the case, they are dark gray and grayish-black.

While the psephites are most frequently calcareous, the psammites show an almost entire absence of calcareous matter. They are also non-oleiferous. They show more indications of organic remains, particularly of vegetable origin, as the remains of casts of trunks of trees, the impressions of reeds and leaves, which are occasionally converted into coal, lignite or mineral charcoal, in the carbonaceous rocks.

3. *Slates and Shales.* The argillaceous sandstones are gradually passing into real argillaceous or micaceous slates by the degradation of their materials into the finest particles. Some are entirely free of grit, passing into vitrified clay, shale, or fire-clay. Some of them retain a tolerably firm laminated structure, which in some instances may be carried to a great degree of divisibility. But they are, nevertheless, unfit for slating, being too much affected by the weather. In other instances, the slates fall into thin angular fragments soon after being exposed to the air. The shales of a very fine texture are characterized by soon falling into irregular fragments, and by decomposing readily into a good clay for ceramic purposes. The color of the slates is variously gray, greenish, and bluish-gray, dark drab, brown, and nearly black; in the western districts, red shales are also found. The shales are generally of light-gray or ash-color.

Some of the dark-brown and black slates contain considerable carbonaceous and bituminous matter, and some would yield a large quantity of illuminating material. Some of them when cut by the knife appear almost like brown coal, or the impure qualities of the Kanawha cannel.

Iron pyrites, in a finely divided state, as well in concretions and large crystals, is frequently met with in the black and brown slates; also carbonate of lime in concretions, some of fibrous texture, and some in scales and small seed-like grains: the remains of a species of *Cythere* occur in some of the strata.

In regard to the organic remains the slates, and particularly the black slates, offer the greatest treasury among all the rocks. The impressions of whole fish, multitudes of scales, small bones, and saurian teeth, two species of *Estheria*, *Cythere*, reeds and stems of *Equiseta* and *Calamites*, and also, but more rarely, various leaves occur, principally in smooth, divisible, most argillaceous, but also most fragile, slates. In consequence of the bituminous and pyritical nature of the same, they possess in a high degree the property for spontaneous combustion (*Brandschiefer*).

4. *Limestones.* They are confined to a few distinct strata of considerable thickness. But they occur not unfrequently in the form of scales and crystals of calcites, in streaks, seams and concretions of more or less magnitude and in spherical or lensiform shapes.

They are generally of a close texture or arenaceous, but occur also as fibrous and crystallized calcite. The color is principally light or dark gray, brownish, or ash-color. A notable quantity of carbonate of iron is found in some of the limestones, but not in sufficient quantity to make it a carbonaceous iron ore. Upon some of the slabs of limestone perfect crystals of gypsum and iron pyrites are found in considerable profusion.

5. *Coal.* The coal which occurs in this formation is mostly of a highly bituminous character, and must be classed amongst the coking and gas coals, both of which qualities it possesses in a very high degree. Still at certain localities a less bituminous and even non-bituminous coal, carbonite, semi-anthracite, and natural coke are met with.

Physical Characters of the Coals.

a. *Bituminous Coal.* It is highly laminated, bright black

jet, highly resinous, thick laminæ, generally in thick layers, alternating with dull black laminæ of less dimensions. On the fresh fracture, which is more or less conchoidal, it is jet black; lustre resinous, splendent; it splits readily parallel to its stratifications, which are strongly marked by the appearance on the surface of the dull variety mentioned above in a thin film. Its specific gravity, according to Professors O. P. Hubbard and B. Silliman, is 1.292; according to Professor Johnson, specific gravity, 1.246, and the weight of one cubic yard, 2075 lbs.

It contains, on an average, from 30 to 38.5 per cent. of volatile matter; 59 to 66 per cent. of fixed carbon; 2 to 10.8 (average of twenty-one analyses, 5.58) per cent. of ash, and 0.6 to 1.7 per cent. of sulphur.

b. *Carbonite.* The true carbonite is probably only a semi-bituminous coal, generally with a large amount of earthy impurities.

In appearance it is of a dark iron-gray or grayish-black color, dull, or semi-metallic lustre, compact and even very tough, but not hard to cut. Hardness,—2.5. Specific gravity,—1.323 (Professor Johnson).

It contains about 11 per cent. of volatile (scarcely bituminous) matter, 80 per cent. of fixed carbon, and from 9 to 22 per cent. of ash, also considerable sulphuret of iron.

In certain instances it has the property of decrepitating very badly. Slickensides are not unfrequently noticed upon it.

c. *Natural Coke.* The true natural coke, although the carbonite is also generally termed natural coke, differs materially in aspect from the preceding.

It is of a dark iron-black color, of more metallic lustre, porous, and has, in general, more the aspect of an artificial coke than the former. It is found at such places where igneous rocks influenced the bituminous coal and deprived it of its bitumen.

d. *Semi-anthracite.* Under the same conditions as the former a volatilization of bituminous matter has taken place, producing in some cases an anthracite coal, which much resembles the true anthracite, particularly in the Dan River deposits. It is hard, of iron-black color, submetallic lustre, and conchoidal fracture.

6. *Igneous Rocks.* Penetrating the sedimentary rocks, igneous rocks are occasionally met with in the form of dikes. They are generally dolerite, but in some instances euphotide (feldspar-euphotide, containing sphærosiderite flourspar in crystals and epidote-euphotide). The former are generally dark gray or greenish-black, the latter light gray or yellowish-gray, very compact, hard, and crypto-crystalline. Amygdaloids are also found with their cavities filled by epidote, quartz, and chalcedony.

7. *Accessory Minerals.* Among the occurring minerals but few can be noticed, none being of any importance in a practical point of view.

Malachite, *Libethenite*, and *Copper Pyrites* are sometimes met with as thin incrustations between the strata of the sedimentary rocks; also some of the fossil remains are incrusted by them.

Gypsum. This mineral is found in the coal mines of the James River basin, in a profusion of well-formed crystals upon the surface of limestone strata. The crystals lie flat upon the joints of the slabs, and in some instances, where space admits, they stand in erect positions, but inclining at an angle to the main axes, leaving the distinct tracing of the section of the crystal as a print upon the surface of the limestone when detached from it.

Iron Pyrites. It occurs as the cubic pyrites and marcasite in well-defined crystals, also finely disseminated through the slates and upon the stratification planes of the coal. It also occurs in spherical masses of more or less magnitude, termed "sulphur balls."

Carbonate of Iron. Among the calcareous concretions and small limestone strata, we may notice some which contain notable quantities of carbonate of iron. They are of a dark grayish-black color, compact in texture and of an earthy appearance, differing by nothing else apparently from the other calcareous concretions except their great weight. Samples have yielded as much as fifteen per cent. of peroxide of iron.

[TO BE CONTINUED.]

ray,
oth,
Mr.

880.
,811
,662
,871
,988

344

,481
,277

,484

the

0
0

,0

M
D

M

1879

80.
,579
,862
,901
76
,359
151
,648

,641
,918

,438

the

I.

28
47

81

the
plint
and
ying
to
of

lley
that
sue.
rta-
por-
g a
ver-
ient
ced
Any
tion
ver-
are
ther
ope
d it

geological sur,

*, *

ropn
calit
whic
quar
disea
mus
inva
psan
mica
in th
are
yell
bons
gray
W
psan
The
orga
mai
leav
mine
3.
grad
the
Som
or fl
stru
degr
slati
insta
bein
are
by d
The
gray
trict
ligh
S
ble
yiel
whe
imp
Ir
and
bro
fibr
the
Ir
the
The
and
sten
vari
argi
the
in
tion
4.
con
the
and
lens
T
cur
cips
qua
ston
iron
of g
of a
the
in
mir
cite

The Montgomery, Va., Gold Field.

An open letter from Prof. JOHN L. CAMPBELL.

Maj. Henry Fink, Receiver A. M. & O. RR.

Sir:—Among the many and valuable sources of mineral wealth within reach of your line of railway, "Brush Creek Gold Field," in Montgomery county, merits at least a passing notice. Through your courtesy and kindness I have recently been placed in convenient circumstances for visiting the locality in question. The place was visited in company with the Rev. Chas. Miller of Christiansburg—a gentleman thoroughly familiar with the topography of the whole region where the gold is found.

The area within which the metal has been found lies along the S. E. base of Pilot Mountain, chiefly in Montgomery, though partly in Floyd county, in what is known as the "Brush Creek Valley." "Prospecting" has been extended for some distance along the valley, and gold is said to have been detected at numerous points over an area 20 miles long and 4 miles wide—80 square miles; but the "washings" hitherto have been limited chiefly to one small branch of Brush Creek on the lands of Mr. John Walters, near the line of Montgomery and Floyd counties, and about 12 miles south of Bang's, the Christiansburg depot.

The gold region is beyond the limits of our Great Valley, the S E. boundary of which at this place is Pilot Mountain, a Primordial ridge that separates the Valley limestones along its N. W. base from the metamorphic rocks that border it on the S. E. The country rocks of the gold region are all *metamorphic*, and are traversed by numerous veins of white and mottled quartz, from one or more of which the gold has been derived. This is evinced by the fact that many fragments of the quartz have been found that contain just such particles of the metal as are washed from the alluvium along the banks of the little streams where it is obtained; and by the additional fact that little particles of the quartz are sometimes found adhering to some of the little nuggets of gold.

At the period of my visit the gold-bearing rock had not been found *in situ*, but was obtained solely from the alluvial deposits along the banks of the one little branch above mentioned, and within a space of less than half a-mile in length, and only a few yards in width. Preparations, however, were in progress for working in other localities, at which there were promising indications that the precious metal would be obtained in paying quantities.

The particles of gold are generally very small, and are disseminated through large quantities of the debris of the quartz and other rocks of the region. The washing and panning, by which the metal is separated, are conducted after a very primitive fashion, and must fail to secure anything like the whole of the gold. Improved methods will doubtless be introduced, if the workable area is found to be large enough to encourage a sufficient influx of capital.

I was informed that a few individuals commenced work there in May last, and that the number had since increased to about 35 to 40. They are steady, earnest men who seem to pay all due regard to the rights of one another, and of the owner of the land on which they are operating. The value of gold (containing a considerable percentage of silver) obtained up to the date of my visit, July 29th, was estimated, by some of those engaged in the mining, at about $2,500, obtained in two and a half months.

If the alluvium of many of the branches of Brush Creek, along which gold is said to have been discovered, should be found worth working, or should the gold-bearing vein or veins be discovered—as will doubtless be the case when a proper system of exploration has been tried—the introduction of suitable appliances for a more complete extraction of the metal will soon follow, and this may ere long become an important point of industry within reach of your great line of transportation. The field is certainly not unworthy the attention of those who have capital to invest in mining operations.   Yours very respectfully,

                                       J. L. CAMPBELL,
                        Prof. Chemistry and Geology.
Washington & Lee University,
Lexington, Va., Aug. 10th, 1880.

The Coal and Coke movement over the Chesapeake & Ohio Railway, for the months of May and June and for the 6 months ending June 30th, 1880, and for the corresponding periods of 1879, in tons of 2,000 lbs., by Mr. Charles M. Gibson, Fuel Agent of the Company, is as follows:

	May.		June.	
	1879.	1880.	1879.	1880.
Fuel for use of Company	8,559	11,540	8,187	13,811
Shipped at Huntington on Ohio River	12,627	12,046	8,086	8,663
Delivered on line of road west of Richmond	1,583	1,837	587	1,871
" at Charlottesville to Va. Mid. RR.,	2,039	4,418	2,051	2,968
" at Gordonsville to do.	12	....	12	....
" at Junction of R., F. & P. RR.,	86	1,010	241	344
" at Richmond for consumption, including steam tugs and dredges,	5,265	9,973	3,358	2,481
Shipped at James River wharves	15,339	16,639	17,236	24,277
Total,	45,060	50,460	39,760	54,484

The character of the coals moved during the same period is shown in the following exhibit:

For the Month ending	Cannel.	Splint & Bit's	Coke.	Total.
May 31, 1880,	3,714	44,473	2,973	50,460
Same period, 1879,	2,397	38,899	3,754	45,050
Increase, 1880	1,317	5,574	....	5,410
Decrease, 1880,	....	....	1,481	
June 30, 1880,	4,549	47,634	2,301	54,484
Same period, 1879,	3,493	34,180	2,187	39,760
Increase, 1880,	1,056	13,554	64	14,674

The following is the movement for the first 6 months of the years 1879 and 1880:

	1879.	1880.
Fuel for use of Company	41,945	63,579
Shipped at Huntington on the Ohio River	37,361	67,862
Delivered on line of road west of Richmond	18,030	13,901
" at Staunton to Valley Railroad	211	76
" at Charlottesville to Va. Midland RR.,	12,911	20,353
" at Gordonsville	138	151
" at Junction to R. F. & P. RR.,	1,107	6,548
" at Richmond for consumption, including steam tugs and dredges,	24,046	23,841
Shipped at James River wharves	63,798	81,318
Total,	195,347	279,428

The character of the coals moved during the same period is shown in the following exhibit:

From 1st January to	Cannel.	Splint & Bit's	Coke.	Total.
June 30, 1880,	20,415	242,550	16,463	279,428
Same period, 1879,	9,087	173,786	13,474	195,347
Increase, 1880,	11,328	69,764	2,989	84,081

So far the movements of 1880 are largely in excess of those of 1879, for the same period. That of cannel coal increased over 124 per cent; that of splint and bituminous coals over 40 per cent.; that of coke over 22 per cent.; and the total movement is more than 43 per cent. greater. This is a gratifying exhibit and it explains why the C. & O. has recently been compelled to increase the number of its coal cars, which it has done from the shops of the Tredegar Company, at Richmond, Va.

Attention is invited.—To the excellent, Shenandoah Valley home, on the Valley Railroad, but a few miles from Staunton, that Dr. Eichelberger offers for sale by advertisement in this issue. This is an every way attractive place, highly improved, comfortable, convenient, easy of access, and in one of the best of neighborhoods. We commend it to the attention of any one wanting a good country home.——The terms of Washington and Lee University have been reduced for the coming session, as its advertisement shows. This is not only one of the best institutions for advanced instruction in all the land, but it is also one of the cheapest. Any young man with capacity enough to acquire a college education can readily find a way for acquiring it by applying to this university.——The James River Steel Work, near Lynchburg, Va., are now in successful operation. It advertises its specialties in another column. We know that it does none but good work and we hope our patrons requiring such railway supplies as it makes will send it their orders and so sustain this Virginia enterprise.

The Iron Ores of Virginia and West Virginin.

By·Prof. William B. Rogers.

Editorial Note.—In the year 1835 the State of Virginia, (then embracing what is now Virginia and West Virginia,) organized a Geological Survey and appointed William B. Rogers, at that time Professor of Natural Philosophy in the University of Virginia, State Geologist and put him in charge of that work. Prof. Rogers, aided by a number of assistants, began this geological survey in 1835 and, zealously and with wonderful ability, carried it on until 1841-2, exploring, more or less, every portion of this great State, from the Atlantic to the Ohio; and gathering the materials for a Geological Map of Virginia—a reduction of which, by himself, was given in the June, 1880, No. of The Virginias—and for a full report on its geology. During the progress of that survey he furnished to the Board of Public Works of Virginia, the body having supervision of that work, annual reports, as follows : (1) For 1835, "Report of the Geological Reconnoissance of the State of Virginia," published in 1836 in 52 quarto pages. (2) "Report of the Progress of the Geological Survey of the State of Virginia for the year 1836," published in 1837 in 14 quarto pages. (3) "Report of the Progress of the Geological Survey of the State of Virginia for the year 1837," published in 1838 in 24 quarto pages. (4) "Report of the Progress of the Geological Survey of the State of Virginia for the year 1838," published in 1839 in 32 quarto pages. (5) "Report of the Progress of the Geological Survey of the State of Virginia for the year 1839," published in 1840 in 161 octavo pages. (6) "Report of the Progress of the Geological Survey of the State of Virginia for the year 1840," published in 1841 in 132 octavo pages.

These *six* "Reports of Progress" were the only reports on the geology of Virginia that Prof Rogers ever published, for soon after the publication of that for 1840 the survey was discontinued, and his final report, in the preparation of which he had made much progress, was never completed, and the world of science as well as the State of Virginia thereby suffered an irreparable loss.

These published reports, unlike most preliminary ones, have and always will have a permanent value, and yet they are inaccessible, since not more than three or four complete sets of them exist.—The eminent Professor of Geology in the University of Virginia, in his introductory lecture, last year, said, "I have been told that a complete copy of the reports of Prof. Wm. B. Rogers would command its weight in gold. It cannot be obtained."

In view of this rarity of Prof. Rogers' reports and of the present value of their statements in the interest of development in these states, we propose to present to our readers, from time to time, extracts from these reports, *in the exact words of the author,* grouped by subjects and arranged in the order of their publication, with some explanatory notes made necessary by the changes and developments that have taken place in the 40 odd years that have passed since their appearance.

We now begin, and will continue until completed, the publication of *all that is said in Rogers' reports about the iron ores of Virginia and West Virginia,* arranging the statements, as far as may be, topographically as well as geologically; an arrangement that can be readily comprehended if reference is made to Rogers' Geological Map of the Virginias that is already in the hands of our readers, and that will be, substantially, as follows :

1. The Tertiary iron ores; those of Tidewater in Va.
2. The Archæan iron ores; those of Midland, Piedmont and the Eastern Blue Ridge, in Va.
3. The Mesozoic iron ores; those in Mesozic areas of Midland, in Va.
4. The Primordial iron ores; those of the Western Blue Ridge, in Va.
5. The Middle and Upper Cambrian iron ores; those of The Great Valley, &c., in Va. and W. Va.
6. The Silurian iron ores; those of Apalachia, in Va. and W. Va.

7. The Devonian iron ores; those of Apalachia, in Va. and W. Va.
8. The Lower and Middle Carboniferous iron ores; those of Trans-Apalachia, in Va. and W. Va.
9. The Upper Carboniferous iron ores; those of Trans-Apalachia, in Va. and W. Va.

In group (1), are those of Dana's formations 19 and 20 ; in (2), Dana's 1 ; in (3), Dana's 17 and 18 ; in (4), Dana's 2, Rogers' I or Primal ; in (5), Dana's 3 and 4, Rogers' II and III ; in (6), Dana's 5, 6, 7 and 8, Rogers' IV, V, VI, and VII · in (7), Dana's 10, 11 and 12, Rogers' VIII and IX ; in (8), Dana's 13, Rogers' X and XI; in (9), Dana's 14, Rogers' XII, XIII, XIV, XV, and XVI.

N. B.—First the page and then the year of the report quoted will follow the quotation in brackets. The small figures above words refer to notes at end of article.

1. The Tertiary Iron Ores of Virginia.—These are the ores of the Tertiary in Tidewater Virginia.—"Occasional bands of iron ore occur in connection with one of the fossiliferous deposits of this region" [4-1835].

In the Miocene Marl District.—"A thin stratum of red ferruginous stone, containing a large proportion of oxide of iron, is found in this region, running horizontally below, and sometimes in the beds of clay before described, and generally separated by only a few feet from the underlying masses of shells. This stratum, which is very generally present, varies in thickness from an inch to a foot. Its texture is sometimes cellular, sometimes compact and fibrous, like that of certain varieties of hematite. In the more eastern portions of the Miocene district the peculiar structure of which will be hereafter described, much ore of this description lies loosely scattered on the surface : while in the more elevated parts of the country, its invariable position is such as above described. The character of the ore in many localities is such as to promise great facility in reducing it to the metallic state, together with a large percentage of resulting metal. A specimen obtained from above the marl on the cliff at Mount Pleasant, Surry county, yielded by analysis in the 100 grains, Peroxide of iron 72.40 ; Alumina 3.90 ; Silica 7.71 ; Water 14.35 ; Loss 1.64. With a sufficient quantity of ore like this, accompanied with the advantage of a shell limestone, sometimes beautifully crystalline, in its immediate vicinity, the manufacture of iron would promise a high degree of productiveness; and it is by no means improbable that in some parts of this region the supply of the ore may be found sufficient to make such an enterprise not only safe but profitable. The subject is at all events worthy of some attention. Indeed it appears not a little surprising that this rich mineral seems hitherto to have escaped observation, or at least to have been regarded as undeserving of an especial notice". [6-1835.]

In the Miocene Tertiary "frequently much oxide of iron is mingled with the earthy matter, giving it more or less of a yellow or brown appearance, and this is the aspect which the upper beds containing shells most usually present. [8-1835.]

"Throughout all the upper fossiliferous strata, as well as in the argillaceous beds just mentioned, will be found disseminated greenish black grains of silicate of iron and potash, identical with those already described as existing in the stratum immediately overlying the shells, and having the same form and composition with the granules contained very abundantly in an older formation both in this country and in Europe. In some of the beds of marl or shells, these particles so abound as to give a very decided color to the whole mass." [7-1835.]

Near Yorktown "a narrow layer of iron ore extends along the cliff, with occasional interruptions, at a small distance above the fossiliferous strata." [10-1835]

"*Sulphate of iron and sulphur.*—In some parts of the Miocene district, there occur beds of clay more or less sandy, and usually of a dark color, containing these substances in a minute but still appreciable quantity. Such matter, there is reason to believe would not in general prove directly beneficial to the soil. The former

has been thought positively detrimental to vegetation, and certainly when applied in considerable quantity this is its effect. What agency it might exert in a more diluted state, and mingled with other matter, we are without the means of determining. Probably under such circumstances it might operate as a stimulant, and thus contribute to the growth. The same doubts are also applicable to the other substance above mentioned. Yet in some well authenticated cases, the action of these *copperas and sulphur* clays has been found strikingly beneficial. In these instances, however, it would seem that much if not all the benefit was produced by the effectual protection which even minute quantities of these substances, especially the latter, afford against the attacks of insects. In a cotton field in which all the alternate rows were lightly sprinkled with earth of this description, the plants so treated grew up vigorous and healthy, while the others became sickly and were nearly devoured by insects. Much careful observation is required to determine the kind and mode of influence which these substances exert, and it would be premature, in our present ignorance of the matter to assert any convictions on the subject." [13–1835.]

In the tables of analyses of Miocene Marls [14 and 15–1835.] "peroxide of iron" and "oxide of iron" are named as ingredients of those marls.

"Sulphate of iron, or copperas," is spoken of [16–1835.] as a common ingredient in the clay beds of the Miocene, helping to make the water obtained from them unfit for use, and contributing to the decay of the fossil shells imbedded in those clays, converting their carbonate of lime into sulphate, or gypsum and thus improving the character of the soil.

The third bed of the Miocene from the top, near Piping Tree on the Pamunkey, is a "ferruginous stratum abounding in casts, and occasionally containing the shells themselves." [18–1835.] The same "thin band of ferruginous rock or clay was generally observed to be interposed between the bluish marls and the diluvial sand and gravel" on the Potomac and the Rappahanock as on the James and the York. [3–1836.]

The Upper Miocene beds of the Northern Neck "rarely contain an appreciable amount of carbonate of lime, but are impregnated with sulphate of lime, (gypsum), together with sulphate of iron (copperas), sulphate of alumina, sulphur and sometimes even a sensible amount of sulphate of magnesia (Epsom salts)." There "the cause of the extensive destruction of shelly matter once imbedded in these clays, was clearly traced to the sulphuric acid originating in the decomposition of sulphuret of iron, which permeating the beds of marl converted the carbonate into sulphate of lime. This being in part retained, formed the crystals of gypsum now discovered in these strata. At the same time, that by the decomposition of the sulphuret, the sulphate of iron and other ingredients above noticed were brought to light; and the overlying layer of ferruginous rock or clay most probably owes its origin to the same source." [4–1836.]

"Ferruginous sand" is mentioned in "observations" on Miocene Marls. [4 to 8–1837.]

Between the Miocene and the Eocene "is very commonly met with a ferruginous stratum, sometimes having the hardness of a rock, consisting usually of coarse sand and some pebbles, cemented by oxide of iron." [22–1839.]

"The yellow marls owe their hue to an intermixture of oxide of iron, which even in the small proportion in which it is mingled with the other matter of these beds, is capable of imparting a bright ochrous yellow or a deep brownish tinge. The source of this ferruginous matter so generally present in the upper marls beds, as well as in the clays and sands which rest immediately upon them in numerous places, is for the most part to be sought for in a peculiar condition of the waters at the time in which these beds were forming, and not in the penetration of ferruginous matter from the overlying diluvium. Such a condition would naturally result from the extensive prevalence of a turbid state of the sea, like that so often witnessed in the waters of James River, when heavy rains have conveyed into them the red earthy matter met

with so extensively on the surface of that portion of the state lying between the head of tide and the Blue Ridge." [33–1839.]

The termination of the Eocene outcrop on the Potomac, near Mathias' Point, shows a lower, fossil bearing bed 8 or 9 ft. thick ; this is separated from the heavy bed of red clay forming the upper portion of the bank "by a thin band of ferruginous gravel and sandstone, such as is often seen occupying a similiar position on the Pamunkey, or in other localities." [12–1840.]

On Snow Creek, below Fredericksburg, in the second Eocene stratum from the bottom "the shelly matter has almost entirely disappeared and its place is now occupied by oxide of iron of a deep brown color presenting the most perfect casts, both of the interior and exterior of the shells." The stratum of yellowish white sand, some 20 feet thick, over this is "variegated with numerous bright yellow blotches, faintly representing the figures of the shells which they have replaced. These blotches are principally composed of oxide of iron." [14–1840.]—In general, the upper beds of the Miocene on The Peninsula contain proportions of "sulphate of iron." [16–1840.]

On the Northern Neck, in the Miocene "Besides the overlying band of ferruginous rock there occurs, in some places, another similar stratum, nearly on the top of the diluvium. This, of course, presents no marks of organic remains, and is generally but an aggregation of coarse gravel and sand, cemented by ferruginous matter." At the base of the Stratford and Chantilly cliffs, in Westmoreland, there is a stratum of blue sandy clay extending to the height of from 50 to 70 ft. "Upon the surface of this clay, especially where it projects from the general cliff, a copious efflorescence of sulphate of iron is usually found, imparting a greenish yellow color to the surface." [17–1840.] "This stratum is overlaid by a band of indurated ferruginous clay, approaching to the hardness of rock, and filled with a material closely resembling pipe-ore. This is about 2 ft. thick." "Next above is a stratum consisting, alternately, of sand and ferruginous mottled clay, extending to a height of about 40 ft." [17–1840.] Under the Chantilly cliffs 2 miles below Stratford "The beach is strewed with fragments of ferruginous sandstone, which have fallen from the upper portion of the cliff, where a band of this material overlies the shelly strata of the Miocene." [18–1840.]

In the bank of the Potomac below Cole's Point in Westmoreland, there is "A band of iron sandstone 3 inches thick ;" in the Rappahannock cliffs, in Richmond county, some 36 ft. above the water, there is "A band, of 12 inches, of a ferruginous aspect ;" in a stratum of that are spiculæ of gypsum which are generally painted over with brown oxide of iron. In many places, sulphate of iron and sulphate of alumina effloresce upon the surface." [19. 1840.] "Irregular nodules of ferruginous clay are found imbedded in the other materials." In the cliffs of Lancaster county, about 8 miles above the mouth of Curratoman, heavy beds of clay "rest upon a stratum of soft ferruginous sandstone, graduating into a sandy clay, and sometime a yellowish sand, mottled with ferruginous spots;" further down the river is a "rocky layer, consisting entirely of shells, converted into brown oxide of iron, situated at the base of the cliff," forming a "ferruginated, shelly rock 4 ft. in thickness," over which is "five ft. of sand, with ferruginous blotches and streaks." [20. 1840.] In the cliffs of the Rappahannock in Lancaster county near Cherry Point the 4th stratum from the water is "A layer of ferruginous sandstone, in bands alternating with thin seams of sand, 3 ft. thick," under the diluvium. In a ravine, 1½ miles E. of Lancaster C. H., the 4 ft. thick stratum next the surface is "A layer of ferruginous matter abounding in he casts and impressions of shells. There casts are usually found in the interior of spheroidal nodules, or geodes of oxide of iron, and consist of this oxide replacing the shelly matter, and covered with a beautiful shining covering of the carbonate or velvet iron ore." [21. 1840.] "A layer of ferruginous sandstone" is exposed in a hollow 4 miles S. W. from Northumberland C. H. [22. 1840.]

On the Peninsula, in the Eocene, the upper stratum is, frequently, "more or less impregnated with sulphates of lime, iron and

alumina," and "a thin band of ferruginous gravel, sometimes partially cemented, frequently overlies these beds, and forms the boundary between them and the Miocene." [24. 1840.] On the Potomac, at Eagle's Nest and Mount Stuart, the banks, 20 to 25 ft. high, are composed of two strata, the lower, about 12 ft. thick, is "dark bluish clay and sand strongly imbued with copperas, and containing a little gypsum; and the upper, of coarse ferruginous sand and gravel." [25. 1840.]   (*To be continued.*)

The Mineral Traffic of the Atlantic, Mississippi & Ohio Railroad for the first 6 months of 1880, in tons of 2,000 lbs., by Col. E. E. Portlock, the Auditor of that road, is given below. The first table is that of Virginia minerals from the line of this railway, giving kinds, quantities, and destination; the second is the mineral traffic from beyond Bristol, the western terminus of this railway, giving kinds and quantities.

DESTINATION.	Barytes.						Copper, Lead and Iron Ore.						Pig Lead.						Mar bls.	Zinc Spelter						Copper Ingot.						Coal.						Pig Iron.						Plaster.						Salt.					
	Jan.	Feb'y.	March.	April.	May.	June.	Jan.	Feb'y.	April.	May.			Jan.	Feb'y.	March.	April.	May.	June.		Jan.	March.	April.	May.	June.	Jan.	Feb'y.	March.	April.	May.	June.	Jan.	March.	June.				Jan.	Feb'y.	March.	April.	May.	June.	Jan.	Feb'y.	March.	April.	May.	June.
Boston		8	18	26	49	22	53	1		10	10	18			10																																		
New York......	131	123	71	49	68	76			10					33			22		12	21	72	10		119								11	41	36														
Philadelphia...	34	92	53	102	73	130		1						10		39				13	10				16	22	33	22	33																			
Baltimore......	4	21	19		12			1		16		39											20	20		168	179	190	125	202	459																	
Lynchburg ...																									42	58					6		1		11												
Way Stations.							206	80																148	162	86	96	50						130	262	847	872	118	3	11	60	107	94	83	61
Norfolk																																10				10									
Richmond																																33	113	33	80	67									
Va. Mid'l RR.																																						13		10	2						
South'rn States																																					80	527	538	323	30	9	812	696	351	432	342	215
Total........	185	254	150	78	198	237		23	307	21	90	36	16	36	19	35		80	22	23	92	22	73	10	30	126	190	195	83	108	50	336	234	340	180	612	594	210	758	1297	1206	159	12	893	736	298	457	435	277
Aggregate for six months...			1147						451						114				18		69						256						636						2205						3742					3095

Minerals received from beyond Bristol, via E. T., V. & Ga. RR.

	Jan.	Feb'y.	March	April	May.	June.	Total.
Marble, ...	148	181	112	214	222	552	1409
Barytes, ...		10	30	80	40	80	140
Zinc Ore, ...	364	540	744	240	84	...	1872
Manganese, ...				20	..	20	40
Salt, ...			9	12	..	12	33
Coal, ...	44	9	408	492	332	358	1743
Pig Iron, ...	14	68	17	155	92	13	459
Total, ...	470	808	510	1163	770	885	5696

A comparison of these tables with those given in the June number shows the introduction of a new traffic, that in "pure spelter" or metallic zinc, a result of the opening of the Bertha Zinc Works at Martin's Station; this also shows a movement of pig iron and plaster to Richmond, of pig iron to Norfolk, and of plaster to the line of the Va. Midland. The movement of Virginia marble to Boston indicates that some of the beautiful, and even rare, marbles of S. W. Va. are attracting attention. The steady increase in the transportation of pig iron shows that there is a steady demand for the superior charcoal irons of Wythe that find their way to market over the A. M. & O.

The Virginias.

A Mining, Industrial and Scientific Journal:
Devoted to the Development of Virginia and West Virginia.

Vol. I, No. 9. }   Staunton, Virginia, September, 1880.   { Price 25 Cents.

The Virginias,

PUBLISHED MONTHLY,

By JED. HOTCHKISS, · · · Editor and Proprietor,

At 346 E. Main St., Staunton, Va.

Terms, including postage, per year, in advance, $2.00. Single numbers, 20 cents. Extra copies, $20.00 per 100. Back numbers, from the first, can be had at 25c each. Advertising, per inch of length of single column (3 columns to a page, as on advertising pages), one month, $2.00; two months, $4.00; three months, $5.50; six months, $7.50; nine months, $10.00, and twelve months, $12.00; payable in advance.

Specimen Numbers of this journal are sometimes sent to parties supposed to have an interest in the development of the Virginias, or a desire to be informed in reference to their resources, improvement, etc.; they will please consider this an invitation to become subscribers and so help to sustain a paper devoted to their interests.

On sale at Hunter & Co.'s Bookstore, Main Street, Staunton, Virginia.

Mining Statistics of the Virginias for the Tenth Census.—Gold and Silver have been withdrawn from the list of substances published in our August number as those of which Maj. Jed. Hotchkiss is gathering the statistics in these States,—a special agent has been appointed for those metals. Nor does he gather the statistics of coal mines *of which the entire product is coked*, though he does of all others, even of the small ones mined for home and neighborhood use.

In gathering the statistics of these substances—Apatite, Asbestos, Arsenic, Asphaltum, Antimony; Barytes, Buhrstones, Borax, Bismuth; Chrome, Cobalt, Copper, Corundum and Emery, Cements (Hydraulic); Fluor Spar, Feldspar (for potash); Grahamite, Graphite, Gypsum and Plaster, Grindstones, Glass Sand, Green Sand; Honestones, Hydraulic Cement; Infusorial Earth, Iron Ores, Iron Pyrites; Kaolin; Lead, Lignite, Lithium; Manganese, Mica, Millstones, Molybdenum, Mercury; Nitre, Nickel, Novaculite; Ochres; Peat; Quartz; Roofing Slates, Serpentine, Slate, Slate Pencils, Soapstone (Steatite), Soda; Talc, Tin, Tungsten; Zinc;—Prof. Raphael Pumpelly, the Expert Special Agent in charge of Statistics of Mining Industry east of the Mississippi, instructs, (August 31st, 1880.):—

1st. Collect specimens of raw and finished product of each grade, to be carefully labeled and sent to his office,

2nd. Enter in the note books:—(1) A description of the method of mining or quarrying;—(2) Of the method of preparing the material at the quarries for the market;—(3) Of the geological age of the material;—(4) The names of the associated rocks;—(5) The form of the deposit;—(6) The manner of the occurrence of the material in the deposit;—(7) The distinguishing characteristics of different grades and the methods used in testing qualities.

In reference to the small neighborhood diggings of coal, where the product is worth less than $500 a year, it is important to have the facts so that the agent can report, by counties, (1) The amount, and (2) the value of the coal so mined; and also (1) The method of working these mines; (2) The kind of labor; (3) The usual wages paid; (4) Under what circumstances they are worked and under what they are idle.

It is proposed to construct a *Map showing in detail, the Movement of the Iron Ores of the Country to Meet the Coal.* For this purpose it becomes necessary to obtain a statement of the ore used at each Furnace, Forge, or Direct Process works, during the year ending June 1st, 1880, the *names and locations of the mines,* and the *aggregate amount* from each mine.—This has reference to *Total Consumption,* and includes *all ore* smelted, without reference to the state where mined.

Owners and managers of mines, furnaces, Catalan forges, etc., will confer a great favor if they will send me any of this information.

In reply to an application to the Census Office at Washington for the returns of population of the counties of these States, the Superintendent informs us (Sept. 8), "That the population of Virginia and West Virginia for 1880 has not yet been ascertained, but when it is, the information will be sent at the earliest practicable date."—We desire to present our readers the population of the counties of Virginia in Natural Grand Divisions, as in Hotchkiss' Summary of Virginia, for the last three decades, 1860, 1870, and 1880, with comments on the changes and movements of our population; but shall not do so until we have the *official returns* for 1880. None of those that have as yet been published are such,

The following Special Agents have been appointed in Virginia and West Virginia "to collect the Manufacturing Statistics of their respective cities," —D. P. Morris of Norfolk and Portsmouth; D. M. Dabney, of Lynchburg;

S. S. Northington of Petersburg; F. F. Bowen, of Danville; and James Alston Cabell, of Richmond; in Va.; and Dana L. Hubbard, of Wheeling, W. Va.

Blast Furnaces.—The new Ferrol Furnace, of the Pennsylvania and Virginia Iron and Coal Co., Augusta county Va., Maj. J. F. Lewis Supt., was lighted by Mrs. Lewis at 10 p. m. August 31st, and is making a good run. It is making 15 tons per day, getting 46 per cent. from the ore put in.— The Quinnimont, W. Va., Furnace of the same Co. which Mrs. L. lighted over 22 months ago is still running. At this furnace they are making thirty tons per day. May the same "good luck" follow the blowing in at Ferrol.—The Buffalo Gap Furnace was ready to blow in on Sept. 1st, but the high water did some slight damage that will delay a few days.—Pittsburg, Pa., and Youngstown, Ohio, gentlemen, among them Caleb B. Wick of the latter place and Mr. Wilson of the former, have made a con ditional contract for the purchase of the Rippetoe iron ore lands, just beyond Buffalo Gap, Augusta Co., Va. It is understood that these gentlemen will erect a first-class furnace there, between the Buffalo Gap and Ferrol furnaces, as soon as their purchase is perfected.

The James River Steel Works, above Lynchburg, Va., began on the 6th, rolling the iron for the Va. Midland R. R. bridge over the James at Lynchburg, says *The Virginian.*

Iron Ore.—A vein of Magnetic iron ore, called the "Shepherd" vein, from 3.5 to 4 ft. wide, yielding 64.1 per cent. of metallic iron, is said to have been opened 4.5 ms. west of Ca Ira, on the Buckingham road, in Buckingham Co., Va. Another vein, from 10 to 20 ft. thick, is reported to have been uncovered by P. A. Hubard on the waters of Whispering Creek, in the same county, some 3 miles west of and parallel to the "Shepherd" vein.—Prof. Shaler and party have examined the region of Willis' Mountain and called attention to a rich outcrop of Magnetic iron ore in a ridge a half mile east of the "Shepherd" vein, on the line between R. T. Hubard and J. J. Guthrie, which has been traced for nearly a mile.—*Farmville Mercury.* (A reference to the article on the Archæan Iron Ores, in this number, which we have compiled from Prof. Rogers' reports, will show that all the above "finds" were "found" long ago by Prof. Rogers. We trust they will not only stay "found" but also prove a valuable "find" now that men are beginning to know that our mineral wealth has a commercial value.—Ed.)—Mr. Sadler is now delivering on the C. & O. Ry., at Backbone, 30 miles west of Low Moor, 5,000 tons of lump ore from the "Stack" mine near that station, which he has sold to the Low Moor Iron Co., and which the railway is delivering and adding to the large "stock pile" that Company is accumulating preparatory to blowing in their every-way first-class furnace a few days hence.

Gold.—Prospecting on and near Brush Creek in Montgomery and Floyd counties, Va., develops pay earth over a considerable area. Capt. J. T. Hart, of Martin's, Va., for himself and associates, has just purchased, of John Walters 7 acres of gold-bearing land for $300 per acre ; of Cummings and Wimmer (?) 15 acres for $4,500; of John Wimmer and Charlton 36.15 acres for $11-895; and of Sallust Lawrence 12.3 acres for $900 per acre;—so writes us Maj. Wm. F. Guerrant, August 30th.—The *Floyd Reporter* of Sept. 10, states that the gold discoveries on Laurel Creek, in Floyd county, are proving valuable. The yield more than doubling the richest on Brush Creek in Montgomery.— The old Garnett and Mosely mine, 3 miles west of Willis' Mountain, in Buckingham, is now worked energetically by the Morrow Co.,—says the *Farmville Mercury.*

The American Manufacturer and Iron World, of Pittsburg, Pa., in its issue of Sept. 3rd, *copies in full,* and with the courtesy of credit that it never forgets,from our August number, articles on the "Excelsior Iron Mine" and on "The Bedford Iron Mining and Manufacturing Company," thus giving them the benefit of its wide circulation among all the iron-workers of the country.

Zinc.—A correspondent says, Zinc ore has been found on Roanoke River, about 2 miles above Alleghany Springs, Montgomery Co.,Va., near the western foot of the Blue Ridge.

Asbestos, of fine quality, a correspondent writes us, has been discovered on the Blue Ridge, near the line of Floyd and Franklin counties, about 30 miles from Christiansburg.

Sketch of the Present Condition of the Great Kanawha River Improvement.

Written for THE VIRGINIAS,
By Lieut. Thomas Turtle, of the U. S. Engineers.

The object of the present improvement of the Great Kanawha River, in West Virginia, is to obtain a constant navigable depth of at least 7 feet from the coal-field of the Great Kanawha to the Ohio River. This object is to be obtained by a series of dams with locks from the upper limit of this coal-field to the mouth of the river. The dams, from the foot of Paint Creek shoal upward, are to be the ordinary fixed dams, and all navigation through them will have to pass through the locks. The river below these fixed dams is to be improved by the construction of locks with movable dams; when the stage of the water is low, boats and barges will pass through the locks, but when the stage of water permits navigation in the open river for heavily laden boats all traffic will pass unimpeded through openings in the dams, provided for that purpose.

The movable portion of each dam consists of a series of wickets 3 ft. 4 inches in width and about 13 ft. in height (wooden frame work) rotating about their middle line, i. e. half way of their height. At this point of rotation, when raised, each wicket is supported by an iron frame-work which consists of a prop supported at its lower end, and of a "horse" formed by two uprights which act as ties to overcome the tendency of the entire system to rotate about the lower end of the prop,—a cross-head, passing through the head of the prop and the two uprights of the horse, working loosely in the former, forming a journal, and fixed to the horse, has its ends embraced by journal boxes in the frame work of the wicket. The wicket is thus free to swing on the line half way of its height. The horse has an axis of rotation, at the lower ends of its uprights, in journal boxes which are firmly anchored in the masonry of the foundation, as in the dam near Brownstown, or to the solid rock by wedge bolts, as in the dam below Cabin Creek shoal. The centre of pressure being two-thirds the depth of the water from the surface, and the wicket when up resting against a sill at its lower end and against the cross-head at its middle point, the equilibrium is stable until the water in the pool rises to a certain height above the top of the wicket. If, however, the prop be deprived of its point of support at its lower end, the entire system is free to rotate down stream about the lower axis of rotation of the horse. The wicket will then settle down to the floor of the pass and the entire depth of water lying above will be available for navigation draft. The level of the wicket when down, with reference to the water surface, is lower than the crests of the shoals in the vicinity, so all the draft that can be taken in the river will clear the pass floor.

The props of the pass wickets are deprived of their supports by pulling them sidewise by two rods which are operated by gearing in the wall of the lock at one end of the pass and in the masonry of a pier at its other end.

Up stream from the wickets is a movable bridge formed of trestles about 17 feet in height. These trestles when upright are joined at their upper ends by "T" beam rails. Upon the railway thus formed a car and winch travel for raising the wickets when down. A chain attached to the butt of the wicket and passing round the drum on the winch is wound in; this operation raises the wicket, with its end and lower side only exposed to the force of the current, by causing the horse to rotate up stream about its lower journal. The prop, in the mean time, sliding on the floor in a groove, finally falls into its rest against the "heurter," an iron abutting piece fastened to the floor. If now the chain be secured to the trestle the wicket may be kept swung to about a horizontal position and it will, while so swung, contract the water-way but very little. In this manner all the wickets of the pass may be "placed on the swing" without creating a "head-" or "back-water" to impede the raising of the last wickets. All the wickets being so placed the chains may, successively, be detached from the trestles and the wickets permitted, one by one, to swing downward until they rest against the sill. In this operation the winch is again used; the chain is attached to the drum, hauled taut, detached from the trestle and then unwound firmly, so

as not to permit the wicket to swing against the sill with a shock. The wickets are thus "righted," one by one, the pass is closed and a dam is formed.

The passes on the Kanawha consist of 62 wickets. When these wickets are down the opening in the dam is 248 feet wide. Between each two wickets is a space 4 inches in width. When the river is very low these spaces may be covered, making the dam as "tight" as necessary.

When the dam is opened the rails are removed from the trestles, one set at a time, and the trestles are rotated across the current, about their lower ends in journal boxes, and lie upon the floor of the pass out of the way. The tops of the trestles are connected by chains so that one being raised the chain of the next trestle is brought to the top of the bridge by which this next trestle can be raised.

The lock and pass occupy about half the width of the stream. The remainder of the width is occupied by the "weir," extending from the pier, mentioned above, to the abutment. The weir consists of a masonry foundation from the bed-rock to within 5 or 6 ft. of the level of the top of the dam. This 5 or 6 feet is occupied by a movable dam having wickets and trestles similar to the pass, but of less height. The movable top of the weir provides escape for the surplus water at the stages when the river is not sufficiently high for the pass to be opened. The top of the weir wickets are at the same level as the tops of the pass wickets. The aim is to prevent the water in the pool from rising higher than the tops of the wickets and still keep the pool at the proper height to give the required depth upon the mitre-sill of the lock above and on the crests of the shoals between. How this is done is shown by the following instructions to the lock-keepers for the regulation of the levels of the pools:

"**To regulate the levels of the pools.**—At dead low water all the wickets of pass and weir will be up, with a certain number of joint covers over the spaces between the pass wickets. At this stage the pool must be kept level with the tops of the wickets. Whenever the dam is up the winch will be kept habitually upon the weir bridge. When the river commences to swell, remove sufficient joint covers to reduce the level of the pool to the top of the wickets. If the removal of all the joint covers be not sufficient to reduce the level of the pool to the top of the dam, the wickets of the weir must be placed 'on the swing' in sufficient number to keep the pool down to its proper level. When the river is falling, a number of weir wickets being 'on the swing,' it will be necessary to right these wickets, one by one, to keep the pool up to its proper level. When all the weir wickets are righted, if the pool still continues to fall it will be necessary to place joint covers upon the pass wickets."

The weir is again of service when the operation of raising the pass wickets is in progress.—The following instructions are issued to lock-keepers:

"**Order of Operations in Raising a Dam.**—After a flood, or at the end of the high-water season, the dam is to be raised. Ordinarily instructions will be awaited, from the engineer in charge, to begin.

The preliminary operations may begin when the seats of the trestle bridges are exposed.

First. The foot-bridge of the weir will be raised, planked, and the winch placed upon it.

Second. The wickets of the weir will be raised and kept 'on the swing.'

Third. The foot-bridge in the pass will be raised. This will not be done till navigation in the open river is to be abandoned. The engineer in charge will give notice of this period.

Fourth. The wickets of the pass will be raised and 'kept upon the swing.'

Fifth. The pass wickets will be righted.

Sixth. The wickets of the weir will be righted, one by one, as may be necessary to keep the pool at its proper level."

It will be seen by the above instructions that when the pass wickets are about to be raised, the weir is practically open for the discharge of the stream, and as the righting of the pass wickets causes a "head-" or back-water," the open weir insures escape for the water and prevents too great pressure against the pass wickets whilst the men are handling them.

The axis of rotation of the weir wickets is also above the

point two-thirds their length from the top, to insure stability when the water is as high as the tops of the wickets; but is below the middle point, so that their equilibrium may be destroyed, if the pool rises much too high, and the wickets tip spontaneously while the pass wickets are yet in a condition of stable equilibrium. This insures an automatic lowering of the pool, if for any reason the keepers should fail to swing the wickets of the weir. At time of high water the wickets and trestles of the weir should be lowered.

The movable dam at the head of the Charleston pool (Dam No. 5), is now (August, 1880,) practically ready for use, and the passing of boats through the lock has commenced. The pool formed by this dam, which overcomes Oat-Fish and Witcher's Creek shoals, is 6¼ miles in length. It will enable all the coals between Cabin Creek and the head of the Charleston pool inclusive, and from Witcher's Creek and Fields' Creek, to reach the Charleston pool at all seasons,—through the lock, if the water be low, and through the pass, without detention, if the river be sufficiently high.

The Charleston pool is an important point to reach. It bears the same relation to the Kanawha coal-field that the harbor at Pittsburg does to the Monongahela coal-field. This pool is about 10 miles in length, with sufficient depth, throughout nearly its entire extent, for the harboring of heavily loaded barges and boats at the lowest stage of the river.

From the "Great Falls" of the Kanawha to the foot of Paint Creek shoal, the river falls an average 3.5 feet to the mile; thence to the head of the Charleston pool 1.5 feet per mile; while from the lower end of this pool to the Ohio the fall is only 0.8 of a foot per mile. From this pool boats drawing 5 feet can run out to the Ohio on an average of 909.8 days in a year (average of 7 years); and those drawing 6 feet, can run out on an average of 159.5 days per year.—This compares favorably with the Ohio River at Pittsburg, where on an average (22 years) the Ohio river is 155.9 days in the year above 6 feet. The Ohio at Pittsburg is 80 days per year below the 3 feet stage, while the Kanawha at Charleston is but 51 days below that stage.

The movable dam just below Cabin Creek shoal (Dam No. 4) is also practically ready for use, and boats are now being passed through the lock. The pool of this dam, which overcomes Cabin Creek shoal and Banseman's ripple, is 6.2 miles in length, and, with the Brownstown dam, will permit all coals, from the foot of Paint Creek shoal (21.4 miles above Charleston) to Cabin Creek inclusive, and from Kelley's Creek, to reach the Charleston pool at all seasons, through the locks or through the passes, according to the stage of the river.

Lock and dam No. 3, at the foot of Paint Creek shoal, are now in process of construction, and it is expected that they will be complete for low water next year. This dam is not movable. The lock is of 12 feet lift. Locks 4 and 5 are of 7 feet lift. The abutment of Dam No. 3 is complete, and the delivery of the timber for the dam is in progress. The masonry of the lock is entirely built to above the ordinary stage of the river, and the setting of the coping of the land wall is about to begin. The pool of this dam will overcome Paint Creek, Windsor and Hunter's shoals and will, with dams Nos. 4 and 5, below, permit all coals, from Cannelton to Paint Creek, and from the tributary streams between these points, to reach the Charleston pool at all seasons.

Possession is about to be obtained of the site for lock and dam No. 6, about 4 miles below Charleston, and the lock will be placed under contract this season. The pool of this dam will back the water to No. 5, about 13 miles, and will increase the depth upon the mitre-sill of the lock, just above Charleston on Elk River (Elk River Manufacturing Company's) to 5.95 feet.

The site for lock and dam No. 2, near Cannelton, will soon be obtained by purchase or condemnation, when work upon the lock will begin. The pool of this dam will overcome Lykens' shoal and will extend up to the foot of Loup Creek shoal, about 31.5 miles above Charleston.—When this lock and dam are built, all the coals from Loup Creek and below can reach the Charleston pool at all seasons.

Already inquiry has been made by the Gauley River interests to learn when the Kanawha will be slack-watered to the Great Falls. To do that it would be necessary to build lock and dam No. 1, which will be required when the Great Kanawha becomes a link in the "central water line." As this latter project has not been entered upon, the construction of lock and dam No. 1 on the Kanawha is not now contemplated.

THOMAS TURTLE,
First Lieut. U. S. Engineers.
Charleston, W. Va., August, 1880.

Broadway, Rockingham County, Va., on the line of the Valley Branch of the great Baltimore & Ohio R. R., is very properly called an "enterprising little town," by Prof. Campbell in the interesting, valuable, and suggestive article on the "Resources of "Brock's Gap," one of the regions tributary to this village, that, with a most excellent geological section, he contributes to this number of The Virginias.

Broadway is one of the scores of attractive and flourishing villages that have developed along the lines of the Virginian railways in the last ten years. Situated at the junction of Linvill's Creek and the North Fork of the Shenandoah, near the middle of the Western Central Valley of the Shenandoah—(See its position, on the Geological Map, in The Virginias of June last, just over the last letter in the word "Rockingham,")—it has all the advantages that result, and will result, from being the depot of a rich surrounding limestone region, and also of a large area of Apalachian country abounding in resources as yet mostly undeveloped. Linvill's Creek is a springs-fed perennial stream, and the North Fork has a large gathering ground on the lee side (so far as the most rain-bearing winds are concerned), of the Shenandoah, or Great North Mountain, a range that has an average altitude of over 4,000 ft., (3,000 above The Valley at Broadway), making it, at the same time, a shield against the cold winds from the northwest and a barrier to arrest the water-laden winds from the southeast and condense and gather their waters to make full-volumed the streams that flow from it. From Broadway upward both the Creek and the River fall at the rate of 40 feet or more to the mile, so that a slight dam across either, a mile away, would afford a "head" that would be over the tops of the buildings along the railway. Some of this great waterpower is now used, most of it runs away. The mountain country, having its outlet along North Fork and through Brock's Gap, abounds in white pine, tulip-poplar, the oaks, and other timber trees; the logs from these could be easily "flushed" to Broadway and its fine water-powers, giving it abundant advantages for a lumber making centre and the manufacture of articles made of wood.

The piles of chestnut oak bark that are always awaiting shipment there suggest that the half dozen mountain ranges in sight abound in this best of tannin-furnishing trees, and that great tanneries could be profitably located here, or at the mouth of Brock's Gap.

The near mineral resources Prof. Campbell has sufficiently mentioned. An inspection of the Geological Map of The Virginias (see our June No.) reveals the fact that it is less than 50 miles, as the crow flies, from Broadway Depot to the famous Cumberland coal-field; and those familiar with the topography well know that there is a perfectly feasible route, for a railway that shall have moderate grades and a length of less than a hundred miles, hence to that great bed of superior coal, and through a region rich in timber, mineral, cattle and other wealth. In fact this place is nearer, by a feasible route, to the great coal-field than any other in The Valley. The enterprising men of Broadway procured from the last Legislature a charter for a railway in the direction indicated, and the free railroad law of West Virginia will give them right of passage to the coal-field, Cumberland or elsewhere. The same charter conveys the privilege of extending this railway to Washington, D. C., on the north-east, and to the city of Petersburg, Va., on the south-east. From our local stand-point we see that a line from Broadway to Cumberland and its coal-field would give to Staunton, by the Valley RR. and that line, a short and quite direct route, not only to that important railway centre and its stores of coal, but also to Central Pennsylvania and to Pittsburg.

We think the day is not distant when a railway will follow the North Fork of the Shenandoah, through Brock's Gap, to its head, then down Lost River, thence by "The Glades" to Romney, and thence down the South Branch Valley to the B. & O. RR. or across to Keyser on the same railway. Nature has opened the way by eroding the valleys and cleaving the mountains.

We commend Broadway to those seeking favorable locations for the manufacture of iron, lumber, leather, etc.

The Gold Regions of the Atlantic States.—In June, 1834, James Dickson, F. G. S., of London, England, who had spent three years in examinations of the gold belt extending from the Rappahannock River, in Virginia, to the Coosa River, in Alabama, read an elaborate paper before the Geological Society of Pennsylvania, which was published in its "Transactions," which he styled "An Essay on the Gold Region of the United States," meaning thereby the gold belt of the Atlantic States, for no other was then known. Among other things, he called attention to the fact that "some had succeeded and others failed in mining operations;" that the advantages of this mineral region are "thick forests, navigable rivers, inland seas and bays, cheap machinery, a well organized and numerous population, and, above all, a stable government and institutions, a mild and genial climate and great agricultural prosperity,—the necessaries of life being within the reach of all," and therefore "that if the ores and mines here are equal to, or as productive as those elsewhere, then they are superior."

He had visited the gold mines of many regions, from those of Russia to those of the Spanish colonies, and stated that "There are richer ores of gold and diluvial deposits here in the United States than are to be met with at Gorgo Soco in the Brazils, or in the Uralian chain of mountains." He had met in the United States, "principally in Virginia, numerous instances where the weight of specimens of solid gold, and their character had been much superior to any of those he had met elsewhere."

He said that "only the lower mineral belt is met with in Virginia," but just what he meant by that he did not explain. "Felt sure that these gold deposits are from the decayed gold-bearing veins. Found the richest mines where water-courses run along the strike of a vein. Thought $6-millions of gold had been taken from these mines, and that the most of that had gone abroad for jewelry."

Said "the gold leads of the United States had not been fully explored, as the greatest depth of shafts did not exceed 150'. Veins are abandoned on too slight grounds." "In Virginia, where the granite and talcose slate form the respective walls of the vein of quartz containing gold, masses of decomposed granite are to be found sometimes in the slate of the opposite wall and *vice versa*; seams of red clay also traverse the respective walls. In fact the whole of the formation is in a crude and confused state. The vein itself consists of disjointed masses of ore with seams of clay intermingled; its dip and inclination varying from one point of the compass and from one angle to another, every 4 or 5 ft. in depth or horizontality. One fact is apparent, the formation has been once softened by the superincumbent water, from a depth varying from 50 to 100 ft.; that it has been almost in a state of suspension in water, as the muddy sediment of a pond; that while it continued in this state, it has been frequently violently agitated and waved to and fro, like a field of grass in a high wind; and that these various changes in the position of the vein and the lead itself, thus originated, is self-evident."

"When the gold loads consist of auriferous vein ore, or a quartz vein containing a large proportion of sulphuret of iron and native gold, changes have taken place above the depth of 100 ft., which could alone have originated in the action of water for a lengthened period on the sulphuret. The pyritical cubes have been converted into brown, red and purple hydrates of iron; sometimes a cube is found only half decomposed. In the centre of the solid quartz itself, cavities are met with resembling a honey-comb entirely empty, but which bear the impress of the shape of the pyritical cube, and coating richly the interior of each minute cavity is found a quantity of gold. There is one point clearly shown: it is, that all the gold which is obtained by amalgamation from these pyritical ores of gold is that portion which has been disintegrated, and left isolated in its native state by the decomposition of the sulphuret. The residue of the metallic sulphuret, if collected and concentrated, would yield and does by experiments frequently repeated by the writer of this essay, afford a large portion of the precious metal by fire assay."

"Pyritical ores of gold constitute the mass of the loads of Colombia, the Brazils and the United States; if then a process was employed which would in the first place obtain by amalgamation nearly all the disintegrated gold, and the balance of metallic matter was concentrated, many rich mines which at present are considered to consist of very intractable ores, would yield vast profits."

He then treats of the processes in use for extracting the gold.

Personal, Geological, etc., for August.—Prof. J. L. Campbell has been making a geological exploration of the Rich-Patch chain of mountains, in Alleghany and Botetourt counties, Va., the 100 square miles of iron land extending southwest from Clifton Forge, the junction of the Chesapeake & Ohio and Richmond & Alleghany railways and lying in a triangle between those roads. This is one of the most remarkable, and has and will continue to be one of the most productive *iron ore* regions in Virginia, including, as it does, the great iron estates known as Clifton Forge, Kayser's, Callie Furnace, Reynolds, Parsons or Alleghany Coal and Iron Co., Low Moor Iron Co. of Va., H. Robertson, Low, and Roaring Run Furnace,—*nine great iron properties*, any one of which in Pennsylvania or Ohio would be considered a great fortune. In some future issue of THE VIRGINIAS we shall have detailed reports on this region, fully illustrated by maps and geological sections.—One of Prof. Shaler's parties, consisting of G. H. Squier, in charge, Ro. Swift, and L. B. Squier, is now in Botetourt county, having completed the geological survey for the Richmond & Southwestern Ry., from the border of the great coal-field in Russell to the Blue Ridge. His party that started from Chandler (Gloucester Point), will meet this one at Fincastle about the 15th of September.—Maj. Morrison, of the Virginia Militry Institute, Lexington, Va., and Hugh Blair, Esq., of Richmond, Va., have been making geological observations around Richmond, and the latter has published in *The Standard* (the sprightly and every-way successful literary, historical, etc., weekly of J. Watson James, Esq.), a very valuable "Discourse about the geology of Richmond," which we propose to reproduce in THE VIRGINIAS, along with some other papers on the same subject, that, with fine illustrations, we have in hand awaiting room.

Lieut. Turtle's article on The Improvement of the Great Kanawha River

is illustrated by the following figures, the execution of which was so delayed as to prevent their introduction in the text.

We are under many obligations to this every-way capable and efficient officer for this timely contribution. It is a matter of daily repeated regrets among the substantial citizens of the Kanawha Valley that Lieut. Turtle has been taken from the immediate charge of this great work, up to this time he has supervised, and all hope that his absence may be but temporary.—We have not room for comments on this improvement, but will make them in our next. It will place the Great Kanawha Coal-field in its proper commercial position.

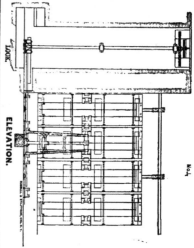

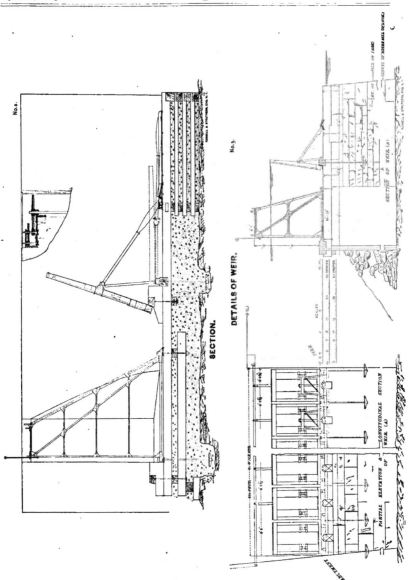

SECTION.

DETAILS OF WEIR.

No.2.

No.3.

The Iron Ores of Virginia and West Virginia.

By Prof. WILLIAM B. ROGERS.

(CONTINUED FROM PAGE 130.)

2. The Archæan or Metamorphic Iron Ores of Virginia.—
These are the magnetic, specular, limonite, (brown hematite), etc.
iron ores of the Archæan or Metamorphic area of Virginia, which
is by far the larger portion of Midland and Piedmont and all of
the Eastern Blue Ridge of Virginia. (See the Geological map in
the June No. of THE VIRGINIAS.)

"Much oxide of iron and some lime" are mentioned as contained in hornblende, which decomposes into a deep red earth,
which, in virtue of its composition, is generally found productive.
[27-1835]. In the rocks of the "gold belt," the gold-bearing
ones, "the cavities are often filled with a bright yellow ochre, or
hydrated peroxide of iron which generally contains gold in a state
of minute division. Sulphuret of iron (Pyrites) is another accompanying mineral, which in many mines occurs in considerable
quantities. At Morton's mine, (Buckingham,) it is peculiarly
abundant, and there, as in other places, generally contains a portion of combined gold. In the Union mine, near the Rappahannock, some of the auriferous veins consist largely of the Pyrites,
which here contains so much of the precious metal as to render the
extraction of it an object of profit. This Pyrites, in all probability, was, at some former period, more generally diffused throughout
all the auriferous veins, and by its decomposition, gave rise to the
peroxide of iron, with which the quartz is always more or less imbued, while the gold existing in it was deposited in the cells and
fissures of the quartz." [29-1835.]

The micaceous garnet slate, at New Canton in Buckingham,
which was used as an auxiliary furnace flux, "yields a considerable
amount of iron." [30-1835.]

"Several veins or beds of iron ore exist in Buckingham in the
region of the gold veins and slates, and ore of similar description
makes its appearance in Fluvanna, Louisa, &c. In the former
county indications of this deposit have been distinctly traced
throughout a line of seven miles, and the proprietors of the furnace
at New Canton have assured themselves of its continuity for two
miles. West of the principal vein is another at the distance of 100
yards : a vein of friable slate dipping east occupying the interval.
In the first or principal bed a continuous mass of ore has been uncovered, whose length is about 60 feet, and average breadth 15.
As yet no certain opinion exists as to the depth to which it reaches
below the surface. This ore is generally embedded in a brownish
yellow ferruginous clay, and fragments lie scattered over the surface
in the neighborhood of the bed. Through a long but narrow belt
in Louisa, Fluvanna and Buckingham, and in fact throughout the
whole length of the gold region, so called, these surface indications
may be traced. The ore is a *hematite*, in irregular masses, sometimes cellular and frequently mammillary. The cells often contain acicular white crystals of great lustre. The color of the ore
varies from a yellowish to a blackish brown. Its hardness in
different localities also differs, and in the immense mass above
described, is such as to require blasting necessary. There is some
difference as to the proportion of oxide of iron contained in the
ore from the two veins near New Canton, and a mixture of both
varieties of ore has been advantageously used in the furnace now in
successful operation. As early as the Revolutionary war iron was
manufactured from the Buckingham ore, but until recently this
valuable resource has been almost entirely neglected. The limestone on the western edge of the county furnishes the flux employed
in the smelting of this ore, which, under the superintendence of
Mr. Dean of New Canton is now conducted on a scale of such extent as to give a weekly product of between 30 and 40 tons of 'pig
metal, much of which is of a superior quality. Ore of precisely
the same description is found likewise in the gold region above
Fredericksburg, and as in present instance, in the vicinity of the
garnet slate. From the curious association of this ore with the
auriferous rocks, it might be expected that in the operations of the

furnace a portion of the precious metal would occasionally appear,
and accordingly it has been discovered in fine specks in the cinder
of the Buckingham works. Magnetic iron ore of a very valuable
quality occurs at the base of Willis' Mountain in Buckingham,
and is found at several other places in corresponding position.
[31-1835.]

"In the immediate neighborhood of the veins of this material,
(quartz and greenstone) abestos, iron pyrites and other minerals
occur, which are known to be thus developed in various rocks by
veins of intensely heated matter injected into them in a state of
fusion." [33-1835.]

"Throughout the South-West Mountain and its prolongations,
but especially on Buffalo Ridge, micaceous and magnetic iron ore
occur. In the neighborhood of Stonewall Mills, and near the
Buffalo Ridge Springs these ores are peculiarly abundant. They are
also met with in the vicinity of the Folly. Hematite containing
some manganese is seen also apparently in veins in a slaty rock at
Reuben Carver's, near the above named mills, and has been supposed by some to be an ore of silver. The micaceous oxide is generally blended more or less intimately with the substance of a
talcose and siliceous schist, and appears to exist in beds of considerable breadth amid these rocks. Hitherto, little value appears
to have been attached to the magnetic oxide or oxidulated iron ore
which is thus abundant throughout this region ; and yet, judging
by the experience of other counties where this ore is smelted in
great quantities, there can be but little doubt that under a judicious
system of operating it might be found a highly valuable material
for the manufacture of iron. In the highlands of New Jersey, so
noted for the quality and amount of their forged as well as cast
iron, an ore of precisely the same character is used, and the difficulties in smelting which appear to have deterred our iron masters
from its employment, are completely overcome." [34-1835.]

"Sulphuret of iron, in cubical and other forms," is very frequent
in Buckingham and Amherst. [35-1835.]

"The slates of the gold region, together with the iron ores occurring in them" to the N. W. of Fredericksburg, were examined.
[6-1836.] "The iron ore from the site of the old works at Chan-
cellor's, was examined and found to be of good quality." [7-1836.]
The Report for 1837 makes no mention of the iron ores of the
Archæan,—the Primary as it was then called.'

"Among the useful results of these researches may be mentioned
the determination of the *composition* and consequent *value* of
numerous specimens of *iron ore*, either from localities already
known and resorted to by the furnaces of the State, or from such
as have been discovered in our explorations, and which hold out
the promise of becoming valuable at a future day, when the importance of this branch of manufacture shall be so appreciated
as to attract a just share of the growing enterprise of the community." [4-1838.]

"The deposits of iron ore, some of which are of important extent
and favorably situated for manufacturing purposes, together with
the veins or beds containing other minerals of economical or
scientific value have also been subjects of very special examination." [36-1839.]

In Piedmont "the red color of the soil, derived from Epidote
and Hornblende, is due to the large proportion of oxide of iron
they contain, sometimes amounting to 30 per cent." [40-1839.]

"The principal components of Schorl are silex, alumina and oxide
of iron. "It occurs at numerous points in Mecklenburg, Lunen-
burg, Amelia, Buckingham, &c." [41-1839.]

"The constituents of Garnet are silex, alumina, lime and oxide
of iron ; the lime 20, the oxide of iron 16 per cent. From the
large quantity of lime present, it is a comparatively fusible mineral,
and hence some of the rocks in which it abounds may be used as
an auxiliary flux for iron ores, having the additional advantage of
themselves furnishing a considerable amount of iron. It occurs in
some of the primary and metamorphic rocks very abundantly, and
is met with in the southern region, particularly in rocks of the latter
class in numerous places. The neighborhood of New Canton in

Buckingham county, may be mentioned as an interesting locality." [42–1839.]

"In many varieties of gneiss displayed throughout this region, a very marked amount of sulphuret of iron (iron pyrites) exists in the form of brilliant crystals disseminated through the mass. This as a general rule, impairs the durability of the rock when used as a building material, because of the readiness with which these crystals are decomposed by the atmosphere, and the softened condition of the mass they thus induce. Such rocks, however fresh and clear their surfaces when first removed from the quarry, in process of time become studded with small brown ferruginous specks, which gradually extend themselves so as to injure the appearance as well as the solidity of the mass." [45–1839.]

"Gray gneiss containing white kyanite, tinged red by iron," is mentioned as occurring at Willis' Mountain. [45–1839.]

The limestone belt south of the James "possesses great importance, not only on account of its extent, but its contiguity to the extensive beds of rich iron ore which are used at Ross' Furnace, the limestone lying a little east of the most eastern band of ore." [58–1839.] "Iron pyrites" are named as among the ingredients of the "bluish or clouded" limestones of Campbell county. [59–1839.]

"*Iron Ores.*—On this head only a few observations can be usefully presented at the present time, as the chemical examinations relating to these materials are as yet too little advanced to furnish a body of analytical results sufficient to illustrate their composition and probable economical value. The extensive beds of these ores found at some points in the southern region, their great richness in iron, and their proximity in several instances to some of the beds of limestone above described, together with the favorable position in which some of them are placed as regards water-power and facilities of transportation, give them a not unimportant rank among the mineral resources of this portion of the State. These deposits are by no means so numerous in this region, as from the deeply ferruginous tinge of the soil over extensive districts and the frequent occurrence of loose fragments of ore upon the surface, ordinary observers have been led to imagine. All the slaty rocks of which I have treated above are more or less impregnated with iron, usually showing itself in the undecomposed rock in the form of crystallized sulphuret of iron or iron pyrites, and in many instances bearing a large proportion to the other materials with which it is intermingled. Nor is it exclusively confined to the class of rocks in question, occurring sometimes in equally marked amount in beds of Gneiss and in veins of Quartz, particularly such as have been found to contain gold. This mineral may be known by its yellowish metallic lustre, and the generally cubical or square form of its crystals. Though worthless in itself, it would appear to have been the source whence some of the most valuable and extensive ore beds of this region have been supplied. The beds referred to are those consisting of the brown and ochrous ores hereafter to be mentioned.

A few remarks upon what would seem to be the theory of their formation will, I hope, not be deemed inappropriate as a part of the present brief sketch of the geology of our southern region. The brown and ochrous ores contain the metal in the state of an oxide, and are made up of this oxide, together with silex, alumina and water. The oxide contains 70 per cent. of metallic iron, so that were the ore composed of this alone, each hundred pounds ought to yield 70 pounds of metal. In the richer ores as much as 85 per cent. of the oxide is sometimes found, the remaining 15 per cent. consisting principally of water. This would correspond to about 60 lbs. in the 100 of ore, and is an amount scarcely ever obtained in the operations of the furnace. The ores in question are uniformly found associated with Micaceous or Talcose slates or Gneiss in which the sulphuret is or has been present in great quantity. In the immediate vicinity of the bed, these rocks are seen in a decomposing condition, and impregnated with ochreous matter, which is the material of the ore. In fact, with a little attention, the various gradations may be traced from the unchanged rock, at some distance from the bed, to the softened and decomposing material in which the sulphuret has disappeared and the dark brown stains of oxide are presented, and thence to a mixed substance consisting of the matter of the rock, with a predominance of the oxide, from which we pass into the massive and comparatively pure ore. Of the stages of chemical change by which this conversion would seem to have been brought about, the first is obviously the decomposition of the sulphuret of iron, and the production of copperas or the sulphate of iron, an effect continually witnessed where moisture and air have access to the sulphuret, and the second the separation of the brown oxide from the copperas, probably in some measure by the action of the magnesia and potash present in the Mica, Talc and Felspar of the adjacent rock. In this view of their production, the ores in question are to be regarded as of much later origin than the adjacent rocks, and indeed as being in some places in progress of formation now. Striking examples might be referred to of beds of Micaceous and Talcose slates, in which knots of such ore are to be met with disseminated through the mass, and still in part retaining the structure of the slate, so as to exemplify one of the stages of change before noticed, in which the production of the bed of ore has not yet been carried to its completion.

Besides the brown and ochreous ores, there occur also two other varieties, viz. : the Micaceous oxide and the Magnetic oxide. The former is not unfrequently associated in small quantity with the ores first mentioned, but most commonly occurs in small veins included in Quartz. It is distinguished by its glistening scaly crystals, not unlike those of a dark brown Mica, but unlike these it yields a bright reddish brown powder when bruised, and will stain the fingers of this hue when rubbed. Though of common occurrence it is not found in large quantities. The composition of this ore is the same as that of the pure brown oxide, but unlike that variety it is never united with water.

The Magnetic oxide, when pure, is richer in iron than either of the preceding, containing within a small fraction of $72\frac{1}{2}$ per cent. of metallic iron. It is distinguished by its nearly black color in mass as well as when reduced to powder, and its strong action on the magnetic needle, attracting one extremity and repelling the other. It is from ore of this description that nearly all the Swedish iron, so celebrated for its excellent qualities, and so well suited for conversion into steel, is extracted. This variety of ore occurs at several points in the southern region in the form of beds or strata of considerable thickness and of good quality.

The following enumeration of some of the exposures of these ores may serve to indicate their geological position as well as their general extent and characters :

1. In Buckingham county an extensive bed of the brown and ochreous ore has been traced for many miles in a direction southwestwards of the furnace near New Canton. Of this deposit some account was given in my first report. Omitting further details at this time, I would merely remark that from its continuity and thickness, and from the general richness of its contents, this bed deserves to be considered as of high economical value. The iron made from it is for many purposes regarded as of good quality, though like most of the metal manufactured from the ores east of the Blue Ridge, it requires the admixture of a softer material in converting it into bar iron. The position of this bed between Micaceous slates, and the graduation of the ore into slate along the sides of the bed, afford good illustrations of what has been said in regard to the origin of these ores.

2. In the same county a bed of the brown ore is extensively exposed on Stonewall Creek in sight of Mr. Ross' new furnace, and shews itself at several other places in the neighborhood. At the furnace it has a width varying from 10 to 15 feet—at Mr. Yeatman's, half a mile below, its width is 12 feet. Its position is nearly vertical, included in yellowish Talcose slate, and its range or bearing is N. 20° E. The ore is generally compact and dense, but sometimes cellular and containing ochre. Higher up the hill and eastwards of the former, another parallel bed occurs, consisting chiefly of a yellow ochreous oxide of iron with numerous and large cavities. Still more towards the east we meet with the range of

limestone formerly spoken of, furnishing a flux to be used with the ores.

3. Near the mouth of Elk Island Creek in Amherst county, two or more considerable beds of ore are met with, the more eastern of which, about half a mile above the mouth of the creek and a quarter of a mile above the furnace, is from 4 to 8 feet in thickness where explored, and is a brown oxide of iron, sometimes Micaceous, contained in Micaceous and Talcose slates. Half a mile westward occurs another bed, consisting principally of slaty and Micaceous ore, and at various points in the vicinity bog ore is abundantly met with, serving a useful purpose in union with the compact and Micaceous ores. As already stated, beds of limestone are found within a short distance of the ores.

4. A little east of the belt of grey granite, formerly described as ranging through Campbell county near the Charlotte line, and crossing the Staunton river at Brooknead, there occurs a prolonged bed of ore, similar in character to those above described. About a mile N. E. of Col. Hancock's dwelling, the width of the bed is 8 feet, but there is reason to believe that at some points it swells out to more than double this amount. It here ranges in a N. N. E. direction, has a high eastern dip and is associated with Mica slates. The ore is a brown oxide. sometimes quite compact, sometimes ochreous and occurs in large masses on the E. side of Hot (Hat ?) creek, (one of the branches of Falling river,) near its mouth, much ore is seen on the surface, and has been exposed by diggings—apparently the continuation of the bed explored on Col. Hancock's land and its vicinity.

5. Near Rocky Mount in Franklin county, a little north of the bed of Steatite formerly described, the Magnetic oxide occurs in sufficient quantity to supply a furnace in the vicinity. The ore is granular, of a black and greenish black color, and is associated with decomposing Micaceous slates—width of the bed varying from 4 to 6 feet. Another bed of the same description, several feet in width, is met with a little north of the village. Impure bog ore occurs in the neighboring meadows, yellow and ochreous, accompanied on the surface with the grains called shot ore. Seven miles west of the village we meet with the brown oxide in Mica slate.

6. In Patrick county, a little west of Goblintown Creek and on the east side of Stewart's Knob, we find the Magnetic oxide exposed at several places, the main deposit supplying the Union Iron Works in the vicinity, being a bed of from 3 to 6 feet wide, of a fine grained, generally black ore, sometimes having a greenish tinge from the intermixed scales of Talc, and sometimes red and ochreous.

7. In Buckingham county, about a mile east of Whispering Creek, and nearly in a line with Willis' Mountain, a heavy bed of the Magnetic oxide crosses the road leading from Maysville to Ca Ira, and may be traced for some distance in a N. E. and S. W. direction. It is from 6 to 8 feet in width, solid and dense, generally bright and specular, though sometimes dull. It affects the needle powerfully, and is evidently a very rich ore.

Further details in regard to these, and a similar full account of other localities are reserved for a future time, when the chemical examinations connected with the subject shall have been brought to maturity. But it will be seen from the particulars which have now been stated, that the portions of the southern region referred to are by no means wanting in supplies of this mineral, and that some of the most extensive beds are very favorably situated, both as regards the limestone so essential in the manufacture of iron and an easy conveyance of the products of the furnace to market." [63–66–1839.]

The Gneiss of Piedmont "with comparatively little Mica, contains more or less Talc, occasionally Chlorite, and in a great number of cases, Hornblende and Iron Pyrites, the latter aiding its disintegration, and along with the Hornblende imparting more or less of a reddish tint to the soil into which it is resolved." [45—1840.]

"The Hornblende slates and Hornblendic Gneiss rocks" "forming the margin of the primary on the east" frequently contain "beds and veins of Quarts," "and beds of a coarse description of Iron Ore have been found in them at a few localities." [47–1840.]

In the dark, argillaceous slates on the Rappahannock, in Fauquier, a mile south of the White Sulphur Springs, "many of the seams and joints are stained of a yellowish brown by the iron deposited from the decomposing Iron Pyrites, of which small crystals are seen dispersed through the rock. It is this ingredient also that produces the little knots or tubercles frequently seen on the surface of the laminæ ; and thus aided by some slight irregularities of lamination, causes the rock to split with surfaces a little rough and uneven." [50–1840.]

Near the Potomac, in Fairfax county, "between Difficult Creek and Still House Creek, the greenish Talcose slate is seen to include heavy beds of Serpentine and Steatite rock, including several interesting minerals, among which is Chrome-Iron ore."—In the Serpentine quarry near Dranesville, associated with the Serpentine,

are "Talc, Asbestos, Carbonate of Copper, Chrome-Iron, and Magnetic Oxide of Iron." [52–1840.]

"At Taylorstown, on Kittoctin Creek, the calcareous masses are enclosed in greenish, slaty Talcose rocks, containing iron pyrites and Magnetic Oxide of Iron in small octahedral crystals. [58–1840.]

In the analyses of "limestones from the Primary," the "Alumina and Oxide of Iron" in that from Whitley's and Gibson's in Fauquier, were 0.40 per cent. ; that from Gibson's, south-side of Rapid-Anne River, 0.52 ; that from Colby Cowherd's, 1.5 ms. from Gordonsville, and that from Rawlings', near Orange C. H., 0.80 ; that from Rapid-Anne, 300 yds. E. of Gibson's vein, 0.92 ; that from Todd's, 5 ms. from Gordonsville, 1.28 ; and that in some thin layers in mica slate, 0.44. [108–109–1840.]

ANALYSES OF IRON ORES FROM THE PRIMARY.

LOCALITIES.	Peroxide of iron.	Per cent, metallic iron.	Alumina.	Lime.	Silica & insoluble matter.	Water.	Loss.	Manganese Oxide.
No. 1. Ross Furnace, Hopewell Creek	84.11	56.77	0.28	....	6.54	11.10	0.97	....
" 2. Yeatman's, Stonewall Creek	76.00	53.20	0.50	....	13.00	10.00	0.50	....
" 3. Elk Creek, ¼ mile above mouth	84.00	58.80	0.85	trace	7.60	7.10	0.45	....
" 4. Col. Hancock's, E. of Falling River	84.20	58.94	0.56	trace	4.50	10.00	0.74	....
" 5. 6 Miles S. W. of New Canton	64 95	45.49	2.65	....	23.30	10.00	0.20	trace
" 6. Six miles S.W. of New Canton	73.00	50.40	1.33	....	16.47	10.04	....	trace

No. 1. "Hematitic brown oxide. Structure somewhat fibrous and cellular, interior of cells coated with a bluish crust : color clove brown, lustre glimmering and resinous."
No. 2. "Brown hematite and silicious brown oxide. Structure externally hematitic, fibrous ; internally amorphous, granular ; color blackish brown, lustre glimmering."
No. 3 "Structure amorphous, cellular ; color chestnut brown ; general aspect earthy, in spots glimmering."
No. 4. "Structure amorphous ; compact ; fine grained ; fracture somewhat conchoidal ; color chestnut brown, without lustre."
No. 5. "Associated with Talcose slate. Structure massive, compact and silicious, color clove brown ; surface presenting glimmering points of quartzose particles."
No. 6. "Structure cellular, cells minute : color light brown ochreous ; contains small specks of quartz." [116–117–1840.]

The Resources of Brock's Gap, Va.

Written for THE VIRGINIAS,
BY PROF. J. L. CAMPBELL.

The name Brock's Gap is applied, not simply to a gap in Little North Mountain, but also to an interesting region of country, of considerable extent, in the northern corner of Rockingham county, Virginia. Let us take a view of it with its surroundings in reference to (1) Its Geography and Topography ; (2) Its Geological features ; (3) Its Mineral and other Resources ; (4) Its facilities for utilizing these resources.

1. *Geography and Topography.*—By referring to the accompanying map the village of Broadway may be found on the line of the Valley RR., at the junction of Linvill's Creek and the North Fork of the Shenandoah River in Rockingham county Va. This enterprising little town is the centre of trade for one of the finest agricultural regions in the Great Valley ; it is also the mart of that beautiful mountain country, called the "Brock's Gap Settlement" or "Little Germany." It carries on several manufacturing industries.

After traveling about four miles up the North Fork, we come to a narrow pass in Little North Mountain, where that river has cut a way for its waters that are gathered from the little mountain valleys beyond. This pass is Brock's Gap, and it gives name to the thickly settled region, drained by North Fork through it, made up of many mountain valleys terminating along the banks of the river. This settlement is bounded on the S. E. by Little North Mountain, and on the N. W. by Shenandoah Mountain. Some intervening ridges divide the whole area into several subordinate valleys. Of these ridges Church Mountain is the most important.

Topographically the region is hilly or mountainous, with some fine alluvial bottoms along the streams. The soil on the hills is generally slaty or pebbly ; but where the limestones,

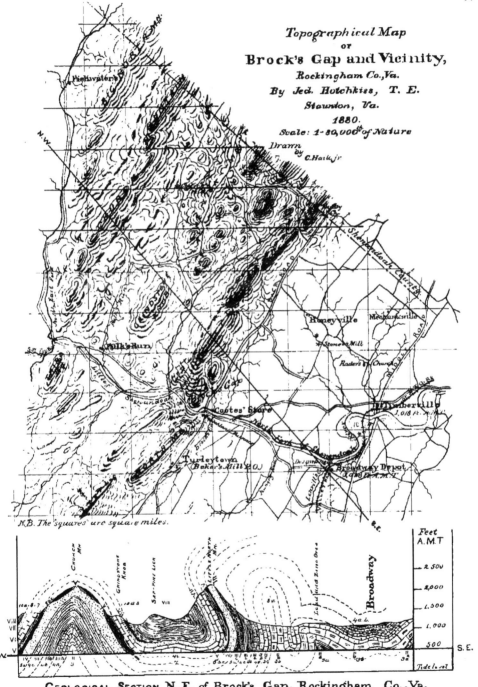

Topographical Map
OF
Brock's Gap and Vicinity,
Rockingham Co., Va.
By Jed. Hotchkiss, T. E.
Staunton, Va.
1880
Scale: 1-80,000ᵗʰ of Nature
Drawn by C. Hall, jr.

N.B. The 'squares' are square miles.

GEOLOGICAL SECTION N. E. of Brock's Gap, Rockingham Co., Va.
By J. L. Campbell, Washington and Lee University.

that here belong to the Upper Silurian (Helderberg, or No. VI) crop out along the bases of some of the ridges they give a good soil; and in all cases they have contributed largely to the fertility of the bottom lands. The whole settlement is well watered, and well wooded; while the landscape views in many parts of it are not easily surpassed in beauty and variety.

2. Turning now to the geological section accompanying the map; conceive the line marked S.E.—N.W. on the map, to lie several hundred feet beneath the surface of the river, and imagine the "section," as a vertical plane 2,500 feet high, with its lower edge resting upon this line. Such a plane would cut all the hills, valleys and mountains from a little S. E. of Broadway to the N. W. base of Church Mountain. On it are represented, by differently marked bands, the ideal edges of the various strata of rocks through which it is supposed to cut. The limestones are "blocked," and the different varieties distinguished by ruling or dotting the blocks. Shales or slates are indicated by "ruled," and sandstones by "dotted" bands Ruling and dotting combined mark sandy slates, or slaty sandstones.

Broadway stands in a sort of double trough of what are known in geology as Trenton Limestones (III a. Rogers). Along the creek near the town the lowest and hardest beds are exposed; of the hills on each side the more shaly rocks form the surface and give good soils. As we go towards the mountain, a little more than half a mile, we find the older and harder limestones, (II b.c. Rogers), coming to the surface, but dipping S. E. beneath those we have passed. Still nearer the mountain the strata are turned upon their edges and closely folded, as seen on the "section," while the Little North Mountain, with all the strata resting against its eastern base, has evidently been inverted, so as to put the older rocks above the newer. Some of these inverted strata are strikingly exhibited in the gap where the river passes out of the mountain region.

Tracing the "section" still farther N. W. we find the shales of No. VIII (Devonian) occupying a trough of the Upper Silurian beds (IV, V, VI and VII. R.), and covering the whole valley between Little North and Church mountains. They rise in such mass along one part of their hilly range as to constitute what the maps call "Sap-pine Lick Mountain." N. W. of this trough we find Church Mountain formed of the same strata as Little North, but here giving us a series of concentric arches; the upper limestones, sandstones and shales broken away from the top of the ridge, but left cropping out along both bases, as seen on the "section."

3. *Mineral and other Resources.*—The foregoing brief geological sketch will aid in a proper understanding of both the position and extent of the valuable minerals found in a region covering several miles on both sides of the line of the "section." The minerals are among the most important features of value, especially in the mountainous portions of the area we have under discussion.

Lead and zinc ores have been found in the older limestones, marked II b. Rogers, or 3 b. Dana. *Galena,* with a small percentage of silver in it, was mined to some extent many years ago, at a point two miles north of Broadway; it has been attracting renewed attention recently. *Zinc ore* of promising quality, but undetermined as to quantity, is found contiguous to, and sometimes mingled with the lead ore.

The iron ores of Brock's Gap, both on account of *quantity* and *quality*, demand our earnest attention. The extent of their developments may be inferred, in a general way, from a simple inspection of the map and section; on both of which the *red lines* mark beds of iron ore. Two of the great iron-bearing formations—the Clinton, No. V., and the Oriskany, No. VII.,—are conspicuous in this region; and the ore of No. III is said to have been once worked on Little North Mountain.

I have carefully traced the ores of the No. V shales along the western face of Little North Mountain; and have examined in person, and learned from others, the character of their outcropping on both faces of Church Mountain. On the former some of the ore is inferior, but some of it is of fine quality. It is from a part of this formation that the Messrs. Pennybacker are reported to have been mining a superior ore when the price of iron compelled them to stop their furnace (the old "Oakland") in this neighborhood, many years ago. They also mined ores on both sides of Church Mountain, where, their former manager told me, they worked beds 10 feet in thickness, of ore that, by their crude process, yielded them 40 per cent. of pig iron. This No. V bed, extending for miles along the mountain, could be readily opened by a proper system of mining; it evidently contains a vast quantity of an ore (the red-shale) that has long been famous for the quality of its iron.

The Oriskany formation (No. VII) is, throughout this region, chiefly a heavy bed of coarse sandstone; but it evidently contains some beds of rich ores that have not been developed to any great extent, though the outcroppings along the eastern base of Church Mountain are promising. Like beds will doubtless be found elsewhere in the neighborhood. The ores of this formation are generally more or less silicious, while those of formation V. are argillaceous. Hence the two are well adapted for *mixing*,—both together fluxing better than either does separately. The sand of the one and the clay of the other both combining at the same time with the lime of the flux, make a slag that is readily fused in the furnace.

Variegated marble is another object of interest here. A quarry has been partially opened on lands belonging to Dr. J. Q. Winfield of Broadway, that promises to yield encrinal and shell marbles equal in texture and beauty to those so extensively quarried at Craigsville, in Augusta county, Va. Both are from the same geological formation, No. VI (Helderberg) —a limestone of a later geological age than those of the Great Valley. The same beds of limestone among which the marble is found will also yield inexhaustible supplies of limestone, for furnace flux, for building stone, and for the manufacture of lime.

Clay, of a very infusible character, has been found at several places, and is worthy of a fair trial for fire-bricks, tiles, terra-cotta work, &c.

4. *Timber* suitable for various kinds of lumber—oak, pine, tulip-poplar, walnut, ash, maple, &c.—abounds at many points easy of access. There are also large tracts of unbroken forests adapted to coaling, whenever it becomes desirable to make charcoal iron.

5. *Ample water-power* for furnaces, mills and other kinds of machinery, can be secured, either within the mountain region or at Broadway, by utilizing the natural fall of the North Fork of the Shenandoah River and its tributaries.

For use in a charcoal furnace the ore, limestone and charcoal can be procured in abundance, at points not very remote from a common point on the river, at which a furnace could be conveniently located, and to which all the material consumed could be brought by a descending grade.—If *coke* is wanted for fuel, it seems to me that a point on the Valley RR., near Broadway, would afford a most appropriate location. Furnace sites and water-power are there, limestone is at hand in great abundance, coke can easily be brought from Connellsville, Pa., or from New River, W. Va., by rail; while the ores could be brought down from Brock's Gap by a tram-way, or a narrow-gauge RR. at a very moderate cost beyond that of constructing the track. The iron could be utilized on the ground, or shipped off by rail without the cost of any intermediate transportation.

This section of country is well worthy of the attention of capitalists, who desire to make safe investments. Those who desire more specific information in regard to the Brock's Gap region, can obtain it from Dr. J. Q. Winfield of Broadway, or from Rev. R. C. Walker (P. O. Stover's Shop, Augusta Co., Va.). These gentlemen either own, or control, several large and important tracts embraced within the region above described, and any statement they make may be safely relied upon.   J. L. CAMPBELL,
                                    Prof. Chem. and Geology.

Washington & Lee University,
Lexington, Va., Aug., 1880.

The Mesozoic Formation in Virginia.

By Oswald J. Heinrich, Mining Engineer.

Continued from Page 126.

III. General Geological and Stratigraphical Characters of the Formation.

It has already been stated that the sedimentary deposits participating in this formation, when exhibited upon a topographical map, appear either as isolated basins or unconnected strips, passing in the latter instance below the Tertiary formation, which in this state immediately succeeds the Triassic deposits of the Mesozoic formation. But by a closer examination regarding the present topography of the country, some interesting deductions may be drawn, which by proper interpretation may have considerable practical value.

Assuming an imaginary line parallel to the course of the Blue Ridge Mountain in this State, which in its main bearing will be from N. 35° to 48° E., not taking in consideration the deflected portion of the southeastern extremity, we will find the axis of the isolated patches of more or less magnitude, to conform to two double ranges, two eastern and two western, which have been termed respectively the Eastern, Middle-eastern, Middle-western and Western deposits (see Map). Proceeding from the southern extremity we will notice that the extreme northern parts of three of the divisions, namely: the Eastern, Middle-eastern, and Middle-western, underlie in their eastern extension the Tertiary strata in this State, which formation is fully distinguished by its different stratigraphical, lithological, and palæontological characters, while the Mesozoic formation itself rests upon Eozoic rocks, the precise age of which has not been defined in all instances. The southern extremities on the contrary, as well as the entire western range, rest also entirely upon the Eozoic rocks, but are mostly deprived of their incumbent Tertiary strata, most of the covering being Quaternary deposits. Within the lines of bearing of the different ranges we find considerable intervals, where even the Mesozoic formation has partially disappeared. The question of interest would be to ascertain if a former connection of all the separate deposits did exist, and if the present position warrants such a supposition.

In the absence of a full series of altitude and observations, we will depend principally upon the natural system of drainage, as now noticed upon the map, to ascertain the summits and general declination in the State, with such numerical data as have been collected to test the point in question.

On a general view of the map we will notice three main channels of drainage in that part of the State east of the Blue Ridge. In the southwestern extremity of the State we have the most southern channel, formed by the Dan and Staunton rivers, with all their tributaries, flowing east or southeast to form the Roanoke, and passing thus through the Albemarle Sound into the Atlantic. The elevation of the headwaters of those streams along the Alleghany, or rather eastern base of the Blue Ridge Mountain, is about 900 feet at the passage of the Roanoke or Staunton River. Its extreme northern summit will be, about the base of the Peaks of Otter, over 1,000 feet above tide, Liberty being 947 feet.

In the central part of the State we have the James River channel, with its tributary rivers as far north as the headwaters of the Rivanna. The elevation of the James River at Balcony Falls is 706 feet, at Lynchburg 513, Scottsville 275, Columbia 205, Dover 145, and Richmond 30 feet. With its southern summit at the former base of the Peaks of Otter, its northern will be at the headwaters of Swift Run, south of Swift Run Gap, probably over 900 feet, this being the elevation at Rockfish Gap, southwest of it. The direction of the James River from Balcony Falls, at the foot of the Blue Ridge, to Lynchburg, is about southeast, but takes at this point an abrupt turn at right angles into a northeast course for about 40 miles, then resumes its southeast course to Richmond. Along this line of northeastern direction a summit is distinctly visible, at Concord, 833 feet, and Appomattox Courthouse, 835 feet, dividing the waters of the Appomattox from those of the southern line of drainage on the south side of James River, and a similar summit between Fredericksburg, 48 feet, and Gordonsville, 498 feet, turning the waters of South Anna, North Anna and Mattapony rivers respectively, with those of

the James River and its tributaries, into the Chesapeake Bay. All those streams have a more or less southeast course. The most northern line of drainage is effected by the Potomac River. At an elevation at Harper's Ferry of 205 feet, it takes up all the waters from north of Manassas Gap to the Potomac. The headwaters between Manassas Gap and Swift Run Gap run, in part, in a southeasterly course directly into Chesapeake Bay, through the Rappahannock and its tributaries, the Robertson, Hazel, and Hedgman rivers; another portion running likewise in a southeast direction discharges through the Occoquan River into the Potomac; while a third portion, running northeasterly, reaches the Potomac, and ultimately the Chesapeake, through the Kittoctan, Goose, Broad Run, and Difficult creeks.

Let us now observe the position of the various tracts covered by the Mesozoic formation (see Fig. III, Plate II), and also notice a few items in regard to the Eozoic rocks upon which the former were deposited. Passing up the James River or from Richmond to Scottsville, the average course of which, N. 67° W., coincides tolerably well with the dip of the strata, we have a fair sectional view. At and beyond Richmond we notice the prevailing southeast dip in the granitic rocks, probably in part Laurentian. The Mesozoic formation, with a similar but by far less steep dip, reposes upon the same again, being covered by the Tertiary sands, clays, and gravel-beds conformably. About seven miles west of Richmond the first change in the dip occurs, marking an anticlinal in the older rocks. The northwest dip now continues until the Mesozoic rocks belonging to the Richmond deposits are reached, reposing upon the older rocks also with a westward dip, but generally not conformably, the older rocks again having the greater pitch. Passing over them for nearly six miles, we come to the western edge of the same formation, but now assuming the southeast dip, as also noticed in the Eozoic rocks, until about seven and a half miles, between Little Beaverdam and Beaverdam Creek, and again six miles farther west, at Little Lickinghole Creek, we pass two anticlinal axes in the Eozoic rocks, consisting mostly of gneiss, mica, and hornblende slates. The western dip continues to Byrd Creek, about forty miles (in a direct line) west of Richmond, where the strata are almost perpendicular; reclining now again to a steep southeast dip, they continue so beyond the Rivanna River at Columbia, Scottsville, and Carter's Mountain, a high mountain ridge northwest of the river. The last remarkable ridge is then west of Charlottesville, through the country called North and South Garden, Butler, and Ragged Mountain, which shows several pronounced anticlinal wrinkles at considerable heights above the general elevation of the country. If we continue along the banks of the James River, after its remarkable turn, previously noted, towards Lynchburg, we notice again, in the section of country southeast of the river and west of Maysville and Slate River, the continuation of the anticlinal, rather more distinctly marked, existing along the James River.

The position of the first anticlinal is west of Richmond Falls, therefore, between the Eastern and Middle-eastern deposits; the second (two) between the Middle-eastern and Middle-western; the third nearly in the line or slightly east of the Western deposits, and evidently the most marked along the James River in its north-eastern deviation below Lynchburg, in the great gap between the two principal Western deposits; the fourth and last is west of the Mesozoic deposit, at least as far as developed, and about the line of Bull Run and Kittoctan Mountain. It is, therefore, not unreasonable, reflecting upon all points enumerated, to suppose the following former connections.

The most southern and eastern exposures on Meherrin River at Hicksford, and west of it, as well as those at Petersburg, Richmond, South Anna River, Fredericksburg, and Mount Vernon, may be designated as the remaining parts of the former principal border line of the Mesozoic sea along the Atlantic. From the Taylorsville deposits (South Anna River), Middle-eastern division, an estuary or former valley extended in the direction of the Deep Run and Richmond basin, in a southwest course, even as far as North and South Carolina, including the Deep River coal basin.

Another extended from the Aquia deposits (Fredericksburg), Middle-western division, in a similar direction as the former, as far south as the Farmville basin.

The last and most extensive of the estuaries extended from Maryland across the Potomac River entirely through the State of Virginia, terminating in the State of North Carolina, at the Dan River basins.

The formations along the Potomac, and at Fredericksburg, Richmond, Petersburg, etc., expose rocks, which according to localities further south of it appear to belong to a geological horizon higher up in this series, while in their respective altitudes they assume a level even below that of the surface at the Richmond and Farmville basins, which unquestionably represent the lowest rocks in the series. They have also a more gentle dip to the southeast, and are capped by the Tertiary rocks directly. At Mount Vernon they are lost in their passage across the Potomac. No other Mesozoic rocks have been as yet developed in the States north of Virginia along the Atlantic, which exhibit a decided permanent southeast dip for a long line of bearing until we reach Connecticut and Massachusetts. No positive connection can be proved to exist between these two extreme points. But from observations by soundings, a map, prepared by the Coast Survey along the coast of New Jersey and Staten Island, indicates that the position of the beds on the Atlantic border on this part of the continent was nearly at its present level, and therefore, dry land stretched farther to the eastward than now, and that sea-shore deposits were formed which are now submerged (Man. of Geol., by J. D. Dana, p. 423). If we assume a steep escarpment of the Eozoic rocks along that part of the former coast line, depositions of Mesozoic rocks could have been formed along this escarpment until the level of the same was reached and the former outcrop, which butted against it, was ultimately covered by more recent depositions, as in Maryland and New Jersey, hiding the continuation of the extreme points of the formation below the sea-level. Upon a small scale such is the case in some parts of the Richmond coal basin, where the rocks below the coal and the coal strata themselves do not appear upon the surface, but butt against the Eozoic rocks forming the base of the trough, while at other points they lap farther out, over 1,500 feet, showing the outcrop of the coal that much farther (apparently) inside the basin. Such a supposition would, therefore, indicate the connection of the border line of the Mesozoic rocks of Virginia, including the two estuaries of the Middle-eastern and Middle-western division.

The Western division shows a continuation from the Potomac through Maryland, Pennsylvania, and New Jersey to the Hudson River, uninterruptedly. Throughout New Jersey, and particularly along the Hudson River (the most eastern part of that section), and again in Connecticut, on the western part of the Mesozoic rocks, heavy outbursts of trap rocks are known to exist. May not then the gap in the formation along the Hudson River at West Chester have been formed by causes similar to those forming the gap through which the James River now passes, destroying the former connection between the two great areas?

The destruction of a connection formerly existing between all the Mesozoic depositions along the Atlantic States might, therefore, be attributed to a slow and unequal rising of Eozoic rocks after the deposition of the former upon the uneven floor of the latter, noticed in the anticlinals of the latter, and producing an unequal denudation of the Mesozoic deposits. The rising of these older rocks upon one side may also have produced subsequent partial depression of the section along the Atlantic.

The elevation, now exhibited by the summits southwest and northeast of the James River, exposed the central part of that long western basin more to the denuding action of the atmosphere, leaving only the vestiges in the small patches along the James River.

The anticlinals exhibited in the elevations along the table-lands of the James River, at Buffalo and Slate rivers, divided the Middle-western deposits, and the denudating forces have acted most forcibly at the southern extremity, where an entire new line of drainage, strongly southeast, was created; consequently but little of the formation remains, particularly south of Farmville. It appears that similar summits are indicated north of the Potomac, at New Market, Westminster, and Strasburg, Maryland, and across the Susquehanna above Castleton, to Pennington, Waynesburg, and Norristown, all southeast of the great western belt of the Mesozoic.

Denudations are less noticed in the arm of the Mesozoic ex-tending from the South Anna to the Appomattox, until we pass south of the latter. Although less perceptible, the summits are noticed to exist between Keysville and Burkaville (527 feet), west of the deposits, at Swift Creek east, and at Blacks and Whites (A. M. & O. R. R.) south of the belt. The most remarkable summit in that direction exists near Oxford, in Granville County, North Carolina, dividing the northern part of that arm from its southern extension into Granville, Chatham, and Moore counties (Geol. Rep. of North Carolina, 1856, E. Emmons). Along the most eastern belt from Richmond to the Roanoke River, the courses of all the rivers are nearly the same, due east or slightly southeast. A regular denudation at intervals, according to the individual depressions of the various water courses, may account count for the now disconnected patches remaining along the borders of the Tertiary, but would indicate the continuity of the Mesozoic below in its orignal linear extent.

The frequent occurence of trap rocks throughout the Mesozoic, particularly noticeable at such points where considerable stratigraphical and metamorphic changes in the sedimentary rocks have occurred, as for example in the Dan River belt; at the Rapid-Anne River, and southwest of it; at Warrenton, and the western boundary along the Bull Run and Kittoctan Mountain, and across the Potomac deposits at Leesburg; along the eastern border of the Richmond deposits, north and south; about the James River, at Hall's mill, at the more southern portion; also in the Deep River deposits of North Carolina; but principally at the northern extremity in New Jersey, Connecticut, and Massachusetts, gives rise to the hypothesis of a gradual elevation of the older rock floor. The time must have been between the close of the Mesozoic and the beginning of the Tertiary, since the latter, and probably even the upper part of the Mesozoic along the former shore, has not been affected by the penetration of the trap rocks. In many instances in Virginia, the influence is only noticed upon the sedimentary deposits, while the trap itself is often invisible, not having risen to the surface, but produced saddle-shaped flexures.

In regard to the superposition of the strata composing the formation, it is rather difficult to obtain complete series in sectional views in consequence of the topography of the country, the similarity of the material composing the formation, and the extreme scarcity of characteristic accessories and fossil remains.

The predominating rocks are sandstones of various grades, slates and shales, occasionally, also, conglomerates of a coarse character. The limestones exist in very small proportion in the series, and in consequence offer the best landmarks. Similarity in appearance of related species of rock, and rapid changes in the various stratifications of the most hetrogeneous materials are frequently noticed. Almost white sandstones of the arkose species alternate in small strata with those of a gray or darker color, and again with the finest bituminous black shale of the softest character. It is also noticed that the material constituting the rocks differs according to the nearest source from which it was derived. This may furnish additional proof of the isolated position each estuary occupied at the time of deposition, receiving in all instances its materials directly from the nearest Eozoic or Silurian rocks, in which the troughs were carved out previous to the deposition of the Mesozoic. Accordingly, we notice the difference in the material of the more brownish-tinged ferruginous sandstones and shales in the western or extreme southern parts, which derived their materials from the older slates and schists, including ferruginous materials in deposits and as accessory minerals. In the eastern basins, the predominating lighter-colored granites furnished the principal material, and produced the predominating arkose or feldspathic sandstones in those deposits.

Very little has been done in the last thirty-eight years to develop the geology of the State of Virginia, since the arduous labors of Prof. W. B. Rogers were abruptly terminated by the legislature in 1840. While all the other States in this country have commenced, or at various times continued and revised geological surveys, we may have to wait in patience until the next century for the accomplishment of this important work by State appropriations, and must, in the meantime, look to private observations. Having the opportunity recently of exposing to ocular examination, through the deep borings with the diamond drill, and the sinking of shafts, at least a large portion of the formation, for the purpose of establishing the existence

and further continuity of the coal deposits in the Richmond coal basin, the results of the same will be first given to form a true basis of comparison hereafter, and they are of especial value, as such extensive explorations may not be made again at an early day. The results are carefully computed from a number of borings near the granite for over 1.1 mile upon the line of dip, from 8) to 1142 feet deep, and also from the section of the two shafts, 640 and 1338 feet deep (including 322 feet of borehole at the bottom of deepest shaft.) The whole explorations extended over an area of two square miles, and are verified at the various points.

The results obtained, demonstrated in the 1518 feet of section passed perpendicularly (see Fig. II, Plate II), justify the conclusions that from the granite base upwards at least seven divisions may be distinctly noticed. They consist of:

I. *Boulder formation*, 36 feet, resting upon a coarse-grained, hard granite, resembling the red Scotch granite, composed of gray quartz, rod feldspar (orthoclase), and a little black mica. Seams of satinspar penetrate the granite in various directions. Spathic iron ore, in small crystals, and fluorspar are found in the base rock.

Character of the Strata.—Hard, but principally soft ferruginous sandstones, containing much *red feldspar*, black mica, chloritic minerals (altered), and iron pyrites. Lower down, boulders of granite and quartz. Granite boulders of the same material as the basin floor, but altered by atmospheric exposures, imbedded in a ferruginous, highly calcareous cement.

II. *Lower sandstone group*, 251 feet.

Character of the Strata.—The larger portion (71½ per cent.) consists of *sandstones*, grayish-white or gray and reddish-gray, feldspathic, feldspar occasionally red, also black mica. Upper strata more frequently coarse, and in smaller benches in frequent alternations. Occasionally brownish-tinged and carbonaceous sandstones, the former in the lower strata, very slightly coherent, containing sometimes specks of specular iron ore. The sandstones are less calcareous, only about 57 per cent., except in the lower part of the group, which is more calcareous. They contain obscure carbonized vegetable remains, and in one instance the fragments of a small tooth of a saurian was found. Two oleiferous strata occur near the central part of the group.

Slates, only 28½ per cent. of the group, are mostly black or brownish-black, some highly bituminous, also less calcareous (43 per cent. not calcareous at all), mostly fossiliferous, containing obscure vegetable impressions; occasionally a *Calamite*, *Cythere*, and *Estheria*, scales of fish (*Dictyopyge*), particles of saurian teeth, and small coprolites occur near the lower portion of slates. *Limestone*, in thin sheets, in the slate, and as concretions, also in small seams, is found ; the former in the upper part, the latter nearer the bottom of the group.

III. *Lower calciferous group*, 245 feet.

Character of the Strata.—The largest portion of the group, 72 per cent., consists of *sandstones*, more or less feldspathic; about 29 per cent. of it consists of the lighter arkose, the balance is argillaceous, schistose, carbonaceous, or of various shades of gray. The larger portion, about 61 per cent., is calcareous; some 4 or 5 benches are rather coarse, and a few fossiliferous, containing obscure vegetable impressions and *Calamites*. Near the top of the group a brownish-gray sandstone occurs, very strong in oil, about two to three feet thick.

The *slates*, 27 per cent. of the group, are generally dark gray and brownish-gray, bituminous, and also black. Ash-colored shales and fireclay are also found, particularly near the top of the group ; fully half of the slates are calcareous, containing concretions and streaks of carbonate of lime. At the bottom of the group they are also pyritiferous, containing *Estheria* and fish-scales (*Dictyopyge*), which is also the case near the top of the group, where impressions of long vegetable stems and coprolites are found. The limestones occur principally in four divisions, either in concretions or in strata of arenaceous gray limestone, attaining sometimes the thickness of from one to three feet, but generally interstratified with other rocks. The first is about 16 feet from bottom of group, the next two respectively 60 feet and 75 feet above.

IV. *Carbonaceous group*, 150 feet.

Character of the Strata.—The larger portion of the group, 59 per cent., consists of *sandstones*. About half of them are light-colored, feldspathic, arkose, but generally contain blotches of gray and black slate. The other half are of gray, or even black color, argillaceous, schistose, and frequently carbonaceous. At the top and bottom of the group a coarse feldspathic sandstone will generally be noticed. The argillaceous and carbonaceous sandstones are fossiliferous.

The *slates*, about 19 per cent., are generally more or less dark-drab-colored, except at the top of the group, and at the partings of the coal seams, where black slates predominate. They are fossiliferous and pyritiferous.

Three distinct coal seams exist in this group, about 22 per cent., but they are not always present throughout the formation as such, deteriorating often into highly bituminous slates. They are also sometimes split, forming more than three seams.

In the upper twenty or twenty-five feet of the group, *Tæniopteris*, *Equisetum*, and carbonaceous stems are found, and also *Cythere* and *Estheria*. In the coal slates only *Equiseta* and *Calamites* are noticed.

The first coal seam is at 566 feet from the granite floor, 3½ to 5 feet thick ; the second coal seam at 599 feet from the granite floor, 1 foot thick ; and the third coal seam, at 618 feet from the granite floor, 20 to 50 feet thick, but sometimes split into two seams.

Near the top, as well as near the bottom of the group, oleiferous sandstones are generally found. Except at the top of the group, where limestone is sometimes found, but which probably belongs rather to the next group, it is perfectly void of calciferous rocks. Sometimes a little carbonate of lime, in scales and crystals, is found in the coal, generally at disturbed points, saddles, etc.

V. *Oleiferous group*, 191 feet.

Character of the Strata.—To a great extent it consists of sandstones, 64 per cent. of it, in heavier strata, mostly nearly white or light gray arkose, and sometimes tolerably coarse ; also schistose sandstones with slaty partings occur. About one-half of the sandstones are slightly calcareous.

The most characteristic strata are the first occurrence of *oil rocks*, generally three, greenish-spotted, feldspathic sandstones in the upper, middle, and lower part of the series. The *slates*, 36 per cent., are mostly black and greenish-gray ; nearly all of them are calcareous, containing also concretions and benches of limestone, as also concretions of sulphuret of iron (sulphur balls, as they are called). At 708 to 730 ft. from the granite, a black slate containing fish-scales (*Tetragonolepis*), *Cythere*, and *Estheria*, and six inches of gray limestone, containing crystals of gypsum and iron pyrites, is very permanent, fairly exposed at all points, and generally over or near a very coarse arkose. Whilst the sandstones are free of fossils the slates are rich in *Calamites* and other vegetable impressions, fish-scales of *Tetragonolepis* and *Dictyopyge*, *Cythere*, and *Estheria*.

VI. *Upper calciferous group*, 334 feet.

Character of the Strata.—They consist to a great extent of sandstones (57 per cent.), generally light gray, feldspathic, arkose, principally fine-grained ; about 30 per cent. of them calcareous. Three coarse sandstones occur at 958, 1081, and 1193 feet from the granite; in the last mentioned *Calamites* occur.

Slates (42 per cent.) principally dark gray and black, about 50 per cent. of them calcareous, containing small seams and concretions of limestone ; towards the bottom of the group also gypsum and iron pyrites. *Calamites*, slender vegetable stems, fish-scales, principally *Dictyopyge*, and *Estheria* occur in the slates.

The upper half of the group is characterized by thick strata of slate and fewer sandstones, and by the occurrence of *Calamites*. The lower half contains more sandstones and a large number of small benches of slate containing *Calamites* and slender stems, but particularly fish-scales, *Estheria*, and also most of the limestones. The latter occur principally in two distinct beds, from 6 inches to nearly 4 feet. The last is the most regular, and is of brownish-gray color; the first is associated with fossiliferous slates ,about 984 and 1079 feet above the granite floor.

VII. *Upper sandstone group*, 291 feet, as far as exposed by the geological column of this section. The extreme western point of this section is yet two and a quarter miles from the centre of the basin. Consequently the upper sandstone group, or any subdivisions in it, could gain a thickness of 1500 to 2000 feet, which has not yet been settled by positive facts.

Character of the Strata.—Principally sandstones, 80 per cent. of what has been exposed ; buff-colored at top, but most-

ly fine-grained gray, argillaceous, and light-gray feldspathic (arkose); most of them are non-calcareous and coarser near the top of the section, containing at the bottom of group the remains of *Calamites*.

Slates, about 20 per cent., generally light gray or ash color, non-calcareous, except a few layers which contain calcareous concretions; also a small stratum of gray micaceous limestone, with crystals of calcite and thin strata of marly limestone at 1204 and 1321 feet from the granite. A thick stratum of indurated clay and shale, with traces of obscure vegetable impressions, is found at 1357 feet from granite. At 1490 feet from the granite floor a small coal seam, 5 inches thick, occurs.

The Mesozoic rocks are covered by level strata of more recent origin, consisting of a soft buff-colored conglomerate of red clay, with friable quartz pebbles; at the elevated summit it is from 5 to 46 feet in thickness.

How far the groups characterized above will be verified in other sections of this basin, or even other belts of the same formation in this State, will be, of course, a matter for future determination. But as they are the results of diligent explorations, which are not likely to be soon repeated, they may serve as a useful guide hereafter. To this end a more minute record for public use will therefore be admissible.

Section of the Mesozoic Rocks in the "Richmond Belt," at the Old Midlothian Coal Mine, from the Granite upwards (see Fig. I, Plate I).

Total dis. from granite.

I. Boulder formation, 36'.

Feet	In.	Description	Feet	In.
36		Conglomerate, yellowish-brown, marly, friable rock, highly calcareous, containing boulders of granite with orthoclase feldspar, ...	36	

II. Lower sandstone group, 251'.

Feet	In.	Description	Feet	In.
54		Sandstone, feldspathic brown ferruginous, with small seams of carbonate of lime, particles of specular iron ore, red feldspar, and quartz pebbles, ...	90	
5		Brownish-gray argillaceous sandstone and drab-colored slate containing vegetable impressions,	95	
19	8	Sandstone, arkose, white, containing blotches of clay, slightly ferruginous, and red feldspar in part, ...	114	8
6		Slate, drab-colored, containing vegetable impressions, ...	120	8
3		Sandstone, arkose, gray, containing fragments of teeth, (saurian) and red feldspar, ...	123	8
8	6	Slate, gray and black, some highly bituminous, arenaceous, containing *concretions of limestone*, vegetable impressions, teeth and coprolites, . .	132	2
9	6	Sandstone, brownish-gray, oleiferous, containing red feldspar, ...	141	8
7	4	{ Sandstone, schistose, containing mineral charcoal at top of strata, and Slate, black, bituminous, containing vegetable impressions and coprolites,	149	
30		Sandstone, arkose, white, slightly calcareous, partially coarse in smaller strata, with slaty bands at bottom of strata, ...	179	
11		Sandstone, brownish gray and arkose; white, hard, *oleiferous* at bottom, ...	190	
13	6	Slate, black, highly bituminous, calcareous, containing *Calamites, Cythere, Estheria,* and carbonaceous sandstone containing slender vegetable stems, ...	203	6
23	5	Sandstone, arkose, white, coarse, slightly calcareous, and pyritiferous argillaceous sandstone, containing carbonaceous vegetable fossils, *red feldspar,*	226	11
20		Slate, black, bituminous, calcareous, containing fish-scales (*Dictyopyge*), *Cythere,* mineral charcoal, and vegetable stems; also carbonaceous sandstone, *red feldspar,*	246	11
17	4	Sandstone, arkose, light gray, coarse, slightly calcareous, containing black mica; also arenaceous, dark drab-colored slate containing carbonaceous particles. *Red feldspar* makes its first appearance in this stratum, ...	264	3
23		Sandstone, arkose, white, coarse, slightly calcareous, containing black mica; also drab colored calcareous slate and carbonaceous sandstone, containing streaks of carbonate of lime, . . .	287	3

Total dis. from granite.

III. Lower calciferous group, 245 feet.

Feet	In.	Description	Feet	In.
2		Slate, black bituminous, containing streaks of *carbonate of lime, fish-scales, Estheria,* iron pyrites, and carbonaceous inclosures, ...	289	3
21		Sandstone, arkose, light gray, coarse, with blotches of clay, oleiferous at top of strata; also argillaceous sandstone containing carbonaceous fossil stems, ...	310	3
9		Dark-gray carbonaceous *sandstone, slate and limestone, fish-scales, (Dictyopyge),* in black bituminous slate at bottom of strata, ...	319	3
22		Sandstone, arkose, white, coarse at top of strata, calcareous, ...	341	3
10	10	Sandstone, dark brownish gray, carbonaceous, and slaty, containing carbonized fossil stems, . .	352	1
11		Sandstone, arkose, white and reddish gray, coarse and argillaceous; sandstone containing mineral charcoal, ...	363	1
3		Sandstone, drab-colored, micaceous and arenaceous *limestone,*	366	1
20		Sandstone, arkose, light gray, partially coarse and calcareous, containing mineral charcoal and *Calamites,*	386	1
4	9	Sandstone, gray, carbonaceous, *slate* and limestone,	390	10
15	3	Sandstone, arkose, light gray, calcareous, . .	406	1
3		Sandstone, dark gray, carbonaceous, *slate and limestone,*	409	1
23	8	Sandstone, arkose, light gray, mostly very coarse and hard, calcareous, containing blotches of clay and small strata of black slate, ...	432	9
13		Sandstone, light gray, carbonaceous and slaty, strata containing mineral charcoal, ...	445	9
14	6	Sandstone and *slate,* drab-colored, containing long vegetable stems, carbonaceous particles, pyritiferous slates and small strata of *limestone,* . .	460	3
18		Sandstone, arkose, grayish white, coarse, *conglomerate,* slightly calcareous, ...	478	3
17	6	Sandstone and *slate,* strata of gray and drab-colored argillaceous micaceous sandstone and slate, calcareous, containing coprolites; also some arkose, ...	495	9
6		Sandstone, dark, brownish gray, carbonaceous, argillaceous, containing carbonaceous inclosures, also arenaceous *slates,*	501	9
11		*Oil rock,* strong, brownish-gray sandstone, . . .	503	9
	7	Sandstone, argillaceous, light gray, calcareous and arenaceous *limestone;* fire-clay at bottom of strata, ...	515	4
16	3	Slate, black, highly bituminous, containing *fish-scales, Estheria,* bony coal, and concretions of limestone, ...	531	7

IV. Carbonaceous group, 150 feet.

Feet	In.	Description	Feet	In.
34	9	Sandstone, arkose, light gray, hard, partially coarse, containing an oil-bearing stratum near the bottom, ...	566	4
5		First coal seam, 3½' coal, 1½' slate, . . .	571	4
6	2	Slate and schistose sandstone, dark gray, pyritiferous, ...	577	6
4	3	Sandstone, arkose, light gray, partially schistose, containing mineral charcoal, ...	581	9
8		Slate, dark gray, vegetable impressions, . . .	589	9
9	10	Sandstone, arkose, gray, with argillaceous blotches,	599	7
1		Second coal seam, ...	600	7
9		Slate, gray, containing carbonized vegetable stems,	609	7
9		Sandstone, arkose, gray, hard, containing carbonaceous blotches, ...	618	7
12		Third coal seam, divided by slaty bands, from 2" to 24", }		
10	3	Sandstone, gray, silicious and gray slate, containing Calamites, }	655	4
14	6	Coal seam divided by various slaty bands, . . }		
4		Slate, black and argillaceous sandstone, micaceous, containing crystals of calcite and thin sheets of the same; Equiseta, particles of coal, . . .	659	4
11		Sandstone, arkose, grayish white and drab-colored, argillaceous, slightly calcareous blotches of clay, . .	670	4
12		Slate, black, bituminous, containing remains of fish (Tetragonolepis), Cythere and Estheria, and a stratum of limestone (sometimes 2 feet thick); carbonaceous sandstone in part, containing Tæneopteris and Equisetum, . . .	682	4

To be Continued.

Prof. Wm. B. Rogers.—Dr. J. A. Broadus, of Louisville, Ky., one of the associate editors of the ably-conducted *Religious Herald*, of Richmond, Va., in a letter to that paper of Sept. 9, 1880, writes :—

"We called on the celebrated scientific man, Wm. B. Rogers, who lives in Boston, but has his summer cottage at Newport. I had never seen him since he resigned the chair of Natural Philosophy and Geology in the University of Virginia, twenty-seven years ago. He must now be a very old man, but is beautifully well preserved, with the same tall, erect and slender figure, the same not handsome but engaging features, the same musical voice, and the same winning kindliness of manner, that are associated with some of the brightest hours of my student life. And the pleasure of finding him at home was heightened by finding there also his brother, Dr. Robert E. Rogers, with whom I studied chemistry at the University, in experiments that never failed and lectures that sparkled with interest, who has for nearly thirty years been professor in one of the great medical schools of Philadelphia, and seems still full of strength and vivacity. Ah ! as we grow old, how dear to us become the teachers of our youth."

The *Mining Record* of New York,—one of the best-informed and most reliable exponents of mining industries,—in its issue of August 28, has this item :

"INCREASED IRON PRODUCT.—The August number of *The Virginias*, published in Staunton, Va., overflows with valuable reports and statistics as to the iron resources of the two Virginias. Generally, their statements are too voluminous for our columns. They exhibit the steady growth of the output."

Quinnimont Furnace of the Pa. & Va. Iron & Coal Co., on the C. & O. Ry., is now, in its 22nd month of run, producing about 30 tons per day of chiefly "foundry" pig. This furnace is now in the immediate charge of Mr. Moses Harris, from Troy, N. Y.,—one of a family of well-known furnace men. Quinnimont will probably see the winter through under his excellent management. We welcome the addition of Mr. Harris to the iron-working corps of the Virginias.

The bee-hive coke ovens at Quinnimont produced 65.3 per cent. of coke for all the coal consumed in the 3 months from June 1st, to Sept. 1st. Ten ovens are to be immediately added to the 100 now in use there, to enable the company to supply the increased demand incident to the running of its new 15-ton furnace at Ferrol, on the C. & O. Ry., in Va., at its iron mines, which, under the immediate management of Mr. C. A. Rundel, another New Yorker, and by the new name of Grace, (in honor of the sprightly adopted daughter of Maj. J. F. Lewis, the efficient General Manager of this Co.) is, as elsewhere stated, now "in full blast."

The Virginias.

A Mining, Industrial and Scientific Journal:
Devoted to the Development of Virginia and West Virginia.

Vol. I, No. 10. }   Staunton, Virginia, October, 1880.   { Price 25 Cents.

The Virginias,

PUBLISHED MONTHLY,

By JED. HOTCHKISS, - - - Editor and Proprietor,

At 346 E. Main St., Staunton. Va.

Terms, including postage, per year, in advance, $2.00. Single numbers, 25 cents. Extra copies, $20.00 per 100. Back numbers, from the first, can be had at 25c each. **Advertising,** per inch of length of single column (3 columns to a page, as on advertising pages), one month, $2.50; two months, $4.00; three months, $5.50, six months, $7.50; nine months, $10.00, and twelve months, $12.00; payable in advance.

Specimen Numbers of this journal are sometimes sent to parties supposed to have an interest in the development of the Virginias, or a desire to be informed in reference to their resources, improvements, etc. they will please consider this an invitation to become subscribers and so help to sustain a paper devoted to their interests.

On sale at Hunter & Co.'s Bookstore, Main Street, Staunton, Virginia.

Attention is invited to the advertisement of a "*Gold Mine for Sale or Lease*." In the Geology of North Carolina, published in 1875, page 261, Prof. Kerr says :—"An immense quantity of gold has been obtained from the mines of this section, since their opening about 1829, probably between two and three millions of dollars. The most noted localities,—the richest and most extensive beds of auriferous gravel lie on the head waters of Silver Creek," etc. "As much as $10 a day to the hand has often been made in the early workings of these deposits, and I am informed by some of the older citizens, that just before the California gold deposits began to attract attention, as many as 3,000 hands might have been seen at work on one of the above-named streams.—There is still a large amount of gold in the beds which remain untouched, as well as in those which have been rudely and carelessly worked over, some of them more than once. Indeed some of the richest of these deposits have remained unworked," etc.

It is now well understood that gold is always accumulating or becoming "free" in all these beds of gold-bearing gravels from the disintegration and decay of the gravels themselves, so beds that formerly paid well will in due time do so again.

Furnaces in blast on the Chesapeake & Ohio Railway.—Never before has there been as much iron manufactured on the line of this great mineral traversing road as is being done now. Beginning at Buffalo Gap, at the border of the Appalachian country, 147 miles west from Richmond, and going westward, the following furnaces are now in blast:

(1) Buffalo Gap Furnace of the N. Y. & Va. Iron and Coal Co., Buffalo Gap, Augusta county, Va., 147 miles from Richmond and 274 from Huntington. Using brown hematite ores from its own mines and limestone from its own quarry near at hand and some ore from Hebron Church 5 miles eastward in The Valley, on the C. & O., and coke made at Fire Creek mines 168 miles farther west. Now making about 10 tons a day.

(2) Grace Furnace of the Pa. & Va. Iron and Coal Co., at Ferrol, Augusta county, Va., 153 miles from Richmond and 268 from Huntington. Using brown hematite ores from its own mines and limestone from its own quarries, near the furnace, and some red-shale ore from Clifton Forge 39 miles farther west, and coke from its own mines and ovens at Quinnimont, 141 miles farther west. It now makes 15 tons a day.

(3) The Lucy Selina Furnace of the Longdale Iron Co., Alleghany county, Va., 8 miles, by the Co's narrow-gauge railway, from Longdale station which is 190 miles from Richmond and 231 from Huntington. Using brown hematite iron ores (Oriskany) from its own mines 4 miles distant by extension of its narrow-gauge railway, limestone (Lower Helderberg) from its own quarry on line of its railroad, and coke from its own coal mine and ovens at Sewell 128 farther west. Its product is about 30 tons a day.—A second furnace is nearly completed that will make from 50 to 60 tons a day.

(4) Callie Furnace, of Hileman, Cook & Co., Botetourt county, Va., (P. O. Williamson's) 5.5 miles, by Co's standard gauge railway, just completed, from Callie Switch 194 miles from Richmond and 227 Huntington. Using brown and red hematite ores (Oriskany) from its own mines and limestone (Lower Helderberg) from its own quarries in the immediate vicinity of the furnace.— Is now drifting in a stratum of ore 45 ft. thick, as far as penetrated, within 900 ft. of furnace.—Uses coke from the Nuttallburg mine and ovens 123 miles farther west. After thorough repairs and additions went into blast Monday, Oct. 11th, and is now making about 15 tons a day.

(5) Low Moor Furnace of the Low Moor Iron Co of Va., at Low Moor 197 miles from Richmond and 224 from Huntington. Using brown hematite ore (Oriskany) from its own mines 2 miles distant by Co's standard gauge railroad, and some from Stack's mine 19 miles farther west (but will use only from its own mines), limestone (Lower Helderberg) from its own quarries, ¼ of a mile distant by rail. Buys coal from Beury, Cooper & Williams, at the Elm Colliery, 118 miles farther west, and makes its own coke in ovens alongside the furnace. A new, first-class, modern furnace, just completed, having a capacity of 80 to 100 tons a day, was blown in on Monday, Oct. 11th, made a first cast, of 15 tons, Tuesday night, and made near 50 tons on Wednesday.

(6) The Quinnimont Furnace of the Pa. & Va. Iron and Coal Co., Quinnimont, Fayette county, W. Va., 294 miles from Richmond and 127 from Huntington. Uses brown hematite ores (Oriskany) from its own mines at Ferrol, 141 miles, and from Peter's Mountain 85 miles eastward, and red-shale ore (Clinton) from Clifton Forge 102 miles eastward. Limestone (Greenbrier or Carboniferous) is obtained from Fort Spring, 49 miles to the east. It uses coke made at its own mines a mile, by branch of C. & O., from the furnace. Is producing 30 tons a day, now, in the 23rd month of its present run.

These six furnaces now in blast, all using coke made from the New River or Lower Measure coals, are making about 180 tons a day, and by the time this reaches our readers their product will probably be near 200 tons daily, or over 60,000 tons a year.—This is but a small beginning of the manufacture of iron in this most highly favored field for that industry. Other new furnaces are already projected and the idle old ones are to be renewed and put in operation.

Emigration to Virginia.—A telegram of Oct. 12, from London, gives the following as one of the resolutions recently passed by the Committee of the Virginia Bond-holders of the Council of Foreign Bond-holders in that city :—

"That the Committee of Virginia Bond-holders, having learned with satisfaction that a society, comprising some of the most prominent citizens of the State, has been formed, under the title of the 'Virginia Immigration Society,' for the purpose of attracting emigrants with capital to settle in the State, and that arrangements have been made by the said society for establishing an agency in London for the United Kingdom of Great Britain and Ireland, hereby resolve to give the said society and its agents here its cordial support."

We are gratified to see that this powerful corporation, one that virtually controls all the foreign movements of British capital, has at last removed its embargo on the movement of capital for investments in the Virginias.''

When (Feb. 21, 1873) by invitation of the Society of Arts, of which the Prince of Wales is President, the editor of this journal read before it, in London, a paper "On the Virginias; their Agricultural, Mineral and Commercial Resources," which that Society printed in full, in 11 solid pages of its Journal and circulated by thousands, and which was reproduced, in full also, in the great mining journals of London, and commented on favorably by the leading dailies, the "Times" included,—the Secretary of the Council of Foreign Bond-holders (who was also Secretary of the Committee of Virginia Bond-holders), Mr. Hyde Clark, was present and was the first to enter upon a "discussion" of the paper that had been read. After remarking upon the sympathy that in all past time had been felt by the Society of Arts for Virginia, he felt it his duty to say that "Virginia must set her affairs in order before she could apply to England for further assistance."—From that day to this the Council of Foreign Bond-holders has opposed all investments here, in one case inducing the recall of a million dollars, with which work on the Norfolk & Great Western Railway was to have been begun. This opposition was provoked because the English holders of Virginia bonds were excluded from the benefits of the "Funding Bill," by its repeal, before they had time to exchange their bonds. They are probably better satisfied with the "McCulloch Bill," hence the resolutions.

The long continued stagnation in business in England has caused a vast accumulation of idle money, money seeking paying investments, and now that this investment controlling power approves of Virginia as a field for such purposes, we may confidently look for a large and active investment of capital in this direction. We shall be glad to see it and will be on the alert to warn against its waste in investments that must prove unprofitable and in the promotion of schemes that have not a substantial character.

Mr. Addison Borst, the Secretary of the "Virginia Immigration Society," has been for some time in England on business for his Society, and he is entitled to much of the credit of this revival of interest in reference to Virginia.

The "Low Moor Iron Company of Virginia."—On Monday, Oct. 11th, 1880, the largest and most thoroughly well appointed blast furnace ever constructed in Virginia or West Virginia, that of the Lowmoor Iron Company of Virginia, at Low Moor station of the Chesapeake & Ohio Railway, 197 miles from Richmond and 224 from Huntington,—was blown in and a new era in the manufacture of iron in these states inaugurated.

The "Low Moor Iron Company of Virginia" was organized under a charter granted by the state of Virginia, July 5th, 1873, "to mine, ship and sell iron ores, and to manufacture iron and steel in all its branches." Its minimum capital stock was fixed at $500,000, "divided into shares of the par value of $100 each," and it can hold real estate up to 10,000 acres. Its principal office is located at Staunton, Va.

The "owners, corporators and directors" of this Company at the time of its organization were, and at the present time are, John Means, of Ky., President; Maj. H. M. Bell, of Va., Vice-President; A. A. Low, of N. Y., Treasurer; John F. Winslow and E. H. R. Lyman, of N. Y., and A. S. Winslow, of Ohio, Directors; and George T. Wickes, of Va., Managing Director. John F. Winslow is also Chairman of the Executive Committee.

John Means is the president of the company that owns the Ashland, Ky., furnace, of which he is manager, which has an annual capacity of 15,000 net tons; he was also the president of the Lexington and Big Sandy R. R., which has recently become a part of the Elizabethtown, Lexington & Big Sandy R. R., the westward extension of the Chesapeake & Ohio; he is also connected with other large iron works in Kentucky.—Maj. H. M. Bell is a well-known lawyer of Staunton, Va., a member of the enterprising firm of Echols, Bell & Catlett, which he represents in this Company, a firm that has been more successful than any other in the introduction of capital into the iron and coal regions of Virginia and West Virginia, and in the establishing of manufactures, especially on the line of the C. & O. R'y.—A. A. Low, the head of the great importing house of A. A. Low Brothers, of New York City, so extensively and successfully connected with the China and Japan trade, and who has recently given fresh evidence of his sagacity by purchasing thousands of acres of coal lands in West Virginia.—E. H. R. Lyman, of New York City, is also a prominent member of the house of A. A. Low Brothers; he also has invested in W. Va. coal lands.—John F. Winslow, of Poughkeepsie, N. Y., one of the founders and presidents of the noted Rensselaer Polytechnic Institute, of Troy, N. Y.; was long the leading spirit of the great steel works at Troy, N. Y., and was a member of the firm of Cornell & Winslow, that purchased the right for the Bessemer Process in the United States, introducing to this country that great industry, the manufacture of Bessemer steel, in which we now rank the second in the world, producing yearly over 1,750,000 tons.—A.S.Winslow, a brother of John F., is vice-pres. of the First National Bank of Cincinnati.—George T. Wickes, brother-in-law of J. F. Winslow, and an engineer graduate of the Rensselaer Polytechnic, is from New York, but has been connected with mining operations in N. C., and elsewhere; he has, from the first, had charge of the extensive operations, both of mining and construction at Low Moor, managing the affairs of the company with great energy and skill.

The Low Moor Company began by purchasing some 4,118 acres of mineral and farming lands lying on the western ranges and slopes of the Riteh patch chain of mountains, where broken and drained by Karnes' Creek, and extending to Jackson's River and crossed by the Chesapeake & Ohio R'y, in Alleghany county, Va. After extended explorations of the extensive iron ore beds that there outcropped, it constructed a branch railway, of standard guage, 2½ miles long, from Low Moor station of the C. & O., southward to its mines, where a well built mining village soon sprung up and where machinery for washing a large quantity of ore was erected.

Regular mining operations, on a large scale, began in 1875, the company making the mining and selling of ores its business. From that time to the present it has mined some 85,000 tons of brown hematite iron ore, a large portion of which was sold to Quinnimont Furnace, on the C. & O. R'y, 97 miles farther west, and to Wheeling, Steubenville, the Hanging Rock region, and other points on the Ohio. About 53,000 tons were shipped in 1875, '6 and '7, but little in 1878, and some 9,000 tons in 1879.

In 1878 this company decided to build a first-class modern blast furnace, nearly, if not quite, as large and about equal in capacity to any in the United States. Having purchased 800 acres of land, adjoining the first purchase, some 230 of which are in a broad bottom extending to Jackson's River and intersected by the C. & O. R'y, furnishing the best of sites for furnaces, rolling mills, etc., and for a manufacturing village; it increased its capital stock to $600,000, all paid up, and procured plans for the furnace and its appurtenances. In July, 1879, the work of collecting materials and of construction began, and has been continued, almost uninterruptedly—so favorable is our climate for out-of-doors and all-the-year-round operations—to the recent completion of this extensive blast-furnace plant,—representing an expenditure of some $300,000 in about 15 months. The result is a 100-ton furnace in blast, 104 coke ovens, 44 of which are in operation, a neatly built and comfortable looking village of 115 houses, a large depot, store, shops, numerous railway tracks, storage platforms for ore and bins for coal, etc., etc., all constructed and finished in the best manner.—The furnace made 75 tons on the 8th day after it was blown in.

The furnace is an iron-cased stack, 75 feet high, having an inside diameter of 9 feet at both bottom and top; it rests on a cast iron ring supported by 8 columns, It is 18 feet in the bosh and has 8 tueyres. The lining is two-thirds Mt. Savage and one-third Sciotoville fire brick. There are 3 Whitwell hot-blast stoves, brick-lined sheet iron cylinders with vertical flues. It has 2 engines and 12 cylinder boilers; the steam cylinder is 3 ft. in diameter, the blowing one 84 inches, stroke 4 ft.; the 2 fly-wheels are each 10 ft. in diameter. The elevator is 75 ft. high, made by Otis & Bro., New York. The casting house is 60 ft. by 116 and the engine room 34 by 40. Six large weighing scales are in use. About 4 miles of railway track belong to the place, 2½ of which lead to the iron mines and the limestone quarry. Water, in abundance, is obtained from Jackson's River by about 1,000 ft. of 12 inch iron pipe; by a small engine it is forced into two reservoirs, one elevated about 100 ft., the other a storage one in the yard. Some 400 laborers are employed in mining, quarrying, transportation, furnace and other work.—The assistant manager, in charge of the furnace, is Mr. Richards, from the Edgar Thompson Furnace near Pittsburg.

The ore beds, decayed, stratified deposits and strata in place, are on the company's land, 2 miles, by rail, from the furnace; the limestone is ¾ of a mile in the same direction. The company makes its own coke, having built 104 beehive ovens, having a capacity for 1½ tons each a day, alongside the furnace, and purchasing coal from the Elm Colliery of Beury, Cooper and Williams, at Elm station, of the C. & O. R'y, 118 miles farther west, at a cost of $1.80 per ton delivered at the furnace;—analyses of this coal and the coke made from it are given elsewhere in this number.

The Iron Ores used at Low Moor are from the Oriskany, Rogers' No. VII, and the Clinton, Rogers' No. V, beds on the company's land, about 2 miles, by branch railway, south from the furnace. Their character may be judged of from the following analyses:—

DR. OTTO WUTH. Jan'y 14th, 1875.	DR. OTTO WUTH. Feb'y 16, 1875.	PROF. C. E. DWIGHT. June 13th, 1876.	PROF. C. E. DWIGHT. July, 1876.
(1)	(2)	(3)	(4)
Water............ 9.14	Water............ 9.57	Silicic Acid......14.54	Sesquioxide Iron 53.230
Silicic Acid..... 10 16	silicic Acid..... 7.13	Alumina.......... 2.526	Peroxide of Iron 1.804
Alumina.......... 6.8	Alumina.......... 1.41	Sesquioxide Iron 79.266	Manganese....... 0.484
Peroxide of Iron. 73.84	Peroxide of Iron .75.84	Lime............. 0.266	Alumina.......... 3.305
Sesquioxide " 0.00	Lime............. 1.04	Phosphoric Acid. 0.664	Lime............. 1.028
Lime............. 1.05	Magnesia......... 0.42	Undetermined } 9.436	Magnesia......... 0.317
Magnesia......... 0.54	Manganese........ 2.93	Matter....... }	Silicic Acid..... 8 490
Manganese........ 3.14	Phosphoric Acid. 1.21		Phosphoric Acid. 0. 75
Phosphoric Acid.. 0.45	Sulphur.......... trace		Sulphuric Acid.. 0.21
Sulphur.......... trace			Moisture........ 0.826
			Loss............ 0.149
100.00	100.00	100.000	100.3
Metallic Iron... 51.68	Metallic Iron.... 53.13	Metallic Iron. 59.586	Metallic Iron...38.770
Phosphorus 0.19	Phosphorus 0.53	Phosphorus.... 0.290	Sulphur......... 0.04
			Phosphorus...... 0.101

The first, second and third of the above analyses are of the brown hematite ore, of which there are about 3.5 miles of length outcrop, exposed by the undulations or upheavals of the strata, (one bed of which is shown in the "section" by Mr. Wickes, published in the January No. of THE VIRGINIAS.) In

the "Prospectus," by G. T. Wickes, Engineer and Managing Director, 1878, (to which we are indebted for many of the facts here published), in reference to the quantity of these ores, on the Low Moor lands it is stated,—"Thus far, in mining these Hematite ores, the rule has been found to be unvarying, that, as the workings deepened, the vein has widened and the quality has improved ; in one instance, where the vein of ore was 16 ft. wide at the surface, 280 ft. down from *this* surface the vein was 70 ft. wide, while at this depth it was only 90 ft. below the surface of the main valley ; and the ore is mined here not by sinking shafts, but by 'drifts' run in from the hill side." —Mr. W. enumerates 11 "drifts" and "open cuts" that, to 1878, had been made, without making any "rooms" in the ore-beds, aggregating 4,441 ft. of *drifts*, and 1,547 feet of *open cuts*, "actually in the ore, varying from 9 to 70 ft. in thickness and extending downward to an unknown depth." He estimated, from surveys and test-holes, that "1,500,000 tons of marketable ore" was then "in sight and accessible from these *drifts* and open cuts." "Nor do these include more than one-twentieth part of the accessible portion of this first bed or vein upon the company's property, as proven by numerous test-holes ; and when we add to these the contents of the second bed or vein (not shown in the section), we think we may prudently say that the quantity of this kind of ore on the property is practically inexhaustible."

The third analysis given above was made at the instance of the Riverside Iron-works Co., of Wheeling, W. Va., to test the quality of Low Moor ore before a proposed purchase ; after working in their furnace they reported "that it yielded 53 per cent. of pig-iron of very satisfactory quality."

The fourth analysis is of what Mr. Wickes calls a "*Block ore* that lies to the right of and below the fossil ore, as shown on the section (given in THE VIRGINIAS for Jan., 1880), equal in lineal extent to the latter, and varying from 4 to 6 ft. in thickness. It contains too large a proportion of silica for profitable working alone, but in connection with argillaceous ore could be advantageously used. It can be mined very cheaply, and at some future day may prove a valuable accession to the company's mineral resources."

Fossil ore on these lands is mentioned by Mr. Wickes as follows :—"By referring to the section it will be seen that this ore lies on the right, and underneath the sandstone formation marked thereon as No. V. Upon a part of the property the position of the veins is nearly vertical, while at other points it is nearly horizontal. Some 8 drifts and galleries have been put in on the veins, aggregating 3,000 feet in length, and about 5,000 tons of ore taken out, most of which was marketable. The vein shows from 6 inches to 2 ft. in thickness, and extends the entire length of the property, a distance of 4 miles across the widest part."—"As an ore it is a favorite with iron smelters for mixing with the brown hematite ; it yields 50 per cent. of metallic iron.

The limestone of this property, belonging to the Lower Helderberg (Va. No. VI), is thus mentioned in the "Prospectus."—"There is an almost unlimited quantity of this material so indispensable as a flux in ore smelting. It may be very cheaply quarried, and is of excellent quality, as shown by the following analyses. Lying, as it does, immediately adjoining the rail track, it can be put into cars without additional cost beyond the quarrying. It is shown as No. VI, veins No. 1 and 2 on the section.

The analyses of samples from the two veins, made by Prof. C. E. Dwight, of Wheeling, W. Va., August 22, 1876, gave the following :—

	Vein No. 1.	Vein No. 2.
Carbonate of lime	97.632	93.440
" " magnesia	0.113	1.337
" " iron	0.014	1.049
Alumina	0.301	0.368
Silicic acid	1.530	3.086
Phosphate of lime	0.023	0.014 .
Sulphate of "	0.102	0.021
Organic matter and water	0.260	0.548
Loss	0.025	0.137
	100.000	100.000

The cost of making a long ton of pig-iron at Low Moor was estimated in this "Prospectus," Oct. 1, 1878, as follows :—

1.5 tons coke, at $2.85 per ton, ...	$ 4.27
2.25 tons ore, at $2.05 per ton, ...	4.61
1 ton limestone, at 40 cents per ton, ...	0.40
Labor	1.75
Extras	0.47
Total	$11.50

The comments on this estimate are :—"At this price for ore a profit on it is allowed the mines, while 2.25 tons to the ton of iron is probably more than would be currently used. Then, again, a saving will doubtless be made ultimately in the cost of coke, so that we regard these figures as being quite up to, if not beyond what will be the regular practice."

We shall watch, with very great interest, the workings of this Low Moor Furnace, confident that it will satisfy the expectations of those that have invested in it, and, in all possible ways, "devised liberal things" in its construction. We look to it to demonstrate that good iron can be made more cheaply in the iron regions of Virginia than at any other points in the United States.—The ores, the limestones, the fuel, the labor, the climate, the midway station between Eastern and Western markets with ample transportation outlets to both, are all there, and nothing is wanting but energized capital, energized as it has been at Low Moor, to prove that nowhere will the iron-master be more liberally rewarded for his expenditures than in the Virginia iron-belts.

The "Old Dominion Land Company" has just been incorporated at Richmond, Va.; the corporators are C. P. Huntington, Harvey Fisk, A. S. Hatch, James H. Storrs and J. E. Gates, all of New York city. C. P. Huntington is president and Frank Storrs secretary. The capital stock of this Co. is from $2000,000 to $4,000,000. Its object is to mine and own and develop land in Virginia.—These gentlemen are connected with the Chesapeake and Ohio Ry., and, doubtless, one of the objects of the O. D. L. Co. is laying out and building up a city at Newports-news.

Amherst Furnace, Amherst Co., Va., is now making 6 tons of charcoal iron a day, using 200 bushels of charcoal, made near the furnace, to the ton. Its ores are Primordial (No. I) brown hematite, brought from its Buena Vista mines, on the Western Blue Ridge, in Rockbridge Co., 22 miles by canal and ¼ of a mile in carts from the ore bed.—*Marl* is used for flux in a one-eight proportion ; it is dug from a bed over 20 ft. thick, on the bank of North River and the canal, 23 miles above the furnace, in Rockbridge Co. It is preferred to limestone and costs less.

The Tinsalia Coal and Iron Company, composed of Western Pennsylvania capitalists, has just received its charter from the State of Virginia. The company will build a branch railroad from their works in Wise county to the main line. The capital invested is $500,000. A. V. Tinstman, of Pittsburg, is President of the concern, and E. K. Hyndman, present manager of the Connellsville Coal and Iron Company, is vice-president.—*Pittsburg Telegraph.*

Prof. J. J. Stevenson is now making a geological survey of Wise, Scott, and Lee counties, Va., and a geological section from the Black Mountain (Cumberland of the maps) to Bristol, on the A. M. & O. RR, for the Tinsalia Coal and Iron Co., as Gen. Imboden writes us from Big Stone Gap, Wise Co., whither he has lately removed in the interests of that company.

The "Powhatan Coal and RR. Co." was incorporated at Richmond, Va., Oct. 19. Its office is to be at Richmond. Frederick Wolffe, of Montgomery, Ala., is president, and James R. Werth, of Richmond, secretary. Its capital may be from $20,000 to $400,000. It will operate, chiefly, in Powhatan Co., Va.

The Lynchburg Iron, Steel and Mining Co. is not only running its iron-works—the products of which are advertised in THE VIRGINIAS—on full time, but has recently completed and put in blast a new furnace, fed by ores from its James River mines, below Lynchburg.

The Iron Ores of Virginia and West Virginia.

By Prof. William B. Rogers.

(Continued from Page 140)

3. The Mesozoic Iron Ores of Virginia.—These ores are found in the Upper Jurassic beds that are exposed along the eastern border of Midland Virginia, projecting, in places, into the Tidewater country, in the areas colored a light red on the Gological Map (in The Virginias for June); and in the Lower Jurassic beds that occur as isolated and somewhat oval patches in Midland Virginia, in the areas colored a deep red on the Geological Map;—they are within the Archæan and along its eastern border. In his reports Rogers called these formations the Middle and the Upper Secondary,—in a recently published table (see page 14 of The Virginias) he classes them as the Lower Mesozoic (17, 16), or Jurasso-Triassic, the Middle Secondary Sandstones and Coal Measures; and the Upper Mesozoic, or Jurasso-Cretaceous, the Upper Secondary Sandstones.—These are coal, rather than iron-bearing formations.

"While referring to the valuable character of the rich deposits of bituminous coal I am anxious again to call attention to the *iron ores* which accompany them in several place. Since the former report, in which allusion was made to the probable importance of these ores to the manufacturing industry of eastern Virginia, several specimens have been submitted to chemical analysis, and from the results obtained, the really valuable character of the ore may be considered as satisfactorily established. A specimen of hematitic ore, from the neighborhood of Tarbue's pits, in Chesterfield, gave in the 100 grains the following ingredients: Peroxide of Iron, 85.15; Silica, 4.20; Alumina, 4.00; Water, 6.50.

The existence of this mineral in immediate contiguity with the coal is a fact of such obvious importance, that no commentary is needed to make it deeply interesting to persons of capital and enterprise, who may be concerned in developing the resources of this portion of the State." [6–1836.]

"Micaceous iron in small scales" is mentioned as found in the "igneous" or "altered rocks," near Goldsby's Falls of the James, in Buckingham. [83–1839.]

The quarries of Upper Secondary Sandstone of Francis Taliaferro, on the Rappahannock, below Fredericksburg, are said to furnish a "rock varying from a nearly white to a light brownish-gray color. The latter tint is generally developed after exposure to the air, and is obviously due to the decomposition of the embedded particles of iron pyrites present in the strata of this as well as other localities." [83–1840.]

"Iron ore from the Chesterfield coal basin.—Structure massive, somewhat slaty; texture coarse; color brownish black, with glimmering quartzose points. Composition in 100 parts: Peroxide of Iron, 66.00; Alumina, 7.10; Silica and insoluble matter, 14.30; Water, 12.50; Loss, 0.10; Percentage metallic iron, 46.20. [121–1840.]

Note.—We have now given all the iron items in Rogers' reports relative to all that part of Virginia lying eastward of the Blue Ridge, and in the Archæan or Metamorphic portion of that chain, the Eastern Blue Ridge. The rocks of that extensive Archæan region (see Geological Map) have not, as yet, been classified, nor has the order of their succession been determined or agreed upon by the leading geologists. Rogers, in his notes for Macfarlane's Geol. Ry. Guide (1877), does not attempt to classify them; he merely says (p. 181): "The letters A, B, C, D mark four rather distinct groups of Archæan rocks found in Virginia, of which the first three may probably be referred to the Laurentian, Huronian and Montalban periods respectively, and the fourth to an intermediate stage—the Norian or Upper Laurentian." And Lesley, in the same work, says: "All beneath the Potsdam is

styled Azoic, because no survey has yet sufficiently differentiated the mass into its several systems."—Which is equivalent to saying, as said above, that as yet we know nothing definite about the order, etc., of these rocks, and that we have here a large field for the exercise of geological talents of the highest order. But, the Eastern Blue Ridge fairly crossed to the westward and the old shore of the Paleozoic sea reached—a sea that in old time extended from the long Archæan island, the western border of which remains as the Eastern Blue Ridge, to the Rocky Mountains, and from the Laurentian Highlands to those that encompass the Gulf of Mexico on the south—we come to where the order and succession of the rocks are well known, and their structure, position and extent are, in a general way, determined, and have been since 1836 when Prof. Rogers announced that, "After much toil and perplexity, occasioned by the rugged features and complicated structure of the mountainous districts which were examined, the true relations of the rocks and minerals of this portion of the state were satisfactorily determined." [8–1836.] Especially so since 1837, when they were grouped and named, in the report, after the statement "that the determination of the order in which the several members of our geological series are arranged throughout the region west of the Blue Ridge, constitutes one of the most interesting and valuable results yet developed by the labors of the survey, not only leading to curious and important conclusions of a strictly scientific nature, but furnishing a sure guide to researches of economical value." [13–1837.] This is the grandest geological discovery that has been made on this continent, and it has furnished the key for all subsequent ones. The honor of its inception belongs to the Virginia of 1835 and to her State Geologist, who was then just entering his 30th year, and in part, also, to his co-working and since jointly famous brother.

The fact of succession in the rocks discovered, Rogers proceeded to divide the rocks themselves,—which he had studied through a mile of thickness in the upheaved and eroded Apalachian region extending from the western Blue Ridge to the Ohio, but really containing many miles of thickness of displaced strata—into groups or "formations," putting together those having common resemblances or that he found entering into common topographical features. Recognizing the great value of the order of numbers, he marshaled his groups and designated them by numbers, calling that which he found at the bottom, the one that rested on the broken and unordered rocks of the eastern Blue Ridge, *Formation No. 1;* the next, *Formation No. 2*, and so on to No. 12, which lay "immediately beneath and incorporated with the widely extending coal measures of the west."—This in 1837. In 1838, having extended his observations, Prof. Rogers adopted Roman numerals, an obvious advantage in writing, for his formations, and, as before, designating them *Formation No. I, Formation No. II,* etc., up to Formation No. XIII. In 1840 he divided No. XIII, which included the Middle and Upper coal-measures of The Virginias, into Nos. XIII, XIV, and XV; in his recent table (The Virginias, p. 14) he has a No. XVI, but he did not use that in his Virgiia Reports.

These numbers are used by Rogers in his reports, and they furnish the most convenient names for the field observation and study of the rocks *in the Virginias*, and for communicating, locally, information concerning the position of the rocks and that of the mineral treasures associated with them, as the writer has found in an experience of many years and with people of all degrees of intelligence. They number all the groups of rocks here that have now a determined order, giving the succession *of the whole series of conformable rocks* as displayed in these states. Until the geologists have agreed amongst themselves which is the *foundation rock*, the *No. I* that is not to be changed in the next generation, we may as well adhere to the old shore-line of Prof. Rogers for our zero and westward ascending scale, and thus, while courteously, but parenthetically, using the New York names and the Dana changed scale numbers, enjoy the orderly and readily recalled classic Virginia and Pennsylvania names, and, by so doing, continually suggest that from that same old shore line there lies an unexplored geological world to the eastward for some coming man—perhaps some Virginian trained in the school that Corcoran and Rogers have so generously endowed, and that has its seat amid those

rocks—to explore and do for the east-lying regions what Rogers did for the west, and become another honored benefactor to the state by so doing.—ED.

"*Of the twelve rocks, each marked by certain distinctive characters, composing the mountains and valleys of this region, it has been determined that at least eight are accompanied by beds of iron ore.* Each ore has distinctive marks by which it may be recognized, and peculiarities of composition, fitting it for certain uses to which others would be less happily adapted. Thus, in the quantity and variety of this material, in all its valuable forms, our state is now proved to have no rival, unless, perhaps, Pennsylvania may be such. Looking to the immense extent of the region over which these rock are spread, and to the structure of its mountains and valleys—bringing to light at various points each of the twelve principal strata which it comprises—freighted, in great part, with the most inestimable of metallic products, it becomes evident at once that the topography of the rocks and mineral resources of this region, as it will be exhibited in the general geological map, is destined to bestow upon it a new and almost unhoped for interest. With such incentives, and with such a guide, enterprise directed to this portion of the state can neither falter nor be disappointed. Anticipation, confiding in the certain deductions of cautious scientific research, already begins to sketch the gladdening picture of successful industry—crowding population and wide-spreading improvement, which at no remote day, it will be its happy lot to realize. [8–1836.]

In his preliminary report, commenting generally on the mineral resources of Virginia, Rogers says: "The iron ore of the Valley constitutes another of its most valuable possessions. This, although manufactured into iron in numerous places, has as yet been the subject of no systematic geological and chemical examination, further than the determination of its general features, and some of its qualities in the furnace. An examination of the composition of all the principal varieties now in use, as well as the determination of the relations of the deposit, geologically, with the rocks among which it is found, would furnish matters of enquiry, whose practical bearing upon a valuable branch of industry in this region will be promptly and fully recognized by all who are interested in its success. For, although the tact of the operator in this, as in almost all the department of the arts, is necessary to the profitable pursuit of the manufacture, those engaged in the smelting of iron have long been sensible, at least in other countries, of the high importance of such suggestions as are furnished by a chemical examination of the ores upon which they operate, and a geological investigation of the positions in which the beds of ore occur. The ores almost exclusively in use are hematites of various aspects, known under the name of Honeycomb and Pipe ores—many of which yield a metal of the very finest character. The facility of smelting, as well as the quality and amount of product, varies of course with the description of ore employed—and from the want of such knowledge as has been just referred to, the difficulties of the process in some places have almost put a stop to the operations of the furnace." [39–1835.] And in the same connection mention is made of "octahedral and dodecahedral sulphuret of iron" as objects interesting to the mineralogist, found in that region. [39–1835.]

In 1838, in presenting analyses "of the iron ores of the Valley and its mountains," given hereafter, Rogers gives the following general statements in reference to these ores:—"In describing the geological structure of the Great Valley of our state, and of the mountains rising within it or forming its western border, some account was given of the localities and extent of the various beds of iron ore associated with the several formations. I proceed now to add a few chemical details in regard to the composition of these ores, confining myself to those varieties which are of most importance, as well from

the extent in which they are found as from their intrinsic excellence. Numerous other analyses of the ores of this region have been completed, and many yet remain to be executed, of which it is designed at a future day to make a detailed report. Similar examinations have also been made of a large number of ores associated with the strata of the mountainous region lying to the northwest, of which many are from the same formations as occur in the Valley. Of these general mention was made in the report of last year, in treating of the eleven successive formations comprising the Apalachian series. The minute investigation of the geological position, as well as the extent of the ore in question, zealously prosecuted during the past year, has brought to light the important fact that throughout a large portion of the middle district of the Apalachian zone, as well as in various parts of its two other subdivisions, the most abundant, continuous and valuable deposits of this material are to be found in formation VII, the coarse sandstone near its upper boundary, being frequently replaced by the ore for a great thickness and over a wide extent.

In announcing the discovery of the geological connection here mentioned as one of much *economical interest*, it is proper to repeat the remark often made on previous occasions in my reports, that such a *general* fact claims a high consideration for utility from the extent of area over which it becomes applicable as the guide to individual exploration through all future time. To discover every accessible deposit of ore within the wide expanse of our Apalachian zone, would obviously be impracticable with any scheme of geological investigation, however ample and complete. Ages must elapse before all the available localities of this widely disseminated material shall have been explored, yet, by determing *now* the law concerning it in position with rocks conspicuously exposed and readily identified from the minute description of them already given, a safe guide is placed in the hands of the enquirer, with which and the geological details of structure, revealing the order and position of the formations in each ridge and valley he can hardly fail in reaching a satisfactory result. On this account it was that much, and perhaps a seemingly undue importance was attached in my last year's report to the discovery of the *fossiliferous and calcareous iron ore* associated with formation V. Yet of the practical value of this generalization, I may cite as proof that during the last season it has led to the observation in numerous places in the mountains of the southwestern counties, of the very same ore in the same geological position, when, but for the direction thus given to our enquiries, many of these localities would necessarily have been overlooked." [1838, p. 28.]

4. The Primordial Iron Ores of Virginia and West Virginia.

There are the iron ores of the Primordial or Potsdam formation, Rogers' No. I; those found in and along the broken ranges of foot-hills lying west of the Blue Ridge proper, the Eastern one, and along the eastern border of The Great Valley,—the ranges that from their relations to the Blue Ridge chain of mountains may, with great propriety, be called the Western Blue Ridge. These ores are only found on the eastern borders of the Valley counties, and perhaps to some extent in the western borders of Floyd, Carroll and Grayson, and in the out-of-place Valley area of Bedford, the Buford valley.

Rogers included this in his "Third general division" of Virginia in his first report, in which he mentions "iron ore" as one of "the valuable materials included in that section of the state." [5–1835.]

CONTINUED ON PAGE 160.

Analyses of West Virginia Coals and Cokes.—A Most Important Work.—Arrangements have been effected by which full analyses are to be made of samples of all of the coals and cokes of West Virginia now available from along the line of the Chesapeake & Ohio Railway, and the results published.

The samples will be carefully selected by the Editor of THE VIRGINIAS who will see that they are proper averages, truly representing the fuel as it is prepared for market: each point of shipment will be visited by him, and the selections made in regular order

The analyses will be made by Mr. J. Blodget Britton of the Iron-Masters' Laboratory, of Philadelphia, and reported from time to time as they are severally completed.

This work, it is believed, will reveal the existence, in quantity, in West Virginia, of some of the best, if not the very best coals for coking and iron-manufacturing purposes in the United States. It will be proceeded with as rapidly as its nature will permit.—Already Mr. Britton has made two analyses, and the following are copies of his report:

"IRON-MASTERS' LABORATORY,
WARRENTON, VA., BRANCH, Oct. 16, 1880.

Results of analysis of Coal (Bituminous), from *Elm Colliery*, Fayette Co., W. Va.—Sample, received from Jed Hotchkiss, Esq., was pounded up and weighed 1 lb., 10½ oz.

Water, expelled at 212° Fah.	2.41
Volatile combustible matter,	24.43
Fixed carbon,	71.82
Ash,	1.34
	100.00

Included in the above; { Sulphur, ... 0.371
{ Phosphorus, . . . a trace.

Result of analysis of Coke produced from Coal from *Elm Colliery*, Fayette Co., W. Va.—Sample, received from Jed. Hotchkiss, Esq., was pounded up and weighed 1 lb., 2 oz.

Moisture (absorbed from the air after coking,)	1.49
Volatile combustible matter,	0.58
Fixed carbon,	94.03
Ash,	3.90
	100.00

Included in the above; { Sulphur, ... 0.494
{ Phosphorus, . . . a trace.

The coke could not have been made from coal identical with the sample analysed; coal like the sample would have made a still purer coke, though the one now reported is undoubtedly a superior article."

Elm Colliery, that of Messrs. Beury, Cooper & Williams, from which this coal came, is at Elm station of the Chesapeake & Ohio Ry., Fayette Co., W. Va., west 315 miles from Richmond and 118 from Low Moor, and 106 east from Huntington on the Ohio. (See map in THE VIRGINIAS of Feb. 1880.) The coal is from a bed of the Lower Coal Measures, Rogers' Formation No. XII, (Dana's 14 a.) which is there 55" thick, of clean coal. This bed is probably the same as that mined at Nutallburg,—59 of Page's section on page 22 of THE VIRGINIAS.—This coal was selected as the first to be analysed because it is the one from which is made the coke used at the largest blast furnace in the Virginias, that at Low Moor, Alleghany Co., Va., which, as stated elsewhere, has just gone into blast.

The sample analysed was taken from the stock pile, of some 2,000 tons, at Low Moor, whither the coal, as mined, had been recently shipped. A bushel of fragments was picked from every part of the stock pile, so as to secure, beyond question, a bushel that would truly represent the commercial character of the coal; this bushel was then pounded up and shaken together, and from it a pounded-up sample of 1 lb., 12.5 oz., was taken and at once sent to Mr. Britton and by him analysed, with the utmost carefulness, within the following week.

Coke from the Elm Colliery coals, selected, in the same manner as the coal in the preceding analysis, from the stock pile of some 500 tons, or more, at Low Moor Furnace, lying alongside the coke ovens at that furnace where it had just been made, was analysed by Mr. Britton at the same time as the coal, a sample of 1 lb., 2 oz. having been sent him.

Iron Ore.—The New York and Ohio Steel and Iron Company, of Ironton, Ohio, has recently purchased a thousand tons of the "Excelsior" iron ore at about $3 per ton, on the C. & O. R'y, at Excelsior Switch, Alleghany county, Virginia,—having had its attention called to these excellent ores by the notice taken of them in the August number (p. 119) of THE VIRGINIAS.—The prices at which these and other Virginian ores, that contain over 51 per cent. of metallic iron, can be bought, are in striking contrast with those paid for Western ores in the same region; for among the "mining news" of our recent exchanges is this item:—"The Missouri ores are an expensive material just now, costing, per ton, $13 for Iron Mountain, $9 for Meramac, and $6 for Pilot Knob, and $2.65 more for freight to the Hanging Rock region of Ohio." According to the official Geological Reports of Missouri, (See Vol. on Iron Ores, 1872) the Iron Mountain ores contain from 65.16 to 68.53 per cent. metallic iron, from 0.03 to 0.11 phosphorus, and from 0.003 to 0.008 sulphur; the Pilot Knob ores contain from 36.52 to 64.93 per cent. metalliciron, 0.015 to 0.044 phosphorus, from a trace to 0.079 sulphur, and from 5.18 to 28.16 silica; the Meramec ores contain from 22.38 to 69.27 per cent. metallic iron, 0.027 to 0.208 phosphorus, and from a trace to 0.126 sulphur.—Two miles north of Covington, Alleghany Co., Va., Ed. Burke, Esq., after three days prospecting on his land struck a solid bed of brown hematite 5 feet thick. Iron men pronounce it of good quality.—*Alleghany Tribune*, Oct. 15.

The Richmond & Alleghany RR Co. is making good progress in track-laying from each end of its line. From the Richmond end the cars are now running 34 miles, to Cedar Point, 114 miles below Lynchburg: from Williamson's, its western junction with the Chesapeake & Ohio, construction trains run over 8 miles of completed track, to where a bridge over James River is nearly completed, that done, in a few days now, track-laying will proceed rapidly to Buchanan. Trains will soon be running over this Williamson's-Buchanan division of the road and the great iron ore beds of Arcadia, Purgatory, Salisbury, Lowry's, and Roaring Run, Parson's, Cook's, Callie and Kayser's, on Rich-patch Mtn., will be put in communication with the railway system of the country and a new and rich iron field be opened for development.

This company has purchased the Clifton-forge property, one mile below Williamson's, which includes the Clifton-forge pass of Jackson's River through Rich-patch Mtn. and its extensive water-power, iron ore and timber lands, and also the riverside portion of the Kayser property below the pass and just east of Rich-patch Mtn. On the broad bottoms and river terraces of the latter the town of "Iron Gate" is to be laid out and at once built up, for there the company will erect its machine shops, a hotel, making it the present western terminus of its road, etc. Mr. Lowry has already opened the old Kayser house there as a hotel.

Awards to Iron Ores and Coals from the Virginias.—At the 8th annual Cincinnati Exposition, closed October, 9th, the highest prize, a silver medal, was awarded to Pleumer & Bramwell, metal and mineral dealers of Cincinnati, for the "*Best display of iron ores any State.*" It was for iron ores from along the C. & O. R'y, in Virginia and West Virginia.—A silver medal was also awarded to the Pennsylvania and Virginia Iron and Coal Co. for the "*Best Display of Iron Ores.*" It is needless to say that these are from the same line,—samples of ores used by that company at its Ferrol and Quinnimont furnaces.—To Pluemer & Bramwell was also awarded the highest prize for coals, gathered also from the Kanawha and New River fields.

The competition for these awards was from all directions, from Kentucky, Pennsylvania, Ohio, Alabama, Tennessee, West Virginia, and Virginia, and it is no small matter that these states have won them.—We ask the attention of those that say that the coals, cokes, and ores of other states are are not equal in quality to those of other states, to these impartial awards.

Hon. W. H. Ruffner, Supt. of Public Instruction in Va., delivered to the Virginia Summer Normal School, lately in 6-weeks session at the University of Va., 13 lectures on geology and mineralogy with special reference to Virginia. In concluding his lectures he advised all those who felt an interest in the subject to subscribe for THE VIRGINIAS.

Sinking Creek Furnace, Craig Co., Va., "is now in blast, making 6 tons charcoal iron a day; could make 10, but have had a long drouth and water very low," writes, under date of October 13, Supt. E. P. Williams.

The Mesozoic Formation in Virginia.

By Oswald J. Heinrich, M. E.

CONTINUED FROM PAGE 145.

Continuation of Old Midlothian Coal Mine Section.

Total dist. from the granite

V. Oleiferous group, 191 feet.

			Ft.	In.
10	6	Sandstone, arkose, gray, hard, and coarse, slightly calcareous and schistose sandstone, . . .	692	10
7		Slate, highly bituminous and carbonaceous sandstone, containing fish-scales and long vegetable stems, ...	699	10
4	6	Oil rock, sandstone, light gray, with greenish blotches, slightly calcareous, ...	704	4
17		Sandstone, arkose, light gray, coarse ; also schistose, ...	721	4
9		Slate, black, containing fish-scales, Estheria, Calamites, and other vegetable impressions ; also gray limestone, ...	730	4
24		Sandstone, arkose, coarse, and carbonaceous sandstone, oleiferous near top of strata, ...	754	4
6	8	Sandstone, coarse and very hard, arkose, white,	761	
6	6	Slate, black, bituminous and greenish, calcareous and arenaceous, micaceous, containing marly limestone, fish-scales (Tetragonolepis), Cythere, Estheria, vegetable impressions and coaly particles, ...	767	6
13	2	Sandstones, gray, argillaceous and schistose ; also feldspathic, containing mineral charcoal, . .	780	8
7	8	Slate, black bituminous, pyritiferous, containing fish-scales (Tetragonolepis), Estheria, Cythere, and long vegetable stems ; also a stratum and concretions of a fibrous nearly black carbonate of lime and carbonate of iron ; also a strong oil rock, ...	788	4
32	8	Sandstone, arkose, grayish white, porous in two heavy strata, containing an oil rock near top of the last bench, ...	821	
3	6	Slate, greenish, dark drab-colored, and black, highly bituminous slate, containing Cythere, fish-scales, and carbonate of lime in thin sheets sometimes oleiferous sandstone at bottom, . .	834	6
20	6	Sandstone, arkose, grayish white and gray argillaceous, partially large quartz pebbles (probably containing teeth of saurians), ...	851	
14	9	Sandstone and slates, drab-colored, arenaceous, and arenaceous limestone, ...	865	9
7	8	Slate, gray and black, containing fish-scales, Cythere, Estheria, Calamites, and other imperfect vegetable impressions, concretions of limestone, and iron pyrites upon the joints of the rock. (Teeth of saurians), ...	873	5

VI. Upper Calciferous Group, 334 feet.

			Ft.	In.
28	7	Sandstone, arkose, light gray and schistose sandstone, with slaty strata, ...	902	
23		Slate, gray, arenaceous and black fissile, containing fish-scales, Calamites, and long vegetable stems and limestone, arenaceous, drab-colored, in small strata ; also some benches of arkose dividing it from the next, ...	925	
7	9	Slate, pyritiferous, containing in addition, Estheria, thin sheets of calcite and gypsum, . . .	932	9
5	9	Sandstone, arkose, light gray, conglomerated and carbonaceous, ...	938	6
3	6	Slate, dark gray, pyritiferous, containing gypsum,	942	
16	9	Sandstone, arkose, light gray, coarse, slightly calcareous, ...	958	9
13	10	Slate, dark gray and drab-colored, containing calcareous concretions, pyritiferous, obscure vegetable impressions, ...	972	7
12	4	Sandstone, arkose, white, slightly calcareous, .	984	11
5	1	Slate, gray, calcareous, and 3' 6" limestone, . .	990	
45	1	Sandstone, arkose, grayish white, calcareous, in heavy benches divided by slaty strata, ...	1035	1
18	2	Slate, black, pyritiferous, calcareous, containing fish-scales, Estheria, and limestone strata from 1' to 4', ...	1053	3
27	10	Sandstone, arkose, light gray, coarse and calcareous, and argillaceous carbonaceous sandstones,	1081	1

Total dist. from the granite.

			Ft.	In.
30	9	Slate, gray and drab-colored, and arkose ; small strata of limestone at the top, larger at the bottom, the latter in slate, containing fish-scales, ...	1111	10
36	9	Sandstone, greenish gray, fine grained and arkose in middle of strata, ...	1148	7
29	9	Slate, black, micaceous and argillaceous micaceous sandstone, obscure vegetable impressions, ...	1178	4
15	1	Sandstone, arkose, grayish white, coarse, calcareous, ...	1193	5
13	7	Slate, black or bluish black, compact, finely laminated and benches of ash-colored sandstone, near top of strata ; obscure vegetable impressions, Calamites in lower part of strata, ...	1207	

VII. Upper Sandstone Group, 291' represented.

			Ft.	In.
30	6	Sandstone, gray schistose, containing micaceous limestone, with crystals of calcite upon bed plains, ...	1243	6
28	5	Sandstone, arkose, principally, and benches of schistose micaceous sandstone, containing vegetable impressions, ...	1271	11
2	6	Slate, dark gray, arenaceous ; Calamites, ...	1274	5
12	11	Sandstone, arkose principally, and dark brownish-gray fine-grained slate, calcareous sandstone, coarser at bottom, ...	1287	4
8		Slate, dark gray, ...	1295	4
26		Sandstone, ash-colored, fine-grained, calcareous,	1321	4
14	11	Slates, dark drab-colored and greenish gray, calcareous concretions at top, 6" marly limestone at middle of stratum ; also greenish-gray argillaceous sandstone in upper part, ...	1336	3
21		Sandstone, arkose, light ash-colored, medium-grained, containing inclosures of clay, decomposed feldspar, calcareous, ...	1357	3
26	4	Shale, gray and drab-colored, obscure traces of vegetable remains, ...	1383	7
37	5	Sandstone, gray, argillaceous, fine-grained, . .	1421	
24	5	Sandstone, arkose, gray, coarse, ...	1445	5
43	5	Sandstone, ash and buff-colored, calcareous in last four feet, ...	1489	10
	8	Coal seam, ...	1490	3
8	5	Shale, buff-colored, approaching fuller's earth. Recent deposits, from 5 to 46 feet, ...	1498	8
20		Surface soil followed by soft buff and pink-colored conglomerate of red clay and quartz pebbles ; also frequently a pure gravel bed,*	1518	8

* Upon the north side of James River the results of this investigation are verified by a section at the Carbon Hill mines given previously by Mr. Werth, Sr., formerly agent of the mines, as the following comparison shows :

Recent formation : Soil, ...	20 feet.	20 feet.

Group No. VI. Upper calciferous.

Alternating shales and sandstones, . . .	450 feet.	335 feet of it.

Group No. V. Oleiferous.

Cinders, so-called, fire-clay, ...		195 feet.
Nodular pyrites, ...	15 feet.	
Shales and sandstones, ...	60 "	

Group No. IV. Carboniferous.

Coke seam, coke (above) 2' 3," coal 3' 6,"	6 feet.	152 feet.
Shale and sandstone, ...	50 "	
Coal seam, ⎫	6 "	
Shales, ⎬ 3d seam, ...	17 "	
Coal seam, ⎭	4½"	
Shales and sandstones containing 6" seam of coal, 2d seam, ...	40 "	
Coal seam, slope seam 8-10', 1st seam, .	9 "	

Group No. III. Lower calciferous.

Sandstones and slates to supposed granite base of coal, ...	160 feet.	140 feet of it.
	837½ feet.	

The coke seams is not represented in the Midlothian mines, except by slates with bony coal.

TO BE CONTINUED.

The "Purgatory" Iron Property, Botetourt Co., Va.

By Prof. J. L. CAMPBELL

HARRISON ROBERTSON, ESQ.

Dear Sir;—At the request of Maj. Charles S. Carrington, I have recently examined with care all the points important in forming a proper estimate of the natural advantages and resources of your Purgatory property, in regard to its geographical position; its geological features, as far as they relate to the position, quantity and quality of its ores, limestones, &c.; the facilities it has for the mining and transportation of its ores; its supply of timber suitable for lumber and charcoal; the natural and well located site it has for furnaces and buildings of any kind; and, finally, its contiguity to a regular line of railway transportation.

Following the outline thus suggested, I propose to give a concise but somewhat detailed description of the property, with an account of what I conceive to be elements of value of no ordinary character.

Position.—By reference to the accompanying map it will be seen that the southern point of your tract of land lies within a few hundred yards of the line of the Richmond & Alleghany Railroad, and about one mile west of Buchanan. From that point its eastern boundary is chiefly along the crest of Purgatory Mountain for about 8 miles. The line then follows the general direction of a short spur connecting Purgatory and Mays' mountains and passes over to the western base of Mays' Mountain, then it turns towards the southwest and south and embraces a considerable area along the west flank of that mountain, until it reaches Roaring Run near its mouth. Thence it turns directly down that Run to its mouth, and then, after following James River for a short distance, it strikes off for half a mile in a northeasterly direction, then it again turns southward and, by a zigzag course, returns to the southern starting point. Thus we see that it embraces all the western slope of Purgatory Mountain and nearly the whole of Mays' Mountain, and also the trough-like valley of Roaring Run lying between those ranges, it also includes a large area of forest land west of the southern half of Purgatory Mountain,—the whole tract covers 5,120 acres.

If Mays' Mountain had its original southward extension, which no doubt was to the River, the two mountains would enclose a canoe-shaped valley through the bottom of which Round Mountain has been thrust upward. But the southern portion of Mays' Mountain has been carried away by the denuding forces of nature, and the Valley limestones have thus been stripped of their original mountain covering, and rendered easy of access for future use. At the same time Purgatory and Mays' mountains may both have extended far to the south of the River.

While a large portion of your tract lies upon the faces of the mountains above mentioned, and is quite rugged in its features, there are also large areas in the valley between the two mountains, and on the outer slopes of the ridges, which consist of long spurs and rounded hills separated by ravines, many of which are traversed by streams of pure mountain water—all running towards the river. The largest of these streams is Roaring Run, which rises about four miles from the river, in the loop of Purgatory and Mays' mountains, and flows down the valley between these ridges until it reaches the southern terminus of Mays' Mountain where it turns abruptly to the west through a deep gorge by which Rich Hill is cut off from the main ridge, and empties its water into the James.

Roaring Run is an important feature of the property, in view of its being extensively utilized in future as a water-power and for washing iron ores.

Nearly the whole of this large tract of land is covered with virgin forest. The lands surrounding it have been extensively cleared, and are now under cultivation; but it has been but slightly culled here and there and its woodlands remain mostly untouched. The timber thus abounding is adapted to the preparation of various kinds of lumber and to the extensive burning of charcoal for furnaces whenever demanded.

The Geology of this region presents a problem hitherto but partially solved, so far as I know; it was therefore a subject of absorbing interest to my mind, viewed not only from a scientific stand-point, but also with reference to its practical bearing upon the relative ages, and hence the probable extent and character of the beds of ore that are found cropping out so extensively along the sides and bases of its mountain ridges.

If we give to Prof. Rogers' brief account of the ores of Purgatory Mountain (Report of 1838) the most obvious interpretation it will bear, we must conclude that he regarded them as belonging to his No. III formation.

[*Note*—In this report the several geological formations are distinguished by the *notation* and *names* employed in Dana's Manual of Geology, in Le Conte's Geology, and by Prof. Rogers himself in Macfarlane's Geological Guide, while the corresponding notation formerly used by Rogers in his Virginia Reports is inserted in parentheses. It is best for us all to become familiar with the *general system* of notation now in very extensive use among our best geologists.]

Rogers says (page 19, Report of 1838):—"The Purgatory Mountain commencing in Camp Mountain, displays for some distance south the regular synclinal structure, formation IV (5 a. Dana) resting on III (4 Dana), and both rocks on the western side dipping to the east, and on the eastern to the west. The dips becoming gentler as we trace the mountain southward, the usual trough-like capping of IV (5 a. Dana) ceases to be exhibited about 6 miles above the termination of the ridge. Here and for some distance towards the south the summit of the mountain presents the upper slates of III (4 c. Dana) with a small and broken remnant of the lowest band of IV—and it is at the junction of the two that exist those ample beds of iron ore, from which the Etna and Retreat furnaces were formerly supplied."

Now it is entirely true, as I discovered from observation and learned from old residents of the neighborhood, that there are "ample beds of iron ore from which the Etna and Retreat furnaces were formerly supplied,"—that ore is at the junction of 4 c. and 5 a. (III and IV R.). But I also discovered, from a careful survey of the whole region, that these same furnaces, at a more recent date, procured still better and more abundant ores from the eastern slope of Mays' Mountain, but from the shales of 5 b. c. (V R.) overlying, geologically, both the formations 4 and 5 a. (III and IV R.).

This formation, 5 a. (No. V R.) is one of the most important iron-bearing ones in Virginia, and nowhere in the State have I seen its ores more largely developed than on the western flank of Purgatory, and on both flanks of Mays' Mountain, so far as these ridges face each other.

The position of the ore beds of this region, as well as their extent, will be better understood and more highly appreciated after a careful inspection of the map and section. The broken red lines on the map follow the outcroppings of the ore beds, and the chief openings that have already been made in them.—A simple inspection is enough to indicate their great extent and continuity.

It is evident, from the position of Roaring Run and tributaries, that all the ores from the northern half of the property can be readily transported by a down grade to a furnace at the mouth of that stream; and that from the southern portion they can also be brought to the railway by descending grades.

The Geological Section accompanying the map is to be viewed as a vertical plane resting upon the line E.—W. of the map, which is supposed to lie 500 feet below the bed of the river. The plane of section is then represented as rising 2,000 feet higher than the line on which it rests, or 2,500 feet above mean tide, and as cutting all the rocks of Mays' and Purgatory mountains and their foot-hills on both sides.

Beginning our examination at the eastern base of Purgatory, we find first the beds of hard limestone of the Great Valley 3 b. c. (II R.) lying beneath the softer and more fissile limestones of 4 a. (Trenton,) and these again passing beneath the shales and shaly sandstones of 4 b. c. (III R.) that form a large portion of the eastern slope of the mountain.—In these are the ores that are found

on the eastern face of Purgatory. At a point a little south of Cartmell's Gap these shales have been pushed up to such a height that they now constitute the most elevated knob of the mountain, while masses of the heavy sandstones of 5 a. (IV R.) have been thrown off from the crest on both the west and east faces. Resuming our examination of the section we find Purgatory Mountain capped with the heavy sandstones of 5 a. (IV R.) which here, and as far north as the junction of the two mountains, have at first moderate and afterwards an increasing dip towards the west, evidently passing beneath the valley of Roaring Run. Against the western slope of these beds of sandstone rest the beds of shales and the lighter beds of sandstones of 5 a., carrying rich and extensive beds of iron ore, and some promising indications of manganese.

Directing our attention to the section where it cuts Mays' Mountain, we have only to visit the gorge cut directly through it by Roaring Run to see a natural series of arches of 5 a. b. (IV and V R.), not unlike those at Clifton Forge, though not on so grand a scale. The section cuts the same arches a little farther north, but at a point where the mountain evidently has the same anticlinal structure. This remarkable form of the ridge with the iron-bearing shales of 5 b. (Clinton) flanking it on both sides, accounts for the extensive lines of outcroppings and openings along its spurs and foot-hills.

At the western base of the arch of Mays' Mountain the strata of sandstone have been pushed over westward until they are nearly vertical—thus presenting another point of anology to the arch at Clifton Forge—but they soon appear again, in the ravines west of the ridge, in a nearly horizontal position, with the shales of 5 b. resting upon them.

Between Mays' Mountain and Round Mountain there is a short abrupt displacement of strata, a "fault," by which Trenton limestones, 4 c. (III A. R.) are brought to the surface on the eastern side of the creek, while the sandstones and shales of Mays' Mountain abut against the limestones, appearing, in fact, to dip beneath them from the western side. Similar irregularities of uplift though of less extent, are not unfrequent in this region; these ought to be carefully studied, as they often give the ore beds an *apparently* abnormal position; as in the case of Round Mountain, the western slope of which consists of the uplifted shales of 4 b. c. (III R.) while on its eastern slope we find the beds of ore that correspond to those on the eastern slope of Mays' Mountain, belonging to No. 5.

South of Cartmell's Gap and Round Mountain the western side of the ancient mountain trough has been swept away by the great floods, perhaps of the Glacial Period, which cut off a considerable part of Mays' Mountain, that as before stated, once extended far south of its present terminus. Here the mountain sandstones and most of the shales, as well as the iron ores, have been carried away, while the underlying limestones are left to form productive soils. Still, however, a very considerable belt of iron ores is left along the western and southern slopes and foot-hills of Purgatory. The exact geological position of these has not been fully determined in every case. Some of them appear to belong to 4 c. (III R.), while others are probably in 5 b.—This latter formation has frequently *two* workable beds running parallel to each other; and in some places, as at the Karnes bank, inversions of the strata have been caused by a strong westward thrust of the mountain.—This tendency to a westward inversion prevails throughout the whole of the Apalachian ranges in Virginia.

These geological details are important for showing the relative position of the several ore beds; at the same time they indicate the almost entire certainty of their continuity, wherever the geological structures continue unbroken. Then the extent, number, and thickness of the several beds thus determined, afford a basis for calculating the quantity of ore within a given range; while the positions of the lines of outcrop indicate the facility with which mining may be conducted.

Quantity of Ore.—I never undertake to calculate with absolute certainty the quantity of ore in any tract like this, unless numerous and extensive exposures of the several beds have been made. But, from the topographical and geological features already given, we may very safely conclude that you have here vast quantities of ore.

Viewing first only what lies north of a line joining the mouth of Roaring Run and Cartmell's Gap, embracing to that extent the western base of Purgatory and the whole of Round and Mays' mountains,—you have at least three and sometimes four continuous beds, with an average length of four miles or more, giving an aggregate extent of at least 12 miles. Where these beds have been opened, as indicated on the map, they are from 6 to 10 feet thick, or *wide*, as it is often expressed. You will be entirely safe, I think, in taking 7 feet as the mean thickness of these several beds. The dip of nearly all of them is high, ranging from 45° to 65°, while in some places they are nearly vertical.

From the foregoing data it requires but a simple calculation to determine the quantity of ore within the reach of mining operations. Suppose, for example, you open only one mile (5,280 feet) of one of these beds 7 feet thick of good ore, and you work to the depth of 50 feet down the slope, you will have 5280 x 7 x 50=1,848,-000 cubic feet of ore. But you can easily increase this quantity ten fold within an area from which the ores can be conveniently transported by tramways to an admirable furnace site on the margin of the River at the mouth of Roaring Run, as more fully described further on.

Then you have along the western base of Purgatory, south of Cartmell's Gap, and on the southern end of the mountain where it slopes off towards the river, evidences of other deposits of ore, both numerous and extensive, the products of which can be easily carried down to the adjacent railroad.

Convenience of Mining.—The situation of all the beds, being on the slopes of the mountain ridges, makes the approach to them convenient, with moderate labor, either by open cut or tunnel; and the mining properly conducted may, for many years at least, be kept free from the annoyances of accumulating water by the simplest kind of drainage.

A tramway, or narrow-gauge railway, could be run up the west side of Roaring Run, with short branches to Round Mountain, and to the Karnes and other contiguous banks that may be opened, and continued, as future demands arise, till it reaches the old Retreat banks in the loop of the mountains. The main stem with its branches would not be more than 6 or 7 miles long. A glance at the map will at once show what a vast quantity of ore would be reached by such a line—the nearest beds being within half a mile of the furnace site. But there would be no necessity for constructing the whole of the line at once. Two or three miles of it would reach ore enough to supply a furnace for many years.

The quality of the ores is superior, not only from their richness in metallic iron, but also on account of their freedom from sulphur, and the very low percentage of phosphorus found in them. I analyzed samples from three beds, remote from one another and so situated as to give a fair mean of the whole, except that the Mays bank is not yet fairly opened, and I have no doubt but that it will prove to be richer in iron at greater depths. These ores all belong to the class known as "Limonite" or "Brown Hematite."

Examined with reference to Iron, Phosphorus and Sulphur, the following are the results of the three analyses made:

	Retreat Bank.	Karnes Bank.	Mays Bank.
Metallic Iron,	54.850	56.550	41.800
Phosphorus,	0.085	0.112	0.094
Sulphur,	A trace.	A trace.	A trace.

Besides the oxygen and combined water, which are necessary constituents of all ores of this class, the foreign matter is chiefly *clay*, with a small percentage of lime and very little silica. The ores are, moreover, sufficiently soft and vesicular to be reduced in the furnace with great facility.

These results indicate a high percentage of iron, a very low percentage of phosphorus, and almost entire freedom from sulphur.

It is not surprising, therefore, that some of these same ores, when formerly worked in the old Retreat Furnace, produced a quality of iron that ranked high in market—as I have been credibly informed.

Limestone, suitable for fluxing in the furnaces, for building stone and for the manufacture of lime, is abundant in the neighborhood, and may be quarried with great facility at numerous points along the line of the R. & A. RR.

The masses of sandstone exposed where Mays' Mountain is cut by Roaring Run afford a most valuable building material for the construction of furnace stacks, for the foundations of houses, for chimneys, and for structures of all kinds requiring the most durable material.

The Timber on this property constitutes one of its valuable features. Oaks of different kinds, suitable for fencing, for railroad ties, and other purposes are very abundant; while tulip-poplar, pitch-pine, ash, walnut and hickory are found in sufficient abundance to more than meet the demands likely to arise for these classes of timber. For coaling, in case you wish to run a charcoal furnace, the supply of wood is large. An unbroken forest covers the greater part of the whole tract.

Coke, from New River or Kanawha, of superior quality, can be brought to this point by rail at a very moderate cost. Thus you can have your choice of fuel, and manufacture, either charcoal iron, which generally commands a high price, or coke iron which is made at less cost; or, by erecting two furnaces, you can make both classes of metal at the same time. By such an arrangement you could readily adapt your operations to the demands of the iron market.

The Furnace Site.—The denuding forces, that have left their marks so distinctly defined along this portion of the James River Valley, have carved out two natural terraces adjacent to the mouth of Roaring Run, both above high-water mark, the upper one rising abruptly for 30 or 40 feet above the lower, as if the latter had been designed for the location of one or more furnace stacks, while the former was to be the platform from which the furnaces could, with the aid of bridges, be most conveniently fed. The lower terrace is but little above the level of the turnpike and the railway, while the upper one may be easily reached by railway line or wagon road.

The water of the creek, by a small dam at its fall in the gorge of the mountain, can be conveniently brought to the furnace, by race and trunk, so as to make a fall of 40 or 50 feet available for producing blast or for working machinery.

Around this furnace site you have more than 70 acres of land well suited for buildings of any description, and for cultivation; while the quantity can be greatly increased, if found desirable, by the purchase of adjacent lands, now offered for sale at moderate prices. In fact there is room here, and the location is very appropriate, for a manufacturing village of considerable extent. By reference to the accompanying map it will be seen that by means of a "turnout," a little over two miles in length, on the R. & A RR., the line of that road could be made to pass the furnace site, and thus furnish most ample facilities for the transportation of coke, and supplies of every kind to the furnace, and for carrying away the metal produced. It might be well in this connection to note the additional fact that when the Valley Railway is completed its line will pass within a few hundred yards of the southern limit of this property, and thus afford a competing line of transportation.

Summary.—Let us now take a general survey of what has been presented.

(1) It is evident that the topographical and geological features of this tract indicate continuity and therefore great extent of ore beds.

(2) While the ores are practically inexhaustible in quantity, their analyses show that they are superior in quality.

(3) The convenience for the mining and transportation of these ores is rarely surpassed.

(4) Limestones and sandstones are abundant and easily quarried.

(5) The large area of unbroken forest will yield coal enough to make many thousand tons of charcoal iron.

(6) The site proposed for furnaces is within convenient reach of ores, fuel and flux, and will have, near at hand, lines of transportation ample for all demands.

It is my candid opinion that no practical man can make a careful and impartial survey of this property, as I have done, and say that I have given an exaggerated representation of its natural resources and advantages   Yours very truly.

          J. L. CAMPBELL,

          Prof. Chemistry and Geology.

Washington and Lee University, Sept., 1880.

Correspondence.

OFFICE OF THE N. Y. AND VA. IRON AND COAL CO.,

        BUFFALO GAP, VA., Oct. 18, 1880.

Maj. Jed. Hotchkiss,

My Dear Sir:—In accordance with my promise to report to you when our furnace went into blast, I have the pleasure of stating that at sunrise, Sept. 25, Capt. D. P. McCorkle, Gen. Supt. of the Co., Mr. Wm. S. King our furnace Manager and myself fired up the furnace. At 8 A. M. of the 26th, blast was put on, and, for the past 17 days we have cast regularly, making in that time 174 tons of fine iron.

We are working our furnace cautiously, increasing the burden gradually. As you well know this furnace has had some mishaps, but owing entirely to incompetent furnace managers. The present manager, Mr. King, has been successful beyond our expectations.

The make so far has been principally from ore from the company's land which analyses from 51 to 55 per cent., and is *superior to any ore in our vicinity.* The furnace could not work better. I hope you will soon come out and see us and we will show you one of the most valuable properties, for its extent, in the state.

     Yours most truly,

         HENRY J. ROGERS, V.-Pres.

We learn from Capt. McCorkle that they are now using (at Buffalo Gap furnace) 1050 lb. charges, using 250 lbs. of ore from the Phillip's bank, in Valley limestone, in connection with the Buffalo Gap ores, and 40 per ct. of limestone, which they will reduce to 35. So far 2, tons of ore have made one ton of iron.—ED.

The Tariff.—"Virginia wants a tariff on ores, not on iron. Her ores need protection, not her metals.—We want capital here to develop our resources. We do not want capital protected and encouraged in other places at our expense."—*The Advance,* Lynchburg, Va.——Protection, and a plenty of it, we want on metals also, so that capital can be induced to come here and make the metals. Capital will not "plant" itself unless it is protected. Go and ask the great capitalists who have invested at Low Moor, and given to Virginia her first great modern iron furnace, if they would have "planted" over a half million dollars there if they had not been satisfied, not only that "protection protects," but that it will continue. All the iron works would have been broken up in the "drop" of a few months ago but for the "brake" of "duty" on foreign iron. —You cannot "Advance" that way; Lynchburg is to be an *iron city,* so no half-way tariff notions, good neighbor. Read again what Gen. Hancock has just written:—

"*I am too sound an American to advocate any departure from the general features of a policy that has been largely instrumental in building up our industries and keeping Americans from the competition of the underpaid labor of Europe.*"

The Danville and New River RR., (narrow-guage) is in process of rapid construction into Henry county, under Major Sutherlin, its untiring president. It has been decided that the present terminus of the road shall be so located at Martinsville, the county seat of Henry county, that when the proper time comes the road can be extended westward. It is expected that it will before long reach the iron region of Patrick county.

"THE VIRGINIAS uniformly maintains its interesting features as a mining, industrial and scientific journal of a good order.— The September number, a valuable one, has been received."— *Spirit of Jefferson,* Charlestown, W. Va.

The Chesapeake & Ohio Railway has purchased some 700 acres of land at Newport's News, on the magnificent harbor of Hampton Ronds, 6 miles southwest from Fortress Monroe, the entrance to Hampton Roads, and but 24 miles, by the ship channel, from the Atlantic at the mouth of Chesapeake Bay. The Chesapeake & Ohio will be immediately extended down The Peninsula to this deep-water terminus, most probably from near Atlee's station, 10 miles north of Richmond, by a line 80 miles long, following the York-James watershed, without crossing a single stream of water, and by grades of from 10 to 30 ft. to the mile, since Atlee's is 201 ft. above tide and the banks at Newport's News are about 21. This will make the C. & O. a road 500 miles long from Hampton Roads to the Ohio at Huntington.

We have always contended that Newport's News was the only proper terminus for this great Virginian and at the same time trans-continental railway, because at no other point can it find convenient and accessible storage and harbor room for the vast outgoing and incoming traffic that, beyond the slightest question, it will have. President Huntington has displayed his usual sagacity in this purchase and fixing of a seaboard terminus. Since he gave his personal attention to the completion of the Chesapeake & Ohio as a through line, he has, in a few months nearly completed it, and now has the cars running to Ashland, Kentucky; and the work is so well under way that by the end of the year it will be finished to Mount Sterling and a connection with the entire railway system of the West. And now he will push the construction of the eastern end—a comparatively easy task over the Tidewater plain—so that, as we predicted months ago, the gathering to the great and last centennial of the Revolution, the Yorktown celebration a year hence, from the Bay of San Francisco to that of the Chesapeake, across Virginia's ancient from sea-to-sea territory, will be by the *through* Chesapeake & Ohio Railway.

In this connection it may be well to emphasize the significance of this Chesapeake & Ohio terminal conclusion by quoting (from Hotchkiss' Physiography of Virginia, p. 126. now in press), the following:—"*The Hampton Roads* expansion of the James, the widening of this river for 11 miles from its mouth upward, in a broad, irregular oval with numerous tidal arms, is one of its most remarkable features; it is also one of the most noteworthy and important features of the eastern coast of the United States, since it forms the largest and most central and commodious land-locked harbor on that coast. This great roadstead is bounded north by the 8 miles of shore between Old Point Comfort and Point Newport's-news, and south by the more than 24 miles of shore between Point Willoughby and Ragged-island Point. It varies in breadth from 2.4 miles at the mouth and some 4.3 between points Newport's-news and Ragged-island, Newport's-news and Pig, Newport's-news and Sewall's, and Comfort and Sewall's, to 8.5 in a north and south course, between the mouths of Hampton Creek and Elizabeth River. Its area is about 400 square miles, or 256,000 acres; some 150 square miles of this, in a continuous belt 11 miles long and from 1 to 2 miles wide, has a depth ranging from 18 to 80 ft. at mean low water, which includes but a single tract, some 200 acres, Newport's-news Middle Ground, having less than 18 ft.,—that having from 12 to 18; this is bordered on each side by belts, having from 12 to 18 feet of depth, that occupy 35 square miles; and these, in turn, by wide belts, in which the depth is from 6 to 12 ft., occupying 160 square miles;—hence, this great anchorage has some 345 square miles of available ship room."

These facts of the condition of this great harbor—the first settled upon in the Union and erelong to be the most resorted to—will be more appreciated if we turn to the U. S. Coast Survey Report for 1871 and read what it says are the requirements of a *great harbor*, requirements that but very few can fill. It says:—"Roominess of length and breadth, in channelways, roadsteads and harbors, is scarcely less important than depth where a trade is to be accommodated that requires fleets of shipping,—for navigable facilities do not vary in proportion to tides and depths. A first-class ship requires a half mile, and a medium sized schooner 600 feet of way, or sea-room, when beating to windward, and in a straight channel steamers and vessels in tow of steam-tugs must have at least 100 feet. In anchorage 2.7 acres of swing-room, beyond the 18-feet curve, are needed for each ship of a coasting fleet, and 32 acres, in

not less than 10 fathoms of water, for a man-of-war,—some of the latter take 44 acres."

"The draught of sailing vessels, taking the registry at Lloyd' for a guide, is over 20 feet for about one-third of all afloat, and over 16 feet for 95 per cent. Of large sailing ships 16 per cent. draw 24 feet and over, while of barks only 3 per cent. draw over 16 feet. Coast-wise, coal-loaded steamers usually draw 16 feet, and coal-loaded schooners 12 feet; the average draught of merchant schooners is only 10 feet, and that of fishing vessels is less."—So, in one or another of the large areas of different depths in Hampton Roads, the largest *fleets* of any class of vessels can have "anchorage" and "swing" room without occupying or obstructing the great channel-ways.

Coke.—At Stone-cliff, on the Chesapeake & Ohio Railway, 116 miles east of Huntington on the Ohio, on Monday, Oct. 11th, the incline to the mine of the Fayette Coal & Coke Co., of which George F Stone of New York is President, was completed and the coke ovens were fired. This company under the management of George W. Bramwell, M. E., has in the last six months built up a neat mining village—now a P. O. and R'y station named for its president, Stone-cliff; opened a coal mine in the New River or Lower Coal Measures, built an incline and 60 first-class beehive coking ovens. It will, at present, make 60 tons a day of 48-hour coke, all of which will be taken by the New York Iron & Steel Co. at its works at Ironton, Ohio. The natural sources of supply of coals, coke and iron ores for the Ohio Valley are in W. Va. and Va., and it is gratifying to be able to record the completion of such arrangements as this between Stone-cliff and Ironton in the inauguration of the coke movement. Whenever the superior character of the Lower Measure cokes become known they will, beyond question, be preferred to any others.

The Virginia Midland RR., officially the Washington City, Virginia Midland & Great Southern, by a recent decree of the Court of Appeals of Va., is to be sold as a whole, the main line and all its branches, to satisfy the claims of its bondholders. This sale, which will probably be made in a few weeks, will convey the 384 miles of railway extending from Alexandria to Danville, via Lynchburg, including the new connecting road known as the Charlottesville & Rapid-Anne, recently completed, the 9 miles of road from Orange C. H. to Gordonsville, the 5 miles of the Warrenton Branch, and the 103 miles of the old Manassas Gap RR., 63 miles of which, from Manassas to Strasburg, is now the Manassas Branch of the Va. Midland, and 30 miles, from Strasburg to Harrisonburg is part of the Valley RR. branch of the Baltimore & Ohio—about 430 miles in all, with all the appurtenances of the road. The Valley portion will, it is most likely, be sold subject to the 99 year lease of the Baltimore & Ohio

The James River Steel, Mining and Manufacturing Co. is now working 75 men at its works above Lynchburg, Va. It is turning out a superior class of rails for the street railway in process of construction at Lynchburg. The *Lynchburg Virginian*, of Oct. 13, says:—

A large number of rails are being shipped to the city from the Rolling Mills, and track-laying for the street railway is progressing as rapidly as possible. These are the first street railway rails ever made in the South—and they are pronounced by judges as being of a very superior quality—which speaks well for this new enterprise in southern industry.

Marble.—*The Valley Virginian* reports the discovery of a "valuable and extensive vein of variegated marble" on the land of Col. John Lewis Peyton near this place. Steps have already been taken to test the character of the quarry and to have slabs of the marble polished. By our next issue we hope to be able to report favorably on this "find."—The Valley is a great limestone region and there is no reason why good marble should not be found here.

The Elizabeth, Lexington and Big Sandy RR., the westward extension of the Chesapeake & Ohio is now completed for 30 miles from Huntington; 16 miles of new road down the Ohio to Ashland, Ky., and 14 miles thence to the Rush coal mines by a RR. already constructed. The remaining gap of 64 miles to make a connection a Mt. Sterling with the western railway system will soon be completed

Dan River is being improved, by a party in charge of Capt. Averill of the U. S. Engineers, under an appropriation from the General Government. It is proposed to make it navigable for small steamers.

Continued from Page 153.

The geological position of the ore of the following extract is not known, as its locality is not given, but it is probably in No. I, as the counties named have their common line in that.—

"Iron ore of a very peculiar character is found in Grayson and Wythe, &c., yielding in some cases by the usual smelting process a metal having all the qualities of steel. The composition of this ore, now not known, would throw great light on this interesting result, and might enable those engaged in the iron works of the country, to secure a uniform production of this more valuable metal, instead of being subject to the capricious results of having cast iron at one time, and at another, without any apparent reason, a superior quality of steel." [47–1835.]

"This rock (Potsdam, or No. I) has in many places been found to contain beds of iron ore, though in general of inferior quality to that met with in the limestones of The Valley." [9–1837.]

"At the junction of these sandstones (No. I) with the limestone of The Valley, deposits of iron ore are occasionally to be found which, although sometimes of a good quality, is often blended with oxide of manganese." [15–1837.]

"This formation (No. I) in Virginia is exclusively confined to the western slope of the Blue Ridge and the narrow belt of rugged hills and mountains extending thence to the commencement of the Valley limestone. Its chief importance in an economical point of view arises from the extensive deposits of valuable iron ore which it contains. These are mostly found high among the reddish shales and therefore near the margin of the limestone." [6–1838.]

"But by far the most important materials associated with the strata of this formation (No. I) are its *iron ores*, which are both rich and of inexhaustible extent. These, as formerly stated, are chiefly confined to the slaty rocks next to formation II. Although another ore, generally of inferior quality, but which has sometimes been worked, is occasionally met with among the silicious strata farther east. Of the importance of the ferriferous bands of this formation, it is hoped more just ideas will be entertained upon duly considering the preceding descriptive account of the continuous extent of the formation itself, as well as the further and more local details which follow.

In tracing the slates in question longitudinally throughout the whole length of The Valley, fragments of iron ore and other indications of the existence of valuable beds of this material are of frequent occurrance—not only in the vicinity of the mines which are or have been actually resorted to, but at innumerable other points, the heavy covering of stony debris from the mountain being the chief cause of the concealment of the massive deposits themselves.

The most northern point at which this ore is mined for the purpose of manufacture is in the neighborhood of the Shenandoah Iron Works. Near the Page and Rockingham line, it is procured from the shales adjacent to the limestone along the base of the ridge called Fox's Mountain, composed of formation I. It is here found in great abundance, and is well adapted to the furnace. This ore is a hydrated peroxide of iron, generally compact and close grained, and exhibiting a smooth fracture. In some specimens it has the mammilary and stalactitic character, and not unfrequently presents on its freshly exposed surfaces a beautiful play of the prismatic colors. For its chemical composition, as well as that of the ores of other localities hereafter noticed, I would refer to a succeeding section of the present report.

From this point southward to the neighborhood of Mount Torrey, in Augusta county, no ore banks are known to have been opened—although at numerous points along the eastern margin of the shales of formation I unequivocal indications of good ore are to be met with. At the locality just mentioned, the remains of a furnace are to be seen, the ore for which was supplied, at least in part, from the same formation. Mount Torrey is itself a mass of the white sandstone, flanked towards the west by the shales which are here of little width and soon give place to the Valley limestone.

From Mount Torrey the ore appears to continue almost uninterruptedly along the margin of The Valley to a point S. E. of the Cloverdale Furnace in Botetourt county, and is mined to some extent in several places for the supply of the contiguous furnaces. At the Cotopaxi works, situated on the head waters of South River (of the James), and immediately at the western base of the white sandstone, flanking the Blue Ridge, the massive white sandstone of I is seen in vertical or inverted sheets forming the western faces of these broken and pointed ridges, while a little west occur the shales, the repositories of the ore, with a south-eastern dip, and as usual, still more towards the west, the limestone. This ore, which is a hydrated peroxide, is irregularly stratified and remarkably various in its character—in some bands being quite soft and argillaceous, in others almost pulverulent, and in others again, nodular, or solid and compact.

The ore continues to show itself on the surface at intervals as we proceed in a southerly direction skirting The Valley, and is found mingled in considerable quantity with the fragments of sandstone along the flanks of the hills situated immediately to the south of Buchanan.

Along the waters of Back Creek, to the south and west of this point, the exposures of ore become numerous and highly interesting. The shales containing the iron, begin here to assume a character very commonly presented by them as they continue their course still further towards the S. W., that of *blending* with the limestone by numerous alternations of the shaly and calcareous rock. The ore is found in a line of hills consisting of these mingled rocks, separated from the Blue Ridge by a valley of about three-quarters of a mile in width, and extending in a broken form from about one mile east of Back Creek to within two miles of Cloverdale Furnace, being in all a distance of about 9 mile. The summits and western slopes of these hills consist in great part of a deposit of the hydrated peroxide of iron, brown and black, with some hematitic surfaces. The whole surface seems to be covered with the ore, projecting frequently in large masses. The soil is highly ferruginous and little or no rock associated with the ore. As well as could be judged the breadth of this highly ferriferous belt is about three-fourths of a mile, and as already mentioned, its length about 9 miles.

A little nearer the Blue Ridge than the preceding, there occurs another variety of ore, associated with the sandstones of formation I. This is well seen at Bear Knob, and in a hill about one mile east of Mr. Wood's. Along the western base of Bear Knob, are seen disintegrating sandstones and slaty rocks, with a S. E. dip. These continue to the opposite side, though with a larger admixture of the sandstone, and at the summit of the ridge the ore occurs. The hill, near Mr. Wood's, consists of siliceous sandstone, sometimes white, though generally ferruginous and containing the ore in beds. Along its base, we meet with the ore in large masses associated with the sandstone. It is also scattered profusely over the western declivity, generally in fragments of great size. This ore is hematitic, and closely resembles that of the shales of the same formation. Higher up the hill towards the summit sandstone prevails again, associated with iron, and containing crystallized quartz coating chalcedony in a stalactitical

arrangement. The supply of ore to be obtained from this ridge would be abundant, but the quality is such as to produce a cold share metal, better suited for castings than for bar iron.

The continuation of formation I. along the southern margin of The Valley in the counties of Roanoke, Montgomery, Floyd, Wythe, Smyth and Washington, is accompanied by similar ore, and judging by the indications upon the surface, and some of the more important exposures which have been observed, in quantities not less abundant than in some of the favored districts heretofore noticed. At present however little or no use is made of any but the limestone ores of that region, nor indeed does it appear that the other ores have ever been resorted to, unless, perhaps, for a partial supply at the old Poplar Camp Furnace. In Carter county, Tenn., it is understood they are extensively applied, and it is hoped, that they may be made equally available at some future day to the growing enterprise of the neighboring portion of our state.

The brief view that has now been given of the continuity of this iron-bearing series of rock, bordering our Great Valley on the east throughout its entire length, is calculated largely to add to our estimate of the manufacturing resources of The Valley. For although numerous localities of the ore have long been known and resorted to, it is only by the evidence of this continuity derived from a careful geological examination that just views of the extent of this item of our mineral wealth could be obtained." [11 and 12-1838.]

Analyses of iron ores, before referred to, and remarks on them, were given in the 1838 report. The following are those there classified as "ores of Formation I."—The composition is that of 30 grains; the proportions can be converted into the 100 or per-cent.-form now used, by multiplying them by 3⅓, or, what is the same thing, by dividing by 3 and pointing off one place instead of two for the fractional part.

No.	LOCALITY	Peroxide of Iron	Silica.	Alumina.	Lime-Carb.	Water.	Loss.
1	Fox Mountain	20.60	5.70	0.40 trace		3.00	0.30
2	"	23.93	0.99	1.07	...	3.93	0.38
3	Cotopaxi Furnace	23.57	1.70	0.28	...	4.24	0.21
4	—McCormick's old bank	24.58	1.70 trace		...	3.47	0.23
5	Vesuvius Furnace—Kelly's bank	24.27	3.00 trace		...	2.43	0.30
6	Back Creek—Wood's lower bank	24.18	2.10	0.36	...	3.36	0.21
7	" " upper "	25.00	0.88 trace		...	3.62	0.30

No. 1.—Iron ore from Fox's Mountain 4 miles from Forrer's furnace, Page county. Color dark brick-red or brown, fracture slaty conchoidal, texture uniform, rather fine, earthy, lustre dull, ochreous. Used at Mr. Forrer's furnace.

No. 2.—Iron ore from the same locality. Color very deep brown, lustre shining, texture compact, fracture irregular, sometimes presenting a velvet appearance on the fresh surface. Very valuable in the furnace.

No. 3.—Iron ore from mine worked for the use of Cotopaxi or McCormick's furnace, Rockbridge. Nodular ore. Color on the exterior light ochreous, in the interior dark chocolate brown, texture rather cellular.

No. 4.—Iron ore from McCormick's old bank. Color dark Spanish brown, texture close grained, structure cavernous, fracture splintery. Not now in use.

No. 5.—Iron ore from Kelly's bank, used at Vesuvius furnace. Color rich reddish brown and chestnut, texture compact, though occasionally porous. Surface sometimes mammillary or covered with projecting bosses and lustrous.

No. 6.—Iron ore from Back Creek near Buchanan, James S. Wood's lower bank. Color dark chestnut, texture fine grained, structure cellular, fracture rough.

No. 7.—Iron ore from Back Creek, Wood's upper bank.

Color of exterior dull black, interior dark snuff color, texture fine grained and porous, sometimes mammillary and lustrous, occasionally crystalized." [29-1838.]

Analyses of iron ores are given in the 1840 report. Those of ores from Formation No. I are as follows:—

No.	LOCALITY	Per cent. Met. Iron	Peroxide of Iron.	Alumina.	Lime-Carb. Matter.	Silica & Insoluble Matter.	Magnesia.	Perox. Manganese.	Water.	Loss.
1	Graham's Bank, Wythe Co.	54.94	70.49	0.75	...	8.40	...		11.00	0.30
2	Forrer's " Page "	55.81	70.74	0.75	...	7.67	...		15.58	0.26
3	do " "	52.19	74.56	4.50 trace		5.80	...		15.00	0.14
4	Augusta Co.—from shales	60.10	80.87	trace	...	2.50	...		10.90	0.73
5	Poplar Camp Furnace— Wythe County	50.42	72.04	1.55	...	4.45	...		11.35	0.61

No. 1.—Honeycomb ore, Graham's bank, Reed Creek, Wythe county. Structure somewhat cellular; walls of cells compact and close grained; aspect of surface earthy, of interior slightly resinous; color chestnut brown.

No. 2.—Iron ore from Forrer's bank, Page county. Structure cellular and hematitic, filled with reddish oxide, very tenacious.

No. 3.—Forrer's bank, Page county. Structure hematitic, in slender stalactical columns; color bluish black; spaces between the columns occupied by a rich orange red oxide; lustre resinous and iridescent.

No. 4.—From shales of Formation I, Augusta county. Structure somewhat crystaline; hematitic, compact; color dark chestnut brown.

No. 5.—Iron ore from Poplar Camp furnace, Wythe county. Structure irregular, nodular; close grained, somewhat cellular; color dull brown, without lustre, earthy." [117-1840.]

Lumber.—A West Virginia correspondent writes as follows: David Ward, of Pontiac, Mich., the pine king of that state, after several visits in company with his son to investigate the timber of West Virginia, has begun making purchases of timber tracts in the white pine region of Pocahontas county, which timber is accessible to the Greenbrier River, and will be floated on that stream to Ronceverte, on the Chesapeake & Ohio Railway, where there are three large mills now manufacturing white pine lumber and room for enlarged operations, the demand from the line of the road and eastern markets being largely in excess of their ability to supply. You published, a few weeks since, rates of freight from Ronceverte to eastern points on white pine lumber which now should be corrected as follows:

Ronceverte to	Cents per 100 lbs.
Staunton	.08
Richmond	.12½
Baltimore and Washington, all rail	.25
Baltimore, via Richmond and vessel	.19
Baltimore, via Richmond and steamer	.20¼
Philadelphia, via Richmond and vessel	.22½
Philadelphia, via Richmond and steamer	.24½
New York, via Richmond and vessel	.22½
New York, via Richmond and steamer	.24½
Boston, via Richmond and vessel	.25¾

This is inclusive of all terminal charges at James River wharves. The New York Hoop Company, after experimenting with rented power for several months at Ronceverte, having satisfied themselves of its durability as a place for the manufacture of machine-made hoops, have nearly completed a fine building 60x100 feet, with two large wings and engine room, and are putting up an 80-horse-power engine and upright boilers, and will have 12 to 15 hoop machines soon in operation.—*Northwestern Lumberman, of Chicago, Oct. 16.*

Callie Furnace RR.—A private branch of the Chesapeake & Ohio Ry., of standard gauge, 5.5 miles long, which Hileman, Cook & Co. have for some time been constructing from near Jackson's River station across Rich patch Mountain to their Callie Furnace, was completed Oct. 16th This gives them railway connection to the superior coking coals of New River and opens to market their grand stratified beds of iron ore that is in thickness range from 10 to 50 ft, or even more. Great credit is due to Mr. D. S. Cook, the managing partner, for his untiring energy in overcoming difficulties in constructing this railway.

The Virginia State Agricultural Society holds its 21st. annual fair at Richmond Octobe 26 to 29. The prospects are good for a fine exhibition of the great resources of the commonwealth. Our people are making great progress in the improvement of farm stock of all kinds and the show of horned cattle, horses, sheep, swine, &c., will be an exceptionally good one. Our manufacturers are in a flourishing condition, and the exhibition of their products will be highly creditable, showing articles of unsurpassed excellence and an increased variety. The samples of our mineral wealth that will be gathered there will give some slight idea of our vast and varied undeveloped wealth of that kind. And then, the exhibition of men, women and children will be one worth going far to see, as it always is; for nowhere is raised a nobler and finer crop of humanity than in the Old Dominion, and at no place does it appear to better advantage than at the State Fair.

We had prepared articles on the Tinsalia Co. that has recently been organized to operate in Wise and adjacent counties, in Va.; on the Oxford Ochre Co. that is operating in Page Co., Va.; on the James River Cement Works, and the Buena Vista Iron Mines, Rockbridge Co., Va., and on the Columbia, Liberty and Van Buren furnaces, Shenandoah Co., V.,—all of which, except the first, we have visited in the last month—but they are crowded out of this issue and must await the next. Columbia, Liberty, Van Buren, and Furnace No. 2, in the Shenandoah Valley, are all in blast, making char coal iron. Mr. W. M. Bowron, F. C. S., is now manager at Furnace No. 2, Hon. Wm. Milnes, Jr's. The Ochre Co. and the Cement Co. are actively at work. Amherst Furnace, that uses the Buena Vista ores, is also in blast making charcoal iron.

The Crop Report for all of Virginia for October, as reported by Dr. Pollard its Commissioner of Agriculture in the Monthly Bulletin, is a very favorable one The corn crop—the great staple crop of the State—is 17 per cent. over an average, and the cotton crop, a somewhat important one in the southern counties, Virginia's portion of the cotton-belt, is 5 per cent. over. Tobacco falls short 31 per cent., Irish potatoes about 18 per cent., and sweet potatoes 3 per cent

---

The Purgatory Iron Property that Prof. Campbell so thoroughly and ably describes in this number, presents very great attractions for one desiring to manufacture a high grade car wheel iron, or, in fact, an iron good for almost any purposes. Any one wishing to know more about this very valuable iron estate can address Col. Chas. S. Carrington, Richmond, Va.—We fully endorse what we publish about it.

The Alleghany Coal and Iron Co., the organization of which we have recently mentioned, has purchased from H. C. Parsons, vice-president of the R. & A. RR., several iron ore mines, slate quarries, etc., in Alleghany, Botetourt, Bedford and Buckingham counties, the sale amounting to $150,000.

Bloomery Furnace, Hampshire Co., W. Va., "is now in blast and doing well," writes Mr. John Withers, the Superintendent, Oct. 21, 1880. Mining operations and repairs began January 1st., 1880. It makes charcoal iron.

Real Estates, Water Power, &c.

SALE OF VALUABLE PROPERTY.

Dr. H. S. Eichelberger offers for sale his handsome residence and beautiful farm at Verona, on Valley RR. The farm contains about 120 or 130 acres, and lies on the west side of the Valley pike. The Doctor is willing, if only a small quantity of land is desired, to sell with the residence 15 or 20 acres, which will embrace all the improvements, the finest young orchard in that section, with a spring not excelled for the coldness of the water in the State, with fine dairy attached. This is a rare chance to secure a quiet, lovely home within a ten minutes ride of the city of Staunton, by rail. Its location adapts it well for a summer resort; it is also a good point for a physician. He would invite any one who wishes a quiet, lovely home, free from the noise of city life, to this handsome property For terms, apply to H. S. Eichelberger, Verona, Augusta county, Virginia, or to Elder & Nelson, Staunton, Virginia The Doctor will take pleasure in showing the property.

RESIDENCE IN STAUNTON FOR SALE.

I offer for sale the Residence of Mrs. Virginia B. Donaghe, fronting on three of the principal streets—Main, Lewis and Frederick—in immediate proximity to business, churches, schools, &c. The improvements are first-class, and the property one of the best, if not the very best in the city, either as a home or a speculative investment. It will be subdivided if not sold as a whole. Examination invited.

Terms:—Ten per cent cash, and balance at one, two, and three years, with semi-annual interest

THOMAS D BANSON.

VIRGINIA WATER-POWER AT DANVILLE.

Persons wishing to purchase the splendid Water-power at Danville, Va., can do so on

VERY REASONABLE TERMS.

This is a fine opening for Rolling Mills, Paper Mills, Foundries, &c., &c. Apply in person or by letter to me as the attorney for the owners   E. E. BOUDIN,
Danville, Va.

THE OLD BLACKFORD FORGE PROPERTY,

Including Water-power and Over 600 Acres of Land,

On Hawksbill Creek, Below Luray, Page County, Virginia,

And on line of Shenandoah Valley Railroad, is hereby offered for sale. For terms, etc., address
Lock Box 231, Staunton, Va.

Coal and Coke Dealers.

FIRE CREEK COAL AND COKE COMPANY,

Fire Creek, Fayette Co., West Virginia,

MINERS OF

Red Ash Bituminous Steam Coal,

and manufacturers of Hard Coke. All correspondence should be directed to   M. ERSKINE MILLER,
Sales Agent and Business Manager,
STAUNTON, VA.

W. A. BURKE,
Staunton, Virginia.

Sole Agent for Nuttallburg Coal & Coke.

The best steam coal on the market; coke superior to Connellsville.

Shipper of Kanawha Splint and Gas Coals.
Points of Shipment.—Richmond, Va., and Huntington, West Virginia.

Railways.

THE CHESAPEAKE & OHIO R'Y

Is the Only Route to and via the

White Sulphur Springs and other Most Famous and Fashionable Watering Places of the Mountains of the Virginias.

It is the unparalleled and unapproachable for the wildness, sublimity and picturesque beauty of scenery, and the healing virtues of its health-giving fountains. It is the **Short Line Between the Seaboard and the Great West,** and is second to none in construction, equipment and appliances for the safety and comfort of its passengers

Through Tickets to all Western towns and cities, and excursion tickets to the watering places and summer resorts, are for sale via this line at all principal ticket offices everywhere.
J. C DAME, Southern Agent, Richmond, Va.; H.W. CARR, G. T. Agent, 285 Broadway, New York. CONWAY R. HOWARD, G. P. & T. A., Richmond, Virginia.

Hardware, &c.

A. E. MILLER,
Staunton, Virginia.

Wholesale and Retail Dealer in

Hardware, Cutlery, &c.,

&c., Miners' Tools and Supplies of all descriptions. Orders promptly filled.

HUGH M. McILHANY,
Wholesale and Retail Dealer in

Hardware, Cutlery, &c.,

Augusta St., opp. Court-house,
Staunton, Virginia.

WIRE TRAMWAYS.

The most economical system for the transportation of ores, coal, lumber and agricultural products,—especially adapted for carrying coals from the New River and Kanawha Coal-fields to places of facilities, or across the Rivers to the Railway, in place of bridges. They avoid gradings, cuttings or embankments, are not affected by floods or a tow. Inclines of 1 in 3 are admissable they can be used to transmit power as well as material.
Send for estimates and other information to
THE AMERICAN WIRE ROPE TRAMWAY CO.,
328 Walnut Street, Philadelphia, Pa.

Banks.

H. W. Sheffey, Pres   Davis A. Kayser, Vice-Pres.
W P. Tams, Cashier.

AUGUSTA NATIONAL BANK,
Staunton, Virginia.

Collections in Virginia and West Virginia promptly attended to and remitted on day of payment, at lowest rates of exchange
New York Correspondent . . . . Chemical National Bank.
Baltimore Correspondent, Farmers' and Merchants' Nat'l Bank.
Cincinnati Correspondent . . . Merchants' National Bank.

John Echols, President   Ro W. Burke, Vice-President.
Thos. A. Bledsoe, Cashier.

NATIONAL VALLEY BANK
of Staunton, Virginia.

Designated Depository and Financial Agent of United States.

Capital Stock, $200,000; Surplus and Undivided Profits, $200,000.
New York Correspondent . . . . . . National Park Bank.
New York Correspondent . . . . . Hanover National Bank.
Baltimore Correspondent, Farmers' and Merchants' Nat'l Bank.
Cincinnati Correspondent . . . . . . First National Bank.

Schools.

WASHINGTON & LEE UNIVERSITY.

GEN. G. W. C. LEE, President.

Full courses in Classical, Literary, and Scientific Studies, including those of the professional degrees of Civil Engineering and of Law.
TERMS.—Tuition and other fees in all the Departments $70. Board, Lodging, &c ; per month, from $12 to $20
The next session begins September 16th, 1880, and ends June 22d, 1881.
For other particulars apply to   J. L. CAMPBELL, Jr.,
Clerk of Faculty, Lexington, Va

Newspapers.

THE VALLEY VIRGINIAN,
Staunton, Virginia.

S. M. YOST & SON, Proprietors.

Terms : $2.00 per year.

THE VIRGINIAN is an independent Republican newspaper, devoted principally to the interests of the Great Valley, and Mineral Regions adjacent thereto. Its circulation is larger than that of any other weekly newspaper published in Virginia. As an advertising medium, especially for farming, grazing, and mineral lands, &c., it has no superior. Parties desiring to buy or sell real estate will find it to their advantage to make use of its columns. Specimen copies free.

THE "STAUNTON SPECTATOR,"
129 E. Main Street,
Staunton, Virginia.

The "SPECTATOR" is published every Tuesday morning, at Staunton, Augusta county, Virginia, and is the best advertising medium in the interior of the State.
The "Spectator" was the first paper established at this place, nearly a century ago, and it is now in its 57th volume, under its present title. Its list of subscribers is larger than that of any other paper west of the Blue Ridge, and is, therefore, the best advertising medium in the Valley of Virginia, or in West Virginia. Address
"STAUNTON SPECTATOR,"
Staunton, Virginia.

The Virginias.

A Mining, Industrial and Scientific Journal:
Devoted to the Development of Virginia and West Virginia.

Vol. I, No. 11. }   Staunton, Virginia, November, 1880.   { Price 25 Cents.

The Virginias,

PUBLISHED MONTHLY,

By JED. HOTCHKISS, - - - Editor and Proprietor,

At 346 E. Main St., Staunton, Va.

Terms, including postage, per year, in advance, $2.00. Single numbers, 25 cents. Extra copies, $20.00 per 100. Back numbers, from the first, can be had at 25c each.
Advertising, per inch of length of single column (3 columns to a page, as on advertising pages), one month, $2.50; two months, $3.50; three months, $3.50; six months, $7.50; nine months, $10.00, and twelve months, $12.00; payable in advance.
Specimen Numbers of this journal are sometimes sent to parties supposed to have an interest in the development of the Virginias, or a desire to be informed in reference to their resources, improvement, etc.; they will please consider this an invitation to become subscribers and so help to sustain a paper devoted to their interests.
On sale at Hunter & Co.'s Bookstore, Main Street, Staunton, Virginia.

The University of Virginia offers special inducements and facilities to every young man that would acquire a thorough education. It is not only the leading institution for higher instruction in all the South, but can rightly claim to be the equal of any in the Union in nearly all respects, especially now that its schools of applied science, as natural history, chemistry, etc., are well equipped for training analysts, mining engineers, &c. We invite attention to what Mr. Stuart, the Rector, so well says in reference to its intentions in teaching both theoretical and practical geology and mineralogy, and to the advertisement of Dr. Harrison, the Chairman of the Faculty. The introduction of the "messing system," has made this great and leading institution of learning one of the cheapest also. No young man can have a worthier aspiration than that of being a graduate of the University of Virginia.

Iron Ores.—Mr. —— Horsford, of the Aetna Furnace, of Bridgeport, Ohio, has been examining ore beds near the line of the Ches. & Ohio R'y and has made some conditional leases, looking to supplying that furnace with Va. ores.——Lewis & Gay ship 2 car-loads a day from their Peters' Mt. mine and W. H. Sadler is now working 15 men and will soon work 30 at the "Stack" mine, says the Alleghany Tribune of Nov. 19.——Capt. C. R. Mason has bought 235 A. of ore land on Big Hill, of Lewis Circle for $6,000, and Dr. Hughes and Col. Lowry have bought Milton Armentrout's farm for $3,500. Both these farms are on the line of the Richmond & Alleghany RR., Botetourt Co., Va., and they both contain beds of iron ore.

The "Amherst & Nelson Mining & Transportation Co." has been chartered for the purpose of developing the iron, copper and other mineral resources of Amherst and Nelson counties, and for constructing a railway from Amherst C. H., on the Virginia Midland, by its iron and copper mines, to Greenway, on the Richmond & Alleghany RR.; Thos. Dunlap and Edgar Whitehead are among the corporators.—The Advance.

The New York & Ohio Iron & Steel Co., of Ironton, Ohio, put its furnace into blast Nov. 4. J. H. Bramwell, formerly of the Quinnimont Furnace, W. Va., is the manager. The coke used is from the Co.'s ovens at Stonecliff, Fayette Co., W. Va., on the C. & O. R'y; the ores used are chiefly native, mined from the Co.'s land near Ironton, but some Va. ores, from Alleghany Co., are mixed with them.

Manganese.—P. D. Sutton, of Warminster, Va., has been developing a mine on the lands of Fletcher B. Moore, in Appomattox Co.—The Frank Cabell mine, in Nelson Co., has not been worked since 1877.——Manganese is mined in large quantities on the Franklin narrow-gauge RR., Pittsylvania Co., Va., by Maj. Mason; some 300 men are now employed.—Big Lick News.

Gold.—W. S. Morrow, Supt. of "Morrow Gold Mining Co.," Buckingham Co., Va., writes to the Mining Record that the Howland pulverizer will crush from 1,800 to 2,000 lbs. of his ore, "which is over the average hard," using a 40-mesh screen, per hour; and that the wear of iron is 50 per cent. less than in the stamp mill.

The Allegany Coal & Iron Co. is collecting at the office of the Richmond & Alleghany RR., in Richmond, samples of Virginia minerals. It proposes to sell or lease lands of all kinds. Mr. Wm. H. Barclay is the land agent of the Co.

The Roaring Run Furnace Property, about 10,000 acres of iron land on the eastern slope of Rich-patch Mountain, Botetourt Co., Va.,— which was purchased not long since by J. H. Bramwell, formerly manager of Quinnimont Furnace, W. Va., but now Vice-President and General Manager of the New York & Ohio Iron & Steel Co., Ironton, Ohio,—bids fair to prove one of the leading iron-ore producing properties of that already noted belt of iron mountain ranges. A letter from Mr. Bramwell, of the 2nd. instant, informs us that Mr. Body, who is superintending some mining explorations there, has just opened a new mine with a stratum of ore 14 ft. thick. The "red-shale" and "fossil" ores of the Clinton (No. V.) and the brown hematites of the Oriskany (No. VII.) both exceptionally thick and favorably disposed for mining at a minimum of cost, outcrop for from 4 to 6 miles in the length of this property, and underlie it for a width of from 1.5 to 4 miles. It has a wonderful water-power in an unfailing spring that falls 800 feet in some 2 miles and has volume enough to fill constantly a pipe 2 or 3 feet in diameter. A small charcoal furnace was in blast there up to 1865, making iron noted for its good qualities. The Richmond and Alleghany RR. is now running its trains along this estate and a branch road, 4 or 5 miles long, is in contemplation to reach its fine ore banks and furnace site.

We understand that a large force will be kept at work at Roaring Run during the winter accumulating a large stock of ore, and that it is likely that a charcoal furnace will be started there, in the spring, and forges put up for making charcoal blooms of a high grade which are so much needed in the Ohio mills for boiler plate and the finer grades of charcoal sheet iron.—It is now 15 years since any wood was cut on this estate, so now it can all be coaled over.

Coke.—In an article in the American Engineer on making Bessemer steel-headed rails at Zwickau in Saxony, it is stated that the coke for blast-furnace work in the process is made from coal washed by a Rexroth machine, driven by a 20-horse power engine, at the rate of 35,000 lbs. in 10 hours. The washed coal is placed in two layers in ovens built after the Haldy-Francois system, the bottoms and side walls traversed by channels to get the best advantage of the heat. One oven produces in 48 hours 4,800 lbs. of coke from a charge of 8,700 lbs. of coal, or 55 per cent. in weight, or 90 per cent. in volume.——It is proposed to resume operations at the Antietam Iron-works, Md., and the owners are negotiating to use New River, W. Va., coke.—— Williams & Winans, near Cannelton, W. Va., are now making a first-class coke from Kanawha coals, coke with over 90 per cent. of carbon,—an iron-master skilled in the use of coke so tells us.—W. N. Page, the manager of the Gauley Mountain Colliery, near Hawk's Nest on the C. & O. R'y, has erected two ovens and is now making coke from the coal there mined from the "12 ft." bed.——All the ovens on the C. & O are worked to their utmost capacity, but cannot meet the demand.—Hon. Wm. Milnes, Jr., has begun using New River coke at his Shenandoah Iron-works, Page Co., Va., now that the Shenandoah Valley RR. trains run to his works from the C. & O.; he has been using some Connellsville heretofore.

Richmond & South-western R'y.—Amherst Co., Va. has voted a subscription of $35,000 to this road. The "order of court" fixes the annual tax that will be imposed for this purpose as not to exceed 10 cts. on $100 of valuation; that the road is to cross the county east and west and go north of Tobacco Row Mountains, and to be completed through the county before any bonds are delivered.

W. H. R. (Hon. W. H. Ruffner, of course,) in a letter to the Central Presbyterian of Nov. 2, writing of a visit to Harvard University (Mass.) says: "I met Prof. Shaler; who is the very pattern of a geologist. He is a friendly Kentuckian with a Virginia wife, and is now helping with a grand scheme, which, when carried out, will immensely benefit Virginia, namely the Richmond & Southwestern RR., which is a bona fide affair, but is waiting to increase its means until after the political fever is over. Prof. S. has lately made the state geological survey for Ky., and has geologized not a little in Va. He is one of the most valued professors at Harvard."

Titaniferous iron ores from Canada are now used for one-tenth of the charges at Belfont furnace, Ohio, making No. 1 mill iron. About one per cent. is all of such ores ever used there before.—The day is not distant when furnace men will not only learn to use such ores, but will be glad to get them. Virginia has an abundance of them of a superior quality; they will not spoil on their owners' hands.

The Gold Gravels of North Carolina—Their Structure and Origin.*

BY W. C. KERR, STATE GEOLOGIST, RALEIGH, N. C.

[NOTE.—The following paper is as applicable to the "gold gravels" of Virginia as it is to those of North Carolina, therefore we reproduce it, in full, for the benefit of those interested in developing the same gold belt in its north-easterly extension through Virginia. EDITOR.]

When Agassiz and his party of geologists commenced their exploration of the interior of Brazil and the Amazon region, one of the first and, to the last, one of the most novel and striking phenomena which met them everywhere was the great depth of decomposed or partially decayed rock *in situ*, which mantles, and for the most part conceals, the underlying strata. The same facts strike all geological observers from the North who happen to penetrate the middle and southern latitudes of the Atlantic States. In North Carolina, *s. g.*, the entire middle and western regions, outside of the Quaternary clays, sands and gravels of the East,—that is, all that portion of the State occupied by the Archæan and Mesozoic rocks,—show everywhere this peculiarity, so new to those accustomed to glaciated surfaces. Not only do the hills and slopes, the mountain chains and spurs, present everywhere to the eye this superficial covering, but even the more level tracts and the valleys. The railroad cuts give very good exposures of this covering, and furnish, everywhere, abundant opportunities for the study of its structure and history. Some of the more obtrusive facts are these: the thickness of this covering varies from a few feet to 30 or 40, and often 60 and 75, and even 100 feet, and bears an obvious relation to the character of the underlying rock, being least where this is most refractory, and *vice versa;* the rock is generally nearest the surface in the crests of the hills. The upper portion of this earthy envelop for several feet beneath the soil is homogeneous and structureless; but lines of structure soon make their appearance, becoming more pronounced with the depth. These lines of structure are commonly coincident with bands and ribbons of differently colored earths, which, on closer inspection, show differences in their materials also, these differences becoming more and more strongly marked as they are traced downward, until they pass by insensible gradations into the solid rock beneath. The obvious and necessary conclusion from these observations gives itself, viz., that the rocks of the region are and have long been undergoing a slow chemical decomposition and disintegration from the action of atmospheric forces, this decay being too rapid, however, to be overtaken by the abrasive and transporting power of these same agencies.

So far the general and obvious facts, plain to be read by the man that runs. A little closer inspection reveals another set of facts. It is easily discovered that these mantles of earth and half-decayed rocks are not strictly *in situ*, but have been subjected to some sort and degree of movement, and that the materials have undergone at least a partial rearrangement in certain situations and under certain conditions. In general on the summits of the hills there has been no change, but

Fig. I.

descending the slope, however gentle, a tendency to a sorting and arrangement of materials appears, and this becomes more observable with the distance. At first the fragments of quartz and other hard rocks are sharply angular, and are distributed equally and irregularly through the mass, or in lines corresponding to the bedding of the rocks. Descending a few rods the rock fragments have "settled" somewhat; they are found

*Read at the New York meeting, Feb., 1880, of the American Institute of Mining Engineers.

more thickly strewn towards the bottom, and are less angular. Descending still further all the coarser fragments are found accumulated in a layer of cobbles or pebbles, with only the interstices filled with earth and gravel.

Combining sections of this covering taken from different points, from the hilltop to the bottom of the slope, which commonly terminates in a ravine or valley, or the bed of a stream, we have the appearance shown in Figure 1.

The obvious interpretation of these facts is that there has been a movement or flux of the earthy mass in the direction of the slope. And this notion is confirmed by an occasional observation which is represented in Figure 2.

The difficulty at once arises how to account for a flow of such materials with such results. The ordinary action of flowing water is, of course, excluded. The mere action of gravitation will not account for the phenomena,—slipping and sliding down hill. This, doubtless, happens on very steep declivities, but such cases are easily distinguished. The movements we are considering have taken place at every decree of inclination, from one degree and less upwards, and occasionally on a level, *or even up hill.*

After puzzling over these phenomena for half a dozen years, and wondering that there is no explanation in the books, or

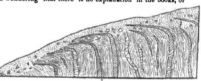

FIG. 2.

even any discussion of the subject or note of the facts, not even in Geikie's *Great Ice Age*, it occurred to me that the only possible solution must be sought in the action of frost. The alternate freezing and thawing of such a mass of earth must needs produce just the effects we have been considering. The earth, saturated with water, in the process of consolidation under the action of cold would, of course, expand just as if it were all water, and in thawing there would be a slight movement of the parts and particles of the mass *inter se*, and of course a settling of the heavier fragments; in other words, the same in kind (though not in amount) as that of a glacier. These masses may be considered earth glaciers. And I have ventured to denominate this group of phenomena, *frost drift.* Now the ordinary glacial phenomena are wanting in North Carolina, with, perhaps, the exception of a few morainal ridges in the gorges of the higher mountains. But during the glacial period, of course, the cold must have been intense enough to account for the depth and extent of action which the theory of *frost drift* supposes.

I was led to these results from the particular study of the gold deposits of the State. They have all been formed in this way. There are probably five hundred square miles of gold drifts in North Carolina. They are found through a range of four hundred miles east and west, from the lower waters of the Roanoke, near Weldon, to the extreme western border, the county of Cherokee. And they belong to all the different subdivisions of the Archæan rocks of the State. The two most extensive deposits are found in the middle region, on the Yadkin and Catawba rivers, among the low ranges and spurs of the mountains. The schistose and slaty rocks, highly inclined and much contorted and dislocated, are in many places penetrated by innumerable small veins and seams of gold-bearing quartz. (See Fig. 3.) In the disintegration and breaking down of these rocks, and the movements of the *debris* in the manner described, it is evident that the gold particles, with the heavier crystalline minerals, will be found accumulated near the bottom of the drifts, on or near the surface of the bed-rock, or "slate," as the miners call it.

The gold mining of modern times began sixty years ago in this region from the accidental discovery of a twenty-eight pound nugget by a boy in one of the streams of this region. Most of the simple and effective appliances now in use every-

Continued on Page 168.

The Mineral Traffic of the Atlantic, Mississippi & Ohio Railroad for July, August and Sept., 1880, in tons of 2,000 lbs., by Col. E. E. Portlock, the Auditor of that road, is given below. The first table is that of Virginia minerals from the line of this railway, giving kinds, quantities, and destination ; the second is the mineral traffic from beyond Bristol, the western terminus of this railway, giving kinds and quantities.

DESTINATION.	Pig Lead.			Barytes.			Copper Ing'ts			Pig Iron.			Zinc Ore.			Coal.			Salt.			Plaster.			Zinc Spelter.			Manganese.		
	July.	August	Sept.	July.	August	Sept.	July.	August	Sept.	July.	August	Sept.	July	August	Sept.	July.	August	Sept.	July.	August	Sept.	July.	August	Sept.	July.	August	Sept.	July.	August	Sept.
Boston		22	10	10	26												12			A						60				
New York	31			134	12	26	31	41	61			47	11			12														
Philadelphia				46	64	125							11	13		12														
Baltimore	23		10	11						771		280	11																16	
Lynchburg										1		12	11	29		22	31	82												
Way Stations																105	934	1266	25	61	80	10	66							
Norfolk																													36	
Richmond	11	67								53		147				1	147													
Va. Midl'd RR.										52		76				513	758	744	25	31	27									
South'rn States												76																		
Total	54	98	20	195	146	221	31	41	31	890	820	530		25		137	955	1266	541	809	929	25	31	93		60			16	
Aggregate for three months		172			567			103			1,950			25			2,380			2,179			102			60			16	

Minerals Received from Beyond Bristol via East Tennessee Va. & Ga. RR.

	July.	Aug.	Sept.	Total.
Barytes	13	40	30	82
Marble	286	387	265	988
Pig Iron	46	74	13	133
Zinc Ore			36	36
Manganese	290	74	116	470
Coal	381	364	464	1059
Total for each month	955	789	1094	2768

A comparison of this table of the traffic of Virginia Minerals over the A., M. & O. RR. with that for the first 6 months of 1880, published on page 130 of our August number, gives these results :—In *pig lead* the increase was large, fully 75 per cent., and Richmond came in for 67 tons ;—In *ingot copper* there was a decrease, and it all went to New York ;—In *pig iron* the increase was over 66 per cent., indicating great activity in the charcoal iron furnaces of the Southwestern Valley (for only charcoal iron is made on this railroad), and quite a change in its destinations, as most of it went to Baltimore and a good amount to the Southern States, indicating an increase in manufacturing in the South ;—Of *zinc ore* there were small shipments, probably single car loads from some of the new mines being opened, as Forney's in Wythe, as samples, to New York and Baltimore ;—In *coal*, from the mines of Montgomery, Pulaski and Wythe, in the lowest (Va.) Coal Measures (No. X) the movement was nearly 8 times as great, probably because of the completion of arrangements to use this coal at the Saltville salt works ;—The *salt* moved was over a 50 per cent. increase ;—That of *plaster* was much less, as this is not the time of year when it is in demand ;—*Spelter*, block zinc, was moved about in the same proportion, but only to New York ;—*Manganese* appears in list, on its way to Liverpool, *via* Norfolk.—On the whole the showing is a good one, indicating a steady development of the mineral interests along this great railway, although the movement is as nothing compared to what it must be from a region so magnificently provided in this respect.

The Southern Planter and Farmer for November is an attractive number for those "devoted to Agriculture, Horticulture, Live Stock and Rural Affairs," and that is the same as saying that it is good, interesting and valuable reading to the majority of our people,—for in 1870 about 59 per cent. of them were engaged in agricultural pursuits. We are gratified to note the sustained vigor of this oldest of Southern agricultural journals. It furnishes in a year some 700 pages of substantial matter for $2. We are sure that anyone interested in any kind of earth tillage will derive more than two dollars worth of information from each number.—Address Southern Planter & Farmer Co., Richmond, Va., or send us three dollars and we will send you both THE VIRGINIAS and *The So. Planter & Farmer* for a year.

COPPER ORE.—Mr. Joseph Pinkham is working a copper mine, on Mr. W. P. Moran's farm, near Guilford, in Loudoun county. We have several specimens of ore from the mine, which those competent to judge, pronounce sufficiently rich to make it profitable to work. A car load of the ore, we are informed, will soon be sent to Baltimore to be tested.—*Reporter.*

The Coal and Coke Movement over the Chesapeake & Ohio R'y,

for the fiscal year ending Sept. 30th, 1880, and for the month of October, 1880, and for the corresponding periods of the previous year, in tons of 2,000 lbs., as reported for THE VIRGINIAS by Mr. Charles M. Gibson, the Fuel Agent for the Co., were as follows :

	Fiscal Year.		October.	
	1879.	1880.	1879.	1880.
Fuel for use of Company	86,618	111,665	8,941	9,923
Shipped at Huntington on Ohio River	88,885	106,891	675	2,092
Delivered on line of road west of Richmond	31,436	35,174	3,452	7,946
" at Stanton to Valley RR	406	381	80	182
" Charlottesville to Va. Mid. RR.	29,746	36,358	3,295	3,850
" Gordonsville do do	950	1,196	319	230
" Hanover June. to R.F. & P. RR.	2,588	18,502	641	1,303
" Richmond for consumption, including steam-tugs and dredges	58,862	48,900	4,537	2,943
Delivered to E. Lex. & Big Sandy RR				87
Shipped at James River wharves	149,506	205,354	26,307	21,528
Total	123,991	559,363	47,347	49,969

This shows that the coal movement for the fiscal year 1879–80 was 135,272 tons, or about 32 per cent more that for 1878–9, and that the movement in October, 1880, was 2,722 more than that for October, 1879. The item of coal delivered to the Elizabethtown, Lexington & Big Sandy RR., in October, indicates the opening of a section of the westward extension of the C. & O. R'y, and marks the beginning of a traffic destined to become one of enormous proportions.

The character of the fuel moved during the same periods, is shown in the following exhibit :

	Cannel.	Splint & Bits.	Coke.	Total.
For the fiscal year 1879–80	46,215	485,566	27,382	559,363
" " 1878–79	30,289	370,357	23,445	423,991
Increase	16,026	115,309	3,937	135,272
In October, 1880	3,750	43,325	2,894	49,969
" 1879	4,040	41,384	1,323	47,347
Increase		1,441	1,571	2,722
Decrease	290			

The above shows an increase during the fiscal year of over 52 per cent. in the movement of cannel coal, of over 31 per cent. in that of splint and bituminous coals, of over 16 per cent. in that of coke, and over 32 per cent. in the whole movement. The October movement shows a decrease of about 7 per cent. in that of cannel coal, but an increase of about 3¼ per cent. in that of splint and bituminous coals, one of nearly 119 per cent. in that of coke, and of nearly 6 in the whole fuel movement.—The large increase of the coke traffic is, of course, in consequence of the recent rapid development in the manufacture of coke iron in Virginia ; but it does not represent the full measure of that development, for in the 23 days in October that Low Moor Furnace ran, it used fully 1500 tons of coke made at the furnace from coals transported over the C. & O., so the real coke movement was 238 per cent. over that for October, 1879.

COPPER MINING in Floyd, Carroll and Grayson counties on the Blue Ridge plateau, in Va., will probably be resumed before long, as parties interested in the Ore Knob mines of N. C. have lately been quietly buying the copper mines in those counties.

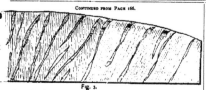

CONTINUED FROM PAGE 166.

Fig. 3.

where for the separation of gold from such deposits—the long tom, the sluice, the riffle-box, etc.—were devised and used in this region, and were carried hence to California when, twenty-five years later, the trained miners of this region emigrated in a body to that newer and richer field. Since that emigration there has been but little placer mining done in North Carolina. Still this sort of mining has never entirely ceased, and in some sections, and by a few families, it has been followed continuously to the present. The richest deposits within reach of water have been worked over, but there are large areas still untouched, because inaccessible to water without considerable outlay for ditching, canalling, and fluming, to which neither the capital nor the enterprise of the region is equal.

The Mica Veins of North Carolina*.

By W. C. Kerr, State Geologist, Raleigh, North Carolina.

A brief sketch only is here intended, with a few illustrations, in order to give a general notion of the character and structure of these veins. I have stated elsewhere, several years ago, that these veins were wrought on a large scale and for many ages by some ancient peoples, most probably the so-called Mound Builders; although they built no mounds here, and have left no signs of any permanent habitation. They opened and worked a great many veins down to or near water-level; that is, as far as the action of atmospheric chemistry had softened the rock so that it was workable without metal tools, of the use of which no signs are apparent. Many of the largest and most profitable of the mines of the present day are simply the ancient Mound Builders' mines reopened and pushed into the hard undecomposed granite by powder and steel. Blocks of mica have often been found half imbedded in the face of the vein, with the tool-marks about them, showing the exact limit of the efficiency of those prehistoric mechanical appliances. As to the geological relations of these veins, they are found in the gneisses and schists of the Archæan horizons, in that subdivision which I have provisionally classed as Upper Laurentian, the Montalban of Dr. Hunt. These rocks are of very extensive occurrence in North Carolina, constituting in fact the great body of the rocks throughout the whole length of the State,—some 400 miles east and west,—being partially covered up, and interrupted here and there by belts of later formation. Mica veins are found here, in fact they may be said to chacterize this horizon everywhere, from its eastern outcrop, near the seaboard, to and quite under the flanks of the Smoky Mountains. It is, however, in the great plateau of the west, between the Blue Ridge and the Smoky, that the mica veins reach their greatest development, and have given rise to a very new and profitable industry,—new and at the same time very old.

It may be stated as a very general, almost universal, fact, that the mica vein is a *bedded* vein. Its position (as to strike and dip) is dependent on and controlled by, and quite nearly conformable with, that of the rocks in which it occurs, and hence, as well as on account of their great size, some observers, accustomed to the study of veins and dikes and the characters of intrusive rocks in other regions, have been disposed to question the vein character of these veins at first. But a good exposure of a single one of them is generally sufficient to remove all doubt on this score. The mica vein is simply and always a dike of *very coarse granite*. It is of the size and shape, from a few inches—generally a few feet—to several rods (in some cases several hundred feet) in thickness, and length from a few rods to many hundred yards, extending in

† the Transactions of the American Institute of Mining Engineers. Read at the New meeting, February, 1880.—The Archæan region of Virginia is a part of the one in North —a, and its mica veins are doubtless in the same condition.—Ed.

some cases to half a mile and more. The strike, like that of the inclosing rocks, is generally northeast, and the dip southeast, at a pretty high angle; but they are subject, in these respects, to many and great local variations, all the conditions being occasionally changed, or even reversed. An idea may be formed of the coarseness of these veins from this statement, that masses of cleavable feldspar and of quartz (limpid, pale yellow, brown, or, more generally, slightly smoky), and of mica, are often found to measure several yards in two or three of their dimensions and weighing several tons. I have found a feldspar crystal from one of these mines of nearly a thousand pounds weight, and I have known a single block of mica to make two full two-horse wagon loads, and sheets of mica are sometimes obtained that measure three and four feet in diameter.

There are many peculiarities about these veins. Among the most important, in a practical sense, is the arrangement of the vein *inter se*. Sometimes the mica, for example, will be found hugging the hanging-wall; sometimes it is found against both walls; again it may be distributed pretty equally through the whole mass of the vein; sometimes, again, it will be found collected in the middle of the vein; in other cases, where the vein varies in thickness along its course, the mica will be found in bunches in the ampullations or bellies of the vein; in still other cases, where the vein has many vertical embranchments, the mica will be found accumulated in nests along the upper faces of these processes or offshoots. These features of structure will be best understood from a few representative diagrams.

Figure 1 is a horizontal section, with several transverse vertical sections, of a typical vein in Yancey County, at the Presnel Mine. The length of the section, i. e. of the portion of the vein that has been stripped, is 125 feet; the thickness varies from 3 to 10 feet, except at a few points, as b, c, where it is nearly 20 feet.

The crystals of mica are found in this mine generally near the foot-wall, in the recesses or pouches; at c, however, as seen in section D, it is found the next hanging-wall.

The inclosing rock in this case is a hard, gray slaty to schistose gneiss. The relation of the vein to the topography is seen in Fig. 2.

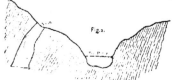

Fig. 2.

Another characteristic vein is well exposed at the Point Pezzle

Mine, in the same county, which has been wrought very success-fully for several years. (Fig. 3.)

Fig 3

The inclosing rock is the same as in the former case The mica here is found mostly next the hanging-wall, and is also in the off-shoots of branches of the vein, as shown in the vertical section at *d*. This vein illustrates the exceeding irregularities which are often found in these intrusive masses,—irregularities in form, size, and position,—and the force with which the inclosing rocks have been crowded and bent and split in the effort of the vein matter to in-sert itself. This vein is 40 feet thick at *b*, and 1 to 2 feet at *c*.

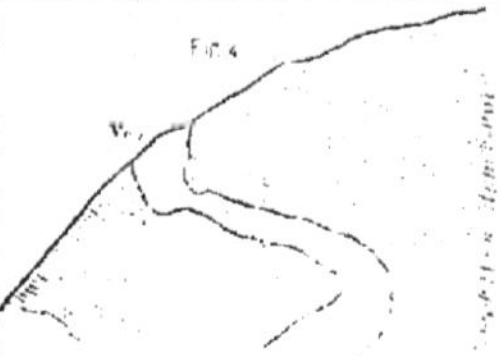

Figure 4 furnishes another illustration of the same points.

Fig 4

Another class of veins is represented by the accompanying cross-section of one of the largest and most pro-ductive veins, on which was opened the first mica mine in this region (Sink Hole) in the bottom of an old pit, partly filled up and overgrown, bottom and top, with heavy forest trees of the age of three to four hundred years. (Fig. 5.)

The lower part of the diagram represents an enlarged cross setion of the vein at *b*. The wall-rock, 1, 1, is a soft, decomposed micaschist. A horse, of this wall-rock, is imbedded in the body of the vein on both sides, 1, 1. At 3, 3, occur interpolations of

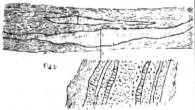

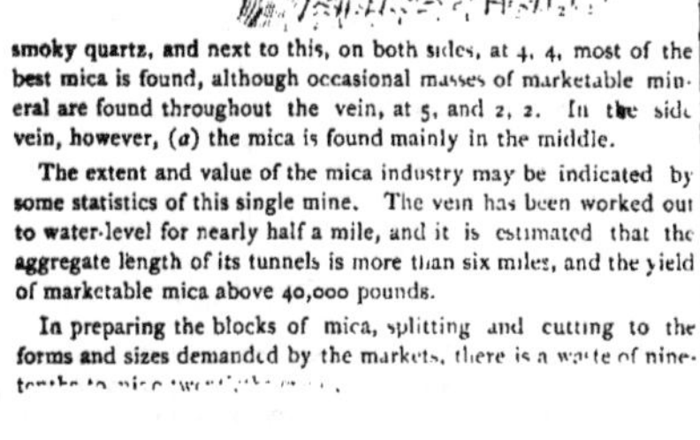

Fig 5.

smoky quartz, and next to this, on both sides, at 4, 4, most of the best mica is found, although occasional masses of marketable min-eral are found throughout the vein, at 5, and 2, 2. In the side vein, however, (*a*) the mica is found mainly in the middle.

The extent and value of the mica industry may be indicated by some statistics of this single mine. The vein has been worked out to water-level for nearly half a mile, and it is estimated that the aggregate length of its tunnels is more than six miles, and the yield of marketable mica above 40,000 pounds.

In preparing the blocks of mica, splitting and cutting to the forms and sizes demanded by the markets, there is a waste of nine-tenths to nine twentieths...

these veins, is often found converted into beds of the finest kaolin; and, curiously enough, this was one of the first and most valuable exports to England in the early part of the seventeenth century, "packed" by the Indians out of the Unaka (Smoky) Mountains, and sold under the name "unakeh" (white). This kaolin, like the mica, will doubtless soon come again into demand,—after lying forgotten for generations.

These are only a few of the more prominent characteristics of these very interesting veins. I have not referred to their singular richness in rare minerals, as samarskite, uraninite, gummite, allan-ite, etc., nor to many curious and unexplained relations between the marketable character of the mica,—size, color, purity, fissility, etc.,—and the special matrix in which the blocks are imbedded. I do not know a better region for the study of the structure and origin of veins in general.

Low Moor Furnace—how it works.—The "stock re-ports" of this leading Virginia furnace show that from the 16th to the 36th days of its present (first) blast—Oct. 24th to Nov. 13th inclusive,—it made 1,266.44 tons of pig iron, 454.71 tons of which were No. 1 and 811.73 were No. 2. The stoppages for various purposes, incident to the getting in full operation of such a large furnace, amounted in this period to 47 hours, or very nearly 2 days, so the average make per day for the days run was 66.65 tons. The consumption of ore was 2,893 tons, one-third of it "wash" and two-thirds "lump," an average of 2.28 tons to the ton of iron. The coke used was 1,373 tons, an average of 1.08 tons to the ton of iron. Of limestone 1,366 tons were used, an average of 1.07 to the ton of iron. The pay roll for labor was $2,452.27, or $1.936 to the ton of iron made. The "charges" were 1,043 in number, 530 in the "morning turn" and 513 in the "evening turn."

Taking the prices of ore, coke and limestone as stated in THE VIRGINIAS for Oct., page 151, as "estimated" by Mana-ging Director Wickes, the *actual results* from the above gives the *cost of making a ton of iron* at Low Moor, exclusive of in-terest, wear and tear, etc., as follows:—

2.28 tons of ore @ $2.05 per ton,		$4.674
1.08 " " coke @ $2.85 " "		3.078
1.07 " " limestone, @ 40 cts. per ton,		0.428
Wages per ton,		1.936
Cost per ton, exclusive of interest, etc.,		$10.116

These results, *from the records of the thing done*, fully con-firm, what we have again and again stated, that nowhere else in the United States, taking into consideration the facilities for reaching all markets, can good iron be made as cheaply as in central Old Virginia, that is where the iron ores and lime-stones of Virginia and the coking coals of West Virginia are near together, when capital and skill combine and there en-gage in this manufacture, as at Low Moor. It is evident that an establishment showing such results in less than a month of "run" and while working at only about two-thirds of its capac-ity, can pay dividends on a half million of dollars of invest-ment such as should satisfy any reasonable investor, and that, with this industry properly protected, it will pay him well un-der all conditions of trade, so that he can afford to reward liberally the labor that helps him to prosper.

Since the above was written the report for the week, Nov. 14, to Nov. 20, inclusive, has been made: it shows a yield of 559 tons. The average quantities to the ton of pig were 2.93 tons ore, 1.04 tons limestone, 1.20 tons coke, 0.02 87 tons Ka-nawha coal added to give more gas, and $1.615 for labor.— Adding this yield to that above makes that for a month of 4 weeks 1,823.44 tons.

Slag-bricks.—A furnace in Saxony makes in 24 hours 1,000 slag-bricks 425 mm long by 210 mm. wide and thick. These have profitable applica-tion in many kinds of building, but do not bear long transportation. The continuous outflowing slag is conducted into square molds where it is mix-ed with clear coke and converted into bricks.—*Am. Engineer.*

The Iron Ores of Virginia and West Virginia.

By Prof. WILLIAM B. ROGERS.

(Continued from Page 161.)

5. **The Middle and Upper Cambrian Iron Ores of Virginia and West Virginia.**—These are the iron ores of what are usually called the *Lower Silurian* valleys of Virginia and West Virginia, those formed from Rogers' formation No. II (embracing 3 a. Calciferous, 3 b. Levis, and 3 c. Chazy of the N. Y. system), and No. III (embracing 4 a. Trenton, 4 b. Utica, and 4 c. Hudson River of the New York system); and found in the areas of these states that are colored blue on the Geological Map (See THE VIRGINIAS, June, 1880,) except a narrow strip of Primordial east of the Great Valley. They may, very properly, be called the *Valley ores*.

NOTE.—In his late writings Prof. Rogers calls his formation No. II Middle Cambrian, and his No. III Siluro-Cambrian or Upper Cambrian, in preference to classing II and III together as Lower Silurian,—following Hunt rather than Dana.

The general references to the Valley ores made in the reports were quoted on page 153 of THE VIRGINIAS. In the report for 1835, p. 45, "iron" is mentioned as one of the products of the Southwest of which "little is known, further than its existence and value."—"Oxide of iron" is mentioned as an ingredient of the Balcony Falls cement. [10–1836.]

"The wide belt of slate (No. III) forming the basis of the sandstones of the Massanutton ranges, and extending in the same general direction into Maryland on the one side, and into the southern parts of the Valley on the other, has been traced throughout a considerable portion of these districts, and its boundaries carefully noted down; at the same time that the iron and manganese ore, which it contains, have been attentively examined." [10–1837.]

In the Massanutton Mountains "the heavy beds of valuable iron ore, of which extensive exposures have already been brought to light in supplying this material to the neighboring furnaces, have been traced for great distances along the borders of the slate (III), subjacent to the massive sandstone (IV), of which the principal ridges are composed." [9–1837.]

"The iron ores associated with the limestone strata (No. II) of the Valley have also been examined at various points, and specimens reserved for similar practical objects,"—that is for systematic arrangement and chemical examination. [10–1837.]

"As conspicuous among the future sources of wealth and prosperity throughout this region (the Southwest Valley), I may be again permitted to call the attention of the board to the extraordinary abundance and excellent qualities of its iron ores. Besides innumerable exposures of this material in various parts of the Great Limestone Valley, and among the ridges lying to the northwest, I would particularly bring to notice the very extensive range of deposits which, commencing at Mack's Run and pursuing a course parallel to the Poplar Camp and Iron mountains, within from two to four miles of their base, continues to the southern boundary of the state. In this region, from two to three miles in width, this ore is found in the flanks of the calcareous ridges in massive beds, frequently enclosed by walls of limestone, and usually of a quality admirably adapted to the uses of the furnace. There is, perhaps, no other portion of the Great Limestone Valley, either in Pennsylvania or Virginia, so bountifully supplied with this material in so available a shape, and none in which this valuable resource has been more indolently improved. A deep sense of the almost unrivalled importance of the iron ores of this and the other districts referred to, must excuse the repeated allusions of which it has been the theme, especially when it is considered, that from the frequency of the occurrence of this material in various parts of the state, the high interest which ought to attach to such a possession does not appear to have been adequately felt." [12–1837.]

"Oxide of iron" is named as one of the ingredients in each of seven analyses given of hydraulic limestone in No. II. [15-16–1837.]

"Another, and by far the most important, of the minerals it (II) contains, is the iron ore, of which several of the most successful furnaces in the state have availed themselves, particularly as it occurs in the southwestern counties of the Valley, some description has already been given. This mineral presents the various forms of compact, earthy, cellular and pipe iron ore, and in general yields a metal of admirable quality." [17–1837.]

In No. III "iron pyrites is of very common occurrence, giving origin to the sulphurous impregnation of numerous medicinal springs, taking their rise in these rocks, some of which, as the Shannondale and Winchester springs, have attained extensive reputation. [17–1837.]

"In an economical point of view, this rock (III) is chiefly interesting, from being the repository of beds of iron ore of great extent and value, and of large deposits of the oxide of manganese. In regard to the former, incalculably the more important ot the two, the extraordinary productiveness of this rock has already been illustrated in sketching some of the results of our researches in the Big and Little Fort valleys of the Massanutton. But I may be allowed again to call attention to the rich abundance and excellent quality of the iron ores appertaining to this member of our series, as forming a part of the structure of those mountains, as well as to the ample deposits exhibited in numerous other localities in connection with the same rock. Though not unfrequently impregnated with manganese, these ores are, for the most part, well adapted to the furnace, and yield a metal of excellent quality. Their position is generally near, or at the upper limits of the slate, or between it and the sandstone, and they seem to have been derived from the ferruginous ingredients of both these rocks, through the influence of slow chemical changes and infiltration." [18–1837.]

"In this group (II) are found several varieties of iron ore, all of good quality." [7–1838.]

"The iron ores of formation II, of which, only a brief notice will be introduced.—Of these ores several important localities have been long known and resorted to, but their quantity is by no means as abundant in this as in some of the superior formations. In the northern and middle counties, they either have been or still are, wrought near Strasburg, Port Republic, Luray, Mossy Creek, &c.; and farther south at Graham's furnace, and several minor establishments. The mines near Luray, from which ore is procured for the Isabella furnace, are situated about two miles west of the Blue Ridge, and within the confines of the limestone, although none of this rock appears either west of them or towards the Ridge.

"The beds of ore occur in clay, and only occasionally at the bottom of the lowest bed is the rock exposed. These beds are not strata interposed between layers of limestone, and cotemporary with them, but rather local and irregular deposits, formed at a later date in the clefts or cavities of the calcareous rock, and such in general appears to be the character of the ores of this formation throughout the Valley. At the mines in question, the ore is mostly in a granular state, slightly coherent, of a reddish brown color, and after being carted to the furnace resembles a heap of reddish earth. In other parts of the deposit it is quite solid, and is extracted in masses of some size. When broken, they somewhat resemble hematitic ore, and contain much ochreous oxide. For their composition, I would refer to a future section of this report.

"A similar ore, highly esteemed for the metal it yields, is found on Mossy Creek, in Rockingham county, under like circumstances to those above described, and again occurs contiguous to a part of the trap dyke before referred to.

"Of the various localities in this portion of the Valley and thence to the southwest no particular description is necessary at present. I will merely add, that they have been met with in Botetourt, Floyd, Montgomery, &c., and that in the most southern counties the extent of the deposit as mentioned in my last year's report is very great. In most cases the limestone contiguous to the ore is cherty or flinty, and sometimes the adjacent rock is chert itself." [16–1838.]

"Of the mineral contents of this formation (III), *iron ore* is by far the most important, and the only one I propose noticing at present. This ore, where found, occupies a position near the upper

limit of the formation (III), and within a short distance of the lower bands of formation IV. As occurring in the Big Fort Valley of the Massanutton Mountain, and on the slope of Caldwell's Mountain, near the Catawba Iron-works, it presents itself in beds of great thickness and length. In the former case, throughout nearly the whole length of the Valley to its termination near Strasburg, traces of the ore may be found, while at Blackford's mines, where it has been extensively excavated for the use of a furnace near at hand, it presents a spectacle truly imposing, from the magnitude of the deposit in which the workings are carried on. At the latter place, the seam of ore gradually sloping up the mountain as it proceeds south, may be traced for perhaps 6 miles with but little interruption.

These ores are the hydrated peroxide, generally dark brown, either cellular or compact, mammillary, and often shewing a play of colors. They are usually a little tainted with manganese, and furnish a brittle metal, which yet is held in high repute." [18-1838.]

"In both these valleys (Big and Little Fort of Massanuttons) iron ore occurs in great abundance, not only in connection with III, as already described, but with V, and is procured from both these formations to supply the two furnaces of Dr. Blackford and Mr. Buck, erected in the neighborhood. The ore from V is found to be peculiarly rich and valuable, and may be traced for several miles. Manganese also occurs abundantly in the Little Fort Valley. Viewing the abundance and excellence of its ores, and the facilities of transportation which it is hoped will ere long be afforded this part of the state, this mountain region would seem to be destined, at no remote day, to become a busy scene of manufacturing enterprise." [18-1838.]

"In Purgatory Mountain and for some distance towards the south the summit of the mountain presents the upper slates of III, with a small and broken remnant of the lowest band of IV, and it is at the junction of the two that exist those ample beds of iron ore, from which the Etna and Retreat furnaces were formerly supplied. Of the extent of the deposits of iron ore above referred to, as also those situated under similar geological circumstances on the west and east flanks of the mountain, the most ample evidence has been procured. At the upper bank, before alluded to, the whole top of the mountain appears to be composed of it, and in numerous other places near the junction of formations III and IV, indications of large deposits are to be met with." [19-1838.]—[See comments of Prof. Campbell on this statement, page 156 of THE VIRGINIAS, and section of Purgatory Mtn.]

"In both the Draper's and Lick ranges *iron ore* occurs at the junction of III and IV, with every indication of being in valuable amount. A locality especially deserving of notice is met with on the side of the peak in ascending from Peak Creek towards the summit. The ore displays itself in a massive bed at or near the commencement of IV, and is of highly promising quality." [20-1838.]

"Oxide of iron" is mentioned as one of the ingredients of No. II limestones in numerous analyses of those rocks. [24-28-1838.]

Analyses of iron ores from formations No. II and No. III are given, pages 30 and 31 report of 1838, as follows:—

	LOCALITY.	Peroxide of Iron.	Silica.	Alumina.	Water.	Loss.
No. II.	No. 1. Isabella Furnace—Blackford's bank,	82.19	8.61	trace	4.00	0.9
	2. Lexington, 1 mile W.,	85.60	0.98	trace	3.46	0.1.
	3. Limestone Hill, N and Short's Hill,	82.58	0.07	0.59	3.61	0.1.
	4. Graham's Furnace—Reed Cr.,	84.81	1.16	0.58	1.40	0.3.
	5. Big Fort Valley—Blackford's bank, W.,	82.30	3.15	0.80	3.05	0.1.
	6. Little Fort Valley—Massanutton Mt.,	90.70	5.48	0.21	3.40	0.0.
No. III.	7. Retreat Furnace—Purgatory Mt.,	81.20	5.40	0.73	1.77	0.1.
	8. " "	84.06	8.43	0.50	1.74	0.0.
	9. Catawba Furnace—E. side Crawford's Mt.,	84.10	1.97	0.16	3.66	0.0.
	10.	84.35	1.47	0.12	3.98	0.0.

FROM FORMATION No. II.

No. 1—"Iron ore from Blackford's bank, Page county, used a Isabella furnace. Color light ochreous brown; texture earthy, friable, light, mixed with slaty clay."

No. 2—"Iron ore, one mile west of Lexington, Rockbridge county. Color ochreous on the exterior, dark lilac brown within; texture very close grained, cellular."

No. 3—"Iron ore Limestone Hill, near N. end of Short Hill, and contiguous to Buffalo Creek. Color light brownish yellow; texture earthy, porous."

No. 4—"Iron ore near Reed Creek, Wythe county—Graham's furnace. Honey-comb ore. Color light brown, inclining to orange; texture fine grained; structure cavernous."

FROM FORMATION No. III.

No. 5—"Iron ore, Blackford's mine, west side of Big Fort Valley, Massanutton Mountain. Color dark brown; texture compact; structure largely cavernous, the hollows frequently filled with white siliceous clay, surface sometimes mammillary, often iridescent or having a rainbow coloring."

No. 6—"Iron ore, Little Fort Valley, Massanutton Mts. Color dark brown; texture fine grained, generally quite compact, but sometimes cellular."

No. 7—"Iron ore, top of Purgatory Mountain, near Retreat furnace. Color dark brown; texture porous and cavernous, the cavities occasionally filled with siliceous clay."

No. 8—"Iron ore same locality. Color dark chestnut, nearly black; texture fine grained, somewhat cavernous."

No. 9—"Iron ore, east side of Crawford's Mountain, near Catawba furnace. Color dark chestnut brown; texture fine grained, cellular, the interior of the cells being often coated with black velvet-like films."

No. 10—"Iron ore, same locality, more cellular variety."

Many analyses of the limestones of No. II and No. III are given on pages 109-112 of report of 1840, and "oxide of iron" is named as one of the ingredients in them.

Analyses of iron ores from formation No. II are given, pages 118-119, 1840, as follows:

		Composition in 100 parts.					
	LOCALITY.	Metallic Iron.	Peroxide of Iron.	Alumina.	Siliceous Mat.	Insol. Mat.	Water.	Loss.
No.								
1. Cedar Creek W'ks—(Russell Co.?)		70.65		3.75	11.50	12.00	0.10	
2. Miller's Iron W'ks—Mossy Cr., Augusta Co.,		81.00	trace	trace		9.47	0.23	
3. Silver Creek—		37.40	80.00	trace	8.14	5.27	0.39	
4. Iron Mt.—Wythe Co'.,		64.90	90.00	trace	4.01	3.79	0.71	

No. 1—"Iron ore from Cedar Creek Works, 2 miles from Russell C. H. Structure hematitic, cellular; brown black, interior of cells lined with a dull brown oxide."

No. 2—"From near Miller's, now Kenagay's Iron furnace, Mossy Creek, Augusta county. Structure cellular, cells ochreous, compact, fine-grained, semi-crystalline; color chestnut brown, bright."

No. 3—"Iron ore from Silver Creek, used at Kenagay's furnace. Structure compact, fine grained, surface smooth; color dark reddish brown."

No. 4—"Iron ore from Wythe county, base of Iron Mountain. Structure cellular; color dark dull chestnut brown, semi-crystalline."

6. The Silurian Iron Ores of Virginia and West Virginia.—These are the ores found in or associated with formations IV (5a. Medina), V (5b. Clinton, 5c. Niagara and 6. Salina), VI (7. Lower Helderberg), and VII (8. Oriskany), the rocks that form the Silurian general group of the Paleozoic system,—those embraced in the "Upper Silurian" area of the Geological Map of the Virginias See June No.), that colored a dark brown. They are confined to the Apalachian division of Virginia and West Virginia, that of parallel mountain ranges, and to the detached and broken mountain ranges of the same kind found in the Great Valley. This is one of the most, if not the most, important and valuable of the iron-bearing groups of these states. An inspection of the Geological Map shows that the Silurian (Upper) rocks are disposed in an

CONTINUED ON PAGE 174.

The University of Virginia—how it proposes to aid development in Virginia and the South.

Written for THE VIRGINIAS.

BY THE RECTOR, THE HON. A. H. H. STUART.

Maj. Jed. Hotchkiss, Editor:—

The important service which your journal has rendered to the states of Virginia and West Virginia, in making the public acquainted with their vast mineral resources, merits, and doubtless will receive, the grateful acknowledgments of their people.—In view of this fact, it seems to me that your journal is the appropriate medium through which the people should be informed of the efforts which are now being made by the Rector and Visitors of the University of Virginia towards the same object.

The enlightened liberality of the late W. Lewis Brooks, of Rochester, New York, in establishing, at the University, a splendid museum of natural history, at a cost of about $70,000, and the generous donation, by Mr. W. W. Corcoran, of $50,000, to endow a professorship of Natural History, in connection with that museum, have created new relations between the University and the industrial interests and natural resources of the commonwealth.

In former years the system of instruction in the University was shaped, mainly, with a view to the education of accomplished scholars, in the departments of classics and mathematics, modern languages and literature, and the preparation of young men for what are ordinarily called the learned professions.

The changes which the last two decades have wrought in our political, social and industrial systems have rendered a change necessary in our course of instruction, whereby more prominence shall be given to those branches of study connected with the development of our mining, agricultural and manufacturing interests. The Rector and Visitors of the University, recognizing this important fact, wisely determined, a year ago, to avail themselves of the new Professorship endowed by Mr. Corcoran to meet, to some extent, this requirement. They selected, to fill the new chair, Professor Wm. M. Fontaine, a gentleman of national reputation as a geologist and mineralogist, and they have instructed him to make the new school, mainly, a school of geology and mineralogy. Their principal object in so doing was to contribute, as far as possible, to the speedy development of the mineral wealth of Virginia and the neighboring states, by educating a class of young men who would be competent to explore the hidden mineral resources of our country, its iron and other ores, coals, slates, building-stones, clays and other natural deposits which may be made the sources of wealth and prosperity.—Another purpose was to open to the educated young men of the country a new, honorable and profitable occupation, as mining engineers, mineralogists and practical explorers and miners.

Prof. Fontaine has therefore been instructed not only to teach geology and mineralogy in their theoretical and scientific aspects, but to take his classes into the field and afford them the advantages of practical instruction and observation, whereby they may obtain a familiar acquaintance with all the processes by which mineral substances are discovered, developed and made to possess commercial value.—By the present regulations of the University the course of theoretical instruction commences on the 15th day of October in each year and is continued by lectures, illustrated by reference to specimens collected in the museum and by parallel reading up to the 15th day of April in each year. At that date the Professor and his students are expected to commence active operations in the field, which will continue until the close of the session, on the 30th of June. During this latter period it is expected that many portions of the state will be carefully examined and oral instruction given to the pupils explanatory of the geological structure and the indicia which point to the deposits of different minerals.

By this system of instruction it is hoped, and confidently believed, that in a few years a number of young men will be sufficiently instructed to pursue, successfully, investigations on their own account and thereby obtain honorable and lucrative employment as practical geologists and mining engineers. In a country like ours, which abounds in so many natural resources, a young man possessing such knowledge as he can acquire by a year's study under the instruction of Prof. Fontaine could hardly fail to obtain profitable employment.

The professions of law and medicine are now filled to repletion, while this new and interesting field of employment is comparatively unoccupied. In illustration of this fact I need only refer to the catalogue of the University, from which it appears that there are 117 students in the law school, 57 in the medical class, while only 8 have matriculated in the school of natural history.

This condition of things is greatly to be regretted. A young man entering a profession has a long period of probation to pass through before he can reasonably expect to earn more than a bare subsistence, while one properly instructed in mineralogy and mining can hardly fail to obtain profitable employment in any of our mining districts, and if he chooses to go the Pacific States, or those bordering on the Rocky Mountains, may reasonably expect, in a few years, to acquire a competency, if not a fortune.

The Virginias are destined, at no distant day, to become the theatre of immense mining operations, and there must inevitably be an active demand for the services of those who possess the requisite skill in these branches of knowledge. The Rector and Visitors of the University have, therefore, felt it to be their duty to employ all the means at their disposal to supply this demand by turning out annually a class of thoroughly educated young men, familiar with these subjects.

It is much to be regretted that the people of Virginia and her sister states of the South do not yet seem to have properly appreciated this sort of instruction. They still seem disposed to run along in the old ruts, forgetting that the days of subtle theory and dreamy speculation have passed away and that the present generation need a more practical education, one that will qualify them to deal successfully with physical and material facts.

Your widely circulated journal seems to offer a channel through which the people may be made acquainted with the actual condition of things, and I therefore avail myself of it to appeal to parents and to enterprising and vigorous young men, who have vim and energy enough to think and act for themselves, to lose no time in availing themselves of the opportunities to obtain useful and profitable knowledge in these branches of physical science, which is offered to them by the University. Almost every range of our mountains is pregnant with mineral deposits of some kind and we hardly take up a newspaper without seeing a notice of some new discovery of ores, clays, marbles and other mineral substances which, if we had had among us a class of educated geologists and metallurgists, would long since have been disclosed and made to furnish profitable employment to the labor of our people.

I write this article in the hope of arresting the attention of the young men, especially of Virginia and West Virginia, and inducing them to qualify themselves for the great field of operation which lies before them in the immediate future. Now, if we want an examination made of our mineral resources, we are, in the main, compelled to seek for competent experts in other states; men who, while they are competent enough in their own states, are not familiar with the geological conditions of ours. This is a reproach to our people. It is one that should be promptly removed. If we had but a single man in each county who was a competent geologist and mineralogist, the pecuniary and industrial condition of our state would be revolutionized before the close of another decade. The University of Virginia now opens her doors and invites the young men of the commonwealth to avail themselves of the theoretical and practical instruction which she is prepared to offer them, that they may become leaders in this great era of material development that is now dawning upon us.

ALEX. H. H. STUART.

The Oxford Ochre Co.—One of the important and growing industries of the present is the mining and manufacture of ochre to meet the large and constantly increasing demand for the paints of many colors that are everywhere in use. Hearing that one of the best ochres in the markets of the country came from Page county, Va., the Editor of THE VIRGINIAS recently sought out and visited the beds and mill from which that article came,—those of the "Oxford Ochre Co." on the line of the Shenandoah Valley RR., where it crosses Stony Run, near the western base of the Western Blue Ridge and not far from the little villages of Honeyville, Markeville and Alma. The company is a Michigan one, having its head quarters at Detroit where lives C. S. Foote, its President; the mining, manufacturing and sending to market of the ochre are in charge of C. B. Foote, the son of the President, as Manager, who resides near the beds and works, whom we found a prompt and well informed business man and a communicative and courteous gentleman.

This company takes its name from one in England that furnishes a well known ochre. It began here in June, 1876, by purchasing some 30 acres of land on Stony Creek (which runs into the South Fork of the Shenandoah near Alma), the waters of which had exposed the ochre beds in its somewhat bluffy banks; some 20 acres more were purchased subsequently. The necessary buildings required—a store room and office, a few frames on which to dry the ochreous clay after it is dug, some sheds under which to pile the dried clay, a building for a common mill with ordinary buhr-stones and a portable engine to drive it—were soon erected. In 1876, 200 tons of ground ochre were sent to market; 350 were sent in 1877 and since then about 1,000 tons a year, sending 18 miles by wagons to the Valley RR. of the B. & O. at New Market; hereafter they will ship by the Shenandoah Valley RR., saving some $4 per ton in the cost of transportation and enabling them to do a greatly increased business.

This ochre bed is in the iron-bearing shales of Formation No. I, the Primordial, occupying a defined position, and as that formation has a remarkable development all along the western base of the Blue Ridge in Va., nearly 300 miles, we may confidently look for a large increase in this business here, now that the Shenandoah Valley and other railways are opening this mineral belt to development,—in fact we know a number of localities where excellent beds of ochre are now exposed.

Copper.—The Copper Knob Mining Co. of N. C. had $23,250 of cash receipts in Sept. and Oct., 1880, its expenditures, including a dividend on its stock were $11,787 for the same period.—The Virginia copper mines, in the same Blue Ridge belt as the Ore Knob of N. C., are just now attracting considerable attention and there is some prospect of active operations all along this rich cupriferous belt. The old partially exposed outcrops near Milford, on the S. V. RR., in Warren Co., have lately been examined by a mining engineer and it is probable that considerable explorations will be made to fully test their value.—Parties are at work exploring the copper veins near Linden, Warren, Co., on the Manassas Branch of the Va. Midland.

RECENT LAND SALES IN VA.—The Lynn 100 A. farm, near Bloomfield, Loudoun Co., for $5,000.—The "Powell farm," near Sinckersville, Loudoun Co , 300 A. for $15,250, $10,000 of it "down."—The "Berryman" farm of 200 A. near Rappahannock Station, Fauquier Co., for $4,000 ; the purchaser, Mr. Hoffman, is from The Valley ; he proposes to raise sheep.—The "Kyger" farm, 8 miles S. E. of Harrisonburg, Rockingham Co., 200 A. at $33.855 per A.—Ten conveyances for land were recorded in Warren Co., between its Oct. and Nov. courts.—Twelve deeds for real estate were recorded in Alleghany Co. between the Oct. and Nov. courts.—In Augusta county 26 deeds were recorded between the Oct. and Nov. courts.—Everywhere there is a marked activity in real estate and an appreciation of values.

MARL AS A BLAST FURNACE FLUX.—At the Amherst Furnace on James River, Amherst county, Va., travertine or deposit marl from the Great Limestone Valley, is now and has been for some time the only flux used. The Messrs. Jordan, the operators of the furnace, consider it a better flux than any limestone they can get, because it is, by analysis, equally pure, much more cheaply mined, and is ready for use without breaking. They obtain it from Hamilton's marl bank, on the canal, in Rockbridge county, 23 miles from the furnace, paying 12½ cts a ton royalty and 12½ cts. a ton for digging.

The **Chesapeake & Ohio R'y** is now adding 12 new stalls to its round-house at Huntington, W. Va., more than doubling the present capacity ; a new blacksmith shop, 80 by 160 ft., is also to be built at once ; the old shop is to be used for a boiler shop and the machine shop is to be extended 75 ft.. Such is the urgency for the construction of these buildings a part of the bricks to be used will be brought from Richmond, Va., 420 miles. These additions are for the accommodation of the Lexington & Big Sandy RR., which will be run in connection with the C. &. O.—The Lexington & Big Sandy RR. has leased from the C. & O. the track from Huntington to the Big Sandy, and November and its trains began to run from Huntington to Ashland, 16 miles, in connection with those of the C. & O.—Surveying parties in charge of Maj. McKendree, took the field, the last week in October, to survey the New-port's-news extension.

THE CHESAPEAKE & OHIO A TRANS-CONTINENTAL LINE.—A late *Norfolk Virginian* has a long article recalling the contest over the Texas-Pacific road bill, which, mainly by the efforts of Hon. John W. Johnston of Virginia, in the United States Senate, will be a Southern road, eventually finding its terminus at Memphis, and showing that the Chesapeake & Ohio will be the extension of that railway to the Atlantic seaboard, and not only that, but will also form the same extension for the Central Pacific, since the chief parties interested control all three of these roads.

THE ELIZABETH-CITY & NORFOLK RR., extending from Berkley, a suburb of Norfolk, Va., to Elizabeth-City, N. C., 43 miles, has been graded and track-laying is going on from each end. It is expected this road will be in operation in about two months. It passes through the fine timber region adjacent to the Great Dismal Swamp, and it is said a large colony of Maine and Pennsylvania lumbermen will be located on its line. This railway connects Norfolk with the fine fish, cotton, lumber, naval stores, etc., country around Albemarle Sound.

THE WASHINGTON CITY & ST. LOUIS N.-G. RR. is again attracting attention ; its President, Mr. J. W. F. Allemong, of Bridgewater, Va., has recently returned from interviewing capitalists in New York, and he is of opinion that when he is ready to submit a report on the resources of the country it will traverse, there will be no difficulty in selling its construction bonds. It is the intention of this company to very soon complete the partially constructed portion of its line between Harrisonburg and Elkton (Conrad's Store), and so make a connection between the Valley RR. and the Shenandoah Valley RR., and also to finish the road from Harrisonburg westward towards Monterey. The regions this road will traverse abound in resources of many kinds.

THE RICHMOND, FREDERICKSBURG & POTOMAC RR., during the fiscal year ending September 30th, 1880, had $330,361.80 of gross revenue ; its expenses for transportation, etc., were $174,642.97, leaving a net revenue of $155,718.83, an increase of $662.49 over that of the previous year. After paying its interest account, it had left a net profit of $53,006.77, against $48,863.33 last year. Many improvements to its property were made during the year ; one-third of its track is now steel. The increase in through freights was over 30 per cent., and for the first time the receipts from "through" exceeded those from "local" freights. Passengers paid an average of 3 41 cts. per mile and freight one of 2.21 cts. per mile.

THE VIRGINIA MIDLAND RR.—A big plow, the beam 20 ft. long and other parts proportionately large, and that can make a 2-feet deep furrow, has been made for this RR. by the Watt Plow Co., of Richmond. It is to be used in ditching alongside the track and be drawn by a locomotive. Time, money, and labor are expected to be saved by it.—*The Advance.*

THE ATLANTIC, MISSISSIPPI & OHIO RR. is now advertised to be sold as whole and with all its appurtenances, at the Custom-house, Richmond, Va., February 10th, 1881.

HOOP-POLES, a half million in number, are wanted, by H. J. Skinner at Ronceverte, W. Va., on the C. & O. R'y.

CONTINUED FROM PAGE 171.

irregular, curved and fragmentary belt having the same general direction as the boundary between Virginia and West Virginia, widest in the northeast and wasting away to a few narrow strips in the southwest. The distribution of these rocks on the map shows where these ores may be found.

In Formation No. IV.—"An iron ore is frequently associated with the more slaty atrata of IV, and is of almost invariable occurrence in connection with the ponderous brown sandstone (Medina) which forms the boundary between this and the next superior member of the series." [18–1837.]

"Valuable beds of iron ore occur in the upper part of this group (No. IV), associated with the ferruginous and shaly rocks." [7–1838.]

In Formation No. V.—Among the Massanutton Mountains "an ore of still superior quality, associated with the red and variegated shales (V), higher up in the geological series, has been discovered in many parts of the Big and Little Fort valleys, exposed in layers; which from the extent of the line of their outcrop, are probably continuously associated with the strata to which they appertain." [9–1837.]

Red-shale iron ores of No. V (Clinton).—"Among the facts of economical interest developed in the course of these researches, may be mentioned the determination of the almost uniform occurrence of a peculiarly valuable description of iron ore in connection with a certain member of our series of rocks, frequently displayed for great distances along the sides and summits of the ridges in this region. This ore presents itself in layers arranged parallel with each other, and separated by thin strata of a reddish shale. Though rarely occurring in single beds of great thickness, the multiplication of small seams, exhibited at numerous points, indicate the abundance in which it might be procured, while the friable and yielding condition of the enclosing material would greatly facilitate its removal from the places in which it is imbedded. In the Knobly, New Creek, Patterson's Creek, Capon, North Fork, Props' Gap, South Branch, Warm Spring, Bull-pasture and Back Creek mountains, and in fact a great majority of the more considerable ridges of this region, the presence of this ore has been recognized—either at isolated points or continuously for a length of several miles, exhibiting in all cases the same associated shales, and occupying an invariable station in the geological series. Of the extraordinary value of this ore, the experience of the furnaces in Pennsylvania, where it has recently been brought into use, furnishes the most conclusive evidence. And since the discovery of its admirable adaptation for the furnace, it has been keenly sought after, and thin seams, which if of a different material, would from their thinness have remained unnoticed, have not only been diligently but profitably worked. In alluding to this important fact, the board will permit me to say, that it is not a little gratifying to me to reach a result in illustration of the advantages of the mode of research which has been pursued and of the utility of that systematic delineation of the strata, which it is hoped, will form one of the crowning works of the survey."—In the same connection mention is made of the fact that the limestones of the next higher formation, No. VI, "occur in immediate contiguity with these red shales." [11–1837.]

"From the general uniformity with which particular ores or other useful minerals are associated with particular members of the series or rocks, as already illustrated in the case of the valuable iron ore of Hampshire, Hardy, Pendleton and other counties, it must be apparent that in tracing any individual rock throughout its course, and much more in developing the general order in which the strata are arranged, results of the highest utility are disclosed, illustrating equally the resources of all parts of the region investigated, and furnishing the only safe guide to the more minute examinations which are to form the basis of individual enterprise." [12–1837.]

Red-shale iron ores of V (Clinton).—"As already indicated, these shales (of V), are the repository of the very valuable form of iron ore previously mentioned. From its occurrence in thin beds,

interstratified with the calcareous shales, and from its being usually filled with impressions or hollow casts of shells and other organic remains, and from its resemblance to a dark brown fossiliferous slate or sandstone, it admits of being very readily identified, even by those but little accustomed to the examination of minerals. So uniform appears to be the association of this ore with the present member (No. V) of our series, that besides being exposed in most of the ridges of Hampshire, Hardy, Bath, &c., as formerly stated, it is exhibited at many points in the valleys of the Massanutton, where these shales are brought to light. The observations already made upon the economical importance of this ore, will, it is hoped, invite attention to it, and the above descriptive remarks, in regard to its form and geological relations, may prove useful in aiding its development." [19–1837.]

"Associated with these shales (of V) occurs the remarkable fossiliferous calcareous iron ore referred to in the report of last year. This, from its striking peculiarities, would of itself suffice to identify the present group were it marked by less distinct characters in other respects." [7–1838.]

In the Big Fort Valley of the Massanuttons, on its western side, "apparently dipping beneath the limestone, are dark slates of formation VIII.—beneath which, a little to the west, occurs a small band of formation VI., the intervening VII., if any present, being concealed.' Next come the red shales and accompanying iron ores of V.—and these rest on IV., forming the eastern slope of Kell's Mountain." [18–1838.]

The Little North Mountain from the Potomac to near Jennings' Gap.—"In general the thickness of V, VI and VII, as included in the structure of this mountain, though extremely variable, is much less considerable than in the ridges lying towards the west. The same is also true of IV, though not without important local exceptions. Extensive beds of iron ore, such as accompany these formations, when of greater thickness are not therefore to be looked for generally in the strata of this mountain." [20–1838.]

"South of Jennings' Gap it assumes a new structure in which an irregular synclinal trough of IV makes its appearance upon the mountain top, the western rim of which suddenly bent down into a steep west dip forms the western slope of the mountain. Here IV as well as the superior formations has become more massive, so that in the *double*, as this synclinal trough is called, as well as near the western flank of the mountain extensive and valuable beds of iron have been found associated with IV., V. and VII." [20–1838.]

In the report for 1838, page 29, mention is made of "the discovery of the *fossiliferous and calcareous iron ore* associated with *formation V.*" the previous year.

Analyses of iron ores from Formation V. were given in the report for 1838, p. 32, as follows :—

LOCALITY.	Percentage of Iron.	Silica.	Alumina.	Carb. Lime.	Water &c. loss.
	Composition of 30 grains.				
1. Knobly Mt., W. side—Paddytown Gap	20.50	4.40	1.85	1.32	1.92
2. Powell's Ridge—b. side, near Fish-hook	22.97	5.16	0.67	trace	1.20

1 "Iron ore west side of Knobly Mountain, near Paddytown gap, Hampshire county. Color brownish red, texture soft and argillaceous, structure slaty, apparently composed of minute scales containing flat fossil impressions."

2. "Iron ore south side of Powell's Ridge, near the Fish-hook. Color glossy reddish brown, texture soft scaly, structure laminated, arising from the multitude of flat fossil impressions."

Analyses of iron ores from formation V. were given in the report for 1840, p. 119, as follows :—

LOCALITY.	Metallic Iron.	Peroxide of Iron.	Alumina.	Carbonate of Lime.	Silica and Mag.	Insol. Mat.	Water.	Loss.
	Composition in 100 parts.							
1. Poor Valley Ridge, Cumberland Gap	51.22	76.11	7.60	1.00	11.0	3	21	0.60
2. bloomery—W. side Capon Mt.	69.36	104.80	trace		3.50	12.12	0.58

"1. Iron ore from Poor Valley Ridge, near Cumberland Gap.

Structure slaty, laminated, fossiliferous, color rich brown with a semi-metallic lustre, arising from the micaceous character of the fossil casts which cover the surface." It contains traces of oxide of manganese and of magnesia.

"2. From the Blooming, (Bloomary) south, on western side Capon Mountain. Structure cellular, cells lined with hematite; color dark chestnut brown."

Formation No. VI.—In the analyses of the limestones of this formation (Lower Helderberg) given on page 247, report of 1839, "oxide of iron" is mentioned as a component.

Formation No. VII.—"Iron ores similar to those of the Valley, abound on the flanks of the mountains where the limestone occurs, and many successful furnaces are supplied from this source. At Jordan's Furnace (Lucy Selina), near the Mill Mountain, castings of a very superior quality are made from a hematite procured in the neighborhood of Brushy Ridge; and at no great distance above, on Jackson's River, the enormous water power which is here given by the torrent as it makes its way through the Rich Patch Mountain, is in part applied to give action to the machinery of a large and successful forge. Facts of this kind, though new to very few, are calculated to fix our attention upon the great resources in materials and motive power which these wild districts of the mountains possess, and thence to illustrate the public advantages which are at some future day to flow from the establishment of proper facilities of communication with them, and the direction of wealth and enterprise to the practical development of the riches which they contain." [41--1835.]

"An iron ore has been found in various places in connection with these strata, but of its extent and probable value, I am not yet prepared to speak." [30--1837.]

"Towards its upper boundary it (No. VII) has generally more or less of a ferruginous stain. Indeed this part of it, throughout a large portion of the Apalachian region, is the repository of continuous beds of iron ore of immense extent, which often replace the sandstone for a great depth." [7--1838.]

"The minute investigation of the geological position, as well as the extent of the ores in question, zealously prosecuted during the last year, has brought to light the important fact that throughout a large portion of the middle district of the Apalachian zone, as well as in various parts of its two other subdivisions, the most abundant, continuous and valuable deposits of this material, are to be found in formation VII., the coarse sandstone near its upper boundary being frequently replaced by one for a great thickness, and over a wide extent." [28--1838.]

"These as already stated, are the most abundant ores in the mountainous parts of the middle district, being exposed almost in every ridge of which this formation composes a part. In the Big and Little North mountains, Brown's Hill, Tower Hill, Back Creek Mountain, Brushy Hill, Digg's Mountain, Allen's Mountain, Potts' Creek Mountain, Rich Patch Mountain, Bratton's Mountain, Mill Mountain, &c., &c., these ores are almost invariably to be found replacing the upper strata of VII., and often of enormous thickness. Of the numerous analyses already made of them, two only will be here subjoined, as examples of their composition generally." [32--1838.]

The following analyses of ores from No. V. are given on page 32, report of 1838:—

LOCALITY.	Peroxide of Iron.	Silica.	Alumina.	Water	Loss.
1. Bath Furnace—E. of Bratton's Mt.	94.60	1.22	trace	3.85	0.33
2. Brushy Hill—Alleghany Co.	83.50	9.22	trace	5.60	0.24

"1. Iron ore, Bath furnace, east side of Bratton's Mt. and south of Calf Pasture river. Color chestnut brown, texture compact, structure crystalline and fibrous."

"2. Iron ore, Brushy Hill, Alleghany county, Jordan's mine. Color delicate purplish brown, texture very compact, structure cavernous and cellular, form tending to nodular."

7. The Devonian Iron Ores of Virginia & West Virginia.—These are the ores found in Formation No. VIII.—10 a. Marcellus, 10 b. Hamilton, 10 c. Genesee, 11 a. Portage, and 11 b. Chemung, of the New York Survey,—and in Formation No. IX.—12. Catskill of N. Y. Survey,—those that form the Devonian general group of the rocks; their areas are shown in light brown on the Geological Map (See June No.) intermingled with those of the upper Silurian, Carboniferous Limestone and Coal Measures groups in an irregular central belt, through West Virginia and Virginia, widely expanded in the northeast but contracted and wasted in the southwest. So far this has proven the least productive in iron ores of any of the Paleozoic groups of rocks in the Virginias, although one of the thickest and most widely distributed of the groups of that system and everywhere highly ferruginous; all the springs that flow from it, especially from No. VIII, are more or less chalybeate in character, and nodules and small "pockets" of iron ore are found in all portions of its mass. In Pennsylvania VIII is one of the important iron-bearing rocks.

Formation No. VIII.—Rogers divided this formation into three members; the upper one he named "the ochreous portion of No. VIII," because of "the rusty or ochreous staining of its weathered surfaces." [21--1837.]

"The presence of iron pyrites in nodules, generally of a spheroidal form, or in a disseminated state, especially in the lowest of the subdivisions above described, favors the disintegration of the rock, gives rise to the incrustations of alum, copperas and gypsum, with which its exposed surface is usually overspread, and imparts to the springs arising in it, that sulphureous and chalybeate impregnation for which they are generally remarked." [21--1837.]

"Iron ore and manganese are met with in these rocks." [22--1837.]

In the report for 1838, page 7, the "upper or ochreous slate" of VIII. is again mentioned; and the statement made that "in the lower part of this formation are found found copperas and alum shales and an inferior variety of iron ore."

Formation No. IX.—"Impure iron ore occurs in this member of the series, but in such small deposits and so rarely as to possess little or no economical interest." [8--1838.]

(To be Continued.)

The Commonwealth Mining Company of Virginia, which has opened mines of specular, magnetic, and brown hematite iron ores at Stapleton and Riverville, in Amherst county, and at Greenway, in Nelson county, Va., on James River, again began the shipment of ore to the North on the 22nd, says *The Advance*, of Lynchburg. This Company has accumulated large stocks of fine ore, at each of its three mines, which greatly interested the gentlemen that Vice-President Parsons lately took over the line of the R. & A. RR.—Col. Thomas Dunlap, the efficient general manager of this Mining Company, in a letter transmitting his subscription to The Virginias, writes:—"As a journalist of some twenty-five years experience, I can honestly call The Virginias the most valuable publication of its specialty that I know of. To me, as interested in developing the minerals of this section of Virginia, it is worth fifty times the subscription. I have already obtained very valuable information from it. I wish you all the success you deserve."——We have the promise of a paper on the modes of the occurrence of the ores, etc., in the mines of this company, from Prof. James P. Kimball, the eminent mining engineer and metallurgist of Bethlehem, Pa., who, as the mining engineer of this company, has spent much time in studying the mineral beds on the James; we are sure our readers will look for this with great interest.

Meteorological.--During Oct. 1880, at Richmond, Va., the rain-fall was 2.14 inches, it rained 3 times. The average temperature at sunrise was 46°.4; the lowest temperature was 36°, the highest 83°. The wind, at sunrise, was 15 times from the north quadrants, and 8 times from the south ones; 3 times it was from the east and 2 from the west.—*Richmond Dispatch.*

The Mesozoic Formation in Virginia.

By Oswald J. Heinrich, M. E.

Continued from Page 155.

Comparing the results thus obtained at the Richmond basin with the sections obtained in other parts of this State, but which unfortunately are not yet sufficiently verified for publication, or with those already published from other States, containing the extension of the Mesozoic belts of Virginia, we can trace more or less distinctly the same series of succeeding divisions, although they are sometimes partially obliterated by the changed aspect of material. Commencing at the Mesozoic formation of North Carolina, so ably delineated by Professor E. Emmons in his geological survey of that State, we notice upon the Archæan rocks:

1. *Conglomerate succeeded by the lower sandstones,* generally more red in color, probably 1,500 feet or more, but materially thinning out northward. Conifers most common as silicified trunks. Represented by groups I and II, Richmond section, 287 feet thick.

2. *Coal measures.* Gray and drab-colored sandstones, calcareous shales and slates, lead-colored and black, coal seams, strata containing iron balls (argillaceous iron ore), vegetable and animal remains, consisting of *Equisetum, Calamites,* arenaceous and others, *Estheria,* and *Cythere,* remains of saurians and fish, 1,200 feet thick. Represented by groups III, IV, and V, about 586 feet, of the Richmond section, containing *Tæniopteris, Pecopteris, Tetragonolepis,* and large saurian teeth, *Clepsysaurus* or *Beledon.*

3. *Upper sandstones.* Upper conglomerate in the lower part of the formation, green and dark-colored slates, containing cycads, ferns, and lycopodiacea, also, red and gray sandstones, and marls, more or less mottled with green and white, containing *Estheria.* Represented by groups VI and VII, of which 625 feet are developed in the section, containing fish-scales, *Estheria,* and mostly obscure vegetable remains.

The same observations seem to hold good in the Dan River basin, in North Carolina, as well as in Virginia, and also in the Potomac basin as far as it can be traced at the surface.

Proceeding from the east across the latter basin, we notice sometimes the lower conglomerate, as at Dranesville and other places, but invariably the red and brown sandstones and slates of the lower group, No. II, followed by gray and ash-colored as well as red sandstones, and calcareous shales, their position being partially indicated by the remains of vegetable and animal origin, and their calcareous character. In consequence, probably, of the effect of igneous rocks predominating in that section, we meet sometimes the conglomerate again upon the western margin. It has been known for many years that the Mesozoic sandstones of North Carolina, as well as Virginia, contain workable seams of coal of great economical value. Questions of vital importance are, therefore: *Where is the proper geological horizon of these coal seams? Will they occur at a comparatively permanent position in the series? Are they sometimes disguised by being deteriorated?*

In regard to the State of Virginia, it was generally supposed and so stated, that the seams of coal generally rested immediately, upon, or only divided by a few feet of slate from, the older Archæan rocks forming the floor of the basin. When the subdivisions of the North Carolina series had been laid down conclusively by Professor E. Emmons, it was firmly established in that section of country that a considerable series of sedimentary strata, entirely wanting in Virginia, existed below the seams of coal. Explorers, therefore, naturally looked for the primary rocks as the most permanent landmark for the outcrop of the coal seams. Many a disappointment followed this universal conclusion, and even the continuity of the coal seams in the Richmond basin was doubted. It can now be seen with perfect clearness how that error occurred and was maintained for many years. It so happened that a number of the most valuable discoveries in the early mining in that section of country were upon points where the granite floor, previous to the deposition of the coal, had been carved out at a very abrupt angle. Consequently, the seams of coal, sometimes even at a very steep angle with the granite floor, were considered to conform in deposition with the granite. This error was still more persistently followed, because in many instances where even sedimentary strata underlaid the

coal, they were frequently of the nature of sandstone, hardly distinguishable from true granite, except by diligent and trained observers. It being considered an established fact that no workable seams of coal existed below the main big seams generally mined there, almost no sinking of shafts below that seam of coal was carried on, or the sinking was at least invariably stopped as soon as a hard feldspathic sandstone was encountered, which appeared to be granite to the uninitiated eye.

The above explorations, therefore, establish the following very important points.

1. At least five hundred and sixty feet of purely sedimentary rocks exist in the Mesozoic formation (at least in the Richmond basin) below the last coal seam, or nearly from the bottom of the carbonaceous group.

2. All the workable seams of coal are concentrated within the central part of about one hundred feet of the carbonaceous group, characterized, particularly at the top and bottom, by very coarse, hard sandstones, with highly fossiliferous slates below each of them, containing *Equiseta* and other vegetable impressions, fish-scales, *Estheria,* and limestone, in concretions or small strata.

3. A small seam of coal exists in the upper sandstone group.

4. No true coal seam, only highly bituminous shales have as yet been found in the strata below the carbonaceous group.

5. Oil rocks exist above and below the carbonaceous division, but are more numerous above. In this group may belong the coke seam at Carbon Hill.

In regard to disturbances which occurred subsequently to the deposition of the formation, we may say, that while instances of the kind are by no means wanting, still they are of far less magnitude than might be anticipated.

The unevenness of the floor of the Archæan rocks, no doubt, first effected the deposits above, probably by subsiding, or even by the giving way of the strata, in consequence of shrinkage. These effects may be noticed in small anticlinal and synclinal rolls of the strata, as well as by limited shifting, principally downwards. Two main directions of disturbances may be noticed: One, about parallel with the trend of the formation; the other, and more important, oblique. The former frequently exhibits dislocations of a few feet or more, but the strata almost invariably recur regularly to the dip. The latter class frequently produce disturbances of far more magnitude, pinching strata often entirely out of existence.

The former, therefore, may be due more to the effect of shrinkage, and a consequent slipping or bending of the upper strata. The latter, no doubt, are often due to the influence of eruptive rocks, which more frequently cross the formation obliquely than parallel with the trend. The effects of these eruptive rocks in hardening those adjoining or crushing them into brecciated rocks, or debituminizing the carbonaceous strata, at least for a short distance, are frequently noticed. A remarkable instance of the latter was once visible at the Clover Hill mines, in the Richmond basin, where a dike of dolorite had penetrated the stratification obliquely.

In the slates above the coal the dike had (probably) produced a cavity of considerable magnitude, which was found to be completely lined with perfect crystals of calcite. The coal next to the dike was converted into a coke somewhat resembling artificial coke, but more compact. In about fifty feet or more the coal gradually increased in bituminous matter until it assumed its former state.

IV. *Fossil Remains of the Formation.*

Though not able to do justice to this subject, I cannot pass over it entirely; or refrain from mentioning at least such of the fossil remains as have been so far noticed in the strata. This is the more necessary as some of them appear to define certain geological horizons.

Prof. W. B. Rogers, in his report to the Association of American Geologists and Naturalists, in 1840–42, in which he endeavored to define the geological age of the secondary sandstone formation of Virginia, refers to the following fossil remains:

1. *Remains of Vegetable Origin.*—*Equisetum columnare, E. arundiniforme; Calamites arenaceus, C. planicostatus; Tæniopteris magnifolia; Pecopteris Whitbyensis, P. Munsteri, P. obtusifolia(?); Lycopodites uncifolius; Zamites obtusifolius, Z.* [unclear]

2. *Remains of Animal Origin.*—Teeth probably of saurians. Fish-scales, probably of a new genus of *Catopterus; Posidonia* (now generally recognized as *Estheria*).

The fossil remains collected during the exploration above referred to contain, according to the revised determination of Prof. C. E. Hall, University of Pennsylvania, the following:

1. *Of Vegetable Origin.*—*Equisetum Mongrotii* (internal cylinder, formerly called *Calamites arenaceus*); *E. Gamnianus* (closely allied to *E. Nuzeri*); *E. Munsteri, E. Rogersii* (in part); *Calamites Suckowii;* tubercles of *Equisetum; Schizoneura meriani;* cones of coniferous trees.

2. *Of Animal Origin.* — *Estheria ovata* and *minuta; Cythere; Dictyopyge; Tetragonolepis* (whole specimen of fish, various fragments of bones and bony-plates, scales, probably also fragments of a tooth); *Clepsysaurus* or *Belodon* (large tooth); coprolites.

In the variegated shales of the Potomac basin remains were found by the author, which seem to be the plates of a species of *Sphaerites* (according to Quenstedt). They are about ½ to 1-16 inch in diameter, hexagonal, and apparently without central perforation. They may be more minutely described at a future time, as it will be of considerable interest to distinguish their position in the series, because so far, I believe, the absence of radiata in the Mesozoic formations of America was generally admitted.

Regarding the position which these various remains assume in the geological column, so far as developed by the section at Midlothian, the following statements may be of interest to verify them hereafter at other localities:

Commencing from the granite floor in group I, and lower part of II, no fossil remains so far have been detected for the first 90 to 100 feet. We then meet with obscure vegetable impressions, and at 123 feet the first fragment of a tooth, and coprolites for the next 25 feet. At 200 feet we recognize *Esthere, Cythere,* and *Equisetum Mongrontii,* which continue through the strata above in connection with others. During the next 50 feet we also find the first small scales of fish (*Dictyopyge*). At about this point and a little higher up the last red-colored feldspar has been detected. In group III, at about 500 to 528 feet, the occurrence of a highly bituminous dark drab-colored and black shale, containing fish-scales, *Estheria,* bony coal, and concretions of limestone, is remarkable, because below it a strong brownish-gray oil-rock exists.

No animal remains have been detected within the group IV, except in the top strata of the group. Among the various vegetable remains, near the top of this group, or the lower part of V, *Taniopteris magnifolia* has been found, also, *Schizoneura meriani,* the strata containing also *Cythere, Estheria,* and fish-scales of the genus *Tetragonolepis,* which is now found in several strata. The fossiliferous strata containing more or less the same remains now continue through group V in greater profusion, including also the saurian teeth. After about 1100 feet above the granite no animal remains have so far been detected, but vegetable impressions continue. No attempt will be made here to enter into a dispute in regard to the real geological age which may be assigned to the various divisions laid down in the section. In fact, they have been more sought for to answer the purpose of the practical explorer than the speculative geologist. A distinctive feature seems to be the predominance of the remains of fish and saurians within a certain range of the series. All the fossils so far refer to the Triassic period. Still in Germany at least (Quenstedt, *Petrefactenkunde*), *Tetragonolepis* has never been found in the Solenhofen calcareous slates and limestones, and according to the same authority is hardly found anywhere except in the Lias. It is also frequently noticed in the Richmond coalfield that the strata below the carboniferous area have a more rapid dip, and some cases unquestionably a different bearing. The latter important fact has been variously noticed between the primary border of the basin and the course of the outcrop of coal where exposed or explored for. It has also been frequently noticed in the mines in cases of disturbed ground by the rising of the floor. Of course more evidence from various localities is yet desirable to verify so important a fact. The occurrence of gypsum as far as noticed is confined to strata above the lower sandstone, and principally to the strata above the carboniferous series.

Taking all facts together it is not unlikely that at least the lower groups below the carboniferous are depositions of a different geological area, in which case it would seem to be settled that the carboniferous and oleiferous groups represent the Lettenkohle of the Triassic. But in the upper series of rocks a subdivision may yet be found to exist when the full series can be determined above the 1500 feet represented in the Midlothian series.

To be Continued

Communication from Hon. W. H. Ruffner, LL.D. Supt of Public Instruction in Virginia.

Lexington, Va., Oct. 30, 1880.

Maj. Jed. Hotchkiss:—

Dear Sir—I have received the Oct. No. of The Virginias, and read it with great interest, as indeed I do every number. Prof. Campbell's article on Purgatory Mountain possesses great value, scientific, as well as practical. He differs so modestly from our honored friend Prof. W. B. Rogers in his interpretation of the structure of the mountain, that only the most careful reader will observe that whilst Prof. Rogers declared the mountain to be a syncline with the iron ore of his No. III cropping out on both sides, Prof. Campbell makes it a monocline with the ore of III on the east side and the ore of V on the west, showing thus the typical structure of the North Mountain in Rockbridge. I have the greatest confidence in Prof. Campbell's geologic interpretations, particularly in the Silurian and Devonian formations of Virginia, which he has been studying for 30 years. Indeed with his clear, cautious and thoroughly sound and honest mind, trained in science and field practice from his youth, I know of no man more worthy of confidence as an explorer, delineator and analyst, than Prof. John L. Campbell.

Concerning The Virginias, my estimate of its value increases with every number. Not only is it of special value to scientific men, to miners and manufacturers, to buyers and owners of mineral lands, to railroad people and such like, but it furnishes most interesting and useful reading to all intelligent people, especially to the people of Virginia and West Virginia, and still more especially to school officers and teachers, whose work lies largely in teaching the growing Virginians what a heritage they have, and how they may use it for their own good and the good of the Commonwealth.

Very truly yours,

W. H. Ruffner.

The Gaymont Coal Co., located a mile above Hawk's Nest station of the C. & O. R'y., Fayette Co., W. Va., has completed the incline, etc., of what was begun as the Louisa colliery and has commenced the shipment of Lower Measures or New River coal. It works the same bed as the Hawk's Nest Coal Co., Maj. Echols', 3 ft. in thickness, which, by analysis of Prof. J. W. Mallet of the University of Virginia was found to contain Moisture 0.93 per cent., Volatile Combustible Matter 21.83, Fixed Carbon 75.37, Ash 1.87, and Sulphur 0.26, and which he pronounced "a valuable fuel, especially for metallurgic purposes."

Timber.—"Attention is being attracted to the hard-wood lands of the country as never before, and it will soon be a question whether our own dealers will not find themselves confined to inferior grades of timber in consequence of the extensive purchases which are being made on foreign account. A disposition is manifesting itself very strongly by foreign operators to secure all the good tracts of oak, ash, maple and other hard-woods which they can obtain in large blocks."—*Northwestern Lumberman,* Oct. 30, 1880.

Limestone.—The Low Moor Iron Co. of Va. invites bids for quarrying limestone from its quarry and delivering at least 125 tons a day on its cars broken up ready for use in the furnace.—D. C. Steele is furnishing a part of the limestone used at Low Moor from Steele's Siding about 3 miles S. W. from the furnace, on the railway.

Mica in valuable beds has been found on the farm of John P. Thompson, near New London, Bedford Co., Va., says the Lynchburg correspondent of the Richmond *Dispatch.*

The James River Steel M'f'g & Mining Co. is now filling an order for 500 tons of 45 lb. iron rails for sidings for the Richmond & Alleghany RR.

The Virginia Mining and Manufacturing Co. was incorporated, Oct. 22, with authority to mine and produce for manufacture or market, kaolin, plumbago, coal, iron, lead, gold, silver, &c.; to manufacture or buy and sell the same, to lease, buy and hold lands necessary therefor. The capital stock is to be not less than $10,000 nor more than $200,000, to be divided in shares of $100 each, the stock to be deemed and treated as personal estate. The company can hold real estate not exceeding 25,000 acres, and the chief office is to be in Richmond.

The names and residences of its officers for the first year are: A. S. Buford, president; William H. Haxall, vice-president. Directors: A. S. Buford, William H. Haxall, Thomas Branch, A. Y. Stokes, W. J. Johnson, A. L. Ellett, F. R. Scott, Isaac Davenport, Jr., T. M. Logan, Richmond; C. C. McRae, Manchester, and William G. Taylor, Chesterfield. Mr. W. A. H. Schreiber, of Philadelphia, Pa., who had charge of the Pottery Dept. at the Centennial Exhibition, is the General Manager. Mr. Schreiber called on us a few days ago and showed a sample of white ware made from Virginia kaolin that was superior in character to that made from the kaolins used at Trenton, N. J. He was much pleased with the kaolins, feldspars, ochres, plumbago, etc., that he had seen in Amelia, Goochland, Chesterfield and elsewhere in Va., and is confident that the Co. he has organized must prove a great success with such cheap, abundant and excellent raw materials to work with, and with such advantages for manufacturing as exist at Manchester or Richmond.—Mr. Schreiber has opened an office in the Wilkinson Building, in Richmond.

This Company has all the elements of strength in its organization and there is no reason why it should not meet with great success in its operations.

The *white-ware potteries* of New Jersey in 1879 (Report of State Geologist) produced $2,500,000 worth of wares, five-eighths of the U. S. product, employed 3,000 hands and paid $1,250,000 for wages,—and yet we imported $4,000,000 worth of the same wares that year. The N. J. potteries are at Trenton, Elizabeth and Jersey City.—Richmond has all that they have and some things, as climate and cheaper living, that they have not.

Norfolk, Virginia's commercial city, is developing rapidly. Its *Daily Virginian* recently published a summary of its trade, etc., during the fiscal year just ended, from which it appears that all its trade amounted to $13,789,209; in that are included $13,789,209 for cotton exported, and $2,500 for cotton sent coastwise,—the city holding its rank, which it reached in 1874, as the third cotton-port of the Union, having received in 1879-80 about one-tenth of the crop of the United States, or 597,086 bales. The clearances were 114,500 tons, only 15,499 of which was in American vessels. Its peanut trade was valued at $1,000,000, and its "trucking" business at $949,200.

The Virginias.

A Mining, Industrial and Scientific Journal:
Devoted to the Development of Virginia and West Virginia.

Vol. I, No. 12. }   Staunton, Virginia, December, 1880.   { Price 25 Cents.

The Virginias,

PUBLISHED MONTHLY,

By JED. HOTCHKISS, - - - Editor and Proprietor,

At 346 E. Main St., Staunton, Va.

Terms, including postage, per year, in advance, $2.00. Single numbers, 25 cents. Extra copies, $20.00 per 100. Back numbers, from the first, can be had at 25c each. Advertising, per inch of length of single column (3 columns to a page, as on advertising pages), one month, $2.50; two months, $4.00; three months, $5.50; six months, $7.50; nine months, $10.00, and twelve months, $12.00; payable in advance. Specimen Numbers of this journal are sometimes sent to parties supposed to have an interest in the development of the Virginias, or a desire to be informed in reference to their resources, improvement, etc.: they will please consider this an invitation to become subscribers and so help to sustain a paper devoted to their interests.

On sale at Hunter & Co.'s Bookstore, Main Street, Staunton, Virginia.

The Virginias for 1880, substantially bound, with the 18 extra pages of maps and sections (including a full geological map of Virginia and West Virginia, in 10 colors,), complete, with index and title page, will be sent, by express or mail, prepaid, to any address in the U. S., on receipt of Three Dollars.

The Virginias for 1881.—The second volume of this journal begins with the year 1881. The subscriptions of most of its numerous and widely distributed patrons ends with the present number and with the year 1880; for, although constant additions have been made to our list throughout the year, up to its very close, in almost every case the back numbers for the year were called for. Some, unasked, have already renewed their subscriptions and are on our list for 1881; we now ask for a prompt renewal by all others, that our mailing list for the coming year may be made ready.—Please remember that our terms are: Two Dollars a year, invariably in advance, and at once remit, by check, bank notes, or postal money order. We do not wish to send THE VIRGINIAS to any one that does not want it, nor to any-one that does not comply with our terms; therefore we make this request. Our time and talents are devoted to the publication of our Journal, that we may make it worth even more than we charge for it, and we have none left to devote to looking after small "dues," scattered all over the country. When the money is received the name is entered on the mailing list for the time paid for, and when that expires the paper will stop, unless payment is renewed.

THE VIRGINIAS for 1881 will probably be an improvement on that for 1880. The storehouse of what may may be said concerning the resources of these states and their development is as exhaustless as their vast beds of coals and iron ores, and we have not been able in our full-freighted issues of the past year to sensibly diminish the always accumulating stock of material worthy of publication that is already in hand. Many valuable articles in reference to our mineral wealth, some of them illustrated, for publication in 1881, are already in hand, and others are in course of preparation by capable men. We have awakened an interest in this work, not only in our universities, colleges, and preparatory schools, but all over these states, that has opened thousands of eyes to see what is before them, and made available sources of information that we expect to draw from liberally.

In this number.—The reports of Prof. W. B. Rogers on the Iron Ores of Va. and W. Va. are completed. The one here published is an extremely valuable one in reference to the iron ores found in the coal measures of W. Va. They will be followed by other articles on these ores which just now are attracting a great deal of attention.—The articles of Mr. Heinrich on the Mesozoic in Va. are completed in this issue. They are of very great value, especially to all interested in the Richmond coal basin. We have some criticisms to make in a future number.—The paper by Prof. Campbell on the Rich-patch Iron Region is, beyond question, one of the most valuable contributions that has ever been made to the geology, both scientific and economic, of Virginia. We have no room now for comments, but simply remark that Prof. Campbell's sections and his elucidation of them show a most wonderful basis for operations in iron manufacturing in this region. Our thanks and those of our readers are due to Prof. C. for having, at our request, given us this timely contribution.—Many items of great interest are crowded out. We shall have more room hereafter.

Index and Title-page will be sent in January.

The January, 1881, number will be mainly devoted to giving the results of mining, quarrying, metal-working, etc., in Virginia and West Virginia during the year 1880, and to a presentation of such of their mining statistics from the 10th Census as we can procure. As complete lists as we can obtain will be published of all the iron, coal, lead, zinc, manganese, ochre, barytes, mica, and other mines; of granite, soapstone, slate and other quarries; of all furnaces, forges, etc.; that were worked during that year, with the names and addresses of the operators; the quantities of raw materials raised and manufactured products made; the number of men employed, etc.—We desire to make a complete presentation of the present condition of these industries, and to this end we earnestly request full information, sent as promptly as possible, from all in charge of the operations specified.

Blast-furnace work along the C. & O. Ry.—Buffalo Gap is doing well, making from 10 to 12 tons a day. It is obtaining some ore from Madison Run, Orange Co., Va.——Grace, of the Pa. & Va. Iron & Coal Co., at Ferrol, J. A. Beck foundryman, in the week ending Dec. 18, made 112 tons foundry iron, from Ferrol ores: on the 19th the output was 20.5 tons.—— Lucy Selina, of the Longdale Co., is doing its usual good work; the second furnace there, one of greater capacity, will very soon be ready to be put in blast. A large stock of ore, limestone and coke has been accumulated.—— Callie is now in full blast, making a good run.——Low Moor, as stated elsewhere, is making from 70 to 75 tons a day. Some 20,000 tons of its iron were recently disposed of at one sale in Cincinnati, on the iron grading high.—— Quinnimont, of the Pa. & Va. Iron & Coal Co., completed its second year of its foundry iron,a day. The furnace was lined with "Scioto Star" fire-bricks, which have stood well its remarkably long run.——It is more than probable, from recent transactions, that before long there will be a resumption of work at the Panther-gap Furnace, and that the extensive, iron-ore-abounding old California Furnace property will be extensively utilized.

Low Moor Furnace, Va.—The report in our last issue was to the week ending Nov. 20. For the week ending Nov. 27 the product was about 484 tons, of which 184 were No. 1 and the remainder No, 2, from about 1,185 tons of ore, one-third lump and two-thirds wash, and some 96 tons of coal, 561 of coke and 544 of limestone.—For the week ending Dec. 4 the yield was about 488 tons, divided between "foundry" and "mill," Nos, 1 and 2; from some 1,164 tons of ore, lump and wash, in same proportions as in previous week, 542 tons of limestone, 89 of coal, 555 of coke.—For the week ending Dec. 11 the production was about 465 tons of iron, of various grades, from some 1,269 tons of ore, proportioned as previously, 72 tons of coal, 602 of coke and 592 of limestone. The make for the 21 days, including 23 hours for stoppages, was about 1438 tons; an average of about 71.5 daily for the time actually run. It is reported that the yield has reached 100 tons on some days.

Arragonite.—We find in the Metallurgical Review for May, 1878, the following analysis of Arragonite, containing lead, from Wythe Co., Va.—Ca O 51.819, Pb O 6.087, CO2 41.800, Fe2 O3 0.033, Si O2 0.012, and H2 O 0.070; total 99.321. Its hardness was 3.5 and its specific gravity 3.078. The analysis was made by Prof. F. P. Dunnington of the University of Va.

Lexington, Rockbridge county, Va., is moving vigorously in reference to a railway not only to but from that attractive town. An association has been formed for the promotion of a scheme for a railway via Lexington to Pittsburg, and prevision is being made for a preliminary survey. Hon. W. A. Anderson is the energetic chairman of the association; he is corresponding with all interested parties.

The Pittsburg, Wheeling & Ky. RR. is now completed to Wheeling. W. Va., from Pittsburg; the Register advocates its extension down the Ohio, 220 miles farther, to Huntington, to a connection with the C. & O. and the E. L. & B. S.

Fincastle, Botetourt Co., Va., has, by action of its Town Council, appointed a committee, of which Capt. J. H. H. Figgat is chairman, to gather information and see how a railroad can be secured to that town.

The Iron Ores of Virginia and West Virginia.

By Prof. WILLIAM B. ROGERS.

(CONCLUDED FROM PAGE 175.)

8. The Lower and Middle Carboniferous Iron Ores of Virginia and West Virginia.—These are the ores of Rogers' formation X (Dana's 13a.) the Lower Carboniferous, the Lowest Virginia Coal Measures, those that Rogers recently calls the Montgomery Grits and Coal Measures, the Vespertine Sandstone and Coal of Penn., those of the "white" areas of the Geological Map, (See June No.), and those of Rogers' formation XI, the Middle Carboniferous, (13 b. of Dana), the Greenbrier Shales and Limestones (Carboniferous Limestones), the Umbral Shales and Limestones of Penn., those of the "pink" areas of the Geological Map. They are only found in the Apalachian divisions of Va. and W. Va., as an inspection of the areas indicated on the map will show.

In formation No. XI the Greenbrier limestones and shales.—"Pyritous slate" is mentioned as occurring in fragments mingled with the gypsum and at the salt wells in Smyth and Washington, and a suggestion made that it may have furnished the sulphuric acid that acting on the limestone of XI changed a portion of it into gypsum. [11–1836.]

"As among the valuable materials associated with the limestones and shales just spoken of, I may be allowed again to notice an iron ore of highly promising character, which has been discovered at several points in Greenbrier and Monroe. Should I be correct in my opinion of its good qualities, and of this chemical examination will furnish the means of judging, its value will soon be duly appreciated, as it indicates a character greatly resembling that of the stratified ore of the shales of our No. 5, and I have reason to believe, may be obtained in abundant quantities." [23–1837.]

"Iron ore of good quality is found in the shales of this group. It is of the nodular variety, resembling that associated with the coal measures, and occurs in the shaly beds in layers, alternating with the other materials of the strata." [8–1838.]

"Iron ores are of frequent occurrence near the upper limit of the formation, more especially where it is met with in the ores before spoken of, and often exists in such amount, and of a quality so rich and easily wrought, as to possess a high degree of economical importance. Of the composition of these ores, which are usually proto-carbonates of iron, some examples will be given hereafter, and a large number of further details will be gathered in the progress of our chemical investigations." [93–1839.]

"Oxide of iron" is mentioned as one of the components of each of 12 samples of limestones of XI of which analyses are given. [148-150–1839.]

"In the vicinity of German Settlement, on the summit of a high hill on the northern side of Rhine creek, is the outcrop of a body of *iron ore* of superior quality. It occurs on the surface over a wide area in large fragments, and is also found a short distance beneath. These fragments are evidently in place, and are portions of a bed which occurs near the surface, in the upper part of formation XI." [113–1839.]

"On the summit on the mountain (Laurel Hill in Preston and Monongalia), is a narrow denuded valley, composed of the upper part of XI. The denudation is not here deep enough to expose the red shales and sandstones of this formation, the only rocks laid bare being the black shales which immediately underlie XII. It is among these shales that the ores supplying the Henry Clay and Greenville furnaces are found. These ores occur in three different bands, which are in general included in a section of 20 and always within 30 feet.

The *upper or castile vein*, the most uniform in thickness, varies from 8 to 15 inches, and having but a slight covering of shale, has been less protected than the lower bands from atmospheric agencies. It is therefore usually found in a decomposed state, the whole bed sometimes presenting the condition of a friable shaly oxide, much valued on account of the ease with which it works. Occasionally it occurs in nodules merely encrusted with the oxide, the nucleus being in the original state of proto-carbonate.

Beneath this, 8 or 10 feet, we meet with the *middle or rock vein*, generally 8 or 10 inches thick, though varying from 4 inches to 3 feet. This is for the most part compact and undecomposed, more uniform in character than the other veins, and in general rich and fine grained.

Below this, at a depth of about 8 or 10 feet, is the *lower vein*, varying from 2 inches to 6, and averaging 4 inches. This is usually coarse and siliceous, and chiefly valuable at the outcrop, where it has been decomposed. All these ores contain vegetable impressions." [123–1839.]

In the Report for 1839, pages 153-154, the following analyses of Iron Ores from formation XI are given, in parts of 30 grains:—

LOCALITY IN W. VA.	Carbonate of iron.	Carbonate of lime.	Carbonate of magnesia.	Silica.	Alumina.	Water and bitumen.	Water.	Carbonate of manganese.
1. Greenville Furnace	28.27	trace	trace	1.12	0.20	0.31	....	trace
2. "	16.08	trace	trace	6.80	1.04	0.80	....	trace
3. "	15.15	trace	trace	7.80	0.94	....	0.50	trace
4.	17.79	0.35	5.62	0.74	....		0.41	trace
5. Henry Clay Furnace	22.28	0.90	1.87	0.30	....		0.22	trace
6. Geman Settlement	23.00	0.30	1.02	0.30	....		0.28	trace

1. "Iron ore from Formation XI., from the upper seam at the Greenville furnace, Laurel Hill, Monongalia county. Color reddish brown, or olive, weathered surface light brown or drab, texture compact, grain fine, fracture slightly conchoidal."

2. "Iron ore from XI, average specimen from 'Rock vein,' Greenville furnace. Color bluish, inclining to grey, texture compact, grain rather fine, fracture earthy."

3. "Iron ore from XI, 'Rock vein' at the 'Greenville works,' contains vegetable remains and numerous disseminated scales of mica. Color grey, texture rather compact, grain moderately fine, fracture irregular, earthy."

4. "Iron ore from XI, 'Lower vein' at Greenville furnace. Color dull reddish brown, texture compact, fracture slightly conchoidal, disclosing minute scales of mica."

5. "Iron ore from XI, upper vein, Henry Clay furnace, Monongalia county. Color grey with a reddish brown tint, texture compact, grain fine, fracture conchoidal, weathered surface, ochreous."

6. "Iron ore from XI, German Settlement. Color bluish grey inclining to brown, texture compact, grain fine, fracture irregular, conchoidal. Contains films of carbonate of lime and minute specks of sulphuret of iron, sparsely disseminated." [153-154–1839.]

NOTE.—"It will be remarked of the above analyses, that a trace of carbonate of manganese is stated as generally present, both in the ores of XI and of the coal measures. In only two or three instances was its amount sufficient to be estimated, and in these cases it was found so inconsiderable as to be undeserving of note. With regard to several other specimens yet to be analysed, there are indications of a larger proportion of this ingredient. I would add that a precise determination of its amount will always be given where it is capable of being noted or worthy of mention in an economical point of view." [156–1839.]

9. The Upper Carboniferous Iron Ores of Virginia and West Virginia—mainly of West Virginia.—These are the ores of Rogers' formations Nos. XII, XIII, XIV, XV and XVI, (Dana's 14.), those of the Lower, Middle and Upper Coal Measures of THE VIRGINIAS (See page 18), the Seral group of Pennsylvania,—those of 14 a, the Great Conglomerate and Conglomerate Coal Group (XII), 14 b. Lower Coal Group (XIII), 14 b. Lower Barren Group (XIV), 14 c. Upper Coal Group (XV), and 14 c. Upper Barren Group (XVI), of the former Va. and Pa. Surveys.

In the "Reconnoissance Report," that for 1835, "iron ore" is mentioned, page 48, as one "of the more important deposits of the coal fields; and, by way of illustration, a portion of Hampshire county, now W. Va., is mentioned, "immediately west of the Eastern Front Ridge of the Alleghany," "extending

for a distance of many miles along the Potomac," where five successive tiers of nearly horizontal beds are exposed, from below upwards, as follows:—"Upon a stratum of valuable iron ore, not less than 15 feet in thickness, there rests a bed of sandstone, upon which reposes a coal seam, 3 feet thick; above this another bed of sandstone, then a 2 feet vein of coal, next sandstone, then another coal seam of 4 feet; again a stratum of sandstone, and over it a 7 feet vein of coal; over this a heavy bed of iron ore, and crowning the series an enormous coal seam of from 15 to 20 feet in thickness." On which the comment is,—"A simple enumeration of the strata there exposed will furnish an illustration of the resources of this corner of the state, well calculated to inspire astonishment and exultation." [48-49-1835.]

In concluding his summary of the mineral resources of the great coal field, in his "Reconnoissance," Prof. Rogers uses these words:—"There is no point of view, however, in which the immeasurable riches of this region are rendered more obvious to our minds than that of the uniform and continuous structure which has already been described. For, it is in those widely spreading strata of sandstone that nearly all the boundless treasures of this country are enclosed, and the continuous character exhibited by them, gives the strongest possible assurance of a like uninterrupted extension of the various beds of valuable materials which they include. In this view, how magnificent is the picture of the resources of this region, and how exhilarating the contemplation of all the happy influences upon the enterprise, wealth and intellectual improvement of its inhabitants, which are rapidly to follow the successive development of its inexhaustible mineral possessions. In a country where the channels of nearly all the principal rivers have been scooped out, in part through beds of coal, where some of them are paved with the richest ores of iron, and where the very rock itself, the sterile sandstone of the cliffs and mountains, is enriched at certain depths with abundant stores of salt, what more is needed to fulfill the happy and glorious destinies that await it, than to awaken enterprise to a due appreciation of the golden promises it holds out, and to direct industrious and active research to the thorough investigation of the character, position and uses of the treasures it contains ?" [50-1835.]

In the report for 1839 all the strata over XII were included in XIII, but that was divided, very properly, into the Upper Coal Series and the Lower Coal Series, the *black flint ledge* being the boundary.

In formation No. XIII.—In a general view of the great coal field the statement is made that the coal seams, "iron ores," etc. passed over on its eastern side, appear again, in reverse order, in Ohio. [85-1839.]

The "rich coal seams and iron ores" of the border of the great coal basin in Ky. and Ohio, where cut by the Ohio, are mentioned as "presenting a noble development." [87-1839.]

Speaking of the layers of limestone of the coal measures the report says, "They not unfrequently lose themselves by gradual transition into slate or iron ore, or sandstone. Numerous beds of slate also interpose themselves between the siliceous rocks, presenting for the most part a dark brown or nearly black, and an ochreous greenish color. It is with these, particularly the former, that the coal seams are in general immediately associated. The bands of iron ore also usually occur in or adjoining them, as well as contiguous to the layers of limestone." [96-1839.]

Speaking of the section on the Kanawha from the falls down to Charleston, the report says, "The comparatively small amount of shaly strata along the latter section, though fortunately unaccompanied by any diminution in the thickness or deterioration in the quality of the coal seams there so admirably exposed for long distances continuously in the river hills, would appear to connect itself with the attenuated width of the bands of iron ore occurring among these slates, and therefore would seem to give a general confirmation to the conclusion derived from our observations thus far, that these ores are much less abundant in that than in some of the more northern divisions of the coal field." [97-1839.]

In the report for 1839, page 99, a promise is made that when examining the coal fields in reference to the character of their coal beds "a careful attention will be given to the bands of iron ore, as well as the limestone accompanying the coal."

In the Eastern or Potomac coal basin the bed of "argilla-

ceous shales" underlying coal bed No. 1 at Wilson's mill, about 2 miles below the mouth of Abraham's creek, and at Harvey's, 6 miles below that creek, is spoken of as "containing rich nodular iron ore, the nodules varying from one to 12 inches in diameter." The shales overlying coal seam No. 1, separating it from No. 2, "are siliceous, coarse and lead-colored, and abound in iron ore, rich but of a coarse texture." [107-1839.]

Over coal bed No. 1, near Harvey's, mentioned above, there is a stratum of sandstone 45 feet thick "through which in some places there runs a band of slate containing good iron ore, at some points 18 inches in thickness, though very variable, and thinning out with the enclosing slate." [106-1839.]

"Higher up the river No. 2 coal bed is repeatedly seen from 10 to 12 inches thick, and slaty. The shales both above and below contain the nodular ore, the nodules in the former being sometimes 18 inches in thickness." [107-1839.]

In the Middle Basin, on Stony River about one mile below where the turnpike crosses it, above the upper coal bed of the locality, "occurs a vein of impure iron ore, which for more than a hundred yards presents a uniform thickness of 2 feet. It is however a rather poor one, though not poorer than is often worked." [109-1839.]

On Cunningham's land, north of the turnpike and near Stony River, "a band of impure limestone 2 or 3 ft. thick, including in calcareous, argillaceous slates, and occasionally containing nodules of iron ore," lies 8 or 10 ft. beneath the lower coal seam.—Three miles below the turnpike on Stony River the "beautifully fossiliferous" slates overlying the lower coal seam "contain two bands of very *rich iron ore*, the upper ranging from one to six inches, the lower from two to three."—Four miles above the turnpike the limestone underlying the lower seam "contains nodules of *pure iron ore* near the bottom."—At the falls of the river, 7 miles above the turnpike, above the lower seam of coal, separating it from a calcareous rock, "are shales and shaly sandstones, in the lower part of which, and immediately over the coal, is a rich band of iron ore 4 inches thick."—In the limestone band between the first and the second seams of coal in all this region where it is exposed "is generally included one or more seams of *iron ore*. This band is seen imperfectly exposed on Stony river about 3 miles below the turnpike, but the presence of iron in it could not be satisfactorily ascertained from the obscured condition of the strata. Four miles above the turnpike it is again exposed on the river, overlying the lower coal, and separated from it by 15 or 20 feet of shales and sandstones. It here abounds in a *rich iron ore*, occurring in nodules sometimes 8 and 10 inches in diameter, fine-grained, homogeneous and of a delicate lead color. Besides this variety, it also contains another and coarser kind, quite siliceous and having the aspect of a poor ore when freshly fractured, but upon exposure assuming a deep ferruginous hue. This is irregularly distributed in the shales."

"At the falls of Stony river the same band is again exposed with a thickness of from 15 to 20 feet, in the upper part siliceous, in the lower shaly. Here the coarser variety of ore predominates, and is found in great abundance. At the preceding localities the rocks in question show themselves 30 or 40 feet above the water's edge, but five miles above the turnpike, owing to the rapid rise of the bed of the stream, they are exposed immediately above it, but too imperfectly to ascertain the extent of iron ore included in them."—"The importance of this band, due to the valuable layers of limestone and iron ore it contains cannot fail to suggest to those interested in this region the advantages that may be derived from an examination of its contents wherever it may be exposed." [110-111-1839.]

In the Western Coal Basin, that of the waters of Difficult creek, and the North Branch of the Potomac in its upper reaches, on the west flank of the ridge between Stony river and Difficult creek, "Still lower down the hill, and geologically under the upper seam of coal the calcareous band is exposed, associated with iron ore, which appears by infiltration to have been converted into per-oxide." [111-1839.]

In the Kingwood basin the lowest seam of coal "where formerly opened, at the point (Cheat river), alluded to above, one mile below the Kingwood ferry, the shales which overly it contain *five bands of rich iron ore* within the space of 4 or

Continued on Page 186.

The Coal and Coke Movement over the Chesapeake & Ohio R'y,

for the month of November, 1880, and for the corresponding period of the previous year, in tons of 2,000 lbs., as reported for THE VIRGINIAS by Mr. Charles M. Gibson, the Fuel Agent for the Co., were as follows:

	1879.	1880.
Fuel for use of Company	8.469	11.896
Shipped at Huntington on the Ohio River	4,065	9 100
Delivered on line of road west of Richmond	3,870	10,559
" at Staunton to Valley RR	40	240
" Charlottesville to Va. Mid. RR	2,727	4,222
" Gordonsville to do do	260	339
" Hanover Junc. to R., F. & P. RR	1,564	1,140
" Richmond for consumption, including steam tugs and dredges	4,819	3,759
Delivered to E. Lex. & Big Sandy RR	....	206
Shipped at James River wharves	12,778	24,006
Total	38,112	65,644

The increase in the total movement in Nov., 1880, was over 72 per cent. over that for Nov., 1879.—The large increase in the business of this company is gauged by its consumption of about 42 per cent. more fuel, and the same remark may be made of the Valley and the Midland roads, the former taking 500 per cent., and the latter over 52 per per cent. more coal The quantities shipped west from Huntington and east from Richmond were just about twice as much in 1880 as in 1879, for the same periods.

The character of the fuel moved during the same periods, is shown in the following exhibit:

	Cannel.	Splint & Bits.	Coke	Total
For the month of November, 1880	3,943	56,702	4 999	65,644
" " " 1879	4,132	32,333	1,847	38,112
Increase	....	24,369	3,352	27,532
Decrease	189	....	....	....

The decrease in the traffic in cannel was about 4 per cent., while the increase in splint and bituminous was over 75 per cent. and that in coke was over 203 per cent.—The great increase in the coke movement shows not only the rapid development going on in the manufacture of iron in these states. but also the demand for W. Va. coke elsewhere, especially on the Ohio.

Taking the movement as from Jan. 1 to Dec. 1, of each year, the *increase* in 1880, over 1879, was 12,577 tons of cannel, or 42 per cent.; 115,866 of splint and bituminous, or 32 per cent.; and 9,241 of coke, or 43 per cent.; a total increase of 137,684 tons, or very near 34 per cent. on the entire movement.

The inside coast route.—A late Nautical Gazette contains a letter from Newberne, N. C., which states that a 210 ft. steamer now carries 700 bales of cotton thence to Norfolk on 6 ft. draft, and that by expending a few thousand dollars on Core Sound there would be 7 ft. of depth all the way from Beaufort to New York by way of the sounds, bays and canals of the inside route.

Raleigh County, W. Va. is on the line of the C. & O. Ry., but across New River. The *Index* of Dec. 6 has an editorial on the great improvement being made in the farms of that county; new houses, barns, fences, stores and churches, are seen everywhere and old ones are repaired; there are good school houses and schools in each district; several steam saw mills have been put in operation, orchards have been planted. improved stock introduced; staves, walnut, poplar and oak timber, are gotten out in large quantities and marketed by the railway; and a number of families from other states have recently settled there.

Personals.—W. H. Dewees, has located at Carkin, Kanawha Co., Va., the seat of the Bennington Collieries.—Col. A. K. McClure, the editor-in-chief of the Philadelphia *Times* is now in the South writing about its condition and prospects for his paper. He wrote a long letter from Richmond, Va., full of commendation for its growth and energy.

Immigration.—Mr. A. E. Boulton from England, is now visiting various parts of Virginia to become informed in reference to the inducements it offers for the settlement of English emigrants. He represents a society in London that proposes to promote this movement —A Georgia RR Co. has organized an immigration scheme, having 3.000.000 acres of land in the N E part of the state to dispose of. One hundred Swiss are now on their way there

Valley RR.—An engineer has been ascertaining the conditions the cuts and fills of the uncompleted portion of this road between Staunton and Salem.

The Richmond & Danville RR.,

during the year ending September 30, 1880, earned $1,243,271.23, its expenses were $745,336.96, or $497,934.27 over all expenses; its net revenues from all sources were $555,419 41. This company also operates the North Carolina RR. and the Northwestern N. C. RR., and there is the handsome showing of 59.3 per ct. in the ratio of earnings to expenses for all the railroads managed by this company. The increase in aggregate tonage moved was 19.2 per ct., and in the passenger traffic 33 per ct. The *local travel* is credited with a large portion of the increase, showing an improving condition of the people. The increased traffic made it necessary to purchase eight new and larger locomotives, and to build 200 new freight cars. The company met all its obligations and reduced its loan indebtedness near $80,000. The report of President Buford calls attention to the progress of the South-Atlantic States, those this railroad is most interested in, during the last decade,—their increase in population, the larger areas devoted to the growth of cotton and tobacco, the accumulation of local capital and the employment of it in manufacturing and mining, as "inspiring new energies and promising new rewards to the revived industry of all classes and sections." He also notes "the increase in population, wealth, trade, and manufactures of Richmond and Danville, in Virginia and of towns in North Carolina," on the Piedmont Air-line, as "representing the degree in which the industrial activities of these States are rapidly recovering their former proportions, which are very soon probably to exceed any at any time heretofore attained." Mention is made of the construction of the Richmond & Alleghany, of the extension of the Chesapeake & Ohio both west and east, of the facilities for trade which the York River road has at and from West Point, and of the improvement of the James to Richmond, as "prominent and eventful facts in the history of the State," and as favorably affecting the future prosperity and usefulness of this company.—Increasing the commercial importance of Richmond he declares to be one of the principal objects of this RR. He also refers with satisfaction to the active progress in the construction of the Danville and New River Narrow-gauge RR. "westward into the producer and hitherto isolated border counties of Virginia."—In conclusion, the announcement is made that "this company has united recently with other lines having similar interests in a system of common agencies for the superintendence of the general traffic, both freight and passenger," to save "unnecessary expenditure, friction with the public, and hostility of management," and that "its financial condition being so well established and recognized "from surplus earnings a dividend of $3 a share on the stock (about $4,000,000) is declared.—Authority was given the board of directors to continue the ballasting of the road with granite, to replace the remaining 23 miles of light rail with steel rails, to erect new depots at Richmond and additional shops in Manchester, and to aid, to the extent of $500,000 in all, in the completion of unfinished tributary lines of railroad in Virginia and North Carolina, and in subscribing to the stock of the Richmond and West Point Terminal Railway and Warehouse Company.—The annual meeting of this company was held at Richmond, December 8. The officers elected for the next term were : Col. A. S. Buford, president; A. Y. Stokes, A. J. Cassatt, W. L. Owen, T. M. Logan, W. P. Clyde, Strickland Nace, W. H. Palmer and J. N. Dubarry, directors.

COAL-MINING IN THE RICHMOND COAL-FIELD.—J. T. Jones & Co. are now opening a new mine near Coalfield station of the Richmond and Danville RR., the Midlothian Basin, going down 210 ft. to reach coal They use the engine that was in use at the Ætna mine.

FISH.—Col. J. M. McDonald, the Virginia Fish Commissioner, is in the employ of the United States Fish Commission. He is now experimenting on cod hatching in Massachusetts. He serves Virginia without pay, and has done, already, an important work in stocking her waters with good fish ; he secured a supply of German carp the present year.

"Virginia is booming up as a progressive iron manufacturing state, and the Low Moor Furnace has the proud distinction of having surpassed any previous work by a Virginia furnace." —*Bulletin of Am. Iron & Steel Ass'n*, Nov. 3.

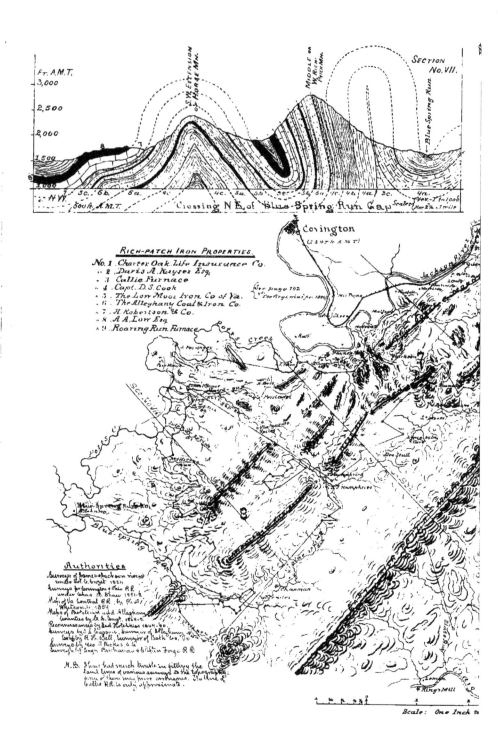

Section No. VII.

Ft. A.M.T.
3,000
2,500
2,000
1,500
1,000

S.W. Extension of Horse Mtn.

Middle or W. Rich-Patch Mtn.

Blue Spring Run

N.W.
800 ft. A.M.T.

7c. 6b. 6a. 4c. 5a. 5b. 5c. 3b. 6m. 1c. 4b. 4a. 3c. 4n.

Crossing N.E. of Blue Spring Run Gap.

Hor. 1 in. to 1000
Ver. 1 in. to 1000
Hor. 2 in. to 1 mile

Covington
(1147 ft. A.M.T.)

Jackson River

RICH-PATCH IRON PROPERTIES.

No. 1. Charter Oak Life Insurance Co.
" 2. Davis A. Keyser Esq.
" 3. Callie Furnace
" 4. Capt. D. S. Cook.
" 5. The Low Moor Iron Co of Va.
" 6. The Alleghany Coal & Iron Co.
" 7. J. Robertson & Co.
" 8. A. A. Low Esq
" 9. Roaring Run Furnace

(See page 192
" Topography map for 1890)

Potts Creek

Humphries

Blue Spring Run R.R.

Blue Spring

Authorities

Surveys of James & Pack own rivers
under Act to Congress 1821
Surveys for Covington & Ohio R.R.
under Cabins B. Shaw 1851-2
Map of Va Central R.R. by P.C. 291
Whitcomb 1859
Maps of Montecure and Alleghany
Counties by L. D. Engle 1864-5
Reconnaissances by Jed Hotchkiss 1864-80.
Surveys by S. Gaugoure, Surveyor of Alleghany
Co by R. H. Bell, Surveyor of Bath Co. Va.
Surveys by Geo J. Meekes & Co
Surveys of Engr Buchanan & Clifton Forge R.R.

N.B. I have had much trouble in fitting the
land lines of various surveys to the topography,
some of them may prove erroneous. The line of
Callie R.R. is only approximate.

Kings Mill

Scale: One Inch to

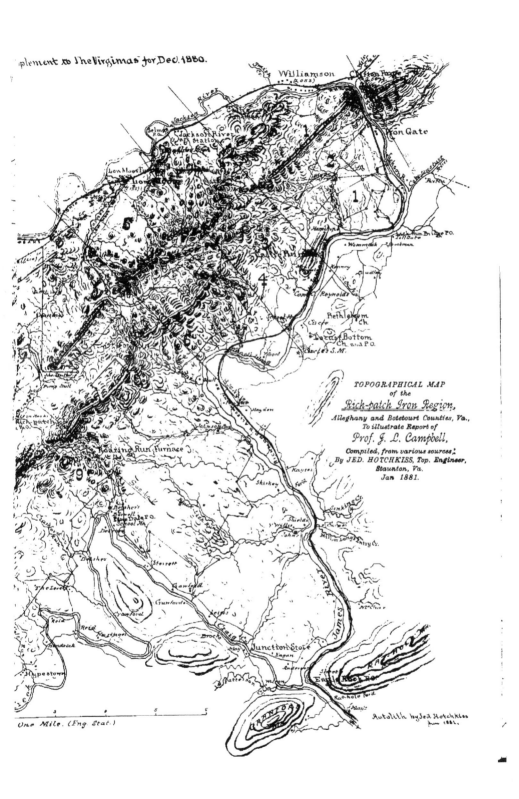

plement to The Virginias for Dec. 1880.

TOPOGRAPHICAL MAP
of the
Rich-patch Iron Region,
Alleghany and Botetourt Counties, Va.,
To illustrate Report of
Prof. J. L. Campbell,
Compiled, from various sources,
By JED. HOTCHKISS, Top. Engineer,
Staunton, Va.
Jan 1881.

One Mile. (Eng. Stat.)

Autolith by Jed Hotchkiss
June 1881.

The Geology, etc., of the Rich-patch, Virginia, Iron Region.

Written for THE VIRGINIAS.

By Prof. J. L. Campbell.

(Illustrated by Map and Sections.)

The little mountain chain, varying in width from one to five miles, and extending from about one mile northeast of Clifton Forge Pass, on the Richmond & Alleghany RR. to a distance of fifteen miles towards the southwest, is rapidly becoming a centre of attraction to manufacturers of iron and to capitalists seeking for iron lands in which to make investments. As Virginia, is destined soon to become the great central iron-producing state of the Union, so this Rich-patch chain is to be *one* of the several great iron centres in Virginia.

This mountain chain lies partly in Alleghany, and partly in Botetourt county, Va.; it is skirted by Jackson River and the Chesapeake & Ohio Ry. on its northwestern border, and by James River and the Richmond & Alleghany RR. for about eight miles along its southeastern border. That the reader may appreciate fully the vast resources of this region in iron ores, limestones and timber, and the facilities for obtaining and utilizing these he must have a clear view of both its *topographical* and *geological* features. We must therefore dwell upon these two important points somewhat in detail.

By reference to the accompanying map it will be seen that the Rich-patch mountain chain is at its northeast extremity, for some miles, a single ridge cut by Jackson River, the main head branch of the James, leaving about a mile of its length as Wilson Hill on the northeast side of the deep gorge through which the river passes. Beyond this single range, extending towards the S. W., the crest of the ridge is depressed into a trough-like shape, so that its cross section is like an inverted arch (See No. II of accompanying sections). Thus we have a double ridge, the eastern one bearing the title of Rich-patch Mtn., while the western one is here called Wait Mtn. After this double ridge has extended a mile or two farther, the trough of sandstone strata that connects its parts together disappears—or rather has been washed away by denuding agencies—and a deep narrow valley, with a limestone bottom and shaly slopes on each side, is left to take its place. This is the beginning of Rich-patch valley, one remarkable for its picturesque scenery, and its fine limestone soils.

This bifurcation of the ranges continues, and gradually widens, for a distance of about 12 miles from its beginning, until the valley is abruptly terminated at the base of Nicholas Knob, a lofty peak of more than 3,000 feet that forms the N. E. end of Potts Mtn. These two leading ridges that border the Rich-patch valley are not equal either in continuity or height. That on the S. E. side, and which is usually called Rich-patch throughout its length, I shall call "*E. Rich-patch Mtn.,*" while the other, which is less continuous, being cut by streams, and having *local names* attached to its several divisions, I shall designate, for present convenience, "*W. Rich-patch Mtn.*"

As long as the mountain is a single ridge, and up to the point at which complete bifurcation takes place, the whole top is composed of beds of coarse sandstones with some interstratified shales. The reason for this condition of things will be seen by looking at Sections I and II. After the ridges have become fairly separated by the upward thrust and subsequent denudation of the intervening limestone valley, each assumes a new structure and has new topographical features. The sandstone beds that hitherto formed the whole top have now a wide gap cut through them lengthwise, and are left to cover only the S. E. face of one, and the N. W. face (and some subordinate outliers) of the other; while the slopes of both ridges facing the valley are composed of limestones and shales extending up to the outcropping sandstone ledges, that come up from the opposite faces of the ridges, and beneath which both the limestones and shales of the valley *dip* and disappear.

Along the outer flanks of these two main ridges there are some special features worthy of note just here. Along the S. E. slope of the E. range, the denuding agencies that have given it its present form have acted very unequally at differ-

ent points. First there are numerous ravines, some of them quite deep, that begin at a considerable height on the face of the mountain and terminate far out among the foot-hills, and slopes that flank its base. Many of these ravines carry streams that can be utilized. Between these ravines are left: *First,* a range of knobs high up on the face of the main ridge, and extending for miles along its general course. These are the outcropping of the more fragile of the sandstone beds (5a.), the still higher parts of which have been worn away. Among these are found thin beds of fossil ore, but not generally very promising, except in a few places to be mentioned hereafter. *Second,* still lower down the slope, is a range of "benches" formed by the wearing down of a ledge of limestone and a contiguous bed of iron ore and sandstone. This limestone is numbered, 7., and this ore bed, 8., on the accompanying geological sections. These are the chief sources of ore and limestone in this region.

Between these rougher features of the mountain and the bottom lands that border on James River, there are many depressed and gradually sloping spurs and rounded hills composed of the dark shales that fill most of the valleys in this region of country, except the Rich-patch valley.

The northwestern slope of W. Rich-patch Mountain has features very similar to those just given for the eastern ridges, as far as Low Moor Furnace, except that the dip of the stratified rocks is towards the N. W., and is less regular than it is on the other ridges, as reference to the geological sections will show. At Low Moor a new feature arises in this part of the chain, in the form of Horse Mountain, which is a subordinate ridge formed by an upward bending of the sandstone strata, so as to leave a trough or narrow valley between it and the main western ridge, making that a *Middle* mountain, as the map shows. This out-lying ridge, broken into parts by two or three streams, extends to several miles beyond Covington. The part embraced between Mill Branch and Hays-gap Run is called Carpenter Mountain. Middle Mountain is a similar undulation of sandstone strata lifted up between Carpenter and Rich-patch mountains.

Its Streams.—The map shows that the Rich-patch region is one common water-shed; sending off its numerous streams into Potts Creek and Jackson River, on the one side, and into Craig Creek and James River, on the other. It is abundantly watered throughout its length and breadth.

For several miles S. W. of Covington, Potts Creek forms a crooked water boundary along the foot-hills of W. Rich-patch Mountain, and affords ample water-power for almost any purpose for which it may be demanded. Then, from the mouth of this stream Jackson River runs with the general trend of the mountain till it reaches the Clifton Forge Pass, or "Iron-Gate," as it is to be called in future, where it turns abruptly to the S. E. through this gorge of the mountain, with a bearing S. 22° E., while the mountain at this point runs about N. 58° E. The ridge, therefore, is not cut at right angles by the river, though it varies from it by only 15°.

Following Jackson River from this point southward we soon reach its junction with the Cow-pasture, from which point onward the combined streams form the James. Here again the course of the river is changed, almost at right-angles, towards the S. W., skirting the foot-hills of the E. Rich-patch range, along its S. E. base for about 8 miles; then it turns southward and makes its way across the Great Valley, and towards the Blue Ridge beyond.

Besides these larger streams, forming a great loop surrounding a large portion of the Rich-patch chain, there are numerous smaller streams, that rise within the chain, on its mountain ranges or in its included valleys, and flow down through the ravines and gaps of these ranges to the main streams just mentioned. Among these are Blue-spring and Hays-gap runs, and Mill Branch, tributaries to Potts Creek; Karnes Creek, which enters Jackson River at Low Moor Furnace, and other like streams—all affording valuable facilitities for washing ores and for other purposes—flowing northwest. On the S. E. face of the range are several tributaries of Craig Creek and James River, capable of being utilized in a similar way. Conspicuous among these is Roaring Run, which has its source in a large and never-failing spring, just in the margin of Rich-patch valley, from which flows an abundant supply of water

Continued on Page 188.

186　　　　The Virginias.　　　　[Number 12.

Continued from Page 183.

5 feet, the lowest band occasionally 4 or 5 inches thick, the upper ones generally about 2 inches." [117–1839.]

South of Kingwood ferry, "The shales overlaying the upper seam of coal abound in nodules of a very *rich iron ore* of a delicate grey color."—"The iron ore found in the overlying shales on the opposite side of the river is here replaced by nodules of impure limestone." [117–1839.]

"About a quarter of a mile west of the ferry the upper seam is worked by Mr. Kelso, and is there covered by shales containing rich nodules of iron ore and rests upon the usual bed of limestone." [118–1839.]

The upper band of limestone between the middle and the upper coal beds at variable intervals "is associated with a white argillaceous clay and shales of a very peculiar character, analogous to those met with in a similar position in the Hardy basins and which there contains iron ore. Here, however, the ore is replaced by nodules of limestone, which are sometimes quite ferruginous, though always containing a preponderating amount of limestone." [118–1839.]

"**Iron Ores.**—The occurrence of iron ore has been alluded to, incidentally, in describing the coal and limestone. Besides the localities thus referred to, several others will now be noticed. One of a very superior quality occurs on Deep Hollow run, a tributary of Muddy creek, near its junction with that stream, which is two and a quarter miles above its mouth. The band varies in thickness from 3 to 12 inches, and apparently over a wide area. Beneath it, a distance of 3 or 4 ft., is a calcareous shale containing nodules of impure iron ore, 8 or 10 inches in diameter. It may be added, as imparting high value to this ore, should it be found to continue of the requisite thickness, that Muddy creek affords a sufficient fall of water and is proverbial for maintaining its stream undiminished throughout the summer.

A very rich ore occurs on the surface, on the estate of Michael Hartman in the Crab Orchard ; the fragments are strewed on the surface, over a wide area, and indicate a continuous vein. It is fossiliferous, of a dark red color, and very pure. Its place is probably either a few feet above or below the second coal seam.

The shales of the coal measures very generally contain iron ore in small nodules, but the indications do not favor the opinion that a large amount of ore is to be met with in this basin. As near Morgantown, and in other parts of the great coal region, the shales immediately succeeding to Formation XII, were found very rich in ore, examinations were made in the corresponding strata of this basin, without discovering any decidedly abundant seam, though small bands were continually met with. It may be well to add that the Bear creek furnace, near Selby's Port was formerly supplied with ore from these shales, which, on the National road, east of Petersburg, appear to contain a band of valuable thickness. It is, therefore, by no means improbable that further investigation may disclose this material in the same geological connection further south, in sufficient amount to be economically valuable." [119–1839.]

"One and a half miles above the bridge on Big Sandy, near Brandonville, Monongalia Co., is a a bed of coarse iron ore which appeared to be upwards of a foot in thickness, and a similar ore is associated with the limestone." [121–1839.]

"*Iron ores on Decker's Creek.*—The ores met with above the conglomerate on the western slope of Laurel Hill, and of which use is made at Mr. Clear's furnace on Decker's Creek, may be considered as occupying two general geological positions, and will be treated of as the lower and upper groups of ores.

Lower Group of Ores.—In the lower part of the shales underlying the lowest coal seam, two bands of iron ore occur, each about a foot in thickness, and separated by about four feet of shales. This ore from its slight protection is generally in a decomposed state, consisting chiefly of per-oxide of a loose shaly texture, and therefore the more easily worked, along with which a nodule of the original carbonate is occasionally found. Beneath the lowest of these two beds of ore is a white sandstone, 4 or 5 feet in thickness, and beneath this is a third bed of ore, generally 6 or 8 inches thick, which, having been defended by the overlying strata, has escaped decomposition, and displays its original character of a compact proto-carbon-

ate. A few inches below this in the shales, a fourth band occurs, 4 inches in thickness. Below this, separated by shales of unknown thickness, probably not more than 3 or 4 feet, occurs a band of limestone 5 feet thick, portions of which are quite rich, but the principal mass impure. From this stratum is procured the flux used at the neighboring furnace. This group of ores occurs very extensively on the western side of Laurel Hill, where, owing to the gentle dip of the strata, being at about the same angle as the slope of the surface, these bands present themselves over a wide area on, the western flank of the ridge, where they have been traced for many miles. As would be expected, owing to infiltrations from above, the ore at the bottom of the hill is generally richest.

Upper Group of Ores.—These ores occur much higher in the series, being above the second seam of coal. They rest upon a lead colored, siliceous and argillaceous sandstone, and are overlaid by siliceous slates of the same color, which being the first rocks of this kind met with above the second seam of coal may serve as a landmark in searching for the ore. This ore is very variable in thickness, usually occurring in large nodules, sometimes fine-grained, though generally coarse and siliceous, occasionally so much so as to resemble a coarse sandstone rather than iron ore. Indeed it frequently gives no indication of the presence of iron until after burning or long exposure. Like the ores of the lower group, it is explored over a wide area, being found within a short distance of the surface from the base of the hills to their summits." [124–1839.]

The limestone not far above the Big Kanawha at Ryder's creek and also below Hughes' creek "is coated with a buff brown ferruginous oxide, giving it the aspect of iron ore." [129–1839.]

On the Big Kanawha, near Cannelton, under the 6 to 7 ft. coal seam that is about 100 ft. above the road, there is a "fine yellowish grey clay, 2 ft. thick, extremely plastic and tenacious," a good fire-brick clay ; *under* that clay are "yellow shales containing a great number of impressions of culmiferous and arundinaceous plants, many of which are enclosed in an oblique direction in the stratum, so as to present a less flattened form than when they repose conformably in their bed. These shales contain also disseminated, flattened and kidney-shaped masses of argillaceous iron ore, but not in sufficient abundance to render it valuable in an economical point of view." [129–1839.]

In Vineyard Hill, near Malden, on the Kanawha, the third stratum, from the river up, is about 40 ft. of bluish drab colored slaty shales and sandstones. In this "The slate, resting directly upon the coal includes a thin seam of nodular iron ore in flattened ovoid masses, and presenting the concentric structure frequently observed to belong to this variety of ore. This is the heaviest bed of slate which occurs along the whole line of the Kanawha as far down as Charleston. The stratum of iron ore assumes in some places above this coal seam the appearance of a ferruginous conglomerate. This is particularly noticed to be the case on Campbell's creek behind the Thoroughfare hill. Indeed the whole of the shale at this point presents more of a ferruginous character than usual. A thin stratum of compact ore is found a few feet above the coal, and a similar ore below it in the bed of the creek." [133–1839.]

In the slates above referred to Prof. Rogers found spheroidal masses of Madreporite, a fossil coral, which are "a tolerably pure limestone." He found the same in slates a few feet above the coal seam worked at Harvey's, 21 or 22 miles up the river from Vineyard Hill, and also on Bell's Creek, doubtless in the same stratum further southeast, and "the same shales which include it (the Madreporite), at these points contain disseminated masses of lenticular iron ore." [133–1839.]

The 6th stratum at Vineyard Hill, 215 ft. of sandstone, "contains in some places, as in Mr. Brooks', drift, irregular nodular masses of compact argillaceous iron ore." [133–1839.]
—The 3½ ft. coal bed in this stratum "in its upper portion contains thin lamina of iron pyrites." [134–1839.]

The *blue* or *black flint*, the 9th stratum at Vineyard Hill, the top stratum of the lower series of coals, (the Middle Measures), is 7 ft. thick. "As seen there, this formation is covered with a thin band of impure iron ore, in kidney-shaped masses, embedded in sandstone—the whole thickness not exceeding 4 inches. Farther down the river the iron disappears,

giving place to ferruginous shales and sandstones, which immediately overlie the siliceous rocks." [185–1839.]

"The section of Vineyard Hill is terminated by a thin capping of about 10 ft. of reddish and yellow shales, the lower portion of which contains disintegrated masses of argillaceous iron." [135–1839.]

"Oxide of iron," is given as one of the ingredients in most of the "limestones of the coal measures." [150-152–1839.]

In the report for 1839, pages 154-156, the following analyses of iron ores from the coal measures are given, in parts of 30 grains:—

LOCALITY IN W. VA.	Carbonate of iron.	Carbonate of lime.	Carbonate of magnesia.	Silica.	Alumina.	Water.	Carbonate manganese.	
1. Hollow Run, Preston. Co............	29.84	0.56	0.94	2.11	0.53	0.26		
2. Stoney Run, Hardy (Grant) Co....	19.99	0.84	0.64	2.54	0.46	0.35		
3. Stoney River Falls,Hardy (Grant)Co	17.75	1.44	1.00	3.05	0.90	0.45		
4. Fairfax's, Preston Co..........	17.14	1.48	3.01.2	82.0.45	0.53			
5. North Branch of Potomac	19.30	0.81	0.76	2.83	0.81	0.38	.3	
6. Crab Orchard, Preston Co.......	18.82	0.15	0.19	6.34.0.97	0.66			
7. Wilson's Mill..................	15.41	0.87	0.56	0.32	1.75	0.51		
8. Valley Furnace, Monongalia Co....	19.18	0.83	0.70	3.18.0.51	0.44			A true or earth.
9............	19.55	1.50	0.75	2.90.0.37	0.50			
10. Brantzburg, N. Branch of Potomac	17.17	0.78	0.15.5.18.0.09	0.49				

1. "Iron ore from Hollow run, a branch of Muddy creek, in Preston county. Color dark blue, texture compact, grain fine, fracture slightly conchoidal, weathered surface, yellowish brown."

2. "Iron ore from Stony run, four miles above the turnpike, Hardy county. Color light grey, weathered surface tinged with per-oxide of iron, texture compact, grain fine, fracture conchoidal."

3. "Iron ore from falls of Stony river, Hardy county. Color dull lead grey, inclining to brown, texture compact, grain rather fine, fracture splintery."

4. "Iron ore from shales above the calcareous band separating the two seams of coal at Col. Fairfax's, Preston county. Color blue in interior, exterior composed of concentric layers per-oxidated by exposure to the atmosphere, texture compact, grain fine, fracture slightly conchoidal."

5. "Iron ore from shales above the lowest seam of coal on North branch of Potomac, 6 miles below the mouth of Abraham's creek. Color dark bluish grey with a brownish tint, weathered surface dark brown, texture compact, grain fine, fracture conchoidal."

6. "Iron ore from the coal measures, M. Hartman's, Crab Orchard, Preston county. Color deep red inclining to brown, texture compact, grain fine, fracture slightly conchoidal, powder dark red, contains vegetable impressions."

7. "Iron ore from Wilson's mill, shales between the first and second seams of coal. Color bluish grey inclining to brown, texture compact, grain apparently coarse, fracture slightly conchoidal."

8. "Iron ore from coal measures, Valley furnace, Monongalia county. Color reddish brown inclining to grey, weathered surface, ochreous, texture rather compact, grain seemingly coarse, but not so to the touch, fracture irregular, contains vegetable impressions."

9. "Iron ore from the Valley furnace as above, called by the miners kidney ore. Color bluish grey, inclining to brown, weathered surface, ochreous, texture compact, grain fine, fracture plane."

10. "Iron ore from shales above the second seam at Brantzburg, North branch of Potomac. Color greyish blue, texture compact, grain moderately fine, fracture irregular, weathered surface tinged with per-oxide of iron."

In the report for 1840, page 73, after giving the general character of the rocks of the "Lower Coal Group," it is stated that "with these are associated beds of limestone and the most important seams of iron are met with in the coal measures."

In describing the section across the Monongalia valley, numbering the strata from formation No. XII upward, the following notes are given in reference to iron ores:—

1. *In the Lower Coal Group, or Formation XIII.*

"Near the bottom of stratum No. 1 is an irregular band of iron ore, sometimes forming a continuous layer, but occurring in the form of nodular masses, varying from 2 to 12 inches in diameter. It is an impure proto-carbonate of iron, covered with layers of hydratic per-oxide, produced by the decomposition of the carbonate. Its color within is grey and greyish dun, on the outside yellowish brown. Its grain is coarse and fracture irregular and sometimes earthy. This ore is generally of interior quality, but has been extensively used at the neighboring furnace. It has been discovered in isolated patches at numerous places on the slope and towards the summit of the mountain, and has been mined at various points along its western base. It disappears below the bed of the creek between Goosenan's bridge and the furnace, from a third or half mile below the former. Its average thickness is estimated at 1 foot, that of the shales in which it is contained being about 6 to 10 feet." [76–1840.]

Stratum No. 2 "is a very good firestone, and has been used for this purpose at the neighboring furnace."—No. 3 is concealed on the line of section, "but there is room to believe that it consists principally, if not entirely, of shales containing some iron ore. Further examination will be required to determine their true nature and extent. And such examination is rendered particularly important by the consideration that this unobserved interval occupies a place in the series analogous to that in which some of the valuable beds of iron ore on Cheat river, resorted to by Henry Clay and other furnaces, are embraced." [76–1840.]

No. 4, a sandstone, "has sometimes a yellow tinge due to oxide of iron." "It has been used for furnace hearths."—No. 5, a shale, is "thought to contain iron ore."—No. 7, flaggy sandstones and shales above 1.5 to 2.5 ft. thick coal bed, is "supposed to include iron ore."—No. 9, flaggy sandstones and shales, above 1 ft. coal bed, "towards the upper part contains nodules of hydrated per-oxide of iron, to what extent remains to be determined."—No. 10 is a limestone, used for lime and for flux. "For a few inches, near its upper surface, it is yellow and so highly ferruginous as in some places to constitute a calcareous iron ore." [77–1840.]—No. 11, a shale, "contains nodular masses of iron ore, consisting of proto-carbonate of iron within, and concentric layers of hydrated per-oxide on the outside. It is of good quality but in too small quantity to be of much value."——The lower part of No. 13, a shale, includes a layer of nodules of iron ore, varying in size from a small pebble to more than a foot in diameter. It is a rich ore, consisting of the proto-carbonate, coated with hydrated per-oxide, and was the material chiefly used at the furnace." "For its composition the reader is referred to my report of last year. It was mined on the side of Laurel Hill, in a southeasterly direction from the furnace. The average thickness of the band of ore is from 6 to 10 inches, that of the shales from 6 to 8 feet."—No. 15 is a shale above 1 to 2 ft. of coal. "It contains a few scattered nodules of iron ore of lenticular form. Parts of its coal bed are rendered impure by the presence of sulphuret of iron." [78–1840.]

In writing of the Lower Coal Group on the Ohio, near the northern extremity of W. Va., the report says:—"This group being the great repository of the iron ores found so abundantly in the coal regions of Ohio and Pennsylvania, at no great distance from the Ohio river, will, on that account, as well as from its valuable beds of coal, demand future minute investigation." [95–1840.]

In the section on the Ohio river a mile above the mouth of Little Beaver, No. 2 stratum in some places contains courses of nodular iron ore of the variety usually found in the coal measures. At the mouth of Little Beaver these nodules vary from 3 to 8 inches in diameter."—No. 6 is "shale with nodules of iron ore."—No. 8, a shale, contains, towards the bottom, nodules of iron ore, though apparently not in large amount." [95-96–1840.]—No. 12, a shale, "contains some nodules of iron ore."

In the section near Wellsville, on the Ohio, on Tomlinson's Run, No. 3, a shale, "contains nodules of iron ore of very good quality, but in what amount remains yet to be determined."—No. 12 a shale, "contains nodular masses of iron ore varying from 2 to 8 inches in diameter, but though they are present in considerable quantity further examination is necessary to ascertain whether they are in sufficient amount to be valuable." [98–1840.]

2. *In the Lower Shale and Sandstone Group, or Form*

-ation XIV.—This group is principally shales; it begins from the quarry sandstone that rises from the river a little below Morgantown, which Rogers made the 18th and top stratum of his No. XIII, or Lower Coal Group.—The strata of XIV are numbered upward in the following:

No. 1, a shale, "near its lower part, contains an irregular band of iron ore, from 6 to 8 inches thick. Like the ore No. 5, preceding, it is a proto-carbonate, covered with a coating of hydrated peroxide. It of a grey color, coarse grained, and rough, irregular fracture. Where mined near the site of the old forge, it is quite impure, nor is it likely to prove of much value at other points, though in mixture with the ores of better quality, it was used at the furnace. At the forge it is from 40 to 50 feet above the bed of the creek, and continues in view to Morgantown, sinking beneath the Monongalia a short distance below the town."
——In the shales of No. 3, "an irregular seam of iron ore occurs towards the bottom of the stratum, of which some use was made at the furnace. Though concealed by the filling up of the pits, the seam as formerly wrought is known to have an average thickness of about six inches and to be of moderately good quality. It is occasionally calcareous. A few feet above this occurs an irregular course of nodules of sufficient thickness in some places to have been found valuable. Both this and the other seam, however, are very variable as to quantity, not unfrequently thinning out entirely."——No. 5 is shales, "sometimes containing nodules composed of calcareous and ferruginous matter blended"——No. 6 is a "ferruginous" limestone, and No. 8 is a "very ferruginous" limestone.——The shales of No. 13 "contains some nodules of impure iron ore," and the coal of No. 14 "contains some sulphuret of iron."——No. 19 is a "ferruginous" limestone, and No. 22 is a "somewhat ferruginous" one.——The shaly sandstone of No. 25 "contains lenticular masses of iron ore, apparently the carbonate, of a bluish tinge, placed with their flattened sides parallel to the lines of lamination, varying from the size of a walnut to masses weighing several pounds."——No. 34 is shale "containing some nodules of iron ore."——No. 41 a shale, "contains some flattened nodules of proto-carbonate of iron, arranged parallel to the lamination." [80-86-1840.]

"Oxide of iron" was found in a "stain" in stratum No. 3, a shale, in the section opposite Steubenville: and in No. 16 of same section, near mouth of Wheeling Creek, a shale, were "some nodules of iron ore." [100-101-1840.]

3. In the Upper Coal Group, or Formation XV.—The bottom of this group is the "Pittsburg" bed of coal, the W. Va. outcrop of which is shown in a dotted line on the Geological Map in THE VIRGINIAS for June, 1880.

Nos. 11 and 12 are coal and shale "containing but little sulphuret of iron."——No. 15 is shale. "The lower part contains a few lenticular nodules of moderately good iron ore of the variety usually found in the coal measures." [89-1840.]

In the report for 1840, pages 120 and 121, the following analyses are given of iron ores from the Western Coal Measures:

LOCALITY IN W. VA.	Per cent. Metallic Iron.	Carbonate of Iron.	Peroxide of Iron.	Alumina.	Lime.	Silica, and Silicate insoluble in acids.	Carbonic Acid and Water.	Water.	Loss.
1. Kelley's Creek, Kanawha Co.,..	39.95	82.55		1.00	trace.	13.05		2.50	0 90
2. Hamilton Place, Nicholas Co.,..	55.55		80 70	1.25		7.40		10.00	0.50
3. Red House Shoals, Kanawha Co.,.	....		58.41	3.45		33.44		4.50	0.35
4. Eighteen-mile Cr., do.	58.10		83.00	3.45		10.00	0.35		0.40

No. 1. "Iron ore from Keller's (Kelley's) creek, Kanawha, interspersed in shales. Structure nodular, compact, close grained; color of the mass dull reddish grey, of crust reddish brown; fracture somewhat conchoidal."

No. 2. "Iron ore on Hamilton Place, Nicholas county, occurs on top of hill in rounded masses. Structure irregularly nodular; texture brittle and somewhat close grained; color chestnut brown, with blackish spots of a dull, resinous lustre."

No. 3. "Iron ore in the red shales, above the blue sandstone at Red House Shoals, Kanawha. Structure compact and somewhat slaty; close grained; color cinnamon brown, without lustre except a few glimmering points.

No. 4. "Iron ore found on dividing ridge between Eighteen-Mile Creek and Kanawha River, one mile from latter, back of Mr. Harvey's, Kanawha. Structure massive, close grained; fracture somewhat conchoidal; color dull brown, with glimmering micaceous points."

Continued from Page 185.

for running a large mill a few hundred yards below, then affords an abundant supply for Roaring Run Furnace, a little lower down the stream.

Geology.—No one can fully comprehend the extent of the mineral resources of a region like this, without at least a general, and at the same time a tolerably full view of its geological features. If, then, the reader will follow me patiently for a little while, and refer occasionally to the accompanying sections, I think he will readily comprehend the geological problems here presented,—problems that he will not find very difficult after he gets the key to their solution. That key may be found in

Section No. 1, which is nothing else than a copy of what the forces of nature have exposed to view in the gorge of "Iron Gate" (Clifton Forge). If a canvas a thousand feet broad were set up in the bed of the river, where it traverses this gorge, and all the protruding edges of the arched sandstones and shales of the adjacent cliffs were projected upon it, they would form the rock picture before us in this section—saving the trees and other minor features. Near the entrance, and the exit of the river, some of the strata that help to form the abutments of the arch—especially near the meeting of Jackson River and Wilson Creek—have been partially cut away; these have been restored in the section, because their representatives are near at hand on both sides of the pass.

The concentric arches pictured on this section should be studied from the bottom upward—the order in which the strata were originally deposited. Imagine all these to have lain originally in horizontal beds, one above another, and while yet in a plastic condition to have been pressed by some powerful lateral force, acting towards the N. W., while an opposing pressure prevented lateral motion in that direction, then an upward curving and arching of the strata would be a natural result. This is the most satisfactory way of accounting for the structure of the mountain at this point.

Sub-divisions of Section No. I —(1) The lowest "course" of the arch, marked 4 c., is a bed of inter-stratified shales and sandstones 185 ft. thick, of a dark brown color, that in all the accompanying sections, underlies the hardest and heaviest bed of sandstone in the whole series of the rocks that enter into the structure of the Rich-patch chain. It is known in the general system as the Hudson River Shales, or the upper member of the Trenton period. In Prof. Rogers' series it is the top of No. III. Its characteristic fossils are less abundant here than in Rockbridge and Augusta counties.—(2) The two courses of the arch, marked 5a. consist of a bed of very hard, light gray sandstone, 90 ft. thick, known in New York as the Oneida Conglomerate or Lower Medina, and above this, a mass of dark brown and reddish purple sandstones, interstratified with beds of shale, sometimes of a greenish tint, having a total thickness of about 300 ft. Both the lithological and fossil features of this bed refer it to what is recognized elsewhere along the Apalachians as the Medina Sandstone. These beds constitute the No. IV. of Rogers' series, in describing which he says: "The thin slabs of buff and olive sandstone lying near the top, are particularly rich in organic remains, among which may be noted as peculiarly abundant a small globose terobratula, and at least two well characterised species of fucoides. * * An iron ore is frequently associated with the more slaty strata, and is of almost invariable occurrence in connexion with the ponderous brown sandstone which forms the boundary between this and the next superior member of the series." This ore has been mined to a considerable extent for use at Quinnimont Furnace. It is generally rather soft and highly colored, though sometimes shaly in structure. It is highly valued for mixture with the silicious ores of the Oriskany bed, 8 (VII. Rogers). The quantity, however, is limited, the bed, as far as opened, not being more than from 1 to 3 ft. thick.—(3.) The courses of 5 b. consist of two beds of quite hard, gray sandstone, with a bed of darker and more shaly between them. The lowest bed of 5 c. is a shaly sandstone, the bottom of which is nearly pure shale. It is the repository of a second bed of fossil ore, that has been mined to a considerable extent near the margin of the river, and also at the Low Moor mines, and, more largely, at Roaring Run Furnace The highest bed of 5 c. is a soft shale that has been disintegrated and removed from the upper

Supplement to "The Virginias" for December 1880. (See page 185.)

GEOLOGICAL SECTIONS, Nos. I to VII, Across Rich-Patch Mountain Chain, Alleghany & Botetourt counties, Va.

By Prof. J.L. Campbell of Washington & Lee University, Lexington, Va.

SECTION No. I.

Equivalents of Numbered Strata of Sec

	J.D. Dana. (Formations)	Roge VIII.
Devonian	10 a,b,c. (Hamilton, etc.)	
	(9.) (Coniferous, etc.) (Montrey?)	VII.
	(8.) (Oriskany)	VI.
	(Lower Helderberg)	
	7. (Salina) (Montrey?)	
	5c. (Niagara)	V.
Silurian (Upper)	5b. (Clinton)	
	5a. (Medina and Oneida)	IV.
	V c. (Cincinnati) (Hudson River)	
	(3d c.) (Utica.)	III.
	(3b.) (Trenton)	
Silurian (Lower)	(3a.) (Chazy)	
	3.a. (Levis or Quebec)	II.

SECTION No. II.

N.B.- Iron-Ore-Bearing Strata are colored "red."

SECTION No. III.

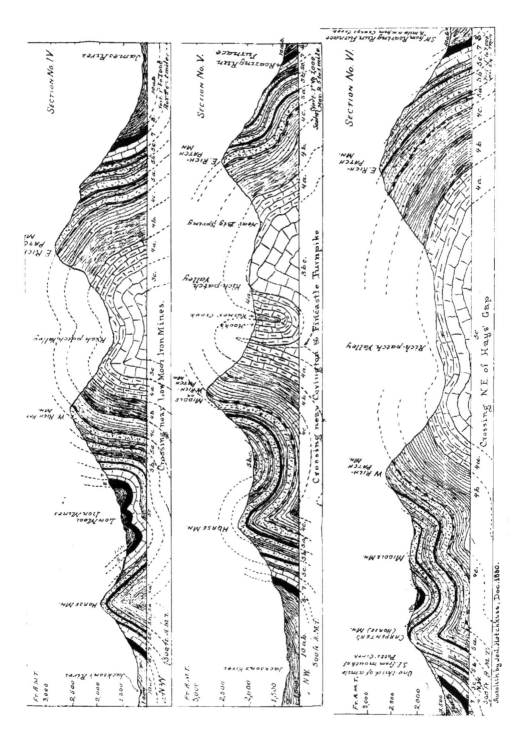

SECTION No. IV

James River

E Rich Patch Mn

Rich patch valley

W Rich Pat Mn

Low Moor Iron Mines

Horse Mn

Jackson's River

Ft. A. M. T.
3,000
2,500
2,000
1,500
1000

10-7. 8 6c. 5b.5a. 4a.
NW

3b. 5a. 4c. 4b. 4a. 3c.

5c. 5b.5c. 7 8
York Fincastle
Rod & 1 mile

Crossing near Low Moor Iron Mines.

(500 ft. 4 M.T.

SECTION No. V

Roaring Run Furnace

E Rich Patch Mn

Near Big Spring

Rich-patch Valley

Hook's Manor Creek

MIDDLE or W RICH PATCH MN

HORSE MN

Jackson's River

Ft. A. M. T.
3,000
2,500
2,000
1,520

NW 500 ft. R. M. T.

10ab. 9-7. 5c. 5b. 5a. 4c.

5b.

4c. 4b. 4a. 3b. 6c.

4a. 4b. 4c. 5a. 5b.5c. 7 8
Scale York 1 to 1000
Scale Hori. 2 to 1 mile

Crossing near Covington & Fincastle Turnpike

SECTION No. VI

SW from Roaring Run Furnace
a mile in from Craney Creek

E Rich-Patch Mn

Rich-patch Valley

W Rich-Patch Mn

Middle Mn

CARPENTERS (HORSE) Mn
One third of a mile
SE from mouth of
Potts Creek

Ft. A. M. T.
3,000
2,500
2,000
1,500
1000

8-7. 5c. 5b. 5a.
NW
500 ft. R. M. T.

4c.

4b. 4a. 5c.

4a. 4b. 5a. 5b. 5c. 7 8
Scale Vert. 1 to 1000
Vert. 1/4 to 1000

Crossing N.E. of Hays' Gap

Autolith. by Jed. Hotchkiss, Dec.1880.

Compliment to The Virginias for December, 1880. (See page 185.)

portion of the mountain by the action of frost, water and ice. It is now found only as a part of the buttresses at the extremities of the arch, and is held between underlying sandstones and overlying limestones. The beds of 5 b. and 5 c. seem to correspond to the "Clinton," and, perhaps, a portion of the "Niagara" epoch of the New York series.

(4.) Outside of this shale of 5 c. (and once overlying it) we have the beds of Lower Helderberg Limestone, 7. (VI. Rog.), at this point 180 ft. thick, but varying from 100 to 200 ft. at other points along the Rich-Patch ranges. This limestone varies very much in quality. Near the bottom, it is frequently argillaceous or slaty, while the highest beds are often silicious, and sometimes abound in concretions of flinty nodules; but among the intermediate beds, *gray limestones* of excellent quality are abundant and sufficiently pure for making good lime and for use as flux in furnaces. This bed of limestone has been cut in grading the R. & A. RR. where it passes out of the gorge, on the lands of Mr. D. A. Kayser. At this point there is a bed of *encrinal and shell marble*, similar to that so extensively quarried at Craigsville, on the C. & O. Ry. At the N. W. limit of the gorge, this Lower Helderberg Limestone is found close to the base of the mountain in a vertical position, while a few yards farther out, it appears, on both sides of Wilson Creek, in a nearly horizontal position, indicating a limited, but very abrupt fracture and slip of the strata at this point.

It will be seen that the strata forming the remarkable arches displayed in this mountain pass are represented on our Sec. No. I as quite symmetrical in structure, except near the N. W. abutments, where the general N. W. thrust, to which the whole mountain has been subjected, has caused a limited rupture of all the beds, with a partial inversion of some of the higher ones. This effect is seen to some extent, even in the lower member of 5 a., where we find a similar crushing and warping of the hardest variety of sandstone.

Outside of the Lower Helderberg Limestone (No. VI. R.), overlying it geologically, we have the Oriskany formation, 8. (No. VII. R.), so remarkable in this whole section of the state for its *extensive deposits of iron ores*. Near the Clifton Forge Pass, it has been opened on both sides of the mountain by the Quinnimont Co. and by Mr. Kayser, and has also been cut in grading the R. & A. RR., near the base of the mountain on the N. W. side, a little way above the entrance to the Pass. Still further along the mountain, the beds of this formation supplied the ores that fed the old Clifton Forge Furnace, once operated here. This same iron ore bed will be seen to constitute a conspicuous feature in all the accompanying sections.

Outside of 8. (9. is wanting in this region), the dark shales of 10 a. and the light colored ones of 10 b. form the spurs and foot-hills of the mountain ranges on both sides, as well as most of the rounded hills that rise as conspicuous features of the landscape in most of the adjacent valleys. These Devonian shales appear at both extremities of all the accompanying sections, except No. VII., extending off for a considerable distance into the neighboring country.

Section No. II.,[*] which cuts the mountain about 2 miles S. W. of Iron-gate, near the crossing of the Callie Furnace Ry., and near Callie Furnace itself, where the chain first becomes double by the up-lift of Wait Mtn., presents one new and striking feature. While all the strata of Sec. I are found here, they no longer form a single regular arch, but may be viewed as two arches, or, perhaps better, as the original arch with its top depressed and still holding, within its trough-like cavity, a portion of the beds of 7. and 8. which here yield both *ore and limestone* in great abundance.

This mountain trough may be regarded as the germ of Rich-patch valley; for the next **Section, No. III**, which crosses not more than 1½ miles S. W. of Sec. II, brings to view the limestones of 4 a., forming the bottom, and the overlying shales of 4 b. and silicious shales of 4 c., forming the mountain slopes on both sides of that valley. Here, then, the mountain assumes a new structure and presents some new features. While the sandstones, shales, limestones and ores of Clifton Forge Pass have accompanied the ranges on both sides, the mountain itself is no longer one double ridge, as at Sec. II., but has become two distinct ridges with a limestone valley

between them. The sandstones and shales of 5 a. b. c., and the limestones of 7. and 8., all dip nearly as they did at the Pass, but the arch connecting them at the top is gone, and on the N. W. and S. E. slopes they still dip with the corresponding faces of the two ridges. Such is the modification of structure here.

The new features here brought to view are—(1) the Trenton limestones, 4 a., forming the bottom of the valley; (2) the Utica shales, 4 b., with the highest Hudson River shales, 4 c., forming the slopes of the mountains on both sides of the valley nearly up to their sandstone crests.

Some of the beds cut by Sec. III are finely displayed at what is known as "White Rock Gap"—a steep, rugged horse-path leading from Callie Furnace and crossing E. Rich-patch Mtn. at an elevation of 2,500 ft. The thickness of 4 a. could not be determined here so well as at points further S. W., but 4 b. displays a thickness of about 500 ft., on the face of the mountain, and 4 c. about 380 ft., while a fine out-crop of the lower bed of 5 a., near the crest of the ridge, is 120 ft. thick—an increase of 30 ft., over its thickness on Sec. I. The limestones that come to the surface in this and other parts of Rich-patch valley must not be confounded with those of 7., for they belong to an older period. They are the same as those that crop out in the Great Valley along the E. base of Purgatory and North mountains, and in many other localities, such as the region in and around Lexington, and along Christian Creek, between Staunton and Fishersville, on C. & O. Ry. They belong to the Lower Silurian age, while the newer Lower Helderberg, 7., belongs to the Upper Silurian.

The Trenton Limestones are everywhere remarkable for the fertile and durable soils produced by their disintegration. They have given the little valley crossed by the several sections under discussion, the title of "The Rich-patch."

On Sec. III the bed of 8., near its S. E. extremity, has its original on the Reynolds property, now owned by Capt. D. S. Cook, of the firm of Hileman, Cook & Co. of the Callie Furnace. The *display of the iron ores* of 8., on both Cook's and the Callie Furnace tracts is remarkable, the whole mass ranging in thickness from 100 to 120 ft.

Section No. IV.—Removing our section plane still farther to the S. W., so as to cut through, or near the Low Moor iron mines, it presents the strata about as they appear on Sec. IV. Here the great N. W. undulation, called Horse Mountain, becomes a conspicuous feature in the geology as well as in the topography of the chain. Its position and relations as an out-lier of the main mountain are here clearly exhibited, with its *limestones* of 7., and *iron ores* of 8. flanking both its sides; then the wrinkles of the strata, that have so remarkably multiplied the ore-beds at this point have been well developed by the mining operations of the Low Moor Co., while Fork Run, a tributary of Karnes Creek here passes through the gorge, once a crevice (?), of W. Rich-patch Mtn., cutting all the strata down to its very base, and affording a striking and instructive display of all the beds that here constitute the ridge. The same general type of structure found in the last section is also displayed at this point. The Trenton limestones, 4 a., of the valley still dip to the N. W. and pass beneath the mountain. The higher limestone and ores, especially on the N. E. side of the gorge, together with the underlying sandstones, have, however, been subjected to a violent thrust towards the N. W., by which they have become considerably warped and broken, and some of the beds partially inverted.

The several undulations of the beds 7. and 8. at the Low Moor mines seem to become a simple syncline towards the S. W. and again to flatten down under the beds of shale, 10 a.b., towards the N. E., while at a short distance above the furnace, they rise and arch over the low long slope by which Horse Mtn. sinks towards the level of the surrounding country. At the point where the limestones of 7. are quarried for use at the furnace, 8. is covered up by the debris that forms the deposits along the banks of Karnes Cr., but appears again along the base of the ridge at points both higher and lower along the stream.

The upper bed of *fossil or red-shale iron ore* has been worked, to a limited extent, at the Low Moor mines, but at the time of my last visit there the ores had not been put to

Continued on Page 192.

[*] Sections II and VII are drawn to a horizontal scale of 2.5 inches to one mile, and a vertical one of one inch to 1,000 ft.

The Mesozoic Formation in Virginia.

By Oswald J. Heinrich, M. E.

CONCLUDED FROM PAGE 177.

V. Economical Products of the Formation.

The variety of useful minerals and rocks which occur in the Mesozoic formation in this State does not appear great, still there are some of such value, that in the hands of men who knew how to develop them to their full extent, they might have been a great source of wealth long ago.

Amongst the most valuable of all must be mentioned the bituminous coal, which exists not only in workable, but in a number of instances in seams of most magnificent size and excellent character. It has been already stated that various kinds of coal occur; still, that of the most practical value is the true and highly bituminous variety.

This coal is known to exist in the Richmond, Farmville, and Dan River basins, but has been principally worked in the first-named, and is therefore best known from that locality. Its existence was known in 1700, and the coal was used as early as that date in the neighborhood.*

At least two workable seams of coal are known to exist in that basin: the lowest seam from three to five feet, and the big, or upper seam, from twenty to forty feet and more in thickness, and occasionally developed in two seams, divided by a series of slates and sandstones from five to ten feet thick. The distance between the upper and lowest seam is about fifty feet. There is no doubt whatever that these carboniferous deposits, geologically speaking, are continuous. But, like many other formations of the kind, they have their deteriorated localities and pinched places, which may, and often have deceived the inexperienced. The coal, although in various instances reaching almost to the surface, has its outcrop excluded from sight by a covering of alluvium, and also probably, to a small extent, by Tertiary strata, ranging from ten to forty feet. The seams pitch variously from 20° upwards. Nearly flat depositions exist in the bottom of the subordinate troughs or synclinal brains, and heavy pitches to 60° and 70° near the anticlinal rolls or saddles; on the average, a pitch of 15° to 35° may be assumed. The course of the coal is about N. 12° to 15° E. The main dip in the Richmond-basin upon the eastern side is northwest, upon the western, southeast.

Where the coal is not so thick, its exploitation offers no material difficulty, but it is often the case that the main seam assumes very considerable dimensions. In such instances, as in many others in this country, much coal has been lost or wasted from the bad system adopted for working the coal. The highly bituminous character of the coal gives rise to an abundance of carburetted hydrogen gases, which render a most thorough system of mechanical ventilation indispensable. Not unfrequently the roof is too defective to stand unsupported for a great length of time, and therefore the main avenues of entrance must be kept in a secure condition, for which timber-work is the cheapest, at present at least, although well-established mines in that district may now more profitably resort to other materials. For the sake of economy, these avenues ought to be reduced to the smallest practical dimensions. Considering all these conditions, it is easily to be seen that no plan for a secure pit could here be adopted by which most of the available coal could be obtained while entering the mine. A certain portion of the ground has to be laid out in such a manner as to avoid all the difficulties mentioned above, and the main bulk of the coal obtained by retreating or working homewards. This can be best accomplished in the thinner seams by a modification of the long-wall system by small-wall faces (*l'exploitation par tailles ascendantes*); in the thicker, by a system of long and strong pillars, which are won on working homeward, the ground behind being gobbed up.† As the seams in this district are generally divided by slates, in connection with other waste, the system will work well in the hands of a careful and experienced manager. Certain precaution must be taken in using the slates for gobbing up. They are liable to spontaneous combustion, the prevention of which must be thoroughly attended to. With such precautions as above mentioned, the yield of these seams is most favorable, and it is astonishing that so little attention has yet been paid to this section of country. According to statements the Mesozoic rocks cover an area of 189 square miles, in the Richmond coal basin, equal to 120,960 square acres. Not over 500 acres of this area has actually been worked, but what is still more important, these 500 acres are principally divided into about six localities, namely, the mines about

---

*I refer here to the historical sketch given in a former paper to the Institute, "The Midlothian Colliery, Virginia, in 1876."—Trans., Vol. IV p. 308.

†See "What is the Best System for Working Thick Coal Seams?" By author.—Trans. Vol. II, p. 105.

Carbon Hill, National, Midlothian and vicinity, and Clover Hill, upon the line of eastern outcrop, at the extreme northern and southern points, and about in the middle of the border line of twenty-eight miles extent; also for about ten to twelve miles upon the extreme northern point of the western outcrop, in the vicinity of Dover, and the mines south of James River; in all, say thirty-eight to forty miles of outcrop, the circumferential line of the basin being about seventy-five miles. The total production from 1822 to 1877 of the Richmond coal field amounted to 5,647,620.61 tons, or without any allowance for years previous to 1822, it would average a yield of 102,684 tons per annum, and 11,295 tons per acre of ground worked. That this is by no means an unreasonable calculation has been practically proved at Midlothian, where, in 1873, from one acre of ground 19,057 tons of coal were raised from a twenty-foot sem, averaging twelve to fifteen feet of coal.— (Transactions, 1874, vol. ii, p. 113.)

According to the statistics given in the "Coal Regions of America," by Macfarlane, from the Cumberland coal region, the aggregate production for thirty years, of 2,525 acres, was 12,953,317 tons, or 5,130 tons per acre, from the big fourteen-foot seam of a very pure coal. In spite, then, of even the inferior mining in Virginia, the results are extremely favorable. A full report of the production of the Richmond coalfield, as far as correct statistics could be obtained, will be found below.

In regard to the quality of the coal, a large number of analyses in the accompanying table may speak for themselves. For the purpose of comparison, a number of analyses of coal, with which the Richmond coal should be in a fair competition, have been included in the same table. The "Committee on Light," from the Richmond Gas-works, reported in 1874 (*Richmond Dispatch*, July 17th), upon coal tested from the Richmond basin and West Virginia, as follows:

KINDS OF COAL USED.	Number of lbs. used.	Yield per lb. cub. ft.	Yield per ton cub. ft.	Candle power.
WEST VIRGINIA.				
Coal Valley.................	40,810	4.11	9,206	14.50
Gordon & Seal..............	35,900	4.06	9,094	15.50
W. C. Robinson.............	26,690	4.05	9,072	13.90
Coalburg...................	28,000	3.78	8,467	13.80
Cannelton..................	34,000	3.97	8,892	13.90
Hampton City..............	20,840	4.10	9,184	14.90
RICHMOND BASIN.				
Clover Hill................	25,650	4.00	8,960	13.90
Marks (Midlothian vicinity)..	26,750	3.98	8,815	13.80
Old Dominion..............	27,810	3.80	8,512	13.80

The price paid at the time was $5.50 per ton, which would be highly remunerative for the Richmond mines, because by reasonable rates of transportation they should be able to deliver coal at Richmond from $2.50 to $3.00 per ton, if large quantities were mined.

From a close observation of the chemical analyses of this coal it will be noticed, that it ranges generally high in ash, which is in consequence of a greater or less amount of slaty substances contained in some of the benches of coal, while others are perfectly pure. This defect could be remedied by the introduction of the hydraulic jigs, now so extensively used in Europe in the bituminous coal fields of the Continent. Particularly all the fine coal, which in bituminous coal forms always a considerable quantity of the whole production, could be purified at low cost, and then converted into a very superior coke, to which this coal is particularly adapted, and for which a market could be established by the erection of furnaces along the James River Canal. (Now the Richmond & Alleghany RR.,—Ed.)

By a close study of this coal it will be noticed that often on the same specimen, as well as in large benches, three varieties exist, which are also noticed in other coal fields.

1. *Glance coal*, of a deep black color, vitreous lustre, and great brittleness; appears like pitch, in thick strata.

2. *Lamellar coal*. Grayish-black, or brownish-black, of a dull resinous lustre, much tougher, generally in thin strata.

3. *Fibrous coal*. A natural mineral charcoal; occurs in very thin film-like layers between the former, also in the form of small pieces; it is much like compressed dust. According to the investigations of Dr. A. Schondorff, in the coal fields of Saarbrucken, the average composition of these varieties is as follows:

	Glance Coal.	Lamellar Coal.	Fibrous Coal.
Water..................	4.26	3.00	0.86
Volatile matter.........	29.00	38.00	7.98
Coke..................	64.74	55.80	83.89
Ash...................	2.00	3.20	7.37

It will be readily perceived that even if much of the fibrous coal should occur, washing will reduce the amount of ash, the fibrous coal being the highest in ash.

This field yielding an excellent gas coal, as well as coking coal, steam coal, and blacksmith coal, its revival in the markets of the United States, which it commanded before the late civil war, will only be a matter of time, because its accessibility to sea-going vessels of 500 to 1000 tons' capacity will fairly counterbalance the moderate cost encountered by deep mining. The average distance from the principal mines now to James River navigation at Richmond, or Osborne's, or Port Walthall below it, is only 13 and 24 miles respectively.

The same coal, but of an inferior character, being very much contaminated with iron pyrites, has been mined near Farmville. Several seams from one and a half to six and a half feet have been partially explored. It has also been found in that part of the western belt extending into North Carolina from Danville.

Although no coal has yet been found in the largest belt in this State, namely the Potomac deposits, it is a matter worthy of inqui-

fuel after proper preparation, it is of importance to look for the other important material for the manufacture of iron. This could be at present found upon two lines of public improvement. The first and most important will be along the James River & Kanawha Canal, (R. & A. RR.) upon the line of which, or close to it, brown and red hematites, specular and magnetic iron ores of excellent quality, from within 50 to 180 miles above the coal-bearing rocks, can be mined in large quantities, at low prices. Upon that line very good limestone can also be obtained at very low cost. The line of the James River would therefore be the most available for the manufacture of iron, at a reasonable cost, along the northern part of the basin. Upon the line of the Richmond and Danville Railroad, in connection with the Atlantic, Mississippi and Ohio Railroad, or the projected branch into the counties of Henry, Patrick and Franklin, are found excellent specular and magnetic ores, which would supply the middle and southern part of the basin, although probably at little higher cost, according to freight charges.

Another material of economical value may be found in the fire-clay and shale, which would form an important item in ceramic

Analyses of Coal from the Richmond Basin.

SOUTH OF JAMES RIVER.

NAME OF PIT.	By Whom Analyz'd	Moisture.	Volat. matter.	Fixed carbon.	Ash.	Sulphur.	Coke.
EASTERN OUTCROP.							
Clover Hill (Coxe's Mines)	Prof. Johnson	1.389	30.984	56.881	10.182	.514	66.963
"	W. B. Rogers	—	29.12	65.52	5.36	—	70.88
"	G. W. Andrews	—	38.50	55.00	6.50	—	61.50
Stiles Henge	W. B. Rogers	—	36.60	58.70	4.80	—	63.50
Creek Company Shaft	Prof. Johnson	1.650	26.786	60.30	8.57	2.89	68.872
Mills & Reed, Creek Shaft	W. B. Rogers	—	38.91	51.07	1.61	—	61.60
Greenhole Shaft	"	—	31.11	57.83	3.00	—	60.83
Midlothian, average	Prof. Johnson	2.458	29.738	51.012	14.737	.058	67.740
" new shaft	"	0.670	31.230	56.40	9.44	2.286	65.840
" screwened	"	1.786	24.296	54.053	8.656	.302	65.718
" 900 ft. shaft	"	1.173	27.279	61.083	10.467	—	71.550
"	B. Silliman and O.						
"	P. Hubbard	2.000	31.62	58.96	7.67	—	66.810
"	J. H. Alexander	—	31.86	61.10	7.10	—	69.20
1875, screened	A. S. McCreath	1.08	36.28	54.27	8.47	1.92	60.74
Midlothian, average	"	1.08	26.49	46.702	13.786	2.23	62.488
Maidenhead	W. B. Rogers	—	22.83	69.97	8.30	—	67.17
English Co., old shaft	"	—	26.93	53.36	10.92	—	64.18
" " middle bench	"	—	26.40	56.50	8.10	—	71.80
" " top bench	"	—	28.40	61.68	9.92	—	71.30
Chesterfield Mining Co.	Prof. Johnson	1.896	25.719	58.794	8.534	1.087	67.439
Willis' Pit (Etna Shaft)	Clemson	—	26.80	56.60	4.60	—	71.90
WESTERN OUTCROP.							
Powhatan Pits	W. B. Rogers	—	22.53	59.97	7.80	—	67.67
Scott's Pit	"	—	33.70	60.86	5.46	—	66.52

NORTH SIDE OF JAMES RIVER.

EASTERN OUTCROP.							
Carbon Hill, bit. upper seam	O. J. Heinrich	1.40	20.80	60.80	17.20	not de-t'm'd	78.00
" second seam	" "	0.40	18.80	71.00	10.00	—	81.00
" carbonate	" "	1.27	9.54	79.93	8.96	consid erable	88.79
" average	Prof. Johnson	1.786	23.069	50.916	14.28	—	74.256
" natural coke	Dr. W. Wallace of	1.115	11.977	75.081	11.826	—	86.907
	Glasgow	1.36	14.36	61.61	02.94	0.38	89.85
WESTERN OUTCROP.							
Anderson's Pits (Dover)	W. B. Rogers	—	28.30	66.76	4.92	—	71.70
"	Clemson	—	26.00	64.90	9.30	—	74.00
T. M. Randolph	W. B. Rogers	—	20.50	66.15	3.58	—	69.50
Coalbrookdale	"	—	29.00	66.48	4.52	—	71.00
" 1st seam	"	—	14.00	70.60	8.30	—	78.00
" 2d seam	"	—	22.83	64.97	09.50	—	77.17
" 3d seam	"	—	24.70	65.80	9.60	—	75.30
" 4th seam	"	—	22.33	56.67	22.50	—	78.87
Cranches, upper seam	"	—	30.00	64.60	8.40	—	70.00
Waterloo	"	—	26.86	55.36	18.00	—	73.70
Deep Run Mines	"	—	15.16	69.95	5.07	—	76.86
FOR COMPARISON.							
Westmoreland, Pa., Gas Coal	Booth & Garrett	1.30	31.45	61.45	5.80	1.04	67.26
Campbell's C'k, W. Va., splint	Riverside Iron Co.	1.86	36.44	61.07	1.41	—	62.48
" 2d seam	W. B. Rogers	—	32.24	64.18	3.60	—	67.78
" 3d seam	"	—	33.68	57.75	8.56	—	66.32
Cannelton, Gas Coal	"	—	56.10	69.90	5.20	—	44.90
Raymond City	Venton	—	35.30	60.10	6.80	—	67.00
Lingan, Cape Breton	Chandler	—	35.20	68.90	4.00	—	64.80
Newcastle, England	"	—	32.75	65.55	1.75	—	67.30
"	McCreath	0.89	30.59	64.69	2.91	1.52	67.50

ry, why should coal not exist in this same formation in so extensive a deposit, when it is found in such small patches as the Deep Run, the Farmville, and in the extreme southern end of the belt in the Dan River deposits? The foregoing may serve as a guide in the investigation of this question. The vital importance of a discovery of coal here can readily be seen by noting the geographical position of the belt, its close proximity to the seat of government, and to excellent deposits of iron ore, which could be reached by railroad improvements already established.

As has been said formerly, no iron ores, at least in sufficient quantity for practicable purposes, have so far been discovered in the Richmond deposits. But since the coal would furnish a good

Annual Production and Shipments of Coal from the Richmond Coal Basin, in Tons of 2,000 Pounds.

*Estimated.

(a) Total amount according to R. C Taylor's and other reports.
(b) Previous to 1841. Deep Run produced about 18,000 tons, taken as average until 1847, when the mines stopped.
(c) Mr. C. & I. M. Co. raised 213,586 tons, from 1841 to 1851, or 21,351 tons, on an average.
(d) Midlothian Co., est. 95,700 tons, on an average, from 1843 to 1862; books burned at the evacuation of Richmond.
(e) Transportation on old Richmond horse RR., up to 1851, from Midlothian district.
(f) Clover Hill RR. books burned at the evacuation of Richmond, amount est., from 1843 to 1862, by the treasurer of the company.
(g) Miscellaneous transportation, estimated by hauling in wagons, during the war.
(h) R. & D. RR., no reports kept in consequence of depreciation of currency during the war.
(i) J. R. & K. Canal, estimated; books being burned with the office at the evacuation of Richmond.
(j) R. & D. RR., the same reason as in 1863.
(k) R. F. & P. RR., no coal shipped during the war, the Deep Run mines belonging to a Northern company.

manufactures. As various qualities, from a light yellowish-gray, or nearly white, to those of red color are found, the manufacture of pottery, firebrick, or common brick and terra cotta, in connection with a low-priced fuel, would be remunerative, and at the same time furnish a new source for the use of coal.

The sandstones of this formation have been used for building purposes, and if selected with proper care, furnish a sufficiently firm material. It is necessary to avoid those in which the feldspar has a great tendency to decomposition, as they will weather and decay more rapidly. Where some of the thicker strata of limestone approach the outcrop use could be made of the same, although, so far, no attention has been paid to it.

A great source of lightning and lubricating material is stored away for future generations in the highly bituminous slates, which

frequently occur in very heavy strata, and near the surface. As long as the petroleum wells furnish this material at so low a price, of course no attempt to compete with them could be successful. But, nevertheless, a test of their real value in carburetted compounds would be a matter of great interest.

The pyritiferous slates, such as occur in this formation, would be used in other countries probably for the manufacture of copperas, alum, etc., as, for example, at Pardubitz, in Bohemia, while here they will for a long time to come only be a source of nuisance.

In concluding this paper I can only heartily echo the expressions of Mr. Macfarlane in "The Coal Regions of America," namely: "We have often turned with a sort of wonder to regard the Richmond coal basin. Its history is very strange. It was one of the earliest turned by the miner. It is the solitary one at tide-water, and near a State capital. It contains several beds of coal, and one of these is sometimes of great thickness; it is mined by shafts, on the English plan, and affords a variety of fuels, ranging from gas coal to native coke. One would have expected its complete development long ere this," etc.

The following statistics from the same volume show how slow its development has been:

	Square miles.	By Railroad from tide-water.		Prod. in	Tons.	Prod. in	Tons.
1. Schuylkill basin, Pa.	.145	93		1822	1,480	1872	6,460,942
2. Lehigh basin, Pa.	..128	113		1820	365	1872	3,743,278
3. Wyoming basin, Pa.	..198	125		1829	7,000	1872	8,812 905
4. Cumberland basin, Md.	27	166½		1852	100,000	1872	2,355,471
5. Richmond basin, Va.	..180	12 to 24					
		from 1822 to 1842			1,925 000		
				1843	95,906	1872	95,278

While the Northern States have kept pace with the times, the Southern States have remained stationary, being satisfied to rest upon the laurels of their forefathers. Therefore this oldest of our coal fields is yet to see its best days.

Imperfect as this present description of the Mesozoic formation must be, it would be gratifying to the author if such practical researches as have been embodied in this paper would be followed up to a thorough and complete knowledge of this formation, which may yet be of great value to the eastern part of the State of Virginia.

Philadelphia, February 21st, 1878.

Continued from Page 189.

any practical use, and I have no information as to whether or not they are now used in the great furnace operated by this enterprising company.

The S. E. end of Sec. IV cuts the *heavy iron ore beds* that seems to form a continuous line of outcrop along the S. E. flank of E. Rich-patch Mountain, from Clifton Forge to and beyond Roaring Run Furnace, crossing near the Wood property, purchased by Col. H. C. Parsons of the R. & A. RR. Co. but now owned by the Alleghany Coal & Iron Co. The *fossil ores* appear at various points along the same face of the mountain, but nowhere of such thickness as to promise very profitable developments, except near Roaring Run Furnace, where they were once largely worked.

Section No. V.—Removing our plane of section, so as to cut the mountain ranges near where the Covington and Fincastle Turnpike crosses them, extending it from a point on Jackson River, near Steele Station, to Roaring Run Furnace, we shall again cut the *bed of 8., iron ore* on the N. W. flank of Horse Mtn., where it has been opened on the lands of H. Robertson, Esq., and also the *fossil ores* that crop out at points on both sides of the same ridge. Here the trough between Horse and Rich-patch mountains has, by denudation, lost its beds of 7. and 8., which, however, re-appear in their usual extent, at points not remote from this line on both sides. There are decided evidences of the fossil beds in this region that indicate sufficient extent to be worked with advantage.

As we cross the mountain and descend into Rich-patch valley, near Hook's, the typical structure is somewhat modified by extensive, and greatly fractured, folds in the Trenton limestones, 5 a., as seen in the section.

The S. E. end of this section cuts the *fine display of iron ore beds* on the Roaring Run property, on the S. E. slope of the mountain. The fossil beds, especially the upper, or red-shale, have been largely opened, and furnished their valuable ores for many years to supply Roaring Run Furnace; but they still seem to be hardly fairly opened. More systematic mining would yet produce these ores in great abundance. The

ores of 8. (VII. R.), crop out on this property in great quantities along the base of the mountain, where they can be mined with convenience and at moderate cost. The limestones of 7. are also very abundant and of good quality at this point.

Section No. VI extends from the loop of Potts Cr., a little way above its junction with Jackson River, to Hays Gap, and thence to a point near Craig Cr. halfway between Grace and Roaring Run furnaces. It cuts the *ores of 8. that crop out abundantly* along the W. base of Horse, here called Carpenter Mountain, and the same bed in the synclinal trough between this and Middle Mtn. This latter ridge here rises as a subordinate undulation between the two higher ridges, and in the ravine traversed by Hays-ap Run, it brings some beds of *fossil ores* within reach of mining operations. The same ores are also found along the N. W. face of W. Rich-patch Mn., in what promises to be workable quantities.

Thus far this section is chiefly on the lands of Robertson & Carrington. After crossing the Rich-patch valley sec. VI cuts the E. Rich-patch Mtn., the main body of which, omitting some minor features on the W. side, has the same general structure presented by it through the whole distance from the line of sec. III to this point.

Section No. VII is designed to show the outcroppings of ores between Hays and Blue-spring run gaps. Two ridges, the main W. Rich-patch and what seems to be in reality a continuation of Carpenter or Horse Mtn., stand up prominently in this section and carry upon their faces, and along their flanks, the *same beds of iron ore* cut by all the other sections. Here the syncline between the two mountains is deeper than we have found it at any other points. This section extends less than half way across the Rich-patch valley, which it enters not far from the base of Nicholas Knob, the southwestern limit of Rich-patch valley. It presents the entire inversion of the strata of the main ridge—a marked modification of what we have seen at the west base of the arch of section, I and in the corresponding strata on section IV near the Low Moor mines.

The lands of A. A. Low, Esq., lie chiefly between sections VI and, VII and, I have reason to believe, contain *all the beds of ore and limestone* represented on these sections N. W. of Rich-patch valley. I was over his lands, but found but few evidences of any explorations having been made.

The Rich-patch Iron Properties.—The region described in this paper, is, as the accompanying map shows, about 18 miles long in a N. E.–S. W. direction and varies in breadth from near 2½ miles in the N. E., between the mouths of Wilson Creek and Cow-pasture River, to one of 9 miles in the S. W., between the mouths of Cole Run of Craig Creek and Blue-spring Run of Potts Creek,—omitting the S. E. salient between Craig Creek and James River. As a whole, it embraces between 50,000 and 60,000 acres of land.

In April, 1795, Virginia granted 14,000 acres to Benj. Martin, that, in a general way, embraced the land lying between Karnes Creek on the N. E. and Blue-spring Run on the S. W., Jackson River and its extension, Potts Creek, on the N. W. and the Rich-patch Valley on the S. E.—The N. E. portion of this patent, about 10,000 acres, extending from near Karnes Creek to Hays-gap Run, with additions along the C. & O. R'y, is now the *property of H. Robertson & Co.*, of Danville, Va. The S. W. portion of this patent, the part that may be said to extend from Hays-gap Run to Blue-spring Run, some 5,000 acres, is the *property of A. A. Low, Esq.*, of New York, N. Y.

In December, 1795, Virginia granted 20,000 acres to Benj. Martin, that included a large portion of the remainder of the Rich-patch region shown on the map. It extended from above the mouth of Cole Run of Craig Creek, running along the foot-hills of the E. Rich-patch range, down nearly to the mouth of Craig Creek, then, in the same way, up James River and Jackson River to about a mile beyond the mouth of Karnes Creek, to the line of Martin's 14,000 acre patent. It included most of the land between the streams named, with the exception of rich bottom and valley lands that had been previously patented —This patent, to which some of the bottoms have been added, is now divided about as follows: The N. E. end, some 1,200 acres, next to Clifton-forge Gap, *belongs*

to the *Charter Oak Life Ins. Co.*, of Hartford, Conn.—S. W of the last, on Jackson River waters (mainly on the waters of Karnes Creek) is the *Low Moor Iron Co. of Virginia estate*, of some 4,500 acres, extending to the Robertson lands.—On the eastward slope of the E. Rich-patch Mountain, beginning at Jackson River, there is: (1) The 840 acres *belonging to D A. Kayser, Esq.*, of Staunton, Va., (he having sold 500 acres to the R. & A. RR. Co. for the site of Iron-gate Station); (2) The *Callie Furnace estate*, some 300 acres, of Hileman, Cook & Co.; (3) The *Reynolds lands*, some 400 acres, of Capt. D S. Cook; (4) The *Wood lands*, 1,233 acres, purchased by Col. H. C. Parsons, now the property of the Alleghany Coal & Iron Co.; and (5) The *Roaring Run Furnace estate*, some 10,000 acres, mainly on Craig Creek waters.

The Resources of this region in iron ores and limestones may be inferred from their extensive outcrops displayed in the several geological sections above described. They point out a continuous bed of the ores of S. (Rogers' VII), of great thickness, cropping out all along the S. E. flank the E. Rich-patch range, beginning on the lands of the Charter Oak Insurance Co. and those of D. A. Kayser, E-q., and extending thence. S. W., through the properties of Callie Furnace, Capt D. S. Cook, the Alleghany Coal & Iron Co., and that of Roari g Run Furnace. These ores have not been explored over the whole of this line, but they have been exposed or outcrop naturally on each of the estates named, and enough is displayed to prove great continuity in this vast bed of at least 10 miles in length. Higher up on the face of the same ridge the fossil and red-shale iron ores are sufficiently promising, as already inti mated, to be worthy of more thorough explorations than have yet been made.

On the N. W. slopes of W. Rich-patch Mountain the bed of S. (Rogers' VII) has been worked on the lands of the Charter Oak Co., on those of Mr. Alexander, and on those of the Low Moor Iron Co. of Va., sufficiently to prove its continuity and thickn ss,—the richness and quality of its ores are no longer a question of doubt, as far as these lands extend.

Advancing farther to the S. W., on the property of H. Rob ertson & Co., we find the same beds that are found on the Low Moor estate, continuing without interruption (except one un-important point already mentioned) all the way to Hays-gap Run, showing ores of great extent and fine quality.

Beyond the last named property, the iron ore beds run into the lands of A. A. Low, Esq., where they are found to show favorable indications, as to quantity and quality, even as far as Blue-spring Run, though they have net, as yet, been well explored.

There are also on the N. W. face of this W. Rich-patch range, and along the faces of its subordinate ridges, many openings in the fossil and red-shale ores that indicate their presence in quantities that will at a future day make them objects of value to the manufacturers of iron.

The *sandstones* of this region—especially those of 5 a.—are unsurpassed for building purposes; they may be obtained within convenient distances of nearly all the numerous furnace sites that may be found throughout this region.

In riding over the several properties here represented, I was struck with the great extent of *virgin forest* still standing and abounding in timber adapted to a great variety of purposes,— timber for charcoal, buildings, fences, railway ties, etc. The fact that three sides of a large portion of the area under discussion, are bordered by railroads already in operation, makes the timber here an object of much greater value than it would be where transportation lines are less contiguous. The demand for railway ties will increase every year in Virginia, and those of best quality will be sought after. No portion of the State can furnish finer young white-oaks of proper size for ties than can be found in this interesting mountain chain.

I traversed this interesting mountain region on or near the lines along which all of the foregoing sections were drawn; and, while no attempt has been made to embrace all the minor features of the areas over which they pass, all that is imp rtant to throw light up n the mineral resources of the region has been carefully preserved in l represented.

Washington & Lee University,   J. L. Campbell.
Lexington, Va., Dec. 188 .

Fat Cattle for England are now being sent from Rock bridge County, Va.

Shenandoah Valley RR.—This company sells ticket books for 500 miles, for the use of families, at 2½ cents a mile ; the result is a large local travel.—Mr. F. J. Kimball, President of the Shenandoah Valley Construction Co., the energetic builders of this road, sailed for England on the 1st of December. It is the opinion of some parties that he has gone to consult with the English bond-holders of the Atlantic, Mississippi & Ohio RR. in reference to a consolidation of interests when that road is sold, in February next. In a short time, by such an arrangement, a new through line from New York to all the southwest could be put in operation.—The *Luray Advance*, the new newsy and sprightly weekly that has recently begun life at Luray, Va., urges the delivery of the Page county bonds to the S. V. RR., that Luray may secure the location of the company's shops there, as promised in that event. A wise urge cy, for the population and business of the town would be doubled as a consequence.—An exchange says the Shenandoah Valley Construction Co. has purchased the famous Luray Caverns.— The engineers are running exp rimental lines between Buchanan, on the R. & A. RR. to the A., M. & O. RR. at Bonsack's or Big Lick. They have completed those between Waynesboro, on the C. & O. R'y, and the mouth of South River of the James, a point on the Lexington branch of the R. & A.

Lime-burning ought to be a great industry in all accessible parts of the Valley of Virginia, where so many varieties of limestone abound and where fuel is plentiful. We are pleased to note that Messrs D C Coffman and R Lee France, the latter from Pa., have erected extensive lime-kilns about a mile N. E. of the Shenandoah Iron-works, on the Shenandoah Valley RR., and are now ready to supply lime for agricultural and other purposes. The name of the firm is the *Rockdale Lime Co.* We wish it abundant success, and hope our farmers learn to know, as they should, [illegible] improve the off days of The Valley as much as [illegible]——Ciss. & Sons ship... 32 [illegible] lime-kilns at Riverton, t e irks

Water-power.—The Upper Appomattox Co. of Petersburg has leased the water-power between the Petersburg Cotton Mills and the river for 10 years at $950 a year.—— Doctor George Washington Bagby, the interesting and philosophising correspondent of *The State*, is one of the best observers and describers of men and manners in the United States, but when he tells us that there is no water-power in all the 80 miles of country between Alexandria and Gordonsville, except at Rapid-Anne (which he barbarously spells *Rapidan*, as though there were no lady in the case), "the streams not affording fall enough to furnish the power needed in mills, etc.," we must set him down as a very poor observer of things and as very badly informed on the water-fall question. We must add that he is good on cats, dogs, and horses.

Virginia Midland RR.—Daily freight trains, instead of tri-weekly, now run over the Manassas Branch, the freightage from the west to Lynchburg is now so heavy.—From the Front Royal and Riverton depots, in Nov., there were shipped, by this RR. 1337 bbls. flour, 11,940 bush. grain, 65,300 lbs. mill feed, 40 tons ground sumac, 54 bbls. wine 7 cars live-stock, and 32 cars (640,000 lbs) lime, the latter from Carson & Sons kilns at Riverton.—*Sentinel.* This RR. and branches is to be sold at Alexandria, Va., Dec. 20.—*Sentinel.*

Barytes.—Mr. John S. Morris of Lynchburg, Va., shipped Dec. 8, to Philadelphia, *via* Norfolk, 300 hundred bbls., 226,350 lbs., of ground barytes from his mills just below Lynchburg.—*Dispatch.*——Betten & Co. are mining barytes on Jos. S. Jackson's farm 4 ms. N. E. of Winchester, on the Martinsburg turnpike.—*Times.*

Mail-matter in Va.—During the first week in Dec. Lynchburg mailed 42,966 pieces.— In Staunton 18,268 pieces were mailed, a gain of 4,767 over the same period in 1879.——Proposals for carrying the Va. mails for 4 years from July 1, 1881, will be received at the Contract Office, P. O. Dept., Washington, D. C., until Jan. 31, 1881.

Religious toleration in Va.—When the Hebrews of Alexandria, Va., learned, recently, that the members of a Presbyterian church in that city had no place of worship they tendered them the use of their synagogue, without charge, until other arrangementi could be made.

The Snow-flake flouring mill at Mt. Meridian, Augusta Co., Va., near the Shenandoah Valley RR., has been renewed and remodeled by Mr. W. B. Felger the Pa. gentleman that has purchased it and the fine estate attached.

Miscellaneous.

THOMAS B. SWANN,

Attorney-at-Law,

Charleston, Kanawha County, W. Va.

W. H. DEWEES,

Carkin, Kanawha Co., W. Va.,

Offers his services in the making of geological examinations, surveys or reports, in superintending the experimental development of mines &c. and in effecting purchases. Agent for Pennsylvania Diamond Drill Co.

Real Estates, Water Power, &c.

SALE OF VALUABLE
　　　　　PROPERTY.

Dr. H. S. Eichelberger offers for sale his handsome residence and beautiful farm at Verona, on Valley RR. The farm contains about 190 or 130 acres, and lies on the west side of the Valley pike. The Doctor is willing, if only a small quantity of land is desired, to sell with the residence 15 or 20 acres, which will embrace all the improvements, the finest young bearing orchard in that section, with a spring not excelled for the coldness of the water in the State, with fine water attached. This is a rare chance to secure a quiet, lovely home within a ten minutes ride of the city of Staunton, by rail. Its location adapts it well for a summer resort; it is also a good point for a physician. He would invite any one who wishes a quiet, lovely home, free from the noise of city life, to this handsome property. For terms, apply to H. S. EICHELBERGER, Verona, Augusta county, Virginia, or to ELDER & NELSON, Staunton, Virginia. The Doctor will take pleasure in showing the property

RESIDENCE
　　IN STAUNTON FOR SALE.

I offer for sale the Residence of Mrs. Virginia B. Donaghe, fronting on three of the principal streets—Main, Lewis and Frederick—in immediate proximity to business, churches, schools, &c. The improvements are first-class, and the property one of the best, if not the very best in the city, either as a home or a speculative investment. It will be subdivided if not sold as a whole. Examination invited.

Terms:—Ten per cent. cash, and balance at one, two, and three years, with semi-annual interest.

　　　　　　THOMAS D. RANSON.

VIRGINIA WATER-POWER
　　　　　AT DANVILLE.

Persons wishing to purchase the splendid Water-power at Danville, Va., can do so on
　　　VERY REASONABLE TERMS.

This is a fine opening for Rolling Mills, Paper Mills, Foundries, &c., &c. Apply in person or by letter to me as the attorney for the owners.　　　　　　E. E. BOULDIN,
　　　　　　　　　　　　Danville, Va.

THE OLD BLACKFORD
　　　FORGE PROPERTY,

Including Water-power and Over 600
　　　Acres of Land,

*On Hawksbill Creek, Below Luray, Page
　　　County, Virginia,*

And on line of Shenandoah Valley Railroad, is hereby offered for sale. For terms, etc., address
　　　　　Lock Box 281, Staunton, Va.

Coal and Coke Dealers.

FIRE CREEK COAL AND COKE
　　　COMPANY,

Fire Creek, Fayette Co., West Virginia,
　　　MINERS OF

Red Ash Bituminous Steam Coal,

and manufacturers of Hard Coke. All correspondence should be directed to　　M. ERSKINE MILLER,
　　　　　　Sales Agent and Business Manager,
　　　　　　　　　　　STAUNTON, VA.

W. A. BURKE,
　　Staunton, Virginia.

Sole Agent for Nutallburg Coal & Coke ;

The best steam coal on the market ; coke superior to Connellsville.

Shipper of Kanawha Splint and Gas Coals.
Points of Shipment:—Richmond, Va., and Huntington, West Virginia.

Banks.

H W. Sheffey, Pres.　　Davis A. Kayser, Vice-Pres.
　　　　　W P. Tams, Cashier.

AUGUSTA NATIONAL BANK,
　　　Staunton, Virginia.

Collections in Virginia and West Virginia promptly attended to and remitted on day of payment, at lowest rates of exchange
New York Correspondent........, Chemical National Bank.
Baltimore Correspondent, Farmers' and Merchants' Nat'l Bank.
Cincinnati Correspondent............. Merchants' National Bank.

John Echols, President　　Ro. W. Burke, Vice-President.
　　　　　Thos. A. Bledsoe, Cashier.

NATIONAL VALLEY BANK
　　　of Staunton, Virginia.

Designated Depository and Financial Agent
　　of United States.

Capital Stock, $200,000; Surplus and Undivided Profits, $200,000.
New York Correspondent...............National Park Bank.
Baltimore Correspondent............Hanover National Bank.
Baltimore Correspondent, Farmers' and Merchants' Nat'l Bank.
Cincinnati Correspondent.................First National Bank.

Hardware, &c.

A. E. MILLER,
　　Staunton, Virginia.
　　Wholesale and Retail Dealer in

Hardware, Cutlery, &c.,

Miners' Tools and Supplies of all descriptions. Orders promptly filled.

HUGH M. McILHANY,
　　Wholesale and Retail Dealer in

Hardware, Cutlery, &c.,

Augusta St., opp. Court-house,
　　　　　Staunton, Virginia.

WIRE TRAMWAYS.

The most economical system for the transportation of ores, coal, lumber and agricultural products,—especially adapted for carrying coal from the Pine River and Kanawha fields to the line of railway, or across the Rivers in the Railway, in place of bridges. They avoid gradings, cuttings or embankments, are not affected by floods or snow. Inclines of 1 in 3 are admissible They can be used to transmit power as well as material. Send for estimates and other information to
　THE AMERICAN WIRE ROPE TRAMWAY CO.,
　　　308 Walnut Street, Philadelphia, Pa.

Newspapers.

THE VALLEY VIRGINIAN,
　　　Staunton, Virginia.
S. M. YOST & SON, Proprietors.
　　　Terms : $2.00 per year.

THE VIRGINIAN is an independent Republican newspaper, devoted principally to the interests of the Great Valley, and Mineral Regions adjacent thereto. Its circulation is larger than that of any other weekly newspaper published in Virginia. As an advertising medium, especially for farming, grazing, and mineral lands, &c., it has no superior. Parties desiring to buy or sell real estate will find it to their advantage to make use of its columns. Specimen copies free.

THE "STAUNTON SPECTATOR,"
　　　129 E. Main Street,
　　　　　Staunton, Virginia.

The "SPECTATOR" is published every Tuesday morning, at Staunton, Augusta county, and is the best advertising medium in the interior of the State.
The "Spectator" was the first paper established at this place, nearly a century ago, and it is now in its 57th volume, under its present title. Its list of subscribers is larger than that of any other paper west of the Blue Ridge, and is, therefore, the best advertising medium in the Valley of Virginia, or in West Virginia. Address　　　　　"STAUNTON SPECTATOR,"
　　　　　　　　　Staunton, Virginia.

Schools.

UNIVERSITY OF VIRGINIA.

Session begins October the First and continues Nine Months. Thorough instruction in the Academic, Engineering, Law and Medical Departments. The Corcoran School of Natural History and Geology, with its full and splendid collection of material in the Brooks Natural Science Museum, affords special facilities for studying Zoology, Geology, Mineralogy and Botany, under the instruction of Professors Fontaine and Page. Apply for catalogues to
　　　　　　JAS. F. HARRISON,
　　　　　　　　Chairman of the Faculty.

WASHINGTON & LEE
　　　UNIVERSITY.
　　GEN. G. W. C. LEE, President.

Full courses in Classical, Literary, and Scientific Studies, including those of the professional degrees of Civil Engineering and of Law.
TERMS:—Tuition and other fees in all the Departments $70. Board, Lodging, &c., per month, from $10 to $20.
The next session begins September 16th, 1880, and ends June 23d, 1881.
For other particulars apply to　J. L. CAMPBELL, Jr,
　　　　　　Clerk of Faculty, Lexington, Va

Railways.

THE CHESAPEAKE & OHIO R'Y

Is the Only Route to and via the

White Sulphur Springs and other Most Famous and Fashionable Watering Places
of the Mountains of the Virginias.

It is the unparalleled and unapproachable for the wildness, sublimity and picturesque beauty of scenery, and the healing virtues of its health-giving fountains. It is the Short Line Between the Seaboard and the Great West, and is second to none in construction, equipment and appliances for the safety and comfort of its passengers
Through Tickets to all Western towns and cities, and excursion tickets to the watering places and summer resorts, are for sale via this line at all principal ticket offices everywhere.
J. C. DAME, Southern Agent, Richmond, Va ; H W CARR, G E. Agent, 315 Broadway, New York ; CONWAY R. HOWARD, G. P. & T. A., Richmond, Virginia.